THE
STYLE
SOURCEBOOK

THE STYLE SOURCEBOOK

THE DEFINITIVE ILLUSTRATED DIRECTORY OF
FABRICS WALLPAPERS **PAINTS** FLOORING **TILES**

REVISED EDITION

JUDITH MILLER

FIREFLY BOOKS

A FIREFLY BOOK

Published by Firefly Books Ltd. 2008
First published in Great Britain in 1998 by Mitchell Beazley, an imprint
of Octopus Publishing Group Ltd.

Revised Edition 2008

Publisher Cataloging-in-Publication Data   (U.S.)
Miller, Judith.
    The style sourcebook : the definitive visual directory of fabrics,
wallpapers, paints, flooring & tiles / Judith Miller.
Rev.ed.
[416] p. : col. photos. ; cm.
Includes index.
ISBN-13: 978-1-55407-359-7 (hard cover)
ISBN-10: 1-55407-359-6 (hard cover)
    1. Decoration and ornament--Directories. 2. Decoration and
ornament--Information services--Directories. I. Title.
745.4/029/4 dc22   NK1705.M56   2008

Library and Archives Canada Cataloguing in Publication
Miller, Judith, 1951–
    The style sourcebook : the definitive visual directory of fabrics,
wallpapers, paints, flooring & tiles / Judith Miller.
Includes index.
ISBN-13: 978-1-55407-359-7 (hard cover)
ISBN-10: 1-55407-359-6 (hard cover)
    1. Interior decoration. I. Title.

NK1705.M54 2008   747   C2007-904734-3

Published in the United States by
Firefly Books (U.S.) Inc.
P.O. Box 1338, Ellicott Station
Buffalo, New York 14205

Published in Canada by
Firefly Books Ltd.
66 Leek Crescent
Richmond Hill, Ontario L4B 1H1

Printed and bound in China

Original edition

Chief Contributor	John Wainwright
Contributors	Chris Blanchett, Penny McGuire, Olga Moyle
Consultants	Jill Draper, David Gunton, Tessa Smith-Agassi, Michael Szell, Christine Woods
Senior Editor	Penelope Cream
Senior Art Editor	Emma Boys
Editor	Julia North
Designer	Kenny Grant
Editorial Assistants	Patrick Evans, Anna Nicholas
Design Assistant	Estelle Bayllis
Production Controllers	Rachel Staveley, Kate Thomas
Picture Researchers	Sally Claxton, Lois Charlton
Executive Editor	Judith More
Executive Art Editor	Janis Utton
Special Photography	Steve Tanner
Special Location Photography	James Merrell

Revised edition

Chief Contributor	John Wainwright
Project Editor	Emma Clegg
Editorial Coordinator	Catherine Emslie
Caption Researcher	Caroline Dyas
Proofreader	Libby Willis
Indexer	Helen Snaith
Executive Art Editor	Auberon Hedgecoe
Designers	Peter Gerrish and John Round
Production Controller	Gary Hayes
Picture Researcher	Emma O'Neill
Special Photography	Roger Dixon

Contents

Foreword

We produced the first *Style Sourcebook* in 1998. Our intention then was to provide something previously unavailable: namely, a comprehensive guide to fabrics, wallpapers, tiles, paints and floor coverings that located particular materials, motifs, patterns and colours within specific historical periods. Judging by our readers' comments and subsequent sales, it proved a major success – a very pleasing, but not surprising outcome. As I noted at the time, there had been a substantial growth of interest in interior decoration since the Second World War. Initially, the opening up of many historically important houses had introduced a wider public to the finest examples of the art. Subsequently, diverse books, magazines and television programmes illustrating both historical and contemporary interiors demonstrated the tremendous decorative potential of all our homes. The result: what in previous centuries had been largely the preserve of a wealthy minority had become the one art form practised by virtually everyone.

Much, of course, has happened in the five years since our initial publication. First and foremost, interest in interior decoration has become even more intense and widespread. Secondly, on-going research has brought to light many new patterns, motifs and colours employed in different historical periods. Thirdly, numerous new designs for contemporary styles of decoration have been conceived. And fourthly, manufacturers have responded by producing the essential decorative media in ever more extensive ranges of historical and contemporary patterns and colourways.

To guide you through all these developments we have produced a thoroughly revised *Style Sourcebook* that encompasses through myriad samples – more than 60 per cent of which are new – fashionable styles of decoration from the Middle Ages to the present day. Judging by the reception of our original title, I am convinced you will find this new book informative, inspirational, user-friendly and, above all, an invaluable guide when choosing decorative schemes for your period or modern home, whether your preferences are historical or contemporary.

Judith Miller

Using *The Style Sourcebook*

Over 2,000 samples, from the widest possible range of international designs, provide inspiration for selecting the ingredients for any interior scheme, from medieval to modern. The Style Guide presents an historical overview of interior design and major stylistic developments, while the chapters that follow contain hundreds of samples of every style, colour and pattern, divided into the main design types, such as florals, geometrics and motifs. Each design type or material is further categorized by period, from medieval to early 21st century, enabling you to select your favourite designs and colours, item by item and era by era.

Useful Features

Various easy-to-use design features on every page make the information in *The Style Sourcebook* highly accessible. Colour-coded bands, each indicating a particular century, lie on the edge of every page to help you to turn instantly to a specific era. The same colour is used in the border of the special feature boxes, linking them with their most relevant period.

Each sample is accompanied by a detailed caption listing all the information needed for ordering, such as name, code number (if applicable) and the colourway shown. Sizes, repeat and composition are also indicated, together with any relevant symbols for usage, special applications and other information (*see* Key to Symbols, left).

Further Information

The samples in the book have been obtained from a wide variety of international manufacturers and suppliers, whose details are listed in the Directory of Suppliers (*see* page 401). The Glossary provides further information about the technical, artistic and historical terms mentioned in the book.

STYLE AND DATE HEADING
Every spread of samples is identified by the type of design and the date of the decorative style. A detailed introduction provides an overview of the era.

DESIGN OVERVIEW
Each design type is discussed with reference to its specific use in interior decoration, and is illustrated with colour examples of room settings and furniture.

KEY DESIGNS
The most significant designs are highlighted and their historical, cultural and artistic importance discussed.

COLOUR BANDS
Easily identifiable colour bands represent the different historical periods, allowing designs of a particular era to be found quickly across all chapters.

CAPTIONS
Every sample illustrated has a detailed caption that provides all the information necessary for ordering the featured design and colourway required.

SCALE BAR
A scale bar beneath the sample indicates the size at which it is reproduced. The largest samples are life size, while the smallest are at 25 per cent of their actual size.

BOX FEATURE
Important historical or technical topics are discussed in detail within a box. The box is colour-coded according to the appropriate corresponding date.

The Samples

FABRICS

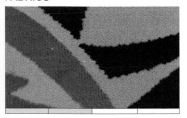

Osborne & Little/Dufy Velvet F5151 Colour **01**
Alt. colours **yes** Composition **59% viscose,
41% cotton** Width **132cm/51¼in** Repeat
59cm/23in Price ★★★★

Price Guide	per metre/yard
£1–20	★
£21–50	★★
£51–100	★★★
£101–150	★★★★
£150+	★★★★★

The samples shown in the Fabrics section (*see* pages 60–201) are categorized by design or pattern type and historical period. The composition of each fabric is shown by fibre type and expressed in terms of percentages.

The price of each fabric is given by the metre/yard; this may vary slightly depending on where and when it is bought. Suggested uses and any special features are indicated at the end of each caption.

Also included in the Fabrics section are the Braids & Trimmings pages. Described here are the different types of braids, ribbons, fringes and tassels.

WALLPAPERS

Bradbury & Bradbury/Glasgow Panel Colour
natural Alt. colours **yes** Width **68.5cm/27in**
Length **2m/2⅛yd** Repeat - Price ★

Price Guide	per metre/yard
£1-5	★
£6–10	★★
£11–20	★★★
£21–35	★★★★
£35+	★★★★★

The Wallpapers section (*see* pages 202–283) is divided by design type and then by historical period. Full-size wallpapers as well as borders and friezes are illustrated, and the latter can be combined with plainer designs.

Prices for wallpapers are shown by the metre/yard, and the symbol ♣ indicates those that are hand-printed or hand-blocked (these are generally more expensive than the machine-printed designs).

Certain wallpapers need painting or finishing after hanging, and this requirement is also indicated by the relevant caption symbol.

PAINTS & FINISHES

Liberon Waxes Colour **gilt cream chantilly**
Composition and finish *spirit-based:* **satin
sheen** Price ★★★★

Price Guide	per litre/gallon
£1–5	★
£6–10	★★
£11–30	★★★
£30+	★★★★

The divisions within the Paints & Finishes section (*see* pages 284–309) concentrate on the application material, such as regular paints, special paints and wood finishes, which is then categorized by date where applicable.

Prices for the samples in this section are per litre/gallon; however, certain finishes such as gilt waxes are needed only in tiny amounts and so may be supplied in smaller quantities.

The composition and finish of each paint is given; many colours are available in a variety of finishes, each suitable for a different use.

TILES

Original Style/Rose and Trellis 6970A Colour
multi Alt. colours **no** Composition **ceramic** Size
15 x 15cm x 7mm/6 x 6 x ¼in Price ★ W

Price Guide	per tile/set
£1–5	★
£6–10	★★
£11–20	★★★
£21–35	★★★★
£35+	★★★★★

The measurements given for the samples in the Tiles section (*see* pages 310–359) signify the longest side by the shortest side(s). This is not an indication of which way up a tile should be positioned – some tile designs can be placed horizontally, vertically or even diagonally.

Prices are given for each tile, or, where the design consists of a number of tiles, for the price of the total set or panel. The tiles are shown without scale bars, and wherever possible each tile is shown in its entirety. Some tiles are available in a variety of sizes and this is indicated by the symbol ⊞.

FLOORING

Kahrs/Alder Monte Carlo Colour **natural**
Alt. colours **no** Composition **alder** Width
20cm/8in Repeat – Price ★★

Price Guide	per square metre/yard
£1–20	★
£21–50	★★
£51–100	★★★
£101–150	★★★★
£150+	★★★★★

The Flooring section (*see* pages 360–397) is split first into the type of flooring material – wood, carpet, matting and sheet flooring – and then into different historical periods. Certain types of flooring were available earlier than others, and this is reflected in the era divisions.

Prices in this section are given per square metre/yard (except in the case of some of the borders, which are sold by the linear metre/yard, so check with the supplier before ordering). Inlaid wooden flooring is often made up on commission to fit the area required, so is priced according to space and type.

USING THE SCALE BAR

Most of the samples in the book, apart from those such as tiles and paints that may vary in size or are not measured by area, have a scale bar beneath them. This scale bar has four divisions which are shaded according to the relative size of the sample shown, in proportion to its actual size.

A single shaded division indicates that the sample is illustrated at a quarter (or 25 per cent) of its full size; two shaded divisions mean that the sample is at half

(or 50 per cent) its actual size; three shaded divisions indicate that the sample is at three-quarters of its actual size (or 75 per cent), while a completely shaded bar means that the sample is shown at actual size (100 per cent).

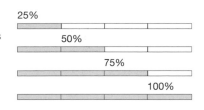

Style Guide

Medieval to pre-16th Century

During the Middle Ages, interior decoration was the preserve of the seigneurial classes. They alone had the money and time to devote to this domestic preoccupation, and what is now called "Medieval style" was confined to their stone-built or timber-framed castles and manor houses.

Medieval interiors were sparsely furnished, so the architectural shell played a major role in the decoration. Floors at ground level consisted of bricks, stone flags or tiles, and upper floors of oak or elm boards. Ceilings were often coffered, and the stone walls left exposed or covered with coarse plaster (the latter limewashed and often painted with stencilled motifs). The wooden studs and braces of timber-framed walls were exposed and the wattle-and-daub panels in between were limewashed and sometimes stencilled. Battened plank doors were set under flat or four-centred arches – as were most mullion windows.

Furniture was mostly of oak, elm or chestnut. Tables were wooden boards supported on trestles, seating largely consisted of benches and stools, and beds were simple pallets or canopied four-posters. Soft furnishings included silk, woollen and tapestry bed- and wall-hangings, embroidered quilts, floor cushions, rush- and straw-matting floor-coverings and, in the grandest households, oriental carpets which were used as table-coverings.

Throughout the Middle Ages, the decorative motifs that adorned furniture, woodwork, tiles and textiles were derived from three vocabularies of ornament: Romanesque, Gothic and Heraldic. The Romanesque combined Classical Roman, oriental, pagan and Christian motifs, and included chevrons, foliage, people and beasts. Gothic ornament included architectural elements such as lancets, foils and tracery, as well as flora and fauna and human figures. Heraldic decoration consisted of motifs and emblems such as cyphers, the "Tree of Life", and human and animal figures.

ABOVE & RIGHT
Monogrammed silk bed- and wall-hangings, and a matching hand-woven rug and chair throw, dominate this Medieval-style bedroom at Leeds Castle, in Kent, England. Prior to the 18th century, monograms were the preserve of the aristocracy and were used to denote ownership or patronage. The colourways here are typical of grand Medieval and early Renaissance interiors.

LEFT Limewashed walls and monogrammed silk hangings provide the backdrop for a military-style, sheer-draped tented washtub at Leeds Castle, England. The woven rush matting provides a near-authentic substitute for the loose rushes that were often laid over wooden floorboards before the 17th century.

16th & 17th Centuries

During the 16th and 17th centuries, interior decoration was marked by an ever-increasing emphasis on domestic comfort, reflecting the spread of prosperity beyond the nobility to the rapidly expanding merchant classes of both Europe and the newly established American colonies. Stylistically, the most significant development was the widespread adoption of Classical (mainly Roman) forms of ornament. Originating in Renaissance Italy, the Classical style was often loosely interpreted in Europe (and later America) via engraved treatises and pattern books. Classical ornament was sometimes combined with Medieval (especially Gothic and Heraldic) types during the 16th century, but virtually supplanted them in the elaborate Baroque interiors of the 17th century. Oriental styles of decoration became popular in the late 17th century as trading links with China and India strengthened.

Architecturally, the 16th century saw the incorporation of geometrically patterned marble, and elaborate marquetry and parquetry floors on the ground level of grander houses; bricks, tiles, stone flags and wooden boards were still in widespread use in most homes. Ceilings still consisted of exposed beams and joists, infilled with limewashed plaster panels. Coarse-plastered and limewashed stone walls were much in evidence, as was exposed studwork in timber-framed houses. However, there was a much greater use of wainscoting throughout the period, either full height or to frieze or dado level. Carved or applied decoration was highly fashionable, with linenfold patterns, arabesques, strapwork and roundels being especially favoured. Panelling made from hardwoods was either left untreated, stained or limed; softwood panelling (particularly prevalent in America) was either flat-painted or, especially in the 17th century, grained in imitation of expensive hardwoods. By the late 16th century transomed

ABOVE The hangings and draperies on this 16th-century bed at Parham House, in Sussex, England, include flamestitch-pattern drapes (*c.* 1615) on the posts, and an embroidered coverlet, back, canopy and mattress valance hand-stitched by Mary, Queen of Scots, *c.* 1585.

RIGHT This wall at St Mary's in Sussex, England, features wood-grained, *trompe l'oeil* arcading, executed by a Flemish painter-stainer for the visit of Queen Elizabeth I of England in 1585.

FAR RIGHT Set against limed oak doors and panelling, the 17th-century furniture at Parham House includes an armchair upholstered with Flemish needlework. The pictorial covering features designs typical of the period.

windows had become as common as Medieval mullions, with diagonally arranged quarries being superseded during the 17th century by larger, rectangular panes.

The most significant development in furniture design was the introduction of upholstery, mostly in the form of back stools and armchairs covered in turkeywork, leather, velvet or tapestry. Such fabrics, together with elaborate crewelwork, damasks, lace and, in the late 17th century, imported cottons (*indiennes*), were also in widespread use as bed- and wall-hangings. Although rush matting was the main form of floor-covering, oriental carpets began to appear on floors at this time, having previously been confined to tabletops.

ABOVE Upholstered seating first appeared in Europe in the 1620s. Favoured fabrics during the 17th century included leather, velvet and, as shown here, flame-stitched tapestry.

LEFT Pale burgundy-painted wall-panelling and stained and polished wooden floor-boards provide a foil for gilt and ebony framed portraits, *chinoiserie* lacquered chairs and Chinese vases.

Early 18th Century

ABOVE Pale colours, such as straw and pearl grey, were popular in the first half of the 18th century. In this New York apartment they provide an understated backdrop for a symmetrical display of botanical watercolours and Queen Anne walnut furniture.

LEFT Rococo elements in this early 18th-century English interior include silk *chinoiserie* upholstery, a swagged nut garland, scallop-shell candle shields and Classical carvings on the furniture and woodwork.

Two quite distinct styles of architecture and decoration dominated the first half of the 18th century. The first, Palladianism, was derived from the writings and engravings of the 16th-century Italian architect Andrea Palladio, and was especially popular in Europe and, from the 1740s, the United States. Classical Roman in origin, the style in its purest form was characterized by bold, austere and, in the grandest houses, large architectural elements, such as Venetian windows. It was also notable for its harmony of proportion and detail. Floorboards were bare wood, augmented with sisal matting or with oriental or turkeywork carpets, and ceilings were plain-plastered or coffered with plaster mouldings. Walls were fully panelled and flat-painted (often in grey and green), wood-grained, or plaster-covered with either silk hangings or hand-painted wallpapers – all providing the backdrop for paintings, prints or engravings. Furniture, much of it made of solid or veneered walnut, was generally sparse. Typical pieces included bureau-bookcases, tripod tables, upholstered armchairs, and occasional and dining chairs. The seating was often upholstered in a fabric that co-ordinated with the window treatment.

In continental Europe, the austerity of Palladian Classicism was superseded from as early as the 1720s by the second distinctive style – Rococo. This was a lighter, exotic, even frivolous look that first appeared in informal buildings such as tea pavilions and garden grottoes. Primarily decorative rather than structural, Rococo was characterized by the use of *rocaille*, *chinoiserie*, *singeries* and Turkish and Indian figures, combined with flowers and foliage, and with light scrollwork and diaper patterns. In England, Rococo was combined with Gothick style, a romanticized revival of elements of Gothic style, such as ogee arches and quatre-foils. However, neither pure Rococo, nor Rococo-Gothick, made a significant impact in America.

ABOVE The window and bed draperies in a bedroom at the Château de Morsan in France are embellished with patterns and motifs inspired by Indian styles of ornament. The walls are hand-painted with delftware-style designs.

RIGHT This painted Rococo settee with ornate *rocaille* and scrolled-leaf carvings has a buttoned velvet squab and is flanked by pairs of topiary sentinels and Kang Hsi vases. The Classical window treatment is typical of early to mid-18th-century reception rooms, and incorporates swagged pull-up sheers, pleated and tied-back yellow silk drapes and a swagged and tailed pelmet embellished with bullion fringing, tassels and fabric rosettes. The plain panelled walls are painted a light yellow – a fashionable colour of the era.

Late 18th Century

ABOVE The most striking feature of this late 18th-century-style New York apartment is the brightly coloured wallpaper. Exotic blooms, birds and insects characterize *chinoiserie* papers of this period.

LEFT Classical Roman motifs embellish the gilded architectural fixtures and fittings and furniture in the French Empire-style *faux*-marble-walled Grand Salon at the Château de Compiègne.

RIGHT Here the bare pine floorboards, grey-white walls divided with cobalt-blue stripes, furniture and striped bed- and window-hangings epitomize late 18th-century Swedish style.

While *chinoiserie* and Gothick remained much in evidence during the second half of the 18th century, especially in Britain, the predominant style of ornament and decoration during this period was Neo-classicism. It emerged in Europe in the 1750s as a reaction to the flamboyant and often frivolous Rococo style, and reached the United States in the 1780s. In many respects it can be seen as a natural development of early 18th-century Palladianism. Like Palladian style, Neo-classicism drew for inspiration on Classical Roman architecture but, unlike Palladianism, it also encompassed ancient Greek ornament. Neo-classicism was drawn from direct observations of Roman and Greek architecture and ornament, made possible by a series of archaeological excavations – notably in Rome, Pompeii and Herculaneum – and the subsequent publication of the illustrated accounts and pattern books of influential architects and designers, such as Robert and James Adam, who visited these sites.

Neo-classical interiors were characterized by an elegance and lightness of style, and a general preference for linear decoration – in marked contrast to the heavier, sculptural qualities of Palladian interiors. For example, plain butt-jointed wooden floorboards, which had been in widespread use in upper storeys for centuries, were now used at ground level. When made from finely figured hardwoods, they were often stained and polished and left uncovered; when of softwoods (such as pine or fir) they were invariably covered with pile carpet which, in the grandest of houses, came from the factories at Savonnerie or Aubusson in France, or Wilton in England. Ceilings were usually smooth, painted plaster, augmented with simple cornice mouldings. However, the grandest featured Neo-classical motifs on painted and gilded plaster panels. Most walls were divided by a dado rail, and either flat-painted or covered

with intricately patterned papers also displaying Neo-classical imagery. Engravings or prints, as well as traditional gilt-framed portrait and landscape paintings, were hung on the walls.

The lightness of ornament that characterized Neo-classicism was mirrored in the furniture of the period – the leading designers of which were Thomas Sheraton and George Hepplewhite. The most fashionable pieces were veneered in satinwood; the most decorative embellished with painted swags of flowers, ornamental bows, and cupids and other mythological or pastoral scenes set in panels. Pieces were usually made from solid or veneered mahogany.

The influence of Neo-classicism spread to 18th-century soft furnishings. Swagged-and-tailed drapes were a common window treatment, while Neo-classical motifs and patterns were featured on both window- and bed-hangings and on upholstered furniture whenever plain fabrics were not used. However, the most striking characteristic of the soft furnishings of the period was the eschewing of lavish, heavyweight fabrics – such as tapestries and woollen velvets – in favour of lightweight silks, printed cottons and sheers.

FAR LEFT Floral-patterned tile slips were often fitted in later 18th-century chimney-pieces, and usually either matched or echoed the floral designs found on upholstery and textile hangings.

CENTRE LEFT Chinese and European styles of ornament are evident in the upholstery and wallpaper in this reconstruction of a late 18th-century French interior. Highly fashionable at the time were flowers, birds and animals, set against vivid yellow grounds.

LEFT The curtain and upholstery fabrics in this late 18th-century drawing room are embellished with plant-form imagery typical of the period. While the top-covers on the painted and gilded chairs and settee show intricate and stylized floral and vegetal patterns, the curtains display naturalistic floral forms that were fashionable from the late 1760s onward.

PREVIOUS PAGES This late-18th-century, Rococo-style French bedroom has been reconstructed in a New York mansion apartment. The pale green walls and ceiling provide a complementary backdrop for a display of engraved fashion plates (published during the reign of Louis XVI of France) and embroidered silk panels. The tasselled draperies on the *lit à la polonaise* are striped and floral Belgian cotton, taken from a documentary design, and are colour co-ordinated with the walls and the floral-patterned table cover.

Early 19th Century

ABOVE Striped fabrics, often embellished with trailing flowers or floral repeats, were the height of fashion in Neo-classical American, English and, as here, French interiors during the early 19th century.

RIGHT & LEFT These two early 19th-century interiors at the Morris Jumel Mansion in New York are decorated and furnished in Empire style. Both feature Neo-classical wallpapers, applied to make a tripartite division of the walls. The day-bed and *lit-en-bateau* are decorated with Classical and Egyptian motifs.

During the early 19th century, interior decoration was still essentially Neo-classical. However, the predominant styles of the period – Empire and Regency – contrasted with the often intricate detailing of late 18th-century Neo-classicism in their employment of purer, simpler Classical forms. They drew inspiration not only from ancient Roman and Greek ornament, but also, in celebration of Napoleon's conquests, from ancient Egyptian and contemporary military motifs.

Empire style originated in France during the late 1790s in the post-revolutionary restorations of French palaces. The basic architectural style of these palaces was Classical, and mostly derived from Imperial Roman rather than Greek examples. Typical motifs applied to architectural fixtures and fittings, furniture and drapery included laurel wreaths, medallions and imperial eagles, as well as animals such as swans and lions.

From *c*. 1820, regional variations began to appear. These included the gradual transformation of American Empire style into a Greek Revival, in which motifs and imagery of Roman origin were supplanted by those of Greek derivation, and, in Britain, the introduction of Regency style, which had much in common with French Empire but which drew more heavily on Greek ornament and incorporated elements of *chinoiserie*. In Austria and Germany a simpler, more functional version of French Empire – known as Biedermeier style – grew in popularity.

A key element of these early 19th-century Neo-classical styles included an increase in the use of fitted cut-pile or Brussels-weave carpets. In most houses, ceilings were generally lower than before and of plain plaster, embellished with a central medallion or garland (from which a chandelier was hung). In larger houses, walls were often divided into frieze, field and dado; in smaller ones the frieze was often omitted in favour of a simple cornice.

Fashionable wall-coverings included flat paint, textiles and wallpapers (mainly pictorial). Swagged and tailed or festooned draperies were also popular, and were usually tied back to flank embroidered lace under-curtains or plain silk blinds. Favoured fabrics for draperies included lightweight silks and floral-patterned chintzes, while damasks and reps proved popular for upholstered seating. Painted *faux* finishes – marbles, porphyries, bronze and woodgrains – were also much in evidence.

Neo-classical furniture was mostly made from mahogany, maple and rosewood. Popular styles included sofa, Pembroke, Loo, and combined work-and-games tables, bow-fronted sideboards and *chiffoniers*, sabre-leg chairs, and *lit-en-bateau* and *chaises-longues*. A new development was the permanent groupings of chairs and tables in reception rooms to facilitate conversation.

ABOVE Re-decorated in its original colour scheme of mauve and yellow, this bedroom in an early 19th-century American mansion in New York features a Federal four-poster bed with an elegant tented and swagged silk canopy.

RIGHT A collection of Duncan Phyfe furniture stands on a hand-woven fitted Savonnerie carpet. The Neo-classical furnishings are enhanced by *faux* marble panelling on the walls.

PREVIOUS PAGES This Welsh interior features a velvet-upholstered *chaise-longue* and a floral-patterned French Aubusson carpet.

FOLLOWING PAGES Vivid yellow walls, drapes and upholstery provide strong colour contrast to the mahogany and ebony furniture in this typical early 19th-century reception room.

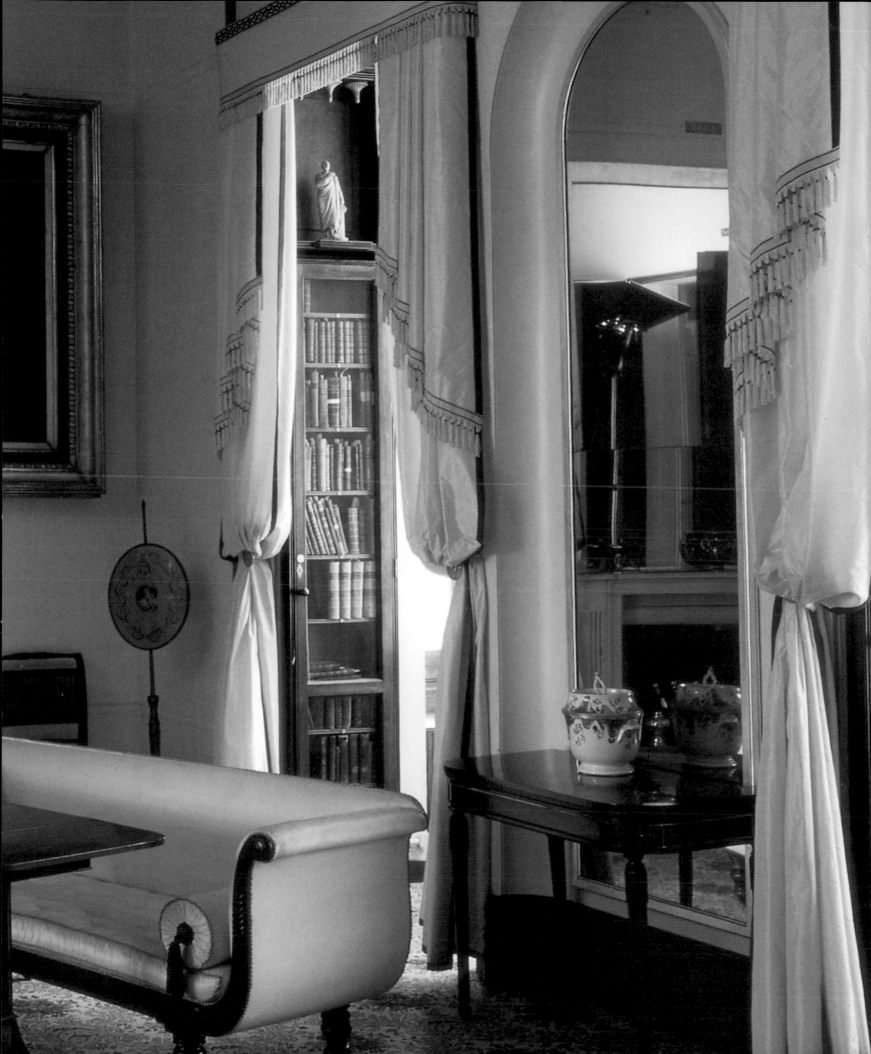

Mid-19th Century

During the middle of the 19th century, an eclectic mix of decorative styles was fashionable on both sides of the Atlantic, the majority of which were revivals of popular styles from previous centuries. They included a Renaissance Revival, based on the 16th-century use of Classical forms (mainly Roman) and relics of Medieval Gothic style; a Baroque Revival (known as Second Empire style in France), which followed the Renaissance Revival and employed Classical architectural detailing, imagery and motifs that were very similar to those employed in the original Baroque style of the 17th century; and a Rococo Revival, derived from the flamboyant 18th-century French Rococo, especially favoured in boudoirs, bedrooms and ladies' drawing rooms. There was also a Greek Revival, a strand of early 19th-century Neo-classicism particularly fashionable in the United States and Britain, and a Gothic Revival, which, unlike the romanticized Gothick style of the late 18th century, was characterized by historically accurate re-creations of Medieval Gothic styles of ornament. In addition to these historic revivals, styles appeared that included motifs and imagery derived from Chinese, Persian, Indian and Arabic ornament, and from primitive African and South American art. These were brought about through increased trade, as well as the travels of architects and ornamentists such as Owen Jones, whose *Grammar of Ornament* (1856) was highly influential.

Although the range of revival or "historical" styles was extensive, and different styles were often employed in different rooms within the same house, most mid-19th-century interiors incorporated a number of common decorative elements. For example, in grander houses, marble slabs or tiles were used on the floors of entrance areas, while in less affluent dwellings simulations of these in linoleum provided a cheaper alternative. However, in most rooms, wooden floorboards were the norm;

ABOVE The smoking room at Cedar Grove, a mid-19th-century American mansion, features a pair of deep red, gold-fringed velvet drapes with elaborate swagged and tailed valances. The carpet is also red and gold – a popular colour combination in mid-Victorian interiors.

RIGHT Ceramic tiles and marble slabs were often employed as floor-coverings in the entrance areas and ground-level hallways of Victorian houses. Geometric patterns were fashionable in the mid-19th century.

LEFT Eclectic groupings of red and yellow damask and striped plush upholstered chairs were often to be found in mid- and late Victorian interiors. However, the dominant feature of this English, Gothic Revival room is the magnificent chimney-piece with its gilded wood and plaster mouldings.

RIGHT Large-scale panoramic or scenic papers were very popular in grander houses in the United States during the middle of the 19th century. Most of them were designed in France by companies such as Zuber, and they were exported in considerable numbers after the fall of Napoleon in 1815. This example shows a sight-seeing tour on a steamboat to the bottom of Niagara Falls.

LEFT The parlour of the 19th-century Monmouth House, in Natchez, Mississippi, USA, is furnished with mid-19th-century mahogany furniture. This armchair, like the rest of the suite, is upholstered with a pale blue silk damask patterned with vases, urns and plant forms derived from Graeco-Roman Classical ornament. The drapes behind are made from the same fabric and secured with rope-and-tassel tie-backs.

these were covered with either a centrally placed, patterned carpet or floorcloth, with the borders stained and polished, stencilled, flat-painted or laid as parquet. Plaster mouldings (cornices and central medallions) – often highly elaborate – also came back into fashion and, while many were flat-painted in a single colour, others were vibrantly polychromatic.

After *c.* 1860, most walls were divided into the classic division of frieze, field and dado. Silk hangings remained a fashionable, if expensive, choice in affluent households, and flat-painting (often augmented with repeat stencil motifs at dado- and picture-rail height) was also employed. However, wallpaper was the principal form of covering following the development of mass-production printing techniques, which made it affordable for the rapidly expanding middle classes.

Faux marble and woodgrained finishes were much in evidence on doors and other woodwork, and on softwood fire-surrounds – the latter a more economical substitute for surrounds made of marble, granite, cast iron and hardwoods such as mahogany. Solid and veneered hardwood furniture was also produced in vast quantities during this period to complement the numerous historical styles. However, the most characteristic pieces were upholstered chairs, settees and sofas, mostly sumptuously stuffed, often deep-buttoned and augmented with cushions, and found in large numbers. The fashion for heavyweight fabrics was extended to the elaborate, layered window treatments of the period, with lined damask, velvet (or plush) and rep much in evidence, topped by large pelmets and drawn or tied back over lace or muslin insertions (either plain or intricately patterned). There was also a profusion of paintings, prints and collections of decorative artefacts, the latter displayed on mantelshelves, in glass-fronted cabinets or on built-in open shelving.

ABOVE This New York interior bears all the hallmarks of the mid-19th-century American Gothic Revival style: these include subdued lighting and ranks of gilt-framed paintings hung against a diaper-pattern wallpaper.

LEFT Standing on a tiled floor in the hall of a manoir near Bordeaux in France, this mid-19th-century mahogany armchair retains its original floral-pattern, cut-velvet upholstery.

FAR LEFT Many stair runners in mid-19th-century houses, as in this American example, displayed either stylized or naturalistic floral patterns set within borders that featured repeated geometric motifs.

Late 19th Century

During the last three decades of the 19th century, the fashion for employing different historical or period-revival styles in different rooms of the same house was still prevalent in Europe and America. It was not unusual to find a Medieval dining room, a Louis XIV drawing room, a Rococo parlour, a Gothic library and a Moresque boudoir under the same roof. However, in the late 1860s a reaction to this eclecticism began to emerge among leading artists and designers, such as William Morris and Charles Eastlake. They wished not only to reintroduce a more coherent decorative style, but also to reduce the "clutter" of Victorian interiors and to re-establish the aesthetic and constructional qualities of pre-industrial, hand-crafted furnishings in the wake of the plethora of poorly designed factory-made goods.

The two closely related styles at the forefront of this reaction to eclectism were the Aesthetic and the Arts and Crafts movements. Both were primarily styles of decoration dependent almost entirely for effect upon colour and pattern, rather than on a particular architectural style. They were successfully applied to houses as architecturally diverse as 15th- or 16th-century, stone-built or timber-framed manor houses, 18th-century townhouses and 19th-century terraces.

The motifs and imagery that appeared on Aesthetic and Arts and Crafts wallpapers, tiles, furniture, soft furnishings and artefacts were derived from Classical, Medieval (Gothic), Renaissance and Chinese and Japanese vocabularies of ornament, with oriental artefacts and motifs being especially favoured by Aesthetic movement designers. Apart from design and good craftsmanship, key elements in Aesthetic and Arts and Crafts schemes included a tripartite division of the walls into frieze, field and dado using three interrelated but distinct wallpaper patterns; colour co-ordination of overmantels to match either the walls or furniture; stained or

ABOVE Swagged, bullion-fringed, silk damask drapes hang in the sitting room at the Calhoun Mansion built in the 1870s in South Carolina, USA.

RIGHT A silk canopy, lace hangings and a lace bedspread furnish this rosewood and walnut half-tester bed in the Garth Woodside Mansion, in Hannibal, Missouri, USA.

LEFT The window treatment at the Calhoun Mansion features silk drapes secured with bullion-fringed tie-backs. It has an elaborate pelmet swagged with matching silk. The deep-buttoned upholstery is also typical of later Victorian interiors.

flat-painted woodwork that acted as a foil for brightly coloured, vegetable- and mineral-dyed papers and fabrics; oriental rugs and carpets, or rush matting, laid over bare wooden floorboards; and groupings of furniture, pictures and ornaments.

In the 1890s, Art Nouveau emerged in Europe and Britain. Peaking in popularity around the turn of the century, and generally out of favour by 1910, the movement took two distinct stylistic paths: one based on austerely elegant, elongated rectilinear forms and tight, precise floral ornament; the other composed of wild, flowing curvilinear elements characterized by restless whiplash lines. Design elements included the use of deep friezes and fields, and a revival in the use of stencilled decoration. "Greenery-yallery" colours such as olive, sage green and mustard were employed, as well as browns, lilacs, violets and muted purples. Stylized vegetal and bird motifs were popular, and there was a preference for artefacts such as ceramics and metalware over pictures. Window treatments were simple, with curtains of plain or mute-patterned fabrics, or abandoned altogether.

LEFT The eclectic nature of many Victorian interiors is shown here. Classical influence is evident in the window treatment and plaster mouldings, while Egyptian motifs adorn the canvaswork panel. The pile-woven rug is Middle Eastern and the upholstery is 19th-century European in style. The willow pattern featured on the ceiling paper is derived from Japanese ornament.

CENTRE LEFT This armchair is covered with a printed paisley pattern fabric that was very popular in late 19th-century interiors. The design is based on pinecones and small incidental motifs found on Indian fabrics. The leopard-spot cushion cover is a typical example of the exotic *faux* animal-skin fabrics favoured at this time.

FAR LEFT The late 19th-century fascination with oriental ornament can be seen in Françoise Lafon's Egyptian-style bedroom. The striped wallpaper and flat-weave carpet are inspired by patterns found on Egyptian textiles. The sand-yellow, pale blue and green colour scheme is also quintessentially Egyptian – the green being *eau-de-nil* (Nile-water green).

PREVIOUS PAGES The Arts and Crafts movement was as influential in the United States in the late 19th century as it was in England, its country of origin. The oak furniture and wall-panelling in this American interior are highly representative of the style. The wallpaper frieze illustrates the extent to which Medieval styles of decoration were rekindled in Arts and Crafts designs.

Early 20th Century

ABOVE This Art Deco living room is in the Geffrye Museum in London, England. It includes abstract-patterned carpeting, geometrically patterned upholstery and an asymmetrical, mottled-tile fire-surround.

LEFT Chocolate brown, black, cream and yellow are recurring colours in Art Deco interiors. The zebra-skin rug laid over a complementary coloured carpet is also typical of the style.

A number of revivalist styles were fashionable in the early 20th century on both sides of the Atlantic. However, the two styles that dominated the period were Art Deco and Modernism.

The term Art Deco was first coined in 1925, and used to describe the displays at the *Exposition Internationale des Arts Décoratifs et Industriels Modernes*. The style was derived from elements in the work of the Deutscher Werkbund and the Wiener Werkstätte, from the early 20th-century art movements of Cubism, Expressionism, Futurism and Fauvism, and from African and native South American art. Prior to the mid-1920s, Art Deco was characterized by the use of rounded and romantic motifs such as garlands and rosebuds. However, during the late 1920s and 1930s these were superseded by abstract and geometric motifs, Egyptian imagery, South American stepped shapes and sun motifs, and emblems suggesting speed and dynamism. Art Deco style was epitomized by clean lines and smooth planes in walls, ceilings, floors and joinery; by contrasting-coloured walls and woodwork; by textiles with geometric or bold floral patterns; and by plump, upholstered sofas and armchairs and other furniture, often veneered with exotic woods or lacquered in black, scarlet or pale yellow and embellished with *chinoiserie* motifs.

Modernist architecture and decoration, avidly adopted on both sides of the Atlantic between the First and Second World Wars, was based upon a desire to render the home, in the words of architect and designer Le Corbusier, a "machine for living in". In practice, this involved shunning unnecessary ornament and highlighting the industrial origins of modern building materials, furniture and textiles. Elements included the use of chrome and glass furniture and fittings, pale walls and ceilings, abstract- or geometric-patterned curtains and carpets (often laid over parquet flooring), and the minimum of displayed artefacts.

LEFT Light colour schemes were very fashionable during the early 20th century. In this eclectic interior, the mint-green painted walls and ceiling provide an unobtrusive and complementary background for the furnishings. Oriental influence is evident in the display cabinet, table-covering and in the stylized plant forms on the rug. African ornament is represented by the *faux* leopard-skin lamp shades, and in the Egyptian motifs on the upholstered chair by the fireplace. The latter is also embellished with Neo-classical floral motifs.

RIGHT Traditional striped and floral patterns remained fashionable for wallpapers during the first half of the 20th century. In this bedroom they are combined in a paper that displays broad blue and white stripes embellished with naturalistic blooms and bouquets (some depicted in Classical Graeco-Roman vases) inspired by 18th-century French decoration.

Late 20th and Early 21st Century

Two broad, discernible trends have been apparent in interior design and decoration since the end of the Second World War: one largely retrospective, the other essentially futuristic. Within the latter category, many architects, designers and manufacturers have enthusiastically embraced new imagery to create innovative styles that simply have not been seen before. The most prominent examples of this appeared from the late 1950s to the mid-1970s, and primarily involved the depiction on fabrics and wallpapers of cellular structures newly exposed by microphotography, and of striking figural, geometric and abstract motifs derived from Pop and Op fine art and Psychedelia. At the same time, new synthetic fibres, plastics and alloys were rapidly adapted to the manufacture of not only textiles and wallpaper, but also furniture – a constantly evolving process.

In contrast, the retrospective movement has been both more extensive and diverse. Comprising a range of historical-revival styles that have been either replications, adaptations or reinterpretations of the originals, it was initially fuelled by an aesthetic rejection of the unremitting rationality and

ABOVE Minimalism inspired by traditional Japanese interiors has been fashionable in the West since the late 20th century. This bedroom is characterized by clean lines, simplicity and lack of clutter.

LEFT The walls of Charles Jencks's 1980s Post-Modernist London residence are painted with colours – and stencilled with small motifs – symbolic of the four seasons. Both the fireplace and mantelshelf columns are *faux*-marbled.

RIGHT This Provençal sitting room, with its yellow-painted, rough-plastered walls, rush seating and earth-coloured upholstery, conveys a sophisticated view of rural calm and simplicity.

minimal use of colour and pattern that characterized Modernist interiors earlier in the 20th century. In many cases this has involved restoring period homes to their original decorative styles, and in many others it has taken the form of often strikingly inventive recolouring and patterning of originally plain, unornamented, Modernist architectural shells.

Specific examples of style revivals in Britain and Europe have included an Art Nouveau revival in the 1960s and early 1970s, and an Art Deco revival in the 1970s and 1980s, while in America Colonial and Federal styles proved fashionable once again during the 1980s and 1990s. Less specific examples have included the "country-house" look, based on the comfortable, chintz-covered rural interiors of the late 19th and early 20th century, but now applied to both urban and rural houses, and a general revival of medieval and, especially, Classical motifs and imagery – Classicism, in all its manifestations, being the least faddish and most enduringly fashionable style of the late 20th and early 21st century.

LEFT Colours, textures and geometric forms, rather than applied patterns, lie at the heart of this late 20th-century decorative scheme. The most striking features of the room are a stone-block fire-surround and a pair of storage cabinets finished with gold leaf. These have been set against an unobtrusive backdrop of mottled green and yellow.

CENTRE LEFT Pale colour schemes incorporating plain or delicate floral-patterned fabrics proved a fashionable treatment for bedrooms for much of the 20th century, particularly from the 1980s.

FAR LEFT During the latter years of the 20th century, some fabric manufacturers, such as Liberty, took traditional patterns and motifs and re-presented them in exciting new colourways. The leaf and sprig motifs on the upholstered chairs boast hot pink and yellow grounds, a theme taken up in the bold, floral-striped curtains and in the coordinated floral-check runner on the table.

In addition to the revival of styles associated with a particular historical period or periods, there has also been a surge in the adoption of the traditional decorative styles of other geographical areas or cultures. Notable imports from the 1980s onward include Japanese-style minimalism – the Post-Modern Modernism; the southern Mediterranean palette, with its luminous whites, dusty terracottas and splashes of pure, vibrant colour; the earth tones and hot candy hues of old rural and modern urban Mexican architecture; and the cooling and/or exotic interiors of North and West Africa.

Significantly, successful reinterpretations or re-creations of all these traditional decorative styles have been made ever more feasible by responsive manufacturers and importers. Quite simply, the ranges of suitable fabrics, wallpapers, tiles, paints and flooring – the building blocks of style – are now more extensive than ever before.

LEFT The understated elegance of African Ivory and Gold Coast interiors is recreated by the designer Decarpentrie in his house in Brussels, Belgium. Flagstone floors, off-white walls, muted-colour textiles and dark-brown wooden furniture and architectural fixtures (the latter often intricately carved) create a cool colour scheme that would offer respite in the fiercest of climates.

BELOW LEFT Late 18th- and early 19th-century Neo-classical style is revived in the living room of Bill Blass's New York apartment. The butt-jointed floorboards, dentilled cornice, marble columns, classical busts and late-Georgian furniture (including daybeds upholstered in a typical Regency stripe) are all period authentic. The colour scheme of whites, creams and shades of brown carried over from the architectural shell to the soft furnishings recalls the elegant simplicity of many Directoire interiors.

FAR LEFT North African Moorish style resonates throughout Zaza Van Hulle's Paris apartment. Geometric-patterned floor tiles, brass trays and lamps, Moroccan-style banquettes, vegetable-dyed kelims and floor cushions, and a profusion of towering vegetation transport the owner from temperate, northern European reality.

FOLLOWING PAGES Classical inspiration is also evident in this sitting room by French designer Yves Gastou. Inherent in the linear symmetry of the architectural shell, it is reinforced by marble statuary and wall-hung torchères, and echoed in the scroll motifs of the carpet. The painting firmly establishes the room as late-20th to early 21st century. However, its yellow, mauve and blue colours – like the rust-reds, terracottas, greys and greens of the soft furnishings – also recall the earth and vegetable pigments of classical antiquity.

Fabrics

Plain Fabrics

Single-colour cloths not embellished with woven or printed patterns are known collectively as "plains", their appeal residing in their colour or texture, or both. Plains include taffetas, cambric, canvas, calico and some tweeds, which have a plain ("tabby") weave of uniform warp and weft threads that pass alternately over and under one another. However, many other fabrics traditionally ascribed to the plains category belie the description "plain" in one of three ways.

First, many "plains" are "self-patterned" by variations within their weave: these include seersuckers, in which alternate bands of tight and slack warps create a puckered effect; ribbed fabrics, such as poplin and rep, which have thick and thin yarns; and zig-zag herringbones. Second, many neutral-colour fabrics, such as slubby silks and noiles, display more than one colour as a result of the presence of naturally occurring "specks" in the fibres. And third, some "plains", such as silk moirés, are dyed one colour, but show variations in tone as a result of "hot-pressing" during the manufacturing process.

LEFT A detail of an Empire-style mahogany daybed, made *c.* 1815 in New York for Nathaniel Russell House, in South Carolina, USA. The bed and its matching bolster are upholstered with a plain yellow silk top-cover that complements the carved and gilded panels (scrolling foliage and shell motifs) along the sides of the bed.

ABOVE Tented ceilings were particularly fashionable in France and England in the early 19th century. They have their origins in the military camps and tournaments of the Middle Ages, and were revived during the Napoleonic wars. The ruched yellow silk example shown here is in a 20th-century re-creation of a Regency bedroom.

COTTON DUCK

Although most fabrics are used for the same purposes today as they were in centuries past, some are now employed in ways never originally intended. For example, cotton duck – the name is derived from the glazed surface which sheds water – is a strong, thick cloth (finer than canvas). During the 19th century it was made of linen and was used to make sails, cooks' aprons, tents and physicians' coats. Nowadays, however, it is often made up into durable slip-covers for chairs and sofas.

KEY DESIGNS

1 Plain-woven fabrics have been made from durable coarse and fine linen since the Middle Ages. Slight stiffness and ease of creasing has made linen weaves better suited to upholstery than to draping.

2 Plain or neutral-coloured herringbones are subtly "self-patterned". Usually made from cotton or linen, they have become increasingly fashionable for upholstery and hangings during the 20th century.

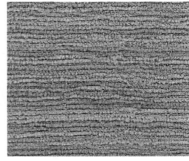

3 Plain-coloured pile fabrics, such as cut or uncut velvets and velours, have been favoured since the Renaissance, and used for upholstered furniture in particular in mid-19th-century interiors.

4 Many plains are employed for their texture as much as for their colour – coarseness of texture being determined by type of weave and thickness of yarn(s), in this case a cotton-viscose mix.

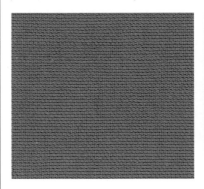

5 Fine plain-weave cottons are well-suited to monochromatic dyeing – both vegetable and synthetic. As they drape well they are often employed for window- and bed-hangings, and for loose covers.

6 Plain-weave silks are also ideal for monochromatic dyeing, and display pure, saturated colours that have been exploited by interior designers from the Renaissance to the present day.

1 De Le Cuona/Hopsack Moss Colour **F4** Alt. colours **yes** Composition **100% linen** Width **140cm/55in** Repeat **–** Price ★★

2 Ian Mankin/Stripe Jacquard Colour **natural** Alt. colours **no** Composition **100% cotton** Width **137cm/54in** Repeat **–** Price ★

3 Jab/Maharadscha Colour **red** Alt. colours **yes** Composition **100% silk** Width **122cm/ 48in** Repeat **–** Price ★★

4 Harlequin/Assisi/Siena Colour **433** Alt. colours **yes** Composition **13% cotton, 87% viscose** Width **140cm/55in** Repeat **–** Price ★★

5 Olicana/Calypso Colour **cayman blue** Alt. colours **yes** Composition **100% cotton** Width **145cm/57in** Repeat **–** Price ★★

6 Seamoor Fabrics/Kaleidoscope Colour **crushed rose** Alt. colours **yes** Composition **100% cotton** Width **120cm/47in** Repeat **–** Price ★

Plains

Some plain neutral-coloured furnishing fabrics are produced by tinting the fibres from which they are made with pale dyes (either vegetable or synthetic). Other "neutrals", such as cambric, are bleached to whiten the fibres. However, many of the "neutrals" considered fashionable in this and previous centuries rely for colour on the natural pigmentation of their fibre(s). Notable examples include unbleached calico, which is a creamy colour relieved by small brown flecks of cottonseed that remain in the cotton yarn; brown Holland, an unbleached, closely woven, pale brown linen popular for window shades during the 18th and 19th centuries; black and white horsehair fabrics, woven from unadulterated horsehair of those colours and favoured for upholstery since the 18th century; neutral-coloured slub silks and noiles, which display the grainy brown specks inherent in natural, unbleached silk fibre; and Tussah silk, produced from cocoons spun by wild silkworms, which produce a textured, pale brown yarn.

1

2

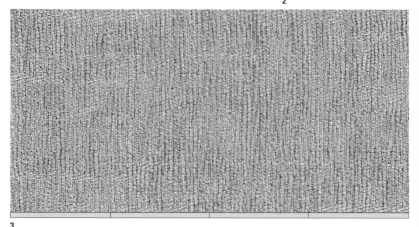
3

1 **De Le Cuona/Storm Italian Straw** Colour **NN2** Alt. colours **yes** Composition **100% linen** Width **140cm/55in** Repeat – Price ★★★ 🛋

2 **De Le Cuona/Peasant Cloth String** Colour **AA1** Alt. colours **yes** Composition **100% linen** Width **135cm/53in** Repeat – Price ★★★ LC 🎴🛋

3 **Harlequin/Assissi/Siena** Colour **431** Alt. colours **yes** Composition **13% cotton, 87% viscose** Width **140cm/55in** Repeat – Price ★★ 🛋🎴

4 **De Le Cuona/Shale Butterscotch** Colour **BB3** Alt. colours **yes** Composition **100% linen** Width **150cm/59in** Repeat – Price ★★★ 🎴

5 **Ian Sanderson/Sophia** Colour **creme** Alt. colours **yes** Composition **83% viscose, 17% cotton** Width **140cm/55in** Repeat – Price ★★ 🛋

4

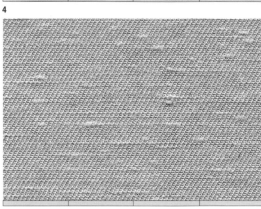
5

6

6 **Malabar/Flote** Colour **Caramel** Alt. colours **yes** Composition **72% cotton, 28% viscose** Width **135cm/53in** Repeat – Price ★★ 🎴⊞�🛋

7 **De Le Cuona/Coast Jade** Colour **H1** Alt. colours **yes** Composition **100% linen** Width **148cm/58¼in** Repeat – Price ★★★ 🎴🛋 LC

8 **Ian Sanderson/Verity Silk** Colour **Duck Egg** Alt. colours **yes** Composition **55% silk, 45% linen** Width **140cm/55in** Repeat – Price ★★ 🎴⊞ W

HORSEHAIR FABRIC

Woven from horse mane and tail hairs on a silk, cotton, linen or wool warp, horsehair fabric has been used for upholstery since the early 18th century, on Chippendale and Hepplewhite chairs notably. Favoured colours have included black, green, grey, gold, red and ivory.

John Boyd Textiles/Ricana RI/620/6 Colour **ivory** Alt. colours **yes** Composition **68% horsehair, 32% cotton** Width **56cm/22in** Repeat – Price ★★★ 🛋 W

John Boyd Textiles/Criollo CR/227 Colour **light grey** Alt. colours **yes** Composition **68% horsehair, 32% cotton** Width **65cm/25¼in** Repeat – Price ★★★ 🛋 W

7

8

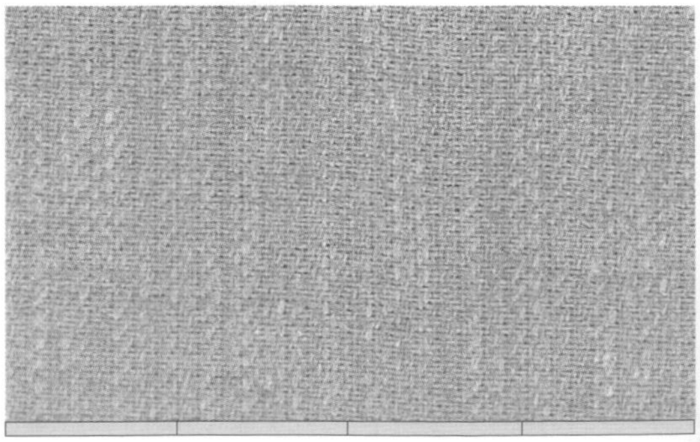

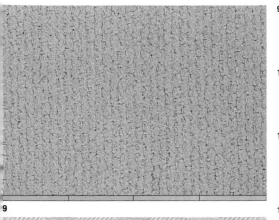

9

9 De Le Cuona/Magma Velvet
Sable Colour **Y2** Alt. colours
yes Composition **100% linen**
Width **140cm/55in** Repeat –
Price ★★★ ⌂⌂⌂⌂

10 Ian Mankin/Pavilion Jacquard
Colour **natural** Alt. colours
no Composition **100% cotton**
Width **137cm/54in** Repeat
2cm/¾in Price ★ ⌂⌂⌂

11 Hodsoll McKenzie/Plain Repp
356/101-106 Colour **natural**
Alt. colours **yes** Composition
76% cotton, 24% silk Width
127cm/50in Repeat –
Price ★★★ ⌂⌂⌂ⓦ

10

12 Brunschwig & Fils/Petassoun
Matelassé **89462** Colour **008
ivory** Alt. colours **yes**
Composition **72% cotton,
28% viscose** Width **147cm/
58in** Repeat **36cm/14in**
Price ★★★ ⌂

13 Marvic Textiles/Misa Moiré
Plain **6565-54** Colour **daisy**
Alt. colours **yes** Composition
52% linen, 48% viscose Width
140cm/55in Repeat –
Price ★★ ⌂⌂⌂

14

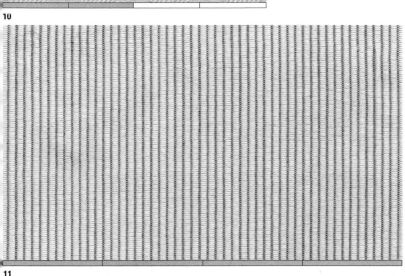

11

14 Olicana/Finistere Colour **white**
Alt. colours **no** Composition
100% cotton Width **130cm/51in**
Repeat – Price ★★ ⌂⌂⌂

15 De Le Cuona/Hornbuckle Milk
Colour **NNN4** Alt. colours **yes**
Composition **50% wool, 50%
polyester** Width **150cm/59in**
Repeat – Price ★★ ⌂

16 De Le Cuona/Shale True Taupe
Colour **BB5** Alt. colours **yes**
Composition **100% linen**
Width **150cm/59in** Repeat –
Price ★★★ ⌂⌂

17 Harlequin/Metzo Colour **690**
Alt. colours **yes** Composition
92% polyester, 8% viscose
Width **140cm/55in** Repeat –
Price ★★ ⌂

18 Larsen/Cybele **L8565** Colour
10 Silver Dust Alt. colours
yes Composition **51% nylon,
49% polyester** Width **150cm/
59in** Repeat – Price ★★ ⌂⌂

19 Marvic Textiles/Moiré Celeste
47-4 Colour **primula** Alt.
colours **yes** Composition
**39% cotton, 35% viscose, 2
6% linen** Width **150cm/59in**
Repeat – Price ★★ ⌂⌂⌂ⓦ

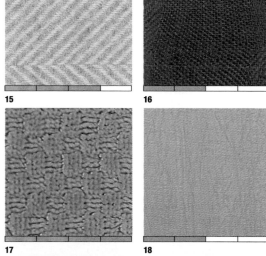

15　16

17　18

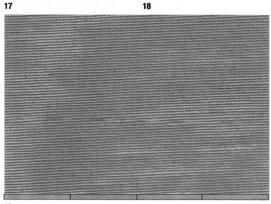

12　13

19

Pre-17th century

17th century

18th century

19th century

20th & 21st century

Plains

Plain fabrics rely heavily on both their colour and their texture for decorative effect. The appearance of any particular colour is affected by a number of factors, ranging from the texture of the fabric and the nature of the weave to the angle and intensity of natural or artificial light to which the fabric is exposed. In other words, the same coloured dye will look markedly different on a ribbed wool or worsted rep (a closely woven ribbed fabric) from how it will on a smooth satin-weave silk. However, the look of colour is affected by more than the physical properties of the fibres to which the colour is applied and the environmental conditions under which the fabrics are used and displayed. The nature of the pigments used also contributes to the appearance of a plain fabric. For example, in the mid-19th century synthetic aniline dyes were developed by extracting benzine oil from coal tar and combining it with acids. The result was a wide range of new, vibrantly coloured pigments that appeared gradually from the 1850s to the 1880s. Notable among them were "mauveine", magenta, various purple-blues and greens, Manchester brown and yellow, Congo blue and a synthetic substitute for indigo.

Jab/Maharadscha 6943-211 Colour **orange** Alt. colours **yes** Composition **100% silk** Width **122cm/48in** Repeat – Price ★★

Osborne & Little/Ghillie Wool F1241 Colour **02** Alt. colours **yes** Composition **92% wool, 8% nylon** Width **140cm/55in** Repeat – Price ★★★

Zimmer & Rohde/Option 1910 Colour **162** Alt. colours **yes** Composition **52% cotton, 48% polyester** Width **140cm/55in** Repeat – Price ★★★

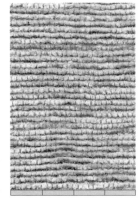

Abbott & Boyd/Albarracin 9740-0 Colour **cream** Alt. colours **yes** Composition **70% cotton, 28% viscose, 2% polyester** Width **138cm/54in** Repeat – Price ★★★

Scalamandré/Adriatic Antique Taffeta 5870-028 Colour **maize** Alt. colours **yes** Composition **100% silk** Width **142cm/55½in** Repeat – Price ★★★

Monkwell/MF 5787 Colour **806 Bison Cherry** Alt. colours **yes** Composition **98% polyester, 2% cotton** Width **137cm/53¾in** Repeat – Price ★

Olicana/Yachting Cotton Colour **red rag** Alt. colours **yes** Composition **100% cotton** Width **137cm/54in** Repeat – Price ★★

Zimmer & Rohde/Priya 6989-226 Colour **tan** Alt. colours **yes** Composition **100% silk** Width **120cm/47in** Repeat – Price ★★★

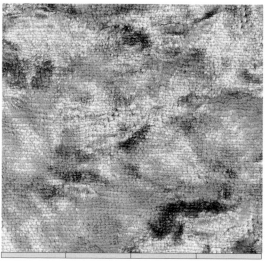

Osborne & Little/Nomad Plain Moiré F1281 Colour **02** Alt. colours **yes** Composition **36% viscose, 32% wool, 16% cotton, 16% polyamide** Width **140cm/55in** Repeat – Price ★★★

Abbott & Boyd/Traviata Colour **05** Alt. colours **yes** Composition **77% viscose, 23% polyamide** Width **140cm/55in** Repeat – Price ★★★★

Harlequin/Assisi/Siena Colour **436** Alt. colours **yes** Composition **13% cotton, 87% viscose** Width **140cm/55in** Repeat – Price ★★

Donghia/Piega 0488/9325 Colour **18** Alt. colours **yes** Composition **55% cotton, 23% polyester, 13% polyacrylic, 9% viscose** Width **133cm/52in** Repeat – Price ★★★★

Osborne & Little/F5023 Colour **05** Alt. colours **yes** Composition **82% (poly)cotton, 18% polyester/viscose** Width **145cm/57in** Repeat – Price ★★★

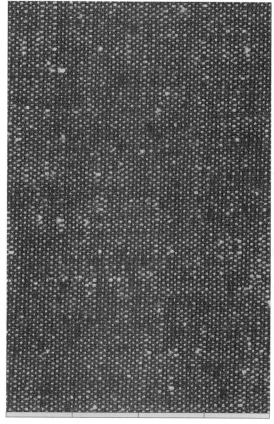

an Sanderson/Sophia Colour **sungold** Alt. colours **yes** Composition **83% viscose, 17% cotton** Width **140cm/55in** Repeat – Price ★★

Jab/Tosca 1-6048 Colour **449** Alt. colours **yes** Composition **100% silk** Width **140cm/55in** Repeat – Price ★★★

Zimmer & Rohde/Tango 9215 Colour **371** Alt. colours **yes** Composition **100% viscose** Width **140cm/55in** Repeat – Price ★★

FABRICS: *PLAINS* **67**

Plains

Synthetic dyes and colours were first introduced in the 1850s and continued to be developed and used during the 20th century. However, many consider that they can never match the chromatic intensity and purity of colour obtained from traditional vegetable dyes – a contemporary view that echoes William Morris's negative reaction to the artificiality and "garishness" of the aniline dyes of the 19th century and his advocacy of a return to the use of vegetable and mineral dyes.

There is no doubt that, when it comes to colour, new technology and increased industrialization do not automatically equate to higher quality. Indeed, the brilliance, intensity, subtle variation and diversity of hue of vegetable dyes used from the Middle Ages to the mid-19th century (and enjoying a revival today) will probably never be matched synthetically. For example, during the 17th century "drugs" from the Orient and the Americas, such as saffron, indigo, quercitron and brazilwood, were employed to produce a vast spectrum of tints, including greens as diverse as parakeet, emerald, carnation, duck and moss, and a palette of 12 different shades of blue.

6

1

2

3

4

7

1 Antico Setificio Fiorentino/ **Tela di Seta T1** Colour **green/gold** Alt. colours **yes** Composition **100% silk** Width **120cm/47in** Repeat – Price ★★★ LC 〔〕 ⌂ W

2 Zimmer & Rohde/**Donna 5083** Colour **583** Alt. colours **yes** Composition **77% cotton, 18% silk** Width **132cm/51¾in** Repeat – Price ★★★ 〔〕

3 Zoffany/**Boston Plain BOS0101** Colour **6** Alt. colours **yes** Composition **95% viscose, 5% silk** Width **144cm/56½in** Repeat – Price ★★ LC 〔〕 ⌂

4 George Spencer Designs/ **Strie 011L/09** Colour **lime** Alt. colours **yes** Composition **79% linen, 21% silk** Width **140cm/55in** Repeat – Price ★★★ 〔〕 ⌂

5 Designers Guild/**Diagonale F563/11** Colour **green** Alt. colours **yes** Composition **100% cotton** Width **140cm/55in** Repeat – Price ★★ ⌂

6 Liberty Furnishings/Savile Weaves/**Plain LF4171** Colour **10** Alt. colours **yes** Composition **100% wool** Width **130cm/51in** Repeat – Price ★★★ LC 〔〕 ⊞ ⌂ W

7 Antico Setificio Fiorentino/ **Spinone Melangé 52** Colour **green** Alt. colours **yes** Composition **60% silk, 40% linen** Width **130cm/51in** Repeat – Price ★★★ 〔〕 ⌂

8 Marvic Textiles/**Misa Moiré Plain 6565-56** Colour **jungle** Alt. colours **yes** Composition **52% linen, 48% viscose** Width **140cm/55in** Repeat – Price ★★ 〔〕 ⌂ W

9 Zimmer & Rohde/**Alto 1928** Colour **718** Alt. colours **yes** Composition **53% cotton, 34% fleece wool, 13% polyester** Width **140cm/55in** Repeat – Price ★★★ ⌂

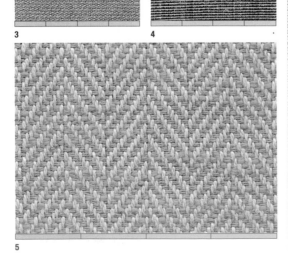

5

8

9

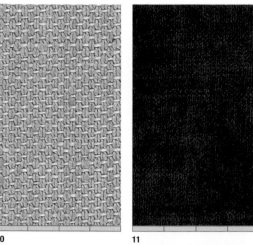

10

11

10 Malabar/Jutka Colour sky
Alt. colours **yes** Composition
50% cotton, 50% linen Width
137cm/53¾in Repeat –
Price ★★ 🗒 ⊞ LC 🛋

11 Today Interiors/Silki SK 23
Colour **windsor blue** Alt.
colours **yes** Composition
**57% viscose, 31% cotton,
12% polyester** Width
140cm/55in Repeat –
Price ★★ 🗒 🛋

12 Zimmer & Rohde/Corela 1913
Colour **663** Alt. colours **yes**
Composition **57% cotton, 43%
viscose** Width **140cm/55in**
Repeat – Price ★★ 🛋

**13 Malabar/Suliman Colour
cochineal** Alt. colours **yes**
Composition **100% silk**
Width **122cm/48in** Repeat –
Price ★★ 🗒 ⊞

**14 Olicana/Calypso Colour
paradisian pink** Alt. colours
yes Composition **100% cotton**
Width **145cm/57in** Repeat –
Price ★★ 🗒 🚗

**15 Liberty Furnishings/Plume
Chenille LF4280** Colour **18**
Alt. colours **yes** Composition
**45% viscose, 30% cotton, 25%
polyester** Width **146cm/57½in**
Repeat – Price ★★ LC 🗒 🛋

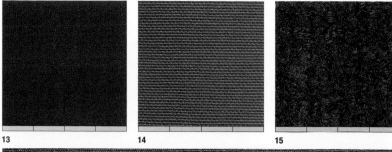

13   14   15

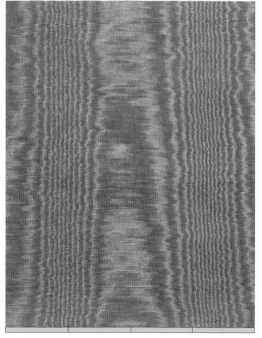

12

16

MOIRÉS

Fashionable since
the early 18th century,
moirés are ribbed
fabrics on to which
clouded or watered
(wave-like) effects are
imposed by passing
them between heavy
iron or copper rollers.
Traditionally, the fabric
is left dry while it is
subjected to intense,
uneven pressure from
the rollers. However,
liquid and heat can
also be applied. Most
moirés are made of
heavy silk, but some
are wool or worsted.
From the 20th century
moirés have often
been made from rayon
or are a mixture of
cotton and viscose.

Marvic Textiles/Marvic Moiré 45-27 Colour **leman** Alt. colours **yes**
Composition **58% cotton, 42% viscose** Width **136cm/53½in**
Repeat – Price ★★ 🗒 🛋 W

17

18   19

**16 Zimmer & Rohde/Idris 6991-
556** Colour **blue** Alt. colours
yes Composition **100% silk**
Width **135cm/53in** Repeat –
Price ★★★ 🗒 🛋

17 Designers Guild/Laelia F558/01
Colour **blue** Alt. colours **yes**
Composition **100% cotton**
Width **137cm/54in** Repeat –
Price ★★ 🛋

**18 Today Interiors/Palio/Drago
CH850027** Colour **27** Alt.
colours **yes** Composition
**40% cotton, 42% viscose,
10% linen, 8% nylon** Width
140cm/55in Repeat **1.7cm/⅝in**
Price ★★ 🗒 🛋

19 Today Interiors/Kariba KB 4078
Colour **green** Alt. colours **yes**
Composition **71% viscose,
21% cotton, 8% polyester**
Width **140cm/55in** Repeat –
Price ★★★ 🗒 🛋

Patterned Pile

Traditionally woven from silk, mohair, wool, worsted or cotton, pile fabrics have been produced for drapery since the Middle Ages, and for upholstery since the 17th century. The best-known are Genoa, Utrecht and *gaufrage* velvets. Related types include moquette ("mock velvet"), chenille ("poor man's velvet"), plush (a wool velvet), Manchester velvet (a cotton variety), velour (cotton) and corduroy (also cotton). All are distinguished by their raised pile, which consists of rows of loops woven into a simple ground weave. The loops can be cut, which gives them a fur-like texture, or left uncut. The direction of the pile, and the angle at which light strikes it, determine the density and sheen of the colours, which can vary from dark matt to bright and shimmering. Patterns are created during weaving, or stamped on afterward with a metal plate or cylinder. If the pattern is woven leaving areas of ground weave exposed, the fabric is referred to as "voided"; alternatively, if the ground is completely covered with patterned pile, the fabric is described as "solid".

LEFT This modern square-framed armchair is covered with "Murskaya" fabric from the Designers Guild Inessa collection. Leaf patterns have been popular for centuries, but this colour combination – a vibrant electric blue against a pale earthy hue – is very 21st century. Typically, the use of a voided ground enhances the three-dimensionality of the raised-pile leaf motifs.

ABOVE This 19th-century painted chair from France has been reupholstered with a flamboyant cut-pile velvet. The naturalistic red and green flower-and-leaf pattern is well defined by a contrasting pale yellow ground weave. The back of the chair nestles into a pair of heavy yellow silk damask curtains.

SELF-PATTERNS

When recreating this typical mid-19th-century interior, Swiss designer Christophe Gollut used a voided cut-pile velvet to upholster the mahogany seating. With the ground weave exposed, a voided pattern will allow the manufacturer to produce a self-coloured pattern in the pile, so creating a damask effect (see pages 76–85), and giving the pattern increased texture and definition.

KEY DESIGNS

1 Naturalistic floral patterns have been a recurring theme in patterned pile fabrics. Here raised-pile flowers and leaves are rendered in golden yellow, sage green and pale brown on a rust-brown ground.

2 Stylized foliage is among the most traditional of pile-fabric patterns. This example has a woven pile, but gaufrage (stamped) foliage patterns have also proved popular since the 16th century.

3 Overall pattern repeats of small motifs, such as the plant forms on this Empire-style chenille, became easier to produce following the invention of the dobby loom in 1824.

4 Such formalized fruit and foliage patterns as this were derived from oriental and classical ornament. They have appeared on patterned pile fabrics since the Renaissance.

5 Inspired by military bunting, striped velvets were very fashionable in the late 18th and early 19th century. This example features a cut blue-stripe pile on a sage-green ground.

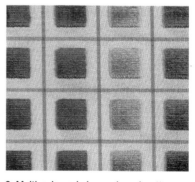

6 Multi-coloured chequerboard-pattern pile fabrics such as this one were popular during the Renaissance, and came back into vogue during the latter part of the 20th century.

1 **Monkwell/MF 5859** Colour **800 rust** Alt. colours **yes** Composition **48% acrylic, 28% cotton, 24% polyester** Width **137cm/53¾in** Repeat **56cm/22in** Price ★★ ⊞ 🛋

2 **Mulberry/Baroque Vine FD338** Colour **J103 cream** Alt. colours **yes** Composition **85% cotton, 10% viscose, 5% polyamide** Width **145cm/57in** Repeat **40cm/15¾in** Price ★★★ LC 🔀 ⊞ 🛋 W

3 **Hodsoll McKenzie/Empire Chenille 093/124** Colour **124** Alt. colours **yes** Composition **100% cotton** Width **127cm/50in** Repeat **5.5cm/2¼in** Price ★★★ 🔀 ⊞ 🛋 W

4 **Lelièvre/Ravenne 647** Colour **02** Alt. colours **yes** Composition **39% cotton, 32% viscose, 29% Bemberg** Width **130cm/51in** Repeat **57cm/22¼in** Price ★★★★★ LC 🔀 🛋

5 **Percheron/Robespierre** Colour **green/blue** Alt. colours **yes** Composition **69% viscose, 31% cotton** Width **130cm/51in** Repeat – Price ★★ 🔀 ⊞ 🛋 W

6 **Old World Weavers/San Marco Square** Colour **multi** Alt. colours **yes** Composition **69% cotton, 31% silk** Width **130cm/51in** Repeat – Price ★★★★★ 🛋

Patterned Pile: **Pre-20th century**

Prior to the 20th century, pile fabrics were produced in numerous colours and patterns. Silk Genoa velvet (made since the Renaissance) has always been the most expensive. It features a multi-coloured pile (cut or uncut) on a satin ground and is patterned during weaving. Less costly Utrecht and *gaufrage* velvets have patterns produced by a stamping process. Alternatives include: moquette (produced since the 16th century), which has a wool warp pile (usually cut) on a linen ground, and woven or stamped patterns; chenille (first seen in the 19th century), a fabric woven from cut and twisted woven cloth, with a fuzzy pile; plush (from the late 17th century), which is a double-warp fabric, of wool and hair (or silk) with woven or stamped patterns and a longer but less dense pile than velvet; and, since the 18th century, Manchester velvet (*see page 70*) and velour (the latter having a short lustrous cotton-warp pile).

1

2

3

5

6

4

7

8

1 Old World Weavers/Sahara SX 02342149 Colour **beige and green** Alt. colours **yes** Composition **47% rayon, 32% acrylic, 21% cotton** Width **140cm/55in** Repeat **47cm/18½in** Price ★★★ 🛋

2 Beaumont & Fletcher/Augustus Chenille 1005C Colour **red/grey** Alt. colours **yes** Composition **90% cotton, 10% wool** Width **140cm/55in** Repeat **28.5cm/11in** Price ★★★ 🛋

3 Hodsoll McKenzie/Turkish Flower 303/101 Colour **coral** Alt. colours **yes** Composition **100% cotton** Width **127cm/ 50in** Repeat **8cm/3in** Price ★★★ 🔲🛋 Ⓦ

4 Lelièvre/Ravenne 647-01 Colour **emeraude** Alt. colours **yes** Composition **39% cotton, 32% viscose, 29% Bemberg** Width **130cm/ 51in** Repeat **57cm/22½in** Price ★★★★★ 🄻🄲 🔲🔳🛋

5 The Silk Gallery/Cantabile Colour **maroon silk, gold chenille** Alt. colours **yes** Composition **83% cotton, 17% silk** Width **127cm/ 50in** Repeat **38cm/15in** Price ★★★ 🔲🛋

6 Old World Weavers/Aracelis Colour **wine** Alt. colours **yes** Composition **54% viscose, 43% acrylic, 3% polypropylene** Width **137cm/54in** Repeat **24cm/9½in** Price ★★★ 🛋

7 Ian Sanderson/Pendragon Colour **coral** Alt. colours **yes** Composition **58% cotton, 24% polyacrylic, 18% viscose** Width **140cm/55in** Repeat **63cm/ 24¾in** Price ★★★ 🔲🛋

8 Old World Weavers/Corda Matisse Colour **gold** Alt. colours **yes** Composition **67% viscose, 33% cotton** Width **130cm/51in** Repeat **66cm/26in** Price ★★★★ 🛋

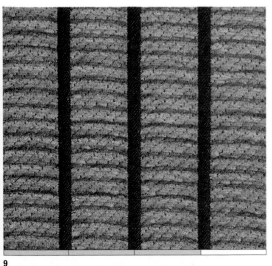

9

10

9 The Silk Gallery/Chenille II
Colour **henna and gold** Alt.
colours **yes** Composition
83% cotton, 17% silk Width
127cm/50in Repeat –
Price ★★★ 🛋

10 Old World Weavers/Leopard
Velvet Y00 6900001 Colour
gold and brown Alt. colours
no Composition **57% silk,
30% cotton, 13% viscose** Width
132cm/51¼in Repeat **73.5/
28¼in** Price ★★★★★ 🛋

11 Hodsoll McKenzie/Star Chenille
301 Colour **106** Alt. colours
yes Composition **100%
cotton** Width **127cm/50in**
Repeat **10.5cm/4in**
Price ★★★ 🎴🛋 W

12 Watts of Westminster/Pine
Colour **brick and leaf green**
Alt. colours **yes** Composition
100% cotton chenille Width
124cm/48¾in Repeat **79cm/31in**
Price ★★★★ 🎴🛋

13 Mulberry/Aubusson Chenille
FD001/508 Colour **S103** Alt.
colours **yes** Composition
75% cotton, 25% wool Width
150cm/59in Repeat **131cm/
51½in** Price ★★★ 🎴⊞🛋

14 Old World Weavers/Velours
Marmara FV6 7028007 Colour
green Alt. colours **yes**
Composition **75% rayon,
25% cotton** Width **135cm/53in**
Repeat – Price ★★★ 🛋

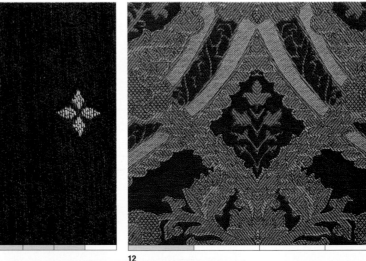

11

12

13

14

15 Zoffany/La Scala VRS
Colour **07** Alt. colours **yes**
Composition **66% linen,
34% cotton** Width **130cm/51in**
Repeat – Price ★★★ 🎴🛋

16 Zimmer & Rohde/Filion 1278
Colour **184** Alt. colours **yes**
Composition **64% polyester,
36% viscose** Width **144cm/
56½in** Repeat **5cm/2in**
Price ★★★★ 🛋

17 Sahco Hesslein/Eroica 04630
Colour **green and yellow**
Alt. colours **yes** Composition
57% cotton, 43% viscose
Width **130cm/51in** Repeat –
Price ★★★★ LC🛋

18 Scalamandré/Billingsley
26594-007 Colour **beige, rust**
Alt. colours **yes** Composition
**55% wool, 45% acrylic
chenille** Width **152cm/
60in** Repeat **59cm/23in**
Price ★★★★ LC🎴🛋

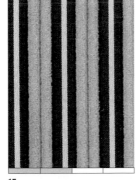

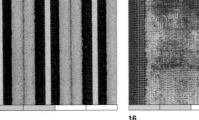

15

16

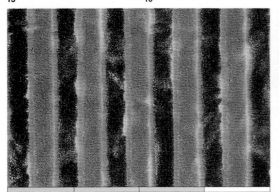

17

18

FABRICS: *PATTERNED PILE*   **73**

Patterned Pile: 20th–early 21st century

Toward the end of the 19th century, patterned pile fabrics suffered a dip in popularity. Because of their densely woven pile, they were viewed by many arbiters of household taste as dust-traps, particularly when heavily draped around beds, over doors or at windows; at the latter, they were also deemed to hinder the entrance of "health-giving" sunlight. In reality, such views were less a concern for health and more an aesthetic reaction to overfurnished and often gloomy "High Victorian" interiors. Patterned pile fabrics enjoyed a resurgence of popularity at the beginning of the 20th century, and, except in minimal Modernist interiors, their use has been sustained to this day.

Manufacturers have continued to produce a wide range of patterned pile fabrics, notably Genoa and *gaufrage* velvets, as well as chenille and velour. Most are intended for curtains and as top-covers for upholstery. Generally, patterns have remained traditional, with floral, leaf or fruit motifs, and stripes and checks being most in demand. As in previous centuries, silk, mohair, wool and cotton yarns are still used in the production of pile fabrics, although, since 1945, synthetic yarns, such as Dralon, have also been employed.

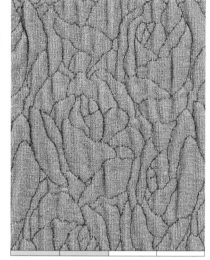

Donghia/Rugose 0556/6480-10 Colour **cavolo-cream**
Alt. colours **yes** Composition **80% viscose, 12% polyester, 8% polyacrylic** Width **133cm/52in**
Repeat **9cm/3½in** Price ★★★★★

Mulberry/Valais Chenille FD348 Colour **J103 cream**
Alt. colours **yes** Composition **100% cotton**
Width **130cm/51in** Repeat **31cm/12in**
Price ★★★

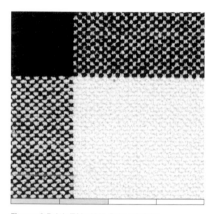

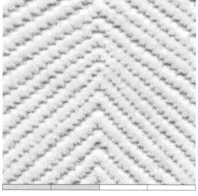

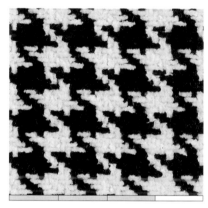

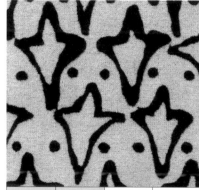

Zimmer & Rohde/Dido 1258 Colour **989** Alt. colours **yes** Composition **100% cotton** Width **140cm/55in** Repeat **22cm/8½in** Price ★★★

Sahco Hesslein/Akka 04614 Colour **cream** Alt. colours **no** Composition **100% cotton** Width **140cm/55in** Repeat – Price ★★★

Zimmer & Rohde/Dina 1260 989 Colour **black and cream** Alt. colours **yes** Composition **100% cotton** Width **140cm/55in** Repeat **2cm/¾in** Price ★★★

Bentley & Spens/Lilies Colour **black/grey** Alt. colours **no** Composition **100% cotton** Width **130cm/51in** Repeat **49cm/19¼in** Price ★★★★★ (special order)

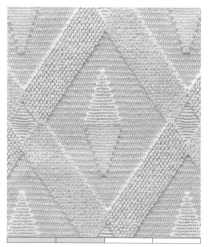

Sahco Hesslein/Akkord 04625 Colour **cream** Alt. colours **no** Composition **68% cotton, 32% viscose** Width **140cm/55in** Repeat **13cm/5in** Price ★★★

POPULAR ANIMAL MOTIFS

Although animal motifs have been regularly used to ornament fabrics since the Middle Ages, they have proved to be particularly popular since the last quarter of the 19th century. The patterned-pile upholstered armchair shown here displays a pride of lions. Although the textile design was created in the late 20th century, it strongly echoes the fabrics embellished with antelopes, gazelles, lions and other exotic African animals that were in vogue throughout much of Europe during the 1920s and 1930s.

Andrew Martin/Pride Colour **taupe** Alt. colours **yes** Composition **face: 100% cotton; back: 72% polyester, 28% rayon** Width **140cm/55in** Repeat **30cm/11¾in** Price ★★

Pierre Frey/Brigitte Bardot/Rivoli 2150 Colour **anthracite** Alt. colours **yes** Composition **77% viscose, 23% cotton** Width **130cm/51in** Repeat **2cm/¾in** Price ★★★

Glant/Labyrinth 9020 Colour **aqua** Alt. colours **yes** Composition **100% cotton** Width **130cm/51in** Repeat – Price ★★★★

Brunschwig & Fils/Altena Velvet 53293 Colour **01** Alt. colours **yes** Composition **78% polyester, 22% cotton** Width **140cm/55in** Repeat **23cm/9in** Price ★★★★

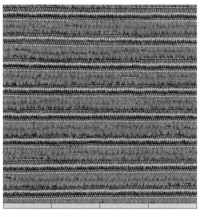

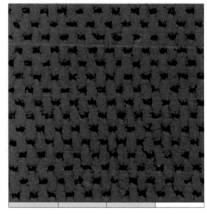

Brunschwig & Fils/Bichon Chenille Plaid 46091 Colour **02** Alt. colours **yes** Composition **60% rayon, 40% cotton** Width **142cm/55¾in** Repeat **15cm/6in** Price ★★★★

Jab/Studio 1-3024-138 Colour **green 138** Alt. colours **yes** Composition **100% cotton** Width **140cm/55in** Repeat – Price ★★★

Jab/Tampa 1-2011-581 Colour **green and blue** Alt. colours **yes** Composition **100% cotton** Width **140cm/55in** Repeat – Price ★★★

Glant/Chaine 3050 Colour **grape 08** Alt. colours **yes** Composition **100% cotton** Width **130cm/51in** Repeat – Price ★★★★

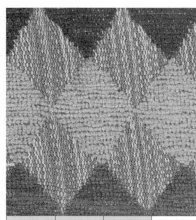

Zimmer & Rhode/Bamboo 5096 Colour **349** Alt. colours **yes** Composition **83% viscose, 17% cotton** Width **138cm/54in** Repeat **34cm/13½in** Price ★★★★

Ian Sanderson/Jester Colour **Harvest** Alt. colours **yes** Composition **84% viscose, 16% cotton** Width **140cm/55in** Repeat **42cm/16½in** Price ★★★

Old World Weavers/Cubic PW0 0930005 Colour **rust/putty** Alt. colours **yes** Composition **60% cotton, 40% rayon** Width **140cm/55in** Repeat – Price ★★★

Brunschwig & Fils/Brigham Mohair Figured Velvet 32 38 01 Colour **5** Alt. colours **yes** Composition **50% cotton, 50% mohair** Width **130cm/51in** Repeat – Price ★★★★

Damask & Brocade

Damasks were first produced in the Syrian capital, Damascus, during the 4th century AD. The first European damasks were made in Italy during the 15th century, and thereafter mostly in the Netherlands, France, Ireland, Switzerland and Britain. True damask is a monochrome reversible fabric displaying fluid but formal patterns created by the contrast between a shiny satin-weave ground and matt sateen-weave figuring. However, damasks incorporating two or more colours have also been produced. Originally, damasks were made of silk, but linen, wool, cotton and man-made fibres have also been used. Traditional motifs include stylized flowers and leaves, and exotic fruits such as the pomegranate.

Brocatelle is a variant of damask and incorporates a satin or twill figuring that is contrasted with a plain- or satin-weave ground.

Brocade is also damask-based, but is distinguished from true damask by the figured patterns raised against the ground by the embroidery-like technique of spooling additional coloured threads through the weave.

ABOVE Residing in the drawing room of a house in Charleston, South Carolina, USA, this pair of 18th-century French gilt armchairs have been re-covered in a 20th-century, chequer-pattern silk damask – the geometric design inspired by upholstery fabrics fashionable in France since the 17th century.

FLORAL DAMASK

The late 18th-century French armchair shown here has been sympathetically reupholstered in a rose-pattern silk damask. Floral patterns have proved to be among the most enduringly popular of damask designs since they were first produced in Europe during the early Renaissance. Many of the examples produced since then have featured designs of stylized and often exotic flowers and vegetation. However, during the late 18th century the floral patterns, as here, tended to be more naturalistic depictions of cultivated and wild flowers that were native to the European countryside.

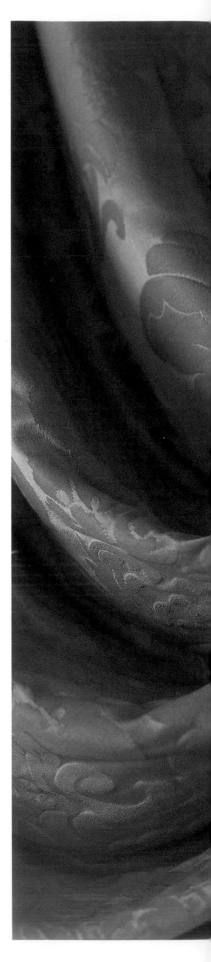

RIGHT A detail of one of a pair of heavy yellow silk damask curtains, with silk rope-and-tassel tie-backs, in Rosalie, a mid-19th-century house in Natchez, Mississippi, USA. The floral-pattern damask is late 20th century, but copied from the fabric originally used in the house when it was first furnished and decorated.

KEY DESIGNS

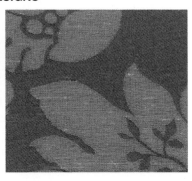

1 Stylized interlaced foliage patterns (arabesques) were derived from Near-Eastern ornament, and favoured on European (and later American) damasks since the mid-16th to early 17th century.

2 Vegetal patterns incorporating ripening fruit or berries (as here), or seed pods, are among the most traditional of damask designs. They were first used during the early Renaissance.

3 While shading has sometimes been employed on damasks to give the design a more naturalistic "three-dimensional" quality, most flower and leaf patterns are flat and highly stylized.

4 Damasks and brocades embellished with small repeated motifs became increasingly popular from the early 19th century – particularly on fabrics intended for use on upholstered seating.

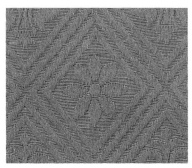

5 Diaper-patterned damasks, such as this small trellis design with stylized flowers, have been produced since the Renaissance, but were a notable feature of 19th-century Victorian interiors.

6 While true damasks are monochromatic, multi-coloured examples are also produced. On floral or faunal patterns, the use of multiple colours almost invariably enhances the naturalistic qualities.

---

1 Lelièvre/Damask Orion 4120 Colour **05 agate** Alt. colours **yes** Composition **65% cotton, 35% silk** Width **130cm/51in** Repeat **80cm/31½in** Price ★★★★ 🔲 ▦

2 Scalamandré/Newport Damask Colour **vermeil** Alt. colours **yes** Composition **100% silk** Width **140cm/55in** Repeat **47cm/18½in** Price ★★★★★ 🔲 W

3 Zoffany/Tours DUP7400 Colour **3** Alt. colours **yes** Composition **100% cotton** Width **138cm/54in** Repeat **64cm/25in** Price ★★ 🔲

4 John Wilman/Laurel Colour **celadon** Alt. colours **yes** Composition **63% cotton, 37% polyester** Width **137cm/54in** Repeat **7cm/2¾in** Price ★ 🔲 🛋

5 Gainsborough Silk Weaving/F841 Colour **gold** Alt. colours **yes** Composition **100% cotton** Width **127cm/50in** Repeat **9.5cm/3¾in** Price ★★★ LC 🔲 ▦ 🛋

6 Brunschwig & Fils/Lady's Slipper Lampas 89481 Colour **876** Alt. colours **yes** Composition **55% silk, 45% cotton** Width **140cm/55in** Repeat **41cm/16in** Price ★★★★★ 🔲 🛋 ▦

Damask & Brocade: **Pre-18th century**

During the Renaissance, Italy led the way in the production of silk damasks and heavier silk brocatelles and brocades, the latter often being augmented with gold and silver thread. Favoured designs – stylized flowers, fruits and leaves – had large pattern repeats particularly suitable for wall-, bed-, window- and door-hangings in grander interiors. After the Netherlands began large-scale production in the late 15th century, less expensive linen weaves became fashionable. During the 16th century, Flemish weavers also introduced new designs, such as hunting scenes, and made traditional patterns with smaller repeats, better suited for upholstery. By the early 17th century, production had spread to France, notably the Huguenot city of Lyons, and, following the emigration of the Huguenots to England, Ireland and Switzerland in the late 17th century, these countries also began to produce large quantities of silk, linen, and even cheaper woollen and worsted weaves for use as both hangings and upholstery.

4 Gainsborough Silk Weaving/
F832 Colour **8** Alt. colours
yes Composition **85% cotton,
15% viscose** Width **127cm/
50in** Repeat **66cm/26in**
Price ★★ 🛋

5 Watts of Westminster/Crevelli
Colour **gold and pearl** Alt.
colours **yes** Composition
**51% cotton, 29% lumiyarn,
20% silk** Width **124cm/48¾in**
Repeat **88cm/34½in**
Price ★★★★★ 🪟 🛋

6 Ian Sanderson/Fontaine
Colour **cranberry** Alt. colours
yes Composition **54% cotton,
46% viscose** Width **140cm/
55in** Repeat **62cm/24¼in**
Price ★★★ LC 🛋

7 Stuart Interiors/Fiori Colour
burgundy and gold Alt. colours
yes Composition **60% wool,
40% linen** Width **175cm/68¾in**
Repeat **60cm/23¾in**
Price ★★★★ LC 🪟 🛋 W

8 Stuart Interiors/Medici Colour
gold, red/gold Alt. colours
yes Composition **100%
wool** Width **170cm/67in**
Repeat **47cm/18½in**
Price ★★★ LC 🪟 🛋 W

1 Claremont/Stanhope Damask
Colour **eau de nil** Alt. colours
yes Composition **100% silk**
Width **130cm/51in** Repeat
55cm/21½in Price ★★★★ 🪟

2 The Silk Gallery/Ceres Damask
Colour **ivory/antique green**
Alt. colours **yes** Composition
82% silk, 18% cotton Width
127cm/50in Repeat **38cm/15in**
Price ★★★★ 🪟 🛋

3 Antico Setificio Fiorentino/Doria
D1 Colour **green on green**
Alt. colours **yes** Composition
100% silk Width **120cm/47in**
Repeat **55cm/21½in**
Price ★★★★★ 🪟 🛋 W

BIRDS
Usually shown in flight or sitting in foliage, birds are among the most traditional of damask and brocade motifs. "Uccellini" dates from the 16th century and is typical of Florentine Renaissance design – similar examples being found in the drapery of paintings by Domenico Ghirlandaio or Benozzo Gozzoli. "Love Bird" is from the 17th century and is representative of the symbolism of birds in fabric patterns. For example, two birds in a tree were emblematic of the Holy Ghost and the Virgin Mary.

Antico Setificio Fiorentino/Uccellini UC1 Colour
silver/green Alt. colours **yes** Composition
100% silk Width **130cm/51in** Repeat
11cm/4¼in Price ★★★★★ 🪟 🛋 W

Scalamandré/Love Bird 1098m Colour **old ivory**
Alt. colours **yes** Composition **100% silk**
Width **127cm/50in** Repeat **46cm/18in**
Price ★★★★★ 🪟 🛋

9 **Crowson/Rousillon Damasks/
Ferdinand** Colour **7** Alt.
colours **yes** Composition
100% cotton Width **137cm/
54in** Repeat **42cm/16½in**
Price ★★ ⬚ ⊞ ⌂

10 **Stuart Interiors/Genoa** Colour
blue and rust Alt. colours
yes Composition **100%
wool** Width **124cm/48¾in**
Repeat **88cm/34½in**
Price ★★★ LC ⬚ ⌂ W

11 **Zoffany/Flower 334405**
Colour **blue** Alt. colours
yes Composition **61% wool,
29% cotton, 10% nylon** Width
145cm/57in Repeat **10.5cm/4in**
Price ★★ ⌂

12 **Zimmer & Rohde/Evangeline
9204** Colour **813** Alt. colours
yes Composition **60% linen,
40% cotton** Width **140cm/
55in** Repeat **21cm/8¼in**
Price ★★★ ⬚

13 **Jab/Adora 1-7327** Colour **180**
Alt. colours **yes** Composition
**65% cotton, 26% silk, 9%
polyester** Width **140cm/55in**
Repeat **44cm/17in**
Price ★★★★ ⬚

13

14

15

16

14 **Sahco Hesslein/Lilian 08888**
Colour **red and gold** Alt.
colours **yes** Composition **57%
linen, 43% cotton** Width **140cm/
55in** Repeat **68cm/26¾in**
Price ★★★ ⬚ ⌂

15 **Watts of Westminster/Holbein
F0012-02/G4** Colour **Canterbury
blue** Alt. colours **yes**
Composition **100% silk**
Width **124cm/48¾in** Repeat
33cm/13in Price ★★★★ ⌂

16 **Sahco Hesslein/Eleganza 1806**
Colour **02** Alt. colours **yes**
Composition **73% wool, 27%
silk** Width **138cm/54in**
Repeat **84cm/33in**
Price ★★★ ⬚ ⌂

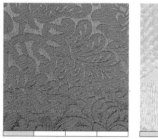

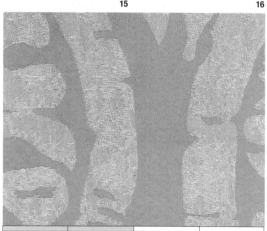

17

17 **Zimmer & Rohde/Solista
5077** Colour **184** Alt. colours
yes Composition **24% silk,
24% linen, 20% acetate**
Width **140cm/55in** Repeat
55cm/21½in Price ★★★ ⬚

18 **Zoffany/Knole Drawing Room
NTF0200** Colour **5** Alt.
colours **yes** Composition
100% cotton Width **138cm/
54in** Repeat **82cm/32½in**
Price ★★★ ⬚ LC ⌂

11

18

Damask & Brocade: **18th century**

The increased production of damasks during the second half of the 17th century was sustained throughout the 18th century. Silk and linen damask upholstery was a feature of Palladian, Rococo-style and Neo-classical interiors in Britain and Europe, and often employed *en suite* with wall-hangings and curtains. Damask upholstery and hangings, mostly of a woollen or worsted variety imported from Britain, were also fashionable in North American Adam-style interiors of the late 18th century.

Favoured colours of the period included magenta and crimson, deep green, dark blue, and pastel pinks and blues. Flower, leaf and fruit patterns remained fashionable, although pastoral designs in which traditional motifs were combined with musical instruments and birds also came into vogue. In grander interiors silk brocade hangings were much in evidence. Many were multi-coloured, with exotic designs such as coral motifs and Indo-*chinoiserie* patterns featuring elephants and buddhas.

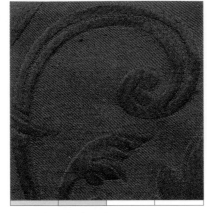

Donghia/Sogno 0387/9315 Colour **09** Alt. colours **yes** Composition **38% silk, 35% linen, 27% cotton** Width **137cm/54in** Repeat **79cm/31in** Price ★★★★★

Andrew Martin/Avignon Colour **black** Alt. colours **yes** Composition **100% cotton** Width **136cm/53½in** Repeat **67cm/26¼in** Price ★★

Scalamandré/Wicklow 20427 Colour **Red Strie** Alt. colours **yes** Composition **83% silk, 17% cotton** Width **140cm/55in** Repeat **60.5cm/24in** Price ★★★★

Beaumont & Fletcher/Marlowe 1012b Colour **gold/red** Alt. colours **yes** Composition **92% wool, 8% nylon** Width **140cm/55in** Repeat **45cm/17½in** Price ★★★

Gainsborough/S590 Colour **22** Alt. colours **yes** Composition **61% cotton, 39% silk** Width **127cm/50in** Repeat **69cm/27in** Price ★★★★★

John Wilman/Laurel 170177 Colour salmon Alt. colours yes Composition 63% cotton, 37% polyester Width 137cm/54in Repeat 7cm/2¾in Price ★★ 🗌🛋

Garin/Anna Maria 3589 Colour rojo
Alt. colours yes Composition 100% cotton
Width 140cm/55in Repeat 69cm/27in
Price ★★ 🗌🛋

Marvic Textiles/Damask Rosario 5210-4
Colour rose Alt. colours yes Composition 71% cotton, 29% silk Width 130cm/51in Repeat 47cm/18½in
Price ★★★ 🗌🛋

Hodsoll McKenzie/Turkish Tulip 357/101-109
Colour natural Alt. colours yes Composition 100% silk Width 127cm/50in Repeat 65cm/25½in
Price ★★★★ 🗌🛋 W

Gainsborough/F954 Colour 1 Alt. colours yes
Composition 61% cotton, 39% silk
Width 127cm/50in Repeat 51cm/21in
Price ★★★★★ T LC 🗌🛋

Warner Fabrics/Hilliard T 114004 Colour cedar
Alt. colours yes Composition 100% silk
Width 140cm/55in Repeat 38cm/15in
Price ★★★ 🗌🛋

The Silk Gallery/Campana Colour henna/cedar ground
Alt. colours yes Composition 82% silk, 18% cotton
Width 127cm/50in Repeat 60cm/23¾in
Price ★★★★ 🗌🛋

Hodsoll McKenzie/Venetian Damask 352/101 Colour dusty pink Alt. colours yes Composition 61% flax, 26% cotton, 13% silk Width 127cm/50in Repeat 66cm/26in Price ★★★★ 🛋

FABRICS: *DAMASK & BROCADE* **81**

Damask & Brocade: Early 19th century

The most significant development in the production of woven fabrics during the first half of the 19th century was technological. The invention, in 1805, of the automated Jacquard loom resulted in a speeding up of the weaving process and, by reducing the number of operators needed, a cut in labour costs. Damasks, brocatelles and, to a lesser extent, partly hand-worked brocades, therefore became more affordable than before, and damask-covered upholstery gradually found its way into middle-class homes – particularly on sofas and chairs. The "dobby" loom, invented in 1824 and designed to supplement the Jacquard loom, also made it easier to produce patterns with smaller repeats – the type most suited to upholstering furniture.

While linen, woollen and worsted damasks, brocatelles and brocades became cheaper and more accessible, more expensive silk versions continued to be produced not only for upholstery but also for wall- and bed-hangings, curtains and lambrequins. During this period, the new looms of Genoa in Italy, Lyons in France and Spitalfields in England turned out increasingly complex and elaborate patterns well suited to the grander French Empire, English Regency and American Federal interiors.

1 **Watts of Westminster/Gaheris F0048-01/N6** Colour **rose/linen** Alt. colours **yes** Composition **64% cotton, 36% linen** Width **140cm/55in** Repeat **18cm/7in** Price ★★★

2 **Guy Evans/Palmerston Damask** Colour **red/gold** Alt. colours **yes** Composition **50% wool, 50% silk** Width **107cm/42in** Repeat **49.5cm/19¼in** Price ★★★★

3 **Garin/Beatriz** Colour **azul** Alt. colours **yes** Composition **55% cotton, 45% viscose** Width **140cm/55in** Repeat **57cm/22in** Price ★★★

4 **Scalamandré/Kilfane 26531** Colour **lime 007** Alt. colours **yes** Composition **38% linen, 34% cotton, 28% silk** Width **144cm/56½in** Repeat **67.3cm/26½in** Price ★★★★

5 **Jab/Mornay 7233** Colour **blue** Alt. colours **yes** Composition **52% cotton, 48% polyester** Width **140cm/55in** Repeat **53cm/21in** Price ★★

6 **Garin/Anna Maria 3591** Colour **crudo** Alt. colours **yes** Composition **100% cotton** Width **140cm/55in** Repeat **69cm/27in** Price ★★

2

3

5

1

4

6

7 Today Interiors/Court Weaves FRW 1332 Colour **gold** Alt. colours **yes** Composition **52% modacrylic, 36% cotton, 12% nylon** Width **140cm/ 55in** Repeat **6.5cm/2½in** Price ★★

8 Harlequin/Assisi/Castina Colour **709** Alt. colours **yes** Composition **13% cotton, 87% viscose** Width **140cm/ 55in** Repeat **57.5cm/23in** Price ★★

9 Northwood Designs/Jupiter Colour **7863** Alt. colours **yes** Composition **100% Trevira CS** Width **280cm/ 110in** Repeat **37cm/14½in** Price ★★★

9

10

11

12

10 Watts of Westminster/Giovanna Damask F0052-01/B4 Colour **white/butter** Alt. colours **yes** Composition **100% silk** Width **124cm/48¾in** Repeat **20cm/8in** Price ★★★★

11 Dedar/Paris Colour **04** Alt. colours **yes** Composition **70% cotton, 30% viscose** Width **140cm/55in** Repeat **56cm/22in** Price ★★

12 Mulberry/Lysander Weave FD403 Colour **oyster blue** Alt. colours **yes** Composition **73% cotton, 20% rayon, 7% nylon** Width **127cm/50in** Repeat **106cm/42in** Price ★★

13 Crowson/Rousillon Damasks/ Corin Colour **10** Alt. colours **yes** Composition **100% cotton** Width **137cm/54in** Repeat **15cm/6in** Price ★★

13

FABRICS: *DAMASK & BROCADE* **83**

Damask & Brocade: Late 19th–21st century

From the mid-19th century to the present day, damasks, brocatelles and brocades have remained in widespread use, with coloured damasks particularly favoured for upholstery, and brocades primarily produced as curtain fabrics. Traditional white linen damask tablecloths and napkins, the preserve of the aristocracy during the 16th and 17th centuries, can also now be found in numerous households. However, damask wall-, bed- and door-hangings tend to be confined to grander period-style interiors.

Over the past 150 years, silk, linen and wool have continued to be used for the manufacture of these fabrics, although cotton damask has become increasingly popular (particularly for upholstery). Traditional designs have also remained fashionable: stylized flowers and leaves, pomegranates and acorns, and, recently, Napoleonic motifs (such as swans, bees and Ns encircled by laurel wreaths) are all much in demand. However, there have been design innovations of note, including late 19th-century Gothic-style polychrome brocatelles incorporating traditional motifs set within geometric grids, 1920s gold brocades featuring stylized floral motifs overprinted with Jazz Age motifs in black, and post-1940s damasks with abstract figuring and designs inspired by 16th- and 17th-century needlework patterns.

Nina Campbell/NCF3440 Falaise Colour **07** Alt. colours **yes** Composition **65% viscose, 19% polyester, 16% cotton** Width **134cm/52½in** Repeat **71cm/28in** Price ★★★ LC ⊡ ⊞⊟

Watts of Westminster/Hilliard F0011-07/J4 Colour **old gold and Medici** Alt. colours **yes** Composition **100% silk** Width **124cm/48¾in** Repeat **22cm/8½in** Price ★★★★ ⊡⊡

Scalamandré/20432 Colour **005** Alt. colours **yes** Composition **72% linen, 28% silk** Width **140cm/55in** Repeat **15cm/6in** Price ★★★ ⊡⊟

Garin/Damjan 97985051 Colour **Barquillo** Alt. colours **yes** Composition **70% cotton, 30% viscose** Width **140cm/55in** Repeat **56cm/22in** Price ★★ ⊡⊟

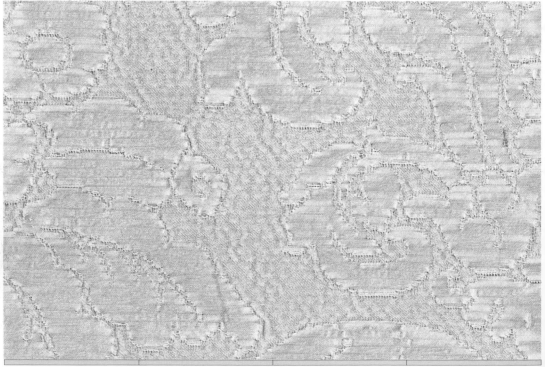

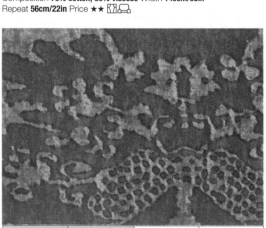

Claremont/Fortuny/Corone Colour **Bayou green and beige** Alt. colours **yes** Composition **100% cotton** Width **120cm/47in** Repeat **100cm/39¼in** Price ★★★★★ LC ⊡

Scalamandré/Lucia 26476 Colour **001** Alt. colours **yes** Composition **100% silk** Width **130cm/51in** Repeat **36.5cm/14¾in** Price ★★★★★ ⊡⊟

19th century

20th & 21st century

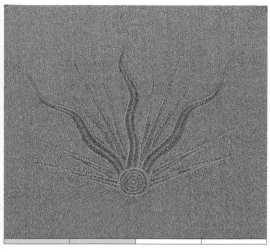

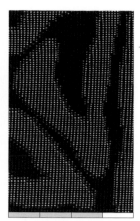

Watts of Westminster/Flame F0007-02/J17 Colour **gold** Alt. colours **yes** Composition **51% cotton, 29% lumiyarn, 20% rayon** Width **124cm/48¾in** Repeat **21cm/8¼in** Price ★★★★ 🎨🛋️

Donghia/Omen 9418 Colour **taupe** Alt. colours **yes** Composition **59% cotton, 29% viscose, 15% polyester** Width **137cm/ 53¼in** Repeat **30cm/11¾in** Price ★★★★ LC 🎨🛋️

G.P. & J. Baker/Arabica K0240 Colour **118** Alt. colours **yes** Composition **57% cotton, 43% modacrylic** Width **145cm/57in** Repeat **2cm/¾in** Price ★★ 🎨🛋️

MATELASSÉ

Derived from the French verb *matelasser*, which means to quilt or wad, matelassé is a term used to describe double-woven damasks (and other fabrics) that incorporate raised figures or motifs on their surface. The decorative puckered effect, which looks like machine quilting, is achieved by weaving in an interlocking "wadding weft" to accentuate relief. The "Magnolia" design shown here is typical of the floral patterns fashionable during the 19th, 20th and early 21st centuries.

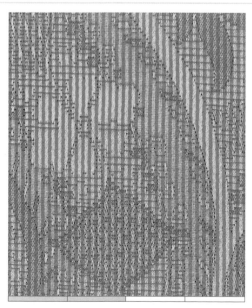

Northwood Designs/Magnolia 18184 Colour **tourmaline 018** Alt. colours **yes** Composition **100% cotton** Width **280cm/110in** Repeat **81cm/32in** Price ★★★ LC 🎨🛋️

Gainsborough Silk Weaving/S590 Colour **19** Alt. colours **yes** Composition **61% silk, 39% cotton** Width **127cm/50in** Repeat **69cm/27in** Price ★★★ 🛋️

Jab/Rigaud 7232 Colour **blue** Alt. colours **yes** Composition **52% cotton, 48% polyester** Width **140cm/55in** Repeat **6cm/2½in** Price ★★ 🎨

Jab/Janai 1-7243 Colour **254** Alt. colours **yes** Composition **86% silk, 14% wool** Width **140cm/ 55in** Repeat **66cm/26in** Price ★★★ 🎨

Bentley & Spens/Day By Night BS09 Colour **natural** Alt. colours **no** Composition **50% linen, 50% cotton** Width **135cm/53in** Repeat **71cm/28in** Price ★★ 🛋️

FABRICS: *DAMASK & BROCADE*

Tapestry

A heavy, durable material, similar in appearance to embroidery, tapestry has been used since the Middle Ages for wall-hangings, bed-hangings, portières, screens and cushion covers; since the 17th century it has also been utilized as a top-cover for upholstered furniture. Tapestry consists of different-coloured warp and weft threads woven to form motifs or, more commonly, narrative accounts of important religious or historical events or scenes from everyday life. The designs were often based on drawings or paintings that were followed as a guide. Prior to the late 19th century, all tapestry was hand-woven with bobbins, and worked on a loom, but since then many tapestries have been machine-made (jacquard-woven).

The traditional yarns used include wool, linen and cotton. The grandest tapestries incorporate silk or gilt thread, while in recent years man-made fibres, such as viscose, have also been employed. The number of colours in any one tapestry can range from as few as eight to as many as 300.

LEFT A pictorial tapestry portière hangs in an arch-top doorway at Parham House, in Sussex, England. Since the Middle Ages, heavier-weight fabrics, including tapestry, velvet and brocatelle, have been favoured for portières because of their draught- and sound-proofing qualities. However, lighter fabrics, such as chintz and silk taffeta, have also been employed, particularly in the better-insulated houses of the 20th century.

ABOVE The tapestry upholstery on this 19th-century painted French canapé, temporarily displayed on the terrace of a medieval *manoir* in Monflanquin, France, is original and particularly well preserved. The floral rose pattern is typical of the period.

KEY DESIGNS

1 Over the centuries many tapestry wall-hangings have featured patterns simulating architectural fixtures and fittings, such as pilasters, cornices, dados or, as here, windows.

2 Scenes of Indian origin, such as these elephants, first appeared on early 17th-century tapestries, and were fashionable again during the second half of both the 18th and the 19th centuries.

3 Elaborate floral-patterned tapestries designed for hangings and upholstery were especially popular during the 17th, the first half of the 18th, and the second half of the 19th century.

4 Tapestries feature an array of heraldic motifs; the lion, featured on medieval, Renaissance, early 18th-century and 20th-century Classical Revival tapestries, symbolizes majesty, courage and pride.

1 **Brunschwig & Fils/Tristan Figured Woven 89528** Colour **833** Alt. colours **yes** Composition **100% spun rayon** Width **140cm/55in** Repeat **50cm/19½in** Price ★★★ 🛋️ LC

2 **Nobilis-Fontan/Les Animaux 8071** Colour **amber on green** Alt. colours **yes** Composition **89% cotton, 11% polyester** Width **130cm/51in** Repeat **78cm/30¾in** Price ★★★★★ 🛋️

3 **Brunschwig & Fils/Animalitos Woven Tapestry 89477** Colour **150** Alt. colours **yes** Composition **100% cotton** Width **145cm/57in** Repeat **74cm/29in** Price ★★★ LC 🛋️

4 **Watts of Westminster/Parisian Lions** Colour **rust** Alt. colours **yes** Composition **58% viscose, 21% polyester, 21% cotton** Width **140cm/55in** Repeat **59cm/23in** Price ★★★ 🛋️

TAPESTRY UPHOLSTERY

When chairs with upholstered seats and backs, such as English "farthingales", first appeared in the 1620s, many were covered with hand-woven tapestry. Providing comfort and durability, tapestry remained a popular top-cover on chairs and settees until the Classical and Neo-classical Revivals of the late 18th century and early 19th century. Tapestry-upholstered seating came back into fashion in Gothic Revival, Arts and Crafts and Jacobean Revival interiors from the 1860s to the 1920s, and has remained popular ever since.

ABOVE Classical mythology and pastoralism are combined in the 19th-century scallop-edged tapestry that extends the canopy to the headboard of this fruitwood four-poster. The bed resides in an 18th-century French hunting lodge.

Tapestry: **Pre-19th century**

Prior to the 17th century, the majority of tapestries were narrative pictorials produced for wall-, bed- and door-hangings. However, non-narrative tapestries were also woven, with fashionable patterns including animals, scrolled ribbons and *mille fleurs*. During the 17th and 18th centuries, tapestry also became a popular top-cover on upholstered furniture. Production increased throughout the world – notably in Flanders, at Aubusson, Gobelins and Beauvais in France, and at Mortlake and Worcester in England. "Picturesque" designs ranged from military conflicts, cities and castles to scenes from nature and Aesop's fables. Elaborate floral arrangements also remained fashionable, while in the 18th century *chinoiserie* and *verdure* tapestries came into vogue.

Changing tastes and the preference for wallpaper over wall-hangings resulted in a decline in tapestry production toward the end of the 18th century that was to last until the second half of the 19th century.

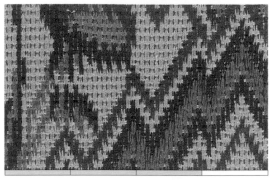

Brunschwig & Fils/89381 Alt. colours **yes** Composition **12% cotton, 87% viscose, 1% polyester** Width **140cm/55in** Repeat **39cm/15¼in** Price ★★★★★ LC

Watts of Westminster/Tea Rose BCF0045-01/J25 Colour **multi** Alt. colours **no** Composition **66% cotton, 34% acrylic** Width **135cm/53in** Repeat **34cm/13⅜in** Price ★★★ ⊞ LC

Fired Earth/Carolean Colour **red** Alt. colours **no** Composition **100% cotton** Width **146cm/57½in** Repeat **45cm/17½in** Price ★★ ⊞

Turnell & Gigon/Perceval 14862 Colour **blue** Alt. colours **yes** Composition **73% cotton, 25% acrylic, 2% rayon** Width **130cm/51in** Repeat **38cm/15in** Price ★★★★

Watts of Westminster/Jacobean Brocade Colour **beige and terracotta** Alt. colours **yes** Composition **66% viscose, 34% cotton** Width **136cm/53½in** Repeat **61cm/24in** Price ★★★★ LC

Stuart Interiors/Rose & Pansy Colour **gold background** Alt. colours **yes** Composition **100% wool** Width **145cm/57in** Repeat **29cm/11¼in** Price ★★★★ LC ⊞ W

AUTHENTIC EARLY COLOURS

The design of this tapestry-woven fabric is based upon an early 17th-century embroidered bed-hanging. The pattern is produced in a limited colour range on a plain ground and contains rudimentary areas of shading. In these respects it bears a much closer resemblance to the flat and highly stylized tapestries of the Middle Ages than to the multi-coloured and subtly shaded "three-dimensional" realism of the style of tapestry that began to be produced during the Renaissance. The thistles and birds-of-prey depicted in the pattern of this fabric are motifs that recur frequently in English and French medieval tapestries.

Watts of Westminster/Windsor F0033-01/23 Colour **Windsor** Alt. colours **yes** Composition **100% cotton** Width **124cm/48¾in** Repeat **57cm/22½in** Price ★★★

Stuart Interiors/Tree of Life Colour **D** Alt. colours **yes** Composition **60% wool, 40% cotton** Width **125cm/49¼in** Repeat **90cm/35½in** Price ★★★★ 🛋️🔲🔳🏠

Fired Earth/Medieval Rose FE9021 Colour **1** Alt. colours **no** 53% polyester Composition **25% cotton, 18% modacrylic, 4% polypropile** Width **138cm/54in** Repeat **34cm/13½in** Price ★★🛋️

Northwood Designs/Fidelio M063N2 Colour **06** Alt. colours **yes** Composition **56% cotton, 44% polyester** Width **140cm/55in** Repeat **36.5cm/14⅜in** Price ★★★ 🔲🔳🔳🏠

Fired Earth/Sunflower Colour **1** Alt. colours **no** Composition **100% cotton** Width **147cm/58in** Repeat **39cm/15¼** Price ★★ 🔳🔲

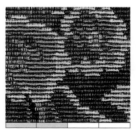

Old World Weavers/Beethoven BD648/0001 Colour **brown** Alt. colours **no** Composition **86% cotton, 14% rayon** Width **140cm/55in** Repeat **86.5cm/34in** Price ★★★ 🛋️

John Lewis/Dean Fr 1 V1229-44 Colour **reds on sand** Alt. colours **yes** Composition **66% cotton, 34% modacrylic** Width **140cm/55in** Repeat **42cm/16½in** Price ★★★★★ **(special order)** 🛋️

Old World Weavers/Clermont ND495 40088 Colour **gold/green/beige** Alt. colours **yes** Composition **100% cotton** Width **127cm/50in** Repeat **72cm/28¼in** Price ★★★★ 🛋️

Tapestry: **19th–early 21st century**

After a 50-year decline, tapestry production enjoyed a resurgence during the late 19th century. Medieval-style designs were predominant, although hanging baskets of flowers set within scrolling wreaths and cartouches also proved highly popular.

Most 20th- and early 21st-century tapestries are machine-made. Heavy and durable, they tend to be more flexible than their hand-woven counterparts and are thus suitable for curtains, although they are also designed specifically for upholstery. Many of the *verdure* tapestries favoured in the early 20th-century Baronial-style and Jacobean Revival interiors featured foliage in soft greens, tans and browns on a dark blue background. Similarly, numerous contemporary tapestries display stylized floral-and-trellis or geometric patterns. Machine-made and hand-woven pictorial tapestries are still produced, primarily as wall-hangings. However, in terms of artistic approach, hand-woven designs have changed. Instigated early in the century at Aubusson, by Frenchman Jean Lurçat, there has been a gradual move away from narrative pictorial realism. Many designs rely on the interaction between the textures and colours used, and in this respect mirror the innovation and developments of modern art.

1 Marvic Textiles/Criss Cross 3903-5 Colour **russet** Alt. colours **yes** Composition 100% cotton Width **140cm/ 55in** Repeat 7cm/2¾in Price ★★★ LC 🛋

2 Marvic Textiles/Maple Leaf 3902-5 Colour **russet** Alt. colours **yes** Composition **100% cotton** Width **140cm/ 55in** Repeat **8.5cm/3¼in** Price ★★★ LC 🛋

3 Watts of Westminster/Parisian Lions Colour **green** Alt. colours **yes** Composition **58% viscose, 21% polyester, 21% cotton** Width **140cm/55in** Repeat **59cm/23in** Price ★★★ 🪟

4 Fired Earth/Mulberry Tree Colour **1** Alt. colours **no** Composition **100% cotton** Width **140cm/55in** Repeat **69.5cm/27¼in** Price ★★ 🪟 ⊞ 🛋

5 Old World Weavers/Boboli TV 25240001 Colour **cinnabar** Alt. colours **yes** Composition **50% rayon, 47% acrylic, 3% cotton** Width **140cm/55in** Repeat **119cm/46¾in** Price ★★★★ 🛋

6 Watts of Westminster/Flora Colour **multi** Alt. colours **no** Composition **100% cotton** Width **138cm/ 54in** Repeat **61cm/24in** Price ★★★ 🛋 LC 🪟

7 Watts of Westminster/Benson Colour **Westminster** Alt. colours **yes** Composition **62% cotton, 38% silk** Width **124cm/48¾in** Repeat **63cm/ 24¾in** Price ★★★★★ 🪟

8 **Watts of Westminster/Damme**
Colour **multi** Alt. colours **no**
Composition **86% cotton,
12% viscose** Width **140cm/
55in** Repeat **69cm/27in**
Price ★★★ LC [icons]

9 **Brunschwig & Fils/89477**
Colour **333** Alt. colours
yes Composition **100%
cotton** Width **145/57in**
Repeat **74cm/29in**
Price ★★★ [icon]

10

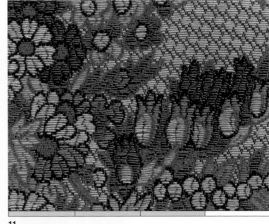

11

9

10 **Brunschwig & Fils/89247**
Colour **402** Alt. colours
yes Composition **100%
cotton** Width **150cm/59in**
Repeat **100cm/39¼in**
Price ★★★★ [icon]

11 **Brunschwig & Fils/89528**
Colour **239** Alt. colours
yes Composition **100%
spun rayon** Width **140cm/
55in** Repeat **50cm/19½in**
Price ★★★ [icons] LC [icon]

12 **Fired Earth/Oakleaf** Colour **1**
Alt. colours **no** Composition
100% cotton Width **157cm/
61¾in** Repeat **45cm/17½in**
Price ★★★ [icons]

13 **Brunschwig & Fils/Jacinthe
Tapestry 53122.01** Colour
ultramarine Alt. colours **yes**
Composition **100% cotton**
Width **137cm/54in** Repeat
11.5cm/4½in Price ★★★ [icon]

14 **Marvic Textiles/Grapes 3901-3**
Colour **yellow** Alt. colours **yes**
Composition **100% cotton**
Width **140cm/55in** Repeat
23cm/9in Price ★★★ LC [icon]

ART NOUVEAU

The revival in tapestry
production that took
place during the Arts and
Crafts movement was
also evident in the output
of the designers who
were working in the Art
Nouveau style from the
late 19th century to the
early years of the 20th
century. Liberty of
London commissioned a
number of designs, one
of which was the late
19th-century tapestry-
weave "Ianthe", shown
here. Typical of Art
Nouveau and its strong
fascination with the forms
of nature, the pattern
depicts stylized stems,
roots, elongated blooms
and foliage within highly
sinuous, interlaced lines.

Arts and Crafts Home/Ianthe 1095022 Colour **E** Alt. colours
no Composition **53% linen, 35% cotton, 12% nylon**
Width **137cm/54in** Repeat **31cm/12in**
Price ★★ LC [icons]

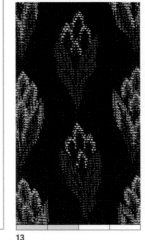

13

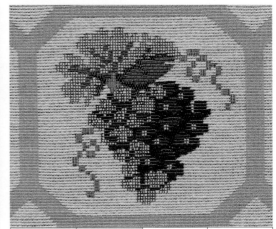

14

Motif Fabrics

Woven and printed cloths displaying patterns made up of systematically repeated images are traditionally referred to as "motif fabrics". Their enduring appeal through the centuries is largely explained by decorative qualities such as strong visual repetition, and by the ease with which they allow hangings, upholstery and floor-coverings to be coordinated *en suite* not only with each other, but also with architectural fixtures and fittings and pieces of furniture embellished with the same motifs. The attractiveness of such fabrics also resides in the huge variety of motifs that can be represented; a catalogue of architectural, mythological, animal and plant-form imagery, both stylized and naturalistic, steadily accumulated from around the globe from the Middle Ages onward, much of it being disseminated via pattern books in circulation from the late Renaissance until the early 20th century.

The inherent symbolism of most motifs is particularly appealing to fabric designers because it allows them to convey "hidden meanings" via the pattern. For example, a wreath motif is not merely a "still life" of bound laurel, oak or olive leaves – it is also a symbol of sovereignty, honour, glory, poetic achievement or victory over death.

ABOVE The silk top-cover of this early 19th-century sabre-legged mahogany "tub" chair from France features a repeat wreath motif. Consisting of a garland or crown of leaves (laurel, oak or olive), the wreath was a popular motif during the early Renaissance, and was revived under the Neo-classical Empire style of the late 18th and early 19th centuries – the Emperor Napoleon chose a golden wreath of laurel for his coronation to recall the sovereignty, honour, glory and victories of the ancient Roman emperors.

LEFT "Palmiers", the yellow linen-cotton top-cover on this late 18th-century French settee and footstool, displays a repeat palm tree motif. The pattern was derived and adapted by Comoglio from an 18th-century Marseilles pattern book. Naturalistic and stylized palm trees – a species native to North Africa – became fashionable fabric motifs during the late 18th and early 19th centuries following Napoleon's military campaigns in Egypt.

CYPHERS

Traditionally, cyphers – initials interwoven to form a flat linear design – are used on fabrics to denote ownership or patronage. Prior to the 18th century, they were the almost exclusive preserve of monarchies – a notable example being the interlaced Ls of Louis XI of France. However, following the publication in 1726 of Samuel Sympson's *A New Book of Cyphers*, which contained "every possible combination of two intertwining scrolling letters embellished with flourishes of foliage", they were increasingly commissioned by other sections of society on both sides of the Atlantic, and proved especially popular in 19th-century Gothic Revival interiors.

KEY DESIGNS

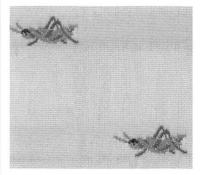

1 Used primarily as symbols of nature and the cycle of life, insects such as grasshoppers, bees, butterflies, moths and beetles have been popular motifs ever since the Middle Ages.

2 Originally from France, the fleur-de-lis (a stylized three- or five-petal lily) has been one of the most popular of all motifs, and was prominent in medieval, Renaissance and Gothic Revival interiors.

3 The wreath – a crown or garland of leaves – symbolized sovereignty, honour, glory and victory in ancient Greece and Rome. Fashionable in the Renaissance, it was revived under Empire style.

4 The swan was associated with Apollo (music) and Venus (love) in classical mythology, and was widely used as a motif on medieval, Empire, Biedermeier, Regency and Art Nouveau fabrics.

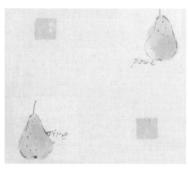

5 This pear motif is early 21st century, but pear and other fruit motifs – from apples and raspberries to figs and pineapples – have been favoured on textiles since the Middle Ages.

6 The oak leaf symbolizes civic virtue and steadfastness and has appeared on numerous fabrics, notably in ancient Roman, Gothic, Renaissance, Neoclassical and Arts and Crafts interiors.

1 **Brunschwig & Fils/89518** Colour **005** Alt. colours **yes** Composition **71% cotton, 29% rayon** Width **140cm/55in** Repeat **6cm/2¼in** Price ★★★ ⬚ LC ⬚

2 **Warner Fabrics/Poitiers T6800** Colour **red** Alt. colours **yes** Composition **69% viscose, 31% cotton** Width **140cm/55in** Repeat **–** Price ★★ ⬚

3 **Scalamandré/Rosecliff NW Bedroom 20221** Colour **cranberry** Alt. colours **yes** Composition **100% silk** Width **140cm/55in** Repeat **16.5cm/ 6½in** Price ★★★★★ ⬚ ⊞ ⬚ W

4 **Stuart Interiors/Medieval Swans** Colour **blue and gold** Alt. colours **yes** Composition **100% wool** Width **145cm/57in** Repeat **16cm/6¼in** Price ★★★★ ⬚ ⊞ ⬚ W

5 **Harlequin/Notebook/Poire 00181** Colour **181** Alt. colours **yes** Composition **36% cotton, 52% linen, 12% nylon** Width **137cm/54in** Repeat **91.5cm/36in** Price ★★ ⬚ ⊞ ⬚

6 **Lee Jofa/Oak Leaf Weave 854252** Colour **hunter green** Alt. colours **yes** Composition **85% rayon, 15% cotton** Width **132cm/51¼in** Repeat **8cm/3in** Price ★★★★ ⬚ ⊞ ⬚

Motifs: **Pre-18th century**

In addition to Islamic ornament, such as arabesques, favoured European motifs of the Middle Ages included stylized heraldic decorations and naturalistic depictions of animals and plant forms – particularly *mille fleurs* (roses, violas, anemones, pinks and columbines), ivy, grapevines, wild strawberries, chestnuts and acorns. Heraldic motifs remained fashionable during the Renaissance, as did military and emblematic symbols. However, Renaissance fabrics were largely characterized by sculptural-like classical forms, such as swags, festoons, dolphins and scallop shells, and realistically depicted acanthus leaves, scrolling foliage, pomegranates, thistles and other plant forms. During the later Renaissance rambling foliage, luxuriant blooms and exotic fruits and birds also embellished imported Indian chintzes. The classical ornamentation of the Renaissance was further consolidated in the Baroque interiors of the 17th century, with fabric motifs including angels, cupids, human figures, scrolls, urns, flaming torches, swags and leafy scrolls. Vying with the classical, however, were *chinoiserie* pagodas, bells, mandarins, dragons and birds, which were very popular in the late 17th century following the publication in several languages of J. Nieuhof's illustrated travel book, *Atlas Chinois* (1665).

1

2

3

1 The Silk Gallery/Fleur Weave
Colour **antique gold and green** Alt. colours **yes**
Composition **68% silk, 32% polyester** Width **127cm/ 50in** Repeat **6cm/2½in**
Price ★★★

2 Elizabeth Eaton/Saighton
Colour **green on white** Alt. colours **yes** Composition **100% linen** Width **122cm/ 48in** Repeat **5cm/2in**
Price ★★

3 Les Olivades/Indianaire
TRT 0064 Colour **yellow/blue** Alt. colours **yes** Composition **100% cotton** Width **150cm/ 59in** Repeat **3cm/1¼in**
Price ★★

4 Stuart Interiors/Heraldic Beasts Colour **rust/beige** Alt. colours **yes** Composition **70% wool, 30% linen** Width **172cm/ 67½in** Repeat **89cm/35in**
Price ★★★★

4

5 Stuart Interiors/Fleur de Lys
Colour **blue** Alt. colours **yes** Composition **75% wool, 25% silk** Width **145cm/ 57in** Repeat **25cm/9¾in**
Price ★★★★

6 Jason D'Souza/Siena SIE01
Colour **coral** Alt. colours **yes** Composition **51% modacrylic, 37% cotton, 12% nylon** Width **135cm/53in** Repeat **4cm/1½in**
Price ★★

7 Zoffany/Rosa GRD8600
Colour **1** Alt. colours **yes** Composition **37% cotton, 13% linen, 50% viscose** Width **140cm/55in** Repeat **14cm/5½in**
Price ★★★

8 Andrew Martin/Parasol
Colour **Alloy** Alt. colours **yes** Composition **56% polyester, 44% viscose** Width **140cm/ 55in** Repeat **10.5cm/4in**
Price ★★★

6

7

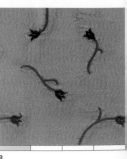

8

9

10

9 **Zoffany/Leaf PCW0300** Colour **1** Alt. colours **yes** Composition 73% cotton, 14% viscose, 12% nylon, 1% silk Width **145cm/ 57in** Repeat **4.5cm/1¾in** Price ★★ ⌷⌷ ⌷⌷⌷

10 **Zoffany/Este DUP7600** Colour **2** Alt. colours **yes** Composition 100% cotton Width **138cm/ 54in** Repeat **32cm/12½in** Price ★★ ⌷⌷

11 **The Silk Gallery/Dis Print** Colour **stone 235** Alt. colours **yes** Composition 100% silk Width **127cm/50in** Repeat **14cm/5½in** Price ★★★ ⌷⌷

12 **Bernard Thorp & Co/Daisy Time** Colour **blue** Alt. colours **yes** Composition 100% jute Width **120cm/47in** Repeat **53cm/21in** Price ★★ ⌷⌷ ⌷⌷

13 **Zoffany/Hardwick High Great Chamber NTF0100** Colour **1** Alt. colours **yes** Composition 47% cotton, 53% viscose Width **141cm/55½in** Repeat **81cm/32in** Price ★★★ ⌷⌷ ⌷⌷

14 **Harlequin/Navaril/Nadir** Colour **736** Alt. colours **yes** Composition 100% cotton Width **137cm/54in** Repeat **64cm/25in** Price ★★ ⌷⌷ ⌷⌷

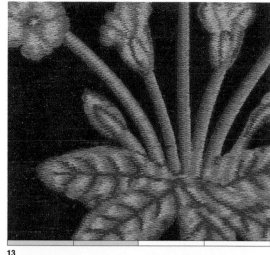

13

11

12

14

HERALDIC MOTIFS

First used in the 12th century to denote position and status in a feudal society, heraldic emblems rapidly became a form of decoration that also conveyed pride of ownership and pedigree. Typical motifs, often within achievements-of-arms, include helmets and shields, cyphers and draperies. Stylized beasts, such as stags, dogs, porcupines or lions, griffins or harpies, unicorns, and enfields or ypotrylls were also very popular.

Andrew Martin/Magna Carta Colour **red** Alt. colours **yes** Composition 100% cotton Width **133cm/ 52in** Repeat **112cm/44in** Price ★★ ⌷⌷ ⌷⌷

Heraldic motifs have been frequently utilized by manufacturers as inspiration for their fabric designs. The central shield on the fabric shown here bears a Latin inscription that translates as: "One does not value things easily obtained."

Motifs: **18th century**

Access to the numerous pattern books in international circulation during the 18th century enabled fabric designers to draw on a rich and varied catalogue of historical ornamentation. Early in the century, fabrics adorning Palladian interiors featured herms, eagles, dolphins and masks inspired by classical Roman and Renaissance ornament, while fabrics in Picturesque schemes displayed pastoral and rustic scenes and *fêtes galantes* – the latter also appearing on the Rococo-style fabrics in vogue until the middle of the century. Other motifs typical of the Rococo period included *singeries*, *rocaille*, scrollwork and *chinoiserie* birds and lanterns. In the Neo-classical Adam- and Federal-style schemes of the late 18th century, Roman motifs – lion masks, rosettes, urns, vases, griffins and delicate scrolling foliage – were prevalent, while the Gothick Revival at the end of the century saw Gothic ornament, such as flora, fauna, the seasons and portraits of masons and clerics, portrayed in an historically accurate manner.

1

2

3

5

6

7

5 **Colefax and Fowler/Osterley 2063/03** Colour **coral and green** Alt. colours **yes** Composition **52% linen, 36% cotton, 12% nylon** Width **134cm/52½in** Repeat **41cm/16in**
Price ★★

6 **G.P. & J. Baker/Pineapple** Colour **2** Alt. colours **yes** Composition **60% linen, 20% cotton** Width **134cm/52½in** Repeat **56cm/22in**
Price ★★

7 **Busby & Busby/Amaretti 4913** Colour **gold, crimson and stone** Alt. colours **yes** Composition **100% cotton** Width **140cm/55in** Repeat **64cm/25in**
Price ★★

1 **Hodsoll McKenzie/Toile d'Avignon 221/105** Colour **red/blue** Alt. colours **yes** Composition **50% rayon, 50% cotton** Width **127cm/50in** Repeat **40.5cm/16in**
Price ★★★

2 **Brunschwig & Fils/Canton Cotton Print 79512.04** Colour **blue fish on white** Alt. colours **yes** Composition **100% cotton** Width **134cm/52½in** Repeat **64cm/25in**
Price ★★

3 **Timney Fowler/Ornamental Stripe** Colour **01 black & white** Alt. colours **yes** Composition **100% cotton** Width **140cm/55in** Repeat **90cm/35½in**
Price ★★

4 **Mulberry/Oberon Chenille/FD402** Colour **stone/jade** Alt. colours **yes** Composition **87% cotton, 13% viscose/flax** Width **127cm/50in** Repeat **165cm/67in**
Price ★★★

4

8

9

11   12

8 **Apenn/Hampton Linen**
LN 476-8/9 Colour **red-blue**
Alt. colours **yes** Composition
100% linen Width **125cm/49¼in**
Repeat **20cm/8in**
Price ★★ 🪑🛋

9 **The Isle Mill/Red Fintry/FIN006**
Colour **red** Alt. colours **yes**
Composition **100% wool** Width
137cm/54in Repeat **6cm/2½in**
Price ★★ LC 🪑🛋

10 **Thomas Dare/Providence 958**
Colour **234** Alt. colours **yes**
Composition **93% cotton, 7%**
rayon Width **137cm/54in**
Repeat **32.5cm/12¾in**
Price ★★ 🪑 ⊞🛋 W

11 **Brunschwig & Fils/89513**
Colour **647** Alt. colours **yes**
Composition **100% Trevira CS**
Width **140cm/55in**
Repeat **63cm/24¾in**
Price ★★★ 🪑 LC W

12 **Brunschwig & Fils/89511**
Colour **409** Alt. colours **yes**
Composition **100% Trevira CS**
Width **140cm/55in**
Repeat **4cm/1½in**
Price ★★★ 🪑 LC🛋

13

   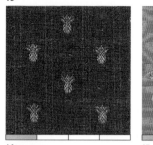

14   15

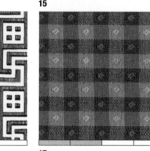

16   17

13 **Bennison Fabrics/China Birds**
Colour **1** Alt. colours **yes**
Composition **70% linen, 30%**
cotton Width **118cm/46¼in**
Repeat **43cm/16¾in**
Price ★★ 🪑🛋

14 **Marvic Textiles/Pineapple Plaid**
414-10 Colour **holly** Alt. colours
yes Composition **62% linen,**
23% cotton, 15% viscose Width
130cm/51in Repeat **6.5cm/2½in**
Price ★★ 🛋

15 **Scalamandré/Strawberry Design**
205-003 Colour **multi on blue**
and ivory Alt. colours **yes**
Composition **100% silk** Width
127cm/50in Repeat **6.5cm/2½in**
Price ★★★★★ 🪑🛋

16 **Timney Fowler/Scroll Stripe**
TF0304 Colour **black & white**
Alt. colours **yes** Composition
100% cotton Width **140cm/55in**
Repeat **21.5cm/8½in**
Price ★★ 🪑 ⊞

17 **Ian Sanderson/Amy Check**
Colour **brick** Alt. colours **yes**
Composition **37% polyester,**
35% cotton, 28% viscose Width
135cm/53in Repeat **1.5cm/⅝in**
Price ★★ 🪑🛋

18 **Timney Fowler/Roman Heads**
TF0027.04 Colour **red and ecru**
Alt. colours **yes** Composition
100% cotton Width **120cm/47in**
Repeat **108cm/42½in**
Price ★★ 🛋

NEO-CLASSICISM

This Louis XVI-style
lampas was designed
in 1779 and used to
upholster chairs in Marie
Antoinette's apartments
at the Château de
Versailles near Paris,
France. In 1859 it was
reproduced for Empress
Eugénie's apartments in
the Palais des Tuileries.
The predominantly floral
pattern, in the centre
of which lies an oval
medallion encompassing
a stylized fluted torch
encircled with flowers
and entwined with
crumpled ribbons, is
typical of late 18th-
century Neo-classicism.

Lelièvre/Lampas – Marie Antoinette 10481 Colour **2** Alt. colours
yes Composition **100% silk** Width **130cm/51in** Repeat **2cm/¾in**
Price ★★★★★ 🪑🛋

18

Motifs: Early 19th century

Underpinning the Empire, Regency and Federal styles of decoration prevalent during the early 19th century was a revival of Classicism in its original purity. Initiated in France by architects Percier and Fontaine (under the patronage of Napoleon), Empire style was encapsulated in their influential book *Recueil des Décorations Intérieures* (1801), rapidly spread to Federal America and was strongly reflected in the Regency interiors of England. Early 19th-century Classicism was made up of two major historical strands: "le Style Etrusque" and Roman. Favoured Etruscan motifs for fabrics included palmettes, palm leaves and anthemions, as well as vases, medallions, winged lions and eagles. Roman motifs and emblems proved even more popular, especially in France, largely owing to Napoleon's desire to identify the country with the greatness of the Roman Empire. Therefore laurel and oak wreaths, lances, arrows and fasces, griffins, winged torches, and figures of victory and fame were much in evidence. An additional historical influence was fuelled by archaeological excavations in Egypt and by Napoleon's Nile campaign, ancient Egyptian motifs, such as scarabs, sphinxes, lotus flowers and hieroglyphics appearing soon after being copied from drawings in Baron Denon's *Voyages dans la Basse et la Haute Egypte* (1802–3).

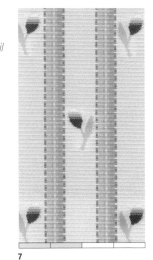

7

6 **Ramm, Son & Crocker/Floris**
Colour **aqua** Alt. colours **yes**
Composition **52% linen, 36% cotton, 12% nylon** Width **140cm/55in** Repeat **10cm/4in**
Price ★★ LC

7 **Scalamandré/26546** Colour **005**
Alt. colours **yes** Composition **50% cotton, 50% viscose** Width **130cm/51in** Repeat **8cm/3in**
Price ★★★★

8 **Today Interiors/Samadhi/Tulipa**
Colour **SAF308** Alt. colours **yes** Composition **88% linen, 12% nylon** Width **137cm/54in** Repeat **48cm/19in**
Price ★★

9 **Lelièvre/Prudhon 4147 07**
Colour **marine** Alt. colours **yes** Composition **55% cotton, 45% silk** Width **130cm/51in** Repeat **22cm/8½in** Price ★★★

1

2

6

8

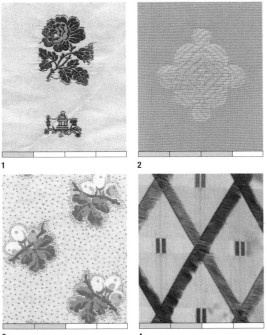

3

4

1 **Brunschwig & Fils/Lindsey's Garden Lisère 53451** Colour **01**
Alt. colours **yes** Composition **55% cotton, 45% rayon** Width **137cm/54in** Repeat **17cm/6¾in**
Price ★★★

2 **Northwood Designs/Romeo/ M061Y6** Colour **pistache** Alt. colours **yes** Composition **100% cotton** Width **290cm/114¼in** Repeat **8.5cm/3¼in**
Price ★★ LC

3 **Warner Fabrics/Little Acorns CS 336080** Colour **petrol/buff** Alt. colours **yes** Composition **100% cotton** Width **137cm/54in** Repeat **10cm/4in** Price ★★
LC

4 **Mulberry/Signal Silk/FD421** Colour **yellow/pink T125** Alt. colours **yes** Composition **83% acetate, 17% silk** Width **148cm/ 58¼in** Repeat **24cm/9½in** Price ★★★★

5 **Laura Ashley/Marlborough** Colour **raspberry** Alt. colours **yes** Composition **70% viscose, 20% cotton, 10% nylon** Width **130cm/51in** Repeat **44cm/17in** Price ★★

5

9

11

10

12

10 Scalamandré/Lampas – Rosecliff Laurel 20221-007 Colour **cranberry** Alt. colours **yes** Composition **100% silk** Width **140cm/55in** Repeat **17cm/6¾in** Price ★★★★ ▨▱

11 G.P. & J. Baker/Laurel Colour **red** Alt. colours **yes** Composition **67% cotton, 33% modacrylic** Width **140cm/55in** Repeat **6cm/2⅜in** Price ★★ ▨▦▱

13

12 Lelièvre/Vernet 414606 Colour **bleu** Alt. colours **yes** Composition **55% cotton, 45% silk** Width **130cm/51in** Repeat **16cm/6¼in** Price ★★★★ ▨▱

13 G.P. & J. Baker/Eccleston Colour **terracotta** Alt. colours **yes** Composition **100% lightly glazed cotton** Width **137cm/54in** Repeat **81cm/31¾in** Price ★★ ▨▦▱

14 Zoffany/Neo Classique Colour **red** Alt. colours **yes** Composition **53.9% viscose, 46.1% cotton** Width **142cm/55¾in** Repeat **86cm/33¾in** Price ★★▱

14

NAPOLEONIC MOTIFS

Three recurring Napoleonic motifs are the bee, the swan and the palm tree. Napoleon adopted the bee as his emblem primarily because it was an ancient Greek symbol of order and industry, but also because metal bees found in the tomb of Chilperic I (a 6th-century Frankish king) provided a link with early French rulers. The black swan was the Empress Josephine's emblem, chosen because swans pulled the chariot of Venus. The palm tree was an emblem of fame and victory, and, being indigenous to Africa, served as a symbol of Napoleon's Egyptian campaigns.

1

2

3

1 Scalamandré/Bee 213-002 Colour **multi on cream ground** Alt. colours **yes** Composition **100% silk** Width **127cm/50in** Repeat **5.5cm/2¼in** Price ★★★★★ ▨

2 Turnell & Gigon/Les Cygnes 18429 Colour **green and red** Alt. colours **yes** Composition **60% viscose, 40% cotton** Width **130cm/51in** Repeat **32cm/12½in** Price ★★★★★ ▨▱

3 Pierre Frey/Palmiers 2525 Colour **original** Alt. colours **yes** Composition **64% linen, 36% cotton** Width **136cm/53¼in** Repeat **25.5cm/10in** Price ★★★★ ▨▱

Motifs: **Mid-19th century**

The majority of fabric motifs favoured in the middle of the 19th century fell into one of two stylistic categories – Classical Revival and Gothic Revival – and in this respect mirrored the "battle of the styles" that was taking place in contemporary architecture. Typical Gothic Revival motifs – employed by noted designers such as the English architect A.W.N. Pugin – included stylized scrolling leaves and heraldic motifs (such as fleur-de-lis), usually set within a flat pattern of basic ogival structure. Mythical beasts, gargoyles and patrons of the arts, presented within medallions, were also recurring motifs of the style.

Classical ornamentation of the period was wide ranging. In Renaissance Revival interiors, Roman-influenced acanthus leaves, scrolling foliage, swags and festoons vied with grotesques and *grisaille* panels incorporating the Elements and the Muses; while in the Baroque Revival (Second Empire) designs that followed, leafy scrolls, swags, urns, flaming torches, angels and putti were all much in evidence. Further enriching the ornamentation of fabrics during this period were Moorish motifs, such as arabesques, and Indian designs, such as the paisley patterns derived from Kashmiri shawls and consisting of formalized representations of pine cones, palms and almonds.

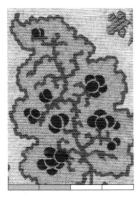

Borderline/Forget Me Not Colour **A** Alt. colours **yes** Composition **100% cotton** Width **137cm/54in** Repeat **37.5cm/14¾in** Price ★★ 🛋

George Spencer Decorations/ Elizabeth 017L Colour **apricot** Alt. colours **yes** Composition **60% cotton, 40% linen** Width **138cm/54in** Repeat **20cm/8in** Price ★★★★ 🛋🪑

Donghia/Vicenza/4906 Colour **10 silver** Alt. colours **yes** Composition **81% viscose, 19% linen** Width **140cm/55in** Repeat **43cm/16¾in** Price ★★★★ LC🪑

Jab/Mukarnas CA 7212 Colour **003** Alt. colours **yes** Composition **46% cotton, 30% viscose, 12% polyacrylic, 12% linen** Width **140cm/55in** Repeat **73cm/28½in** Price ★★★ 🪑

Sheila Coombes/Lindale Colour **76 Sea Holly** Alt. colours **yes** Composition **47% wool, 31% cotton, 12% viscose, 10% nylon** Width **137cm/54in** Repeat **7cm/2¾in** Price ★★ LC🛋🪑W

Bennison Fabrics/Jubilee Stripe Colour **red** Alt. colours **yes** Composition **70% linen, 30% cotton** Width **139cm/54¾in** Repeat **43.5cm/17in** Price ★★★ 🛋🪑

Watts of Westminster/Tudor Badge
F0026-01/U1 Colour **lichen/old gold**
Alt. colours **yes** Composition
100% cotton Width **124cm/48¾in**
Repeat **14cm/5½in** Price ★★★

Watts of Westminster/Wexford Welby 21WWB/3 Colour **Geneva** Alt. colours **yes** Composition **100% cotton** Width
124cm/48¾in Repeat **21cm/8¼in** Price ★★★

Mary Fox Linton/Fedra Colour **01**
Alt. colours **yes** Composition **54%
cotton, 28% viscose, 18% polyester**
Width **140cm/55in** Repeat
16cm/6¼in Price ★★★

Watts of Westminster/Trellis Z1TR/M30FR Colour **bottle green**
Alt. colours **yes** Composition **56% cotton, 44% polycotton** Width
140cm/55in Repeat **18cm/7in** Price ★★★

Mulberry/Cartouche FD336 Colour **T31 gold/blue** Alt. colours **yes**
Composition **65% viscose, 25% cotton, 10% polymide** Width **146cm/57½in**
Repeat **30cm/11¾in** Price ★★

Abbott & Boyd/Objetos Colour
blue/red Alt. colours **yes**
Composition **100%** Width
155cm/61¼in Repeat **19cm/7½in**
Price ★★

Weymss Houlès/Minster/Canterbury
Colour **303** Alt. colours **yes**
Composition **56% linen, 33%
cotton, 11% nylon** Width
137cm/54in Repeat —
Price ★

Zoffany/Dup7600 Este Colour **1** Alt. colours **yes** Composition **100% cotton** Width **138cm/54in**
Repeat **32cm/12½in** Price ★★

Zuber/Chateau de Blois/Alcove Chambre de la Reine T9222 Colour **1** Alt.
colours **no** Composition **100% cotton** Width **130cm/51in** Repeat
74cm/29in Price ★★★★

Motifs: Late 19th century

The diversity of fabric motifs in evidence during the late 19th century was as wide ranging as the contemporary styles of architecture and decoration. On both sides of the Atlantic, an eclectic mix of revivalist styles, such as Gothic, Louis XIV, Rococo and Pompeiian, were often employed in different rooms throughout the same house. However, a reaction to this jumbled diversity of ornamentation set in, and more uniform decorative schemes derived from the Aesthetic, Arts and Crafts and Art Nouveau movements emerged.

Fabric motifs favoured by the Aesthetic movement included flowers (particularly sunflowers), mostly depicted in a conventionalized, flat, circular form, but sometimes with almost botanical accuracy; Japanese-style sparrows, kingfishers and peacocks; Renaissance-style putti, dolphins and grotesques, and scrollwork inspired by Turkish, Persian and Cretan embroideries. Arts and Crafts fabrics – the most popular of the period – featured flowers and birds, rhythmically presented within a medieval-style pattern structure. Stylized birds, and floral and vegetative motifs, notably scrolling acanthus leaves, were also favoured by Art Nouveau designers. However, these were more sinuously illustrated than their Arts and Crafts counterparts.

1 **Bennison Fabrics/India Stripe**
Colour **red** Alt. colours **yes**
Composition **70% linen,
30% cotton** Width **122cm/
48in** Repeat **49cm/19¼in**
Price ★★★

2 **Watts of Westminster/Malvern
WF0016-03/T5** Colour **brick/
rust/old gold** Alt. colours **yes**
Composition **63% cotton,
37% flax** Width **130cm/51in**
Repeat **124cm/48¾in**
Price ★★★★

3 **Kravet/Joseph Abboud/
Cavendisa 19836** Colour
916 mink Alt. colours **yes**
Composition **100% cotton**
Width **137cm/54in**
Repeat **68cm/26¾in**
Price ★★★★★ LC

4 Liberty Furnishings/Allerton
LF4190 Colour **06** Alt. colours
yes Composition **91% cotton,
9% nylon** Width **140cm/55in**
Repeat **62cm/24¼in**
Price ★★ [LC] [sofa]

5 Hodsoll McKenzie/Small
Ottoman **263/101-106** Colour
blue Alt. colours **yes**
Composition **100% cotton**
Width **127cm/50in** Repeat
21cm/8¼in Price ★★★ [sofa]

6 Liberty Furnishings/Lodden
1069622 Colour **C** Alt. colours
yes Composition **100% cotton**
Width **137cm/54in**
Repeat **46cm/18in**
Price ★★ [sofa] [LC] [cut]

7 Scalamandré/Coeur de Lion
26315-002 Colour **crimson**
Alt. colours **yes** Composition
52% acrylic, 48% cotton Width
142cm/55¾in Repeat **18cm/7in**
Price ★★★ [cut] [sofa]

8 Watts of Westminster/Memlinc
F0017-07/A5 Colour **taupe/
oatmeal** Alt. colours **yes**
Composition **100% cotton**
Width **124cm/48¾in**
Repeat **98cm/38¾in**
Price ★★★ [cut] [sofa]

9 Warner Fabrics/Etiennes Folly
CS 8060 Colour **stone/cream**
Alt. colours **yes** Composition
68% linen, 32% cotton Width
137cm/54in Repeat **62cm/24¼in**
Price ★★ [cut] [sofa]

4

5

6

7

8

9

Motifs: Early 20th century

For the first five years of the 20th century, Art Nouveau motifs such as stems, roots, elongated blooms and dream-like figures of women retained their popularity, while Arts and Crafts fabrics, featuring daisies, wild roses and medieval motifs such as the fleur-de-lis, remained fashionable well into the 1930s. Tudor Revival and Jacobean Revival fabrics were also in vogue, ornamented with birds of paradise, the "Tree of Life", Tudor roses and furled, banner-like ribbons.

Less revivalist and more innovative were the designs on the Art Deco fabrics. The earliest examples were embellished with rounded and romantic motifs, such as garlands and baskets of flowers, stylized rosebuds, fawns, doves and ropes of pearls. Such images were gradually superseded by Egyptian motifs, including the scarab, and Aztec symbols, such as stepped shapes and sun motifs. However, these motifs were in turn supplanted by streamlined geometric and abstract images that provoked French designer Paul Iribe to observe: "They [have] sacrificed the flower on the altar of Cubism and the machine."

1

2

1 The Arts and Crafts Home/Mackintosh/Tulip and Lattice Colour **C** Alt. colours **yes** Composition **100% cotton** Width **122cm/48in** Repeat **16cm/6¼in** Price ★★★ LC 🛋

2 The Arts and Crafts Home/Mackintosh/Rose and Teardrop Colour **D** Alt. colours **yes** Composition **100% cotton**, Width **122cm/48in** Repeat **24cm/9½in**
Price ★★★ LC 🛋

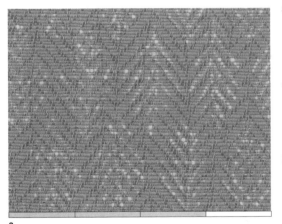

3 Wemyss/Earlswood Colour **1P.172** Alt. colours **yes** Composition **49% modacrylic, 39% cotton, 20% nylon** Width **140cm/55in** Repeat **19cm/7½in** Price ★★ LC 🕅 ⊞ 🛋

4 Lee Jofa/Gadesden HAD Colour **1210** Alt. colours **yes** Composition **100% linen** Width **132cm/51¾in** Repeat **96cm/37¾in** Price ★★★ 🕅

5 Today Interiors/Samadhi/ Samara Colour **SAF3079** Alt. colours **yes** Composition **88% linen, 12% nylon** Width **137cm/54in** Repeat **62cm/ 24¼in** Price ★★ 🛋 LC W

6 Mulberry/Daisy Daisy FD084 Colour **J103 Cream** Alt. colours **yes** Composition **75% cotton, 25% viscose** Width **150cm/59in** Repeat **13.5cm/5¼in** Price ★★★ 🕅 ⊞

7 Hill & Knowles/Lorian/Oakham C4265 Colour **65** Alt. colours **yes** Composition **52% linen, 48% cotton** Width **140cm/ 55in** Repeat **63cm/24¾in** Price ★★ 🕅 LC ⊞ 🛋

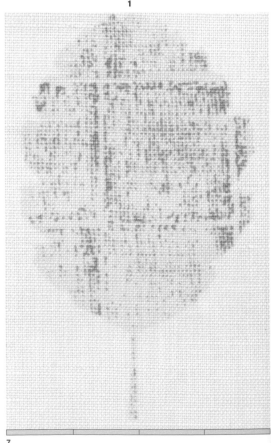

3

4

5

6

7

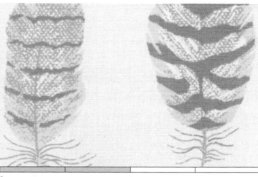

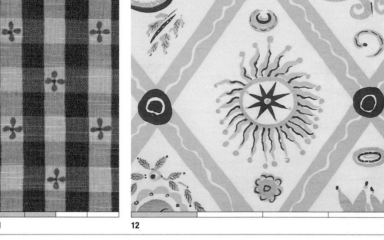

8   10

11   12

13

14

15

8 Donghia/Fleur d'Hiver 0475/ 3310 Colour **01** Alt. colours **yes** Composition **88% cotton, 12% viscose** Width **137cm/ 54in** Repeat **68cm/26¾in** Price ★★★★

9 Hill & Knowles/Lorian/Teal C4482 Colour **82** Alt. colours **yes** Composition **52%linen, 48% cotton** Width **140cm/ 55in** Repeat **35.5cm/14in** Price ★★

10 Brunschwig & Fils/Sycamore Floral Plaid 53373.01 Colour **mandarin plaid** Alt. colours **yes** Composition **100% cotton** Width **130cm/51in** Repeat **16cm/6¼in** Price ★★

11 Zoffany/Provence Check PLP0500 Colour **1** Alt. colours **yes** Composition **100% cotton** Width **137cm/ 54in** Repeat **6cm/2½in** Price ★★

12 Celia Birtwell/Orphée 1013 Colour **beige** Alt. colours **yes** Composition **100% silk** Width **140cm/55in** Repeat **91cm/35¾in** Price ★★★

13 Abbott & Boyd/Medina Colour **verde** Alt. colours **yes** Composition **100% cotton** Width **160cm/63in** Repeat **40cm/15¾in** Price ★★

14 Zoffany/Florette PLP0100 Colour **1** Alt. colours **yes** Composition **100% cotton** Width **137cm/54in** Repeat **21.5cm/8½in** Price ★★

15 J. Robert Scott/Floating Petals 3451 Colour **green tea** Alt. colours **yes** Composition **66% wool, 34% silk** Width **135cm/53in** Repeat **45.5cm/ 17¾in** Price ★★★

THE OAK LEAF

The fabric shown here is adapted from a hand-blocked tapestry woven in the Arthur H. Lee factory in Birkenhead, England, until the early 1970s, when the factory closed. The pattern dates from the early 20th century. However, the oak-leaf motif was first used much earlier than that – for example, in ancient Rome as a symbol of civic virtue, and in naturalistic decorations of the Middle Ages and the Renaissance. Similarly, the acorn – a symbol of life, fecundity and immortality – notably recurs in ancient Roman, Celtic and Scandinavian designs, and has been consistently favoured since the Middle Ages.

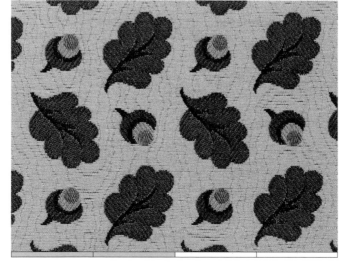

Lee Jofa/Oak Leaf Weave 854252 Colour **carmine** Alt. colours **yes** Composition **85% rayon, 15% cotton** Width **132cm/51¾in** Repeat **8.5cm/3¼in** Price ★★★★

Motifs: Late 20th–early 21st century

Fashionable fabric motifs of the 1950s included abstract, geometric and Cubist-inspired images, as well as crystal-like shapes derived from scientific observations under the microscope and produced by designers working in a style known as Organic Modernism. Small repeat motifs of fruits such as apples and pears were also popular. Depicted in both stylized and naturalistic form, and often set on a plain background, they remained in demand for much of the rest of the century.

The 1960s gave rise to a profusion of decorative styles and accompanying motifs: Art Nouveau fabrics (harbouring sinuous plant stems and roots and elongated blooms) enjoyed a great revival; foliage, flowers, animals, birds and insects appeared in repeating patterns taken from Persian paintings and ceramics; Renaissance-style classical figures, vases and urns – sometimes set within geometric patterns and sometimes in mosaic form – came into vogue, and Pop Art crossed over from canvas and concrete to textiles. As the 1960s drew to a close, a new ruralism emerged, significant consequences of which were the enduring "country-house look" and the accompanying revival in the manufacture of chintzes incorporating traditional foliage, flower, fruit and bird motifs.

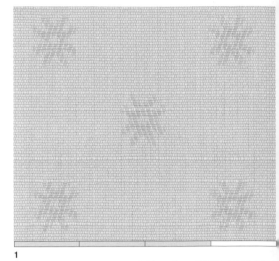

1

2

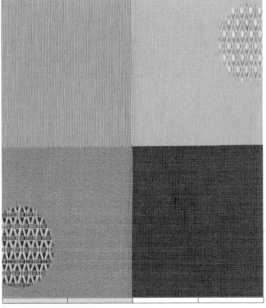

3

4

1 Monkwell/Estrella MF5821
Colour **sand 404** Alt. colours
yes Composition **47% modacrylic, 43% cotton, 10% nylon** Width **137cm/ 54in** Repeat **6cm/2½in**
Price ★★ 🔲 🔲🔲 LC

2 Knowles & Christou/Posey
Colour **porceline** Alt. colours
yes Composition **100% silk** Width **152cm/59¾in**
Repeat **40cm/15¾in**
Price ★★★ 🔲

3 Sahco Hesslein/Minerva 1831
Colour **03** Alt. colours **yes**
Composition **74% cotton, 18% silk, 5% acrylic, 3% viscose** Width **130cm/51in**
Repeat **25cm/9¾in**
Price ★★★ 🔲 LC

4 Nina Campbell/Nina's Garden/
Rock Pool NCF3133/03
Colour **red** Alt. colours **yes**
Composition **100% cotton**
Width **140cm/55in** Repeat
30cm/11¾in Price ★★ 🔲

5 Malabar/Bo Leaf TAPR22
Colour **silver** Alt. colours
no Composition **100% silk**
Width **140cm/55in**
Repeat **49cm/19¼in**
Price ★★★ 🔲 🔲

6 Brunschwig & Fils/89418
Colour **honey beige 069**
Alt. colours **yes** Composition
100% cotton Width **137cm/ 54in** Repeat **63.5cm/25in**
Price ★★ 🔲 LC 🔲

5

6

7

10

11

8

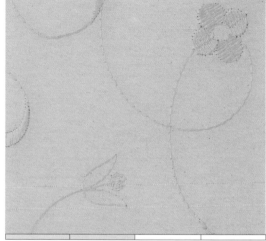

12

7 Donghia/Crown Jewels 2000
Colour **18** Alt. colours **yes**
Composition **81% rayon,
19% polyester** Width **137cm/
54in** Repeat **32cm/12½in**
Price ★★★★★ 🪑🛋

8 Textra/Okaya Colour **cream,
orange** Alt. colours **yes**
Composition **100% linen**
Width **138cm/54in** Repeat
32cm/12½in Price ★★ 🪑🛋

9 Abbott & Boyd/Est Complemento
Flora Colour **antillana verde**
Alt. colours **no** Composition
100% Width **150cm/59in**
Repeat **35cm/13¾in**
Price ★★ 🪑⊞

10 Nina Campbell/Manihiki
Prints/Vanuta NCF3362-04
Colour **04** Alt. colours **yes**
Composition **100% cotton**
Width **140cm/55in**
Repeat **45cm/17½in**
Price ★★ 🪑🛋

11 Osborne & Little/Rondo F1413
Colour **02** Alt. colours **yes**
Composition **57% cotton, 43%
viscose** Width **140cm/55in**
Repeat **36cm/14in**
Price ★★★ 🛋

12 Montgomery/Jasmine
Colour **beige 12** Alt. colours
yes Composition **67% polyester,
26% viscose, 7% linen** Width
140cm/55in Repeat **64cm/25in**
Price ★ 🪑 ⊞

13 Harlequin/Notebook/Tilia Colour
apple green 177 Alt. colours **yes**
Composition **36% cotton,
52% linen, 12% nylon** Width
137cm/54in Repeat **64cm/25in**
Price ★★ 🪑🛋

9

13

Motifs: Late 20th–early 21st century

Many of the fabric motifs favoured since the late 1960s have reflected a widespread nostalgia for previous eras and the accompanying boom in "period-style" interiors. Apart from chintz-style flowers, foliage and birds, revivals have included late 19th-century William Morris- and other Arts and Crafts-style flowers, animal motifs derived from 16th- and 17th-century needlework patterns and, in America, "Native Orders", first popular in the late 18th and 19th centuries. Significant among the latter were corncobs, tobacco and cotton balls, stars, turkeys and bald eagles, as well as Native American motifs including feathered arrowshafts, bison and bison horns. Some of the most striking motifs are classical architectural elements rendered in black and white. At the same time, more short-term nostalgia resulted in "space age" motifs inspired by the Apollo programme and the moon landings.

Internationally, the late 20th and early 21st century also witnessed a further consolidation of the links between contemporary fine art and fabric design, with fashionable motifs featuring artistic images of fruits and berries, a diverse range of domestic artefacts ranging from crockery to buttons, and photographic images and photocopied prints.

Pierre Frey/Minton 1962 Colour **rose ancien 5** Alt. colours **yes** Composition **100% cotton** Width **138cm/54in** Repeat **77cm/30¼in** Price ★★★★ 🗘

Mulberry/Tea Rose/FD441 Colour **red** Alt. colours **yes** Composition **61% silk, 39% polyester** Width **127cm/50in** Repeat **13cm/5¼in** Price ★★ 🛋

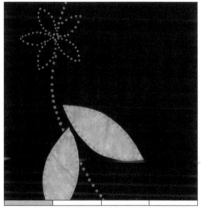

Harlequin/Divine/Sense Colour **197** Alt. colours **yes** Composition **100% cotton** Width **137cm/54in** Repeat **64cm/25in** Price ★ 🗘 🛋

Timney Fowler/Porticos TF0203/03 Colour **03** Alt. colours **yes** Composition **100% cotton** Width **137cm/54in** Repeat **96.5cm/38in** Price ★★ 🗘 🛋

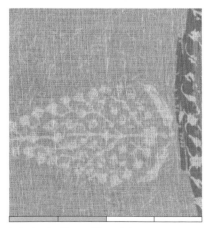

Today Interiors/Aymara/Mirage Colour **3313** Alt. colours **yes** Composition **52% linen, 48% cotton** Width **137cm/54in** Repeat **50.5cm/20in** Price ★★ LC 🗘 🛋

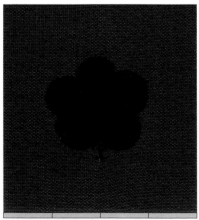

Today Interiors/Taffetas/Pensee Colour **4041** Alt. colours **yes** Composition **100% acetate (flowers - polyester/viscose)** Width **150cm/59in** Repeat **20cm/8in** Price ★★ ⊞

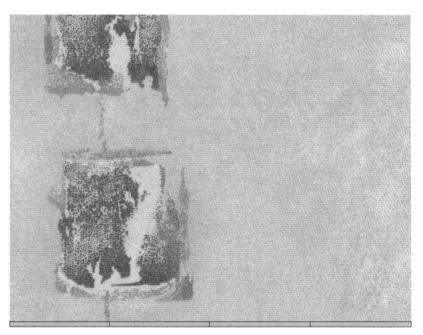

Montgomery/Samurai Colour **12** Alt. colours **yes** Composition **100% cotton** Width **140cm/55in** Repeat **64cm/25in** Price ★ 🗆 ⊞

Brunschwig & Fils 79529 Colour **761** Alt. colours **yes** Composition **100% cotton** Width **142.5cm/56in** Repeat **46cm/18in** Price ★★ 🗆🗆 🗆

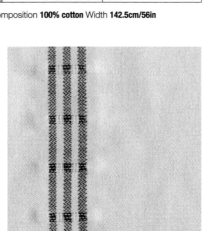

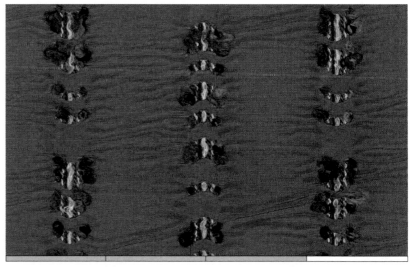

Manuel Canovas/Tilda 4423/21 Colour **rose/jaune** Alt. colours **yes** Composition **73% viscose, 27% cotton** Width **140cm/55in** Repeat **8.5cm/3¼in** Price ★★ 🗆🗆

Malabar/Jutis Colour **01** Alt. colours **yes** Composition **90% cotton, 10% jute** Width **137cm/54in** Repeat – Price ★★ 🗆🗆 ⊞

Liberty Furnishings/Bellini LF4290 Colour **03** Alt. colours **yes** Composition **45% polyester, 35% viscose, 15% acrylic, 5% polyamide** Width **144cm/56½in** Repeat **10cm/4in** Price ★★ 🗆 ⊞

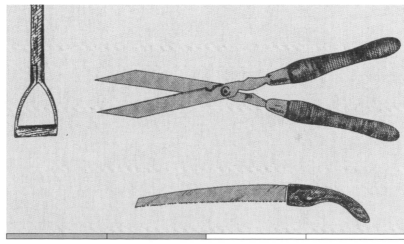

Malabar/Alula Colour **02** Alt. colours **no** Composition **80% silk, 20% wool** Width **140cm/55in** Repeat **70cm/27½in** Price ★ 🗆

Abbott & Boyd/Est el Jardin Verde Colour **green on cream** Alt. colours **no** Composition **100% cotton** Width **160cm/63in** Repeat **66cm/26in** Price ★★ 🗆 ⊞

Anna French/Chalice Colour **28** Alt. colours **yes** Composition **100% cotton** Width **137cm/54in** Repeat **64cm/25in** Price ★★ 🗆 🗆

20th & 21st century

Floral Fabrics

Throughout history, textile designers have made extensive use of plant motifs and floral subjects. In Europe, before the end of the 16th century, floral patterns were featured on a wide variety of fabrics, including tapestry, embroidery and woven damasks and velvets. However, the accurate depiction of the many and diverse plants in existence was restricted by the limitations of early weaving techniques and by a lack of botanical reference material.

Two events were to occur that resulted in a proliferation of floral-patterned fabrics that has endured to this day. The first event was the publication in 1586 of *La Clef des Champs*, by French artist and traveller Jacques le Moyne de Morgues. Depicting flowers, fruits and animals in a simple but accurate style, this early pattern book provided textile designers with a wealth of inspiration, and also set the precedent for more extensive publications in the future. The second was the importation of the first colourfast, hand-blocked calicoes (*indiennes*) from India, which confirmed that floral decoration could be most dramatically exploited on printed fabrics.

LEFT Printed cotton curtains grace the window of a medieval house in a *bastide* in the Lot-et-Garonne region, France. The floral design, augmented with a pattern of foliage and birds, is elegantly rendered in white, red and shades of pink.

BELOW LEFT *Chinoiserie* patterns on 17th- and 18th-century delftware provided the inspiration for the bed-hangings and upholstered seating in this bedroom at the Château de Morsan, France.

BELOW The walls of this room, designed by Roger Banks-Pye, are decorated with a machine-woven, crewelwork fabric, its stylized floral pattern inspired by 17th-century Eastern designs. The various blue-and-white and black-and-white checks covering the cushions and screen stand out sharply against this contrasting background.

ROSE MOTIFS

Rich in symbolism, the rose has been one of the most enduringly popular of the floral motifs. In Christian iconography it is an attribute of the Virgin Mary and paradise, while in classical mythology it is a token of Venus (and love), and of secrecy (*sub rosa*). Other notable associations of the rose include martyrdom (red rose) and piety (white rose). Over the centuries wild and cultivated roses have inspired fabric designs, wild roses being closely associated with medieval, Jacobean and Arts and Crafts fabrics and cultivated roses appearing on Victorian and Edwardian designs.

KEY DESIGNS

1 Naturalistic floral patterns were especially popular in the 18th and 19th centuries, but first began to appear in the 17th century as designers gained access to illustrated botanical studies.

2 Flowering-vine patterns were prevalent in ancient Egyptian, Roman and early eastern Mediterranean decorations, and were favoured on Renaissance and 17th-, 18th- and mid-19th-century fabrics.

3 Stylized floral patterns have been seen since the Middle Ages. They were particularly popular during the late 19th century, and were a feature of Arts and Crafts and Art Nouveau fabrics.

4 Flowers are a feature of *chinoiserie* and *japonaiserie* fabrics, many of which were derived from traditional porcelain designs. Popular imagery included blossom sprigs, peonies and chrysanthemums.

5 Patterns of densely packed blooms and foliage were highly fashionable in Victorian interiors, especially on chintzes, and were to come back into fashion in the Art Deco schemes of the 20th century.

6 Since the Middle Ages, typical embellishments to naturalistic and stylized floral patterns have included trelliswork, hanging baskets and, as in this rose pattern, decorative ribbons.

1 Bennett Silks/Basket and Ribbon Colour **multi** Alt. colours **yes** Composition **100% silk** Width **130cm/51in** Repeat **61cm/24in** Price ★★★

2 Schumacher/Imperial Vine 168360 Colour **document cream and multi** Alt. colours **yes** Composition **100% cotton** Width **137cm/54in** Repeat **64.5cm/25¼in** Price ★★★

3 Morris & Co/Golden Lily PR7702 Colour **4** Alt. colours **yes** Composition **53% linen, 35% cotton, 12% nylon** Width **137cm/54in** Repeat **53cm/21in** Price ★★

4 Old World Weavers/Lasalle Colour **multi/ brown** Alt. colours **yes** Composition **100% rayon** Width **140cm/55in** Repeat **64cm/25in** Price ★★★

5 Jason D'Souza/Blenheim Colour **plum/rust** Alt. colours **yes** Composition **64% linen, 36% cotton** Width **135cm/53in** Repeat **92cm/36in** Price ★★★

6 Lelièvre/Watteau Colour **ivoire** Alt. colours **yes** Composition **68% viscose, 32% silk** Width **130cm/51in** Repeat **8cm/3in** Price ★★★

Florals: **Pre-18th century**

With the notable exception of the often highly naturalistic *mille fleurs* in medieval tapestries, the majority of floral-patterned fabrics produced before the 17th century featured stylized flowers. Most Renaissance damasks and velvets employed symmetrical floral designs, and the brightly coloured calicoes (*indiennes*) imported from India at the end of the 16th century portrayed stylized flowers (as did the European copies that followed). However, during the 17th century naturalistic renderings of an ever-greater number of flowers became increasingly common as knowledge of plant forms grew and pattern books on the subject proliferated. Influential publications included Pierre Vallet's *Le Jardin du Roi* (1608), which introduced many species, such as the tulip, and P.A. Ducerceau's *Bouquets Propres pour les Etoffes de Tours* (c.1660–70). The latter was specifically intended for silk designers and included species as diverse as narcissi, snake's-head and crown fritillaries, lilies, orchids, roses, pinks, clematis and campanula.

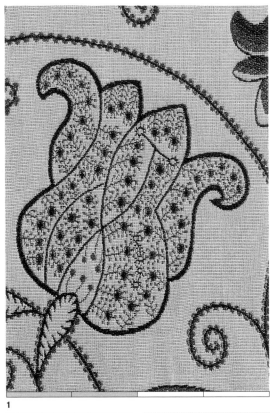

1

2

3

1 **Hodsoll McKenzie/English Crewelwork 220/103** Colour **olive** Alt. colours **yes** Composition **60% rayon, 40% cotton** Width **127cm/ 50in** Repeat **62cm/24¼in** Price ★★★ 🔲 W

2 **Chelsea Textiles/Queen Anne F101A** Colour **rust** Alt. colours **yes** Composition **60% linen, 40% cotton with cotton crewelwork** Width **114cm/ 44¾in** Repeat **107cm/42in** Price ★★★★ LC 🔲 ⊞ W

3 **Zimmer & Rohde/Zagara 5093** Colour **214** Alt. colours **yes** Composition **80% cotton, 20% viscose** Width **140cm/55in** Repeat **116cm/45¾** Price ★★★ 🔲

4

5

4 **Watts of Westminster/Langton F0064-01/ZIF** Colour **natural** Alt. colours **yes** Composition **100% linen** Width **125cm/ 49in** Repeat **80cm/31½in** Price ★★★ 🔲

5 **Jane Churchill/Florian Damask J254F** Colour **caramel** Alt. colours **yes** Composition **100% cotton** Width **143cm/ 56in** Repeat **28cm/11in** Price ★★ LC 🔲

6 **Chelsea Textiles/Grapes Fine Crewelwork F032** Colour **multi** Alt. colours **yes** Composition **100% cotton with wool crewelwork** Width **150cm/ 59in** Repeat **96cm/37¾in** Price ★★★★ 🔲 ⊞

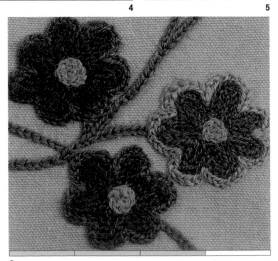

6

SYMBOLISM

The inspiration for "Darnley" came from a 16th-century needlework panel attributed to Mary, Queen of Scots and now part of the historic Hardwick Hall collection in Derbyshire, England. It features interlaced lilies, thistles, and roses, symbolic respectively of Mary's double crown of France and Scotland and of her claim to the throne of England. The fabric is woven in muted shades of the original (but now faded) ivory, gold, rose and green.

Stuart Interiors/Darnley Colour **ivory** Alt. colours **yes** Composition **60% wool, 40% cotton** Width **125cm/ 49in** Repeat **30cm/11¾in** Price ★★★★ LC 🔲 ⊞ W

7

CREWELWORK

A form of outline embroidery, crewelwork was fashionable during the 17th and 18th centuries and enjoyed revivals in the late 19th and 20th century. Stitched with crewel, a loose-spun worsted yarn, on a linen or cotton ground, crewelwork is traditionally used for bed furnishings and cushion covers, and sometimes rugs. Popular stitches for outlining include stem, double-back or chain, while satin, buttonhole, rope coral or French knot are used for fillings. Motifs are generally Eastern in origin, and include naïvely depicted flowers, leaves, animals and birds.

Marvic Textiles/Purna Colour **1213-1 red** Alt. colours **yes** Composition **58% wool, 42% cotton** Width **150cm/59in** Repeat **71cm/28in** Price ★★★★ ⌘ ⊞

10

12

7 **Jason D'Souza/Medici MED03** Colour **burgundy/ blue** Alt. colours **yes** Composition **70% linen, 30% cotton** Width **136cm/ 53½in** Repeat **49.5cm/19¼in** Price ★★★ ⌘

8 **Bernard Thorp & Co/Jane** Colour **blue and red** Alt. colours **yes** Composition **100% jute** Width **120cm/ 47in** Repeat **84cm/33in** Price ★★ ⌘ Ⓦ

9 **Zimmer & Rohde/Perle d'Or 9210 371** Colour **red and cream** Alt. colours **yes** Composition **100% cotton** Width **140cm/55in** Repeat **61cm/24in** Price ★★★ ⌘

10 **Beaumont & Fletcher/Tyger 2337a** Colour **madder/indigo** Alt. colours **yes** Composition **52% linen, 36% cotton, 12% nylon** Width **133.5cm/52½in** Repeat **80cm/31½in** Price ★★★ ⌘ ⌘

11 **Liberty/Moray LF4010** Colour **02** Alt. colours **yes** Composition **100% cotton** Width **140cm/ 55in** Repeat **39cm/15¼in** Price ★★ ⌘

12 **Abbott & Boyd/Floralia Barroca 45314-5** Colour **deep multi on grey** Alt. colours **no** Composition **100% linen** Width **140cm/55in** Repeat **110cm/43in** Price ★★★ ⌘ ⌘

13 **Fired Earth/FE9013 Papaver** Colour **6 Coral** Alt. colours **yes** Composition **60% linen, 20% cotton, 20% modal** Width **134cm/52½in** Repeat **50cm/9½in** Price ★★ Ⓛⓒ ⌘ ⊞ ⌘

1

13

Florals: **Early 18th century**

The first half of the 18th century saw developments in the design of floral-patterned fabrics. A new influence came from the East in the form of Chinese lacquer wares and ceramics showing exotic floral ornamentation. These provided the inspiration to copy unfamiliar flowers, such as the chrysanthemum, and to produce *chinoiserie* designs that imitated oriental compositions, notably the *famille rose* and *Kakiemon* patterns. During the Rococo period pursuit of the exotic even extended to the devising of imaginary species, such as the "umbrella" flower.

Running parallel to the adoption of Chinese forms of decoration was a growth in the production of French and English floral chintzes (developed from the imported Indian calicoes, or *indiennes*, of the previous century). By 1721 these printed cotton fabrics were sufficiently popular to threaten the future of woven fabrics, and in England an Act of Parliament forbade their manufacture for the home market. However, owing to popular demand, the English cotton industry was allowed to renew production in the 1730s (restrictions being removed totally in the 1770s), using a linen-cotton cloth known as fustian. Similar legislation was introduced in France in the 1680s but rescinded in 1759.

5

1

2

3

4

6

1 **Beaumont & Fletcher/Aubusson Rose 2209** Colour **coral** Alt. colours **yes** Composition **52% linen, 36% cotton, 12% nylon** Width **133.5cm/52½in** Repeat **84cm/33in** Price ★★★

2 **Jab/Excelsa-Rose 1-7318** Colour **cream 270** Alt. colours **yes** Composition **100% silk** Width **135cm/53in** Repeat **19cm/7½in** Price ★

3 **Hodsoll McKenzie/Indian Iris 105/501** Colour **red/blue** Alt. colours **yes** Composition **52% linen, 36% cotton, 12% nylon** Width **137cm/54in** Repeat **20cm/8in** Price ★★

4 **Marvic Textiles/Baronscourt 474** Colour **4** Alt. colours **yes** Composition **35% viscose, 39% cotton, 26% linen** Width **136cm/53½in** Repeat **150cm/59in** Price ★★

5 **Scalamandré/Louis XV 2770M-005** Colour **Chinese red** Alt. colours **yes** Composition **100% silk** Width **140cm/55in** Repeat **53cm/21in** Price ★★★★★

6 **Zoffany/Gold Flowers AMB0500** Colour **1** Alt. colours **yes** Composition **100% cotton** Width **138cm/54in** Repeat **73cm/28½in** Price ★★

7 Jason D'Souza/Verona Colour **pink and blue** Alt. colours **yes** Composition **70% linen, 30% cotton** Width **136cm/ 53½in** Repeat **74cm/29in** Price ★★★

8 Garin/Janini 96455041 Colour **rojo** Alt. colours **yes** Composition **69% cotton, 21% viscose, 10% linen** Width **150cm/59in** Repeat **56cm/ 22in** Price ★★★

9 Lee Jofa/Hollyhock Minor Print 849010-16 Colour **mocha** Alt. colours **yes** Composition **100% cotton** Width **132cm/ 51¾in** Repeat **58cm/22¾in** Price ★★

10 Zoffany/Emily FRN0100 Colour **1** Alt. colours **yes** Composition **51% linen, 49% cotton** Width **137cm/ 53¾in** Repeat **56cm/22in** Price ★★

11 Jason D'Souza/Colonne Fleurie CF1 Colour **tonal pink** Alt. colours **yes** Composition **70% linen, 30% cotton** Width **121cm/47¼in** Repeat **47cm/ 18¼in** Price ★★★

7

8

10

12 Zimmer & Rohde/Adrastos 2556 Colour **184** Alt. colours **yes** Composition **70% cotton, 30% viscose** Width **138cm /54in** Repeat **36cm/14in** Price ★★★

13 Colefax and Fowler/Lincoln 2061/03 Colour **cream and aqua** Alt. colours **yes** Composition **60% linen, 20% cotton, 20% modacrylic** Width **135cm/ 53in** Repeat **35cm/13¾in** Price ★★

14 Chelsea Textiles/Wisteria Pink F057P Colour **pink** Alt. colours **yes** Composition **55% linen, 45% cotton with cotton embroidery** Width **120cm/47in** Repeat **20cm/8in** Price ★★★ LC W

15 Old World Weavers/Lisere Romano II AO 27513222 Colour **rose/green** Alt. colours **yes** Composition **100% silk** Width **50cm/ 19½in** Repeat **35cm/13¾in** Price ★★★★★

16 Hodsoll McKenzie/English Ribbon 223/101-108 Colour **blue** Alt. colours **yes** Composition **61% spun rayon, 39% cotton** Width **127cm/50in** Repeat **20.5cm/ 8in** Price ★★★ W

15

12

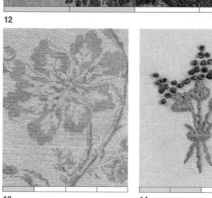

13

14

16

Florals: Late 18th century

The proliferation of floral-patterned fabrics in Europe was further fuelled during the latter half of the 18th century by the British government's removal, in the 1770s, of previously imposed restrictions on the manufacture of cotton chintzes. Moreover, the development of copperplate printing in the 1750s had revolutionized the fabric industry by increasing output, reducing costs and improving the quality of designs. By the end of the 18th century, Americans were also producing their own chintzes thanks to the emigration of a number of English printers to Philadelphia.

Aesthetically, floral patterns of the second half of the century were characterized by a move away from the exotic toward naturalistic renditions of less complicated (often wild) flowers. Typical examples included larkspurs, roses, carnations, poppies and cornflowers, as well as the daisies, stocks, violets and anemones embellishing many of the fabrics used in 1768 to decorate Marie Antoinette's bedroom at the Petit Trianon in Versailles, France.

1

2

4

5

6

3

7

1 **Wemyss Houlès/Wellbeck** Colour **18** Alt. colours **yes** Composition **53% viscose, 35% cotton, 12% nylon** Width **140cm/55in** Repeat **24cm/9½in** Price ★★ 🔲🛋

2 **Lennox Money/Miramar 2433C** Colour **green and yellow** Alt. colours **yes** Composition **100% cotton** Width **136.5cm/53¾in** Repeat **119cm/46¾in** Price ★★ 🔲🛋 W

3 **Bennison Fabrics/Corne Fleurie** Colour **blue and yellow** Alt. colours **yes** Composition **70% linen, 30% cotton** Width **129cm/51in** Repeat **42cm/16½in** Price ★★★ 🔲🛋

4 **Watts of Westminster/Edenwood F0063-02/N15** Colour **Dorchester** Alt. colours **yes** Composition **100% linen** Width **127cm/50in** Repeat **76cm/30in** Price ★★★★ 🔲

5 **Zoffany/China Rose FRN0300** Colour **1** Alt. colours **yes** Composition **100% cotton** Width **138cm/54in** Repeat **55cm/21½in** Price ★★★ 🔲

6 **Hodsoll McKenzie/Roots 926/502** Colour **blue** Alt. colours **yes** Composition **52% linen, 36% cotton, 12% nylon** Width **137cm/53¾in** Repeat **13cm/5in** Price ★★★ 🔲🛋 LC

7 **Brunschwig & Fils/65346.01** Colour **6** Alt. colours **yes** Composition **100% cotton** Width **137cm/54in** Repeat **151cm/59½in** Price ★★★★ 🔲🛋 LC

8 Jane Churchill/Rose Toile J240F Colour **03 Aqua** Alt. colours **yes** Composition **100% cotton** Width **137cm/54in** Repeat **18cm/7in** Price ★★ LC ⬚ ⬚

9 Zoffany/Sweet Briar FRN0500 Colour **1** Alt. colours **yes** Composition **100% silk** Width **136cm/53½in** Repeat **84cm/33in** Price ★★★ ⬚

10 Anne & Robert Swaffer/Amy Colour **32** Alt. colours **yes** Composition **100% cotton** Width **140cm/55in** Repeat **22cm/8½in** Price ★ ⬚ ⬚ ⬚

11 Brunschwig & Fils/36465.01 Colour **5** Alt. colours **yes** Composition **100% wool** Width **122cm/48in** Repeat **16cm/6¼in** Price ★★★ ⬚ LC ⬚

12 Bennison Fabrics/Wheatflower Colour **1** Alt. colours **yes** Composition **70% linen, 30% cotton** Width **126cm/49in** Repeat **57.5cm/22½in** Price ★★★ ⬚ ⬚

13 Brunschwig & Fils/Empress of China Stripe 51305 Colour **01** Alt. colours **yes** Composition **100% cotton** Width **140cm/55in** Repeat **107cm/42in** Price ★★★ ⬚ ⬚

14 Lennox Money/Chekian Lotus Colour **1** Alt. colours **no** Composition **100% cotton** Width **135cm/53in** Repeat **64cm/25in** Price ★★★ LC ⬚ W

8

9

10

11

12

13

14

DOCUMENTARY DESIGNS

A "document" is used to describe an historic fabric that serves as the source for a reproduction – a documentary fabric. In its purest form a documentary fabric is an exact copy of the fibres, width, repeat, colours and every detail of the original design. However, if one or more of the original elements is altered (as is often the case), the reproduction is referred to as an "adaptation". Typical examples include a change from silk to synthetic fibres, adjustments of scale to accommodate modern power looms, and variations in colour caused by different dyes or printing techniques.

The fabrics below are based on the original documents shown above, with some modifications: alteration to the size of the pattern and, in the case of "Tulip Stripe", replacement of some of the roses with a broken stripe.

Apenn/Surrey Rose Garland AV464-1/2/3 Colour **1** Alt. colours **yes** Composition **100% cotton** Width **122cm/48in** Repeat **48cm/19in** Price ★★ ⬚ ⬚

Apenn/Tulip Stripe AV466-1/2/3 Colour **red and blue** Alt. colours **yes** Composition **100% cotton** Width **124cm/48¾in** Repeat **23cm/9in** Price ★★ ⬚ ⬚

FABRICS: *FLORALS* **117**

Florals: **Mid-19th century**

Two technological developments served to expand the production and popularity of floral-patterned fabrics during the middle of the 19th century. The first was the introduction of the power loom, which had come into widespread use during the mid-1820s and served to increase the speed as well as reduce the costs of production. The second development was the discovery of coal tar and aniline dyes in the mid-1850s, which enabled manufacturers to produce deeper and more vivid colours. The result was an outburst of naturalistic, often overblown, floral ornament. For example, many Rococo-style ("Louis Quatorze") fabrics displayed floral patterns augmented with scrolls and cartouches shaded for "three-dimensional effect". Similarly, a typical mid-19th-century chintz incorporated "three-dimensional" scrolling acanthus leaves and flowers in various shades of green, blue, white, violet and yellow. The rationale of this heightened naturalism was expressed by the Jury of the Great Exhibition, held in London, England, in 1851: "The task is to cover the surface almost entirely with large, coarse flowers: dahlias, hollyhocks, roses, hydrangeas, or others which give scope for strong or vivid colouring, and which are often magnified by the designer much beyond the scale of nature."

5

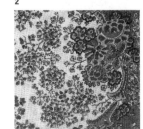

1 Nina Campbell/Rosenkavalier NCF3432 Colour **04** Alt. colours **yes** Composition **84% linen, 16% nylon** Width **140cm/ 55in** Repeat **62cm/24¼in** Price ★★ LC ▨ ⊞⌂

2 Beaumont & Fletcher/Baroque Floral 2239b Colour **rose** Alt. colours **yes** Composition **52% linen, 36% cotton, 12% nylon** Width **133.5cm/ 52½in** Repeat **52cm/20½in** Price ★★★ ▨ ⌂

3 Borderline/Indica 2463 Colour **blue and yellow** Alt. colours **yes** Composition **100% wool** Width **137cm/54in** Repeat **24.5cm/9¾in** Price ★ LC ▨ ⌂

4 George Spencer Designs/ Thistle 108L Colour **red** Alt. colours **yes** Composition **100% linen** Width **120cm/47in** Repeat **47cm/18½in** Price ★★★ ▨ ⌂

5 Lee Jofa/Floral Bouquet 889300 Colour **white** Alt. colours **yes** Composition **100% cotton** Width **134cm/ 52½in** Repeat **84cm/33in** Price ★★★ ▨ ⌂

6 Sanderson/Bloom PR8510 Colour **2** Alt. colours **yes** Composition **100% cotton** Width **137cm/54in** Repeat **32cm/12¼in** Price ★★ ▨ ⌂

7 Colefax and Fowler/Coniston F1314/01 Colour **stone** Alt. colours **yes** Composition **52% linen, 36% cotton, 12% nylon** Width **135cm/ 53in** Repeat **43cm/17in** Price ★ ▨ LC ⌂

8 Warner Fabrics/Montpelier Chintz CS8611 Colour **blue ribbon** Alt. colours **yes** Composition **100% cotton** Width **137cm/54in** Repeat **44cm/17¼in** Price ★★★ 🛋️⊞

9 Jane Churchill/Country Rose Stripe J237F Colour **red/ green 01** Alt. colours **yes** Composition **37% cotton, 51% linen, 2% nylon** Width **140cm/55in** Repeat **34cm/ 13½in** Price ★★ 🛋️ LC 🛋️

10 Brunschwig & Fils/79489 Colour **015** Alt. colours **yes** Composition **100% cotton** Width **137cm/ 54in** Repeat **107cm/42in** Price ★★★ 🛋️ LC 🛋️

11 Jim Thompson/Montague 1055 Colour **04** Alt. colours **yes** Composition **100% silk** Width **122cm/48in** Repeat **46cm/18in** Price ★★★★ 🛋️🛋️

FADED CHINTZ

One of the most attractive characteristics of chintz is that its original bright colours gradually mellow and fade – a process that is caused by exposure to sunlight, laundering and general usage. This explains why 18th- and 19th-century chintzes are sought after today, and why, since the 1970s, designers and manufacturers have been producing "artificially aged" chintzes to meet the demand. Soaking the fabric in a weak solution of tea is a simple method of achieving subtle discoloration, and sandwashing produces fading. However, most manufacturers make adjustments in the dyes they use and employ chemical solutions to achieve the desired effect.

Bennison Fabrics/Rosevine Colour **faded pink, green** Alt. colours **yes** Composition **70% linen, 30% cotton** Width **132cm/51¾in** Repeat **49cm/19¼in** Price ★★★ 🛋️🛋️

Bennison Fabrics/Damask Rose Colour **green/pink** Alt. colours **yes** Composition **70% linen, 30% cotton** Width **119cm/46¾in** Repeat **63cm/24¾in** Price ★★★ 🛋️🛋️

Hodsoll McKenzie/Faded Bouquet 110/403 Colour **blue** Alt. colours **yes** Composition **100% cotton** Width **137cm/54in** Repeat **59.5cm/23¼in** Price ★★★ 🛋️🛋️ W

Florals: **Late 19th century**

The last two decades of the 19th century witnessed a reaction to the highly naturalistic floral patterns favoured earlier. For example, the Aesthetic movement espoused the use of simple flowers, such as the lotus (a Japanese influence), pinks and sunflowers – the latter appearing as a recurring motif in the designs (some highly stylized, some botanically accurate) of Walter Crane. Similarly, William Morris and the Arts and Crafts movement promoted a return to simple, uncomplicated flowers – as illustrated in medieval herbals – and the use of traditional vegetable, rather than chemical, dyes.

Morris's designs included columbines, poppies, honeysuckle, pinks, anemones, marigolds, daisies and jasmine, and had a rhythmical, sensuous quality absent from the flat, static patterns produced by many followers of the Aesthetic movement. This sensuousness was later reflected in the work of some Art Nouveau designers. Many of them had rejected floral forms altogether and turned to vegetal motifs (roots, buds and seedpods) to fit the dynamic lines of Art Nouveau. However, others – such as E.A. Séguy in his *Les Fleurs et Leurs Applications Décoratives* (1899) – employed a wide selection of sinuous plant forms, such as passionflowers, poppies, wisteria and waterlilies.

5

1

1 **Morris & Co/Fruit RR8048** Colour **1** Alt. colours **yes** Composition **100% cotton** Width **137cm/54in** Repeat **64cm/25in** Price ★

2 **G.P. & J. Baker/Avalon R1285 02** Colour **greens** Alt. colours **yes** Composition **60% linen, 22% cotton, 18% viscose** Width **137cm/54in** Repeat **62cm/24¼in** Price ★★

3 **Old World Weavers/Vera Linen B1886L01** Colour **07 multi** Alt. colours **yes** Composition **58% linen, 42% cotton** Width **140cm/55in** Repeat **96cm/37¾in** Price ★★★★

4 **Lee Jofa/Kingsworthy Print 929070** Colour **eggshell** Alt. colours **yes** Composition **100% linen** Width **132cm/51¾in** Repeat **50cm/19½in** Price ★★★★

2

6

7

5 **Brunschwig & Fils/Ogden House Cotton Print 79308** Colour **176 pomegranate** Alt. colours **yes** Composition **100% cotton** Width **138cm/54in** Repeat **38cm/15in** Price ★★★

6 **Borderline/Pomegranate 2170B** Colour **jade/pink** Alt. colours **yes** Composition **60% linen, 40% cotton** Width **14.5cm/5¾in** Repeat **30cm/11¾in** Price ★

7 **Beaumont & Fletcher/Wistaria & Rose 2196A** Colour **rust/tan** Alt. colours **yes** Composition **52% linen, 36% cotton, 12% nylon** Width **134cm/52½in** Repeat **71cm/28in** Price ★★★

3

4

8 **Lelièvre/Bouquet Champêtre 4317** Colour **ivory 01** Alt. colours **yes** Composition **100% silk** Width **130cm/51in** Repeat **103cm/40½in** Price ★★★★★ ⬚

9 **Lelièvre/Les Tulipes 4138** Colour **ivoire 01** Alt. colours **no** Composition **100% silk** Width **130cm/51in** Repeat **53cm/21in** Price ★★★★★ ⬚ ⬚

10 **Scalamandré/Newport – Moiréd Lisère 96495** Colour **multi on beige and salmon stripe** Alt. colours **yes** Composition **100% silk** Width **127cm/ 50in** Repeat **8cm/3in** Price ★★★★★ ⬚ ⬚

11 **Lee Jofa/Southdown Rose 909403** Colour **03** Alt. colours **yes** Composition **100% cotton** Width **132cm/ 51¾in** Repeat **45cm/17½in** Price ★★ ⬚ ⬚

12 **Jim Thompson/Botanica PDB 3014** Colour **A** Alt. colours **yes** Composition **100% silk** Width **122cm/48in** Repeat **91.5cm/36in** Price ★★★★ ⬚ ⬚

13 **Marvic Textiles/Baudouin 8247** Colour **blue 6** Alt. colours **yes** Composition **52% linen, 48% viscose** Width **140cm/ 55in** Repeat **69cm/27in** Price ★★ ⬚ ⬚ ⬚

11

9

10

12

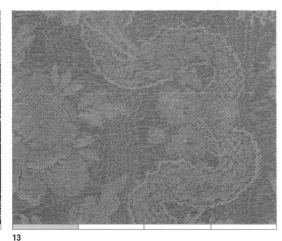

13

ARTS & CRAFTS STYLE

"Anyone wanting to produce dyed textiles with any artistic quality in them must forego the modern and commercial methods in favour of those that are at least as old as Pliny, who speaks of them as being old in his time" (William Morris). For Morris (and the other Arts and Crafts designers) this meant using block- rather than roller-printing, and vegetable rather than chemical dyes. The rhythmical and elaborate patterns of these designers incorporate simple but sinuous flowers and other plant forms, and have remained fashionable to the present day.

Liberty Furnishings/Burnham 1064616 Colour **L** Alt. colours **yes** Composition **100% cotton** Width **137cm/54in** Repeat **51cm/20in** Price ★ ⬚ ⬚

Liberty Furnishings/Snakeshead 1095020 Colour **blue/green** Alt. colours **yes** Composition **53% linen, 35% cotton, 12% polyacrylic** Width **137cm/54in** Repeat **44cm/17in** Price ★★ ⬚ ⬚ ⬚

Florals: Early 20th century

Despite the earlier protestations of the Aesthetic movement, largely on the grounds of "poor taste", naturalistically depicted floral chintzes remained highly popular among the general public around the end of the 19th century. However, the majority of the Art Deco fabrics that were fashionable during the early 20th century incorporated stylized flowers – although they were usually confined (in the "classical style") to baskets, festoons or garlands, or were densely packed. For example, E.A. Séguy's highly influential *Bouquets de Fronaisons*, first published in Paris, France, in 1927, showed illustrations of tightly packed rosebuds and composites such as daisies, marguerites and zinnias.

William Morris's floral designs (*see* pages 122-3) remained fashionable in the later Arts and Crafts interiors of the first three decades of the century, as did the cheaper, machine-printed copies of his designs that were produced. However, the designers of fabrics in the Modernist style largely rejected floral ornamentation altogether.

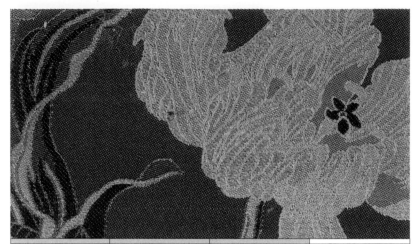

Mulberry/Parrot Tulips FD309/713 Colour **Light Red V139** Alt. colours **yes** Composition **51% silk, 49% cotton** Width **127cm/50in** Repeat **59cm/23in** Price ★★★★

Clarence House/Flowering Quince 33944 Colour **green** Alt. colours **yes** Composition **100% linen** Width **137cm/54in** Repeat **100cm/39¼in** Price ★★★

Ramm, Son & Crocker/Iris & Geranium Colour **red/taupe** Alt. colours **yes** Composition **84% linen, 16% nylon** Width **140cm/55in** Repeat **65cm/25½in** Price ★★

Mulberry/Secret Garden Linen Union FD181 Colour **Red V106** Alt. colours **yes** Composition **51% linen, 37% cotton, 12% nylon** Width **137cm/54in** Repeat **61cm/24in** Price ★★

G.P. & J. Baker/Peony & Blossom R1368 Colour **6** Alt. colours **yes** Composition **100% linen** Width **137cm/54in** Repeat **80cm/31½in** Price ★★

Brunschwig & Fils/79494.051 Colour 4 Alt. colours yes Composition 100% cotton Width 135cm/53in Repeat 106cm/41½in Price ★★★ 🛋🗐⊞

Brunschwig & Fils/Sconset Quilted Floral 32833.01 Colour gold and red Alt. colours yes Composition 100% cotton Width 140cm/55in Repeat 48cm/19in Price ★★★ 🗐🛋

Brunschwig & Fils/Highland Rose 7989.04 Colour ivory Alt. colours no Composition 100% cotton Width 137cm/54in Repeat 36cm/14in Price ★★ 🗐🛋⊞

Anna French/Rosebud Colour 71 Alt. colours yes Composition 100% cotton Width 137cm/54in Repeat 14.5cm/5¾in Price ★ 🗐🛋

Lee Jofa/Harrogate Handblock 697115 Colour natural Alt. colours no Composition 100% linen Width 122cm/48in Repeat 76cm/30in Price ★★★ 🗐⊞🛋

Manuel Canovas/Serendip 11300 Colour Ecru/95 Alt. colours yes Composition 100% cotton Width 135cm/53in Repeat 155cm/61in Price ★★★★ 🗐🛋🅆

Warner Fabrics/Edwardian Roses CS 336910 Colour pink/blue/cream Alt. colours no Composition 100% cotton Width 137cm/54in Repeat 64cm/25in Price ★★ 🗐 LC

Jane Churchill/Country Rose Sprig J238F Colour 05 Russet Alt. colours yes Composition 100% cotton Width 137cm/54in Repeat 20cm/8in Price ★ LC 🗐🛋

Florals: Late 20th–early 21st century

Floral chintzes became less popular after the Second World War, fading away as abstract and geometric patterns started to come into vogue. Chintzes remained largely out of favour for some 40 years, but during the late 1980s there was a revival of interest in them, particularly for use in bedrooms. Consequently, many companies are now producing reproductions of 19th-century chintzes, with original patterns and colours virtually unchanged, while many contemporary designers have returned to nature for inspiration and are producing floral chintzes in "new" pastel colourways. Demand for woven floral damasks has also increased recently, especially for use in upholstery. William Morris designs are highly fashionable once again, as are some of the designs originated by Sybil Colefax and John Fowler in the mid-20th century. Also epitomizing late 20th and early 21st-century tastes in florals are flowerheads, petals, posies and garlands rendered in bright, strong colours.

1

2

3

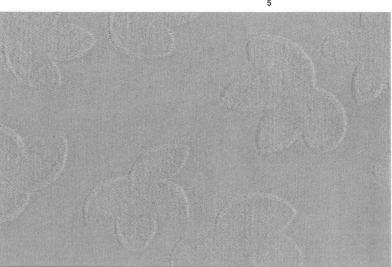

1 **Manuel Canovas/Clelia** Colour **celadon** Alt. colours **yes** Composition **100% cotton** Width **146cm/57½in** Repeat **68cm/26¾in** Price ★

2 **Laura Ashley/Charlotte** Colour **cowslip/multi white** Alt. colours **yes** Composition **100% cotton** Width **122cm/48in** Repeat **32cm/12½in** Price ★

3 **Laura Ashley/Kelmscott** Colour **delphinium** Alt. colours **yes** Composition **100% cotton** Width **138cm/54⅛in** Repeat **57cm/22½in** Price ★★

4 **Nicholas Herbert/Toile de Rosa 121** Colour **03 green** Alt. colours **yes** Composition **100% cotton** Width **137cm/54in** Repeat **25cm/9¾in** Price ★★

5 **Nina Campbell/Manihiki Prints/Futuna NCF3364** Colour **03** Alt. colours **yes** Composition **84% cotton, 16% nylon** Width **140cm/55in** Repeat **62cm/24¼in** Price ★★

6 **J. Robert Scott/Floating Petals 3452** Colour **cardamom** Alt. colours **yes** Composition **66% wool, 34% silk** Width **135cm/53in** Repeat **44cm/17in** Price ★★★

7 **Lelièvre/Nougatine 5983** Colour **ivoire** Alt. colours **yes** Composition **90% viscose, 10% linen** Width **138cm/54in** Repeat **68cm/26¾in** Price ★★★

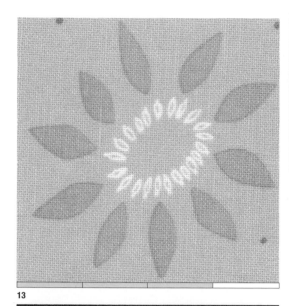

8 Manuel Canovas/Pali 11146
Colour **bleu 59** Alt. colours
yes Composition **100%
cotton** Width **130cm/
51in** Repeat **103cm/40½in**
Price ★★★★★ 🪟🛋️ⓦ

9 Brunschwig & Fils/78790
Colour **04** Alt. colours
yes Composition **100%
cotton** Width **137cm/
54in** Repeat **69cm/27in**
Price ★★★ 🪟 LC🛋️

10 Claremont Fabrics/Sunbury
Colour **wine** Alt. colours
yes Composition **100%
polyester** Width **140cm/
55in** Repeat **60cm/23¾in**
Price ★ 🪟⊞

11 Mulberry/Tuileries FD341
Colour **natural K101** Alt.
colours **yes** Composition
**55% cotton, 45% viscose
spun rayon** Width **145cm/
57in** Repeat **26cm/10¼in**
Price ★★ LC🪟⊞🛋️

12 Fired Earth/Autumn Fall
Colour **coral** Alt. colours
yes Composition **89% cotton,
11% nylon** Width **136cm/
53½in** Repeat **63cm/24¾in**
Price ★★ LC🪟⊞🛋️

13

14

13 Laura Ashley/Roundswood
Colour **pale lavender** Alt.
colours **yes** Composition
68% cotton, 32% linen
Width **140cm/55in** Repeat
32cm/12½in Price ★ 🪟

14 Claremont Fabrics/Octavia
P99013 Colour **sapphire** Alt.
colours **yes** Composition
100% cotton Width **137cm/
54in** Repeat **68cm/26¾in**
Price ★ 🪟🛋️

15 Claremont Fabrics/Sunbury
Flower S03 Colour **wine**
Alt. colours **yes** Composition
100% polyester Width **140cm/
55in** Repeat **45.5cm/17¾in**
Price ★ 🪟⊞

16 Osborne & Little/Turfan F1162
Colour **04** Alt. colours **yes**
Composition **100% cotton**
Width **140cm/55in** Repeat
44cm/17in Price ★★ 🪟🛋️

11

12

15

16

Pictorial Fabrics

Pictorial fabrics have appeared in various guises since the Middle Ages. The best known are woven tapestries and printed *toiles de Jouy*; others of note include Chinese and Middle-Eastern pictorial silks, Indonesian batiks, Indian calicoes (*indiennes*), European chintzes, ethnic African weaves and prints, and European and American hand-blocked or screen-printed synthetics.

Long regarded as a mirror of civilization, narrative pictorial fabrics depict a wide range of human activities (both real and mythical) from biblical scenes, military conquests and political events, to harvesting, hunting, pastoral gatherings and theatregoing. However, this reflection of life is also evident in non-narrative pictorials, such as "still-life" fruits and flowers, views of animals on the move, birds in flight and "drawings" of architectural components. In each case the subject matter, the manner in which it is portrayed and the techniques used to reproduce it reflect both the preoccupations of, and the styles of ornament available to, different cultures at different times.

LEFT A detail of a late 18th-century oval-back, gilt open armchair in a manor house in Norfolk, England. The top-cover is original, exquisitely worked in petit-point, and depicts cherubs at play – a popular subject for the pictorial fabrics used in classical interiors on both sides of the Atlantic during the latter part of the 18th century.

INDUSTRIAL ESPIONAGE

Toile de Jouy fabrics originated in 1770, in a factory established by the German Oberkampf brothers in the French village of Jouy-en-Josas. Intent on expansion, the brothers travelled to England in 1810 in an attempt to find out the secret advances made in copperplate printing techniques. They managed to smuggle out the information by writing it on cotton percale fabric using an alum solution tinted with madder dye, then dipping the fabric in vinegar to render the writing invisible. Once back in France, they immersed the fabric in madder dye to retrieve the concealed information.

ABOVE This late 20th-century settee is upholstered with a hand-printed, modern pictorial fabric designed by Janet Milner. The hairdressing imagery, particularly the exaggerated "beehive" hairdo, is wryly amusing, but the design is potentially classic – largely thanks to the sophisticated combination of black, cream and caramel colouring.

KEY DESIGNS

1 Historically significant naval and land battles were popular subjects for pictorial fabrics, particularly medieval and Renaissance tapestries and 18th- and 19th-century printed toiles.

2 Oriental scenes incorporating human figures, buildings and exotic animals, birds and plant forms, appeared on numerous European textiles from the mid-17th century to the late 19th century.

3 Printed cottons and linens featuring pictorial patterns copied from or inspired by Chinese export porcelain and delftware were highly fashionable in Europe during the 18th century.

4 Fabrics patterned with a series of scenes, framed within decorative plaques or cartouches, have been popular since the Renaissance. This Empire-style print displays classical imagery.

5 Ethnic weaves and prints have been a recurring source of inspiration for 20th- and early 21st-century European and American pictorial textiles.

6 This playing-card pattern is early-21st century, but its portrayal of royalty and theatrical figures is within a genre that extends back to the Middle Ages.

1 Manuel Canovas/Hispaniola Colour **groseille/ ecru 05** Alt. colours **yes** Composition **100% cotton** Width **178cm/70in** Repeat **96cm/37¾in** Price ★★ ⬚ ⬚

2 Apenn/Chelworth Linen Colour **heather/navy blue** Alt. colours **yes** Composition **60% linen, 30% cotton, 10% nylon** Width **122cm/48in** Repeat **83cm 32½in** Price ★★★ ⬚ ⬚ ⬚

3 Bennison Fabrics/Chinese Toile Colour **blue and white** Alt. colours **yes** Composition **70% linen, 30% cotton** Width **122cm/ 48in** Repeat **45cm/17½in** Price ★★★ ⬚ ⬚

4 Marvic Textiles/Empire 5220-007 Colour **red on sand** Alt. colours **yes** Composition **100% cotton** Width **140cm/55in** Repeat **74cm/ 29in** Price ★★ ⬚ ⬚ ⬚ ⬚

5 Fired Earth/Indienne Sapphire Colour **sapphire blue** Alt. colours **yes** Composition **44% viscose, 41% polyacrylic, 15% modacrylic** Width **141cm/55½in** Repeat **33cm/13in** Price ★★ ⬚ ⬚ ⬚ ⬚

6 Scalamandré/Royal Flush 16392-003 Colour **red and brown** Alt. colours **yes** Composition **100% linen** Width **138.5cm/54½in** Repeat **86.5cm/34in** Price ★★★ ⬚ ⬚ ⬚ ⬚

Pictorials: **Pre-18th century**

Medieval pictorial fabrics – mostly tapestry wall-hangings – depicted subject matter from and were executed in a style that bore close resemblance to illustrated manuscripts of the period. Typical subjects ranged from ecclesiastical scenes and narratives of significant matters of state, to everyday life at court. Pageantry was also shown, including military sieges, parades and tournaments (often augmented with motifs such as coats-of-arms). Hunting scenes, featuring stylized heraldic beasts, such as stags, dogs, lions, griffins, unicorns and enfields, were also widely portrayed.

Much of the subject matter of medieval pictorial fabrics, particularly hunting and battle scenes, also appeared during the Renaissance. However, biblical stories, classical mythology and pastoral images became increasingly fashionable, and all images were rendered with a much greater use and understanding of perspective. By the 17th century, pictorial wall-hangings had become even more spectacular and sophisticated in terms of both colour and realism – especially in the grandest French and English Baroque interiors, where classical, mythological, historical, religious and pastoral images remained popular (and often appeared *en suite* on upholstered furniture).

3

3 **Mulberry/Medieval Alphabet F142/608** Colour **red, blue, gold and green** Alt. colours **yes** Composition **100% cotton** Width **132cm/51¾in** Repeat **21cm/8¼in** Price ★★

4 **Brunschwig & Fils/Palio Cotton and Linen Print 79821.04** Colour **rosso** Alt. colours **yes** Composition **54% linen, 46% cotton** Width **137cm/54in** Repeat **46cm/18in** Price ★★★★

5 **Fired Earth/Calligraphy** Colour **red** Alt. colours **yes** Composition **44% viscose, 41% polyacrylic, 15% modacrylic** Width **140cm/55in** Repeat **68cm/26¾in** Price ★★ LC

1

4

5

1 **Claremont Fabrics/Merrydown C74 M53** Colour **chintz** Alt. colours **yes** Composition **100% cotton** Width **137cm/54in** Repeat **68cm/26¾in** Price ★

2 **Fired Earth/Gryphon** Colour **cream on red** Alt. colours **yes** Composition **75% cotton, 25% wool** Width **155cm/61in** Repeat **60cm/23¾in** Price ★★★ LC

2

BATIK STYLE

During the 17th century, imported Indonesian cottons displaying pictorial patterns of stylized buildings, human figures, animals and birds came into vogue in Europe. These fabrics were produced by "batik", a form of printing that involves applying hot wax to the cotton around the pattern before applying dyes or inks. The wax resists the dyes or inks, which adhere to the unwaxed areas, and the pattern is revealed once the wax is removed with hot water.

Monkwell/Batumi 09358 Colour **5** Alt. colours **yes** Composition **100% cotton** Width **137cm/54in** Repeat **62cm/24¼in** Price ★★

6

**11 Monkwell/Tamburlaine
09370** Colour **red and green**
Alt. colours **yes** Composition
100% cotton Width **137cm/
54in** Repeat **64cm/25in**
Price ★★ LC 🛋️ 🛋️

**12 Abbott & Boyd/Caciera
Medieval 49009** Colour
yellow/beige ground Alt.
colours **no** Composition
100% cotton Width **160cm/
63in** Repeat **68cm/26¾in**
Price ★★ 🛋️ 🛋️

**13 Abbott & Boyd/Cenera
Medieval 49131** Colour
yellow/beige ground Alt.
colours **no** Composition
100% cotton Width **160cm/
63in** Repeat **96cm/37¾in**
Price ★★ 🛋️ 🛋️

14 Brunschwig & Fils 89496
Colour **940** Alt. colours **yes**
Composition **65% cotton,
26% silk, 9% polyester** Width
140cm/55in Repeat **62cm/
24¼in** Price ★★★ 🛋️ LC 🛋️

**15 Lee Jofa/Stuart Tree Print
858271** Colour **tapestry blue**
Alt. colours **yes** Composition
100% linen Width **137cm/
54in** Repeat **73cm/28½in**
Price ★★★ 🛋️ 🛋️

11

12   **13**

**Stuart Interiors/English
Needlework Design** Colour
multi Alt. colours **no**
Composition **40% cotton,
60% wool** Width **126cm/
49¾in** Repeat **57cm/22½in**
Price ★★★★ 🛋️ ⊞ 🛋️

**Mulberry/Tudor Animals
FD101/521** Colour **natural**
Alt. colours **yes** Composition
**56% linen, 22% cotton, 22%
viscose** Width **137cm/54in**
Repeat **82cm/32½in**
Price ★★★ 🛋️ 🛋️

Celia Birtwell/Beasties
Colour **green** Alt. colours
yes Composition **100%
cotton** Width **140cm/55in**
Repeat **64cm/25in**
Price ★★ 🛋️ 🛋️

**Abbott & Boyd/Escritura
47658** Colour **4** Alt. colours
yes Composition **100% cotton**
Width **160cm/63in** Repeat
64cm/25in Price ★★ 🛋️ 🛋️

**Monkwell/Salamanca
09371CU/004** Colour **gold
on blue/green** Alt. colours
yes Composition **100% cotton**
Width **137cm/54in** Repeat
82cm/32½in Price ★★ 🛋️ 🛋️

7

8

10

14

15

Pictorials: Early 18th century

Stylistically, some of the pictorial fabrics produced during the early 18th century were rather heavy and sombre in appearance, and echoed the Baroque ornamentation of the previous century. The vast majority, however, increasingly reflected the lighter-hearted and less formal, more colourful and often frivolous approach of the Rococo style that became fashionable across most of Europe as the century progressed.

Much of this change of style can be attributed to an expansion of trade with the Orient and the importation of Chinese silks, ceramics and wallpapers, and hand-painted and hand-printed Indian calicoes (*indiennes*) – all of which provided inspiration for European pictorial silk, cotton and tapestry hangings. Typical subject matter included interpretations of Chinese, Indian, Arabian, Moorish and Persian landscapes filled with indigenous flora and fauna. Also common were native figures engaged in a diverse range of activities including hunting, fishing, harvesting, tax collecting, taking tea, playing musical instruments and bartering with colonial traders. Trading ships in the South China seas were much in evidence, then, and, as the first half of the century drew to a close, images of life in the English countryside began to appear.

1 Brunschwig & Fils/Clipper Ships 79680.04 Colour **cream** Alt. colours **yes** Composition **55% linen, 45% cotton** Width **135cm/53in** Repeat **113.5cm/44½in** Price ★★★

2 Clarence House/Las Palmas 33976/2 Colour **green** Alt. colours **yes** Composition **100% cotton** Width **137cm/54in** Repeat **86cm/33¾in** Price ★★★★★

3 Timney Fowler/Librarian TF0175 Colour **15** Alt. colours **yes** Composition **100% cotton** Width **133cm/52in** Repeat **58cm/22¾in** Price ★★★

4 Timney Fowler/Studies TF0177 Colour **15** Alt. colours **yes** Composition **100% cotton** Width **133cm/52in** Repeat **73.5cm/28¾in** Price ★★★

5 Brunschwig & Fils/Fishing Lady 79654.04 Colour **stone green** Alt. colours **yes** Composition **65% linen, 35% cotton** Width **137cm/54in** Repeat **81cm/31¾in** Price ★★

6 Rubelli/Vasco Da Gama 7469 Colour **1 rosso/verde** Alt. colours **yes** Composition **100% cotton** Width **140cm/55in** Repeat **100cm/39¼in** Price ★★

EASTERN INFLUENCE
Inspired by imported Chinese goods, 18th-century designers such as Antoine Watteau and Jean Pillement devised *chinoiserie* patterns for textiles and wallpapers. Their popularity at the time was reflected in Lady Mary Wortley Montagu's observation of 1740: "Sick of Grecian eloquence and symmetry or Gothic grandeur, we must all seek the barbarous gaudy gout of the Chinese." Similar designs, suitable for 18th-century interiors, are being produced today.

Nina Campbell/Zembla/Manchu NCF3403 Colour **01** Alt. colours **yes** Composition **100% linen** Width **140cm/55in** Repeat **88cm/34½in** Price ★★ LC

18th century

7 Old World Weavers/Voyage en Chine FBA 02A 0002 Colour **black** Alt. colours **yes** Composition **59% linen, 41% cotton** Width **137cm/ 54in** Repeat **114cm/ 44⅞in** Price ★★★

8 Brunschwig & Fils/Chinoiserie Glazed Chintz 75460.04 Colour **lacquer red** Alt. colours **yes** Composition **100% cotton** Width **122cm/ 48in** Repeat **91.5cm/36in** Price ★★

9 Rubelli/Planter Café 7135 Colour **tabac/blue** Alt. colours **yes** Composition **100% cotton** Width **135cm/ 53in** Repeat **96cm/37⅞in** Price ★★★

10 Zoffany/Reveillon Miniature PLP0700 Colour **5** Alt. colours **yes** Composition **100% cotton** Width **137cm/54in** Repeat **50cm/19½in** Price ★★

11 Rubelli/Tea Introduction 7134 Colour **famille rose** Alt. colours **yes** Composition **100% cotton** Width **135cm/ 53in** Repeat **12cm/4¾in** Price ★★★

12 Brunschwig & Fils/West Indies Toile Cotton 79522.04 Colour **blue on white** Alt. colours **yes** Composition **100% cotton** Width **134cm/52⅛in** Repeat **87cm/34¼in** Price ★★

13 Busby & Busby/Serenata 4956 Colour **red/gold** Alt. colours **yes** Composition **100% cotton** Width **140cm/55in** Repeat **91cm/35⅞in** Price ★★

14 Brunschwig & Fils/Bromley Hall Toile 50151.01 Colour **red** Alt. colours **yes** Composition **100% cotton** Width **106.5cm/ 41¾in** Repeat **91.5cm/36in** Price ★★★

Pictorials: Late 18th century

As pictorial tapestry production declined during the second half of the 18th century, the manufacture of pictorial silks and printed calicoes (particularly from Jouy in France) increased. Much of the subject matter favoured in earlier Rococo interiors remained fashionable, except in America where the style never really took root. The *chinoiserie* and Indian scenes produced were more authentically depicted than previously, because fabric designers now had greater access to the illustrated recollections of Europeans who had travelled to the Orient.

In addition, pastoral and rustic images, such as *fêtes galantes*, were much in evidence. This was also the case with theatrical scenes and accounts of contemporary events, such as the American War of Independence, the French Revolution and the first ascents by hot-air balloon. Mythological and ancient Roman and Greek subjects also returned to favour in the Neo-classical interiors that came into vogue during the latter part of the century.

Anne & Robert Swaffer/Boulebard/Valencay 440 Colour **440** Alt. colours **yes** Composition **100% cotton** Width **140cm/55in** Repeat **64cm/25in** Price ★★

Timney Fowler/Draughtsman's Collage TF0172 Colour **20** Alt. colours **no** Composition **100% cotton** Width **133cm/52in** Repeat **110cm/43in** Price ★★★

Abbott & Boyd/Elefantes 47654 Colour **2** Alt. colours **yes** Composition **100% cotton** Width **145cm/57in** Repeat **56cm/22in** Price ★★

The Design Archives/Stove Tiles 54139 Colour **blue on cream** Alt. colours **yes** Composition **100% cotton** Width **137cm/54in** Repeat **80cm/31½in** Price ★★

Brunschwig & Fils/79575 Colour **829** Alt. colours **yes** Composition **100% cotton** Width **131cm/51½in** Repeat **91.5cm/36in** Price ★★

Mulberry/Flights of Fantasy FD140/604 Colour **navy/red F108** Alt. colours **yes** Composition **100% cotton** Width **135cm/53in** Repeat **50cm/19½in** Price ★★

The Design Archives/Gustavian Cameo Colour **black and grey on yellow** Alt. colours **yes** Composition **100% cotton** Width **137cm/54in** Repeat **49cm/19¼in** Price ★★

Brunschwig & Fils/79327.01 Colour **331** Alt. colours **yes** Composition **100% cotton** Width **137cm/54in** Repeat **42cm/16½in** Price ★★★

Marvic Textiles/Le Jardin Anglais 7702-4 Colour **dusky rose** Alt. colours **yes** Composition **100% cotton** Width **138cm/54in** Repeat **79cm/31in** Price ★★

Nina Campbell/Canton Cargo NCF674 Colour **02** Alt. colours **yes** Composition **100% cotton** Width **140cm/55in** Repeat **91cm/35¾in** Price ★★

TOILE DE JOUY

The majority of printed cottons, or toiles, made at the famous Jouy factory in France prior to 1775 were one of two design types – either striped or floral. After this time, however, an enormous variety of narrative patterns were produced. Apart from *chinoiserie*, the most popular subject matter for the fabric designs included idealized or romanticized depictions of rural life and well-known scenes from the theatre. Such patterns were to remain popular in both Europe and America well into the 19th century.

The Design Archives/Pavilions 54138 Colour **red and green** Alt. colours **yes** Composition **100% cotton** Width **137cm/54in** Repeat **62cm/24¼in** Price ★★

Lee Jofa/Chanteloup Brocade 2000182 Colour **pomegranate 19** Alt. colours **yes** Composition **52% cotton, 34% viscose, 14% silk** Width **139cm/54¾in** Repeat **46.5cm/18¼in** Price ★★★★★

Laura Ashley/Toile Colour **raspberry** Alt. colours **yes** Composition **100% cotton** Width **140cm/55in** Repeat **46cm/18in** Price ★★

Marvic Textiles/Les Fables de La Fontaine 7704-3 Colour **carmine** Alt. colours **yes** Composition **100% cotton** Width **137cm/54in** Repeat **59cm/23in** Price ★★

Timney Fowler/Passage of Time TF0200/02 Colour **neutral** Alt. colours **yes** Composition **100% cotton** Width **137cm/54in** Repeat **84cm/33in** Price ★★

The Design Archives/Liaisons 54044 Colour **brown on cream** Alt. colours **yes** Composition **100% cotton** Width **137cm/54in** Repeat **46cm/18in** Price ★★

Marvic Textiles/Les Enfants 5440-005 Colour **black on sand** Alt. colours **yes** Composition **100% cotton** Width **140cm/55in** Repeat **88cm/34½in** Price ★★

Pictorials: Early 19th century

The first three decades of the 19th century saw a further expansion of the printed-cotton industry to meet the ever-increasing demand for pictorial *toiles* (and floral chintzes). Moreover, advances in copperplate printing techniques, when combined with traditional pigments, such as madder (pinks and reds), indigo and woad (blues), and newly discovered mineral dyes, such as manganese (bronze) and antimony (orange), enabled manufacturers to produce increasingly ambitious and sophisticated images.

Chinoiserie, Indian and similarly exotic scenes retained their popularity from the previous century, while narratives depicting Napoleon's campaigns in Egypt became widespread. However, in keeping with the Neo-classical styles of decoration fashionable on both sides of the Atlantic, mythological and classical subjects proved the most popular. Typically elaborate toiles consisted of medallions or cartouches incorporating classical figures or ancient buildings, framed by allegorical figures, animals, scrolls and trophies of arms, linked by scrolling flowers or sheaves of wheat – imagery that drew heavily on the motifs and styles of ornamentation that had been unearthed during archaeological excavations at Pompeii and Herculaneum in the late 18th century.

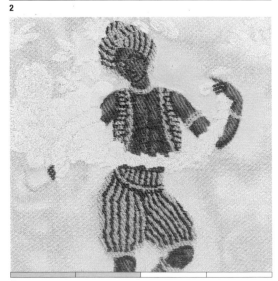

1 **Timney Fowler/Diana TF0300** Colour **01** Alt. colours **no** Composition **100% cotton** Width **140cm/55in** Repeat **105cm/41¼in** Price ★★

2 **Timney Fowler/Regency Toile TF0302** Colour **01** Alt. colours **no** Composition **100% cotton** Width **140cm/ 55in** Repeat **102cm/40in** Price ★★

3 **Rubelli/Bises Novità/Maradjah 21883** Colour **avorio** Alt. colours **yes** Composition **78% cotton, 18% silk, 4% viscose** Width **130cm/ 51in** Repeat **64cm/25in** Price ★★★

4 **Marvic Textiles/Les Amours 5330-007** Colour **blues on off-white** Alt. colours **yes** Composition **100% cotton** Width **140cm/55in** Repeat **50.5cm/20in** Price ★★

5 **Marvic Textiles/Les Vues de Paris 6203-6** Colour **charcoal** Alt. colours **yes** Composition **100% cotton** Width **140cm/ 55in** Repeat **47cm/18½in** Price ★★

6 **Brunschwig & Fils/Mount Vernon 79668.04** Colour **wheat** Alt. colours **yes** Composition **100% cotton** Width **137cm/ 54in** Repeat **91.5cm/36in** Price ★★

7

7 Brunschwig & Fils/79584 Colour **845** Alt. colours **yes** Composition **100% cotton** Width **137cm/54in** Repeat **75cm/29½in** Price ★★

8 Brunschwig & Fils/Hunting Toile 70932.04 Colour **blue** Alt. colours **yes** Composition **50% cotton, 50% linen** Width **122cm/48in** Repeat **28.5cm/11in** Price ★★★

9 Brunschwig & Fils/Bunny Business Glazed Chintz 79781 Colour **04** Alt. colours **yes** Composition **100% cotton** Width **137cm/54in** Repeat **71cm/28in** Price ★★★

10 Busby & Busby/Amaretti Colour **blue/stone** Alt. colours **yes** Composition **100% cotton** Width **140cm/55in** Repeat **64cm/25in** Price ★★

11 Nicholas Herbert/Le Pecheur 113 Colour **01** Alt. colours **yes** Composition **100% cotton** Width **100cm/39¼in** Repeat **65cm/25½in** Price ★★

12

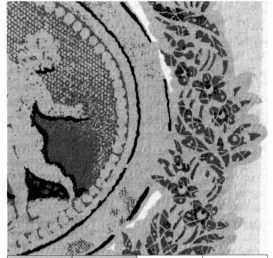

10

13

11

12 G.P. & J. Baker/Directoire Parrot B0849 Colour **01** Alt. colours **yes** Composition **100% cotton** Width **137cm/54in** Repeat **64cm/25in** Price ★★

13 Nicholas Herbert/Corinthia 109 Colour **05** Alt. colours **yes** Composition **100% cotton** Width **130cm/51in** Repeat **94cm/36½in** Price ★★★

14 Timney Fowler/Lady in Waiting Colour **multi** Alt. colours **yes** Composition **100% cotton** Width **133cm/52in** Repeat **117cm/46in** Price ★★

8

9

BRIGHTON

The printed cotton fabric shown here was inspired by fabric wall-panels commissioned in 1801 by the Prince of Wales (subsequently Prince Regent, and then George IV, of England) for the Brighton Pavilion. Like many French and English printed cottons of the late 18th and early 19th centuries, the pattern includes "birds of paradise", exotic insects (dragonflies and butterflies), colourful flowers and luxuriant foliage. They are depicted in a style that owes much to contemporary imported Indian textiles and even more to the ornamentation found on imported Chinese artefacts.

Scalamandré/Brighton 16121-002 Colour **multi on framboise** Alt. colours **yes** Composition **100% cotton** Width **137cm/54in** Repeat **101cm/39¾in** Price ★★★★★

14

19th century

Pictorials: Mid-19th century

To meet the requirements of the increasingly numerous middle classes on both sides of the Atlantic, printed pictorial cottons continued to be produced in quantity in the mid-19th century. However, one consequence of the Gothic Revival was a renewed demand for woven pictorial fabrics – notably tapestries – depicting medieval images. Gothic-arched windows with elaborate tracery provided typical subject matter, and were often augmented with heraldic motifs such as banners, emblems and achievements-of-arms.

As far as printed pictorials were concerned, *chinoiserie*, Indian and African scenes maintained their popularity, and featured exotic and indigenous figures, animals, birds and plant forms. In grander European and American Renaissance Revival interiors, classical ornamentation was the height of fashion, with some of the most interesting pictorial hangings inspired by della Robbia earthenware plaques (made in 15th-century Florence and decorated with festoons of fruit and flowers and white figures on pale blue grounds). Garish in comparison were the pictorial designs of children and animals that found favour in more ordinary households, but were despised for their sentimentality by the emerging Aesthetic and Arts and Crafts movements.

2

3

4

5

6

1

1 **Scalamandré/Daktari 26270** Colour **002** Alt. colours **yes** Composition **65% cotton, 30% rayon, 5% polyester** Width **137cm/54in** Repeat **41cm/16in** Price ★★★ 🛋

2 **Nicholas Herbert/Hunting Lodge 117** Colour **red** Alt. colours **yes** Composition **100% cotton** Width **139cm/ 54¾in** Repeat **51cm/20in** Price ★★★ 🏷 LC ▦🛋

3 **Timney Fowler/Parks & Gardens TF0204** Colour **03** Alt. colours **yes** Composition **100% cotton** Width **137cm/ 54in** Repeat **84.5cm/33in** Price ★★★ 🏷 ▦

4 **Nina Campbell/Sir Oliphant NCF 3124** Colour **04** Alt. colours **yes** Composition **60% linen, 20% cotton, 20% viscose** Width **140cm/55in** Repeat **50cm/19½in** Price ★★ 🛋

5 **Nina Campbell/Lord Lyon NCF 3120** Colour **06** Alt. colours **yes** Composition **100% cotton** Width **140cm/ 55in** Repeat **64cm/25in** Price ★★ 🛋

6 **Marvic Textiles/Vivarais 7542-001** Colour **blue on red** Alt. colours **yes** Composition **100% cotton** Width **150cm/ 59in** Repeat **28.5cm/11in** Price ★★ 🏷 ▦

7

8

9

10

**12 G.P. & J. Baker/The Floating
Pavillion A2109** Colour **4** Alt.
colours **yes** Composition
60% hemp, 40% silk Width
140cm/55in Repeat **115cm/
45in** Price ★★★

13 Timney Fowler/Dante TF0198
Colour **yellow** Alt. colours
yes Composition **100%
cotton** Width **133cm/52in**
Repeat **80.5cm/31¾in**
Price ★★★

14 Bentley & Spens/Animal Magic
Colour **pale green** Alt. colours
yes Composition **70% linen,
30% cotton** Width **135cm/
53in** Repeat **106cm/41½in**
Price ★★ LC

12

13

7 Busby & Busby/Fête 4936
Colour **charcoal** Alt. colours
yes Composition **100% cotton**
Width **140cm/55in** Repeat
91cm/35⅞in Price ★★

**8 G.P. & J. Baker/Blush China
R1361** Colour **1** Alt. colours
yes Composition **100% linen**
Width **137cm/54in** Repeat
69cm/27in Price ★★

9 Rubelli/Black Pepper 7137
Colour **jaune/rose** Alt. colours
yes Composition **100%
cotton** Width **135cm/53in**
Repeat **112cm/44in**
Price ★★★

**10 Abbott & Boyd/Flora Antilana
48076** Colour **9** Alt. colours
no Composition **100% cotton**
Width **150cm/59in** Repeat
96cm/37¾in Price ★★

**11 Timney Fowler/Adam & Eve
TF0197** Colour **blue** Alt.
colours **yes** Composition
100% cotton Width **133cm/
52in** Repeat **79cm/31in**
Price ★★★

11

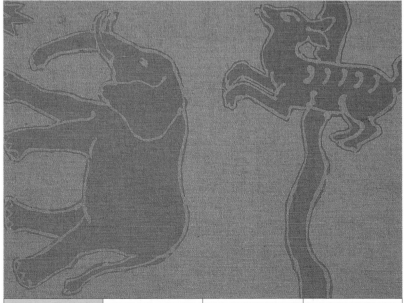

14

Pictorials: Late 19th century

Although the leading exponents of the Aesthetic and Arts and Crafts movements dismissed many of the mass-produced, aniline-dyed pictorial fabrics fashionable since the mid-19th century as garish and sentimental, such designs still found favour outside the confines of these aesthetic elites. Woven and printed pictorials of cats, dogs, horses, children and railway trains were still much in evidence in ordinary homes until the end of the century. Conversely, Aesthetic movement *japonaiserie* fabrics, displaying images of dragons, birds (sparrows, kingfishers, peacocks) and flowers (chrysanthemum, prunus blossom) derived from *Kakiemon*-pattern porcelain, were rarely admired except by the artistically minded.

More universally popular were the Gothic Revival pictorials that drew inspiration from medieval ornamentation. Notable among these were the vegetable-dyed Arts and Crafts designs, many of which depicted human figures set against a floral ground. Similarly, *chinoiserie*, Indian and African pictorials remained in vogue, as did classically inspired architectural prints rendered in black and white. The most innovative pictorials were produced by Art Nouveau designers: dream-like figures of women, set among sinuous, entwining plant forms (*femmes fleurs*), became a recurring theme of their work.

5

1

6

7

3

4

1 **Brunschwig & Fils/79561-207**
Colour **207** Alt. colours **yes**
Composition **59% linen,
41% cotton** Width **137cm/
54in** Repeat **64cm/25in**
Price ★★★

2 **Jim Thompson/Chinoiserie PMS
2991** Colour **B** Alt. colours
yes Composition **100% silk**
Width **122cm/48in**
Repeat **91.5cm/36in**
Price ★★★

3 **Dedar/Dulcina** Colour **02** Alt.
colours **yes** Composition
100% cotton Width **140cm/
55in** Repeat **132cm/51¾in**
Price ★★★

4 **Marvic Textiles/Elizabeth 5205**
Colour **gold 2** Alt. colours **yes**
Composition **60% cotton,
40% viscose** Width **140cm/
55in** Repeat **76cm/30in**
Price ★★★

5 **Colefax and Fowler/Ditchley
F1508/06** Colour **yellow** Alt.
colours **yes** Composition **52%
linen, 36% cotton, 12% nylon**
Width **136cm/53½in** Repeat
71.5cm/28¼in Price ★★

6 **Abbott & Boyd/Pentagramma
45832** Colour **8** Alt. colours **yes**
Composition **100% cotton**
Width **150cm/59in** Repeat
96cm/37¾in Price ★★

7 **Timney Fowler/Agra Ironwork
TF0004** Colour **black & white 01**
Alt. colours **yes** Composition
100% cotton Width **140cm/
55in** Repeat **28cm/10¾in**
Price ★★

8 **Timney Fowler/Ceiling Rose
TF0218** Colour **01** Alt. colours
yes Composition **100% cotton**
Width **140cm/55in** Repeat
69cm/27in Price ★★

9 Borderline/Palmyra 2303 Colour
A Alt. colours **yes** Composition
52% linen, 48% cotton Width
137cm/54in Repeat **56cm/22in**
Price ★★ 🗔

10 Mulberry/Doublet Silk FD089-
675 Colour red **V106** Alt.
colours **yes** Composition
62% silk, 38% polyester
Width **130cm/51in**
Repeat **15.5cm/6⅛in**
Price ★★★ 🗔

11 Timney Fowler/Tunnel Plan
TF0055 Colour **black and white**
Alt. colours **yes** Composition
100% cotton Width **120cm/47in**
Repeat **53cm/21in**
Price ★★ 🗔🛋

12 Borderline/Samarkand 2341A
Colour **burgundy** Alt. colours
yes Composition **52% linen,
36% cotton, 12% nylon** Width
137cm/54in Repeat **52cm/20½in**
Price ★★ 🗔🛋

9

10

11

12

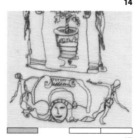

13

13 Borderline/Water Garden Colour
blue Alt. colours **yes**
Composition **100% cotton**
Width **125cm/49¼in** Repeat
42.5cm/16¾in Price ★ 🗔🛋

14

15

14 Mulberry/Final Furlong FD200
Colour **parchment J107** Alt.
colours **yes** Composition
64% linen, 36% cotton Width
139cm/54¾in Repeat **60.5cm/
24in** Price ★★ 🗔⊞🛋

15 Mulberry/Gazebo Sheer FD423
Colour **moss R107** Alt. colours
yes Composition **100% linen**
Width **330cm/130in** Repeat
125cm/49¼in Price ★★★ 🗔

16 Borderline/Otaka 2424 Colour
blue/pink Alt. colours **yes**
Composition **100% cotton**
Width **137cm/54in**
Repeat **48cm/19in**
Price ★★ 🗔

17 Mulberry/Naval Ensigns
FD116/569 **V113** Colour
red/navy Alt. colours **yes**
Composition **100% cotton**
Width **135cm/53in** Repeat
66cm/26in Price ★★ 🗔🛋

16

17

Pictorials: Early 20th century

Although rarely employed in Art Deco and Modernist interiors, pictorial furnishing fabrics continued to be produced in considerable quantities and in a diverse range of styles during the first half of the 20th century. Prominent examples included chintzes that were either reproductions of or inspired by the "Tree of Life" and "birds of paradise" designs favoured during the 17th and 18th centuries. Primarily used in Jacobean Revival interiors, they tended to be made in more sombre and muted colours than the flamboyant originals. Pictorial tapestries also appeared in some Jacobean- and Arts and Crafts-style schemes, although most of the tapestries created during this period departed from the pictorial tradition and displayed geometric and abstract designs. In addition to birds of paradise, animals and fish also proved fashionable in scenes. Especially popular were printed examples primarily intended for use in kitchens and bathrooms, many of them appearing in stylized form and often humorously augmented with pertinent objects, such as items of kitchenalia and vegetables, or perfume bottles, tablets of soap and shaving equipment. Exotic animals, notably African elephants and Indian tigers, were also in vogue, as were groups of "humanized" animals derived from nursery stories, designed for children's rooms.

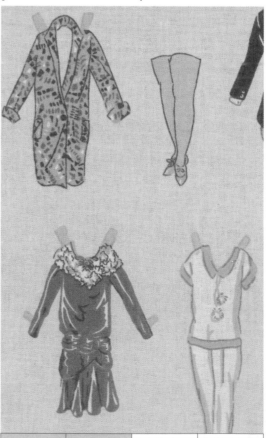

3

4

1

1 Liberty Furnishings/Dante
1095015 Colour **A** Alt. colours **yes** Composition **53% linen, 35% cotton, 12% polyacrylic** Width **137cm/54in** Repeat **33cm/13in** Price ★★ 🎨🛋

2 Scalamandré/Under the Ice
16263-003 Colour **multi on sky blue** Alt. colours **yes** Composition **51% linen, 37% cotton, 12% nylon** Width **138.5cm/54½in** Repeat **88cm/34½in** Price ★★★ 🎨🛋

3 Warner Fabrics/Souvenir d'Afrique CS6140 Colour **straw yellow** Alt. colours **yes** Composition **100% cotton** Width **137cm/54in** Repeat **64cm/25in** Price ★★ 🎨🎨▦

4 Scalamandré/Kilkenny Cats
16259-004 Colour **pink** Alt. colours **yes** Composition **100% cotton** Width **137cm/54in** Repeat **88cm/34½in** Price ★★ 🎨

5 Lee Jofa/Delia's Trousseau Print
2000224 Colour **715 pastel** Alt. colours **yes** Composition **100% cotton** Width **137cm/54in** Repeat **46cm/18in** Price ★★ 🎨

6 Mulberry/Round the Island FD201 Colour **marine blue** Alt. colours **yes** Composition **62% cotton, 38% jute** Width **143cm/56in** Repeat **82cm/32⅓in** Price ★★ 🎨▦

2

5

6

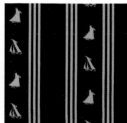

7 **Rubelli/Friday 7470** Colour **oceano 1** Alt. colours **yes** Composition **100% cotton** Width **140cm/55in** Repeat **96cm/37¾in** Price ★★★ LC

8 **Scalamandré/Akbar's Stables 6236-004** Colour **tan and black** Alt. colours **yes** Composition **100% cotton** Width **140cm/55in** Repeat **68.5cm/27in** Price ★★★

9 **Celia Birtwell/Mademoiselle/ Isabella** Colour **red/white/ grey/aqua** Alt. colours **no** Composition **100% cotton twill** Width **140cm/55in** Repeat **42cm/16½in** Price ★★

10 **Mulberry/Jibe Stripe FD153-661** Colour **marine blue H103** Alt. colours **yes** Composition **100% cotton** Width **142cm/ 55¾in** Repeat **15.5cm/6⅛in** Price ★★ LC

11 **Clarence House/Jungle Book 33977** Colour **sand 1** Alt. colours **no** Composition **100% cotton** Width **137cm/ 54in** Repeat **99.5cm/39in** Price ★★★★

TREE OF LIFE

This hand-blocked linen fabric incorporates an early 20th-century version of the "Tree of Life" design. The original pattern, which has at its centre a tree symbolizing the "life force", was first seen in ancient Persian and Indian fabrics. However, the manner in which it is depicted here – with branches and shoots, and with exotic flowers and fruits interwoven with birds of paradise – is in the style of the English "Tree of Life" designs developed during the 17th century and most commonly found on contemporary Jacobean crewelwork and on 19th-century Jacobean Revival chintzes.

Lee Jofa/Tree of Life 667069 Colour **multi** Alt. colours **no** Composition **100% linen** Width **127cm/50in** Repeat **252cm/99in** Price ★★★★★ W W

Pictorials: Late 20th–early 21st century

Much of the subject matter depicted in the pictorial fabrics favoured during the first half of the 20th century has remained popular to the present day – particularly stylized and naturalistic, and Indian-influenced, animal scenes and Persian-style hunting scenes. Printed classical and Neo-classical images inspired by or adapted from designs that were first produced during the Renaissance and the 17th and 18th centuries have also come into vogue. Typical examples include ancient biblical events, as well as ancient Roman and Greek figures in architectural settings – many of which have been produced in black and white or shades of grey. A large number of fabric manufacturers have also mass-produced machine-printed pictorials in the style of 18th- and 19th-century hand-printed toiles (see pages 134–7). Innovations include highly stylized medieval scenes (such as knights on horseback), nursery stories, diverse landscapes and still lifes in styles that mirror the developments of 20th-century fine art.

1

2

3

4

5

6

1 Bentley & Spens/Fruit with Bowls Colour **red** Alt. colours **yes** Composition **55% linen, 34% cotton, 11% nylon** Width **117cm/46in** Repeat **162cm/ 65in** Price ★★★

2 Timney Fowler/Draughtsman's Collage TF0172/20 Colour **multi** Alt. colours **yes** Composition **100% cotton** Width **133cm/ 52in** Repeat **110cm/43in** Price ★★

3 Turnell & Gigon/Newmarket 10005 Colour **1** Alt. colours **yes** Composition **100% cotton** Width **133cm/52in** Repeat **61cm/24in** Price ★★★

4 Ivo Prints/Cox Colour **black, white and green** Alt. colours **yes** Composition **100% cotton** Width **120cm/47in** Repeat **40cm/15¾in** Price ★★ LC

5 Timney Fowler/Madonna TF0196 Colour **black and white** Alt. colours **yes** Composition **100% cotton** Width **133cm/ 52in** Repeat **65cm/25½in** Price ★★

6 Osborne & Little/Toad Hall F1178 Colour **2** Alt. colours **yes** Composition **100% cotton** Width **140cm/55in** Repeat **91cm/35¾in** Price ★★

Sandberg/Saga 300 Colour **24** Alt. colours **yes** Composition **100% cotton** Width **147cm/ 58in** Repeat **90.5cm/35⅝in** Price ★★

Jane Churchill/Jousting JY32F- 03 Colour **dark red** Alt. colours **yes** Composition **100% cotton** Width **141cm/ 55½in** Repeat **40.5cm/16in** Price ★★

Anna French/Treasure Island Colour **24** Alt. colours **yes** Composition **100% cotton** Width **137cm/54in** Repeat **82cm/32¼in** Price ★★

7

10

9

11

12

14

10 Anna French/Fairies Colour **33** Alt. colours **yes** Composition **100% cotton** Width **137cm/ 54in** Repeat **82cm/32¼in** Price ★★★

11 Anna French/Tea for Teddies Colour **22** Alt. colours **yes** Composition **100% cotton** Width **137cm/54in** Repeat **82cm/32½in** Price ★★

12 Donghia/Housepets 0450/5850- 18 Colour **nana** Alt. colours **yes** Composition **100% cotton** Width **137cm/54in** Repeat **34cm/13½in** Price ★★★★★

13 Andrew Martin/Mungo Park Colour **blue and red** Alt. colours **yes** Composition **60% cotton, 40% jute** Width **132cm/51¾in** Repeat **94cm/ 36½in** Price ★★

14 G.P. & J. Baker/Tiger Tiger J0248 Colour **green** Alt. colours **yes** Composition **100% silk** Width **140cm/ 55in** Repeat **63cm/24¾in** Price ★★★★

20th & 21st century

Overall Pattern

ABOVE A flame-stitch pattern fabric has been glued to the walls in this contemporary re-creation of a turn-of-the-18th-century English interior. Hand-woven flame-stitch fabrics were fashionable, especially in America, during the late 18th and early 19th centuries. The example shown here is machine-woven.

BLOCK-PRINTING

One of the oldest methods of printing designs on textiles (and still used today) involves hand-pressuring wooden blocks against the surface of the fabric – the pattern having been carved in relief on to the underside of the blocks, and the dyes or inks being carried on the raised sections of the carving. The number of blocks required depends on the complexity of the design, and can range from one for a simple repeat monochrome to up to a thousand or more for incredibly complex, multi-coloured pictorial patterns. Many scrolling, vegetal patterns have been produced in this way.

Of all the imagery that has provided inspiration for fabric patterns from the Middle Ages to the present day, organic forms – especially plants – have proved the most universal. Fabrics with floral patterns have been produced in such diverse styles that they merit discussion and illustration elsewhere (*see* pages 110–27). However, running a close second to floral designs are the patterns based on fruits, buds, stems, leaves, shoots, roots and organic forms such as animal skins and bird feathers.

Most plant ornament – both naturalistic and stylized – can be traced to specific cultures or periods. For example, the pomegranate is Middle Eastern in origin, the palm Asian and African, and the anthemion ancient Greek and oriental. Since the Renaissance, however, the expansion of export trade in fabrics has "internationalized" these forms, a development that has also been fuelled by archaeological discoveries of ancient civilizations, more extensive travel overseas and the publication of botanical studies and pattern books.

RIGHT The windows and seating in this 19th-century interior are furnished with late 20th-century woven and printed fabrics. The window sheers, the jacquard-woven top-covers on the daybed and oval-back painted armchair, and the jacquard-woven curtains all feature traditional trailing-foliage patterns. The fabrics covering the screen and foreground cushion display fruit-and-foliage patterns printed in complementary colourways.

KEY DESIGNS

1 Stylized interlaced foliage, scrolling or trailing, has been one of the most popular fabric patterns since the late Middle Ages. This scrolling leaf pattern was designed in the late 20th century.

2 Paisley patterns – stylized pinecones surrounded by vegetation – are derived from oriental decoration. Paisley fabrics have been fashionable on both sides of the Atlantic since the mid-19th century.

3 Historically, most interlaced foliage patterns have been highly stylized. However, naturalistic renderings have also been produced, particularly during the early 19th and 20th centuries.

4 Symbolizing immortality, foresight and beauty, peacock feathers are often found on oriental textiles. Other notable applications include Renaissance silks and Aesthetic movement fabrics.

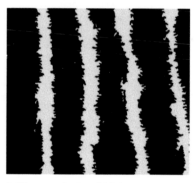

5 Fabric designers have often drawn inspiration from decorative architectural mouldings. Typical examples since the Renaissance include fluting, *guilloche*, and as here, S- and C-scroll patterns.

6 Woven and printed fabric patterns simulating exotic animal skins, such as zebra, tiger and leopard, became fashionable from the middle of the 19th century onward, particularly in Europe.

---

1 Nina Campbell/Wilingdon NCF3411 Colour **06** Alt. colours **yes** Composition **56% rayon, 44% cotton** Width **129cm/51in** Repeat **22cm/8½in** Price ★★

2 De Le Cuona/Grosvenor No11 Colour **coffee** Alt. colours **yes** Composition **60% wool, 40% cotton** Width **140cm/55in** Repeat – Price ★★★

3 Bennison Fabrics/Oakleaf Colour **green** Alt. colours **yes** Composition **70% linen, 30% cotton** Width **141cm/55½in** Repeat **28.5cm/11in** Price ★★★

4 Liberty Furnishings/Hera Colour **green** Alt. colours **yes** Composition **53% linen, 35% cotton, 12% nylon** Width **137cm/54in** Repeat **36cm/14in** Price ★

5 Sahco Hesslein/Tidepool 1871 Colour **01** Alt. colours **yes** Composition **75% silk, 25% wool** Width **140cm/55in** Repeat **32cm/12½in** Price ★★★

6 Chase Erwin/Ultrasuede Colour **zebra** Alt. colours **yes** Composition **100% polyester** Width **120cm/47in** Repeat **76cm/30in** Price ★★★

Overall Pattern: **Pre-18th century**

Prior to the 18th century, the vast majority of overall-patterned fabrics were decorated with stylized or naturalistic plant forms. During the Middle Ages, the ability of European fabric designers to depict such images accurately was restricted by the limitations of early weaving techniques and by a scarcity of botanical reference material (medieval herbals). Nevertheless, patterns based on grapevines, ivy, parsley, water leaves, oak leaves and acorns were much in evidence, as were palms – which were adopted as an heraldic emblem after the Crusades.

During the Renaissance, European fabric designers began to gain access to a much wider catalogue of plant ornament, notably those forms used in classical Graeco Roman and Middle-Eastern decoration. These included the stylized pomegranate and pine forms set within repeat leaf patterns, favoured for damasks and velvets, and classical scrolling foliage patterns based on the acanthus leaf. In the 17th century, the proliferation of botanical pattern books, such as Guillaume Toulouze's *Livre de Fleurs, Feuilles et Oyzéaus* (1656), further fuelled the fashion for overall plant-form patterns, and made possible highly naturalistic renderings of fruit and extravagant scrolling foliage.

1 Warwick/Marseille 105461506-**620** Colour **burgundy** Alt. colours **yes** Composition **100% cotton** Width **137cm/54in** Repeat **64cm/25in** Price ★★

2 Bernard Thorp & Co/Faisan Colour **multi** Alt. colours **yes** Composition **88% flax, 12% silk** Width **120cm/47in** Repeat **96.5cm/38in** Price ★★★

3 Jason D'Souza/Riccio RIC04 Colour **peach** Alt. colours **yes** Composition **50% linen, 50% cotton** Width **136cm/53½in** Repeat **17cm/6¾in** Price ★★

4 Ramm, Son & Crocker/Fontaine R12074 Colour **willow** Alt. colours **yes** Composition **84% linen, 16% nylon** Width **140cm/55in** Repeat **49cm/19¼in** Price ★★

5 Bernard Thorp & Co/Lucien Colour **multi** Alt. colours **yes** Composition **58% flax, 42% cotton** Width **120cm/47in** Repeat **37cm/14½in** Price ★★

6 Montgomery/Kashmir Colour
gold 03 Alt. colours **yes**
Composition **53% polyester,
47% cotton** Width **137cm/
54in** Repeat **21cm/8¼in**
Price ★

7 Garin/Samarkanda Colour
oro/azul Alt. colours **yes**
Composition **75% cotton,
25% viscose** Width **140cm/
55in** Repeat **47cm/18½in**
Price ★★★

8 Rubelli/San Marco 1220
Colour **blue 5** Alt. colours
yes Composition **100%
silk** Width **125cm/49¼in**
Repeat **63cm/24¾in**
Price ★★★★★

6

8

7

MORESQUE

The fabric shown here is
derived from a panel of
English, ivory and white
silk damask overworked
in embroidery, dated
c.1554. The pattern is
"moresque", a term used
to describe the stylized
foliage patterns that
were fashionable in
Europe from the mid-16th
century to the early 17th
century. Also known as
"arabesques", these
patterns originated in
the damascened and
engraved metalwork of
Mesopotamia, Persia
and Syria, and were
introduced into Europe
by Muslim craftsmen who
settled in Venice during
the 15th century.

Stuart Interiors/Walsingham MC/LA Colour **ecru, bottle and cherry**
Alt. colours **yes** Composition **60% wool, 40% cotton**
Width **145cm/57in** Repeat **60cm/23¾in**
Price ★★★

Overall Pattern: **18th century**

The library of plant forms utilized by fabric designers was substantially augmented during the 18th century. The factors fuelling this included a greater understanding of plant ornament used in classical Rome and Greece, following significant archaeological discoveries; the importation of Chinese silks and ceramics and Indian chintzes decorated with oriental plant forms; and the increasing fashionableness of horticulture and gardening, and the attendant publication of botanical pattern books such as J.G. Huquier's *Nouveau Livre de Trophées de Fleurs Etrangers* (*c.* 1750) and Philip Miller's *Figures of the Most Beautiful and Uncommon Plants* (1752). Many plant-form patterns on fabrics in Palladian interiors were based on the acanthus and the water leaf, while in Rococo schemes designs were based on light, scrolling foliage, palms, *chinoiserie* and Indian lotus leaves, artichokes and cauliflower florets. In the Neo-classical interiors of the second half of the century, anthemia, laurels, lotus leaves, oak leaves, palmettes and seaweed were fashionable – the latter often combined with coral on silk damasks. Ivy patterns also became popular in Gothick schemes, as the plant's association with ruined buildings made it well suited to the Gothick taste for images of rustic decay. *Guilloche* patterns (*see* page 160) were also very popular.

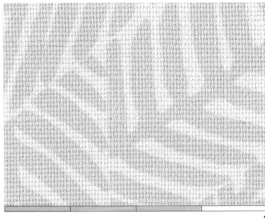

1 The Silk Gallery/Persephone Colour **new gold 278** Alt. colours **yes** Composition **100% silk** Width **127cm/ 50in** Repeat **90cm/35½in** Price ★★★ 〖〗

2 Knowles & Christou/Ferns Colour **fudge** Alt. colours **yes** Composition **100% linen** Width **132cm/51¼in** Repeat **67cm/27in** Price ★★★ 〖〗 ⊞

3 Zoffany/Silk Lampas SLA68 Colour **003** Alt. colours **yes** Composition **84% viscose, 16% silk** Width **128cm/50½in** Repeat **85cm/33½in** Price ★★★ 〖〗 ⊞

4 Timney Fowler/Agra Ironwork **TF004/3** Colour **green and ecru** Alt. colours **yes** Composition **100% cotton** Width **135cm/ 53in** Repeat **28cm/11in** Price ★★ 〖〗 ⊟

5 Watts of Westminster/Alwyne Zial Colour **beige/oatmeal** Alt. colours **yes** Composition **100% cotton** Width **124cm/ 48¾in** Repeat **96.5cm/38in** Price ★★★ 〖〗 ⊟

6 Apenn/Hayward AV469-1
Colour **green** Alt. colours **yes**
Composition **100% cotton**
Width **121cm/47½in** Repeat
8cm/3in Price ★★ 🛋️

**7 Brunschwig & Fils/Benoa
Contrefond Cotton Print 51251**
Colour **01** Alt. colours **yes**
Composition **100% cotton**
Width **135cm/53in** Repeat
17.5cm/7in Price ★★ 🛋️

8 Marvic Textiles/Oakley 7335
Colour **juniper** Alt. colours
yes Composition **74% cotton,
26% viscose** Width **142cm/
55¾in** Repeat **16.5cm/6½in**
Price ★★ 🛋️ LC 🛋️

9 Zoffany/Vine 347706 Colour
Swedish blue Alt. colours **yes**
Composition **45% modacrylic,
41% cotton, 14% nylon** Width
137cm/54in Repeat **10cm/4in**
Price ★★ 🛋️

**10 Brunschwig & Fils/Rampur
Stripe Cotton Print 79637**
Colour **04** Alt. colours **yes**
Composition **100% cotton**
Width **137cm/54in** Repeat
46cm/18in Price ★★ 🛋️

11 Bennison Fabrics/Cinnabar
Colour **sienna on beige** Alt.
colours **yes** Composition
70% linen, 30% cotton
Width **138cm/54in**
Repeat **49cm/19¼in**
Price ★★★ 🛋️

12 Warner/Templeton Field
Colour **grass** Alt. colours
yes Composition **100%
cotton** Width **137cm/
54in** Repeat **2cm/¾in**
Price ★ 🛋️

13 Zoffany/Mirandola DUP7100
Colour **1** Alt. colours **yes**
Composition **100% cotton**
Width **131cm/51½in**
Repeat **46cm/18in**
Price ★★ 🛋️

6

7

8

10

11

9

12

13

FABRICS: *OVERALL PATTERN*   **151**

Overall Pattern: Early 19th century

In early 19th-century Neo-classical interiors, fashionable plant-form-patterned fabrics were based on stylized anthemia (especially popular in France and America), laurels, Egyptian-style lotus and palm leaves, seaweed and the water leaf. However, as the century progressed increasingly naturalistic renderings of plant patterns were produced. Sometimes "sculptured" with shading, favoured patterns included acanthus leaf, grapevine, oak leaf, thistle and various fruits.

Around the middle of the century, there was a reaction to naturalistic patterns, with influential designers such as A.W.N. Pugin and Owen Jones producing heavily stylized designs. For example, many of the fabrics designed by Pugin in the 1840s were "flat-patterned" with a basic ogival structure featuring scrolling leaves and fleurs-de-lis, while Jones's designs incorporated stylized classical and Moorish ornament. Abstract patterns derived from motifs were also popular at this time, as were "ironwork" designs.

1

2

3

5

1 Nicholas Herbert/Loose Leaves **104** Colour **blue** Alt. colours **yes** Composition **66% linen, 34% cotton** Width **130cm/ 51in** Repeat **8.5cm/3¼in** Price ★★★

2 Wemyss Houlès/Kingsbury/ Kensington Colour **18** Alt. colours **yes** Composition **43% cotton, 43% modacrylic, 14% nylon** Width **138cm/ 54in** Repeat **32cm/12½in** Price ★★

3 Lennox Money/Araz **2149A** Colour **beige on green** Alt. colours **yes** Composition **100% cotton** Width **140cm/ 55in** Repeat **120cm/47in** Price ★★

4 Brunschwig & Fils/Coraux Glazed Chintz **62702.01** Colour **blueberry** Alt. colours **yes** Composition **100% cotton** Width **140cm/55in** Repeat **14cm/5½in** Price ★★

5 Hodsoll McKenzie/Arabesque **222/105** Colour **green** Alt. colours **yes** Composition **56% cotton, 44% rayon** Width **127cm/50in** Repeat **36.5cm/ 14¼in** Price ★★★

6 Marvic Textiles/Astor 4557
Colour **cardinal** Alt. colours
yes Composition **100%
cotton** Width **140cm/55in**
Repeat **70cm/27½in**
Price ★★★ 🔲 LC 🛋

7 Busby & Busby/Fontmell 6476
Colour **stone** Alt. colours **yes**
Composition **100% cotton**
Width **140cm/55in** Repeat
64cm/25in Price ★★ 🔲

8 Anne & Robert Swaffer/
Cotterstock/Allington Colour **19**
Alt. colours **yes** Composition
100% textured cotton Width
140cm/55in Repeat **64cm/25in**
Price ★★ 🔲 LC 🔳 🛋

9 Nina Campbell/Ferronnier
Chenilles/Rateau NCF3350
Colour **02** Alt. colours **yes**
Composition **51% rayon,
49% cotton** Width **132cm/
51¼in** Repeat **71cm/28in**
Price ★★★ 🔲 🔳

10 Rubelli/Bises Novità/
Sheerazade 2193 Colour
crena 1 Alt. colours **yes**
Composition **41% linen,
25% cotton, 20% silk, 14%
viscose** Width **130cm/51in**
Repeat **50cm/19½in**
Price ★★★ 🔲 🔳

11

12

19th century

11 Andrew Martin/Cabaret/
Arabesque Colour **arabesque**
Alt. colours **no** Composition
100% viscose Width **132cm/
51¾in** Repeat **41cm/16in**
Price ★★ 🔲 🔳 🛋

12 Montgomery/Halkidiki Colour **6**
Alt. colours **yes** Composition
100% cotton Width **140cm/
55in** Repeat **64cm/25in**
Price ★ 🔲 LC 🛋 🔳

13 Howe/Hydrangea Colour
hydrangea Alt. colours
no Composition **100%
cotton** Width **125cm/49¼in**
Repeat **40cm/15¾in**
Price ★★ 🔲 🔳 🛋

7
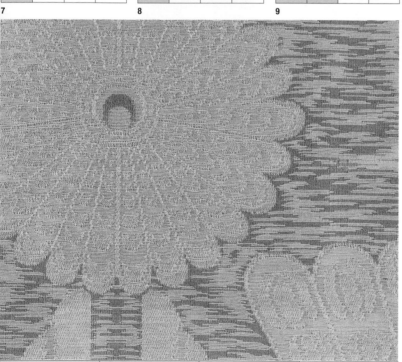
8

9

10

13

Overall Pattern: Late 19th century

Although naturalistically rendered plant-form patterns continued to appear on fabrics during the second half of the 19th century, stylized versions proved more fashionable. For example, designers of the Aesthetic movement drew inspiration from classical, medieval, Renaissance, Middle-Eastern and Japanese flat-patterns and plant motifs. These include E.W. Godwin's rigid geometric designs that incorporate highly conventionalized flowers and leaves reduced to flat, circular forms, and Christopher Dresser's formalized lotus patterns. Many Arts and Crafts fabrics also featured stylized, rhythmical plant forms, such as the willow, worked within medieval-style pattern structures, while Art Nouveau fabrics displayed sinuous vegetal patterns based on pomegranates, thistles, buds and seedpods, and leaf-like peacock feathers.

Of special note during the second half of the century were the paisley-pattern fabrics widely employed in English and American Victorian interiors, and also popular in France. Inspired by imported Kashmiri shawls, they featured formalized representations of pine cones infilled with small, incidental motifs commonly found in Indian textile designs, and surrounded by stylized vegetation based on palms, cypress and other plant forms.

4

1

1 **Lennox Money/Mangosteen 2152c** Colour **dark green on beige** Alt. colours **yes** Composition **100% cotton** Width **138cm/54in** Repeat **113cm/44in** Price ★★

2 **Zoffany/Palmette AMB0300** Colour **1** Alt. colours **yes** Composition **60% linen, 20% cotton, 20% modacrylic** Width **138cm/54in** Repeat **104cm/40½in** Price ★★

3 **Zuber/Arabesque/Volutes 30005** Colour **celadon** Alt. colours **yes** Composition **100% cotton** Width **130cm/51in** Repeat **43.5cm/17in** Price ★★★

4 **Watts of Westminster/Bodley F0041** Colour **English beige** Alt. colours **yes** Composition **54% cotton, 46% Velicren** Width **140cm/55in** Repeat **36cm/14in** Price ★★★

5 **Watts of Westminster/Grange Grosmont Shrewsbury F0040-01/M7** Colour **bottle green** Alt. colours **yes** Composition **54% cotton, 46% Velicren** Width **140cm/55in** Repeat **79cm/31in** Price ★★★

2

3

5

19th century

6 **Borderline/Juniper 2528a**
Colour **red** Alt. colours **yes**
Composition **100% wool**
Width **137cm/54in** Repeat
44cm/17in Price ★★ LC

7 **Bennison Fabrics/Pacific Willow**
Colour **beige** Alt. colours **yes**
Composition **70% linen, 30%
cotton** Width **133cm/52in**
Repeat **13cm/5in**
Price ★★★

8 **Nina Campbell/Curzon Chenilles/
Dalhousie/NCF3412** Colour **02**
Alt. colours **yes** Composition
**74% rayon, 23% cotton, 3%
polyester** Width **131cm/51½in**
Repeat **70cm/27½in**
Price ★★★

6

7

8

9

10

9 **Marvic Textiles/Khaipur 5818-1**
Colour **claret** Alt. colours **yes**
Composition **40% acryllic, 40%
viscose, 20% cotton** Width
150cm/59in Repeat **35.5cm/
14in** Price ★★★

10 **Morris & Co/Garden Tulip
PR8539** Colour **1** Alt. colours
yes Composition **53% linen,
35% cotton, 12% nylon** Width
137cm/54in Repeat **44.5cm/
17¼in** Price ★★

11 **Liberty Furnishings/Hera
1067032** Colour **G** Alt. colours
yes Composition **100% cotton**
Width **137cm/54in** Repeat
36cm/14in Price ★

12 **Mulberry/Cartouche FD336**
Colour **soft green/brick** Alt.
colours **yes** Composition
**65% viscose, 25% cotton, 10%
polyamide** Width **146cm/
57½in** Repeat **30cm/11¾in**
Price ★★★

11

FLAME STITCH

The flame stitch pattern
enjoyed a resurgence of
popularity during the late
19th century and, as a
consequence, machine-
made versions were
produced to meet the
demand. A form of
embroidery that was
primarily used as a cover
for chairs, sofas and fire-
screens, flame stitch
consists of "flames" of
colour. The technique, by
which large areas of
backing canvas can be
covered rapidly and to
dramatic effect, was a
fashionable pastime in
Britain and America
during the 18th century.

Brunschwig & Fils 89381 Colour **M46** Alt. colours **yes** Composition
87% viscose, 12% cotton, 1% polyester Width **140cm/55in** Repeat
39cm/15¼in Price ★★★★★

12

FABRICS: *OVERALL PATTERN* **155**

Overall Pattern: **Early 20th century**

Woven and printed fabric patterns consisting of stylized plant forms remained very fashionable during the first half of the 20th century. For example, sinuously depicted foliage was an important element in later designs of the Art Nouveau period, and thistle, poppy, wisteria and waterlily patterns were especially favoured. Similarly, Arts and Crafts designers continued to explore new areas of plant ornament. L.F. Day, whose influential *Nature and Ornament* was published 1908–9, noted: "The rose has been variously treated but comparatively little use has been made...[to date]...of the fruit, or of the thorns, or of the broad stipules at the base of the leaves."

More traditional plant-form patterns were also much in evidence during the first half of the century. Significant examples included the Renaissance-style pomegranate- and acorn-patterned damasks that were found in Tudor Revival and Jacobean Revival interiors. Also prevalent were the classical Graeco-Roman palms and palmettes that appeared on some of the Art Deco fabrics. However, the increasing influence of fine art on textile design resulted in the appearance of radically new organic forms, such as abstract depictions of aquaria and pond life.

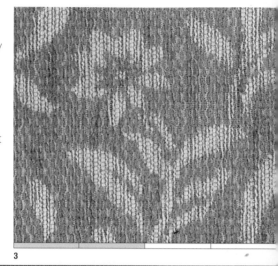

3

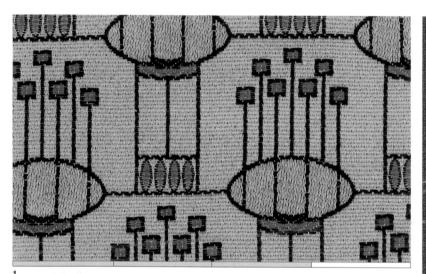

1

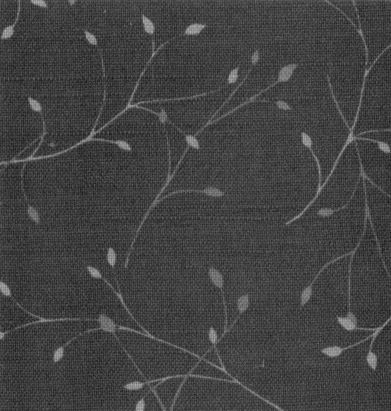

2

4

1 Northwood Designs/Lampen M06352 Colour **03** Alt. colours **yes** Composition **61% cotton, 39% viscose** Width **140cm/ 55in** Repeat **10.5cm/4in** Price ★★★

2 Zuber/Tissus Anciens III/ Chambord Brodé 10174 Colour **white/gold** Alt. colours **yes** Composition **100% cotton** Width **140cm/ 55in** Repeat **67cm/26¼in** Price ★★★★★

3 Monkwell/MF 5883 Colour **ananda** Alt. colours **yes** Composition **37% acrylic chenille, 27% polyester, 14% viscose, 14% polyester chenille, 8% cotton** Width **140cm/ 55in** Repeat **46cm/18in** Price ★★

4 Monkwell/MP 9556 Colour **brick** Alt. colours **yes** Composition **58% linen, 31% cotton, 11% nylon** Width **137cm/ 54in** Repeat **11cm/4¼in** Price ★★

5 Nina Campbell/Ferronnier Chenilles/Poiret NCF3352 Colour **03** Alt. colours **yes** Composition **66% cotton, 34% rayon** Width **137cm/ 54in** Repeat **19cm/7½in** Price ★★★

6 Donghia/Magic 0392/5725-03 Colour **harvest** Alt. colours **yes** Composition **100% silk** Width **140cm/55in** Repeat **13cm/5in** Price ★★★★★

5

6

7 **Lee Jofa/Pardah Print 919301**
Colour **persian red/indgo** Alt.
colours **yes** Composition
**52% linen, 36% cotton,
12% nylon** Width **137cm/
54in** Repeat **72cm/28¼in**
Price ★★ 〔〕🛋

8 **Brunschwig & Fils/89507**
Colour **247** Alt. colours
yes Composition **100%
rayon** Width **140cm/
55in** Repeat **18.5cm/7¼in**
Price ★★★ 〔〕⊞🛋

9 **Warner Fabrics/Aquarium
GW32903** Colour **orange** Alt.
colours **yes** Composition
100% cotton Width **137cm/
54in** Repeat **72cm/28¼in**
Price ★★ [LC] 〔〕⊞🛋

10 **Scalamandré/16316** Colour **001**
Alt. colours **yes** Composition
100% cotton Width **54cm/
21½in** Repeat **25cm/10in**
Price ★★★★★ 〔〕⊞🛋

11 **Zimmer & Rohde/Lyra 6997**
Colour **717** Alt. colours **yes**
Composition **100% silk** Width
140cm/55in Repeat **9cm/3½in**
Price ★★★★ 〔〕🛋

12 **Northwood Designs/Spirale
P074B7** Colour **03** Alt.
colours **yes** Composition
100% cotton Width **140cm/
55in** Repeat **32cm/12½in**
Price ★★★ 〔〕⊞🛋

13 **Brunschwig & Fils/Involve
Silk Texture 53462.01** Colour
imperial blue Alt. colours
yes Composition **76% silk,
24% cotton** Width **140cm/
55in** Repeat **31cm/12in**
Price ★★★ 〔〕🛋

14 **Osborne & Little/Dufy Velvet
F5151** Colour **01** Alt. colours
yes Composition **59% viscose,
41% cotton** Width **132cm/
51¾in** Repeat **59cm/23in**
Price ★★★★ 〔〕[LC]🛋

9

10

11

12

13

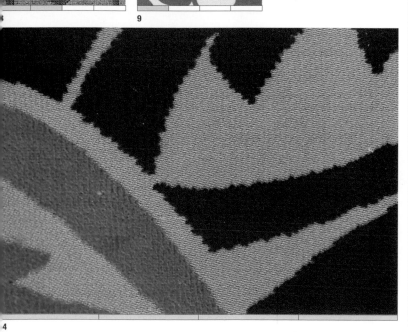

4

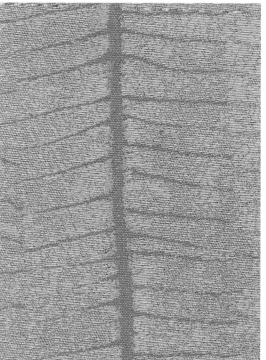

15

15 **Malabar/Taprabane/Rubra Leaf**
Colour **silver** Alt. colours **no**
Composition **100% silk** Width
140cm/55in Repeat **12cm/4¾in**
Price ★★★ 〔〕⊞

16 **Manuel Canovas/Kapsan
1420** Colour **36** Alt. colours
yes Composition **100% cotton**
Width **139cm/54¾in** Repeat
36.5cm/14¼in Price ★★ ⊞

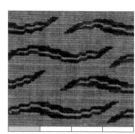

16

FABRICS: *OVERALL PATTERN* **157**

20th century

Overall Pattern: **Late 20th–early 21st century**

Woven and printed fabrics with traditional-style leaf patterns have been much in demand during the late 20th and early 21st century. Highly stylized – sometimes shaded, sometimes flat – they have often been presented on a contrasting plain ground to give them a contemporary feel. Sinuous Art Nouveau and rhythmical Arts and Crafts plant-form patterns (see pages 154-7) came back into fashion in the 1960s and the 1980s respectively. Pointillist-style patterns comprising small repeated fruit motifs such as strawberries and raspberries have also found favour, while stylized and naturalistic animal prints have proved popular, especially as top-covers for upholstered seating.

Among recent and important additions to the catalogue of organic ornamentation are colourful woven fabrics showing stylized "three-dimensional" wickerwork patterns, and literally three-dimensional fabrics that are comprised of plain- or neutral-coloured grounds "embroidered" with highly textured threadwork.

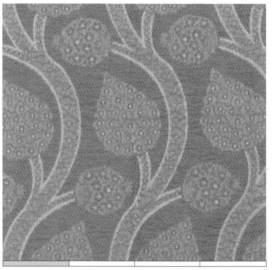

1

4

2

5

6

3

7

1 Clarence House/Zambezi 33975/3 Colour **multi** Alt. colours **yes** Composition **72% linen, 17% cotton, 11% polyester** Width **130cm/51in** Repeat **94.5cm/36½in** Price ★★★★★ 🛋

2 Nya Nordiska/Pavonia Colour **bronze 06** Alt. colours **yes** Composition **40% polyester, 30% polyamid, 30% acetate** Width **160cm/63in** Repeat **21cm/8¼in** Price ★★★ 🪟🛋

3 Monkwell/Vellum MP 9495 Colour **baked** Alt. colours **yes** Composition **100% cotton** Width **137cm/54in** Repeat **32cm/12½in** Price ★★ 🪟▦

4 Garin/Kaisery Colour **arena** Alt. colours **yes** Composition **100% cotton** Width **140cm/55in** Repeat **47cm/18½in** Price ★★★ 🛋 LC

5 Donghia/Casino 10025 Colour **01** Alt. colours **yes** Composition **56% rayon, 44% cotton** Width **140cm/55in** Repeat **18.5cm/7¼in** Price ★★★★ 🪟🛋 LC

6 Knowles & Christou/Cabouchon KG403a Colour **opal and lilac** Alt. colours **yes** Composition **100% cotton** Width **132cm/51¾in** Repeat **10cm/4in** Price ★★★ 🪟🛋 W

7 Galbraith & Paul/Mosaic Colour **silver** Alt. colours **yes** Composition **100% shantung silk** Width **134cm/52½in** Repeat **46cm/18in** Price ★★★★ 🪟

8 Mulberry/Ice Dance FD387
Colour **pink W106** Alt. colours
yes Composition **73% cotton,
20% rayon, 7% nylon** Width
130cm/51in Repeat **43cm/16¾in**
Price ★★★ LC ⬚ ⊞

9 Lelièvre/Damasquine 909
Colour **cuivre 02** Alt. colours **no**
Composition **95% cotton, 5%
polyamide** Width **136cm/53½in**
Repeat **12cm/4¾in**
Price ★★★ ⬚ ⊞

10 Jim Thompson/Image 1023
Colour **07** Alt. colours **yes**
Composition **100% cotton**
Width **142cm/55½in** Repeat –
Price ★★★ ⬚ 🛋

11 Knowles & Christou/Wicker
Colour **blue** Alt. colours **yes**
Composition **100% linen** Width
132cm/51¾in Repeat **3cm/1¼in**
Price ★★★ ⬚ 🛋 W

12 Marvic Textiles/Le Croc/5924-2
Colour **blue** Alt. colours **yes**
Composition **100% cotton**
Width **136cm/53½in** Repeat
27cm/10¾in Price ★★★ 🛋

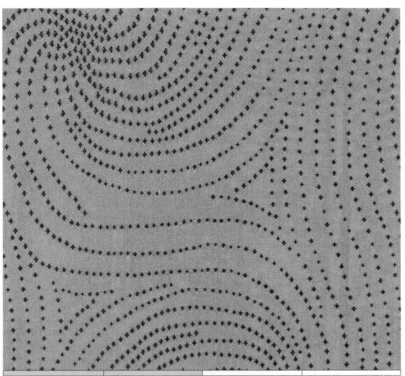

8

9

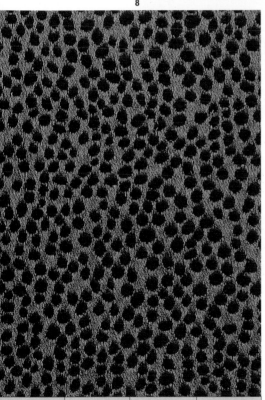

10

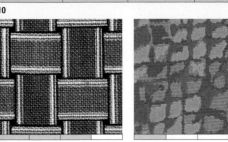

11   12

"ANIMAL SKIN" FABRIC

Distinctively patterned animal skins provided fashionable covers for chairs and sofas during the 19th century, particularly in Britain and France as they expanded their empires into Africa. However, even then demand outstripped supply and thus *faux* skins made of both woven and printed fabrics were also produced for upholstery.

With animals such as the leopard, tiger, panther and some species of zebra now hunted close to extinction, it is the fabric substitutes that have enjoyed a resurgence in popularity during the second half of the 20th century.

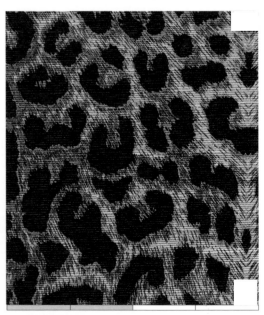

G.P. & J. Baker/Panther J0257-220 Colour **black and cream** Alt. colours **yes** Composition **86% cotton, 14% polyacrylic** Width **138cm/54in** Repeat **38cm/15in** Price ★★ LC ⬚ 🛋

Jim Thompson/Leopard PDB 2798A Colour **A** Alt. colours **no** Composition **100% silk** Width **122cm/48in** Repeat **46cm/18in** Price ★★★★ ⬚ 🛋

Geometric Fabrics

A wide range of geometric-patterned fabrics, woven and printed, has been produced from the Middle Ages to the present day. Much of the geometric ornament employed originated in ancient classical and oriental civilizations or in medieval Europe.

Stylistically, fabrics with geometric patterns can usually be divided into two basic categories. In the first the pattern consists of geometric or linear forms; in the second a basic geometric pattern, sometimes comprised of non-geometric repeat motifs, frames the non-geometric imagery or provides the ground against which it is set.

Patterns classified as "pure" geometrics include woven or printed stripes; checks, such as woven tartans and printed madras; and combinations of irregular geometric forms that were inspired by Cubist art. "Loosely" geometric-based patterns include trellis- or latticework, and *guilloche* – an overall repeating pattern (*see* pages 146–59) of interlacing curved bands, sometimes forming circles enriched with floral motifs.

LEFT The squab seat of the lyre-back chair in the background is upholstered with a red horsehair-weave, cut-pile velvet, while the armchair in the foreground is covered with a red-and-gold trellis-pattern silk lampas by Scalamandré. Both chairs date from the early to mid-19th century, and are in the parlour of the 19th-century Andrew Low House, Georgia, USA.

ABOVE Linear-stripe patterns are particularly suitable for pull-up, pull-down window blinds, and were very fashionable in late 18th- and early 19th-century interiors. These Roman blinds are in a late Georgian house in Brighton, England.

TICKING

This 19th-century French wirework child's bed has been converted into a small bench seat – with a bolster added for extra comfort. The squab and bolster are both covered with a modern blue-and-white striped bed ticking – a fabric that has been produced in various patterns over the centuries, although striped examples are certainly the most common. Blue-and-white striped ticking such as this, woven in either cotton or linen, has changed very little in appearance since the late 18th century, and has remained fashionable on both sides of the Atlantic for a variety of uses.

KEY DESIGNS

1 Popular since the 19th century, checked ginghams have vertical and horizontal stripes of equal width. They are woven from only two colours, but display a third colour where these overlap.

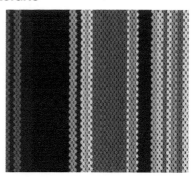

2 Thick-textured, multi-coloured fabrics patterned with woven stripes of various alternating widths were much in evidence during the Renaissance, as well as appearing in 20th-century interiors.

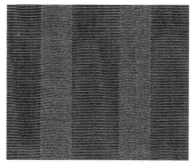

3 Striped fabrics incorporating alternating weaves and colourways have been popular since the Middle Ages, but were especially fashionable during the late 18th and early 19th centuries.

4 Tartans have been widely used as furnishing fabrics since the 19th century. They are produced in various patterns and colourways ("setts"), each associated with a particular Scottish clan.

5 Diaper patterns have consistently appeared on fabrics since the Middle Ages. Favoured designs include trellis or lattice frameworks containing repeated geometric or non-geometric motifs.

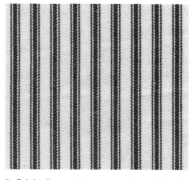

6 Originally a mattress covering, striped herringbone-weave ticking is now widely employed for hangings and upholstery. Classic colourways are black, green, blue or red on white or beige.

---

1 Manuel Canovas/Passy 4261 Colour **96** Alt. colours **yes** Composition **100% viscose** Width **130cm/51in** Repeat **2cm/¾in** Price ★★

2 Thomas Dare/Sarawak Colour **multi/orange** Alt. colours **yes** Composition **100% cotton** Width **137cm/54in** Repeat **–** Price ★★

3 Nobilis-Fontan/Rodolphe 9937 Colour **red** Alt. colours **yes** Composition **56% cotton, 44% viscose** Width **130cm/51in** Repeat **–** Price ★★★

4 The Isle Mill/Tullochcan STR009 Colour **multi** Alt. colours **yes** Composition **100% wool** Width **140cm/55in** Repeat **25cm/9¾in** Price ★★★

5 G.P. & J. Baker/Roi Soleil Colour **green** Alt. colours **yes** Composition **57% cotton, 43% modacrylic** Width **145cm/57in** Repeat **6cm/2½in** Price ★★

6 Ian Mankin/Ticking 01 Colour **black** Alt. colours **yes** Composition **100% cotton** Width **137cm/54in** Repeat **–** Price ★

Geometrics: **Pre-18th century**

During the Middle Ages, diaper patterns were often employed on woven fabrics, and usually took the form of trellis grounds filled with motifs, such as lozenges, squares, scales or formalized flowers and leaves. Chequer patterns – regularly spaced squares of alternating colours – were also popular, as were chevrons (V-shapes, used either singly in vertical series, or strung to form zig-zags), nailheads (small pyramid forms) and powdered ornament (evenly spaced scatterings of small flowers or stars).

Diaper, chequer and nailhead patterns continued to appear on Renaissance fabrics. Strapwork patterns (twisted and intertwined bands similar to ribbons or strips of leather) were also fashionable, and Islamic influence was notable in *guilloches* (repeated interlacing curved bands, sometimes forming circles and usually enriched with floral motifs). However, aside from tartans (*see* opposite), which were primarily used for clothing and blankets during this period, the most notable late 16th- and 17th-century addition to this rich catalogue of geometric ornament was jewelled strapwork: an elaboration of its plainer forerunner in which increasingly intricate banding was embellished with studs or lozenges shaded in imitation of faceted, prismatic jewels.

5

1   **Jason D'Souza/Stripe 561**
Colour **green** Alt. colours yes
Composition **50% linen, 50% cotton** Width **137cm/54in**
Repeat **8cm/3in**
Price ★★

2   **Today Interiors/Checkmate/ Check FR3501** Colour **1** Alt. colours **yes** Composition **100% cotton** Width **137cm/54in** Repeat **51cm/20in** Price ★★

3   **Jason D'Souza/San Marco SAN 01** Colour **walnut and coral** Alt. colours **yes** Composition **50% linen, 50% cotton** Width **133cm/52in** Repeat **5.5cm/2¼in** Price ★★

4   **John Boyd Textiles/Squares 682/5** Colour **purple/black** Alt. colours **yes** Composition **68% horsehair, 32% cotton** Width **56cm/22in** Repeat **-** Price ★★★

5   **John Boyd Textiles/Jutland JU/609** Colour **brown/black** Alt. colours **yes** Composition **68% horsehair, 32% cotton** Width **65cm/25½in** Repeat **-** Price ★★★

6   **Zoffany/Cottage Garden ORC0500** Colour **1** Alt. colours **yes** Composition **56% linen, 36% cotton, 8% nylon** Width **138cm/54½in** Repeat **8cm/3in** Price ★★

1

2

3

4

6

10 Zoffany/Mosaic VEN9600 Colour **1** Alt. colours **yes** Composition **37% wool, 3% nylon, 60% modacrylic** Width **137cm/54in** Repeat **13cm/5in** Price ★★ LC 🛋

11 Anta/Ballone 955 Colour **blue/green** Alt. colours **no** Composition **100% wool** Width **90cm/35½in** Repeat **50cm/19½in** Price ★★★★ 🛋

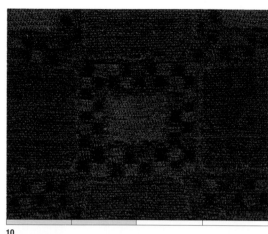

10

7 Wemyss Houlès/Minster/ Winchester Colour **blue** Alt. colours **yes** Composition **56% linen, 33% cotton, 11% nylon** Width **138cm/54¼in** Repeat - Price ★★ 〔✂〕 LC 🛋 ⊞

8 Montgomery/Dot.Com Colour **blue 1** Alt. colours **yes** Composition **53% cotton, 47% polyester** Width **137cm/54in** Repeat **2cm/¾in** Price ★ 〔✂〕 ⊞

9 Zoffany/Bark NAT2900 Colour **1** Alt. colours **yes** Composition **52% polyester, 48% cotton** Width **125cm/49¼in** Repeat **23cm/9in** Price ★★ 〔✂〕

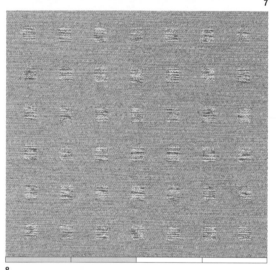

8

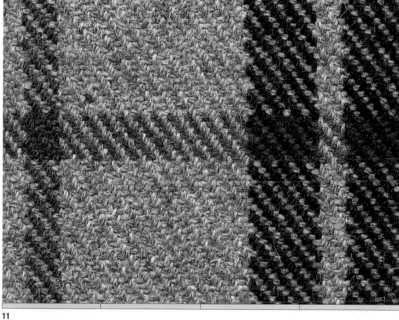

11

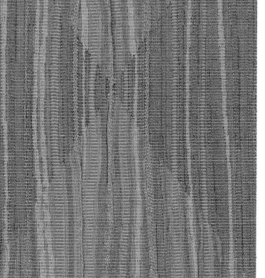

TARTAN

In the 19th century, when tartans became fashionable furnishing fabrics, many manufacturers outside Scotland produced them in setts (patterns and colours) that sometimes bore little resemblance to the authentic designs of the Scottish clans. This development was fuelled by three factors: financial opportunism, the use of synthetic aniline rather than vegetable dyes, and a lack of knowledge. Many of the pre-18th-century setts were never recorded, but were instead passed down by generations of Scottish dyers and weavers.

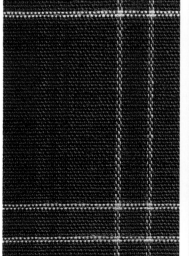

Seamoor Fabrics/Hay Tartan 96720/22 Colour **red and black** Alt. colours **no** Composition **100% cotton** Width **140cm/55in** Repeat **11cm/4¼in** Price ★ LC 〔✂〕 🛋 W

Seamoor Fabrics/Macalpine Tartan 96720/27 Colour **green and cream** Alt. colours **no** Composition **100% cotton** Width **140cm/55in** Repeat **11cm/4¼in** Price ★ LC 〔✂〕 🛋 W

Geometrics: **Early 18th century**

Diaper ornament continued to appear on furnishing fabrics produced during the first half of the 18th century. Indeed, early Rococo-style fabrics were characterized by trellis and latticework patterns (often constructed from leaf motifs), while bandwork (the 18th-century term for strapwork) was also much in evidence, and usually provided the ground for light, scrolling foliage. Other medieval and Renaissance geometric patterns that either remained popular or were revived included V-shape chevrons (particularly prevalent in mid-18th-century Gothick interiors), dogteeth (symmetrically arranged, star-like decorations developed from pyramid-shaped nailheads – *see* page 162), and, to a lesser extent, tartans.

Also increasingly popular during the early 18th century were vertical-stripe patterns. Varied in width, alternated in two or more colours and sometimes incorporating additional small motifs, the stripes either made up the main body of the pattern, or were superimposed over other patterns (often floral) in the weave.

Crowson/Valentino Santi Colour **4** Alt. colours **yes** Composition **38% cotton chenille, 32% polyester, 30% acetate** Width **137cm/54in** Repeat **stripe** Price ★★

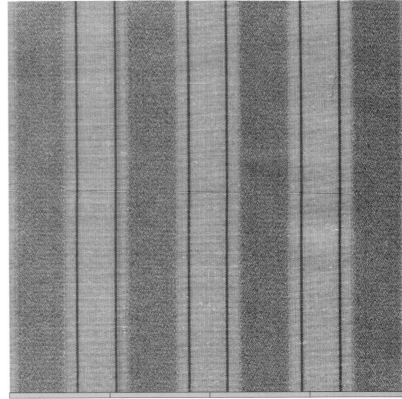

Scalamandré/Province 154-007 Colour **yellow and pale blue** Alt. colours **yes** Composition **100% silk** Width **127cm/50in** Repeat **2.5cm/1in** Price ★★★★★

George Spencer Decorations/Check 001C/11 Colour **green/plum** Alt. colours **yes** Composition **100% cotton** Width **120cm/47in** Repeat **2cm/¾in** Price ★★

Bennett Silks/Manhattan/Waldorf Colour **65** Alt. colours **yes** Composition **100% silk** Width **140cm/55in** Repeat – Price ★★★

John Wilman/Aida 888201 Colour **petrol** Alt. colours **yes** Composition **100% cotton satin** Width **137cm/54in** Repeat **2cm/¾in** Price ★

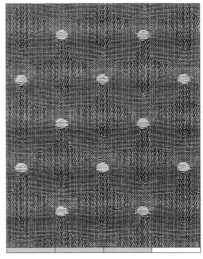

The Isle Mill/Black Watch MW 801 Colour **black and green** Alt. colours **no** Composition **100% wool** Width **140cm/55in** Repeat **25cm/9¾in** Price ★★★ LC ⊞ 🛋

The Isle Mill/Campbell Ancient Muted MW 1203 Colour **green and blue** Alt. colours **no** Composition **100% wool** Width **140cm/55in** Repeat **30cm/11¾in** Price ★★★ LC ⊞ 🛋

Zimmer & Rohde/Arena 6996 684 Colour **green and yellow** Alt. colours **yes** Composition **54% cotton, 46% viscose** Width **140cm/55in** Repeat **3cm/1¼in** Price ★★★ 🗔 🛋

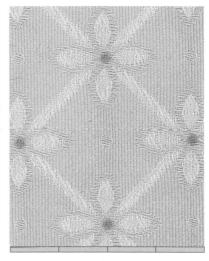

Zoffany/Petites Fleurs FWE3100 Colour **1** Alt. colours **yes** Composition **69.2% cotton, 18.8% viscose, 12% nylon** Width **142cm/55¾in** Repeat **14cm/5½in** Price ★★ 🗔 LC 🛋

Jab/Ragione 1-2300 Colour **117** Alt. colours **yes** Composition **55% polyester, 37% cotton, 8% polyacrylic** Width **140cm/55in** Repeat **3cm/1¼in** Price ★★★ 🛋

Brunschwig & Fils/89511 Colour **409** Alt. colours **yes** Composition **100% Trevira CS** Width **140cm/55in** Repeat **4cm/1½in** Price ★★★ LC 🗔 🛋

TRELLIS PATTERNS

The trellis pattern was a much-favoured fabric design in both Rococo and Neo-classical interiors throughout the 18th century, most notably in Sweden and especially for upholstered furniture. Although the majority of trellis designs were made up of small interlocking leaves, some consisted of small interlaced flowers or buds or, more exceptionally, feather-like motifs. Particularly fashionable colours throughout the century included pale shades of brown or green, straw yellows, pearl greys and muted dark or pale blues.

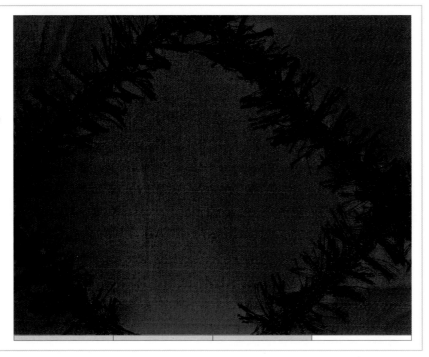

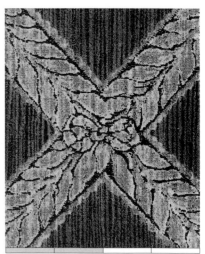

Today Interiors/Taffetas/Frou Frou TAF4025 Colour **25** Alt. colours **yes** Composition **100% acetate; nylon yarn trim** Width **150cm/59in** Repeat **15cm/6in** Price ★★ ⊞

John Wilman/Figaro 888065 Colour **granite** Alt. colours **yes** Composition **100% cotton** Width **137cm/54in** Repeat – Price ★ 🛋

18th century

Geometrics: Late 18th century

Striped fabrics were found in many Neo-classical interiors during the second half of the 18th century. The alternation of the widths and colours of woven stripes also became increasingly sophisticated following technical improvements made to the looms. Typical designs included thin bands of vertically stacked single chevrons alternating with contrasting-coloured wider bands of horizontally linked pairs of chevrons; Etruscan-style vertical stripes composed of leaves, tripods, urns, chimeras, half-figures and other classical motifs; and overall *guilloche* patterns (*see* pages 150–1).

In Greek Revival interiors, the Greek key pattern was often used as a border on fabrics – the interlocking right-angled and vertical lines often doubled up to create a perspective effect – sometimes intermittently embellished with either *paterae* or rosettes. Latticework patterns were also fashionable, often as grounds for *chinoiserie* and Indian motifs, as were multi-coloured woven checks, their squares sometimes decorated with small classical or floral motifs. Toward the end of the century, ticking, too, became popular. Initially employed as a cover for feather mattresses – its herringbone-weave stripes designed to keep feathers in and ticks out – its use subsequently spread to furnishings.

4

1

5

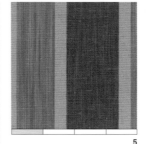

6

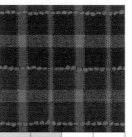

7

1 **Wemyss Houlès/Kingsbury/ Windsor** Colour **05** Alt. colours **yes** Composition **43% cotton, 43% modacrylic, 14% nylon** Width **138cm/ 54in** Repeat **32cm/12½in** Price ★★

2 **Sahco Hesslein/Bellevue 14790** Colour **brown** Alt. colours **yes** Composition **71% cotton, 29% silk** Width **130cm/51in** Repeat – Price ★★★★

3 **Ian Sanderson/Pym Stripe** Colour **brick** Alt. colours **yes** Composition **100% cotton** Width **140cm/55in** Repeat – Price ★★

4 **Zimmer & Rohde/Stradino 4818** Colour **245** Alt. colours **yes** Composition **100% silk** Width **140cm/55in** Repeat **2cm/¾in** Price ★★★

5 **Zoffany/Paysanne Stripe FWE3200** Colour **1** Alt. colours **yes** Composition **55.2% cotton, 44.8% viscose** Width **144cm/56½in** Repeat – Price ★★

6 **Ian Sanderson/Laura Stripe** Colour **brick** Alt. colours **yes** Composition **40% polyester, 34% viscose, 26% cotton** Width **135cm/53in** Repeat **6cm/2½in** Price ★★

7 **Zimmer & Rohde/Calicantus 5097** Colour **188** Alt. colours **yes** Composition **82% cotton, 18% silk** Width **140cm/55in** Repeat **35cm/13¾in** Price ★★★

8 **Sahco Hesslein/Etoile 1919** Colour **02** Alt. colours **yes** Composition **67% cotton, 33% nylon** Width **140cm/55in** Repeat – Price ★★★

2

3

8

9 Bennett Silks/Selby Colour 1131 Alt. colours **yes** Composition **100% silk** Width **150cm/ 59in** Repeat **21cm/8¼in** Price ★★★ 🪑 LC 🛋 ▦

10 Zimmer & Rohde/Sciro 4819 707 Colour **13** Alt. colours **yes** Composition **100% silk** Width **140cm/55in** Repeat **16.5cm/ 6½in** Price ★★★ 🪑 🛋

11 Colefax and Fowler/Maplehurst Check F1305/03 Colour **green** Alt. colours **yes** Composition **45% cotton, 47% modacrylic, 8% linen** Width **137cm/54in** Repeat **5cm/2¼in** Price ★★ 🪑 🛋

12 Manuel Canovas/Vivaldi 4464 Colour **22** Alt. colours **yes** Composition **100% silk** Width **138.5cm/54½in** Repeat **35cm/13¾in** Price ★★★ 🪑

13 Today Interiors/Capella/Zaniah ZF2886 Colour **86** Alt. colours **yes** Composition **100% cotton** Width **137cm/54in** Repeat **20cm/8in** Price ★★ 🛋 LC

14 Scalamandré/Roma 1205-001 Colour **multi on ivory** Alt. colours **yes** Composition **100% silk** Width **127cm/ 50in** Repeat **12cm/4¾in** Price ★★★★★ 🛋

15 Old World Weavers/Ombre Thien JN00030001 Colour **multi/gold** Alt. colours **yes** Composition **100% silk** Width **122cm/48in** Repeat **–** Price ★★★★ 🪑 🛋

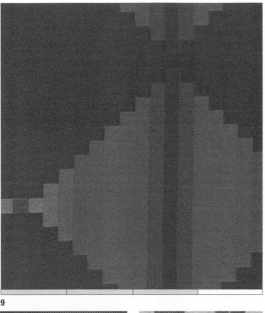

9

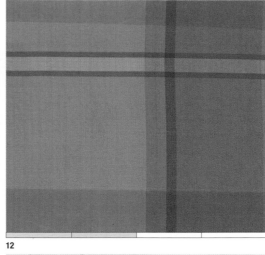

12

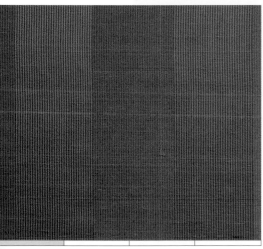

10

11

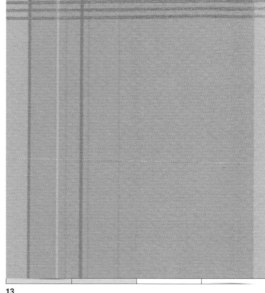

13

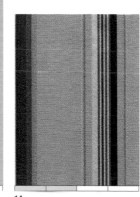

14

ANTICO SETIFICIO FIORENTINO

The Italian cloth factory Antico Setificio Fiorentino has produced woven fabrics since the Renaissance, and makes most of its document fabrics on the original looms – some of which were donated by the Grand Duke of Tuscany in 1780. The factory also retains an ancient thread-winding machine based on a design by Leonardo da Vinci. It is not at all surprising, therefore, that ordering a brocade or damask made there has been described as similar to ordering a custom-made Ferrari.

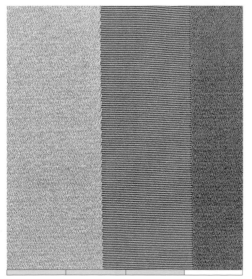

Antico Setificio Fiorentino/Le Roy Colour **gold/orange/bright beige** Alt. colours **yes** Composition **100% silk** Width **120cm/47in** Repeat **29cm/11¼in** Price ★★★ 🪑 🛋 W

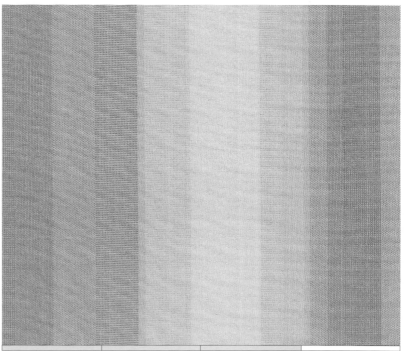

15

Geometrics: **Early 19th century**

Stripes were very fashionable until the 1830s, particularly for upholstered seating (*see* "Striped Fabrics", opposite), while during the 1840s jewelled strapwork patterns and powdered ornament (*see* page 162) reappeared in Gothic Revival interiors. However, in addition, a tremendous range of check-patterned fabrics was produced throughout the first half of the 19th century. For example, rectangular shapes surrounding small Neo-classical and Napoleonic motifs were popular for use in Empire-style interiors, and twill-weave tartans began to be more widely employed as furnishing fabrics in both Britain and America.

Typical of the printed checks that became increasingly fashionable were the imported Indian ginghams. These were lightweight cottons, brightly coloured with vegetable dyes. Unfortunately, they were not colourfast, a problem that also affected silk and cotton, and especially red-and-black-check Indian madras – known as "bleeding madras" because of the instability of its colours.

1

2

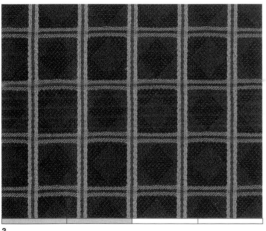

3

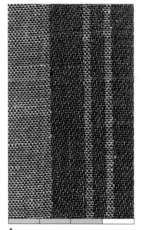

4

5

6

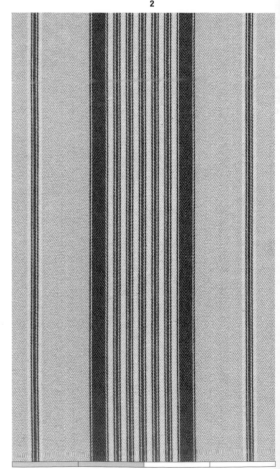

7

1 **The Isle Mill/Macnaughton Muted MW1229** Colour **red and green** Alt. colours **no** Composition **100% wool** Width **140cm/55in** Repeat **25cm/9¾in** Price ★★★

2 **Ian Sanderson/Keswick** Colour **pippin red** Alt. colours **yes** Composition **100% wool** Width **140cm/ 55in** Repeat **17cm/6¾in** Price ★★

3 **Zoffany/Veneto Check CW4700** Colour **1** Alt. colours **yes** Composition **46% cotton, 5% nylon, 49% modacrylic** Width **140cm/55in** Repeat **6cm/2½in** Price ★★

4 **Marvic Textiles/Fabiola 8249-5** Colour **olive** Alt. colours **yes** Composition **52% linen, 48% viscose** Width **140cm/55in** Repeat – Price ★★

5 **Baer & Ingram/Daisy DSF 05** Colour **dark pink** Alt. colours **yes** Composition **100% cotton** Width **140cm/55in** Repeat **11cm/4¼in** Price ★★

6 **Nina Campbell/Violet Plaid NCF3131** Colour **01** Alt. colours **yes** Composition **100% cotton** Width **140cm/55in** Repeat **9cm/3½in** Price ★★

7 **Ian Mankin/Empire 1** Colour **Air Force** Alt. colours **yes** Composition **100% cotton** Width **137cm/54in** Repeat – Price ★

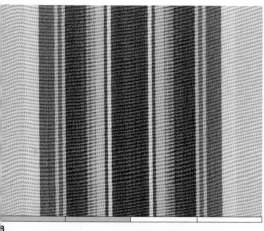

8   Scalamandré/Simbolo 90010-001 Colour **multi on peach** Alt. colours **yes** Composition **100% silk** Width **127cm/50in** Repeat **43cm/16¾in** Price ★★★★ 🪑🛋

9   Garin/Aral Colour **celeste** Alt. colours **yes** Composition **50% silk, 50% cotton** Width **140cm/55in** Repeat **–** Price ★★★ 🪑

10 Brunschwig & Fils/Valmy Lisère Stripe 32482.01 Colour **blue stripe** Alt. colours **yes** Composition **100% cotton** Width **130cm/51in** Repeat **7cm/2¾in** Price ★★★ 🛋

11 The Silk Gallery/Pergamon Colour **henna and Italian gold** Alt. colours **yes** Composition **68% silk, 32% polyester** Width **127cm/50in** Repeat **–** Price ★★★ 🪑🛋 Ⓦ

12 Hodsoll McKenzie/Campaign Stripe 353/103 Colour **red/green** Alt. colours **yes** Composition **76% cotton, 24% silk** Width **127cm/50in** Repeat **–** Price ★★★ 🪑🛋 Ⓦ

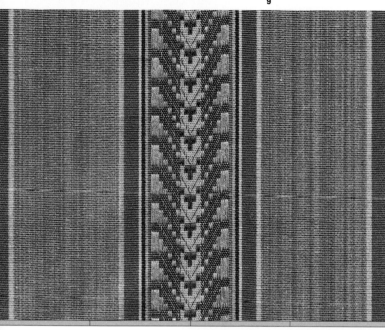

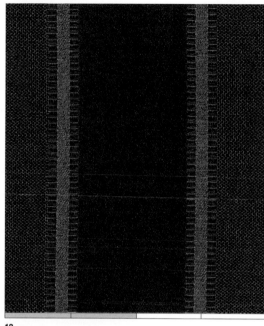

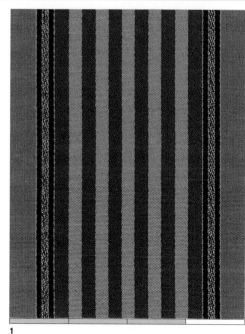

STRIPED FABRICS

Silk, linen and cotton fabrics in striped designs first became fashionable in France during the early years of the 19th century. They were initially inspired by the striped bunting hung from the exteriors of buildings to celebrate the Emperor Napoleon's victories on the battlefield against other European powers.

Striped textile hangings and upholstery fabrics proved just as popular in America and elsewhere in Europe, particularly Britain, until the 1830s. In Britain the range of colourful woven and printed striped fabrics produced during this period (in the Regency and then reign of George IV) came to be known as "Regency stripes".

1   Jim Thompson/Flotilla II 1002 Colour **02** Alt. colours **yes** Composition **100% silk** Width **122cm/48in** Repeat **10cm/4in** Price ★★★ 🪑

2   Marvic Textiles/Emilio FR 1302-7 Colour **red/black** Alt. colours **yes** Composition **63% viscose, 37% modacrylic** Width **140cm/55in** Repeat **–** Price ★★ LC 🪑🛋 Ⓦ

FABRICS: *GEOMETRICS*   **169**

Geometrics: **Late 19th century**

Proposition Eight of Owen Jones's *Grammar of Ornament* (published in 1856 and reprinted until 1910) stipulated that "all ornament should be based on geometric construction". Jones's view, much shaped by his studies of Chinese, Japanese, Indian, Indonesian, African, South American, Celtic and medieval patterns, proved highly influential during the second half of the 19th century, particularly among designers in the Aesthetic and Arts and Crafts movements. Many of Jones's and these designers' theories of ornament also found favour with the general public once translated on to fabrics.

Typical examples included trelliswork, latticework and other diaper patterns, used as frames or grounds for medieval, Jacobean or oriental motifs, such as fleur-de-lis, thistles and pomegranates. Jewelled strapwork, chevrons, stripes and powdered ornament (*see* page 162) were fashionable, as were Celtic triquetra and triskele. Imported Indonesian *ikats*, featuring kaleidoscopic blocks, circles and stripes, and Indian checked gingham and madras were also much in evidence. Extremely fashionable, however, were the striped and checked tartans now widely employed for hangings and covers – a trend fuelled by Queen Victoria's establishment of a royal residence in Balmoral, Scotland.

4

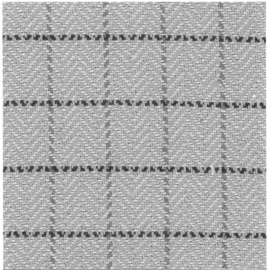

5

1

6

4 **Hodsoll McKenzie/Ottoman Stripe 262/106** Colour **coral/green** Alt. colours **yes** Composition **100% cotton** Width **127cm/ 50in** Repeat **11cm/4¼in** Price ★★★ 🛋🛋 W

5 **Hill & Knowles/Highland/Elgin 01/CA02** Colour **stone** Alt. colours **yes** Composition **100% cotton** Width **140cm/ 55in** Repeat **2cm/¾in** Price ★★ 🛋

6 **John Boyd Textiles/ Fredericksborg FR/605/14** Colour **green and black** Alt. colours **yes** Composition **68% horsehair, 32% cotton** Width **65cm/25½in** Repeat **4.5cm/1¾in** Price ★★★ 🛋

1 **Old World Weavers/Feltre EB35660001** Colour **green and rust** Alt. colours **yes** Composition **50% rayon, 49% cotton, 1% nylon** Width **130cm/51in** Repeat **10cm/ 4in** Price ★★★★ 🛋

2 **Mary Fox Linton/Montallegro** Colour **18** Alt. colours **yes** Composition **60% cotton, 40% viscose** Width **135cm/ 53in** Repeat **2.5cm/1in** Price ★★★ 🛋🛋

3 **Antico Setificio Fiorentino/ Cordellone C1** Colour **ecru, red, pink** Alt. colours **yes** Composition **80% linen, 20% silk** Width **120cm/ 47in** Repeat **14cm/5½in** Price ★★★ 🛋🛋 W

2   3

7 The Isle Mill/Duke of Fife
MW509 Colour **red, green
and black** Alt. colours
yes Composition **100%
wool** Width **140cm/55in**
Repeat **16cm/6¼in**
Price ★★★ 🛋

8 Sahco Hesslein/Duke 1267
Colour **07** Alt. colours
yes Composition **100%
cotton** Width **140cm/
55in** Repeat **17cm/6¾in**
Price ★★★ 🛋 LC

7

8

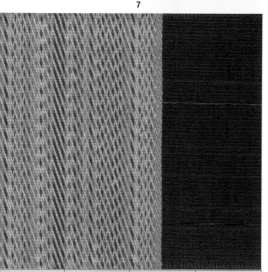

9

9 Zimmer & Rohde/Agave 5091
Colour **387** Alt. colours **yes**
Composition **70% viscose,
30% cotton** Width **140cm/
55in** Repeat **35cm/13¾in**
Price ★★★★ LC 🛋

10 Dedar/Manon Colour
cream and black Alt. colours
yes Composition **50%
cotton, 50% viscose** Width
140cm/55in Repeat –
Price ★★★ ▨

11 Nina Campbell/Stratford
Weaves/Othello NCF3281
Colour **02** Alt. colours **yes**
Composition **62% viscose,
38% cotton** Width **140cm/55in**
Repeat – Price ★★ ▨ ⊞

12 Old World Weavers/Shantung
Albatross SB14862201
Colour **multi** Alt. colours
no Composition **100%
silk** Width **140cm/55in**
Repeat **34cm/13½in**
Price ★★★★★ ▨ 🛋

13 Antico Setificio Fiorentino/
Spinato SP1 Colour **orange,
green, yellow, blue** Alt. colours
yes Composition **70% silk,
30% linen** Width **120cm/
47in** Repeat **16cm/6¼in**
Price ★★★ ▨ 🛋 W

14 John Boyd Textiles/Neapolitan
NE/637/2 Colour **green
and beige** Alt. colours **yes**
Composition **68% horsehair,
32% cotton** Width **65cm/
25½in** Repeat **5cm/2in**
Price ★★★ 🛋

11

12

13

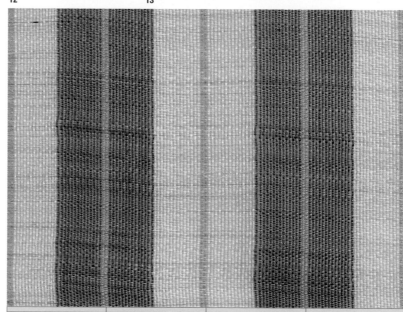

14

Geometrics: **Early 20th century**

Geometrically patterned fabrics remained very fashionable from the end of the 19th century until the outbreak of the Second World War. Many of these had been popular in previous centuries: striped and checked tartans in Baronial-style interiors; strapwork and jewelled strapwork patterns in Elizabethan Revival and Jacobean Revival schemes; and chevrons, Aztec-stepped shapes and prismatic triangles in Art Deco rooms. Herringbone-weave ticking also began to be used increasingly for curtains, upholstery and blinds.

However, the most innovative fabric patterns of the period were designed by artists bridging the gap between fine and applied art. Examples included the woodblock-printed, Cubist-inspired, irregular shapes of Raoul Dufy in the first two decades of the 20th century; the strong geometric forms and bold stripes, often combined with abstract floral forms, produced by Paul Poiret in 1911; and the colourful shapes and lines of Sonia Delaunay in the 1920s and 1930s.

1

2

3

20th century

1 **Bennison Fabrics/Tooth Check**
Colour **greens** Alt. colours **yes** Composition **70% linen, 30% cotton** Width **138cm/54in** Repeat **16cm/6¼in** Price ★★★ 🛋🛋

2 **John Boyd Textiles/Dales**
Colour **black/yellow** Alt. colours **yes** Composition **68% horsehair, 32% cotton** Width **65cm/25½in** Repeat – Price ★★★★ 🛋🛋

3 **G.P. & J. Baker/Gallery J0242**
Colour **755** Alt. colours **yes** Composition **100% silk** Width **140cm/55in** Repeat **18cm/7in** Price ★★★ 🛋🛋

4 **Donghia/Righe 9305** Colour **05** Alt. colours **yes** Composition **100% silk** Width **140cm/55in** Repeat **5cm/2in** Price ★★★★★ 🛋🛋

5 **Ian Mankin/Lincoln Stripe** Colour **slate** Alt. colours **yes** Composition **100% cotton** Width **137cm/54in** Repeat – Price ★ 🛋🛋 LC

6 **Marvic Textiles/Josephine 6102-1** Colour **yellow/leaf** Alt. colours **yes** Composition **100% cotton** Width **140cm/55in** Repeat **4.5cm/1¾in** Price ★★★ 🛋

7 **Manuel Canovas/Vita 4424** Colour **pêche, veronse** Alt. colours **yes** Composition **58% viscose, 42% cotton** Width **130cm/51in** Repeat **4cm/1½in** Price ★★★ 🛋🛋

4

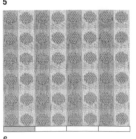

5

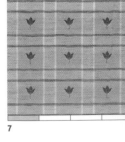

6   7

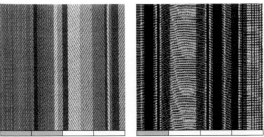

8

9

8 **Brunschwig & Fils/89516**
Colour **235** Alt. colours **yes**
Composition **100% cotton**
Width **142cm/55⅞in** Repeat –
Price ★★ 🛋 LC 🪟 ⊞

9 **Nina Campbell/Wide Stripe NCF
3140** Colour **01** Alt. colours
yes Composition **60% cotton,
40% modacrylic** Width **140cm/
55in** Repeat – Price ★★ 🛋

10 **Sahco Hesslein/Ambassador
15013** Colour **green** Alt. colours
yes Composition **70% wool,
25% silk, 5% polyester** Width
130cm/51in Repeat **22cm/
8½in** Price ★★★★ 🪟 ⊞

11 **Jab/Till 1-7421** Colour **199**
Alt. colours **yes** Composition
100% cotton Width **140cm/
55in** Repeat – Price ★★ 🪟

12 **Garin/Bolero 66754441** Colour
cream, black Alt. colours **yes**
Composition **100% cotton**
Width **140cm/55in** Repeat
1cm/⅜in Price ★★ 🛋

13 **The Isle Mill/Glen Morar GT112**
Colour **blue, red and cream**
Alt. colours **yes** Composition
100% wool Width **140cm/
55in** Repeat **6cm/2½in**
Price ★★ LC ⊞

14 **Osborne & Little/Modello
Trattino F5051** Colour **07** Alt.
colours **yes** Composition
50% cotton, 50% viscose
Width **130cm/51in** Repeat
1cm/⅜in Price ★★ 🪟 ⊞

10

11

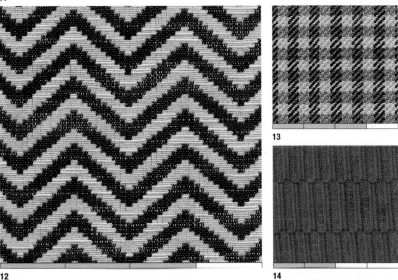

12

13

14

15

15 **Jane Churchill/Carousel Check
J137f** Colour **red** Alt. colours
yes Composition **100% cotton**
Width **140cm/55in** Repeat
1cm/⅜in Price ★★ 🪟

16 **Ian Mankin/Satin Check**
Colour **eau de nil** Alt. colours
yes Composition **100% cotton**
Width **137cm/54in** Repeat
11.5cm/4½in Price ★ 🪟

17 **Bennett Silks/Margot**
Colour **59X** Alt. colours
yes Composition **100% silk**
Width **150cm/59in** Repeat –
Price ★★★ 🪟 ⊞

16

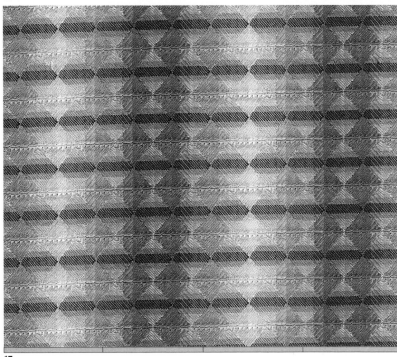

17

Geometrics: Late 20th–early 21st century

Many of the geometrically patterned fabrics that have proved fashionable for drapes and upholstery at the end of the 20th and in the early 21st century have originated from European and American designers. In the 1950s and 1960s, for example, numerous late Modernist-style fabrics were embellished with schematized geometric or abstract patterns; these consisted of modified versions of the irregular geometric forms found in Cubist paintings from earlier in the century. Crystalline structures (such as insulin viewed under a microscope) presented within diaper-ground patterns also provided inspiration for many designs of the period, and symmetrically spaced triangles, squares and dots were much in evidence.

Among the imported fabrics that have become increasingly desirable are ginghams, *ikats* and madras. Indonesian *ikats*, woven in either silk or fine cotton yarn, have been particularly appreciated for the way in which their geometric blocks, circles and stripes are softened by a vegetable-dyeing process – a procedure that feathers the edges of the colours into one another. Similarly, silk, cotton and rayon check madras, at one time dyed only black and red, has become much more popular as other vibrant colourways have been produced.

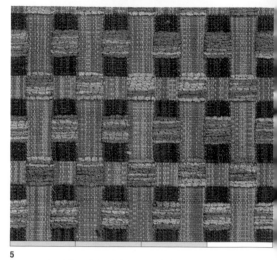
5

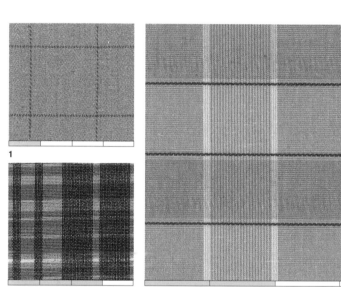
1

2

3

6

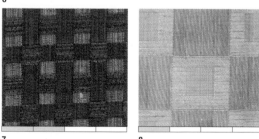
7

8

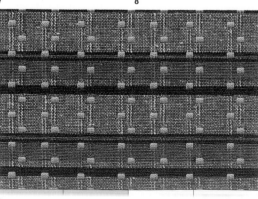
9

1 Thomas Dare/Jermyn 891
Colour **pistachio** Alt. colours **yes** Composition **100% cotton** Width **137cm/54in** Repeat **6.5cm/2½in** Price ★★

2 Brunschwig & Fils/42535
Colour **02** Alt. colours **yes** Composition **86% rayon, 14% dacron** Width **132cm/51¾in** Repeat **4cm/1½in** Price ★★

3 Zoffany/Check PCW0200
Colour **9** Alt. colours **yes** Composition **73% cotton, 14% viscose, 12% nylon, 1% silk** Width **145cm/57in** Repeat **7cm/2¾in** Price ★★

4 Donghia/Quadri 0375/9300
Colour **05** Alt. colours **yes** Composition **100% silk** Width **140cm/55in** Repeat **3cm/1¼in** Price ★★★★★

5 Today Interiors/Palio/Lupa CH85032 Colour **8** Alt. colours **yes** Composition **40% cotton, 42% viscose, 10% linen, 8% nylon** Width **140cm/55in** Repeat **3cm/1¼in** Price ★★

6 Wemyss Houlès/Orient/Java Colour **2E149** Alt. colours **yes** Composition **48% modacrylic, 39% cotton, 13% nylon** Width **138cm/54in** Repeat – Price ★★

7 Today Interiors/Palio/Lupa CH85032 Colour **4** Alt. colours **yes** Composition **40% cotton, 42% viscose, 10% linen, 8% nylon** Width **140cm/55in** Repeat **3cm/1¼in** Price ★★

8 Scalamandré/26656 Colour **007** Alt. colours **yes** Composition **53% cotton, 33% viscose, 14% linen** Width **140cm/55in** Repeat **10cm/4in** Price ★★★

9 Monkwell/Mistri 05413 CU/012 Colour **red and gold** Alt. colours **yes** Composition **88% cotton, 12% polyacrylic** Width **137cm/54in** Repeat **9cm/3½in** Price ★★

20th & 21st century

0 Larsen/Coffee Bean L8680
Colour **07 steel** Alt. colours
yes Composition **51%
polyester, 31% acrylic,
18% silk** Width **123cm/
48½in** Repeat **2.5cm/1in**
Price ★★★ ⊞ 🗹

1 Nya Nordiska/Pila Colour
05 copper Alt. colours **yes**
Composition **50% linen,
40% polyester** Width **155cm/
61in** Repeat **7cm/2¾in**
Price ★★★ 🗹

2 Marvic Textiles/Valencia
Stripe 5013 Colour **browns**
Alt. colours **no** Composition
54% viscose, 46% linen Width
140cm/55in Repeat **–**
Price ★★ LC ⊞ 🛋

3 Turnell & Gigon/Ascot Taffeta
HAP 10001 Colour **cream
ground** Alt. colours **yes**
Composition **57% viscose,
43% cotton** Width **130cm/51in**
Repeat **–** Price ★★ 🗹 🛋

4 The Isle Mill/Kildonan STR016
Colour **blue/gold/rust** Alt.
colours **yes** Composition
100% wool Width **140cm/
55in** Repeat **14cm/5½in**
Price ★★★ LC ⊞

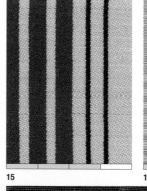
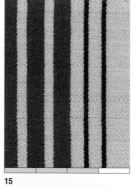
15

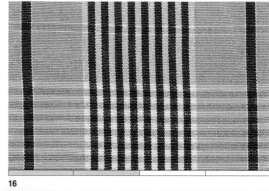
16

11

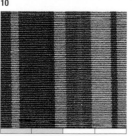
12

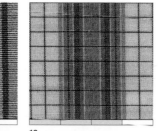
13

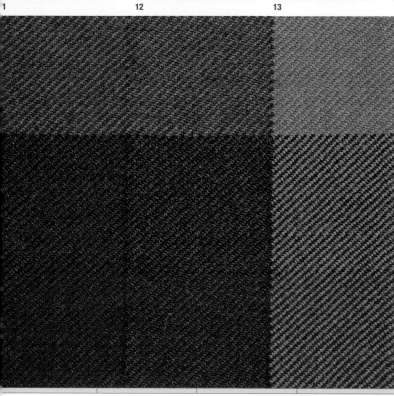
10

17

14

15 John Boyd Textiles/Ardennais
AR/SK 100/72 Colour **beige/
black/red** Alt. colours **yes**
Composition **68% horsehair,
32% cotton** Width **56cm/
22in** Repeat **8cm/3in**
Price ★★★★ 🛋

16 Percheron/Corfu 7246-2 Colour
junior navy 2 Alt. colours **yes**
Composition **43% viscose,
39% cotton, 18% linen** Width
140cm/55in Repeat **12cm/4¾in**
Price ★★★ LC ⊞

17 Zimmer & Rohde/Askuni 2557
Colour **347** Alt. colours **yes**
Composition **52% viscose,
29% cotton, 19% linen** Width
139cm/54¾in Repeat **35cm/
13¾in** Price ★★★ 🗹 🛋

18 Ottilie Stevenson/Monty Check
VF0052 Colour **mustard** Alt.
colours **yes** Composition
100% cotton Width **137cm/54in**
Repeat **–** Price ★★ 🗹 🛋

18

Geometrics: **Late 20th–early 21st century**

The late 20th and early 21st century has seen a strong growth in the number and type of geometric designs. Many of these have been created through innovative weaving techniques, often producing pattern by means of texture and colour. Other fabrics have included several imports, such as the various ethnic weaves and prints from Africa. Notable among these are the woven "kente" silks and cottons, particularly from Ghana and Nigeria, which display brightly coloured, eclectic combinations of stripes, checks, chevrons and other geometric forms. South American weaves, with geometric, abstract and iconographic patterns derived from ancient Aztec and Inca cultures, have been in demand, too, and have provided inspiration for European and North American designers.

Also fashionable during the late 20th and early 21st century have been striped and checked tartans, and printed fabrics embellished with repeat classical motifs framed by traditional diaper grounds, or set within vertical stripes resembling strips of cine-film.

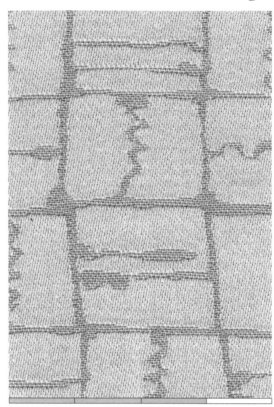

1

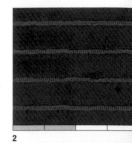

4

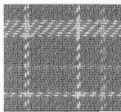

3

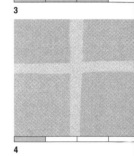

2

1 **Bentley & Spens/New Geometrics** Colour **natural** Alt. colours **no** Composition **50% linen, 50% cotton** Width **135cm/53in** Repeat **42cm/16½in** Price ★★

2 **Today Interiors/Taffetas/Soprano 4055** Colour **55** Alt. colours **yes** Composition **88% acetate, 12% acrylic** Width **150cm/59in** Repeat **2cm/¾in** Price ★★

3 **Thomas Dare/Savile** Colour **teal** Alt. colours **yes** Composition **100% cotton** Width **140cm/55in** Repeat **17.5cm/7in** Price ★★

4 **Today Interiors/Aymara/Axis AYF 3330** Colour **30** Alt. colours **yes** Composition **51% linen, 37% cotton, 2% nylon** Width **137cm/54in** Repeat **40cm/15¾in** Price ★★

5

8

5 **Jim Thompson/Mirage Check P4011** Colour **taupe** Alt. colours **yes** Composition **100% silk** Width **122cm/48in** Repeat **4cm/1½in** Price ★★★★

6 **Lee Jofa/Bill's Plaid 2002194** Colour **8 black** Alt. colours **yes** Composition **100% cotton** Width **143cm/56in** Repeat **19cm/7½in** Price ★★★

7 **Ian Sanderson/Box Check** Colour **cornflower** Alt. colours **yes** Composition **100% cotton** Width **140cm/55in** Repeat **2.5cm/1in** Price ★★

8 **Jim Thompson/Pavilion Cloth 1018** Colour **01** Alt. colours **yes** Composition **60% silk, 40% cotton** Width **122cm/48in** Repeat **1cm/¾in** Price ★★★

6

7

**9 Osborne & Little/Valdepero
F5022** Colour **06** Alt. colours
yes Composition **45%
polyester, 28% viscose,
27% cotton** Width **143cm/
56in** Repeat **31cm/12in**
Price ★★ ⬚ ⊞

10 Nya Nordiska/Baccara Colour
84 purple Alt. colours **yes**
Composition **85% viscose,
15% silk** Width **140cm/
55in** Repeat **31cm/12in**
Price ★★★ ⊞ LC ⬚ 🛋

9

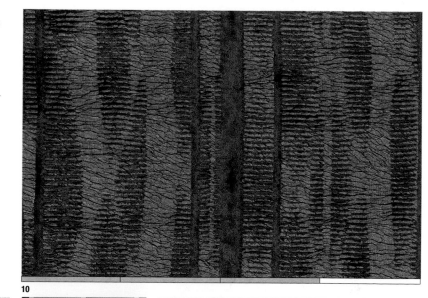

10

**1 Knowles & Christou/Tambour
KG208** Colour **topaz** Alt.
colours **yes** Composition
100% cotton Width **132cm/
51¾in**. Repeat **15cm/6in**
Price ★★★ ⬚ 🛋 W

**2 Knowles & Christou/Taffeta
Silk Stripe** Colour **date** Alt.
colours **yes** Composition
100% silk Width **120cm/
47in** Repeat **16cm/6¼in**
Price ★★★ ⬚ ⊞ W

**3 John Boyd Textiles/Ardennais
AR/SK107/2** Colour **black/
red/beige** Alt. colours **yes**
Composition **56% horsehair,
44% silk** Width **65cm/25½in**
Repeat – Price ★★★★ 🛋 W

4 Anna French/Blanket Colour **29**
Alt. colours **yes** Composition
100% cotton Width **137cm/
54in** Repeat **64cm/25in**
Price ★★ 🛋

5 Nya Nordiska/Trapunta Colour
13 copper Alt. colours **yes**
Composition **50% viscose,
26% polyester, 24% silk** Width
140cm/55in Repeat **8cm/
3in** Price ★★★ 🛋 LC ⬚

6 Larsen/Sugar Cane L8681
Colour **08 amethyst** Alt. colours
yes Composition **51% polyester,
31% acrylic, 18% silk** Width
125cm/49¼in Repeat –
Price ★★★ ⬚ ⊞

11

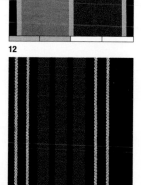

12

13

14

15

16

17 Scalamandré/26577 Colour **001**
Alt. colours **yes** Composition
62% viscose, 38% cotton
Width **137cm/54in** Repeat –
Price ★★★★ 🛋 LC

18 Elizabeth Eaton/Lanka Check
Colour **pink** Alt. colours **no**
Composition **100% cotton**
Width **127cm/50in** Repeat
2.5cm/1in Price ★★ ⬚ 🛋

17

18

Lace & Sheers

Lace is an ornamental openwork fabric that is traditionally made from flaxen thread or silk, wool or cotton yarns. Before the late 18th century it was exclusively hand-made, by buttonhole stitching with a needle and thread ("needle" lace), or by twisting bobbins carrying the threads around pins outlining the pattern and stuck into a pillow ("bobbin" lace). A less expensive alternative is machine-woven Nottingham (or "Swiss") lace, which was first produced in quantity during the early 19th century.

Lace has been used as decorative bed and table covers, but also as bed-hangings and under-curtains designed to diffuse sunlight, provide a degree of privacy and keep out insects. Other materials used for this purpose, known as "sheers", include muslin, a soft, open-mesh fabric woven from finely spun cotton or silk; organza, a stiffer version of muslin; *voile*, a crisp and finely woven fabric made from cotton, silk or synthetics; and leno, a cross-woven gauze made from natural or man-made fibres.

RIGHT The use of lace and sheers as both under-curtains ("insertions") and the main drapes in a window treatment has flourished during the 20th century, especially in bedrooms. Here laces are simply pleated for the insertions, tassel-fringed and tied back for the main drapes, and elaborately swagged and tailed for the heading. They are coordinated with the bed-hangings, cushion covers and bedspread – a fashion that dates back to the late 17th century.

ABOVE These lace under-curtains ("insertions") are in a 19th-century American house. Their sage-green stylized flower-and-leaf pattern was particularly fashionable toward the end of the 19th century. Like much of the lace used in American interiors during this period, these examples are machine-made and imported from Brussels, Belgium.

"ANTIQUING" LACE

Pre-20th-century hand-made lace is highly sought after today; it can be bought from specialist antiques dealers and at textile auctions. However, it is becoming more and more expensive. Consequently, when asked to create a period look on a tight budget, many interior designers mimic the appearance and feel of hand-made antique lace simply by soaking inexpensive, white machine-made lace in a weak solution of cold tea (or coffee). The lace emerges with a subtle, straw-coloured tint and a softer, less crisp texture than it had before the treatment.

KEY DESIGNS

1 While many coloured sheers are literally plain, others – such as this early 21st-century silk sheer – incorporate for decorative effect soft gradations of colour and/or subtle abstract patterns in the weave.

2 Stylized birds, particularly exotic oriental species, as well as architectural components, such as pillars and arches, have been frequent embellishments to lace and sheers since the 19th century.

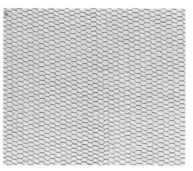

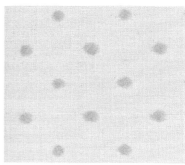

3 Silk bobbin net ("tulle") was first produced in France at the end of the 18th century; it has been used primarily for insertions and bed-hangings, notably in hot climates as an insect barrier.

4 Repeats of small woven or printed dots have been used to embellish sheers and semi-sheers since the 18th century – imported Indian muslins were among the first to display such patterns.

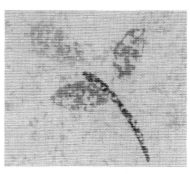

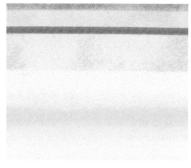

5 During the course of the 20th century, increasingly colourful patterns – mostly printed, like this floral-and-leaf-patterned voile – have been employed on sheers and semi-sheers. They offer a decorative screen that allows light to filter through.

6 Before the 20th century, finely woven voiles were made from cotton or silk; thereafter, synthetic yarns have also been used. Voiles in coloured stripes were especially fashionable during the early 19th century.

1 Nina Campbell/Loire Silks/Touraine Sheer NCF3391 Colour 04 Alt. colours yes Composition 100% silk Width 140cm/55in Repeat 95cm/37in Price ★★ 🗌

2 G.P. & J. Baker/My Lady's Garden Colour white Alt. colours yes Composition 93% cotton, 7% polyester Width 150cm/59in Repeat 64cm/25in Price ★ 🗌

3 Bennett Silks/Annelle Colour 91 Alt. colours yes Composition 100% silk Width 175cm/68¾in Repeat – Price ★★ 🗌

4 Abbott & Boyd/Visillo Plumeti Colour white Alt. colours yes Composition 100% polyester Width 300cm/118in Repeat 2cm/¾in Price ★★ 🗌

5 Anna French/Moss Rose Voile Colour 32 Alt. colours yes Composition 100% cotton Width 137cm/54in Repeat 82cm/32¼in Price ★★ 🗌

6 Liberty Furnishings/Irisa Prints/Isadora LF4202 Colour 02 Alt. colours yes Composition 70% viscose, 30% polyester Width 142cm/55⅞in Repeat – Price ★★ 🗌

Lace & Sheers: **Pre-19th century**

Leading centres of lace production were established in Italy (in Venice, Genoa and Milan), the Netherlands (in Brussels, Mechlin and Antwerp), and Spain and Portugal during the 16th century; then in France (in Alençon, Argenton, Paris and Chantilly) and England (in Honiton) during the 17th century. Lace production in America took hold during the 18th century, notably in Ipswich, Massachusetts. Fashionable needle lace included *punto in aria*, *gros point*, *point plat*, *point de neige* ("Venetian"), *point de France* and *hollie point*. From the early 17th century, bobbin lace was produced in greater quantity and was equally sought after. Popular patterns included stylized flowers linked by scrolling stems, and Moorish geometric designs such as the wheel and the sun.

Throughout this period, hand-made lace was used for bed and table covers and bed-hangings, but rarely for under-curtains. However, many shutterless 17th- and 18th-century windows were covered with "sashes" (thin silks or linens stretched over frames and soaked with oil to make them transparent). Sheers draped at 18th-century windows included "quinze-seize" (thin taffeta), "leno" (a gauze often painted with Indian motifs) and Indian muslin (white or cream and sometimes woven with a ribbed stripe or small motif).

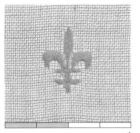
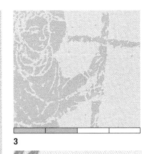
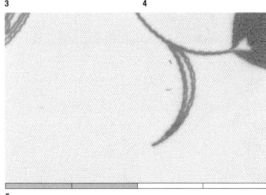

1 Interdesign/Rio Fleur de Lys 2301/3 Colour **white** Alt. colours **yes** Composition **100% linen** Width **210cm/82½in** Repeat – Price ★★★★

2 Knowles & Christou/Cardoban Lion KSC03 Colour **white** Alt. colours **yes** Composition **60% polyester, 40% cotton** Width **120cm/47in** Repeat **24cm/9½in** Price ★★

3 Knowles & Christou/Angels KSC05 Colour **white** Alt. colours **yes** Composition **60% polyester, 40% cotton** Width **120cm/47in** Repeat **24cm/9½in** Price ★★

4 Claremont Fabrics/Campanile JOA COA Colour **green** Alt. colours **yes** Composition **40% polyester, 60% cotton** Width **140cm/55in** Repeat **69cm/27in** Price ★

5 Laura Ashley/Thirlmere Colour **delphinium** Alt. colours **no** Composition **63% polyester, 37% cotton** Width **144cm/56½in** Repeat **71cm/28in** Price ★

6 Larsen/Luminescence L7480 Colour **04** Alt. colours **yes** Composition **70% copper, 18% cotton, 12% polyester** Width **147cm/58in** Repeat **2cm/¾in** Price ★★★

7 Crowson/Script Colour **6** Alt. colours **yes** Composition **67% polyester, 33% cotton** Width **137cm/54in** Repeat **64cm/25in** Price ★

8 Malabar/Indian Organza NSIL28
Colour **gold** Alt. colours
no Composition **100% silk**
Width **137cm/54in** Repeat
2cm/⅞in Price ★★ 🗹

9 Zoffany/Floraison Leaf FRN0700
Colour **1** Alt. colours **yes**
Composition **64% linen,
36% polyester** Width **160cm/
63in** Repeat **10cm/4in**
Price ★★ 🗹

10 Zoffany/Lotus Voile MB0700
Colour **1** Alt. colours **yes**
Composition **100% cotton**
Width **131.5cm/51⅜in**
Repeat **105.5cm/41½in**
Price ★★ 🗹

**11 Rose's Mill/Venus Lace
Panel** Colour **antique ivory**
Alt. colours **no** Composition
100% cotton Width **260cm/102in**
Repeat - Price ★★★★★ 🗹

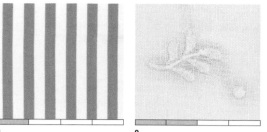

8

9

10

11

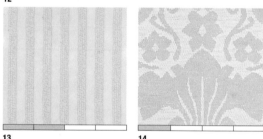

12

13   14

15

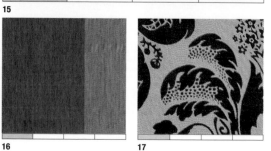

16   17

**12 Today Interiors/Taffetas/Pique
TAF4049** Colour **purple/
burgundy** Alt. colours **yes**
Composition **inner 100%
polyester, outer 77% polyester,
23% nylon** Width **150cm/59in**
Repeat **15cm/6in** Price ★★ 🗹

13 Mulberry/Chenille RIB FD356
Colour **cream J103** Alt.
colours **no** Composition
53% cotton, 47% polyester
Width **300cm/118in** Repeat
1cm/⅜in Price ★★★ 🗹

**14 Bernard Thorp & Co/French
Damask** Colour **white** Alt.
colours **yes** Composition
**91% polyester, 9% flax/
linen** Width **120cm/47in**
Repeat **87cm/34¼in**
Price ★★ 🗹🛋

**15 Rose's Mill/Holyrood Lace
Panel** Colour **pure white** Alt.
colours **yes** Composition
100% cotton Width **91cm/
35⅜in** Repeat – Price ★★ 🗹

16 Mulberry/Venetian Stripe FD377
Colour **red** Alt. colours **yes**
Composition **80% cotton,
20% polyester** Width **322cm/
127in** Repeat **20cm/8in**
Price ★★ ⊞ 🗹

17 Bennett Silks/Como 5111DC
Colour **54/70L** Alt. colours
yes Composition **100% silk**
Width **105cm/41¼in** Repeat
54cm/21½in Price ★★★ 🗹

Lace & Sheers: **19th century**

By the early 19th century, under-curtains had become a fairly standard window treatment in fashionable European (particularly English Regency and French Empire) and American Federal interiors. Thin silks or muslin (the latter by this time made in Europe and America, as well as in India) were the preferred choice, and in many cases they were augmented with delicate fringing or border designs in contrasting colours – green or yellow on white being a popular combination.

The production of lace underwent a revolution throughout Europe and America at the end of the 18th century. Costly hand-made lace was still being manufactured in traditional centres of production (*see* page 180), but the invention of cheaper, machine-woven lace dramatically expanded the market to include less affluent homeowners. Made in large quantities in Nottingham, England, machine-woven lace was largely intended for use as more decorative under-curtains and bed-hangings, and featured exuberant patterns of hothouse flowers and other designs derived from 16th- and 17th-century hand-made lace.

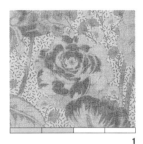

1

1 **Old World Weavers/Vera Sheer B/1886S0108** Colour **multi** Alt. colours **yes** Composition **100% cotton** Width **139cm/54¾in** Repeat **97cm/38¼in** Price ★★★★

2 **Sahco Hesslein/Mizar 16012** Colour **white** Alt. colours **no** Composition **70% cotton, 30% polyester** Width **300cm/118in** Repeat **63cm/24¾in** Price ★★★

3 **Anna French/Fondant Lace** Colour **68** Alt. colours **yes** Composition **100% cotton** Width **150cm/59in** Repeat **72cm/28¼in** Price ★★

4 **Hill & Knowles/Voiles IV/ Feather Dance VF86F** Colour **gold on cream** Alt. colours **yes** Composition **67% polyester, 33% cotton** Width **145cm/57in** Repeat **64cm/25in** Price ★

2

5   **6**

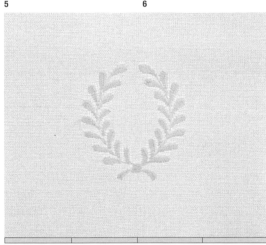

7

5 **Elizabeth Eaton 9550/3609** Colour **white** Alt. colours **yes** Composition **100% cotton** Width **150cm/59in** Repeat **22cm/8½in** Price ★★★

6 **Rose's Mill/Secret Garden Lace Panel** Colour **natural white** Alt. colours **yes** Composition **95% cotton, 5% polyester** Width **137cm/54in** Repeat – Price ★★

7 **Elizabeth Eaton/Muslin 9550/3837** Colour **white** Alt. colours **no** Composition **100% cotton** Width **150cm/ 59in** Repeat **11cm/4¼in** Price ★★

8 **Interdesign/Ric Api 2301/09** Colour **tan** Alt. colours **yes** Composition **100% linen** Width **160cm/63in** Repeat **12cm/4¾in** Price ★★★★

3   **4**   **8**

9 Sahco Hesslein/Mirabelle 16005
Colour **white** Alt. colours **no**
Composition **90% polyester,
10% linen** Width **330cm/130in**
Repeat **5cm/2in**
Price ★★★★ ⟨⟩

10 Bennett Silks/1502 CHR Colour
53/55 Alt. colours **no**
Composition **100% silk** Width
105cm/41in Repeat **34cm/13½in**
Price ★★ ⟨⟩

11 Bennett Silks/1502 CHB Colour
53/55 Alt. colours **no**
Composition **100% silk**
Width **105cm/41in** Repeat
34cm/13½in Price ★★ ⟨⟩

12 Ian Sanderson/Hope Plain
Colour **champagne** Alt. colours
yes Composition **100% linen**
Width **140cm/55in** Repeat –
Price ★★ ⟨⟩

13 Jane Churchill/Country Rose
Sprig Voile J239F Colour
yellow/blue 02 Alt. colours **yes**
Composition **100% cotton**
Width **133cm/52in** Repeat
20cm/8in Price ★★ ⟨⟩

14 Sanderson/Bloom Sheer PR8537
Colour **3** Alt. colours **yes**
Composition **70% polyester,
30% viscose** Width **150cm/
59in** Repeat **60.5cm/24in**
Price ★ ⟨⟩

15 Bentley & Spens/Animal Magic
Sheer Colour **white on white**
Alt. colours **no** Composition
100% cotton voile
Width **135cm/53in** Repeat
106cm/41½in Price ★★ ⟨⟩

16 Bennett Silks/Ravena 5111D101
Colour **89** Alt. colours **yes**
Composition **100% silk** Width
105cm/41in Repeat **18cm/7in**
Price ★★ ⟨⟩

9

10

12

11

13

14

15

16

Lace & Sheers: **Early 20th century**

Around the beginning of the 20th century, a reaction set in to the extensive use of lace and sheers in 19th-century interiors. In some quarters this was an aesthetic judgement – the American writer Edith Wharton dismissed them, particularly at windows, on the grounds that "lingerie effects do not commune well with architecture". Other commentators were more concerned with the welfare of the homeowner. For example, the English architect and writer Charles Eastlake believed it was healthier to sleep without being surrounded by layers of (dust-trap) draperies, and thus recommended metal or wooden bedsteads without hangings – although he did make an exception for warm, humid climates, such as those of Australia and the southern states of America, where muslin or organza could be draped over a four-poster or half-tester, or from a corona, to protect the occupant from mosquitoes and other insects.

However, with the exception of Eastlake, whose views proved highly influential in America, most householders during the first half of the 20th century chose to ignore such arbiters and continued to use sheers such as muslin, organza and voile at windows. Favoured patterns included woven stripes, and woven or printed spots and figurative patterns.

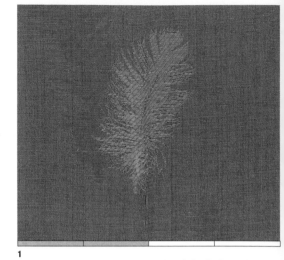

1

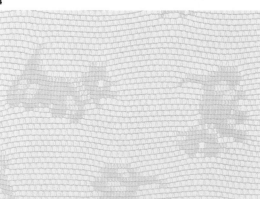

2

3

4

5

6

1 **Marvic Textiles/Plume 4540** Colour **bronze 3** Alt. colours **yes** Composition **50% silk, 50% linen** Width **140cm/ 55in** Repeat **51cm/20in** Price ★★★★ ⌂

2 **Zoffany/Pollen PLP0900** Colour **2** Alt. colours **yes** Composition **67% polyester, 33% cotton** Width **150cm/59in** Repeat **4cm/1½** Price ★ ⌂

3 **Osbourne & Little/Hespera/ Brume F1642/05** Colour **05** Alt. colours **yes** Composition **100% cotton** Width **140cm/ 55in** Repeat **5cm/2in** Price ★★ ⌂ LC ⊞⌂

4 **Osborne & Little/Jivala Silks/Avani Sheer F1963** Colour **01** Alt. colours **yes** Composition **100% silk** Width **137cm/54in** Repeat **40cm/15¾in** Price ★★★ ⌂

5 **Scalamandré/Angus 26366** Colour **white 001** Alt. colours **no** Composition **95% cotton, 5% polyester** Width **151cm/ 59½in** Repeat **–** Price ★★★ ⌂

6 **Scalamandré/Madeira 16318** Colour **swan 001** Alt. colours **yes** Composition **100% cotton** Width **137cm/54in** Repeat **97cm/38¼in** Price ★★★★ ⌂

20th century

10

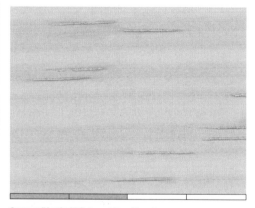

8

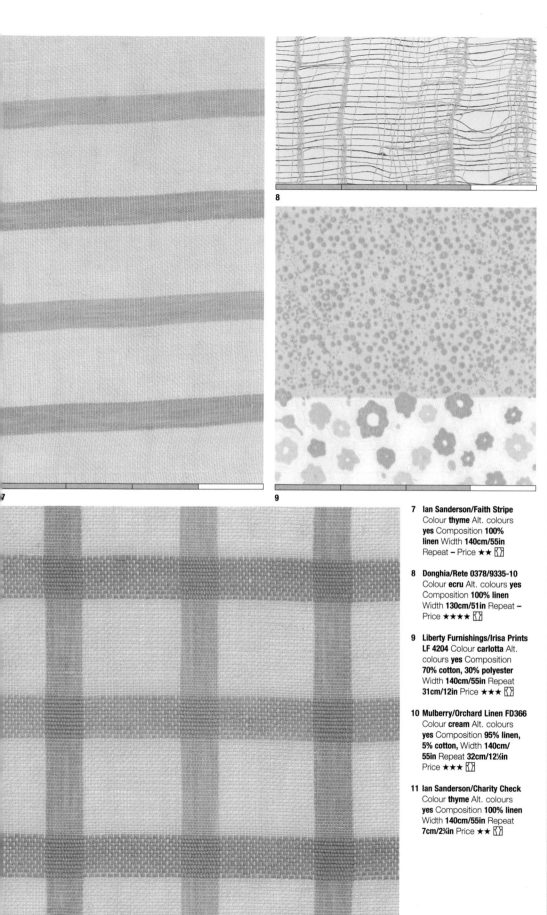

9

COLOURED SHEERS

Historically, most sheers – particularly muslins and organzas – have been produced in either white or off-white colours. However, coloured versions have proved very fashionable, notably during the 20th century. While pale pastel colours are generally widely available, it is worth remembering that when exposed to strong sunlight their colouring can be rendered overly subtle. To compensate for this, slightly stronger tones, such as the yellow and green shown below, can be employed.

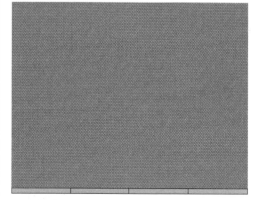

Crowson/Monticelli Colour **yellow** Alt. colours **yes** Composition **100% polyester** Width **150cm/59in** Repeat – Price ★ ⟨⟩

7 Ian Sanderson/Faith Stripe Colour **thyme** Alt. colours **yes** Composition **100% linen** Width **140cm/55in** Repeat – Price ★★ ⟨⟩

8 Donghia/Rete 0378/9335-10 Colour **ecru** Alt. colours **yes** Composition **100% linen** Width **130cm/51in** Repeat – Price ★★★★ ⟨⟩

9 Liberty Furnishings/Irisa Prints LF 4204 Colour **carlotta** Alt. colours **yes** Composition **70% cotton, 30% polyester** Width **140cm/55in** Repeat **31cm/12in** Price ★★★ ⟨⟩

10 Mulberry/Orchard Linen FD366 Colour **cream** Alt. colours **yes** Composition **95% linen, 5% cotton,** Width **140cm/ 55in** Repeat **32cm/12½in** Price ★★★ ⟨⟩

11 Ian Sanderson/Charity Check Colour **thyme** Alt. colours **yes** Composition **100% linen** Width **140cm/55in** Repeat **7cm/2¾in** Price ★★ ⟨⟩

Liberty Furnishings/Zari Weaves/Zari Plain LF4254 Colour **14** Alt. colours **yes** Composition **100% cotton** Width **142cm/55¾in** Repeat – Price ★★ ⟨⟩

Lace & Sheers: **Late 20th century**

During the second half of the 20th century, there was a renewed demand for traditional hand-made lace, particularly for decorative bed covers. Machine-woven lace, notably incorporating floral, animal and bird patterns, was a popular choice for under-curtains in period houses, while plain or patterned muslin, organza and voile sheers (the latter often made from synthetic fibres) were widely employed as bed-hangings.

Although these fabrics had been used to some extent in the first half of the century, manufacturers increasingly produced coloured versions, such as pastel lemons, plaster pinks, pale blues, blue-greys, and warm hues. Other trends included stretching sheers over wooden frames to make screens or room dividers – similar to traditional Japanese *shojis*, and well suited to large warehouse conversions and loft apartments. The 19th-century practice of bordering sheers, such as muslin, with contrasting fabrics was further developed by some 20th-century designers, who alternated and joined strips of semi-transparent muslin with strips of closely woven fabrics, such as damask or leather, to produce web-like effects.

1

1 **Malabar/Tarlatan** Colour **grey 03** Alt. colours **yes** Composition **100% polyester** Width **135cm/53in** Repeat **80cm/31½in** Price ★★★

2 **Elizabeth Eaton/Muslin** Colour **white** Alt. colours **yes** Composition **100% cotton** Width **150cm/59in** Repeat **12cm/4¾in** Price ★★

3 **Bentley & Spens/Cornelli Sheers** Colour **white on white** Alt. colours **no** Composition **100% cotton voile** Width **130cm/51in** Repeat **60cm/23¾in** Price ★★

4 **Laura Ashley/Mimosa** Colour **ecru** Alt. colours **yes** Composition **embroidered voile, 63% polyester, 37% cotton** Width **144cm/56½in** Repeat **15cm/6in** Price ★

5 **Hill & Knowles/Columbine Star VG97F** Colour **gold/ cream** Alt. colours **yes** Composition **67% polyester, 33% cotton** Width **150cm/ 59in** Repeat **32cm/12½in** Price ★

2

3

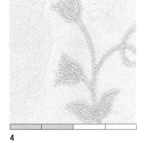

4

5

SEMI-SHEERS

The main difference between sheer and semi-sheer fabrics is a matter of translucency. Sheers such as muslin, organza and voile are highly translucent and allow considerable quantities of diffused light to enter a room. At the same time, sheers can also provide a certain degree of privacy without obliterating the view entirely. The more opaque semi-sheers are generally produced from fabrics such as half-silks and taffetas, as well as open-weave linens, cottons and synthetics.

1

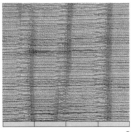

2

1 **Jack Lenor Larsen/ Luminescence** Colour **topaz** Alt. colours **yes** Composition **66% metal, 22% cotton, 12% polyester** Width **140cm/55in** Repeat – Price ★★★

2 **Sahco Hesslein/Caprice 50262** Colour **gold** Alt. colours **yes** Composition **50% viscose, 21% silk, 15% acrylic, 14% linen** Width **140cm/55in** Repeat – Price ★★★

20th century

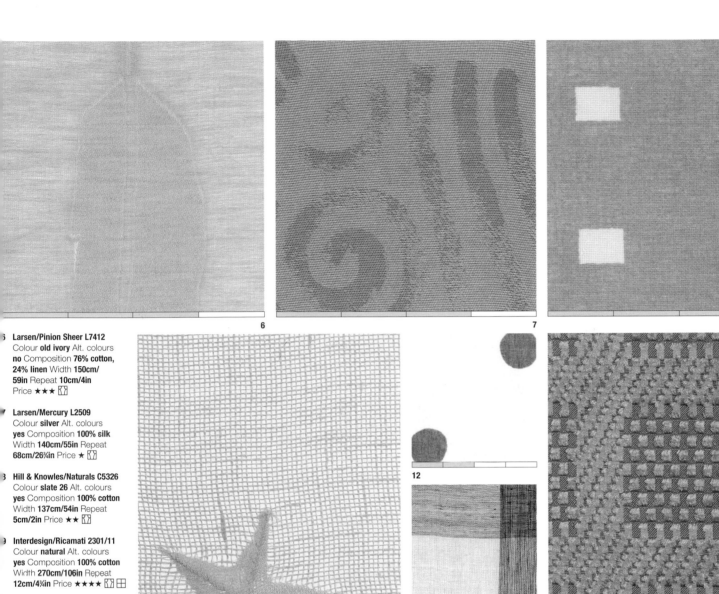

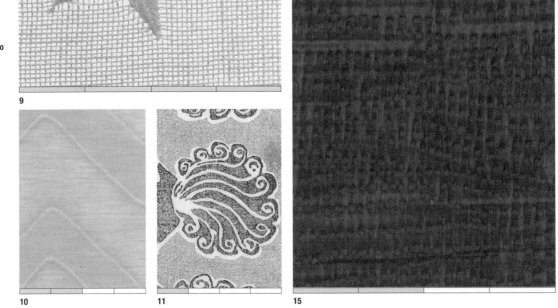

6 Larsen/Pinion Sheer L7412
Colour **old ivory** Alt. colours
no Composition **76% cotton,
24% linen** Width **150cm/
59in** Repeat **10cm/4in**
Price ★★★

7 Larsen/Mercury L2509
Colour **silver** Alt. colours
yes Composition **100% silk**
Width **140cm/55in** Repeat
68cm/26¾in Price ★

8 Hill & Knowles/Naturals C5326
Colour **slate 26** Alt. colours
yes Composition **100% cotton**
Width **137cm/54in** Repeat
5cm/2in Price ★★

9 Interdesign/Ricamati 2301/11
Colour **natural** Alt. colours
yes Composition **100% cotton**
Width **270cm/106in** Repeat
12cm/4¾in Price ★★★★

10 Larsen/Chevalier L7367
Colour **old ivory** Alt. colours
no Composition **51% linen,
49% cotton** Width **150cm/
59in** Repeat **23cm/9in**
Price ★★★

11 Bentley & Spens/Shells
B5044 Voile Colour **bronze,
silver and white** Alt. colours **no**
Composition **100% cotton**
Width **134cm/52½in** Repeat
65cm/25½in Price ★★

12 Anna French/Polka Dot Voile
Colour **red on white V8** Alt.
colours **yes** Composition
100% cotton Width **137cm/
54in** Repeat **10cm/4in**
Price ★★

13 Designers Guild/Oola F495/08
Colour **fuchsia** Alt. colours
yes Composition **100% cotton**
Width **115cm/45¼in** Repeat
10cm/4in Price ★

14 Jack Lenor Larsen/Fielding
7478-01 Colour **hazelnut**
Alt. colours **yes** Composition
100% polyester Width **112cm/
44in** Repeat **6cm/2½in**
Price ★★

15 Marvic Textiles/Raindrop 4541
Colour **damson** Alt. colours
yes Composition **100% silk**
Width **140cm/55in** Repeat
35cm/13¾in Price ★★★

Lace & Sheers: Early 21st century

The late 20th-century revival of interest in lace and sheers has, if anything, gathered further momentum during the early years of the 21st century. In terms of usage, there has been a marked increase in the deployment of sheers as bed-hangings, especially canopied from the ceiling above. Equally, many homeowners who had previously shunned their use at windows on grounds of fashion have come to appreciate the light- and heat-diffusing qualities of sheers in this context; they have also realized that coloured sheers can be called on to subtly alter the colour of natural light and therefore the ambience of an interior.

The majority of new designs that have emerged during the early 21st century have been geometric in pattern. Stripes or bands of subtly contrasting weave or colour have proved particularly popular – both two-tone and polychromatic. Also, whether configured vertically or horizontally, the stripes or bands have rarely been run as neat, crisp parallels: meandering courses, irregular edges and even random acute angles have all been preferred. In contrast to the predominant geometrical patterns (which have also included spherical and rectangular repeats), there has also been a vogue for repeat foliate and insect-like motifs – these often stylized to the point of abstraction.

5

1

1 **Larsen/Hologram Square L7430** Colour **bronze 02** Alt. colours **no** Composition **56% silk, 44% linen** Width **140cm/55in** Repeat **11cm/4¼in** Price ★★★ ⬚

2 **Larsen/Billows L7481** Colour **autumn haze 03** Alt. colours **yes** Composition **100% polyester** Width **165cm/65in** Repeat – Price ★★★ ⬚

3 **Nya Nordiska/Tre-De** Colour **pyrite 05** Alt. colours **yes** Composition **58% viscose, 36% polyester, 6% linen** Width **150cm/59in** Repeat **14-16cm/5½-6¼in** Price ★★★ ⬚

4 **Sahco Hesslein/Ulf Moritz/ Tzar 1842** Colour **01** Alt. colours **yes** Composition **66% horsehair, 23% metal, 11% linen** Width **147cm/58in** Repeat – Price ★★★ ⬚ ⊞

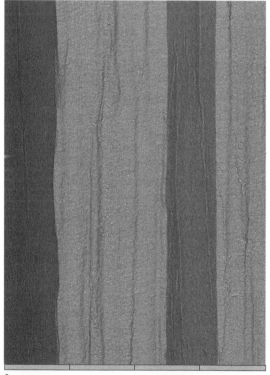

2

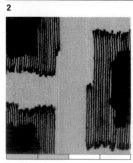

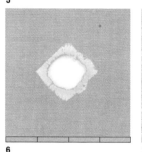

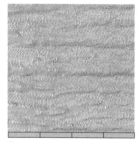

6 **7**

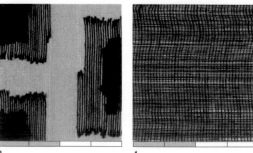

3

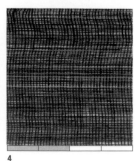

4

8

5 **Interdesign/Missoni Sheers/ Cajun** Colour **51** Alt. colours **yes** Width **295cm/116in** Composition **64% viscose, 36% polyester** Repeat **62cm/24¼in** Price ★★★ ⬚

6 **Osborne & Little/Hespera/ Boreal F1643** Colour **02** Alt. colours. **yes** Composition **65% polyester, 35% cotton** Width **150cm/59in** Repeat **11cm/4¼in** Price ★★ ⬚

7 **Bennett Silks/Kashi/1508C** Colour **54** Alt. colours **yes** Composition **87% rayon, 13% silk** Width **42cm/16½in** Repeat – Price ★ ⬚ ⊞

8 **Sahco Hesslein/Chess 1905** Colour **01** Alt. colours **yes** Composition **65% cotton, 35% polyester** Width **295cm/116in** Repeat **24cm/9½in** Price ★★★ ⬚ ⊞

**Sahco Hesslein/Ulf Moritz/
Tuscany 1883** Colour **01** Alt.
colours **yes** Composition
**47% paper, 33% polyester,
20% viscose** Width
300cm/118in Repeat **–**
Price ★★★★

Larsen/Merlin L2507 Colour
beige 01 Alt. colours **yes**
Composition **100% silk** Width
140cm/55in Repeat **4.5cm/
1¾in** Price ★★★

Larsen/Reflection L7633
Colour **slate 01** Alt. colours
no Composition **60% polyester,
25% linen, 15% cotton** Width
140cm/55in Repeat **–**
Price ★★★

9

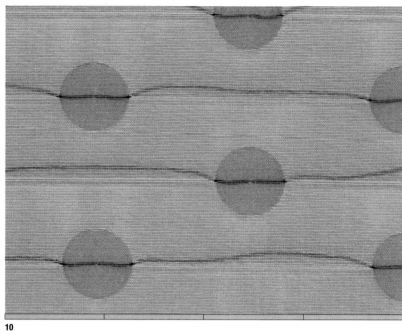

10

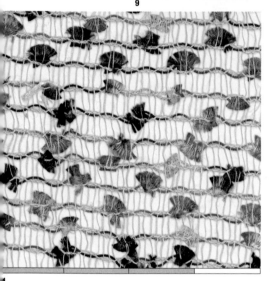

15 **Malabar/Indian Silk/Gold Book**
Colour **NSIL34** Alt. colours **yes**
Composition **100% silk** Width
137cm/54in Repeat **2.5cm/1in**
Price ★★

16 **Liberty Furnishings/Silvani
Weaves/Selkie LF4243**
Colour **06** Alt. colours **yes**
Composition **92% polyester,
8% cotton** Width **300cm/118in**
Repeat **–** Price ★★

17 **Sahco Hesslein/Ulf Moritz/
Azteka 1915** Colour **11** Alt.
colours **yes** Composition
**74% linen, 23% polyester,
3% nylon** Width **168cm/66in**
Repeat **–** Price ★★★

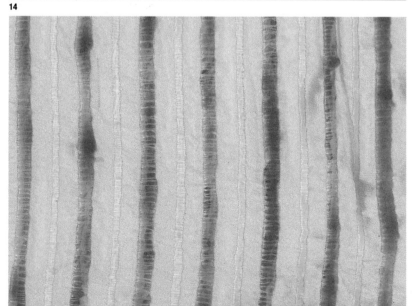

14

12 **Larsen/Cumulus L7456**
Colour **mist 07** Alt. colours
no Composition **80% saran,
20% polyethylene** Width
137cm/54in Repeat **–**
Price ★★★

13 **Chase Erwin/Silk Organza**
Colour **sunset** Alt. colours
yes Composition **80% metallic,
20% silk** Width **110cm/43in**
Repeat **–** Price ★★

14 **Osborne & Little/Hespera/
Cirrus F1640** Colour **05** Alt.
colours **yes** Composition
50% cotton, 50% polyester
Width **140cm/55in**
Repeat **–** Price ★★

16

15

17

21st century

Braids & Trimmings

Decorative hand-sewn trimmings (*passements*), such as tassels, fringing braids and galloons (tapes and ribbons), were originally designed to disguise the seams and edges of wall-, bed- and window-hangings. In the 15th and 16th centuries, *passements* were popular in Italy but rarely used elsewhere. However, following the emigration of skilled Milanese textile workers to the court of Louis XIV of France during the 17th century, *passements* became fashionable among the French nobility.

As window drapes and upholstered furniture became common in the houses of other sections of society during the 17th century, demand for decorative trimmings grew. Much of this was met by the French Huguenot communities who, in order to escape religious persecution, emigrated to England, Ireland, the Netherlands, Germany and Switzerland at the end of the 17th century, taking their skills in the art of *passementerie* with them. The result was a proliferation of intricate trimmings throughout Europe and, later, America, during the 18th and 19th centuries.

LEFT This oval-backed gilt armchair in the Calhoun Mansion in Charleston, South Carolina, USA, features edging braid around the pink moiré silk upholstery. It is coordinated with the wire-braid tiebacks and the deep bullion fringing on the silk damask curtains.

ABOVE These silk damask curtains at the 19th-century Calhoun Mansion were designed to imitate mid-19th-century originals. They are edged with multi-coloured, rope-twist bullion fringing made from silk.

CAMPAIGN FRINGE

Numerous styles of decorative trimmings for drapes and upholstery have been produced since the 15th century, including fringes made up of braid (or sometimes rope), from which hangs a row (or rows) of tassels. Often highly elaborate, most tassels were worked around wooden forms carved in a variety of shapes, such as arrows, domes and balls. However, the most enduringly popular type of edging has proved to be the "campaign" fringe. First devised in Italy in the 17th century, it is so called because the tassels have a bell-like shape – the Italian for bell being *campana*.

KEY DESIGNS

1 While the tops of many of the tassels produced since the Renaissance have been worked around plain wooden forms, some have been enclosed within decorative forms made from carved wood, cut glass, or engraved or plain metal. This tassel is made of jute and bound with a simple tin band.

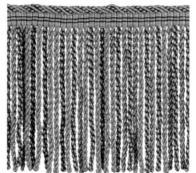

2 Elaborately worked silk-tasselled tie-backs were a favoured means of securing hangings during the 18th and 19th centuries. They remain among the most intricate examples of the *passementier*'s art.

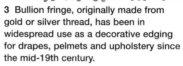

3 Bullion fringe, originally made from gold or silver thread, has been in widespread use as a decorative edging for drapes, pelmets and upholstery since the mid-19th century.

4 Decorative braid edgings, such as this "campaign-fringed" example, featured prominently on curtains, pelmets, upholstery, cushions and lamp shades in Victorian interiors.

5 Ribbons and ribbon-braids (galloons) have been produced in numerous patterns and colourways since the Renaissance. This example is designed as a disguise for upholstery seams.

6 Multi-coloured, interlaced braids were especially popular during the last quarter of the 19th century. This particular design, however, can be traced back to 17th-century France.

1 V.V. Rouleaux/Tin Tassel Colour **jute** Alt. colour **yes** Composition **jute and tin** Depth **15cm/6in** Width – Price ★

2 Scalamandré/T2906-010 Colour **multi** Alt. colour **yes** Composition **90% silk, 10% wood** Depth **60cm/23¾in** Width – Price ★★★

3 Henry Newbery & Co/Melrose/Selkirk **Bullion Fringe** Colour **4** Alt. colour **yes** Composition **mixed fibres** Depth **20cm/8in** Width – Price ★★

4 Henry Newbery & Co/Portobello/Portobello **Tassel Fringe** Colour **12** Alt. colour **yes** Composition **100% viscose** Depth **6cm/ 2½in** Width – Price ★★

5 Abbott & Boyd/Braid Colour **bottle green, golden maize and silver grey** Alt. colour **yes** Composition **100% cotton** Depth – Width **4cm/1½in** Price ★

6 Clarence House/Richelieu Braid 110420 Colour **752** Alt. colour **yes** Composition **100% rayon** Depth – Width **4cm/1½in** Price ★★★★

Tassels & Tie-backs

Decorative tassels and tie-backs have been used to embellish drapery since the Renaissance. At their simplest, tassels are ornamental tufts of thread incorporated into fringing and edgings (*see* pages 196–201) applied to bed-hangings, window drapes, lambrequins, pelmets, portières and upholstery. However, many of the more elaborate tassels – notably those employed as, or as part of, tie-backs for bed- and window-hangings and portières – are among the most intricate examples of the *passementier*'s art. Working around flat-, dome-, arrow-, ball- or screw-shaped wooden forms covered with fabrics such as silk or velvet, the *passementier* could apply a range of embellishments, such as braid or cord edgings, appliquéd motifs and long or short skirts (many of which were made of gold- or silver-thread fringing). During the 18th century, relatively small arrow- and rectangular-shaped heads were popular, as were proportionately short skirts trimmed with appliquéd bows or smaller, fabric-covered wooden forms. Such ornamentation, however, was discreet when compared to the elaborate tassels produced during the 19th century.

3

4

5

6

3 **V.V. Rouleaux/Waxed Turk Hen Knot Tassel** Colour **navy** Alt. colours **yes** Composition **100% acrylic** Depth **3.5cm/1¼in** Width – Price ★★ (special order)

4 **Mulberry/Bishop Tie-back FC004/000** Colour **Natural K101** Alt. colours **yes** Composition **wood and wool** Depth **32.5cm/12¾in** Width – Price ★★★

5 **Mulberry/Hayrick Jute Tie-back FC028/084** Colour **natural K101** Alt. colours **yes** Composition **100% jute** Depth **36cm/14in** Width – Price ★★

6 **Mulberry/Bishop Painted Wood Silky Tie-back FC049/087** Colour **soft gold T106** Alt. colours **yes** Composition **wood & wool** Depth **32.5cm/12¾in** Width – Price ★★★★

7 **Mulberry/Bishop Tie-back FC004/000** Colour **cream J103** Alt. colours **yes** Composition **wood & wool** Depth **32.5cm/12¾in** Width – Price ★★★

8 **Henry Newbery & Co/ Cambridge Tie-back** Colour **wine (1)** Alt. colours **yes** Composition **100% Dralon** Depth **20cm/8in** Width – Price ★★★

7

8

1

2

1 **V.V. Rouleaux/Acorns** Colour **emerald, gold and blue** Alt. colours **yes** Composition **100% polyester** Depth **3.5cm/1¼in** Width – Price ★

2 **V.V. Rouleaux/MOK-05-L** Colour **black and silver** Alt. colours **yes** Composition **70% rayon, 30% polyester** Depth **3.5cm/1¼in** Width – Price ★

RENAISSANCE INFLUENCE

The manufacture of decorative trimmings (known as *passements*) for furnishings has remained a specialist activity since the Renaissance. However, as far as the design of these often exquisite trimmings is concerned, there has always been considerable cross-fertilization of ideas that exist between different areas of textile production. These elaborate tassels are inspired by dressmakers' embellishments and key fobs that were considered the height of fashion in Italy during the Renaissance.

1

2

1 **Wendy Cushing Trimmings/ Traditional Key Tassel 39112** Colour **silver** Alt. colours **yes** Composition **100% cotton** Depth **10cm/4in** Width – Price ★★

2 **V.V. Rouleaux/Terracotta Tassel** Colour **burgundy & gold** Alt. colours **yes** Composition **50% rayon, 50% acrylic** Depth **24cm/9½in** Width – Price ★★★★★

9 **Abbott & Boyd/Single Tassel Tie-back 613** Colour **jute and red** Alt. colours **yes** Composition **50% jute, 50% cotton** Depth **30cm/ 11¾in** Width – Price ★★

10 **Henry Newbery & Co/Fitzherbert Tie-back** Colour **wine and aquamarine** Alt. colours **yes** Composition **100% viscose** Depth **16.5cm/6½in** Width – Price ★★★

11 **Wendy Cushing Trimmings/ Gothic Tie-backs 39033** Colour **black and white** Alt. colours **yes** Composition **100% cotton** Depth **17.75cm/7in** Width – Price ★★★★★

12 **Zoë Barlow Passementerie/ Mexicana Mex/P2/M** Colour **green, blue, yellow and rust** Alt. colours **yes** Composition **cotton and wood** Depth **11.5cm/4½in** Width – Price ★★★★★

13 **V.V. Rouleaux/OP-8612** Colour **light blue 63** Alt. colours **yes** Composition **100% polyester** Depth **14cm/5½in** Width – Price ★

14 **Abbott & Boyd/Double Tassel Tie-back 614** Colour **jute** Alt. colours **yes** Composition **50% jute, 50% cotton** Depth **30cm/11¾in** Width – Price ★★★

ROSETTES

Strictly defined as a circular, formalized flower ornament, but generally accepted as any type of circular ornament with decorative elements radiating from its centre, the rosette has been frequently employed as a trimming for drapery and upholstery since the Renaissance. As shown here, the basic circular shape is frequently augmented with tassels. Since the early Renaissance it has recurred on Classical and Neo-classical furnishing, yet this almost universal motif can be traced back to both ancient Greece and to the Mesopotamian civilization of *c.* 2500 BC, where it was frequently applied to furnishings and other decorative and religious artefacts.

1 **Zoë Barlow Passementerie/ Button and Tassel EP/P20/ Sg/Sp** Colour **pink & green** Alt. colours **yes** Composition **cotton & wood** Depth **55cm/ 21½in** Width – Price ★★★★

2 **Zoë Barlow Passementerie/ Button Med/D10/Sp** Colour **pastel** Alt. colours **yes** Composition **cotton & wood** Depth **30cm/11¾in** Width – Price ★★★

3 **V.V. Rouleaux/Cherry Ball** Colour **neutral** Alt. colours **no** Composition **100% jute** Depth **13cm/5in** Width – Price ★

Tassels & Tie-backs

During the 19th century, tassels generally became more ornate and played an even more prominent role in the furnishing of interiors. As in previous centuries, they were incorporated into fringes and edgings on drapes, lambrequins, pelmets and upholstery. However, the most elaborate examples tended to be reserved for tie-backs and – a new use – bellpulls. In this context their increased complexity mirrored that of related items, such as the bronze and gilt rosettes, discs and cloakpins that were used to secure the tie-backs. Notable examples from the 19th century included multi-tiered tassels worked around a maximum of six carved or turned wooden forms. Arrow- and dome-shaped heads, appliquéd with golden leaves or shells, proved very popular, as did long, onion-shaped skirts.

During the Art Deco and Modernist periods of the 20th century, tassels became smaller and simpler than before, although there were some innovations, including the use of heads made from uncovered cut-glass. More recently, to meet renewed demand, manufacturers and designers have once again begun to produce highly intricate and elaborate tassels, based on, or inspired by, authentic period designs.

1 **Zoë Barlow Passementerie/ Tropical Fish/Purple Angel** Colour **purple, yellow and orange** Alt. colours **yes** Composition **wood, cotton and rayon** Depth **31cm/12in** Width – Price ★★★★★

2 **Scalamandré/Tassel Tie T2906-10** Colour **black and sand** Alt. colours **yes** Composition **100% silk** Depth **15cm/6in** Width – Price ★★★★★

3 **Henry Newbery & Co/Melrose – Single Tassel** Colour **pink** Alt. colours **yes** Composition **100% viscose** Depth **17.5cm/ 7in** Width – Price ★★★

4 **Wendy Cushing Trimmings/ Celtic Tie-back 39063** Colour **blue** Alt. colours **yes** Composition **50% cotton, 50% artificial silk** Depth **23cm/9in** Width – Price ★★★★★

5 **Scalamandré/T2790-12** Colour **green and gold** Alt. colours **yes** Composition **100% silk** Depth **18cm/7in** Width – Price ★★★★★

6 **Henry Newbery & Co/Alpha Tie-back** Colour **green and sand** Alt. colours **yes** Composition **100% viscose** Depth **24cm/9½in** Width – Price ★★★

7 **Claremont/Embrasse Neker Guirlande** Colour **blue and gold** Alt. colours **yes** Composition **100% fibranne** Depth **29cm/11¼in** Width – Price ★★★★★

8 **Zoë Barlow Passementerie/ Tassel Electric Blue** Colour **blue** Alt. colours **yes** Composition **100% cotton, wood** Depth **28cm/10¾in** Width **–** Price ★★★★ 🎨

9 **Henry Newbery & Co/Beta** Colour **bright gold** Alt. colours **yes** Composition **47% cotton, 43% metallic thread, 10% wood** Depth **27cm/10½in** Width **–** Price ★★★★ 🎨

10 **V.V. Rouleaux/Mosaic Tassel** Colour **multi** Alt. colours **yes** Composition **100% acrylic, coloured glass, iron** Depth **to order** Width **–** Price ★★★★★ (special order) 🎨

11 **Zoë Barlow Passementerie/ Double Tie-back Tassel MEX/ P2/M** Colour **blue, green, yellow & rust** Alt. colours **yes** Composition **100% cotton, wood** Depth **11.5cm/ 4½in** Width **–** Price ★★★★★ 🎨

12 **Claremont/Embrasse Raisins** Colour **green** Alt. colours **yes** Composition **100% fibranne** Depth **18cm/7in** Width **–** Price ★★★★★ 🎨 T

13 **Zoë Barlow Passementerie/ Tassel Siamese Fighting Fish (A)** Colour **rusty orange & bottle green** Alt. colours **yes** Composition **100% cotton, wood** Depth **22.5cm/8¾in** Width **–** Price ★★★★★ 🎨

14 **V.V. Rouleaux/Sev – Special** Colour **red and gold** Alt. colours **yes** Composition **100% acrylic** Depth **40cm/15¾in** Width **–** Price ★★★★★ 🎨

TIE-BACKS

Historically, the majority of tie-backs used to restrain window drapes, bed-hangings and portières have been embellished with intricately worked *passements*. However, relatively simple arrangements have also found favour. For example, during the 17th century most tie-backs consisted merely of plaited rope cords made from fibres as diverse as silk, cotton and hemp. Ribbons or "galloons" proved popular during the 18th century, and plain cords re-emerged during the 19th century – albeit some as thick as an elephant's trunk.

1 **Mulberry/'Silk' Sash Tie-back FC056** Colour **soft gold T106** Alt. colours **yes** Composition **100% viscose rayon** Length **85cm/ 33½in** Width **35cm/13¾in** Price ★★★ 🎨

2 **Claremont/S & S Cable Tie-back** Colour **green, pink and white** Alt. colours **yes** Composition **100% cotton** Length **75cm/29½in** Width **5cm/2in** Price ★★★ 🎨 T

3 **Nobilis-Fontan/Embrasses Club 1201.87** Colour **gold and blue** Alt. colours **yes** Composition **70% viscose, 15% silk, 15% cotton** Length **90cm/35½in** Width **3cm/1¼in** Price ★★ 🎨

4 **Abbott & Boyd/211** Colour **58** Alt. colours **yes** Composition **95% cotton, 5% viscose** Length **73cm/28½in** Width **3cm/1¼in** Price ★ 🎨

Fringes

As the influential 19th-century English architect, designer and ornamentist A.W.N. Pugin once noted, fringe was at one time "nothing more than the threads of a silk or woollen stuff knotted together at a ragged edge, to prevent it unravelling further". In terms of its original purpose, this was undeniably true. However, since the 17th century fringe has been produced in a wide variety of styles, some of which have been simple and functional, others highly elaborate and decorative (see pages 198–9).

During the 19th century, extremely ornate upholstery fringing was the height of fashion. Prior to that time, fringes were often relatively plain, with typical examples consisting of braid (or sometimes lace) tops hung with simple tufts or tassels. The depth of such fringes essentially depended on their purpose: shorter versions (which did not droop) were designed for the vertical edges of hangings and upholstered seating, while longer fringes were intended for the bottom edges. Some simple fringes were also made during this period, specifically for the leading edges of mantelshelves (tours de cheminées) and bookcases, the purpose of the latter being to dust a book each time it was removed from and returned to its shelf.

4

1

2

3

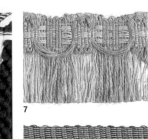

7

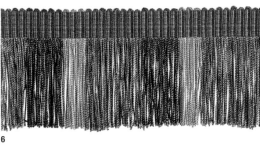

8

9

5

1 **Wemyss Houlès/Toinette 33127** Colour **royal blue (light blue) with white** Alt. colours **yes** Composition **100% viscose** Depth **7cm/2¾in** Width – Price ★ 🛋🛋

2 **Scalamandré/Cut Fringe FC1195** Colour **red and parchment** Alt. colours **yes** Composition **90% silk, 10% rayon** Depth **9.5cm/3¾in** Width – Price ★★★ 🛋

3 **Wendy Cushing Trimmings/Roll Top Bullion Fringe** Colour **black and white** Alt. colours **yes** Composition **100% rayon** Depth **12cm/4¾in** Width – Price ★★ 🛋🛋🛋

4 **Wendy Cushing Trimmings/Silk Bullion with Gimp Heading and Silk Acorns 39120** Colour **silver** Alt. colours **yes** Composition **100% silk** Depth **10cm/4in** Width – Price ★★★★★ 🛋

5 **Mulberry/Cotton Tassel Fringe FC013/000** Colour **gold T102** Alt. colours **yes** Composition **100% cotton** Depth **3cm/1⅛in** Width **7.5cm/2¾in** Price ★★ 🛋🛋

6 **Claremont/Block Fringe Long** Colour **mauve, mustard and green** Alt. colours **yes** Composition **100% fibranne** Depth **6.5cm/2½in** Width – Price ★★ 🛋🛋🛋🛋

7 **Turnell & Gigon/Effilé Naturel 906** Colour **two-tone natural (3)** Alt. colours **yes** Composition **93% linen, 7% viscose** Depth **6cm/2½in** Width – Price ★★ 🛋🛋

8 **Henry Newbery & Co/Portobello/ Bayswater Fan Edge** Colour **12** Alt. colours **yes** Composition **100% viscose** Depth **2.5cm/1in** Width – Price ★ 🛋🛋

9 **Henry Newbery & Co/Opera Fringe/Callas Looped Ruche** Colour **2** Alt. colours **yes** Composition **80% viscose, 20% wool** Depth **5cm/2in** Width – Price ★ 🛋🛋

10

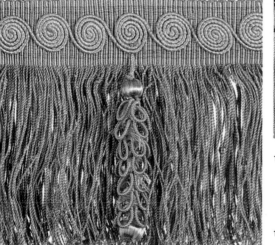

11

12

13

BULLION FRINGE

So called because its twisted lengths of hanging rope were often made from gold, silver or metallic fibres, bullion fringe was particularly fashionable during the mid-19th century. Its primary use was as a skirt for the base of upholstered armchairs and sofas. Single- and multi-coloured linen and cotton versions also proved popular in mid-20th-century "country-house" style interiors.

1

2

1 **Ian Sanderson/Zanzibar Trimmings/Bullion Fringe**
Colour **spice** Alt. colours **yes** Composition **59% viscose, 40% acrylic, 1% polyester** Depth **15cm/6in** Width **–** Price ★★ ⌂⌂ 🛋

2 **Clarence House/Vérone Frange Torse 119612**
Colour **green, gold, red & brown (859)** Alt. colours **yes** Composition **100% viscóse** Depth **12cm/4¾in** Width **–** Price ★★ LC ⌂⌂ 🛋

10 **Claremont/Frange Guirlande**
Colour **blue and gold** Alt. colours **yes** Composition **100% fibranne** Depth **17cm/6¾in** Width **–** Price ★★★★★ ⌂⌂ 🛋 T

11 **Wendy Cushing Trimmings/ Spiral Silk Fringe with Hangers 39121** Colour **grey** Alt. colours **yes** Composition **100% silk** Depth **10cm/4in** Width **–** Price ★★★★★ ⌂⌂

12 **Clarence House/Cut Fringe Richelieu 110421** Colour **navy and gold** Alt. colours **yes** Composition **100% viscose** Depth **12cm/4¾in** Width **–** Price ★★★★ ⌂⌂ 🛋

13 **Wemyss Houlès/Samurai 33063** Colour **9582** Alt. colours **yes** Composition **100% viscose** Depth **6.5cm/ 2½in** Width **–** Price ★★ ⌂⌂

14 **V.V. Rouleaux/Feather Trim** Colour **brown and black** Alt. colours **yes** Composition **100% feathers** Depth **16cm/ 6¼in** Width **–** Price ★★★ 🛋

14

Fringes

During the late 18th and early 19th centuries, fringe was generally regarded as unfashionable. Napoleon I, for example, described it as a "useless" ornament and banned it from his apartments at the Tuileries in Paris. There was also a reaction against it among the followers of the Aesthetic movement during the second half of the 19th century. However, for most of the Victorian era and for much of the 20th century an enormous variety of intricate and highly elaborate fringing was employed on drapes and upholstery. For example, from the 1830s to the 1850s long spiral and bullion fringes, embellished with appliquéd flowers and topped with picot or gimp braids, were very fashionable. In the second half of the 19th century, Persian fringe incorporating a wide braid border supporting fabric-covered balls ("teardrops") was popular, and during the 20th century many Art Deco and Modernist furnishings featured long, skirt-like fringes with deep, crochetwork headings. These are but a few of the many types of fringing that have enjoyed a vogue. Other significant types include "inch", "caul", "block", "campaign", "vellum", "trellis", "butterfly", "snailing", "tufted", "twisted", "knotted", "netted", "fagoted" (sic) and "swagged", all of which are still produced by the *passementiers* of today.

7 **Clarence House/Richelieu – Fringe & Mèches 110422** Colour **752** Alt. colours **yes** Composition **100% viscose** Depth **11cm/4¼in** Width – Price ★★★★ 〔〕 🛋

8 **Wemyss Houlès/Cordelia 33376** Colour **9573** Alt. colours **yes** Composition **85% wool, 15% viscose** Depth **9cm/3½in** Width – Price ★★★★ 〔〕🛋

9 **Wemyss Houlès/Sultane 33379** Colour **9574** Alt. colours **yes** Composition **90% viscose, 5% cotton, 5% metal** Depth **6.5cm/2½in** Width – Price ★★★★ 〔〕🛋

10 **Henry Newbery & Co/Capricorn/ Salvador Bullion Fringe** Colour **rosebud** Alt. colours **yes** Composition **80% viscose, 20% acrylic chenille** Depth **20cm/8in** Width – Price ★★★ 〔〕🛋

11 **Henry Newbery & Co/Capricorn/ Capricorn Tassel Fringe** Colour **rosebud** Alt. colours **yes** Composition **93% viscose, 7% acrylic chenille** Depth **7cm/2¾in** Width – Price ★★ 〔〕

1

2   **3**

1 **Henry Newbery & Co/Blenheim** Colour **green and beige (2)** Alt. colours **yes** Composition **90% acrylic, 10% rayon** Depth **7cm/2¾in** Width – Price ★★ 〔〕⊞

2 **Zoffany/Pompom Tassel Fringe TRM0900** Colour **3** Alt. colours **yes** Composition **100% viscose** Depth **6.5cm/2½in** Width – Price ★★ 〔〕⊞

3 **Scalamandré/Tassel Fringe FT44** Colour **1** Alt. colours **yes** Composition **100% silk** Depth **6cm/2½in** Width – Price ★★★★ 〔〕⊞

4 **Wemyss Houlès/Cap-Ferret 33385** Colour **yellow-maize and green** Alt. colours **yes** Composition **82% viscose, 18% wool** Depth **7.5cm/2¾in** Width – Price ★★ 〔〕⊞

5 **Zoffany/3¼" Tassel Fringe TRM0800** Colour **3** Alt. colours **yes** Composition **100% viscose** Depth **8.5cm/ 3¼in** Width – Price ★★ 〔〕

6 **Brunschwig & Fils/Applause Tassled Fringe 30429-mmm** Colour **multi** Alt. colours **yes** Composition **100% viscose** Depth **8cm/3in** Width – Price ★★ 🛋

4

5   **6**

10

11

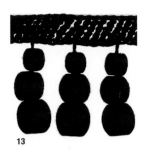

12

14

15

**12 Wendy Cushing Trimmings/
Gilded Bell Hanger Fringe 39045**
Colour **gold** Alt. colours **yes**
Composition **50% cotton, 50%
wool** Depth **10cm/4in** Width –
Price ★★★★ 🛋

**13 V.V. Rouleaux/3-Drop Bauble
Fringe** Colour **terracotta** Alt.
colours **yes** Composition
75% cotton, 25% jute Depth
10cm/4in Width –
Price ★★ 🛋

**14 Brunschwig & Fils/Paulina
Beaded Fringe 905861.05**
Colour **creme** Alt. colours
yes Composition **50% silk,
50% glass** Depth **6cm/2⅜in**
Width – Price ★★★★ 🛋

**15 Scalamandré/Clear Crystal
Fringe ST5401** Colour **white**
Alt. colours **yes** Composition
50% rayon, 50% lucite Depth
4cm/1½in Width –
Price ★★ 🛋

16

**16 Henry Newbery & Co/Carlos
Fringe** Colour **4** Alt. colours
yes Composition **100% acrylic**
Depth **10cm/4in** Width –
Price ★★ 🛋

**17 Brunschwig & Fils/Tourner
Wood Mould Fringe 90580.
05/2** Colour **natural** Alt.
colours **yes** Composition
**74% wood, 25% cotton,
1% metal** Depth **9cm/3½in**
Width – Price ★★★★ 🛋

18 Henry Newbery & Co/Opera
Colour **4** Alt. colours **yes**
Composition **100% viscose**
Depth **5cm/2in** Width –
Price ★★★ 🛋

**19 V.V. Rouleaux/3 Bauble Drop
R5** Colour **oyster** Alt. colours
yes Composition **100%
polyester** Depth **15cm/6in**
Width – Price ★★★★
(special order) 🛋

**20 Wendy Cushing Trimmings/
Classical Hanger Fringe 39052**
Colour **green, red & gold**
Alt. colours **yes** Composition
silk & wood Depth **10cm/4in**
Width – Price ★★ 🛋

17

18

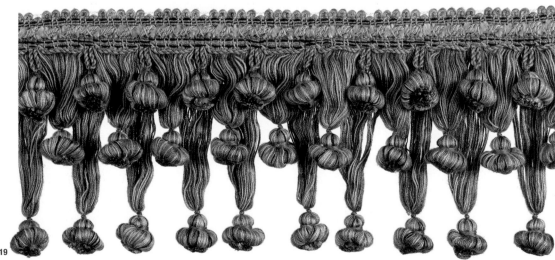

19

20

 placed

Braids & Ribbons

Primarily used to disguise seams and raw edges, braids – flat, narrow, woven textiles – also serve to add decorative embellishments to drapes and upholstery, often in conjunction with tassels and fringing. In the 17th century, braids of plaited silk and gold thread were fashionable, as were velour braids that featured stylized flowers and lozenges. From the 18th century, many tie-backs were edged with substantial braids embellished with flowers, bows, rosettes and butterfly shapes, and picot or gimp braids served as headings for fringing. Early 19th-century braids tended to be delicate, while mid-century examples were generally larger, and end-of-century braids were often multi-coloured, curved and interlaced. In the 20th century, neater, straighter braids with geometric motifs have been favoured.

Decorative ribbons ("galloons") have also been widely used for embellishments. In Paris, France, there were more than 700 *rubaniers* producing bows and artificial flowers from ribbons during the mid-18th century. These were used as trims on drapes, pelmets, valances, tie-backs and table coverings. Many examples, such as "à la cocque", "au mirlton", "à la quadrille" and "à l'allure", took their names from current events, personalities, popular songs and dances, and are still available today.

7

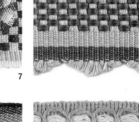

8

9

10

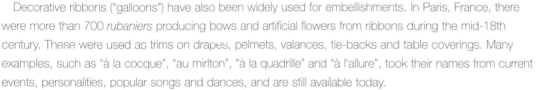

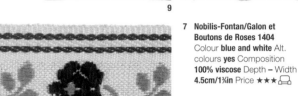

1

11

1 Claremont/Galon Chenille Colour **pink, green, cream and black** Alt. colours **yes** Composition **100% cotton** Depth – Width **5cm/2in** Price ★★ ⊞ 🛋 T

2 Henry Newbury & Co/Windsor Gimp Colour **17** Alt. colours **yes** Composition **70% rayon, 30% acrylic** Depth – Width **1cm/⅜in** Price ★ ⊞ 🛋

3 Wendy Cushing Trimmings/ Tabby Braid 39038 Colour **black and cream** Alt. colours **yes** Composition **50% cotton, 30% silk, 20% rayon** Depth – Width **1.5cm/⅝in** Price ★★ ⊞ 🛋

4 Henry Newbury & Co/Norfolk Picot Braid Colour **16** Alt. colours **yes** Composition **100% cotton** Depth – Width **2.5cm/1in** Price ★ ⊞ 🛋

5 Henry Newbury & Co/Kingston Braid Colour **82** Alt. colours **yes** Composition **80% viscose, 20% cotton** Depth – Width **2cm/¾in** Price ★ 🗺🛋⊞

6 Wemyss Houlès/Cap-Ferret 32179 Colour **9171** Alt. colours **yes** Composition **100% viscose** Depth – Width **4cm/1½in** Price ★ ⊞ 🛋

2

3

4

5

6

7 Nobilis-Fontan/Galon et Boutons de Roses 1404 Colour **blue and white** Alt. colours **yes** Composition **100% viscose** Depth – Width **4.5cm/1¾in** Price ★★★ 🛋

8 George Spencer Designs/ Check Braid 506 Colour **manila and terracotta** Alt. colours **yes** Composition **100% cotton** Depth – Width **6cm/2½in** Price ★★ ⊞ 🛋

9 Scalamandré/Military Ribbon V161-48 Colour **jade green, maize and old glory red** Alt. colours **yes** Composition **100% rayon** Depth – Width **2cm/¾in** Price ★★ 🗺 🛋

10 Abbott & Boyd/Braid 621 Colour **jute and white** Alt. colours **yes** Composition **70% jute, 30% cotton** Depth – Width **3.5cm/1¼in** Price ★ ⊞ 🛋

11 Claremont/Galon Colour **burgundy, green and cream** Alt. colours **yes** Composition **100% fibranne** Depth – Width **13cm/5in** Price ★★★ 🛋 T

12 V.V. Rouleaux/Indian Figure of Eight Colour **jute** Alt. colours **no** Composition **100% jute** Depth – Width **6cm/2⅜in** Price ★ ⊞ 🛋

13 V.V. Rouleaux/Petersham Colour **6** Alt. colours **yes** Composition **64% viscose, 36% cotton** Depth – Width **2cm/¾in** Price ★ ⊞ 🛋

14 Claremont/Greek Key Border Colour **gold, white and black** Alt. colours **yes** Composition **100% fibranne** Depth – Width **5.5cm/2⅛in** Price ★★ ⊞ 🛋 T

13

14

15 Scalamandré/Braid V635-4
Colour seaspray, teal blue and cream Alt. colours yes Composition 100% silk Depth – Width 5cm/2in Price ★★ LC 🛋

16 Brunswig & Fils/30434-M21
Colour wine, red, turquoise, cream and gold mix Alt. colours yes Composition 100% viscose Depth – Width 5cm/2in Price ★ 🛋 ⊞

17 Scalamandré/Braid V713-4
Colour taupe and pink Alt. colours yes Composition 90% silk, 5% rayon, 5% Bemberg Depth – Width 5cm/2in Price ★★★ LC 🛋

18 Scalamandré/Braid V417-12
Colour salmon pink, tarragon and parchment Alt. colours yes Composition 100% silk Depth – Width 4cm/1½in Price ★★★ ⊞ 🛋

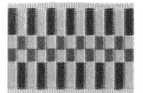

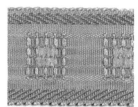

21

23

24

22

25

19 Zoffany/Flower Braid TRM0700
Colour 3 Alt. colours yes Composition 100% viscose Depth – Width 1.5cm/⅝in Price ★ 🛋 ▥

20 Claremont/Galon d'Olives Colour red museum Alt. colours yes Composition 100% wool Depth – Width 3cm/1⅛in Price ★★ ⊞ 🛋 T

21 Claremont/Palmette Colour tan, green and black Alt. colours yes Composition 100% viscose Depth – Width 4cm/1½in Price ★★▥ T

22 V.V. Rouleaux/Mokuba – Flower Tape 9313 Colour yellow, blue and red Alt. colours yes Composition 85% rayon, 15% polyester Depth – Width 7mm/¼in Price ★★ ⊞ 🛋

23 V.V. Rouleaux/1359 No. 12
Colour 7 Alt. colours yes Composition 100% silk Depth – Width 5cm/2in Price ★ 🛋

24 V.V. Rouleaux/Mokuba Ribbon
Colour moss green 16 Alt. colours yes Composition 100% polyester Depth – Width 5cm/2in Price ★ 🛋

25 Ian Sanderson/Etosha Trimmings/Lacy Leather Trim
Colour earth Alt. colours yes Composition 100% leather Depth – Width 4cm/1½in Price ★ 🛋

26 V.V. Rouleaux/Ribbon Picot Edge Colour cayenne, green and cream Alt. colours yes Composition 100% polyester Depth – Width 2.5cm/1in Price ★ ⊞ 🛋

26

UPHOLSTERY BRAIDS

Braid was first extensively employed as a means of decoratively masking the seams and raw edges of drapes and pelmets during the reign of Louis XIV of France. However, the profusion of braid designs that emerged from the late 17th to the end of the 19th century largely resulted from the development of numerous styles of upholstered seating during this period. Braid provided a complementary (or contrasting) edging material, and served to define the diverse shapes of seating as varied as wing and bergère chairs, occasional and corner chairs, and settees and chaise-longues.

1

2

3

1 Henry Newbury & Co/Capricorn/ Phoenix Border Colour leopard Alt. colours yes Composition 90% viscose, 10% acrylic Depth – Width 4.5cm/1¾in Price ★ 🛋 ▥ ⊞

2 Zoffany/Picot Braid TRM1400
Colour 5 Alt. colours yes Composition 100% cotton Depth – Width 1cm/⅜in Price ★ LC 🛋 ▥

3 Scalamandré/Braid V780-7
Colour royal blue, wine and gold Alt. colours yes Composition 90% cotton, 10% rayon Depth – Width 2.5cm/1in Price ★★★ ⊞ 🛋

Plain Wallpapers

Although most wallpapers made since the 15th century have been embellished with patterns and motifs, a significant minority have been produced in plain or mottled colours. The plainest present a solid expanse of a single colour. The types of dyes and inks – animal, vegetable, mineral, aniline and chemical – used to print them, as well as the method of printing, have varied, and have determined the purity, strength and vivacity of colour available (*see* page 206). However, the primary purpose of these plain papers has always been to introduce colour into a room while providing an uncluttered and complementary backdrop for architectural fixtures and fittings, furniture and soft furnishings. Also found within the plains category are those papers that exhibit subtle gradations or mottling of colour. Some are purely abstract, such as many 20th-century Modernist papers, but others are intended as simulations of stone, wood and textiles, such as hessian and tweed. Many papers of this type have been produced since the Renaissance, and a few also exhibit embossing or applied texturing across their surface.

RIGHT In the Victorian era, pictures were often displayed against plain wallpapers. Crimson and magenta papers were deemed appropriate as they accentuated the warm glow of gilded and polished wooden picture frames while providing a contrasting ground for ebony and black-lacquered frames.

PAINT-EFFECT PAPERS

Wallpapers that reproduce the appearance of decorative paint effects have been famously popular since the 1980s. Most are imitations of colourwashing, ragging, rag-rolling, sponging and stippling. Known as "broken-colour techniques", all these effects display, to varying degrees, subtle gradations and patterning of colour. Some – such as sponging or rag-rolling – are often used in re-creations of period interiors. They simulate the mottling that occurred in many pre-20th-century paint finishes as a result of a chemical breakdown in their pigments following exposure to light.

ABOVE Since the late 19th century, dark blue papered walls have often been used as complementary backdrops for displays of silverware and grey marble and granite artefacts.

KEY DESIGNS

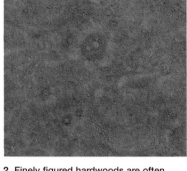

1 Many plain papers have been produced in imitation of plain-woven fabrics. This early 21st-century example imitates the warp and weft of the weave in its two-colour surface printing.

2 Finely figured hardwoods are often simulated in wallpapers. This modern design displays the configurations and mottled colouring associated with stained and polished walnut.

3 During the 19th and 20th centuries, a number of papers were produced in imitation of leather wall-hangings. Some, like this taupe-coloured paper, do actually have the texture of leather.

4 This *faux*-limewash paper exhibits the subtle gradations and luminosities of colour associated with this traditional paint finish. Paint-effect papers have proved very popular since the 1980s.

5 Some plain wallpapers suggest the appearance of stonework or patinated metal surfaces. They can also display subtle and random variations in tonality that can be appreciated in their own right.

6 Grass cloths have been used as wall coverings for centuries, particularly in Japan and Korea. They were very fashionable in Europe and America from the 1960s until the 1980s.

---

1 Harlequin/Notebook Colour **45664** Alt. colours **yes** Width **52cm/20½in** Length **10m/11yd** Repeat – Price ★

2 Maya Romanoff/Patina MR-T35-176-G Colour **golden taupe** Alt. colours **yes** Width **76cm/30in** Length **to order** Repeat – Price ★★★★★

3 Today Interiors/FX/Leather FXV342 Colour **1** Alt. colours **yes** Width **53cm/21in** Length **10m/11yd** Repeat **53cm/21in** Price ★

4 Zoffany/Limewash NTW070 Colour **07** Alt. colours **yes** Width **52cm/20½in** Length **10m/11yd** Repeat – Price ★

5 Osborne & Little/Glissando W1443/01 Colour **silver** Alt. colours **yes** Width **52cm/20½in** Length **10m/11yd** Repeat – Price ★

6 Donghia/Hemps Wallcovering G970/01 Colour **red** Alt. colours **yes** Width **91cm/35¾in** Length **3.5m/3⅞yd** Repeat – Price ★★★★★

Plains

Forerunners of wallpapers, printed with a single block of colour (usually blues, reds and greens), appeared in the 15th century as grounds for paper cut-outs of religious and heraldic imagery. During the 18th century, plain blue, crimson and yellow wallpapers were used in "print rooms" (*see* page 245). In 19th-century interiors, single-coloured wallpapers (especially in shades of red) were favoured for displaying ebony- and gilt-framed pictures, while in the 20th century plain-coloured papers have proved particularly suitable for Modernist and post-Modernist interiors.

Prior to the 1850s, papers that had been hand-blocked with animal, vegetable or mineral dyes exhibited a notable delicacy and purity of colour. In comparison, the hand-blocked or roller-printed aniline dyes of the mid- and late 19th century were more vibrant, but sometimes rather garish. The synthetic chemical dyes of the 20th and 21st centuries have increased the colour range but, partly owing to the slight loss of crispness associated with photogravure and screen-printing, have often failed to match the even coverage given by vegetable dyes – a fact that explains the revival of hand-blocking with traditional vegetable and mineral dyes that began in the late 20th century.

Nina Campbell/Lawn NCW2025/06 Colour **yellow** Alt. colours **yes** Width **52cm/20½in** Length **10m/11yd** Repeat – Price ★

G.P. & J. Baker/Carrara W0110-01 Colour **01** Alt. colours **yes** Width **52cm/20½in** Length **10m/11yd** Repeat – Price ★★

Maya Romanoff/Washi Tsuchikabe MR-RW3018 Colour **green** Alt. colours **yes** Width **93cm/36in** Length **to order** Repeat – Price ★★★★

Zoffany/Stucco PC81905 Colour **05** Alt. colours **yes** Width **52cm/20½in** Length **10m/11yd** Repeat – Price ★

Ornamenta/Lysander Cirrus GIR306 Colour **grey** Alt. colours **yes** Width **52cm/20½in** Length **10m/11yd** Repeat – Price ★★★★★

Today Interiors/FX/Fresco FXV343 Colour **2** Alt. colours **yes** Width **53cm/21in** Length **10m/11yd** Repeat – Price ★

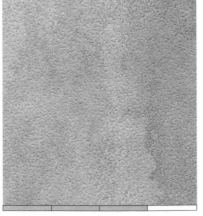

Crowson/Sparta Colour **45** Alt. colours **yes** Width **53cm/21in** Length **10m/11yd** Repeat – Price ★

Maya Romanoff/Patina MR-T35-163 Colour **mustard** Alt. colours **yes** Width **77cm/30¼in** Length **to order** Repeat – Price ★★★★★

Ornamenta/Woodgrain WGR808 Colour **beige, pink and rose** Alt. colours **yes** Width **53cm/21in** Length **10m/11yd** Repeat – Price ★★★★★ ♣

Anya Larkin/Moondust Teapaper Colour **236 pueblo** Alt. colours **yes** Width **102cm/40in** Length **3m/3⅓yd** Repeat – Price ★★★★★ ♣

Andrew Martin/Raffia Medium Colour **natural** Alt. colours **no** Width **91cm/35¾in** Length **6m/6½yd** Repeat – Price ★★

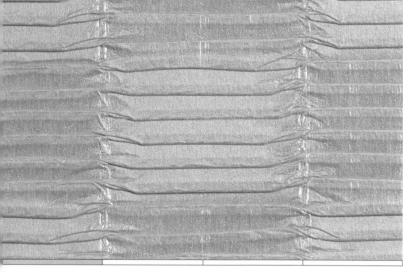

Anya Larkin/Concertina Colour **430 ivory** Alt. colours **yes** Width **74cm/29in** Length **3m/3⅓yd** Repeat – Price ★★★★★ ♣

Harlequin/Navari Colour **45808** Alt. colours **yes** Width **52cm/20½in** Length **10m/11yd** Repeat **52cm/20½in** Price ★

Nobilis/Tassili Colour **TAS214** Alt. colours **yes** Width **68cm/26¾in** Length **10m/11yd** Repeat – Price ★★

Anya Larkin/Flat Teapaper Colour **104 gold** Alt. colours **yes** Width **102cm/40in** Length **3m/3⅓yd** Repeat – Price ★★★★★ ♣

GRASS CLOTHS

Textured wallpapers with a "natural" look have been popular since the mid-1960s, especially in northern Europe and Scandinavia. Typical examples include loose-weave hessian (laminated to a paper backing), suedes and grass cloths (shown here). The latter, which consist of parallel strips of dried grass (or seaweed) glued or woven to a coarse paper ground, had been used as wall-coverings in Korea and Japan for centuries. Many of the grass cloths included in Western interiors are imported from the Far East, but some are produced in Europe (notably France), and these often have a flame-retardant coating.

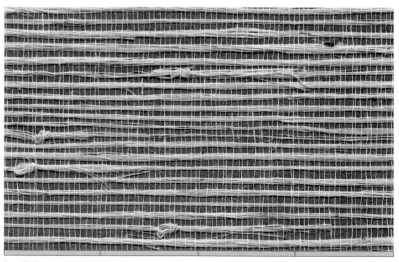

Donghia/Grasscloth G946-04 Colour **04 seaweed** Alt. colours **yes** Width **91cm/35¾in** Length **3.5m/3¾yd** Repeat – Price ★★

Plains

Wallpapers displaying subtle mottling and gradations of colour printed in imitation of stonework, such as marble, limestone, granite and porphyry, were produced in Italy and France as early as the 16th century. As a cheaper substitute for the often unavailable raw material, they have remained in widespread use ever since. Papers simulating the colours, figuring and grain of hardwoods, such as mahogany, oak, maple and birch, have also proved fashionable since the 17th century and have been primarily employed as a substitute for expensive dado panelling, or half- or full-height wall-panelling. Throughout the 20th century and in the early 21st, other special-effect papers have appeared featuring abstract patterns not dissimilar to *faux* stone and wood. Among the most notable and influential are the Modernist papers of the 1930s, which displayed blurred, streaky patches of graduated colour and were sometimes enlivened with gilt powders.

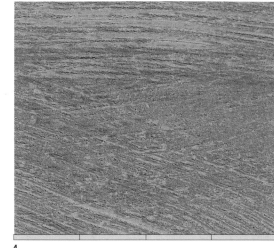

4 **Fardis/Les Ochres 89840**
Colour **54** Alt. colours **yes**
Width **70cm/27½in** Length
10m/11yd Repeat **35cm/
13¾in** Price ★

5 **Graham & Brown 11525**
Colour **yellow** Alt. colours
yes Width **52cm/20½in** Length
10m/11yd Repeat – Price ★

6 **Graham & Brown 11522**
Colour **terracotta** Alt. colours
yes Width **52cm/20½in** Length
10m/11yd Repeat – Price ★

1 **Coloroll/Firenze Texture 27-109B**
Colour **buttermilk** Alt. colours
yes Width **52cm/20½in** Length
10m/11yd Repeat **64cm/25in**
Price ★

2 **De Gournay/"E" Red Silk** Colour
red Alt. colours **yes** Width
93cm/36in Length **3m/3⅓yd**
Repeat – Price ★★★ 👑

3 **Fardis/San Marco/Les Rouges
85800** Colour **031** Alt. colours
yes Width **70cm/27¼in** Length
10m/11yd Repeat **40cm/15¾in**
Price ★

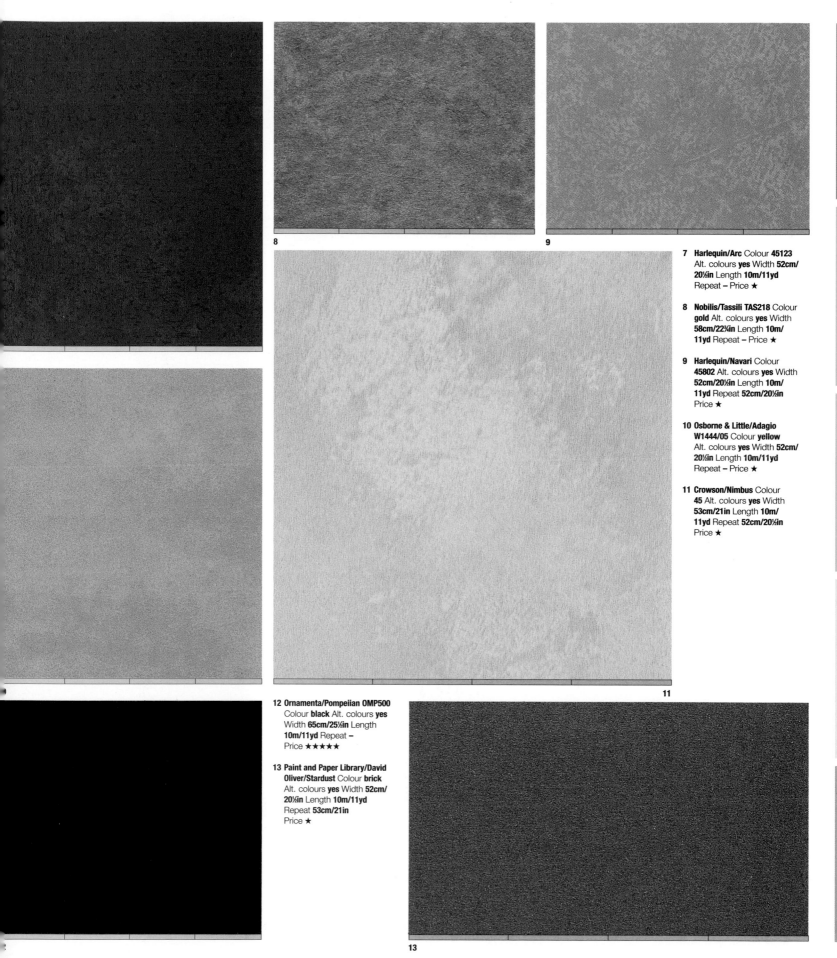

8

9

7 **Harlequin/Arc** Colour **45123**
Alt. colours **yes** Width **52cm/
20½in** Length **10m/11yd**
Repeat – Price ★

8 **Nobilis/Tassili TAS218** Colour
gold Alt. colours **yes** Width
58cm/22¾in Length **10m/
11yd** Repeat – Price ★

9 **Harlequin/Navari** Colour
45802 Alt. colours **yes** Width
52cm/20½in Length **10m/
11yd** Repeat **52cm/20½in**
Price ★

10 **Osborne & Little/Adagio
W1444/05** Colour **yellow**
Alt. colours **yes** Width **52cm/
20½in** Length **10m/11yd**
Repeat – Price ★

11 **Crowson/Nimbus** Colour
45 Alt. colours **yes** Width
53cm/21in Length **10m/
11yd** Repeat **52cm/20½in**
Price ★

11

12 **Ornamenta/Pompeiian OMP500**
Colour **black** Alt. colours **yes**
Width **65cm/25½in** Length
10m/11yd Repeat –
Price ★★★★★

13 **Paint and Paper Library/David
Oliver/Stardust** Colour **brick**
Alt. colours **yes** Width **52cm/
20½in** Length **10m/11yd**
Repeat **53cm/21in**
Price ★

13

WALLPAPERS: *PLAINS* **209**

Plains

Over the centuries, but particularly since the mid-19th century, wallpapers produced in imitation of plain textiles have proved just as popular as those simulating the appearance of wood and stone (*see* page 208).

Favoured "fabrics" during this period have included canvas, cambric, calico, hessian, tweed, seersuckers, moiré silks and lurex. In many cases the simulation is achieved by flat-printing the weave and subtle gradations of colour that characterize the fabrics. Screen-printing and photogravure have proved highly suitable for simulating texture, the latter achieving this *trompe l'oeil* effect by building up the finish with a series of small coloured dots of varying degrees of opacity (*see* page 281).

However, some of the *faux* fabrics produced – notably pile fabrics such as velvet and corduroy – have actually been textured, either by embossing the paper or by flocking it, while other fabric papers, such as Korean and European grass cloths (*see* page 207) are textured in their own right.

1

2

3

1 Today Interiors/FX/Linen FXV345 Colour **8** Alt. colours **yes** Width **53cm/21in** Length **10m/11yd** Repeat – Price ★

2 Graham & Brown 11527 Colour **blue** Alt. colours **yes** Width **52cm/20½in** Length **10m/11yd** Repeat – Price ★

3 Today Interiors/FX/Basket Weave FXV341 Colour **9** Alt. colours **yes** Width **53cm/21in** Length **10m/11yd** Repeat – Price ★

4 Jane Churchill/Eliot JY60W-04 Colour **blue** Alt. colours **yes** Width **52cm/20½in** Length **10m/11yd** Repeat – Price ★

5 Ornamenta/Pompeiian OMP508 Colour **blue** Alt. colours **yes** Width **65cm/25¾in** Length **10m/11yd** Repeat – Price ★★★★★

6 Today Interiors/Zaniah ZW283 Colour **6** Alt. colours **yes** Width **53cm/21in** Length **10m/11yd** Repeat – Price ★

7 Today Interiors/Zaniah ZW2821 Colour **1** Alt. colours **yes** Width **53cm/21in** Length **10m/11yd** Repeat – Price ★

8 Crowson/Eclipse/Moonshine Colour **50** Alt. colours **yes** Width **52cm/20½in** Length **10m/11yd** Repeat – Price ★

9 Crowson/Willowmead Colour **40** Alt. colours **yes** Width **52cm/20½in** Length **10m/11yd** Repeat – Price ★

10 Cole & Son/Jaspé 57/2513 Colour **aqua** Alt. colours **yes** Width **52cm/20½in** Length **10m/11yd** Repeat – Price ★

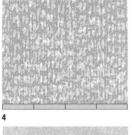

4

5

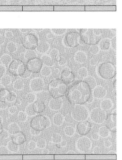

6

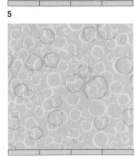

7

8

9

10

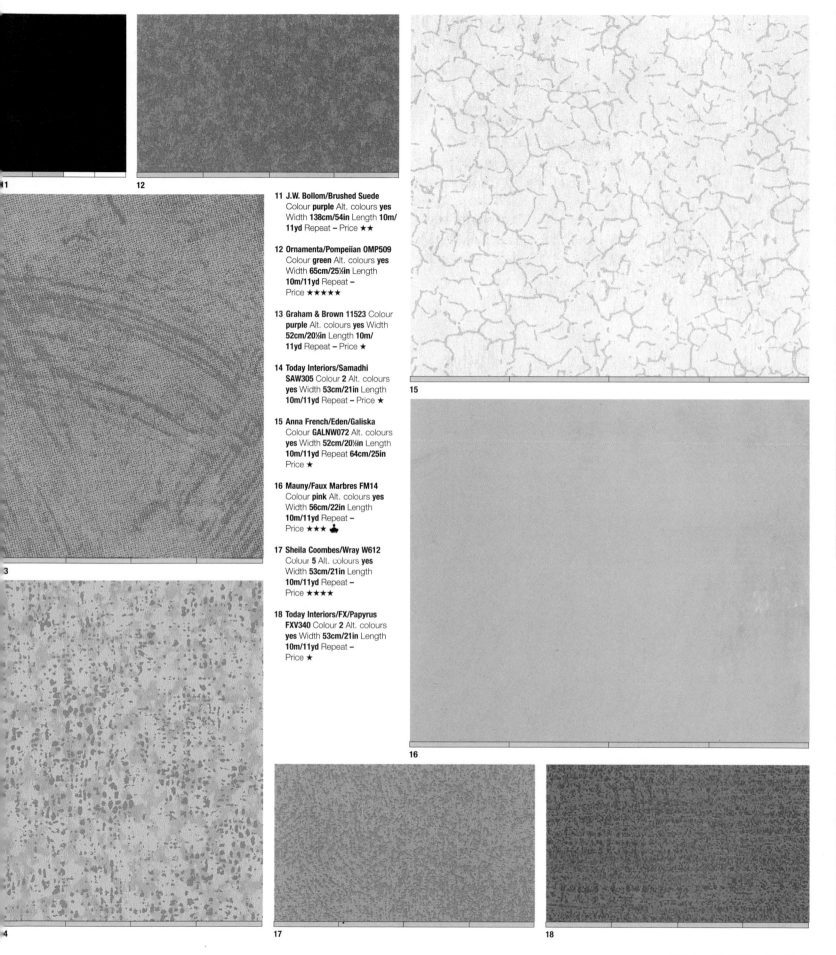

11 J.W. Bollom/Brushed Suede
Colour **purple** Alt. colours **yes**
Width **138cm/54in** Length **10m/
11yd** Repeat – Price ★★

12 Ornamenta/Pompeiian OMP509
Colour **green** Alt. colours **yes**
Width **65cm/25½in** Length
10m/11yd Repeat –
Price ★★★★★

13 Graham & Brown 11523 Colour
purple Alt. colours **yes** Width
52cm/20½in Length **10m/
11yd** Repeat – Price ★

**14 Today Interiors/Samadhi
SAW305** Colour **2** Alt. colours
yes Width **53cm/21in** Length
10m/11yd Repeat – Price ★

15 Anna French/Eden/Galiska
Colour **GALNW072** Alt. colours
yes Width **52cm/20½in** Length
10m/11yd Repeat **64cm/25in**
Price ★

16 Mauny/Faux Marbres FM14
Colour **pink** Alt. colours **yes**
Width **56cm/22in** Length
10m/11yd Repeat –
Price ★★★ ♣

17 Sheila Coombes/Wray W612
Colour **5** Alt. colours **yes**
Width **53cm/21in** Length
10m/11yd Repeat –
Price ★★★★

**18 Today Interiors/FX/Papyrus
FXV340** Colour **2** Alt. colours
yes Width **53cm/21in** Length
10m/11yd Repeat –
Price ★

Motif Wallpapers

The vast catalogue of motifs that wallpaper designers have been able to draw on has accumulated since the late Middle Ages as oriental, Asian and African styles of ornament have gradually been added to those of European origin. In addition, the types of motif favoured at different periods have invariably reflected the cultural, aesthetic and political preoccupations of the time.

For example, heraldic imagery remained much in evidence during the early Renaissance, and resurfaced during the Gothic Revival of the 19th century. Classical motifs began to appear during the Renaissance, and were added to and refined until the mid-19th century as knowledge of ancient Greek and Roman civilizations increased. Chinese motifs were adopted as European fascination with the Orient developed through trade from the late 17th century onward. Egyptian motifs were assimilated during Napoleon's military campaigns in the early 19th century and, during the 20th century, Cubist, Pop Art and Constructivist imagery found its way on to wallpapers.

LEFT This grand, 19th-century American dining room displays the papered tripartite division of walls – frieze, field and dado – that was the height of fashion in reception rooms during this period. The ceiling is also compartmentalized with complementary papers in imitation of polychromatic plaster mouldings. The motifs, which include stars and shells, are of classical origin.

While wallpapers embellished with classical imagery were much in evidence during the late 18th and early 19th century, patterns made up of small, regularly spaced leaf motifs, similar in appearance to medieval powdered ornament, were also fashionable.

WATTS OF WESTMINSTER

The British architects G.F. Bodley, Thomas Garner and Gilbert Scott the Younger founded Watts & Company in 1874 to produce wallpapers, textiles, needlework and furniture in the Gothic Revival and early English Renaissance style – furnishings they were unable to obtain elsewhere. Many of their hand-blocked wallpapers were inspired by A.W.N. Pugin's Gothic Revival designs, of which this diaper-patterned paper with floral motifs is a typical example. It is representative of what was to become the accepted decorative style of the Church of England and the British Establishment.

KEY DESIGNS

1 Highly conventionalized leaves and flowers, combined with repeat geometric motifs in imitation of Islamic tiles, featured on many late Victorian papers, notably those by Christopher Dresser.

2 The stylized, three-petalled lily flower – or fleur-de-lis – is an heraldic motif that has been in widespread use since the Middle Ages. It appeared on many 19th-century Gothic Revival papers.

3 An heraldic symbol, also much used in Islamic ornament, the star has often appeared on papers, notably in Regency England and in America during the early years of independence.

4 Animal motifs, such as those derived from heraldic ornament, were frequently depicted on papers in 18th-century, Neo-classical and Victorian interiors. The lion is a symbol of strength and pride.

5 Medieval and early Renaissance motifs, such as the rose and the coronet, appeared on many Gothic Revival papers of the 19th century. This example was designed by A.W.N. Pugin.

6 Etruscan motifs of urns, festoons, scrolling leaf forms and palmettes were discovered in Pompeiian wall paintings in the mid-18th century and were popularized in England by Robert Adam.

---

1 Bradbury & Bradbury/Algernon AGW Colour **210** Alt. colours **yes** Width **68.5cm/27in** Length **4.5m/5yd** Repeat **34.5cm/ 13½in** Price ★★★ ♣

2 Graham & Brown **12835** Colour **red** Alt. colours **yes** Width **52cm/20½in** Length **10m/11yd** Repeat **16cm/6¼in** Price ★

3 Watts Of Westminster/Cleopatra Star W0012 Colour **Llewellyn** Alt. colours **yes** Width **54cm/21½in** Length **10m/11yd** Repeat **8cm/3in** Price ★

4 Zuber/Documents III/Lions 40028 Colour **gris et vert** Alt. colours **yes** Width **47cm/ 18½in** Length **10m/11yd** Repeat **23cm/ 9in** Price ★★★ ♣

5 Watts of Westminster/Tudor Badge W0058-04/B11 Colour **14** Alt. colours **yes** Width **52cm/20½in** Length **10m/ 11yd** Repeat **13cm/5in** Price ★

6 Laura Ashley/Chaville 3167 759 Colour **raspberry and gold** Alt. colours **yes** Width **52cm/20½in** Length **10m/11yd** Repeat **64cm/25in** Price ★

Motifs: **Pre-19th century**

The most commonly used motifs on late 15th- and 16th-century papers were heraldic and floral, and were mainly woodcut-printed or stencilled. Typical of the heraldic imagery were coats-of-arms, emblems, cyphers and fleurs-de-lis, while notable flowers and plant forms included Tudor roses, anemones, columbines, thistles, chestnuts and acorns, stylized pomegranates and pinecones derived from European damasks. On many papers these motifs were applied to plain grounds, but on others they were printed on *faux*-marble grounds or framed by simple diaper patterns. Heraldic motifs and stylized plant forms remained fashionable during the 17th century. Naturalistic flowers, fruits, caterpillars and butterflies, as found on "Spanish stitch" textiles, were also in evidence, as were classical motifs, such as cupids, putti, vases and urns. Classical imagery remained popular throughout the 18th century, when it also included eagles, dolphins, masks, rosettes, griffins and architectural components inspired by archaeological discoveries at Herculaneum and Pompeii. Also often found in the late 17th and 18th century were motifs taken from oriental pictorials; these included pagodas, dragons and exotic birds and flowers (*see* pages 132–133).

1 **Graham & Brown 12842** Colour **gold** Alt. colours **yes** Width **52cm/20½in** Length **10m/11yd** Repeat **2cm/¾in** Price ★

2 **Hamilton Weston/Archway House** Colour **white, green and black on grey** Alt. colours **yes** Width **52cm/20½in** Length **10m/11yd** Repeat **9cm/3½in** Price ★★ ♟

3 **Elizabeth Eaton/Saighton** Colour **No. 4** Alt. colours **yes** Width **57cm/22½in** Length **10m/11yd** Repeat **5cm/2in** Price ★★

4 **Cole & Son/Temple Newsam** Colour **special** Alt. colours **yes** Width **52cm/20½in** Length **10m/11yd** Repeat **54cm/21½in** Price ★★★ ♟

1

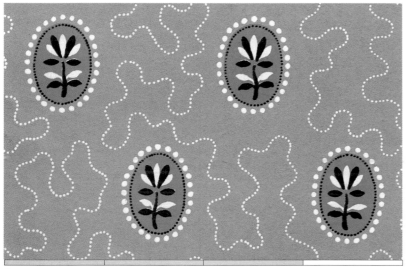

2

3

4

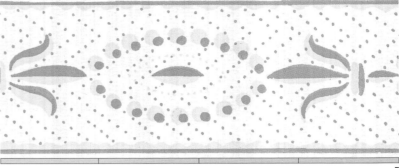

5

7

5 **Hamilton Weston/Guilloche BD43** Colour **document** Alt. colours **yes** Width **4cm/1½in** Length **10m/11yd** Repeat – Price ★ 🖌

6 **The Design Archives/Delphi 58020** Colour **3** Alt. colours **yes** Width **52cm/20½in** Length **10m/11yd** Repeat **4.5cm/1¾in** Price ★

7 **Hamilton Weston/Embroidery BD21** Colour **grey** Alt. colours **yes** Width **4cm/1½in** Length **10m/11yd** Repeat – Price ★ 🖌

8 **Anna French/Eden/Gobi** Colour **GOBNW044** Alt. colours **yes** Width **52cm/20½in** Length **10m/11yd** Repeat **4cm/1½in** Price ★

6

8

10

9 **Ornamenta/Gothick Shadow GTK 408** Colour **beige** Alt. colours **yes** Width **52cm/ 20½in** Length **10m/11yd** Repeat **30cm/11¾in** Price ★★★★★ 🖌

10 **Laura Ashley/Embleton Border 1045 111** Colour **brick** Alt. colours **no** Width **13cm/5in** Length **10m/11yd** Repeat **19.5cm/7¾in** Price ★

11 **Zoffany/Brittany 36BY03** Colour **03** Alt. colours **yes** Width **52cm/20½in** Length **10m/11yd** Repeat **8cm/3in** Price ★

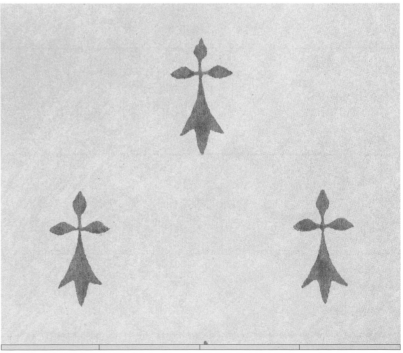

9

11

WALLPAPERS: *MOTIFS* **215**

Motifs: Early 19th century

Many of the early 19th-century papers patterned with repeat motifs were printed in Britain, where, unlike in France, a stringent government tax based on the weight of the wallpaper inhibited the production of large pictorial designs that required heavier paper. The majority of motif patterns that were produced for the French Empire, English Regency and American Federal interiors of the first 30 years of the century were derived from the classical vocabulary of ornament, particularly Roman and Etruscan. Egyptian motifs, including scarabs, sphinxes and lotus flowers, were also much in evidence after the Peninsular War fought between France and England.

Typical Roman motifs, popular in America and Europe (especially in France under the rule of Napoleon Bonaparte), included laurel, oak and olive wreaths, rosettes, arrows and lances, winged torches, lions, eagles and griffins. Favoured Etruscan motifs – which were in fact ancient Greek in origin – included palm leaves, anthemions, festoons, vases, medallions and chimeras, while Egyptian influence was evident in lotus flowers, scarabs and sphinxes. Also liked during this period were *trompe l'oeil* border papers made in imitation of acanthus leaf, Greek key, rope, dentil and egg-and-dart plaster or stucco mouldings.

1

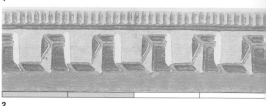

2

3

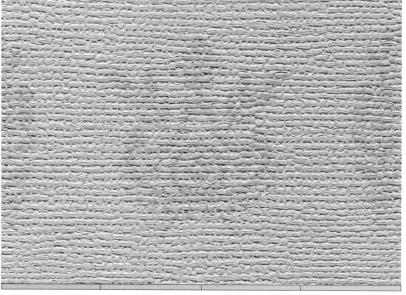

4

5

6

7

1 Alexander Beauchamp/Egg and Dart Border Colour **grey** Alt. colours **yes** Width **6.5cm/2½in** Length **25m/27½yd** Repeat **5cm/2in** Price ★★★★ 👑

2 G.P. & J. Baker/Keystone Border W0122-02 Colour **02** Alt. colours **yes** Width **6cm/2¼in** Length **10m/11yd** Repeat **8cm/3in** Price ★

3 Zuber/Documents III/Petits Lauriers 40084 Colour **JSD** Alt. colours **yes** Width **47cm/18½in** Length **10m/11yd** Repeat **55cm/21½in** Price ★★★

4 Laura Ashley/Burgess Border 1635 275 Colour **gold** Alt. colours **yes** Width **13cm/5in** Length **10m/11yd** Repeat **8cm/3in** Price ★

5 Zuber/Document III 40066 Colour **gold** Alt. colours **yes** Width **47cm/18½in** Length **10m/11yd** Repeat **60cm/23¾in** Price ★★★★★ 👑

6 Laura Ashley/Lexington Border 5417 522 Colour **gold** Alt. colours **yes** Width **8cm/3in** Length **10m/11yd** Repeat **6.5cm/2½in** Price ★

7 Hamilton Weston/Anthemion Border Colour **beige** Alt. colours **yes** Width **4cm/1½in** Length **10m/11yd** Repeat – Price ★ 👑

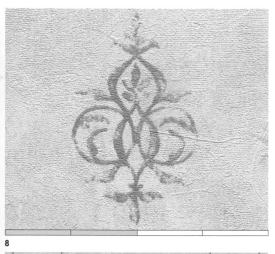

8

8 **Graham & Brown 91204** Colour **terracotta** Alt. colours **yes** Width **13cm/5in** Length **5m/5½yd** Repeat – Price ★

9 **Hamilton Weston/Green Park** Colour **210** Alt. colours **yes** Width **52cm/20½in** Length **10m/11yd** Repeat **4cm/1½in** Price ★★

10 **Jane Churchill/Colbrooke Sprig JY58W-07** Colour **yellow** Alt. colours **yes** Width **52cm/20½in** Length **10m/11yd** Repeat **4.5cm/1¾in** Price ★

11 **G.P. & J. Baker/Heraldic Damask W0113-02** Colour **02** Alt. colours **yes** Width **52cm/20½in** Length **10m/11yd** Repeat **53cm/21in** Price ★

12

9

10

11

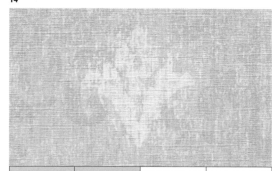

13

12 **Hamilton Weston/Regency Rosette** Colour **mint green on pale green** Alt. colours **yes** Width **52cm/20½in** Length **10m/11yd** Repeat **5cm/2in** Price ★★

13 **Cole & Son/Victorian Star 55/3017/PR** Colour **gold on red** Alt. colours **yes** Width **52cm/20½in** Length **10m/11yd** Repeat **4.5cm/1¾in** Price ★

14 **Zoffany/Blois V322** Colour **01** Alt. colours **yes** Width **52cm/20½in** Length **10m/11yd** Repeat **9cm/3½in** Price ★

15 **Graham & Brown 91186** Colour **beige** Alt. colours **yes** Width **18cm/7in** Length **5m/5½yd** Repeat – Price ★

14

15

WALLPAPERS: *MOTIFS* **217**

Motifs: **Mid-19th century**

The majority of classical motifs that had appeared on wallpapers during the early 19th century also found favour in the Renaissance and Baroque Revival interiors fashionable on both sides of the Atlantic around the middle of the century. In contrast to these predominantly naturalistic and often "three-dimensionalized" classical motifs were the stylized, flat motifs on Gothic Revival wallpapers throughout Europe – notably those devised by influential English designers such as A.W.N. Pugin (*see* opposite) and Owen Jones.

Conventionalized plant forms, often presented within a geometrical pattern structure, lay at the heart of many of Pugin's and Jones's designs. However, while Pugin drew heavily and precisely from the Gothic and heraldic vocabulary of ornament prevalent during the Middle Ages and the early Renaissance, Jones's sources were more wide-ranging; they were primarily oriental – Chinese, Far Eastern, Persian, Indian, Arabic and Moorish – while also embracing medieval imagery and primitive art.

Graham & Brown 11645 Colour **yellow** Alt. colours **yes** Width **52cm/20½in** Length **10m/11yd** Repeat **32cm/12½in** Price ★

Hodsoll McKenzie/Fleur de Lys 504/631 Colour **yellow** Alt. colours **yes** Width **52cm/20½in** Length **10m/11yd** Repeat **7.5cm/2¾in** Price ★

Watts of Westminster/Pineapple W0039-03/I12 Colour **Seton** Alt. colours **yes** Width **54cm/21½in** Length **10m/11yd** Repeat **27cm/10½in** Price ★★

Zuber/Chateau de Blois/Alcove Chambre de la Reine 9222 Colour **gold, terracotta and grey** Alt. colours **no** Width **51cm/20in** Length **9m/10yd** Repeat **88cm/34½in** Price ★★★

Cole & Son/The Strawberry OEW0141 Colour **white** Alt. colours **yes** Width **52cm/20½in** Length **10m/11yd** Repeat **37cm/14½in** Price ★★★★ ♛

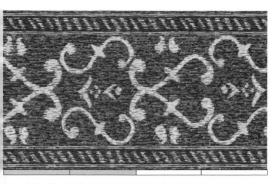

Laura Ashley/Farnley Border 155 241 Colour **dark brick** Alt. colours **no** Width **9cm/3½in** Length **10m/11yd** Repeat – Price ★

Sandberg/Erik 933 Colour **24** Alt. colours **yes** Width **3.5cm/1⅜in** Length **10m/11yd** Repeat **22cm/8⅝in** Price ★

Cole & Son/Block 015 Colour **yellow on green** Alt. colours **yes** Width **52cm/20½in** Length **10m/11yd** Repeat – Price ★★★ ♣

Watts of Westminster/Rose and Coronet Colour **Stuart** Alt. colours **yes** Width **54cm/21¼in** Length **10m/11yd** Repeat **45cm/17½in** Price ★★

Hamilton Weston/Uppark Mock Emboss Colour **document** Alt. colours **yes** Width **52cm/20½in** Length **10m/11yd** Repeat **48cm/19in** Price ★★ ♣

Watts of Westminster/Shrewsbury W0050 Colour **Walton** Alt. colours **yes** Width **54cm/21¼in** Length **10m/11yd** Repeat **47cm/18½in** Price ★★

Osbourne & Little/Durbar/Rajura W1012 Colour **03** Alt. colours **yes** Width **52cm/20½in** Length **10m/11yd** Repeat **20cm/8in** Price ★

Zoffany/Gothic Flower 36GF04 Colour **04** Alt. colours **yes** Width **52cm/20½in** Length **10m/11yd** Repeat **32cm/12½in** Price ★

PUGIN PAPERS

The influential English architect A.W.N. Pugin (1812–52) designed hundreds of wallpapers in the mid-19th century, notably for the New Palace of Westminster, in London, England. Dismissive of eclecticism, and scornful of *trompe l'oeil* papers for creating "dishonest" illusions of depth on two-dimensional surfaces, his flat and conventionalized treatments of imagery were derived from Gothic art. Typical patterns included heraldic emblems and stylized fruit and foliage forms found on medieval manuscripts and textiles, as well as geometric patterns based on medieval tiles and stencilling.

Watts of Westminster/Trellis W0056-06/I12 Colour **Padgett** Alt. colours **yes** Width **54cm/21¼in** Length **10m/11yd** Repeat **18cm/7in** Price ★★

Watts of Westminster/Triad W5057-15/A13 Colour **Amsterdam** Alt. colours **yes** Width **54cm/21¼in** Length **10m/11yd** Repeat **80cm/31½in** Price ★★

Motifs: Late 19th century

The tremendous variety of motifs employed on wallpapers during the last three decades of the 19th century reflected the eclectic mixture of decorative styles favoured at this time in both Europe and America. Classical and Pompeiian motifs typical of the 18th century (*see* pages 214–215) re-emerged, while A.W.N. Pugin's Gothic Revival imagery endured, especially in Britain, and the oriental- and Moresque-based patterns of Owen Jones remained internationally influential.

However, the most distinctive, and in many respects the most innovative, wallpapers of the late 19th century were produced by designers working under the umbrellas of the Arts and Crafts, Aesthetic or Art Nouveau movements. Many Arts and Crafts patterned wallpapers, particularly those devised by William Morris, were characterized by stylized, rhythmical plant forms – usually English, floral and medieval in origin. Conventionalized as well as naturalistic plant forms, together with exotic bird and insect motifs, were also an important feature of both Aesthetic and Art Nouveau papers, and were inspired not only by medieval imagery but also by Renaissance, Rococo, Chinese and, especially, Japanese styles of ornament.

1 **Zuber/Documents III/Fleur de Lys 4805 BRD** Colour **blue** Alt. colours **yes** Width **47cm/18½in** Length **10m/ 11yd** Repeat **33cm/13in** Price ★★★

2 **Hamilton Weston/Victorian Leaf Quatrefoil** Colour **cream, grey and grey/blue** Alt. colours **yes** Width **52cm/20½in** Length **10m/11yd** Repeat **15cm/6in** Price ★★ ♣

3 **Zoffany/Maple V43805** Colour **05** Alt. colours **yes** Width **52cm/20½in** Length **10m/ 11yd** Repeat – Price ★

4 **Zoffany/Lennel BLY02** Colour **02** Alt. colours **yes** Width **52cm/20½in** Length **10m/11yd** Repeat **32cm/12½in** Price ★

5 **G.P. & J. Baker/Fleur de Lys W0097-09** Colour **red** Alt. colours **yes** Width **52cm/ 20½in** Length **10m/11yd** Repeat **5cm/2in** Price ★

6

7

8

6 Bradbury & Bradbury/Roland
RLW-130 Colour **130** Alt.
colours **yes** Width **68cm/
26¾in** Length **4.5m/5yd**
Repeat **27cm/10½in**
Price ★★ ♣

7 Laura Ashley/Ashton 3162
283 Colour **plum and natural**
Alt. colours **yes** Width
52cm/20½in Length **10m/11yd**
Repeat **16cm/6¼in** Price ★

8 Watts of Westminster/Gaheris
WW0017-02/E12 Colour
Garbot Alt. colours **yes**
Width **47cm/18½in** Length
10m/11yd Repeat **19cm/
7½in** Price ★★

9 Cole & Son/Butterflies
54/4717/PR Colour **red
on green** Alt. colours **yes**
Width **52cm/20½in** Length
10m/11yd Repeat **30.5cm/
12in** Price ★

9

10 Today Interiors/Odonata/
Dragonfly ODW 3654
Colour **4** Alt. colours **yes**
Width **53cm/21in** Length
10m/11yd Repeat **52cm/20½in**
Price ★

11 Zoffany/Florentine Lily ZV0503
Colour **03** Alt. colours **yes**
Width **52cm/20½in** Length
10m/11yd Repeat **8cm/3in**
Price ★

10

11

Motifs: Early 20th century

Although plant-form motifs were generally excluded from Modernist designs, they were widely employed in the other fashionable decorative styles of the early 20th century. For example, Art Nouveau wallpapers featured roots, stems and elongated blooms, while small leaves, fruits and cup-shaped blossoms appeared on Deutscher Werkbund papers. Arts and Crafts papers were characterized by conventionalized flowers and leaves, while early Art Deco designs incorporated stylized floral motifs (*see* pages 124–125). Many wallpapers were also produced in imitation of 18th- and 19th-century floral chintzes. Even the highly mathematical Cubist-patterned papers of the 1920s and 1930s were sometimes softened with small flower or leaf motifs.

Egyptian motifs (*see* opposite); heraldic imagery on Tudor Revival papers; and bows, swags, shells, insects and architectural scrollwork inspired by 18th-century, French Rococo and Neo-classical decoration were all to be seen. The majority of other fashionable motifs were either geometric or abstract in form. These included medieval and oriental diaper patterns, the stepped shapes and overlapping squares and oblongs of Art Deco, and the shaded circles, triangles and rectangles inspired by Constructivist principles of painting.

2

1

1 Graham & Brown/51506 Colour **beige** Alt. colours **yes** Width **52cm/20½in** Length **10m/11yd** Repeat **53cm/21in** Price ★

2 Bradbury & Bradbury/Neo-Grecian Dado NGD-210 Colour **210** Alt. colours **yes** Width **69cm/27in** Length **to order** Repeat **35cm/13¾in** Price ★★★ 🖌

3 Coloroll/Ironwork Motif 27-026 Colour **terracotta** Alt. colours **yes** Width **52cm/20½in** Length **10m/11yd** Repeat **64cm/25in** Price ★

4 Alexander Beauchamp/Florence Colour **red, gold and black** Alt. colours **yes** Width **53cm/21in** Length **10m/11yd** Repeat **76cm/30in** Price ★★★ 🖌

3

FINISHING LINCRUSTA

Machine-embossed Lincrusta papers – a composite of linseed oil, gum, resins and wood-pulp on canvas (*see* page 239) – provided a substantially cheaper alternative to traditional wood, plaster, leather and tile panelling and mouldings. Lincrusta was particularly suited to avant-garde use – the example shown here was designed for dado panelling and features a stylized flower and foliage pattern typical of early 20th-century Art Nouveau. Its *faux* tile finish was created by lightly distressing a blue-green oil-based glaze, which was applied over a bronze-gold basecoat.

IHDG/Edwardian Dado RD1950 Colour **white** Alt. colours **no** Width **61cm/24in** Length **102cm/40in** Repeat **–** Price ★★★ 🖻

4

EGYPTIAN MOTIFS

Wallpapers patterned with Egyptian motifs first became fashionable in early 19th-century Neo-classical interiors, particularly in France and Britain, after Napoleon Bonaparte's military campaigns in Egypt. They also appeared on British wallpapers during the last quarter of the 19th century as the British Empire consolidated its rule over Egypt. During the first half of the 20th century, Egyptian motifs, such as scarabs, sphinxes, lotus leaves and (as shown here) palm trees and camels, enjoyed a further revival. Egyptian elements and features were also frequently included in Art Deco schemes of the period.

Andrew Martin/Khartoum Colour **red** Alt. colours **no** Width **52cm/20½in** Length **10m/11yd** Repeat **26cm/10¼in** Price ★

8

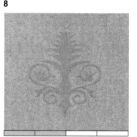

9

10

5 **Alexander Beauchamp/Art Deco Fans** Colour **special** Alt. colours **yes** Width **53cm/21in** Length **10m/11yd** Repeat **55cm/21½in** Price ★★★ ♣

6 **Cole & Son/Alma Trellis 55/3062/PR** Colour **yellow and gold** Alt. colours **yes** Width **52cm/20½in** Length **10m/11yd** Repeat **13.5cm/5¼in** Price ★

7 **Nicholas Herbert/Sherwood W03-08** Colour **beige** Alt. colours **yes** Width **52cm/20½in** Length **10m/11yd** Repeat **13cm/5in** Price ★

8 **Graham & Brown 13105** Colour **white** Alt. colours **no** Width **52cm/20½in** Length **10m/11yd** Repeat **8cm/3in** Price ★

9 **Osborne & Little/Chantilly VW1223/04** Colour **terracotta** Alt. colours **yes** Width **52cm/20½in** Length **10m/11yd** Repeat **11cm/4¼in** Price ★

10 **Zuber/Documents III/Grandes Abeilles 30118V0** Colour **green** Alt. colours **yes** Width **47cm/18½in** Length **10m/11yd** Repeat **24cm/9½in** Price ★★★

7

Motifs: **Late 20th–early 21st century**

During the 1950s and 1960s, wallpapers embellished with geometric and abstract motifs retained their popularity from earlier in the century. Apart from Cubist-inspired squares and oblongs, motif designs of the 1950s included diamonds, suns, stars, checks, "worm-casts", prisms, sound waves, sketchy squiggles and organic shapes based on amoeba and crystalline structures. In the 1960s, sunbursts, giant circles and even flying-saucer shapes appeared.

Plant-form motifs also remained prevalent during this period, especially in America and Scandinavia, where many designers were preoccupied with bringing nature indoors. Papers of this genre, designed to appeal to traditionalists, displayed patterns such as large-scale tropical flowers or leaves, single roses in cartouches, and Victorian sprigs or stylized flowers on diaper grounds derived from Persian art and ceramics, as well as sinuous Art Nouveau-style roots, stems and elongated blooms. More modern designs included wild strawberries, marine fauna and hogweed, while papers intended for kitchens featured not only fruits and vegetables, but also kitchenalia, recipes and bottles of "foreign" wine – the latter reflecting the substantial increase in international leisure travel at this time.

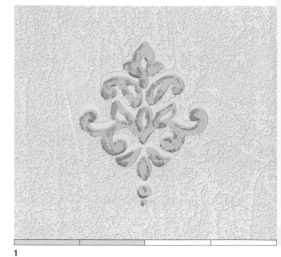

1

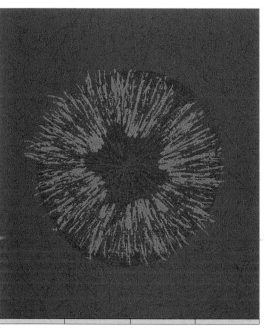

2

4

3

5

6

1 **Coloroll/Firenze Motif 27-108** Colour **beige** Alt. colours **yes** Width **52cm/20½in** Length **10m/11yd** Repeat **64cm/25in** Price ★

2 **Today Interiors/Zaniah ZW2800** Colour **0** Alt. colours **yes** Width **53cm/21in** Length **10m/11yd** Repeat **53cm/21in** Price ★

3 **Zoffany/Star 36ST05** Colour **05** Alt. colours **yes** Width **52cm/20½in** Length **10m/11yd** Repeat **32cm/12½in** Price ★

4 **Graham & Brown 91185** Colour **green** Alt. colours **yes** Width **18cm/7in** Length **5m/5½yd** Repeat – Price ★

5 **Sandberg/Mona 941** Colour **14** Alt. colours **yes** Width **3cm/1¼in** Length **10m/11yd** Repeat **9cm/3½in** Price ★

6 **Zoffany/Palm NC9802** Colour **peach** Alt. colours **yes** Width **52cm/20½in** Length **10m/11yd** Repeat – Price ★

20th & 21st century

7 **Today Interiors/Aymara/Saffir/ AYW339** Colour **2** Alt. colours **yes** Width **53cm/21in** Length **10m/11yd** Repeat **52cm/20½in** Price ★

8 **Zoffany/Coppice WAL0100** Colour **2** Alt. colours **yes** Width **52cm/20½in** Length **10m/11yd** Repeat **52.5cm/ 20¾in** Price ★

8

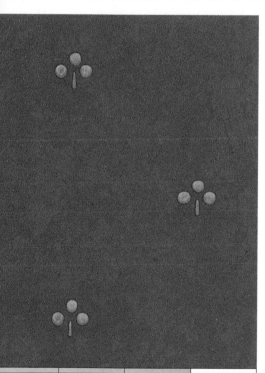

9 **Zoffany/Blois Plain V43005** Colour **05** Alt. colours **yes** Width **52cm/20½in** Length **10m/11yd** Repeat **8.5cm/3¼in** Price ★

10 **Harlequin/Charm** Colour **60307** Alt. colours **yes** Width **52cm/20½in** Length **10m/11yd** Repeat **2.5cm/1in** Price ★

11 **Laura Ashley/Rosie Border** Colour **lavender** Alt. colours **yes** Width **13cm/5in** Length **10m/11yd** Repeat **13cm/5in** Price ★

12 **Sandberg/Albin 711** Colour **24** Alt. colours **yes** Width **53cm/21in** Length **10m/11yd** Repeat **32cm/12½in** Price ★

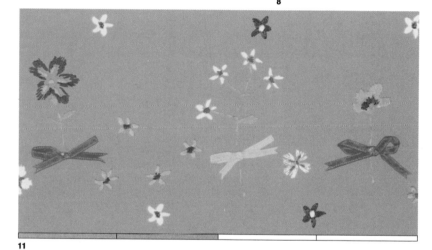

11

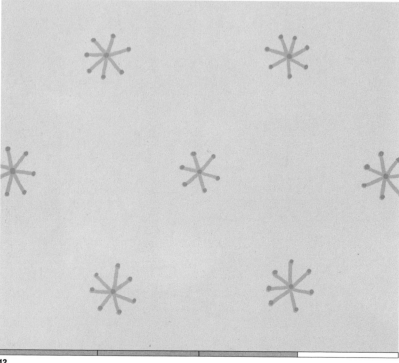

12

20th & 21st century

Motifs: Late 20th–early 21st century

While many new designs have been introduced since the 1970s, there has also been a major revival of interest in the wallpaper patterns of earlier periods. Favoured motifs have consequently been drawn from a rich catalogue of international ornament accumulated since the Middle Ages (*see pages 212–225*), with much of that imagery consisting of plant forms (especially floral motifs), geometric or abstract shapes, various emblems and imitations of architectural mouldings.

In many cases wallpaper companies have reproduced the original designs using traditional dyes and the original method of printing. In other cases, however, designers have adapted and updated the motifs by stylizing and recolouring them to suit a more modern aesthetic. Generally, this reworking has taken the form of a reduction in the numbers of colours used in any one design or pattern. There has also been a distinct favouring of colours that, although saturated, have a noticeably soft, chalky appearance.

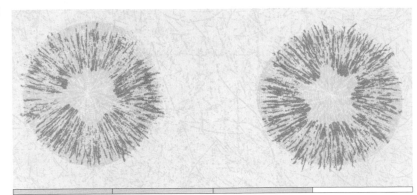

1

2

3

1 Today Interiors/Zaniah/Aphelion **ZW280** Colour **1** Alt. colours **yes** Width **53cm/21in** Length **10m/11yd** Repeat **10.5cm/4in** Price ★

2 Osborne & Little/Durbur/Catalpa **W1010** Colour **06** Alt. colours **yes** Width **52cm/20½in** Length **10m/11yd** Repeat **21cm/8¼in** Price ★

3 Today Interiors/Aymara/Maya **AYW340** Colour **3** Alt. colours **yes** Width **53.5cm/21in** Length **10m/11yd** Repeat **53.5cm/21in** Price ★

4

4 Anna French/Chalice Colour **CHAWP02** Alt. colours **yes** Width **52cm/20½in** Length **10m/11yd** Repeat **46cm/ 18in** Price ★

5 Harlequin/Navari Colour **355908** Alt. colours **yes** Width **52cm/20½in** Length **10m/11yd** Repeat **17.5cm/ 7in** Price ★

6 Osborne & Little/Sundance Border **B854/04** Colour **blue** Alt. colours **yes** Width **11cm/ 4¼in** Length **10m/11yd** Repeat – Price ★

7 Designers Guild/Pushpa **P243/03** Colour **ultramarine** Alt. colours **yes** Width **53cm/21in** Length **10m/ 11yd** Repeat **53cm/21in** Price ★

8 Today Interiors/Samadhi/Tulipa **SAW305** Colour **5** Alt. colours **yes** Width **53cm/21in** Length **10m/11yd** Repeat **26cm/ 10¼in** Price ★

5

6

7

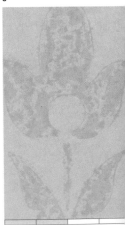

8

9

10

11

15

Harlequin/Notebook Colour **35550** Alt. colours **yes** Width **52cm/20½in** Length **10m/ 11yd** Repeat **52cm/20½in** Price ★

Ornamenta/Elements/22 Carat Gold Leaf Colour **gold on brown** Alt. colours **yes** Width **50cm/19½in** Length **5m/5½yd** Repeat **50cm/ 19½in** Price ★★★★★ 🖌

Today Interiors/Samadhi/Arbus SAW301 Colour **8** Alt. colours **yes** Width **53cm/21in** Length **10m/11yd** Repeat **26cm/ 10¼in** Price ★

Today Interiors/Aymara/Oasis AYW342 Colour **0** Alt. colours **yes** Width **53cm/21in** Length **10m/11yd** Repeat **53cm/21in** Price ★

Mulberry/Royal Palm FG038 Colour **H101** Alt. colours **yes** Width **52cm/20½in** Length **10m/11yd** Repeat **38cm/15in** Price ★

Jane Churchill/Book Eight/ Florian/Florian Leaf J034W-02 Colour **green** Alt. colours **yes** Width **52cm/20½in** Length **10m/11yd** Repeat **20.5cm/ 8in** Price ★

Anna French/Eden/Gobi Colour **GOBNW04** Alt. colours **yes** Width **52cm/20½in** Length **10m/11yd** Repeat **4cm/ 1½in** Price ★

12

16

16 Laura Ashley/Butterfly 3180 659 Colour **pink** Alt. colours **yes** Width **26.5cm/10½in** Length **10m/11yd** Repeat **26.5cm/10½in** Price ★

17 Mulberry/Hedgerow FG037 Colour **S111** Alt. colours **yes** Width **13cm/5in** Length **10m/11yd** Repeat **13cm/5in** Price ★

13

14

17

WALLPAPERS: *MOTIFS* **227**

20th & 21st century

Floral Wallpapers

From the early Renaissance to the present day, flowers that are naturalistic and conventionalized in form have proved to be the most enduringly fashionable and universal form of imagery used on wallpapers. Only in the Modernist interiors of the first half of the 20th century were floral designs not prevalent.

Sources of inspiration for floral wallpaper patterns have been many and varied. For example, before the 19th century numerous papers replicated the floral designs found on textiles, particularly damasks and chintzes.

Throughout the 20th century and into the 21st, the wallpaper industry has avidly imitated the manner in which flowers have been depicted in fine art. Certain wallpaper designers have also produced floral patterns and motifs from their own observations of nature. However, the primary reference material for floral designs has been the pattern books and illustrated botanical studies that have been published since the 17th century, first in Europe and, later, also in America.

LEFT This provincial-style bedroom is in a late 18th-century Parisian townhouse. The wallpaper displays a naturalistic floral pattern printed in shades of red on a pale yellow ground. It echoes the other plant-form motifs on the bedding, and is typical of the horticultural and rustic imagery fashionable in many parts of Europe during the second half of the 18th century.

EMPIRE-STYLE FLORALS

This floral-patterned wallpaper is in a drawing room of the Jumel mansion, in New York, USA. The mansion was decorated and furnished in French Empire style during the 1820s after Madame Jumel returned from a trip to Paris with a collection of hand-blocked wallpapers and other furnishings that were considered the height of fashion and quality on both sides of the Atlantic. Naturalistic bouquets set against contrasting coloured grounds were among the most loved of Empire-style patterns.

KEY DESIGNS

1 Small repeats of native European flowers, such as larkspurs, roses, poppies, daisies, violets and anemones, were generally favoured over exotic oriental blooms in the late 18th century.

2 Uncomplicated floral patterns of delicately trailing flowers printed on pale grounds were very fashionable in France during the 1770s and 1780s, and remained popular until the 1840s.

3 Botanically accurate, large-scale floral patterns, characterized by realistic colours and subtle use of highlighting and shading, appeared in many Victorian interiors in the mid-19th century.

4 From the late 18th century onward, wallpaper manufacturers in both France and England have produced numerous floral-patterned papers that imitate *toile de Jouy* fabrics.

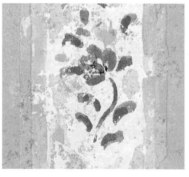

5 Since the early 18th century, many floral papers have been produced in imitation of floral-patterned, silk damask wall-hangings. This English example has a late 18th-century floral pattern.

6 Small repeat floral motifs are often used to embellish striped papers. This example is late 20th century, but floral-decorated stripes were also popular in the late 18th and early 19th century.

---

1 Harlequin/Charm Colour **30003** Alt. colours **yes** Width **52cm/20½in** Length **10m/11yd** Repeat **13cm/5in** Price ★

2 Brunschwig & Fils/Georgette **16171-06** Colour **scarlet on white** Alt. colours **yes** Width **68.5cm/27in** Length **4.5m/5yd** Repeat **64cm/25in** Price ★★★★

3 Nina Campbell/Zembla/Zembla NCW **2222/03** Colour **03** Alt. colours **yes** Width **52cm/20½in** Length **10m/11yd** Repeat **76cm/30in** Price ★

4 Ornamenta/English Musick **EMK702** Colour **blue** Alt. colours **yes** Width **53cm/21in** Length **10m/11yd** Repeat **92cm/36¼in** Price ★★ 🌿

5 Cole & Son/Pompadour/Cadora **58/1001** Colour **blue and cream** Alt. colours **yes** Width **52cm/20½in** Length **10m/11yd** Repeat **43cm/16¾in** Price ★★★★★

6 Anna French/Daisy Rose Stripe Colour **DAIWP077** Alt. colours **yes** Width **52cm/20½in** Length **10m/11yd** Repeat **64cm/25in** Price ★

Florals: **Medieval to mid-18th century**

Many of the black-and-white woodcut-printed papers of the late 16th and early 17th century featured floral patterns based on "black stitch" embroidery (black silk embroidery executed on a white ground). Sophisticated, stylized floral patterns derived from velvets and brocades were also highly fashionable during the 17th century (with many examples featuring additional hand-painted elements), as were naturalistically depicted flowers and fruit in imitation of "Spanish stitch" textiles.

Other 17th-century, floral-patterned papers of note displayed elaborate arrangements of flowers, such as tulips, narcissi, orchids and roses, set in classical vases and surrounded by stylized foliage and strapwork. Such designs were to remain in vogue for much of the 18th century, and became increasingly realistic as knowledge of plant forms grew (via illustrated pattern books) and methods of printing improved. Also fashionable in the first half of the 18th century were English flock papers styled in imitation of floral-patterned damasks, and Chinese and *chinoiserie* papers that displayed flowering shrubs, roses, chrysanthemums, poppies, peonies and bamboo, often accompanied by exotic birds and insects.

1

2

1 Chameleon/Bayley Arms/**Acanthus** Colour **AND 019** Alt. colours **no** Width **50cm/19½in** Length **10m/11yd** Repeat **50cm/19½in** Price ★

2 Alexander Beauchamp/**Ghintez** Colour **green** Alt. colours **yes** Width **47cm/18½in** Length **10m/11yd** Repeat **47cm/18½in** Price ★★★ 🔲

3 Chameleon/Bayley Arms/**Damask** Colour **AND 009** Alt. colours **yes** Width **53cm/21in** Length **10m/11yd** Repeat **27cm/10½in** Price ★

4 Alexander Beauchamp/**Jacobean** Colour **special** Alt. colours **yes** Width **39cm/15¼in** Length **10m/11yd** Repeat **51cm/20in** Price ★★★ 🔲

5 G.P. & J. Baker/**Solomon's Seal W0087-63** Colour **63** Alt. colours **yes** Width **52cm/20½in** Length **10m/11yd** Repeat **53cm/21in** Price ★

3

4

5

6 Sheila Coombes/Heversham **W614** Colour **2** Alt. colours **yes** Width **53cm/21in** Length **10m/11yd** Repeat **53cm/21in** Price ★★★★

7 Hamilton Weston/Twickenham Colour **document grey, black and white on green** Alt. colours **yes** Width **52cm/20½in** Length **10m/11yd** Repeat **21cm/8¼in** Price ★★★ 🖌

8 Jane Churchill/Florian/Book Eight/Florian Damask **J038W** Colour **02** Alt. colours **yes** Width **52cm/20½in** Length **10m/11yd** Repeat **41cm/16in** Price ★

6

9

7

9 Alexander Beauchamp/Melton Colour **green and white** Alt. colours **yes** Width **44cm/ 17in** Length **10m/11yd** Repeat **72.5cm/28½in** Price ★★★ 🖌

10 Nicholas Herbert/Bradenham **W07** Colour **04 green and cream** Alt. colours **yes** Width **52cm/ 20½in** Length **10m/11yd** Repeat **27cm/10½in** Price ★

11 Zoffany/Padova **DWP3100** Colour **6** Alt. colours **yes** Width **68.5cm/27in** Length **10m/11yd** Repeat **51cm/ 20in** Price ★

12 Brunschwig & Fils/Rêve du Papillon **12473.06** Colour **yellow** Alt. colours **yes** Width **69.5cm/27¼in** Length **4.5m/ 5yd** Repeat **98cm/38¾in** Price ★★★★ 🖌

10

8

11

12

WALLPAPERS: *FLORALS*   **231**

Florals: Late 18th century

Floral-patterned wallpapers, like floral-patterned textiles, were very fashionable in the second half of the 18th century. Chinese and European *chinoiserie* floral papers proved immensely popular, and many other papers displayed imagery that was half-Chinese and half-classical in origin – a typical example would combine oriental peacocks and parrots with classical vases of flowers.

Popular French papers included *papiers marbrés* stencilled with floral patterns, floral flocks made from silk shearings in imitation of silk wall-hangings, floral arabesques (see page 247) and papers with patterns composed of flowers bound with ribbons. Fashionable English papers featured flowers with large petals, flowering bushes and diapered bouquets. Leading designers of the period included Jean-Baptiste Réveillon of France and the Englishman John Baptist Jackson. During this period, many papers by these designers, with others from France and Britain, were exported in large numbers to the increasingly prosperous American colonies.

3

5

4

6

7

1

2

FABRIC IMITATIONS

Many of the floral wallpapers that were produced during the 18th century derived their patterns from contemporary textiles – particularly Chinese silks, French and English printed floral chintzes and, above all, woven damasks and brocades. This is not surprising, given that during this period wallpapers were beginning to be employed as a less expensive alternative to textile wall-hangings in all but the grandest of houses. The paper shown here – a late 18th-century design – is an imitation of a typical stylized, floral-patterned damask (*see* pages 80–81).

Zoffany/Damask V2140 Colour 2 Alt. colours **yes** Width **52cm/20½in** Length **10m/11yd** Repeat **23cm/9in** Price ★

8

1 **Hamilton Weston/Mayfair 404** Colour **green** Alt. colours **yes** Width **52cm/20½in** Length **10m/11yd** Repeat **53cm/21in** Price ★

2 **Jane Churchill/Country Garden/ Book Seven/Rose Toile J026W** Colour **02** Alt. colours **yes** Width **52cm/20½in** Length **10m/11yd** Repeat **17.5cm/ 7in** Price ★

3 **Hamilton Weston/Kew Green Border** Colour **pink, dark turquoise on cream** Alt. colours **yes** Width **6.5cm/2½in** Length **10m/11yd** Repeat **34cm/13⅓in** Price ★★★ ♣

4 **Hamilton Weston/Kew Green** Colour **pink, dark turquoise on cream** Alt. colours **yes** Width **50cm/19½in** Length **10m/11yd** Repeat **34cm/13⅓in** Price ★★★ ♣

5 **Brunschwig & Fils/Suffield Arabesque 15690.06** Colour **white** Alt. colours **yes** Width **57cm/22½in** Length **4.5m/ 5yd** Repeat **55cm/21⅓in** Price ★★★★★ ♣

6 **Zoffany/Qing Trellis WAL0600** Colour **1** Alt. colours **yes** Width **68cm/26¾in** Length **10m/11yd** Repeat **60cm/ 23¾in** Price ★

7 **Brunschwig & Fils/Marianthi 13900.06** Colour **white** Alt. colours **yes** Width **68.5cm/ 27in** Length **4.5m/5yd** Repeat **68.5cm/27in** Price ★★★★★ ♣

8 **Zoffany/Floraison Trail FRW0300** Colour **7** Alt. colours **yes** Width **52cm/20½in** Length **10m/11yd** Repeat **64cm/ 25in** Price ★

9 **Zoffany/Floralie FRW0100**
Colour **4** Alt. colours **yes**
Width **52cm/20½in** Length
10m/11yd Repeat **45.5cm/**
17⅞in Price ★

10 **Zoffany/Tours DK0300** Colour
8 Alt. colours **yes** Width
68.5cm/27in Length **10m/**
11yd Repeat **64cm/25⅛in**
Price ★

11 **Nobilis/Bagatelle** Colour **BGL**
316 Alt. colours **yes** Width
52cm/20½in Length **10m/**
11yd Repeat **52cm/20½in**
Price ★

12 **Nobilis/Bagatelle** Colour **BGL**
325 Alt. colours **yes** Width
52cm/20½in Length **10m/**
11yd Repeat **52cm/20½in**
Price ★

13 **Cole & Son/Paradise Tree 2630**
1003 Colour **3** Alt. colours **yes**
Width **52cm/20½in** Length
10m/11yd Repeat **70cm/**
27½in Price ★

9

14

0

15

14 **Alexander Beauchamp/Genoa**
Colour **yellow** Alt. colours
yes Width **53cm/21in** Length
10m/11yd Repeat **72cm/**
28¼in Price ★★★★ ♣

15 **Cole & Son/Chippendale**
58/1020/PR Colour **gold**
on coral Alt. colours **yes**
Width **52cm/20½in** Length
10m/11yd Repeat **100cm/**
39¼in Price ★★★

16 **Zoffany/French/Bergère**
FWP4200 Colour **5** Alt.
colours **yes** Width **52cm/**
20½in Length **10m/11yd**
Repeat **70cm/27½in**
Price ★

1

12   13   16

Florals: **Early 19th century**

At the beginning of the 19th century, some British, French and American manufacturers produced stylized floral-patterned papers in imitation of fashionable glazed floral chintzes. More popular, however, were the naturalistically depicted floral patterns that had first come into vogue in the classical interiors of the late 18th century. Many of these were also inspired by contemporary textiles, such as elaborate floral-patterned silks.

The tendency to represent flowers in a naturalistic way, as opposed to conventionalizing them, became more marked as the century progressed. Apart from aesthetic considerations, the main factors that fuelled this greater realism were the publication of numerous illustrated botanical studies that provided designers with increasingly accurate reference material, and the development of new mineral dyes, including various oranges and greens, that closely resembled the vivid colours displayed in many natural plant forms. Also playing a part was the ever more sophisticated use of woodblock-printing (*see* opposite) to create subtle shading and "three-dimensionality" within patterns – a quality further, and literally, enhanced on the flocked papers that proved highly desirable during this period.

4 **Hamilton Weston/Kingston Market** Colour **8132** Alt. colours **yes** Width **53cm/ 21in** Length **10m/11yd** Repeat **26.5cm/10½in** Price ★★ ♣

5 **Zoffany/Trianon 77010** Colour **03** Alt. colours **yes** Width **52cm/20½in** Length **10m/ 11yd** Repeat **64cm/25in** Price ★

6 **Colefax and Fowler/Sudbury Park 7046/01** Colour **red on red** Alt. colours **yes** Width **52cm/ 20½in** Length **10m/11yd** Repeat **7.5cm/2¾in** Price ★

4

1 **Hamilton Weston/Covent Garden Floral** Colour **red on red** Alt. colours **yes** Width **52cm/ 20½in** Length **10m/11yd** Repeat **28.5cm/11in** Price ★★

2 **Graham & Brown 51026** Colour **aubergine** Alt. colours **yes** Width **52cm/20½in** Length **10m/11yd** Repeat **53cm/ 21in** Price ★

3 **Zoffany/Tulip Panel 326100** Colour **5** Alt. colours **yes** Width **52cm/20½in** Length **10m/11yd** Repeat **64cm/ 25in** Price ★

1

2

3

5

6

7 **Cole & Son/Sweet Pea**
54/4682/PR Colour **yellow**
Alt. colours **yes** Width **52cm/
20½in** Length **10m/11yd**
Repeat **38cm/15in**
Price ★

8 **Chameleon/Traditional Style/
Sonja** Colour **green** Alt. colours
yes Width **53cm/21in** Length
10m/11yd Repeat **76cm/30in**
Price ★

9 **Hamilton Weston/Hortensia
Border** Colour **document**
Alt. colours **yes** Width
10.5cm/4in Length **5m/
5½yd** Repeat **–** Price ★★ ♕

10

8

9

11

10 **Nobilis/Bagatelle** Colour **BGL
317** Alt. colours **yes** Width
52cm/20½in Length **10m/
11yd** Repeat **52cm/20½in**
Price ★

11 **Hamilton Weston/Fuchsia
St. James** Colour **8155** Alt.
colours **yes** Width **53cm/
21in** Length **10m/11yd**
Repeat **27.5cm/10¾in**
Price ★★ ♕

12 **Chameleon/Traditional Style/
Lucy Anne** Colour **mustard**
Alt. colours **yes** Width **53cm/
21in** Length **6.5m/7yd**
Repeat **50cm/19½in** Price ★

13 **Zoffany/Hopetoun Flower**
77040 Colour **04** Alt. colours
yes Width **52cm/20½in** Length
10m/11yd Repeat **26.5cm/
10½in** Price ★

HAND-BLOCKING

Despite the introduction of hand-
operated cylinder printing in 1764,
and machine-driven roller printing in
the 1830s, the best-quality wallpapers
were those that had been hand-
blocked. The subtle shading, purity
of colour and crispness of detail
evident in this early 19th-century
naturalistic floral border paper
epitomizes traditional hand-
blocking. The hand-blocking process
involves each different colour of the
pattern being allotted an individual
wooden block (bearing part of the
pattern in relief). The blocks are then
skilfully pressed into position one at
a time, each in perfect register with
the previous colour.

Scalamandré/Prestwould Saloon Border WB81504/001 Colour **01** Alt. colours **no** Width **55.5cm/21¾in**
Length **6.5m/7yd** Repeat **110cm/43in** Price ★★ ♕

12

13

Florals: Mid-19th century

Although conventionalized flowers figured in the flat wallpaper patterns of internationally influential designers such as A.W.N. Pugin and Owen Jones around the middle of the 19th century, most of the floral-patterned papers produced during this period were naturalistically depicted, and subsequently given far greater depth either by shading and highlighting, or by flocking. Indeed, many floral designs were rendered realistic almost to the point of caricature. This effect was largely the result of designers favouring large coarse flowers, such as dahlias, hollyhocks and hydrangeas, and of manufacturers printing them with new synthetic aniline dyes that yielded sharp yellows, vivid blues and acid greens of a chemical intensity that did not always reflect the natural colouring of the real blooms and foliage. More authentically realistic were many of the popular "satin" papers made in imitation of floral silk hangings; their silk-like appearance was created by polishing the surface with french chalk.

1 **Hodsoll McKenzie/Dorset Rose 502/607** Colour **red** Alt. colours **yes** Width **52cm/20½in** Length **10m/11yd** Repeat **46cm/18in** Price ★

2 **Nobilis/Bagatelle** Colour **BGL 326** Alt. colours **yes** Width **52cm/20½in** Length **10m/11yd** Repeat **52cm/20½in** Price ★

3 **Cole & Son/Madras Violet 54/4625/PR** Colour **cream ground** Alt. colours **yes** Width **52cm/20½in** Length **10m/11yd** Repeat **53cm/21in** Price ★

4 **Graham & Brown 15559** Colour **pink** Alt. colours **no** Width **52cm/20½in** Length **10m/11yd** Repeat **64cm/25in** Price ★

5 **Graham & Brown 91139** Colour **aubergine** Alt. colours **yes** Width **18cm/7in** Length **10m/11yd** Repeat – Price ★

6 **Nobilis/Volubilis BOR3101** Colour **pink, yellow and green on cream** Alt. colours **yes** Width **23cm/9in** Length **9m/10yd** Repeat **47cm/18½in** Price ★★★ 🪑

7 **Jane Churchill/Country Garden/ Book Seven/Country Rose J023W** Colour **01 red** Alt. colours **yes** Width **52cm/20½in** Length **10m/11yd** Repeat **61cm/24in** Price ★

8 **Colefax and Fowler/Geranium Moiré 7402/01** Colour **coral and aqua** Alt. colours **yes** Width **52cm/20½in** Length **10m/11yd** Repeat **45.5cm/17¾in** Price ★

**9 Laura Ashley/Melrose 023
127** Colour **old rose multi**
Alt. colours **yes** Width **52cm/
20½in** Length **10m/11yd**
Repeat **32cm/12½in**
Price ★

**10 Laura Ashley/Freshford 5255
575** Colour **sapphire** Alt.
colours **yes** Width **13cm/
5in** Length **10m/11yd**
Repeat **13cm/5in**
Price ★

**11 Hodsoll McKenzie/Faded
Bouquet 610/601** Colour
pink Alt. colours **yes** Width
52cm/20½in Length **10m/
11yd** Repeat **61cm/24in**
Price ★

12 Coloroll/Shayla Stripe 26-092
Colour **burgundy** Alt. colours
yes Width **52cm/20½in** Length
10m/11yd Repeat **53cm/21in**
Price ★

13 Crowson/Rosehill/Firle
Colour **15** Alt. colours **yes**
Width **52cm/20½in** Length
10.5m/11½yd Repeat **26cm/
10¼in** Price ★

9

10

11

14

12

15

16

**14 Hamilton Weston/Yellow
Bedroom** Colour **document**
Alt. colours **yes** Width **52cm/
20½in** Length **10m/11yd**
Repeat **54.5cm/21½in**
Price ★★★ ♣

**15 Watts of Westminster/Nimue
W0031** Colour **grant** Alt.
colours **yes** Width **47cm/
18½in** Length **10m/11yd**
Repeat **44cm/17in**
Price ★★

**16 Colefax and Fowler/Camilla
7017/03** Colour **yellow and blue**
Alt. colours **yes** Width **52cm/
20½in** Length **10m/11yd**
Repeat **23cm/9in** Price ★

**17 Chameleon/Bayley Arms/
Cabbage Rose** Colour **AND
017** Alt. colours **yes** Width
53cm/21in Length **10m/
11yd** Repeat **25cm/9¾in**
Price ★

13

17

19th century

Florals: Late 19th century

Naturalistically depicted flowers continued to appear on wallpapers produced during the last 30 years of the 19th century. However, as a reaction to the overblown naturalism of many mid-19th-century papers, conventionalized floral patterns were more in evidence, especially in Arts and Crafts, Aesthetic and Art Nouveau interiors, where they were often employed as the field (filling) in a tripartite (frieze-field-dado) division of the walls. Undoubtedly the most popular were the Arts and Crafts papers of William Morris and his followers. These featured relatively simple flowers, such as poppies, daisies, marigolds and jasmine, hand-blocked with traditional vegetable dyes and contained within formal pattern structures.

Aesthetic papers, notably those by the influential English designer E.W. Godwin (publicized in Britain and America by Charles Eastlake), were also characterized by uncomplicated blooms, such as sunflowers, pinks and the Japanese lotus. Although many were botanically correct, they were generally highly stylized and rather static. These were in marked contrast to the sinuous poppy, wisteria and waterlily patterns of Art Nouveau designers, which, while conventionalized, had a marked rhythmical and sensuous quality.

4

4 Brunschwig & Fils/Kyoto 15908-06 Colour **pongee** Alt. colours **yes** Width **68.5cm/ 27in** Length **4.5m/5yd** Repeat **91.5cm/36in** Price ★★★★★ ♣

5 Cole & Son/Special Block Print/Moss Rose 0139 Colour **dark green** Alt. colours **yes** Width **52cm/20½in** Length **10m/11yd** Repeat **12cm/ 4¾in** Price ★★★★★ ♣

6 Cole & Son/Dennis Hall/Pelham 63/7045 Colour **caramel** Alt. colours **yes** Width **52cm/20½in** Length **10m/11yd** Repeat **30.5cm/12in** Price ★★★★★

1

2

1 Colefax and Fowler/Bowood 7401/04 Colour **yellow and blue** Alt. colours **yes** Width **52cm/20½in** Length **10m/11yd** Repeat **30cm/11¾in** Price ★

2 Watts of Westminster/Sunflower W0055-01/P12 Colour **Xanthe** Alt. colours **yes** Width **54cm/21½in** Length **10m/11yd** Repeat **52cm/20½in** Price ★★

3 Colefax and Fowler/Rose Damask 7407/03 Colour **yellow** Alt. colours **yes** Width **52cm/20½in** Length **10m/11yd** Repeat **61cm/24in** Price ★

3

5

6

Alexander Beauchamp/Oleander Trellis 161/20 Colour **multi** Alt. colours **yes** Width **47cm/18½in** Length **10m/11yd** Repeat **46cm/18in** Price ★★★★ ♧

Laura Ashley/Victoria Border 187 187 Colour **burgundy and stone** Alt. colours **yes** Width **13cm/5in** Length **10m/11yd** Repeat **13cm/5in** Price ★

7

8

9 **Graham & Brown/51022** Colour **aubergine** Alt. colours **yes** Width **52cm/20½in** Length **10m/11yd** Repeat **53cm/21in** Price ★

10 **Zoffany/Cottage Flowers WAL0300** Colour **4** Alt. colours **yes** Width **52cm/20½in** Length **10m/11yd** Repeat – Price ★

11 **Elizabeth Eaton/Chinese Poppy** Colour **blue and cream** Alt. colours **yes** Width **57cm/22½in** Length **10m/11yd** Repeat **47cm/18½in** Price ★★★ ♧

12 **Bradbury & Bradbury/Antique Rose Panels ARP-550** Colour **550** Alt. colours **yes** Width **69cm/27in** Length **14m/15¼yd** Repeat **48cm/19in** Price ★★★★ ♧

10

LINCRUSTA & ANAGLYPTA

Lincrusta was developed in 1877 by Frederick Walton, the inventor of linoleum. Made of linseed oil, gum, resins and wood-pulp spread over canvas, its surface was embossed with patterns produced by engraved metal rollers. Waterproof and durable, Lincrusta could be painted, stained or gilded to simulate traditional relief mouldings of wood, plaster, leather or tiles. A cheaper and lighter alternative – Anaglypta – was invented in 1886 by Thomas Palmer. Made from cotton fibre-pulp, its relief patterns were created by hollow moulding. Lincrusta and Anaglypta remain in demand in the 21st century, with both traditional and modern designs still being produced.

IHDG/Italian Renaissance RD1952 Colour **white** Alt. colours **no** Width **52cm/20½in** Length **102cm/40in** Repeat **102cm/40in** Price ★★★ ㄖ

11

12

Florals: Early 20th century

Numerous floral-patterned wallpapers were manufactured during the first half of the 20th century. Designs included the stylized, long-stemmed lilies and poppies that were featured on Art Nouveau papers, and the cup-shaped blossoms favoured by the Deutscher Werkbund. Bizarre, dusty-coloured "magic flowers", with elongated, lancet-shaped leaves and slender blossoms, were characteristic of later Wiener Werkstätte papers, while Arts and Crafts floral patterns (*see* pages 238–239) retained their popularity from the previous century. Roses, daisies and dahlias were also among the floral motifs preferred in Art Deco interiors, their round heads stylized in a two-dimensional fashion, strongly outlined, densely packed and often presented in baskets, festoons or garlands.

Floral-patterned papers featured in early 20th-century interiors inspired by 18th-century French decoration, and took the form of fields in imitation of floral damasks, topped by friezes of swagged roses and ribbons, or of combined friezes and fields in which roses or wisteria cascaded down the wall. The "English country-house" look (fashionable in both Britain and America) also gave rise to many designs based on 18th- and 19th-century floral chintz patterns.

1 **Chameleon/Art Deco/Fleur** Colour **red on gold** Alt. colours **yes** Width **53cm/21in** Length **10m/11yd** Repeat **26cm/10¼in** Price ★

2 **Colefax and Fowler/Jessica 7403/01** Colour **yellow and blue** Alt. colours **yes** Width **52cm/20½in** Length **10m/11yd** Repeat **22.5cm/8¾in** Price ★

3 **Mauny/Bouquets** Colour **document** Alt. colours **yes** Width **55cm/21½in** Length **10m/11yd** Repeat **19cm/7½in** Price ★★★★ 🖌

4 **Baer & Ingram/Cottage Rose** Colour **yellow** Alt. colours **yes** Width **52cm/20½in** Length **10m/11yd** Repeat **26.5cm/10½in** Price ★★★★

2

3

4

5 **Bradbury & Bradbury/Honeysuckle** Colour **HSW-900** Alt. colours **yes** Width **68.5cm/27in** Length **4.5m/5yd** Repeat **40cm/15¾in** Price ★★ 🖌

6 **Colefax and Fowler/Lydia 7611/02** Colour **yellow and sage** Alt. colours **yes** Width **52cm/20¼in** Length **10m/11yd** Repeat **4.5cm/1¾in** Price ★

7 **Jane Churchill/Tulip Sprig JY67W-02** Colour **blue on white** Alt. colours **yes** Width **52cm/20½in** Length **10m/11yd** Repeat **13cm/5in** Price ★

8 **Bradbury & Bradbury/Thistle Wall** Colour **THW-970** Alt. colours **yes** Width **68.5cm/27in** Length **to order** Repeat **53cm/21in** Price ★★ 🖌

5

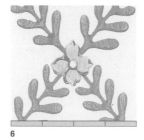

6

7

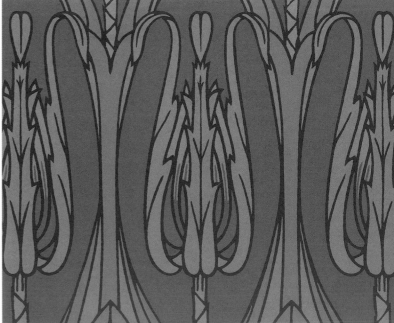

8

9 **Mauny/Tarterres 5044** Colour **document** Alt. colours **yes** Width **47cm/18½in** Length **10m/11yd** Repeat **68cm/ 26¾in** Price ★★★★ ♣

10 **Bradbury & Bradbury/Glasgow Panel** Colour **GWP-970** Alt. colours **yes** Width **68.5cm/ 27in** Length **2m/2⅛yd** Repeat **–** Price ★★★ ♣

11 **Jane Churchill/Country Garden/ Book Seven/Sweet Pea Sprig J025W** Colour **02** Alt. colours **yes** Width **52cm/20½in** Length **10m/11yd** Repeat **26cm/10¼in** Price ★

12 **Laura Ashley/Freshford Border 5094 677** Colour **pumpkin multi nutmeg** Alt. colours **yes** Width **13cm/5in** Length **10m/11yd** Repeat **13cm/5in** Price ★

13 **Mulberry/Honeysuckle FG036** Colour **soft gold T106** Alt. colours **yes** Width **52cm/ 20½in** Length **10m/11yd** Repeat **41cm/16in** Price ★

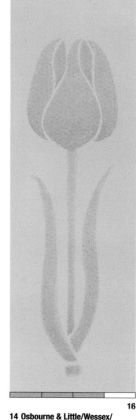

16

14 **Osbourne & Little/Wessex/ Buckton W1500** Colour **01** Alt. colours **yes** Width **52cm/ 20½in** Length **10m/11yd** Repeat **36cm/14in** Price ★

15 **Sanderson/Rose and Peony WR7670** Colour **1** Alt. colours **yes** Width **53cm/21in** Length **10.5m/11½yd** Repeat **53cm/ 21in** Price ★

16 **Crowson/Mackintosh Irvine** Colour **65** Alt. colours **yes** Width **52cm/20½in** Length **10m/11yd** Repeat **53cm/ 21in** Price ★

10

14

1

12

13

15

Florals: Late 20th–early 21st century

The years following the Second World War were characterized by innovative designs as much as by period ones. Frequently seen during the 1950s were large and flamboyantly coloured tropical flowers and, for feature walls, photo-engraved prints of single fantasy flowers; or screen-printed, freely spaced flowers embellished with metallic highlights and displayed on dark grounds. Floral damask and *chinoiserie* patterns were also fashionable, but often recoloured, rescaled and applied over textured grounds – brown, grey or pink flowers on white grass cloth being a typical example.

In the 1960s, Victorian sprigs and floral trails and sinuous Art Nouveau designs vied with sketchily realistic blooms and simplified flowers in bold, bright hues – the latter superseded during the romanticism of the mid-1970s by chalkily rendered, tiny floral repeats. Since the early 1980s there has been a significant growth of interest in documentary floral papers dating from the late Renaissance to the early 20th century; 18th- and 19th-century floral chintz patterns regained appeal (having fallen out of favour from 1945 until the late 1970s). More recently, bright, impressionistic floral designs – inspired by painters such as Monet and Matisse – have come into vogue.

Laura Ashley/Natile 3162 591 Colour **plum and lavender** Alt. colours **yes** Width **52cm/20½in** Length **10m/11yd** Repeat **32cm/12½in** Price ★★★

Jane Churchill/Country Garden/Book Seven/Rose Sprig J024W Colour **02** Alt. colours **yes** Width **52cm/20½in** Length **10m/11yd** Repeat **26.5cm/10½in** Price ★

Designers Guild/Quite Contrary Colour **orange** Alt. colours **yes** Width **52cm/20½in** Length **10m/11yd** Repeat **52cm/20½in** Price ★

Anna French/Eden/Decadence Colour **DECNW024** Alt. colours **yes** Width **52cm/20½in** Length **10m/11yd** Repeat **46cm/18in** Price ★

Brunschwig & Fils/Johanna 16140.06 Colour **ivory** Alt. colours **yes** Width **68.5cm/27in** Length **4.5m/5yd** Repeat **129cm/50¾in** Price ★★★★★ ♣

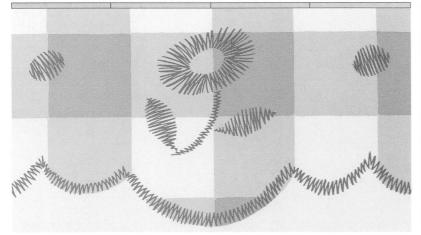

Baer & Ingram/Daisy Border DSB16 Colour **blue** Alt. colours **yes** Width **10cm/4in** Length **10m/11yd** Repeat **9cm/3½in** Price ★

Coloroll/Life Border 355410 Colour **lilac** Alt. colours **yes** Width **13cm/5in** Length **5m/5½yd** Repeat **53cm/21in** Price ★

Nina Campbell/Zembla/Kiku NCW 2226 Colour **08** Alt. colours **yes** Width **52cm/20½in** Length **10m/11yd** Repeat **61cm/24in** Price ★

Anna French/T for Teddy/Rosebud Colour **ROSWP071** Alt. colours **yes** Width **52cm/20½in** Length **10m/11yd** Repeat **15cm/6in** Price ★

Anna French/Eden/Japonica Colour **JAPWP025** Alt. colours **yes** Width **52cm/20½in** Length **10m/11yd** Repeat **61cm/24in** Price ★

Anna French/Isolde Colour **ISOWP063** Alt. colours **yes** Width **52cm/20½in** Length **10m/11yd** Repeat **61cm/24in** Price ★

Baer & Ingram/Cornflower CFW06 Colour **blue** Alt. colours **yes** Width **52cm/20½in** Length **10m/11yd** Repeat **53cm/21in** Price ★★★★

Baer & Ingram/Rambling Rose RMW06 Colour **blue** Alt. colours **yes** Width **52cm/20½in** Length **10m/11yd** Repeat **53cm/21in** Price ★★★★

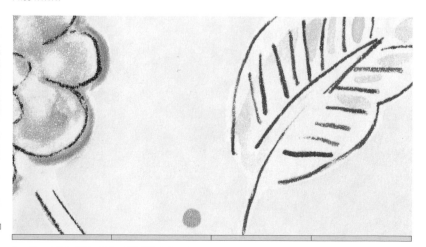

Nina Campbell/Rosenkavalier/Rosenkavalier NCW 2230 Colour **04** Alt. colours **yes** Width **52cm/20½in** Length **10m/11yd** Repeat **72cm/28½in** Price ★

Anna French/Eden/Chinoiserie Colour **CHIWP032** Alt. colours **yes** Width **52cm/20½in** Length **10m/11yd** Repeat **76cm/30in** Price ★

Anna French/Ming Stripe Colour **MINWP069** Alt. colours **yes** Width **52cm/20½in** Length **10m/11yd** Repeat **76cm/30in** Price ★

Pictorial wallpapers were first documented in 1481, when Louis XI paid Jean Bourdichon to paint 50 rolls of paper blue, and to add a Latin inscription held by three painted angels. Coloured papers with pictures of religious and allegorical subjects were also used in Europe during the 16th and 17th centuries. However, it was not until the 18th century that pictorial wallpapers were produced in quantity – many inspired by Chinese wall-hangings.

In England, John Baptist Jackson was the first to use papers in imitation of architectural features, but the finest pictorial papers were hand-printed in France during the late 18th and early 19th century, notably by paper-stainers such as Boulgard, Réveillon, Zuber and Dufour. Many of these papers were exported to Britain and America where, because of their high cost, they firmly remained as the preserve of the wealthy. The introduction of the cylinder-printing process in the 1850s then made possible the manufacture of mass-produced pictorials at more affordable prices thereafter.

LEFT A mid-19th-century Zuber pictorial wallpaper, hung in the Monmouth Mansion, in Natchez, Mississippi, USA. Never having visited America, the French designer painted this scene from his imagination, with Mississippi steamboats at Niagara Falls, Spanish moss at the Boston Tea Party and Native Americans in African dress.

ABOVE Hand-painted *c.* 1830, this paper uses images from the first volume of Audubon's *Birds of America* (1827); a facsimile was hung at Temple Newsam, England, in 1927.

PRINT ROOMS

The fashion for decorating rooms with prints pasted over painted walls originated in the mid-18th century. Many print rooms featured black-and-white prints and borders simply pasted in rows; others, such as those designed by Thomas Chippendale, were more flamboyant and incorporated *trompe l'oeil* paper cut-outs of swags, garlands, bows and chains "supporting" and embellishing the prints. This decorative convention continued well into the 19th century and has recently enjoyed a revival, with books of prints and borders being specifically designed for the purpose.

KEY DESIGNS

1 Human figures engaged in activities as diverse as military battles, hunting, shooting, harvesting, trading, sailing and taking tea have proved popular subject matter for pictorial papers.

2 *Trompe l'oeil* papers produced in imitation of luxuriously swagged, tailed and pleated textile hangings were often employed in grander late 18th- and early 19th-century Neo-classical interiors.

3 *Chinoiserie*-patterned papers were fashionable during the 18th century and early 19th. Much of the imagery was heavily Europeanized by designers who had only scant knowledge of the Orient.

4 Imported Chinese papers and artefacts provided much of the inspiration for bird motifs during the 17th and 18th centuries. Audubon's *Birds of America* (1827) was extremely influential in the 19th century.

5 Pictorial papers with naturalistic "still life" images of fruit and foliage were popular in the late 18th and mid-19th century, and have enjoyed a revival in the late 20th and early 21st century.

6 Nursery motifs were first introduced during the late 19th century. Subjects have included characters from children's tales and nursery rhymes and, since the late 1940s, from films and television.

1 Lewis & Wood/Vauxhall Gardens LW09 Colour **azure** Alt. colours **yes** Width **52cm/20½in** Length **10m/11yd** Repeat **53cm/21in** Price ★

2 Hamilton Weston/Regency Swag Border Colour **yellow and umber** Alt. colours **yes** Width **32cm/12½in** Length **to order** Repeat **24cm/9½in** Price ★★ ♣

3 Scalamandré/Ch'in Ling WP81212-10 Colour **old gold and bark on lacquer red** Alt. colours **yes** Width **61cm/24in** Length **5.5m/6yd** Repeat **96.5cm/38in** Price ★★★ ♣

4 Cole & Son/Humming Birds Colour **white** Alt. colours **yes** Width **52cm/20½in** Length **10m/11yd** Repeat **53cm/21in** Price ★★

5 Brunschwig & Fils/Bartlett 16043-06 Colour **gold** Alt. colours **yes** Width **68.5cm/27in** Length **4.5m/5yd** Repeat **64cm/25in** Price ★★★★★ ♣

6 Paper Moon/Peter Rabbit Border BPC 13045 Colour **sky** Alt. colours **yes** Width **16.5cm/6½in** Length **5m/5½yd** Repeat **24cm/9½in** Price ★ ⊞

Pictorials: **Pre-19th century**

Many pictorial papers of the 16th century and early 17th depicted subject matter similar to that of pictorial tapestries, including figures emblematic of the four seasons surrounded by coats-of-arms, hunting scenes, and characters and events from Christian history and classical mythology. Imported Chinese pictorial papers also became fashionable during the late 17th century. Typical patterns included landscapes of naturalistic flowering plants and trees; rivers and pools and exotic birds and insects; architectural images; and oriental figures engaged in diverse activities – both urban and rural, secular and religious.

These Chinese papers provided the inspiration for the European *chinoiserie* pictorials that proved popular throughout the 18th century, especially in Rococo interiors. Equally fashionable, however, were *chiaroscuro*-printed imitations of fine art (notably the paintings of Titian and Tintoretto) and of Graeco-Roman statuary and architecture. Also liked in the latter part of the century were French arabesques inspired by Roman wall paintings, Gothic ruins and exceptionally large panoramas or "panoramic papers" of subject matter as varied as the Grand Tour, the exploration of the South Pacific, *fêtes galantes* and scenes from the French Revolution.

4

1

1 **Laura Ashley/Toile 1635 150** Colour **delphinium** Alt. colours **yes** Width **52cm/20½in** Length **10m/11yd** Repeat **53cm/21in** Price ★

2 **Zoffany/Réveillon Landscape 81004** Colour **04** Alt. colours **yes** Width **53cm/21in** Length **10m/11yd** Repeat **98cm/38¼in** Price ★★

3 **Timney Fowler/Sphinx Border** Colour **black** Alt. colours **no** Width **11cm/4¼in** Length **10m/11yd** Repeat **61cm/24in** Price ★

4 **Scalamandré/Pillement Toile** Colour **4** Alt. colours **yes** Width **69cm/27in** Length **4.5m/5yd** Repeat **69cm/27in** Price ★★★

5 **Lewis & Wood/Print Room** Colour **legume** Alt. colours **yes** Width **52cm/20½in** Length **10m/11yd** Repeat **60cm/23¾in** Price ★★★★★

6 **Nobilis/L'Arbre Nantais** Colour **red on cream** Alt. colours **yes** Width **55cm/21½in** Length **10m/11yd** Repeat **75cm/29½in** Price ★

2

3

5

6

7 **Baer & Ingram/Summertime Toile SMW06** Colour **mid blue** Alt. colours **yes** Width **52cm/20½in** Length **10m/ 11yd** Repeat **53cm/21in** Price ★★★★

8 **Cole & Son/Les Enfants Des Enfants 53/6074** Colour **parchment** Alt. colours **yes** Width **52cm/20½in** Length **10m/11yd** Repeat **53cm/ 21in** Price ★★

9 **Schumacher/Jungle Kingdom 519011** Colour **document** Alt. colours **yes** Width **68.5cm/ 27in** Length **4m/4½yd** Repeat **93cm/36in** Price ★★

7

8

9

10

10 **Alexander Beauchamp/Hunting Scene** Colour **multi** Alt. colours **yes** Width **50cm/19½in** Length **10m/11yd** Repeat **39.5cm/15½in** Price ★★★★ ♣

11 **Zoffany/Réveillon Mini 8515004** Colour **04** Alt. colours **yes** Width **52cm/20½in** Length **10.5m/11½yd** Repeat **46cm/ 18in** Price ★

12 **Brunschwig & Fils/Yunnan 69344** Colour **190 cinnabar** Alt. colours **yes** Width **68.5cm/27in** Length **10.5m/11½yd** Repeat **182cm/71¾in** Price ★★★ ♣

13 **Hamilton Weston/Lambeth Saracen** Colour **8116** Alt. colours **yes** Width **51.5cm/ 20¼in** Length **10m/11yd** Repeat **20cm/8in** Price ★★ ♣

14 **De Gournay/Askew J-018** Colour **verdigris** Alt. colours **yes** Width **91cm/35¾in** Length **2.5m/2¾yd** Repeat – Price ★★★★★ ♣

11

12

13

ARABESQUES

The term "arabesque" refers to the stylized, interlaced foliage patterns derived from Islamic art. These patterns were introduced to Europe in the engraved metalwork of Muslim craftsmen, who emigrated to Venice during the 15th century, and they subsequently appeared on wallpapers from the 17th century to the early 21st.

In the 18th century, however, arabesques acquired an additional meaning: French designers used the term to describe grotesque patterns, based on Roman wall-paintings, which incorporated figures, vases, bandwork, flowers and scrolling foliage.

Zuber/Documents V/Sully 2402N Colour **black** Alt. colours **yes** Width **47cm/ 18¼in** Length **10m/11yd** Repeat **46cm/18in** Price ★★★

14

Pictorials: Early 19th century

The French panoramics produced during the late 18th century (*see* page 246) became even more popular during the early 19th century, although few were exported until the end of the Napoleonic wars in 1815. Apart from *chinoiserie* designs (*see* opposite), fashionable subject matter included classical deities (in *chiaroscuro*); views of English, European and American cities, monuments and landscapes; hunting and horseracing scenes; wars and battles; and episodes from literature.

Also widespread in the early 19th century were religious pictures portrayed in *grisaille,* and paper friezes designed in imitation of stucco work and sculpture depicting ancient Greek or Roman figures, legends and architectural elements. Of special note were the hand-blocked *trompe l'oeil* papers (*see* right), of mostly French manufacture, that simulated silk and velvet hangings realistically swagged and tailed, pleated or button-backed, and often embellished with decorative *passements,* such as cords, braids and tassels.

1

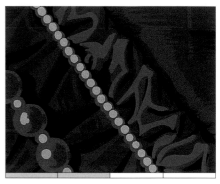

2

1 **Zoffany/Empire Damask 36ED** Colour **05** Alt. colours **yes** Width **52cm/20½in** Length **10m/11yd** Repeat **46cm/18in** Price ★

2 **Brunschwig & Fils/Vaison 15760.06** Colour **sand** Alt. colours **yes** Width **68.5cm/27in** Length **4.5m/5yd** Repeat **46.5cm/18¼in** Price ★★★★ 👑

3 **Brunschwig & Fils/Bunny Business 15892-06** Colour **bluebell** Alt. colours **yes** Width **68.5cm/27in** Length **4.5m/5yd** Repeat **68.5cm/27in** Price ★★

3

TROMPE L'OEIL

A characteristic of many pictorial wallpaper designs produced for Neo-classical interiors of the early 19th century was an enhanced use of perspective. The realistic three-dimensional effect created by these *trompe l'oeil* papers, such as the pleated textile (right) and the Greek frieze (below), was primarily achieved by strengthening both the shadows and the highlights in the pattern.

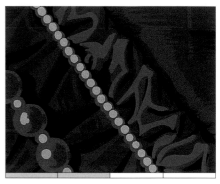

Zuber/Document IV/Eugénie 9013 Colour **rouge** Alt. colours **yes** Width **47cm/18½in** Length **9m/10yd** Repeat **66.5cm/26¼in** Price ★★★

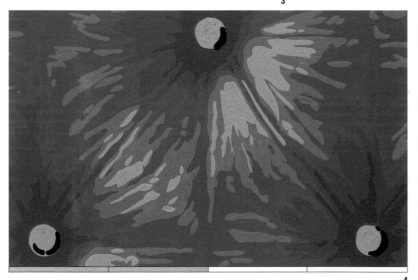

4

4 **Zuber/Document V/Capiton 30023** Colour **rouge** Alt. colours **yes** Width **47cm/18½in** Length **10m/11yd** Repeat **20cm/8in** Price ★★★★

5 **Zuber/Bordures VII/Bordure Draperie Empire 20047** Colour **vert** Alt. colours **yes** Width **34cm/13½in** Length **10m/11yd** Repeat **47cm/18½in** Price ★★★★★

5

Scalamandré/Prestwould Saloon Dado WB81504 Colour **document** Alt. colours **yes** Width **53cm/21in** Length **6.3m/7yd** Repeat – Price ★★ 👑

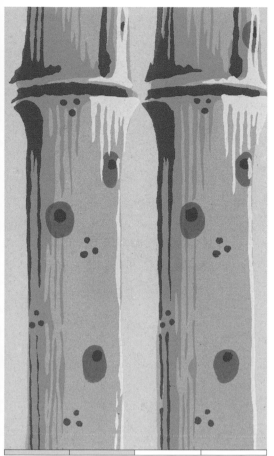

7

6

8

PANORAMIC DESIGNS

During the first half of the 19th century, panoramic wallpapers were very fashionable on both sides of the Atlantic. Some papers were prodigiously large (up to 16m/52½ft long by 3m/10ft high), and the drops were designed to be placed in sequence around the four walls of a room. Some panoramic designs were so complicated that their production required up to 1,500 separate printing blocks. Especially desirable were *chinoiserie* designs, depicting scenes of everyday life in China, and landscapes populated with flowering trees and exotic birds, butterflies and insects.

6 Alexander Beauchamp/Regency Bamboo Border Colour **multi** Alt. colours **yes** Width **16.5cm/ 6½in** Length **10m/11yd** Repeat **68.5cm/27in** Price ★★★★★ ♠

7 Zuber 2369 Colour **blue** Alt. colours **yes** Width **53cm/ 21in** Length **10m/11yd** Repeat **70cm/27½in** Price ★★★ ♠

8 Coloroll/Pitcairn Border 750079 Colour **green** Alt. colours **yes** Width **17cm/6¾in** Length **5m/5½yd** Repeat **53cm/ 21in** Price ★

9 Brunschwig & Fils/Parc de Vincennes 69333 Colour **967 charcoal** Alt. colours **yes** Width **76cm/30in** Length **10m/11yd** Repeat **64cm/ 25in** Price ★

9

De Gournay/Coutts Colour **antique finish** Alt. colours **yes** Width **91.5cm/36in** Length **3.5m/3¾yd** Repeat – Price ★★★★★ (hand-painted) ⊞

De Gournay/Coutts Colour **painted paper** Alt. colours **yes** Width **91.5cm/36in** Length **3.5m/3¾yd** Repeat – Price ★★★★★ (hand-painted) ⊞

De Gournay/Earlham J040 Colour **dark blue** Alt. colours **yes** Width **91.5cm/36in** Length **3.5m/3¾yd** Repeat – Price ★★★★★ (hand-painted) ⊞

19th century

Pictorials: Late 19th century

During the second half of the 19th century, the development of roller-printing and the introduction of new synthetic dyes made it much easier for wallpaper manufacturers on both sides of the Atlantic to produce sophisticated but reasonably inexpensive pictorial patterns. The favoured subject matter was diverse. Notable designs included three-dimensional depictions of animals, flowers, fruits and other plant forms – many indigenous to Europe and America, but others derived from more exotic *chinoiserie*, *japonaiserie*, and Indian and African imagery. Rural landscapes, scenes from industry and commemorative pictorials of significant military and political events also proved successful. Particularly fashionable in the various Classical Revival interiors of grander European and American homes were *trompe l'oeil* simulations of architectural elements, such as statuary, pillars, plaster mouldings and wood carvings. Favoured pictorial papers in Gothic Revival houses, on the other hand, were generally flatter-patterned and incorporated mMedieval imagery ranging from Gothic-arched windows with elaborate tracery to beasts-of-the-field, all invariably augmented with stylized or naturalistic plant forms, or with heraldic motifs, such as emblems and coats-of-arms.

1 Warner Fabrics/Temples of Antiquity Colour **cream** Alt. colours **yes** Width **52cm/ 20½in** Length **10m/11yd** Repeat **41cm/16in** Price ★

2 Morris & Co/Fruit WR8048 Colour **1** Alt. colours **yes** Width **53cm/21in** Length **10.5m/11½yd** Repeat **54cm/21½in** Price ★

3 Watts of Westminster/Bird Colour **blue** Alt. colours **yes** Width **64cm/25in** Length **10m/11yd** Repeat **59cm/ 23in** Price ★★

4 Bradbury & Bradbury/ Pomegranate Panel Colour **410** Alt. colours **yes** Width **68.5cm/ 27in** Length **to order** Repeat **68.5cm/27in** Price ★★★ 🖌

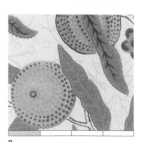

5 Brunschwig & Fils/Bartlett 16043-06 Colour **gold** Alt. colours **yes** Width **68.5cm/ 27in** Length **4.5m/5yd** Repeat **64cm/25in** Price ★★★★★ 🖌

6 Morris & Co/Trellis Colour **document** Alt. colours **no** Width **53cm/21in** Length **10.5m/11½yd** Repeat – Price ★★★★ 🖌

7 Bradbury & Bradbury/Lion and Dove Frieze LDF Colour **001** Alt. colours **no** Width **67cm/ 26¼in** Length **to order** Repeat **117cm/46in** Price ★★★★★ 🖌

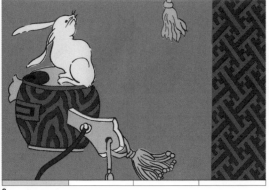

8

9

11

10

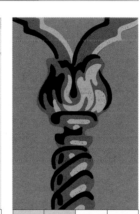

12

13

8 **Brunschwig & Fils/Shimo 15414.06** Colour **green** Alt. colours **yes** Width **64cm/ 25in** Length **4.5m/5yd** Repeat **64cm/25in** Price ★★★

9 **Coloroll/Perfume Bottle Border 37375** Colour **beige** Alt. colours **yes** Width **17cm/ 6¾in** Length **5m/5½yd** Repeat **53cm/21in** Price ★

10 **Alexander Beauchamp/Etienne Frieze** Colour **multi** Alt. colours **yes** Width **53.5cm/21in** Length **10m/11yd** Repeat **25.5cm/10in** Price ★★★★ ♙

11 **Beaumont & Fletcher/Aubusson Rose** Colour **rose and duck egg** Alt. colours **yes** Width **52cm/ 20½in** Length **10m/11yd** Repeat **53.5cm/21in** Price ★★

12 **Sandberg/Altea 956** Colour **06** Alt. colours **yes** Width **3.5cm/1⅛in** Length **10m/ 11yd** Repeat **13.5cm/5¼in** Price ★

13 **Alexander Beauchamp/Moorish Dado** Colour **multi** Alt. colours **yes** Width **47cm/18½in** Length **10m/11yd** Repeat **56.5cm/22¼in** Price ★★★★★ ♙

CEILING PAPERS

Many wallpapers designed specifically for use on ceilings and adjacent cornices were made during the 19th century, and these were widely employed in Classical Revival interiors. As a result of new printing techniques, many examples, especially those of French origin, were sophisticated in terms of colour and shading – qualities exploited to produce *trompe l'oeil* simulations of both floral and faunal imagery, as well as plasterwork moulding, such as fan- and star-shaped roses and geometrical strapwork.

Bradbury & Bradbury/Renaissance Dado RED Colour **550** Alt. colours **yes** Width **68.5cm/ 27in** Length **4.5m/5yd** Repeat **68.5cm/27in** Price ★★★★ ♙

Bradbury & Bradbury/Gossamer Ceiling GSC Colour **610** Alt. colours **yes** Width **68.5cm/27in** Length **4.5m/5yd** Repeat **68.5cm/27in** Price ★★ ♙

Detail of an American Italianate or Second-Empire ceiling. Individual papers include a scrolling foliage Renaissance frieze, Italianate borders and Roman corner fans.

Pictorials: **Early 20th century**

Scenic wallpapers similar to those produced in early 19th-century France enjoyed a revival during the early 20th century, especially in America. Subject matter was diverse and ranged from horseracing to views of important cities and monuments, with woodland and hunting scenes favoured in dining rooms and seascapes appearing in bathrooms. Imitations of both medieval and Renaissance narrative tapestries also proved understandably popular in Arts and Crafts, Tudor and Jacobean Revival interiors.

Apart from nursery papers (*see* opposite), other pictorial-patterned wallpapers of note included designs inspired by 18th-century *chinoiserie* papers, Egyptian desert imagery, and exotic wild animals from the jungles and plains of central and southern Africa. In the 1940s, fine art exerted a strong influence, with manufacturers offering screen-printed mural copies of works by artists such as Henri Matisse, Jean Miró and Raphael, including the latter's decorations for the Loggia of the Vatican.

Osborne & Little/Jester Border B1210/05 Colour **yellow, red and blue** Alt. colours **yes** Width **13cm/5in** Length **10m/11yd** Repeat – Price ★

Scalamandré/Akbar's Stable WP81542-1 Colour **1** Alt. colours **yes** Width **70cm/27½in** Length **4.5m/5yd** Repeat **70cm/27½in** Price ★★★★

Osborne & Little/Toad Hall W1199-03 Colour **green** Alt. colours **yes** Width **52cm/20½in** Length **10m/11yd** Repeat **72cm/28¼in** Price ★★

Sandberg/Felicia 936 Colour **24** Alt. colours **yes** Width **10.5cm/4in** Length **10m/11yd** Repeat **32cm/12½in** Price ★

Mauny/Les Singes 5042 Colour **multi** Alt. colours **yes** Width **47cm/18½in** Length **10m/11yd** Repeat **52cm/20½in** Price ★★★★ ♣

Cole & Son/Pagoda 63/2010 Colour **tomato** Alt. colours **yes** Width **52cm/20½in** Length **10m/11yd** Repeat **61cm/24in** Price ★

20th century

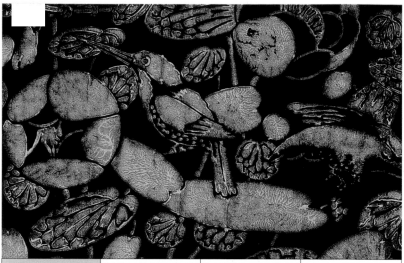

Mulberry/Flights of Fantasy FG034 Colour **F108** Alt. colours **yes** Width **52cm/20½in** Length **10m/11yd** Repeat **53cm/21in** Price ★

Sandberg/Felicia 936 Colour **25** Alt. colours **yes** Width **10.5cm/4in** Length **10m/11yd** Repeat **32cm/12½in** Price ★

Mauny/Martin Pêcheur 5035 Colour **multi** Alt. colours **yes** Width **47cm/18½in** Length **10m/11yd** Repeat **62cm/24¼in** Price ★★★ ♣

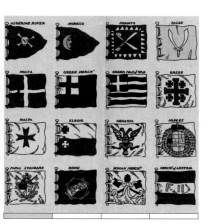

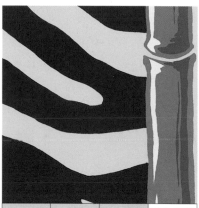

Mulberry/Naval Ensigns FG028/569 Colour **V113** Alt. colours **yes** Width **52cm/20½in** Length **10m/11yd** Repeat **59.5cm/23½in** Price ★

Marthe Armitage/Willow Pattern Colour **multi** Alt. colours **yes** Width **53cm/21in** Length **10m/11yd** Repeat **42cm/16½in** Price ★

Mauny/Chinoiseries 5059 Colour **multi** Alt. colours **yes** Width **47cm/18½in** Length **10m/11yd** Repeat **47cm/18½in** Price ★★★★ ♣

Nobilis/Zèbre et Léopard Colour **BOR2901 black and white** Alt. colours **yes** Width **16cm/6¼in** Length **10m/11yd** Repeat – Price ★★ ♣

NURSERY PAPERS

Pictorial wallpapers designed specifically for children's rooms first appeared in the late 19th century, when leading illustrators of the time (including Walter Crane, Kate Greenaway and Mabel Attwell) devised patterns based on children's stories and nursery rhymes. While the nursery-paper genre was established in the 19th century, it proliferated in the 20th century. Some early 20th-century designs, notably those based on the tales of Beatrix Potter and cartoon characters such as Mickey Mouse™, are still very popular today and compete with subject matter as diverse as soldiers, aeroplanes, vintage cars, farm animals, humorous vegetables and famous film and television characters.

Osborne & Little/Lords and Ladies B1211/02 Colour **blue** Alt. colours **yes** Width **13cm/5in** Length **10m/11yd** Repeat – Price ★

Nobilis/Borders No. 4/Fanny Colour **BOR2102** Alt. colours **no** Width **26cm/10¼in** Length **10m/11yd** Repeat – Price ★★★ ♣

Pictorials: **Late 20th–early 21st century**

The revival of mural wallpapers that took place in the early 19th century has been largely sustained to the present day. However, there have been some significant changes of style and content that reflect the developments in both urban and rural life, and in printing techniques. For example, in America during the 1950s and 1960s fashionable photomurals showed subjects as diverse as the high-rise New York skyline, groups of commuting office workers, and Highway 66 winding its way through its desert landscape. Similarly, the Pop Art and Op Art of the 1960s was readily translated on to visually dramatic still-life pictorial papers.

Nursery papers have also been produced in increasing quantities in the late 20th and early 21st century. Many are photogravure murals designed to cover modern flush doors ("photodoors") in a child's bedroom, and, while some of the subject matter, such as the tales of Beatrix Potter, "life on the farm", Thomas the Tank Engine™ and Disney's Mickey Mouse™, is as popular today as it was earlier in the century, the genre has constantly accommodated new characters – familiar comic-book and cartoon figures including Barbie™, Action Man™, The Simpsons™ and Buzz Lightyear™ being very popular.

4

1

2

1 Crowson/Elephant Border
Colour **10** Alt. colours **yes**
Width **17.5cm/7in** Length
10m/11yd Repeat **17cm/
6¾in** Price ★★

**2 Nina Campbell/Ferronier/
Mirari NCW2195** Colour
04 Alt. colours **yes** Width
52cm/20½in Length **10m/
11yd** Repeat **72cm/28⅓in**
Price ★

3 Vymura/Teddies Border 29616B
Colour **natural medium** Alt.
colours **no** Width **26cm/
10¼in** Length **10m/11yd**
Repeat – Price ★

**4 Marthe Armitage/Italian
Garden** Colour **black and
white** Alt. colours **yes** Width
59cm/23in Length **10m/
11yd** Repeat **42cm/16½in**
Price ★

**5 Vymura/Thomas The Tank
Engine™ Border 19107**
Colour **multi** Alt. colours
no Width **17.5cm/7in** Length
10m/11yd Repeat – Price ★

**6 Baer & Ingram/Country Living/
Kitchen Garden KTW01** Colour
natural Alt. colours **no** Width
52cm/20½in Length **10m/
11yd** Repeat **53cm/21in**
Price ★★★★

5

3

6

7 Baer & Ingram/Country Living/
   Woof! Woof! WFW10 Colour
   tan Alt. colours yes Width
   52cm/20½in Length 10m/
   11yd Repeat 53cm/21in
   Price ★★★★

8 Vymura/Buzz Lightyear™
   09320 Colour bright blue
   Alt. colours no Width 26cm/
   10¼in Length 10m/11yd
   Repeat – Price ★

9 Sandberg/Kaspar 708 Colour
   blue 14 Alt. colours yes Width
   53cm/21in Length 10m/11yd
   Repeat 64cm/25in Price ★

10 Vymura/Action Man™ Border
   09322 Colour extreme orange
   Alt. colours no Width 26cm/
   10¼in Length 10m/11yd
   Repeat – Price ★

11 Vymura/Barbie™ Border 79111
   Colour multi pastel Alt. colours
   no Width 17.5cm/7in Length
   10m/11yd Repeat – Price ★

12 Laura Ashley/Outer Space
   Border 1180 793 Colour multi
   blue Alt. colours no Width
   26.5cm/10½in Length 10m/
   11yd Repeat 26.5cm/10½in
   Price ★

13 Vymura/Fairies Border 29614
   Colour medium pink Alt.
   colours no Width 26cm/
   10¼in Length 10m/11yd
   Repeat – Price ★

14 Laura Ashley/Lemon Grove
   Border 664 888 Colour
   cowslip/multi ivory Alt.
   colours no Width 13cm/
   5in Length 10m/11yd
   Repeat 13cm/5in
   Price ★

15 G.P. & J. Baker/Castle Street
   Border W0117-01 Colour 01
   Alt. colours available Width
   18cm/7in Length 10m/11yd
   Repeat 18cm/7in Price ★

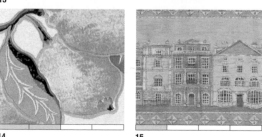

Overall Pattern Wallpapers

Of the countless patterns that have appeared on wallpapers from the late 15th century to the present day, a substantial number have been based on plant forms. Vying for popularity with floral designs have been patterns depicting fruits, nuts, vegetables and foliage. Since the Renaissance, the gradual assimilation of oriental, Middle Eastern, Asian and African styles of decoration into the vocabulary of European and, later, American ornament has resulted in a steady increase in the types of plant form available to wallpaper designers. The vagaries of fashion have also resulted in these organic forms being either conventionalized or depicted naturalistically during different periods. For example, naturalistic renderings were common for much of the 17th century, as well as in the late 18th and mid-19th century, while stylized representations were a feature of the late 19th and early 20th century.

Other popular overall patterns used since the 17th century include imitations of decorative plaster and wooden mouldings, simulations of the figuring and grain of various hardwoods, replicas of the random crazing found on craquelure-varnished panelling, and abstract designs inspired by microphotography and 20th- and 21st-century fine art.

PLANT-FORM REPEATS

Chinese wallpapers that displayed all kinds of exotic oriental imagery were highly sought after in Britain and Europe during the early years of the 18th century. However, they were generally confined to use in reception rooms. In bedrooms of this period it was much more usual to find wallpapers embellished with indigenous plant-form patterns. This example, in the Prince's Room at Temple Newsam, near Leeds, England, has a repeating pattern of leaves, fruit and vegetables, and is a reproduction of the original paper that was hung there in 1827.

ABOVE AND LEFT Large numbers of foliage-pattern papers, designed for use on both ceilings and walls, were produced throughout the 19th century and proved popular on both sides of the Atlantic. Early in the century, laurel-leaf and hart's-tongue patterns were fashionable. By the middle of the century, acanthus leaves, oak leaves, grapevines and ivy were popular, while in the later Aesthetic and Arts and Crafts interiors formalized oak, acanthus and lotus leaves were much in evidence. Colours – mostly shades of green and brown – remained realistic throughout the 19th century.

FAR LEFT Wallpapers produced to imitate stone blocking have been popular since the beginning of the 20th century, particularly in Medieval Revival interiors. Some examples are flat-patterned, and therefore little more than a pastiche of stonework, but others employ subtle highlights and shading in the areas of the mortar joints to achieve quite realistic *trompe l'oeil* effects.

KEY DESIGNS

1 Small-scale leaf patterns have been used on papers since the 17th century. This early 21st-century example is typical of many papers that have been inspired by period fabric designs.

2 The large-scale leaf pattern of this early 21st-century paper is derived from late 17th-century designs. As with many two-tone foliate patterns, it is produced in imitation of a silk damask.

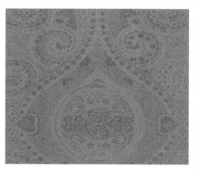

3 Willow-pattern papers for walls and ceilings were especially fashionable during the second half of the 19th and the early 20th century, notably in Aesthetic and Arts and Crafts interiors.

4 Formal, stylized designs of Eastern and Middle-Eastern origin were very fashionable in the late 19th century. This example incorporates the scrolled leaf forms found in paisley patterns.

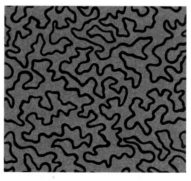

5 Abstract patterns have been popular since the end of the Second World War. Diverse sources of inspiration include rainwater, snowflakes and the microscopic organisms discovered by microphotography.

6 Many overall leaf patterns designed in the late 20th and early 21st century have had a pleasingly understated quality. In most cases this is achieved by using subtly different tones of the same colour.

1 Graham & Brown 17393 Colour **green** Alt. colours **yes** Width **52cm/20½in** Length **10m/11yd** Repeat **32cm/12½in** Price ★

2 Mulberry/Baroque Vine FG039 Colour **biscuit J115** Alt. colours **yes** Width **52cm/20½in** Length **10m/11yd** Repeat **76cm/30in** Price ★

3 Morris & Co//Willow Bough Colour **Morris 210** Alt. colours **yes** Width **53cm/21in** Length **10.5m/11½yd** Repeat **46cm/18in** Price ★ ♣

4 Mulberry/East of Suez FG024/633 Colour **gold T102** Alt. colours **yes** Width **52cm/20½in** Length **10m/11yd** Repeat **64cm/25in** Price ★

5 Chameleon/Traditional Style/Warrington Puddle Colour **WS3018** Alt. colours **yes** Width **53cm/21in** Length **10m/11yd** Repeat **53cm/21in** Price ★

6 Today Interiors/Novus NV322 Colour **4** Alt. colours **yes** Width **53cm/21in** Length **10m/11yd** Repeat **17.5cm/7in** Price ★

Overall Pattern: **Pre-19th century**

From the mid-16th to the late 18th century, most overall-patterned papers depicted conventionalized or naturalistic fruit or foliage, with many of the designs produced in imitation of fashionable textiles such as damasks. Favoured plant forms during the Renaissance and the 17th century included grapevines, ivy, parsley, water leaves, oak leaves and palms, as well as pines and pomegranates (usually set within scrolling acanthus leaves). These were also used during the 18th century, when they vied with plants of oriental origin, such as lotus leaves and artichokes, Neo-classical anthemia, laurels and seaweed.

Apart from fruit and foliage, overall-patterned papers of the 18th century often imitated decorative architectural features traditionally made of plaster or wood. Typical examples, mostly *chiaroscuro*-printed to achieve the required three-dimensional imagery, included elements such as *grisaille* panelling and scrollwork, while in Sweden wood-effect designs were particularly popular.

1

2

4

5

6

1 Hamilton Weston/Royal Crescent
Colour **grey, brown and white on blue** Alt. colours **yes** Width **52cm/20½in** Length **10m/ 11yd** Repeat **53cm/21in** Price ★★★ ♣

2 Nina Campbell/Rosenkavalier/ Mandore NCW 2233 Colour **03** Alt. colours **yes** Width **52cm/20½in** Length **10m/ 11yd** Repeat **26.5cm/ 10½in** Price ★

3 Alexander Beauchamp/Seaton Colour **multi** Alt. colours **yes** Width **46cm/18in** Length **10m/11yd** Repeat **61cm/24in** Price ★★★★ ♣

4 Alexander Beauchamp/ Gainsborough Colour **white on blue** Alt. colours **yes** Width **43cm/16¾in** Length **10m/11yd** Repeat **46.5cm/18¼in** Price ★★★ ♣

5 Coloroll/Mansfield Border 19-176 Colour **blue** Alt. colours **yes** Width **13cm/ 5in** Length **5m/5½yd** Repeat **53cm/21in** Price ★

6 Hamilton Weston/Fynedon Gothick Colour **document red** Alt. colours **yes** Width **47cm/18½in** Length **10m/ 11yd** Repeat **47cm/18½in** Price ★★ ♣

7

7 Sanderson/Chalfont Damask WR8559 Colour **5** Alt. colours **yes** Width **53cm/21in** Length **10m/11yd** Repeat **61cm/24in** Price ★

8 Zuber/Venise Or/Damas Or 40068 Colour **red and gold** Alt. colours **yes** Width **53cm/21in** Length **10m/11yd** Repeat **–** Price ★★★ 🖌

9 Alexander Beauchamp/ Holcombe Colour **red and gold** Alt. colours **yes** Width **50cm/19½in** Length **10m/ 11yd** Repeat **39.5cm/15½in** Price ★★★ 🖌

10 Nicholas Herbert/Lodge W01 Colour **01** Alt. colours **yes** Width **52cm/20½in** Length **10m/11yd** Repeat **18cm/7in** Price ★

11 Alexander Beauchamp/Urn and Acanthus Colour **red** Alt. colours **yes** Width **53cm/ 21in** Length **10m/11yd** Repeat **47cm/18½in** Price ★★★ 🖌

12 Alexander Beauchamp/Italian Damask Colour **green** Alt. colours **yes** Width **53cm/ 21in** Length **10m/11yd** Repeat **60.5cm/24in** Price ★★★★ 🖌

8

10

11

9

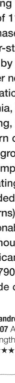

12

SMALL-SCALE DESIGNS

The wallpaper shown here – also known by its original spelling "Sattin Grass" – was one of 11 fine-quality papers purchased from the English paper-stainer James Duppa in 1799 by Lady Jean Skipworth for her new house, Prestwould Plantation in Clarksville, Virginia, USA. It features a striking, interlaced foliage pattern on a highly polished satin ground. It is typical of the simple, small-scale repeating designs (which also included stripes and floral patterns) that became fashionable in grander English townhouses and substantial American mansions during the 1790s and the first decade of the 19th century.

Scalamandré/Satin Grass WP81527-7 Colour **07** Alt. colours **yes** Width **53cm/ 21in** Length **4.5m/5yd** Repeat **53cm/21in** Price ★★★ 🖌

Overall Pattern: **Early 19th century**

In the 1830s and 1840s, cylinder-printed papers with patterns produced in imitation of arabesque-shaped plasterwork and set on *irisé* (blended colour) grounds proved very popular. Also fashionable were abstract-patterned papers in imitation of moiré silks. Nevertheless, as in previous centuries, the vast majority of overall-patterned papers produced during the first half of the 19th century were of the hand-blocked variety with their imagery derived from plant forms, particularly foliage.

In French, British and American Neo-classical interiors at the beginning of the century, favoured forms included laurels, hart's tongue (or water leaf), anthemia and "fibre" (seaweed). Most were conventionalized, but, as the century progressed, more naturalistic imagery, incorporating a greater use of shading (and sometimes flock), came into vogue. Oft-seen patterns included acanthus and oak leaves, parsley, thistles, grapevines, ivy and various fruits. However, by the 1840s, a reaction to highly naturalistic and three-dimensional imagery was beginning to set in, evidenced by the appearance during this period of many flat foliage patterns of stylized palmettes and anthemia derived from classical and Indian ornament.

5

1

2   3

1 Hamilton Weston/Jasmine Colour **red and gold dots on olive green** Alt. colours yes Width **52cm/20½in** Length **10m/11yd** Repeat **30.5cm/ 12in** Price ★★ ♣

2 Hamilton Weston/Covent Garden Floral Colour **red on peach** Alt. colours yes Width **53cm/21in** Length **10m/11yd** Repeat **28.5cm/11in** Price ★ ♣

3 Chameleon/Traditional Style/ Lord Irvine Leaf Colour **WS2358** Alt. colours yes Width **53cm/ 21in** Length **10m/11yd** Repeat **38cm/15in** Price ★

4 Zoffany/Bokhara 9300 Colour **2** Alt. colours yes Width **53cm/ 21in** Length **10m/11yd** Repeat **64cm/25in** Price ★

      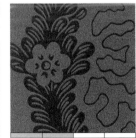

4   6   7

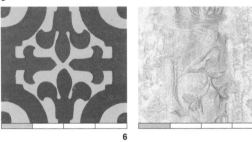

8   9

10   11

5 Hamilton Weston/Uppark Tapestry Room Colour **unfaded document** Alt. colours yes Width **47cm/ 18½in** Length **10m/11yd** Repeat **26cm/10¼in** Price ★★ ♣

6 Hamilton Weston/Charlecote Strapwork Colour **document orange on cream** Alt. colours yes Width **52cm/20½in** Length **10m/11yd** Repeat **91.5cm/ 36in** Price ★★★ ♣

7 Graham & Brown 51063 Colour **yellow** Alt. colours yes Width **52cm/20½in** Length **10m/11yd** Repeat **53cm/21in** Price ★

8 Crowson/Gallery/Matour Border Colour **80** Alt. colours yes Width **17.5cm/7in** Length **10m/11yd** Repeat **17cm/6¾in** Price ★

9 Nicholas Herbert/Bradenham W07 Colour **09** Alt. colours yes Width **52cm/20½in** Length **10m/11yd** Repeat **27cm/10½in** Price ★

10 Hamilton Weston/Carlyle Damask Colour **cream on yellow** Alt. colours yes Width **53cm/21in** Length **10m/11yd** Repeat **53cm/21in** Price ★★ ♣

11 Today Interiors/Carlton Damask/ Ashridge CDV360 Colour **2** Alt. colours yes Width **53cm/21in** Length **10m/11yd** Repeat **26.5cm/10½in** Price ★

12

13

14

15

16

12 Cole & Son/Clandon 52/7000
Colour **yellow and gold** Alt.
colours **yes** Width **53cm/
21in** Length **10m/11yd**
Repeat **14cm/5½in**
Price ★

**13 Jane Churchill/Colbrooke
Trellis JW62W-04** Colour
red Alt. colours **yes** Width
52cm/20½in Length **10m/
11yd** Repeat **17.5cm/7in**
Price ★★★★

**14 Zuber/Arabesques/Volutes
30005** Colour **20** Alt. colours
yes Width **47cm/18½in** Length
10m/11yd Repeat **47cm/18½in**
Price ★★★

**15 Hamilton Weston/Cyfarthfa
Damask** Colour **gold on red**
Alt. colours **yes** Width **52cm/
20½in** Length **10m/11yd**
Repeat **13cm/5in**
Price ★★ ♛

**16 Watts of Westminster/
Kinnersley WW5025-01/B**
Colour **blue** Alt. colours **yes**
Width **54cm/21½in** Length
10m/11yd Repeat **89cm/35in**
Price ★★

17

18

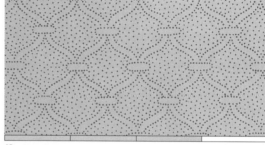

19

20

17 Zuber/Moiré 1265 Colour **rouge**
Alt. colours **yes** Width **47cm/
18½in** Length **10m/11yd**
Repeat **66cm/26in**
Price ★★★

18 Coloroll/Kells Border 29-704
Colour **pink** Alt. colours
yes Width **13cm/5in** Length
5m/5½yd Repeat **13cm/5in**
Price ★

**19 Hamilton Weston/Chester
Square** Colour **green** Alt. ·
colours **yes** Width **52cm/
20½in** Length **10m/11yd**
Repeat **14cm/5½in**
Price ★

**20 Chameleon/Traditional Style/
Fern** Colour **autumn** Alt.
colours **yes** Width **53cm/
21in** Length **10m/11yd**
Repeat **76cm/30in**
Price ★

Overall Pattern: Late 19th century

Victorian designers Owen Jones and William Morris believed that, because wallpaper was intended to cover flat surfaces, the only appropriate form of pattern for it had to be two-dimensional in appearance; any *trompe l'oeil* and other three-dimensional effects were simply "dishonest". Their opinion was to prove remarkably influential during the second half of the 19th century: naturalistic foliage patterns continued to appear, but they were generally supplanted by conventionalized Arts and Crafts, Aesthetic and Art Nouveau designs in which any shading was usually limited to dots, lines and hatching. Arts and Crafts designs, notably those by Elbert Hubbard, were frequently based on willow and acanthus leaves. Aesthetic patterns, such as those by E.W. Godwin and Christopher Dresser, included formalized bamboo and lotus leaves, while many of C.F.A. Voysey's and the Silver Studio's Art Nouveau papers featured sinuously depicted pomegranates, thistles, various roots and leaf-like peacock feathers.

1

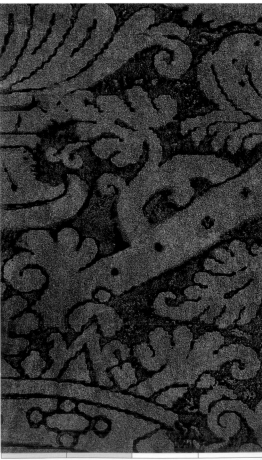

3

1   **Joanna Wood/Bourne Street L/W3354** Colour **Chinese yellow** Alt. colours **yes** Width **52cm/20½in** Length **10m/11yd** Repeat **27cm/10½in** Price ★

2   **Cole & Son/Owen Jones 52/7040** Colour **red** Alt. colours **yes** Width **53cm/21in** Length **10m/11yd** Repeat **7cm/2¾in** Price ★

3   **Alexander Beauchamp/Langley** Colour **blue** Alt. colours **yes** Width **46.5cm/18¼in** Length **10m/11yd** Repeat **48cm/19in** Price ★★★★♣

4   **Zuber/Venise 40068** Colour **130** Alt. colours **yes** Width **55cm/21½in** Length **10m/11yd** Repeat **66.5cm/26¼in** Price ★★★

2

4

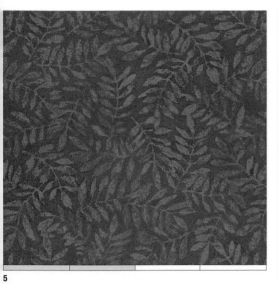

5

6

7

8

9

5 **Coloroll/Laurel Damask 21-027T** Colour **red** Alt. colours **yes** Width **52cm/20½in** Length **10m/11yd** Repeat **53cm/21in** Price ★

6 **Watts of Westminster/Melias W5028-02/A12** Colour **cream** Alt. colours **yes** Width **47cm/18½in** Length **10m/11yd** Repeat **35cm/13¾in** Price ★★

7 **Bradbury & Bradbury/Eastlake Dado ELD** Colour **550** Alt. colours **yes** Width **69cm/27in** Length **to order** Repeat **8cm/3in** Price ★★★ 👑

8 **Hodsoll McKenzie/Fern 616/602** Colour **yellow** Alt. colours **yes** Width **52cm/20½in** Length **10m/11yd** Repeat **53.5cm/21in** Price ★

9 **Watts of Westminster/Clarence W0011** Colour **rose** Alt. colours **yes** Width **54cm/21½in** Length **10m/11yd** Repeat **26cm/10¼in** Price ★★

SANITARY PAPERS

In 1871 the English firm of Heywood, Higginbottom & Smith pioneered the first washable wallpapers. They were known as "sanitaries" because they could be kept clean. They were printed with engraved metal rollers that built up the pattern from a series of small dots of thin, oil-based inks or varnish colours. This technique produced a very smooth surface that was water-resistant, and also allowed for considerable subtlety in the shading and blending of colours.

Watts of Westminster/Cogges Manor Farm W5061-01/B13 Colour **Oxford** Alt. colours **yes** Width **54cm/21½in** Length **10m/11yd** Repeat **53cm/21in** Price ★★★

Overall Pattern: **Early 20th Century**

Botanic and organic forms continued to provide much of the inspiration for overall-patterned wallpapers during the first half of the 20th century. Scrolling acanthus, stylized thistles and sweeping and curving wisteria, and reed and waterlily patterns featured large in Art Nouveau designs, while small leaves with undulating stems articulated the surface of many Deutscher Werkbund papers. Stencilled leaf patterns were characteristic of the later Arts and Crafts papers of the 1920s and 1930s, and numerous early Art Deco designs consisted of fantastically stylized abstractions of plant forms. Also fashionable in the 1930s were realistic sketches of branches, leaves and blossom, and stylized, large-scale leaf patterns rendered in "teastain" colours and sometimes highlighted with silver or gold; in the 1940s ivy-leaf trellis papers proved especially popular.

Also much in evidence during the first half of the 20th century were papers displaying spattered patterns similar to those found on contemporary ceramics. In addition, papers were produced in imitation of 17th-century tooled-leather wall-hangings, classical mouldings, *faux*-marble paint finishes and panelling made of decoratively figured hardwoods such as maple and birch.

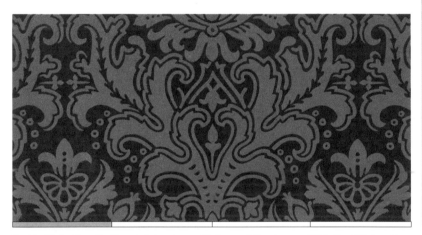

Hamilton Weston/Edwardian Damask Colour **document lustre on red** Alt. colours **yes** Width **61cm/24in** Length **10m/11yd** Repeat **61cm/24in** Price ★★ ♣

Chameleon/Art Deco/Suzzanne Colour **blue, black and gold on brown** Alt. colours **yes** Width **53cm/21in** Length **10m/11yd** Repeat **51cm/20in** Price ★

John Wilman/Figaro 170426 Colour **red** Alt. colours **yes** Width **52cm/20½in** Length **10m/11yd** Repeat **7.5cm/2¾in** Price ★

Osborne & Little/Madrigal W1441/10 Colour **green** Alt. colours **yes** Width **52cm/20½in** Length **10m/11yd** Repeat **–** Price ★

Zoffany/Viola Plain V21704 Colour **04** Alt. colours **yes** Width **52cm/20½in** Length **10m/11yd** Repeat **13cm/5in** Price ★

Zuber/Venise Or/Damas Or 10174 Colour **111** Alt. colours **yes** Width **47cm/18½in** Length **10m/11yd** Repeat **62cm/24¼in** Price ★★★

RAISED RELIEF DESIGNS

White or neutral-coloured wallpapers with raised relief patterns, intended for painting, proved popular throughout the 20th century. Being made of paper (or paper and vinyl), they proved cheaper to produce than Lincrusta and Anaglypta, and thus supplanted these earlier relief coverings in the mass market. Before the 1980s, all raised relief papers were produced by mechanical embossing, but thereafter "blown" vinyl techniques have also been employed. Favoured designs have ranged from traditional geometrics to abstracts such as bubble patterns, impasto-like doodlings and "cracked ice".

IHDG/Arundel RD100 Colour **white** Alt. colours **no** Width **52cm/20⅛in** Length **10m/11yd** Repeat – Price ★

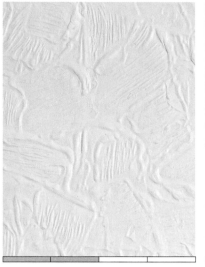

IHDG/Westminster RD101 Colour **white** Alt. colours **no** Width **52cm/20⅛in** Length **10m/11yd** Repeat **53cm/21in** Price ★

IHDG/Berkeley RD125 Colour **white** Alt. colours **no** Width **52cm/20⅛in** Length **10m/11yd** Repeat **13cm/5in** Price ★

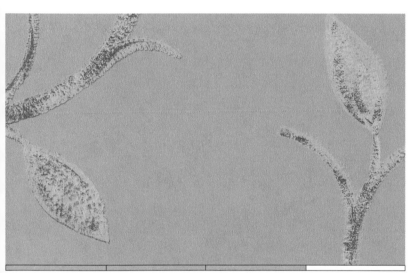

Today Interiors/Samadhi/Aritum SAW 302 Colour **4** Alt. colours **yes** Width **53cm/21in** Length **10m/11yd** Repeat **52cm/20½in** Price ★

Chameleon/Traditional Style/Oliver Colour **moss** Alt. colours **yes** Width **53cm/21in** Length **10m/11yd** Repeat – Price ★

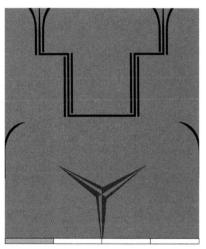

Chameleon/Art Deco/Deco Merc Colour **stone** Alt. colours **yes** Width **53cm/21in** Length **10m/11yd** Repeat **26cm/10¼in** Price ★

Graham & Brown 15069 Colour **white** Alt. colours **no** Width **52cm/20⅛in** Length **10m/11yd** Repeat **32cm/12½in** Price ★

Crowson/Willowmead/Vine Colour **40** Alt. colours **yes** Width **52cm/20⅛in** Length **10m/11yd** Repeat **17cm/6¾in** Price ★

Marthe Armitage/Solomon's Seal Colour **orange** Alt. colours **yes** Width **53cm/21in** Length **10m/11yd** Repeat **43cm/16¾in** Price ★★★★★

Sheila Coombes/Belle Isle W607 Colour **10** Alt. colours **yes** Width **53cm/21in** Length **10m/11yd** Repeat **27cm/10½in** Price ★★★★

Overall Pattern: Late 20th–early 21st century

Conventionalized and naturalistic plant-form patterns seen in the previous century reappeared on numerous field and border papers produced during the 1950s and 1960s. For example, the late 19th-century rhythmical Arts and Crafts designs of William Morris and J.H. Dearle were hand-printed again with the original wooden blocks, and sinuous Art Nouveau vegetal patterns came back into fashion. American designers also created leaf patterns either overlaid with lines, dots, diamonds and checks, or combined with simulations of tweed textiles, while many Scandinavian and other American papers featured intricate patterns depicting marine flora and fauna.

Microphotographic views of the molecular structure of materials such as myoglobin and insulin provided additional inspiration for wallpaper designers during the 1950s and 1960s, and a general preoccupation with naturally occurring forms and phenomena was further evident in those patterns based on wormcasts, spiders' webs, amoeba and rainfall. Also fashionable since then, as in the early 20th century, have been printed replicas of the figuring and grain of various species of wood, as well as realistic and fantastic simulations of decorative stone finishes, such as those seen on marble and porphyry.

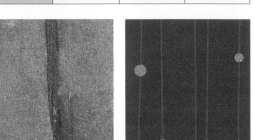

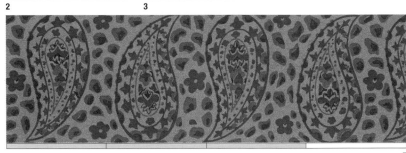

1 **Maya Romanoff/Mica MR-SK-1402** Colour **Ishtar** Alt. colours **yes** Width **93cm/36in** Length **to order** Repeat – Price ★★★★

2 **Donghia/Fluxus 2001** Colour **silver** Alt. colours **yes** Width **102cm/40in** Length **3m/3⅓yd** Repeat **15cm/6in** Price ★★★

3 **Harlequin/Divine** Colour **15255** Alt. colours **yes** Width **52cm/20½in** Length **10m/11yd** Repeat – Price ★

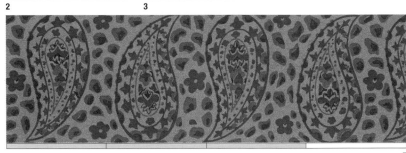

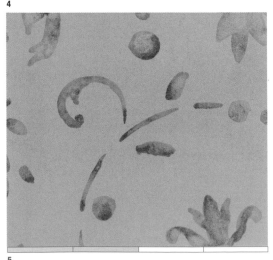

4 **Marthe Armitage/Chestnut** Colour **green** Alt. colours **yes** Width **59cm/23in** Length **10m/11yd** Repeat **81cm/32in** Price ★

5 **Anna French/Fondant** Colour **WP075BI** Alt. colours **yes** Width **52cm/20½in** Length **10m/11yd** Repeat **52cm/20½in** Price ★

6 **Paint and Paper Library/David Oliver/Liberation/Opium 088-OP-DE-B3** Colour **duck egg** Alt. colours **yes** Width **52cm/20½in** Length **10m/11yd** Repeat **53cm/11yd** Price ★

7 **Chameleon/Paisley/Dusty Border** Colour **TC531** Alt. colours **yes** Width **9cm/3½in** Length **10m/11yd** Repeat – Price ★

8 **Ornamenta/Arabesque** Colour **bronze on silver** Alt. colours **yes** Width **53cm/21in** Length **10m/11yd** Repeat **30cm/11¾in** Price ★★★★★♣

9 **Graham & Brown 91154** Colour
beige Alt. colours **yes** Width
18m/7in Length **5m/5½yd**
Repeat – Price ★

10 **Graham & Brown 91152** Colour
green Alt. colours **yes** Width
18cm/7in Length **5m/5½yd**
Repeat – Price ★

11 **Osborne & Little/Oratorio**
W1440/06 Colour **06** Alt.
colours **yes** Width **52cm/**
20½in Length **10m/11yd**
Repeat **53cm/21in**
Price ★

9

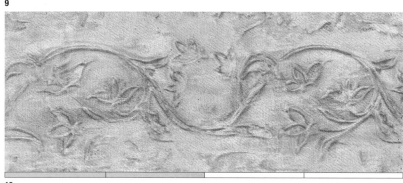

10

11

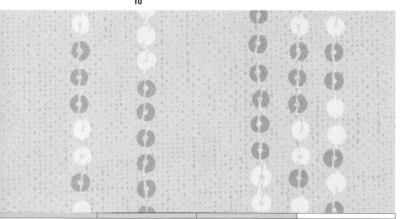

12

13

14

15

12 **Today Interiors/Novus/Saros**
NV320 Colour **2** Alt. colours
yes Width **53cm/21in** Length
10m/11yd Repeat –
Price ★

13 **Nicholas Herbert/Celestria**
W04 Colour **03** Alt. colours
yes Width **52cm/20½in**
Length **10m/11yd**
Repeat – Price ★

14 **Ornamenta/Curve** Colour **silver**
and pearl Alt. colours **yes**
Width **53cm/21in** Length
10m/11yd Repeat –
Price ★★★★★ ♣

15 **Anna French/Eden/Ritz** Colour
RITWP038 Alt. colours **yes**
Width **52cm/20½in** Length
10m/11yd Repeat **61cm/24in**
Price ★

16 **Today Interiors/Novus NV318**
Colour **4** Alt. colours **yes**
Width **53cm/21in** Length
10m/11yd Repeat **26cm/**
10¼in Price ★

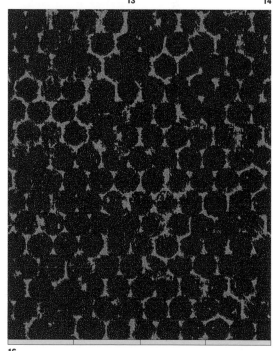

16

Overall Pattern: Late 20th–early 21st century

Many of the plant-form patterns favoured in the 1950s and 1960s (*see* pages 266–267) enjoyed a new lease of life during the late 20th century. This was largely as a result of manufacturers adapting them to suit more contemporary aesthetics. In the early 1970s, for example, some of these papers were reproduced in incandescent or muted colours on shiny or dull metallic grounds – a look that made them perfectly suited to what *Vogue* magazine described as "a Nickelodeon land of Art Deco with potted palms and mirrored halls".

Since the 1970s, metallic finishes have also served as patterns in their own right. Most of these finishes show random mottling across their surface that essentially replicates the appearance of tarnished metals and alloys, such as copper and bronze, in much the same way that some distressed paint finishes do. However, metallic finishes have not dominated wallpaper designs: abstract doodles, snowflakes under the microscope, wave-like patterns, small repeats of fruits and berries, and imitations of limed wood have also been much in evidence. Another trend has been a resurgence of documentary patterns dating back to the 17th century.

Ornamenta/Chinoiserie Colour **CHI 903 chinese red/straw** Alt. colours **yes** Width **52cm/20½in** Length **10m/11yd** Repeat – Price ★★★★★

Harlequin/Arc Colour **60356** Alt. colours **yes** Width **52cm/20½in** Length **10m/11yd** Repeat **52cm/20½in** Price ★

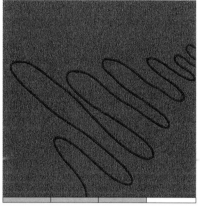

Paint and Paper Library/Hairpin 067-HP-RC-B3 Colour **red chalk** Alt. colours **yes** Width **52cm/20½in** Length **10m/11yd** Repeat **60cm/23¾in** Price ★

Jane Churchill/Esher JY66W-05 Colour **blue** Alt. colours **yes** Width **52cm/20½in** Length **10m/11yd** Repeat **27cm/10½in** Price ★

Paint and Paper Library/Emily Todhunter/Curves 015-CV-MO-S1 Colour **moss** Alt. colours **yes** Width **52cm/20½in** Length **10m/11yd** Repeat **60cm/23¾in** Price ★

Anna French/Eden/Olive Grove Colour **OLIWP096** Alt. colours **yes** Width **52cm/20½in** Length **10m/11yd** Repeat **26.5cm/10½in** Price ★

Today Interiors/Samadhi/Aritum SAW 303 Colour **3** Alt. colours **yes** Width **53cm/21in** Length **10m/11yd** Repeat **52cm/20½in** Price ★

Anna French/Eden/Ritz Colour **RITWP088** Alt. colours **yes** Width **52cm/20½in** Length **10m/11yd** Repeat **61cm/24in** Price ★

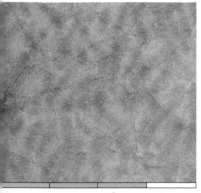

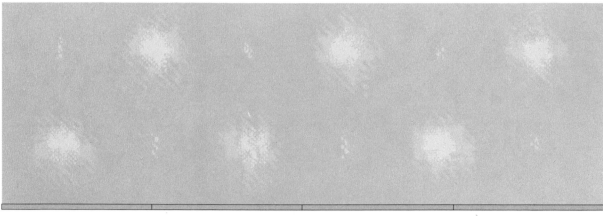

Maya Romanoff/Crushed Pearl MR-P50-971 Colour **medium peach** Alt. colours **yes** Width **79cm/31in** Length **3.6m/4yd** Repeat **69cm/27in** Price ★★★★★

Today Interiors/Novus NV321 Colour **3** Alt. colours **yes** Width **53cm/21in** Length **10m/11yd** Repeat **–** Price ★

Nobilis/Papiers Bois Couleur PBC103 Colour **yellow** Alt. colours **yes** Width **125cm/49¼in** Length **to order** Repeat **–** Price ★★★★

IHDG/Tiger Eye RD841 Colour **white** Alt. colours **no** Width **52cm/20½in** Length **10m/11yd** Repeat **32cm/12½in** Price ★

Coloroll/Wessex Border 29-710 Colour **cream** Alt. colours **yes** Width **17cm/6¾in** Length **5m/5½yd** Repeat **64cm/25in** Price ★

Coloroll/Antonello Damask 16-279 Colour **peach** Alt. colours **yes** Width **52cm/20½in** Length **10m/11yd** Repeat **53cm/21in** Price ★

Anya Larkin/Moondust Teapaper Colour **239 evergreen** Alt. colours **yes** Width **102cm/40in** Length **3m/3⅓yd** Repeat **–** Price ★★★

Coloroll/Mosaic Border 37-372 Colour **dark green** Alt. colours **yes** Width **13cm/5in** Length **5m/5½yd** Repeat **53cm/21in** Price ★

Geometric Wallpapers

Geometric and linear patterns appeared on wallpapers as soon as they were introduced as an alternative to textile wall-hangings during the late 15th century. Most of the geometric designs that were fashionable before the 18th century have been revived, particularly during the second half of the 19th century when designers on both sides of the Atlantic produced patterns based entirely on geometric principles of ornament. The catalogue of geometric patterns available to wallpaper designers has been extensive, steadily increasing since the Renaissance, as oriental, Islamic, African and South American geometric imagery was assimilated into Western culture. Favoured designs have included vertical stripes, checks, powdered ornament (stars and other geometric shapes), diaper patterns (trelliswork, latticework and strapwork) and, during the 20th century, mathematical and abstract shapes inspired by Cubist and Constructivist art. Some of these patterns have been augmented with, or provided the ground for, non-geometric imagery, such as stylized plant forms.

RIGHT Although vertical-striped wallpapers are closely associated with the Neo-classical interiors of the late 18th and early 19th century, they were often fashionable both before and after this period. This contemporary pale blue and white paper imitates painted stripes.

ABOVE The geometric wallpaper on the walls of this bathroom in a French Mediterranean villa is produced in imitation of blue and white gingham.

DIAPER PATTERNS

Trelliswork, latticework and strapwork patterns – collectively known as diaper patterns – have appeared on fabrics since the Middle Ages, and on wallpapers since the 17th century. Diaper patterns, original to both European and oriental decoration, often enclose small motifs. They also provide a ground for, and are often interlaced with, different types of plant-form or floral imagery. However, sometimes these geometric patterns remain unembellished – as with the blue-on-yellow latticework paper in this partly updated, early 19th-century, provincial English drawing room.

1 Diaper patterns have been used on papers since the Renaissance. This stylized flower-and-leaf trelliswork design is typical of both Regency and early 20th-century Classical Revival papers.

2 "Two-tone" striped papers made up of vertical bands of alternating solid colours were especially fashionable in Neo-classical interiors during the late 18th and early 19th century.

3 While many trelliswork patterns are unembellished, others are either entwined with or (as here) enclose or provide a ground for other motifs, such as naturalistic or stylized plant forms.

4 Many striped papers consist of vertical bands of alternating widths and colours. The bands are often embellished with small motifs, or show tonal configurations similar to those of moiré silk.

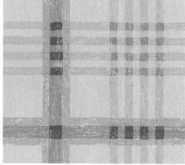

5 Diamond shapes have been an enduringly popular geometric motif on papers. An integral component of most diaper patterns, they are also often used as stand-alone repeat motifs.

6 Checked-and-striped papers produced in imitation of geometrically patterned fabrics, such as gingham and madras, became fashionable during the early years of the 20th century.

1 **Cole & Son/Tavistock 60/7045** Colour **green** Alt. colours **yes** Width **52cm/20½in** Length **10m/11yd** Repeat **20cm/8in** Price ★

2 **Laura Ashley/Colourwash Stripe 35089** Colour **taupe/ivory** Alt. colours **yes** Width **52cm/20½in** Length **10m/11yd** Repeat **–** Price ★

3 **Chameleon/Traditional Style/Gothic** Colour **HC 011** Alt. colours **yes** Width **50cm/19½in** Length **10m/11yd** Repeat **77cm/30¼in** Price ★

4 **Coloroll/Regency Stripe 694847** Colour **green** Alt. colours **yes** Width **52cm/20½in** Length **10m/11yd** Repeat **26.5cm/10½in** Price ★

5 **Today Interiors/Novus NV319** Colour **6** Alt. colours **yes** Width **53cm/21in** Length **10m/11yd** Repeat **–** Price ★

6 **Osborne & Little/Voyage/Parnasse W1120** Colour **01** Alt. colours **yes** Width **52cm/20½in** Length **10m/11yd** Repeat **27cm/10½in** Price ★

Geometrics: **Pre-19th century**

Some of the earliest woodcut-printed papers of the 16th century were patterned with simple repeats of spots or trelliswork, and many French papers of this period displayed rose motifs on vertical-striped grounds. Fashionable patterns of the 17th century included nailheads (small pyramid shapes), powdered ornament (sprinklings of stars or small flowers), trelliswork (often consisting of chevron-shaped pairs of leaves), strapwork (twisted and intertwined bands similar to ribbons or strips of leather), jewelled strapwork (in which the banding was enhanced with imitations of faceted jewels) and *guilloche* (Islamic in origin and consisting of interlaced, curved bands – some forming circular shapes – embellished with floral motifs).

Diaper patterns – mostly trellis- and latticework – were also featured in the Rococo and Gothick interiors of the 18th century. Some were flocked, and many provided the ground for, respectively, *chinoiserie* and heraldic imagery. However, the most prevalent geometric patterns in the Neo-classical interiors of the late 18th century were vertical stripes – consisting of plain bands of alternating widths and colours, or made up of stacked chevrons – or classical motifs, such as leaves, urns or figures.

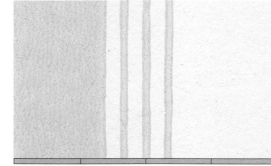

5

6　　　　　　7

5　**Colefax and Fowler/Juliana 7405/02** Colour **yellow** Alt. colours **yes** Width **52cm/ 20½in** Length **10m/11yd** Repeat **–** Price ★

6　**Hamilton Weston/Twickenham** Colour **grey, white and black on red** Alt. colours **yes** Width **52cm/20½in** Length **10m/ 11yd** Repeat **21cm/8¼in** Price ★★★ ♣

7　**Hamilton Weston/Strand Teardrop** Colour **8124** Alt. colours **yes** Width **52cm/ 20½in** Length **10m/11yd** Repeat **3cm/1¼in** Price ★★ ♣

8　**Today Interiors/Carlton Damask/Ashridge CDV359** Colour **8** Alt. colours **yes** Width **53cm/21in** Length **10m/11yd** Repeat **26.5cm/ 10½in** Price ★

1　　　　　　2　　　　　　3

1　**Chameleon/Traditional Style/ Trailing Vine** Colour **NF12** Alt. colours **yes** Width **50cm/ 19½in** Length **10m/11yd** Repeat **77cm/30¼in** Price ★

2　**Zoffany/Silk Stripe 245700** Colour **3** Alt. colours **yes** Width **52cm/20½in** Length **10m/11yd** Repeat **17cm/ 6¾in** Price ★

3　**Zoffany/Welbeck Trellis** Colour **gold and blue on beige** Alt. colours **yes** Width **52cm/20½in** Length **10m/11yd** Repeat **4.5cm/1¾in** Price ★

4　**Zoffany/Ticking Stripe 36TK03** Colour **03** Alt. colours **yes** Width **52cm/20½in** Length **10m/11yd** Repeat **–** Price ★

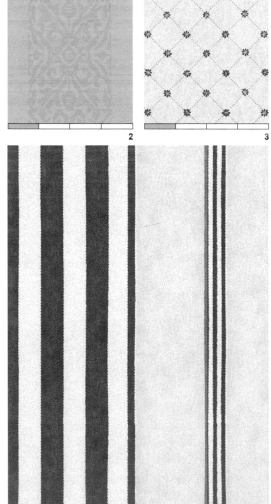

4

8

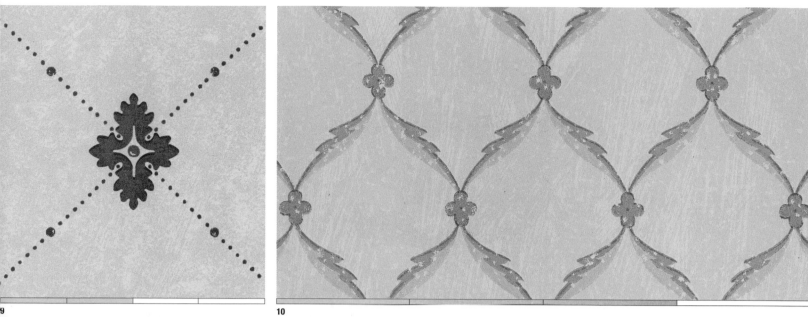

9

10

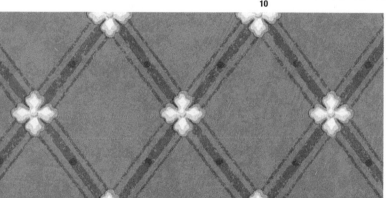

9 Zoffany/Leaf Trellis V433
Colour **01** Alt. colours **yes**
Width **52cm/20½in** Length
10m/11yd Repeat **17cm/**
6¾in Price **★**

10 Osborne & Little/Pipori
W1013/05 Colour **blue/**
pink Alt. colours **yes** Width
52cm/20½in Length **10m/**
11yd Repeat **9cm/3½in**
Price **★**

11 Zoffany/Venetian Grill V434
Colour **05** Alt. colours **yes**
Width **52cm/20½in** Length
10m/11yd Repeat **8cm/3in**
Price **★**

12 Zoffany/Trellis V21502 Colour
02 Alt. colours **yes** Width
52cm/20½in Length **10m/**
11yd Repeat **52cm/20½in**
Price **★**

13 Zoffany/Felbrigg Attic Paper
NTW040 Colour **01** Alt. colours
yes Width **52cm/20½in** Length
10m/11yd Repeat **4.5cm/1¾in**
Price **★**

14 Hamilton Weston/Bedford
Stripe Colour **303** Alt. colours
yes Width **52cm/20½in** Length
10m/11yd Repeat **15cm/6in**
Price **★**

15 Zoffany/End Paper 8600
Colour **7** Alt. colours **yes**
Width **53cm/21in** Length
10m/11yd Repeat **21.5cm/**
8½in Price **★**

12

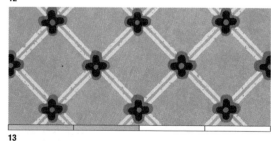

13

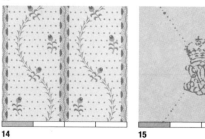

14

15

11

WALLPAPERS: *GEOMETRICS*   **273**

Geometrics: **Early 19th century**

Striped wallpapers inspired by contemporary textiles were highly fashionable in French Empire, English Regency and American Federal interiors during the early 19th century. In many cases the striped pattern consisted of solid vertical bands of alternating widths and colours, while in others some of the bands were made up of stylized foliage patterns or were edged with thin stripes that were similar in appearance to the decorative trimmings used as edgings on curtains.

Other popular geometric wallpaper designs of the first half of the 19th century included Greek-key borders; chequer patterns, brightly coloured in imitation of Indian ginghams and often embellished with small motifs; and oriental diaper patterns. One of the most significant examples of the latter was the three-dimensional *chinoiserie*-latticework design: set on a wave-pattern blue ground, this was devised by Robert Jones and J.G. Grace for the Royal Pavilion, in Brighton, England. Medieval and Renaissance diaper patterns, especially jewelled strapwork, also came back into vogue in Gothic Revival interiors during the 1840s, as did powdered ornament (evenly spaced scatterings of small, stylized motifs).

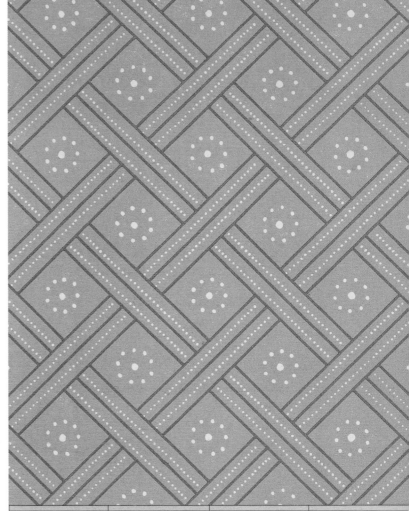

Osborne & Little/Alabaster/Ophite W5035 Colour **07** Alt. colours **yes** Width **52cm/20½in** Length **10m/11yd** Repeat – Price ★

Coloroll/Liberty Stripe 26-019 Colour **blue** Alt. colours **yes** Width **52cm/20½in** Length **10m/11yd** Repeat **26.5cm/10½in** Price ★

Hamilton Weston/Bloomsbury Square Colour **501** Alt. colours **yes** Width **52cm/20½in** Length **10m/11yd** Repeat **4cm/1½in** Price ★

Crowson/Gallery/Viliana Colour **80** Alt. colours **yes** Width **52cm/20½in** Length **10m/11yd** Repeat **52cm/20½in** Price ★

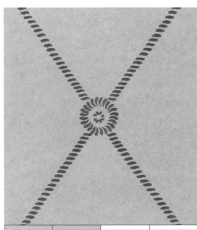

Cole & Son/Georgian Rope Trellis 59/3020 Colour **beige** Alt. colours **yes** Width **48cm/19in** Length **10m/11yd** Repeat **23.5cm/9¼in** Price ★

Hodsoll McKenzie/Scroll Stripe 615/601 Colour **pink** Alt. colours **yes** Width **52cm/20½in** Length **10m/11yd** Repeat **13.5cm/5¼in** Price ★

Hamilton Weston/Empire Stripe Colour **701** Alt. colours **yes** Width **52cm/20½in** Length **10m/11yd** Repeat – Price ★

Zoffany/Regency Trellis 36TR05 Colour **05** Alt. colours **yes** Width **52cm/20½in** Length **10m/11yd** Repeat **10cm/4in** Price ★

Baer & Ingram/Daisy Paper DSW04 Colour **yellow** Alt. colours **yes** Width **52cm/20½in** Length **10m/11yd** Repeat **4.5cm/1¾in** Price ★

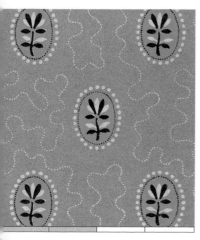

Hamilton Weston/Archway House Colour **blue, black and white on brown** Alt. colours **yes** Width **52cm/20½in** Length **10m/11yd** Repeat **9cm/3½in** Price ★★ ♣

Zoffany/Middle Hertford ZPH220 Colour **05** Alt. colours **yes** Width **52cm/20½in** Length **10m/11yd** Repeat **–** Price ★

Nicholas Herbert/Firle W08 Colour **01** Alt. colours **yes** Width **52cm/20½in** Length **10m/11yd** Repeat **12cm/4¾in** Price ★

Zuber/Rayures à Auge Colour **190 jaune** Alt. colours **yes** Width **47cm/18½in** Length **10m/11yd** Repeat **–** Price ★★

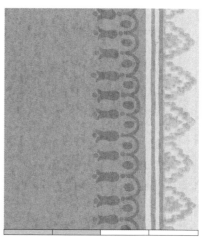

Zoffany/Felbrigg Bedchamber NTW030 Colour **06** Alt. colours **yes** Width **52cm/20½in** Length **10m/11yd** Repeat **4cm/1½in** Price ★

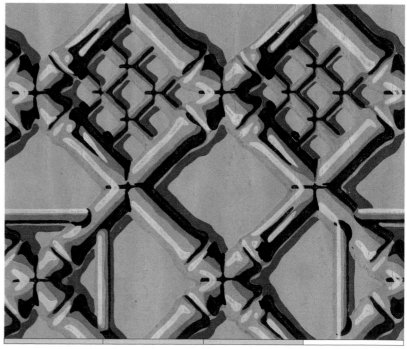

Cole & Son/Brighton Pavilion/Bamboo Trellis Colour **traditional** Alt. colours **yes** Width **53cm/21in** Length **10m/11yd** Repeat **7cm/2¾in** Price ★★★★★

Geometrics: Mid-19th century

Although geometric-patterned wallpapers had proved fashionable during the early part of the 19th century, they were produced in far greater numbers following the publication of Owen Jones's *Grammar of Ornament* in 1856, in which he stipulated that "all ornament should be based on geometric construction". Jones had reached this conclusion partly as a result of a distaste for European pictorial and overblown naturalistic decoration, but mainly through his extensive studies of Egyptian, Turkish, Spanish, Chinese, Persian, Indian and Arabic styles of ornament. Jones's views, and the patterns he devised, proved highly influential with his design contemporaries. Among the numerous geometric patterns produced around the middle of the century were jewelled strapwork and lattice- and trelliswork grounds embellished with stylized plant-form motifs. However, ogival patterns were also successful, while stripes and powdered ornament retained their popularity from earlier in the century.

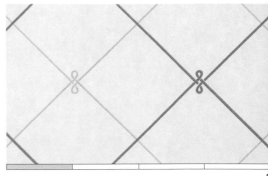

1 Watts of Westminster/ Brandiles ZBR/J001 Colour **khaki** Alt. colours **yes** Width **47cm/18½in** Length **10m/ 11yd** Repeat **29cm/11¼in** Price ★★

2 Hamilton Weston/Charlecote Trellis Colour **metallic gold/ grey on white ground** Alt. colours **yes** Width **52cm/ 20½in** Length **10m/11yd** Repeat **79.5cm/31¼in** Price ★★

3 Hamilton Weston/Richmond Trellis Border Colour **8161** Alt. colours **yes** Width **17.5cm/7in** Length **3m/3⅓yd** Repeat – Price ★★ 🖌

4 Zoffany/Pemberley FRW0200 Colour **4** Alt. colours **yes** Width **52cm/20½in** Length **10m/11yd** Repeat – Price ★★

5 Chameleon/Traditional Style/ Broad Stripe Colour **SAW 3007** Alt. colours **yes** Width **50cm/19½in** Length **10m/ 11yd** Repeat – Price ★

6 Today Interiors/Samadhi/Stripe Colour **taupe** Alt. colours **yes** Width **53cm/21in** Length **10m/11yd** Repeat – Price ★

7 Hamilton Weston/Victorian Leaf Quatrefoil Colour **document (unfaded)** Alt. colours **yes** Width **52cm/20½in** Length **10m/11yd** Repeat **15cm/ 6in** Price ★★★★★ 🖌

8 Cole & Son/Plains and Stripes/ Oxford Stripe 57/2594 Colour **PR** Alt. colours **yes** Width **52cm/20½in** Length **10m/11yd** Repeat **15cm/6in** Price ★★★★★

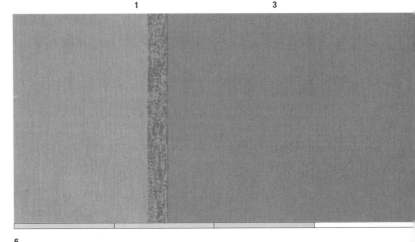

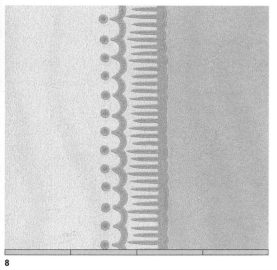

8

10

11

8 Nina Campbell/Sackville
Stripe NCW510/01 Colour
yellow Alt. colours **yes** Width
52cm/20½in Length **10m/11yd**
Repeat – Price ★

9 The Arts & Crafts Home/Audsley
LW5025 Colour **01** Alt. colours
yes Width **52cm/20½in** Length
10m/11yd Repeat **27cm/10½in**
Price ★

10 Zoffany/Middle Hertford **ZV07**
Colour **01** Alt. colours **yes**
Width **52cm/20½in** Length
10m/11yd Repeat –
Price ★

11 Alexander Beauchamp/Greek
Key Border Colour **brown,
black and shades of green**
Alt. colours **yes** Width
18cm/7in Length **10m/
11yd** Repeat **56.5cm/22¼in**
Price ★★★★★ ♣

12 Hamilton Weston/Uppark Trellis
Colour **document** Alt. colours
yes Width **53cm/21in** Length
10m/11yd Repeat **11.5cm/4½in**
Price ★★★ ♣

9

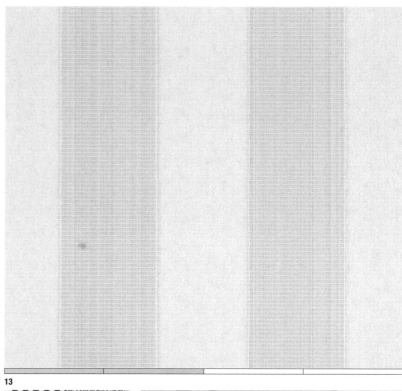

13

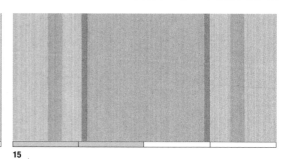

14   **15**

16

13 Cole & Son/Finsbury/Langley
Stripe **59/8048** Colour **8** Alt.
colours **yes** Width **52cm/
20½in** Length **10m/11yd**
Repeat – Price ★★★★

14 Jane Churchill/Langdale
Stripe **JY63W-08** Colour **red**
Alt. colours **yes** Width **52cm/
20½in** Length **10m/11yd**
Repeat – Price ★

15 Zoffany/Pavilion **770800**
Colour **3** Alt. colours **yes**
Width **52cm/20½in** Length
10m/11yd Repeat –
Price ★

16 Colefax and Fowler/Wickham
7610/02 Colour **yellow** Alt.
colours **yes** Width **52cm/
20½in** Length **10m/11yd**
Repeat – Price ★

19th century

Geometrics: **Early 20th century**

Wallpapers presenting geometric patterns were much in evidence during the first half of the 20th century. Many Art Deco papers featured highly mathematical forms, such as overlapping squares or oblongs derived from Cubist paintings, while some were inspired by Constructivist art – circles, triangles or rectangles appearing partly defined (on one side for example) and partly merged (on another side) into the background. Striped papers also proved fashionable during the 1920s, the stripes either plain, hatched or containing small repeat motifs. Also widely seen in the mid-1920s were pastel-coloured geometrics in which stripes, squares and triangles were harmoniously arranged in subtly balanced tones or gradations of a single colour.

In addition to a revival of Victorian striped and diaper-pattern designs, the 1930s witnessed the launch of the Bauhaus papers. Intended to encourage Modernist designers to use papered rather than painted finishes, they displayed shimmering cross-hatching; vertical, horizontal or wavy lines; or delicate latticework in closely related pastel tones. Many of these designs, together with patterns of sparsely arranged arrows, mazes and grids printed in bright colours on pale grounds, retained their popularity throughout the 1940s.

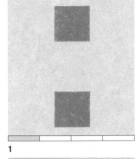

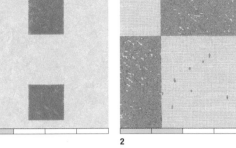

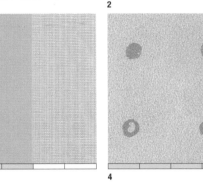

1 **Osborne & Little/Lamorna/ Galena W1677** Colour **05** Alt. colours **yes** Width **52cm/20½in** Length **10m/ 11yd** Repeat **9cm/3½in** Price ★

2 **Anna French/Eden/Aquila** Colour **AQUNW03** Alt. colours **yes** Width **52cm/20½in** Length **10m/11yd** Repeat **53cm/21in** Price ★

3 **Cole & Son/Wide Moiré Stripe 55/3100** Colour **off-white** Alt. colours **yes** Width **52cm/ 20½in** Length **10m/11yd** Repeat **7cm/2¾in** Price ★

4 **Osborne & Little/Tangent/Index CW5162** Colour **03** Alt. colours **yes** Width **52cm/20½in** Length **10m/11yd** Repeat **2cm/¾in** Price ★

5 **Osborne & Little/Axiom/Calculus W1823** Colour **05** Alt. colours **yes** Width **52cm/20½in** Length **10m/11yd** Repeat **2.5cm/1in** Price ★

6 **Jane Churchill/Fernhurst JY61W** Colour **05 stone** Alt. colours **yes** Width **52cm/20½in** Length **10m/11yd** Repeat **7.5cm/2¾in** Price ★★★★

7 **Mauny/Grècque Frieze 506L** Colour **multi** Alt. colours **yes** Width **4cm/1½in** Length **10m/11yd** Repeat – Price ★ ♣

8 **Paint and Paper Library/David Oliver/Liberation/Liberation 005-LIB-BF-S1** Colour **buff** Alt. colours **yes** Width **52cm/20½in** Length **10m/11yd** Repeat **53cm/21in** Price ★

9 **Cole & Son/Pinstripe 55/3043** Colour **PR yellow** Alt. colours **yes** Width **53cm/21in** Length **10m/11yd** Repeat – Price ★

10

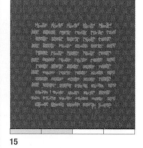

15

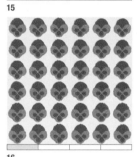

16

17

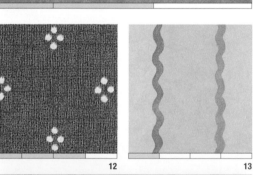

11   **12**   **13**

18

15 Today Interiors/Novus NV317
Colour **0** Alt. colours **yes** Width
53cm/21in Length **10m/11yd**
Repeat – Price ★

16 Mauny/Pensée 5016 Colour
multi Alt. colours **yes** Width
47cm/18½in Length **10m/11yd**
Repeat – Price ★★★ 🖌

**17 Colefax and Fowler/Candy
Stripe 7409/02** Colour **pink**
Alt. colours **yes** Width **52cm/
20½in** Length **10m/11yd**
Repeat – Price ★

18 Nicholas Herbert/Katie W05
Colour **12 cream on moss** Alt.
colours **yes** Width **52cm/
20½in** Length **10m/11yd**
Repeat **5cm/2in** Price ★

10 Zoffany/Fresco Check V436
Colour **04** Alt. colours **yes**
Width **52cm/20½in** Length
10m/11yd Repeat **10.5cm/
4in** Price ★

**11 Jane Churchill/Tamora/Tamora
Stripe JY98W** Colour **08 aqua/
cream** Alt. colours **yes** Width
52cm/20½in Length **10m/11yd**
Repeat – Price ★

12 Graham & Brown 51030
Colour **aubergine** Alt. colours
yes Width **52cm/20½in** Length
10m/11yd Repeat **4cm/1½in**
Price ★

**13 Nina Campbell/Zembla/Rick
Rack NCW 2225** Colour **08**
Alt. colours **yes** Width **52cm/
20½in** Length **10m/11yd**
Repeat – Price ★

**14 Colefax and Fowler/Albemarle
7074/06** Colour **red** Alt.
colours **yes** Width **52cm/
20½in** Length **10m/11yd**
Repeat **8.5cm/3¼in**
Price ★

14

SIMULATIONS

Since the First World War,
many manufacturers have
produced patterned and
plain wallpapers that are
intended to simulate fabric
or leather wall-hangings;
notable examples include
linen, cotton and (as here)
snakeskin. Various methods
have been employed to
achieve the desired effect,
including flocking, screen-
printing and, more recently,
photogravure printing – the
latter building up the
pattern and texture of the
paper by means of a series
of small coloured dots of
varying degrees of
translucency and opacity.

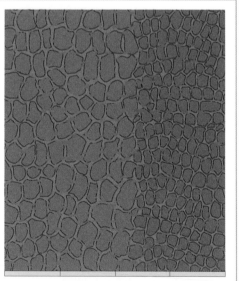

Today Interiors/FX/Snakeskin FXV3445 Colour **5** Alt.
colours **yes** Width **53cm/21in** Length **10m/11yd**
Repeat – Price ★

20th century

Geometrics: Late 20th–early 21st century

During the 1950s and 1960s, the link between wallpaper patterns and the designs employed in contemporary fine art that had been evident early in the 20th century was further consolidated by the appearance of the geometric papers produced by the British designer Lucienne Day, which featured linear patterns and ovoid shapes. The abstract, geometric shapes that appeared on the "Corbusier papers" launched in the late 1950s also revealed the influence of contemporary architecture. Other "modern" or "futuristic" designs of note included, from Scandinavia, giant circles and waving vertical bands displayed on rectangular grids in strong tone-on-tone colours and, in America, France and Britain, patterns made up of small geometric motifs rendered in reds, yellows, greys, mauves and black on dark backgrounds. For the more traditionally minded, striped-and-checked tartan patterns also proved popular during the 1950s and 1960s, while a mid-1960s' and 1970s' Art Deco revival provided more recent nostalgia. However, apart from a substantial increase in the production of documentary geometric papers dating from as early as the 17th century, the latter years of the 20th century were most notable for the arrival of naturalistic photogravure papers produced in imitation of brick walls and stone-blocking.

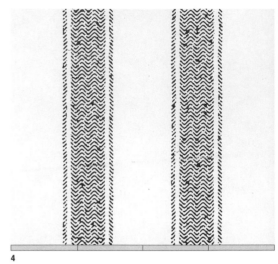

4

1

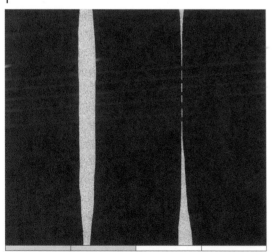

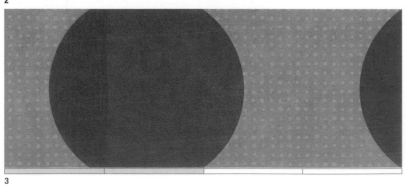

2

3

5

6

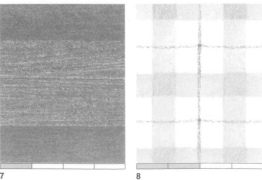

7

8

1 Today Interoirs/Zaniah ZB287 Colour **4** Alt. colours **yes** Width **53cm/21in** Length **10m/11yd** Repeat – Price ★

2 Today Interoirs/Samadhi/Fino SAW304 Colour **3** Alt. colours **yes** Width **53cm/21in** Length **10m/11yd** Repeat **26cm/10¼in** Price ★

3 Harlequin/Divine Border Colour **35361** Alt. colours **yes** Width **13cm/5in** Length **5m/5½yd** Repeat – Price ★

4 Baer & Ingram/Ticking Paper TKW11 Colour **black** Alt. colours **yes** Width **52cm/20½in** Length **10m/11yd** Repeat **4.5cm/1¾in** Price ★

5 Nina Campbell/Ferronnier/ Chareau NCW2193 Colour **04** Alt. colours **yes** Width **52cm/ 20½in** Length **10m/11yd** Repeat – Price ★

6 Coloroll/Harmony Stripe 86226 Colour **red and beige** Alt. colours **yes** Width **52cm/20½in** Length **10m/11yd** Repeat **53cm/21in** Price ★

7 Osborne & Little/Lamorna/ Zennor W1670 Colour **01** Alt. colours **yes** Width **52cm/20½in** Length **10m/ 11yd** Repeat **18cm/7in** Price ★

8 Anna French/T for Teddy/Rug Colour **RUGWP034** Alt. colours **yes** Width **52cm/20½in** Length **10m/11yd** Repeat **2.5cm/1in** Price ★

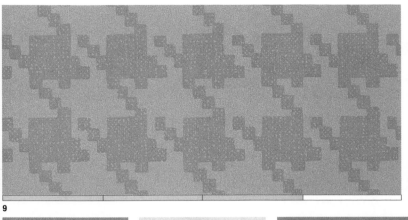

9

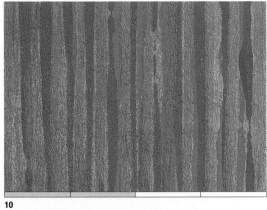

10

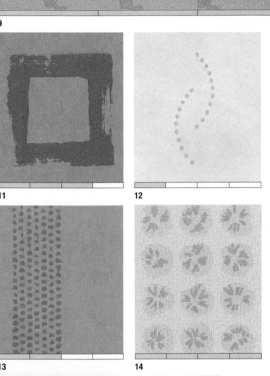

11

12

13

14

15

16

17

9 **Ottilie Stevenson/Houndstooth V0035** Colour **yellow** Alt. colours **yes** Width **52cm/ 20½in** Length **10m/11yd** Repeat **3cm/1¼in** Price ★★★★

10 **Anya Larkin/Artemis AR1** Colour **grey and blue on gold ingot** Alt. colours **yes** Width **76cm/30in** Length **3m/ 3⅓yd** Repeat **23cm/9in** Price ★★★★★

11 **Today Interiors/Samadhi SAW306** Colour **4** Alt. colours **yes** Width **53cm/ 21in** Length **10m/11yd** Repeat **3cm/1¼in** Price ★

12 **Harlequin/Arc** Colour **35023** Alt. colours **yes** Width **52cm/20½in** Length **10m/ 11yd** Repeat **26cm/10¼in** Price ★

13 **Today Interiors/Zaniah/ Electrum ZW282** Colour **6** Alt. colours **yes** Width **53cm/ 21in** Length **10m/11yd** Repeat **52cm/20½in** Price ★

14 **Today Interiors/Aymara/Leo AYW336** Colour **1** Alt. colours **yes** Width **53cm/21in** Length **10m/11yd** Repeat **10.5cm/4in** Price ★

15 **Anna French/Eden/Cupola** Colour **CUPNW01** Alt. colours **yes** Width **52cm/20½in** Length **10m/11yd** Repeat **52cm/20½in** Price ★

16 **Anna French/T for Teddy/Fairy Stripe** Colour **FAIWP093** Alt. colours **yes** Width **52cm/ 20½in** Length **10m/11yd** Repeat **52cm/20½in** Price ★

17 **Nobilis/Tenor Border** Colour **BOR3604** Alt. colours **yes** Width **14cm/5½in** Length **9m/10yd** Repeat – Price ★★ ♣

18 **Nobilis/Lousiaine** Colour **LOSA29** Alt. colours **yes** Width **70cm/27½in** Length **10m/11yd** Repeat – Price ★

19 **Anna French/T for Teddy/ Polka Dot** Colour **POLWP027** Alt. colours **yes** Width **52cm/ 20½in** Length **10m/11yd** Repeat **11cm/4¼in** Price ★

20 **Osborne & Little/Jangala/ Aztec W5106** Colour **06** Alt. colours **yes** Width **52cm/ 20½in** Length **10m/11yd** Repeat **53cm/21in** Price ★

18

19

20

Paints & Finishes

Paints

Prior to the mid-19th century, most paint pigments were derived from clays, vegetable matter and by-products of the mining industry such as copper carbonate, cobalt and iron, and chrome oxides. Until pharmacies began to sell phials of premixed pigments at the end of the 19th century, most paints were prepared onsite by itinerant craftsmen. Although a wide range of hues could be produced from these pigments, many proved unstable, or "fugitive", when exposed to moisture and sunlight. This instability caused bright colours to fade and blotch.

The invention of aniline dyes in the mid-19th century and, more significantly, of synthetic chemical pigments during the 20th century, resulted in more stable, durable paints, and an increase in the range of the colour palette. This mass-production also provided greater consistency of colour. However, recently there has been a reappreciation of the decorative qualities of some of the earlier paints – notably limewash and milk paint – with their constituents moderated to ensure greater stability and longevity than before.

LEFT The linear configuration of the colour scheme in this late 20th-century bathroom echoes some of the Art Deco interiors of the 1920s and 1930s (and revival Art Deco interiors of the 1960s). However, the pale yellow and lilac hues used here are lighter and cooler than the hot, saturated colours often employed in classic Art Deco rooms.

KEY COLOURS

1 Ox blood, burgundy and other dark red paints were a feature of decorative schemes from the Middle Ages to the early 18th century, and enjoyed numerous revivals thereafter.

2 Vegetable- and mineral-pigmented dark green paints were often used on woodwork from the early 17th to the mid-18th century. Acid greens became very fashionable in the Victorian era.

3 Lighter, more muted greens have included grey-green "drab" during the 18th century, olive green ("greenery-yallery") in the late 19th century and eau de Nil during the 1930s and 1940s.

4 Terracotta-coloured paints, tinted with clay pigments, have been produced for thousands of years, but stronger, more vivid mustard yellows emerged only with the invention of aniline dyes in the 1850s.

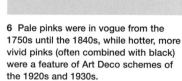

5 Pale blues, such as turquoise and Wedgwood blue, were fashionable from the 1750s until the 1840s, particularly on plasterwork. Light pastel blues have also proved popular since the 1930s.

6 Pale pinks were in vogue from the 1750s until the 1840s, while hotter, more vivid pinks (often combined with black) were a feature of Art Deco schemes of the 1920s and 1930s.

---

1 Finnaren & Haley Colour **Mt. Vernon red 520315** Composition and finish *water-based:* **matt, semi-gloss** *oil-based:* **semi-gloss** Price ★★★ W 🎨 🏠

2 Sanderson/Spectrum Colour **northern pine 56-1U** Composition and finish *water-based:* **matt, silk** *oil-based:* **eggshell, gloss** Price ★★ W C

3 Sigma Coatings/BS4800 Colour Range Colour **Westmorland 12B21** Composition and finish *water-based:* **matt, satin** *oil-based:* **gloss, satin** Price ★ W 🎨

4 Annie Sloan Colour **strong yellow 27** Composition and finish *water-based:* **matt** Price ★★ W 🎨

5 Zest Essentials/Mediterranean Palette 113 Colour **Alexandria** Composition and finish *water-based:* **matt** Price ★★★ W

6 Fired Earth/Kevin McCloud/English Palette Colour **great house pink** Composition and finish *water-based:* **emulsion, eggshell, distemper** Price ★★ W C 🎨 🖼

ABOVE The ambience in this southern Mediterranean hallway is created by the open archway and the juxtaposition of the quarry-tiled floor and staircase with a cool blue colourwash on the walls. Blue is often used in Mediterranean kitchens and hallways because of its cooling effect.

LEFT This is a typical 19th-century Shaker bedroom. The stone-coloured painted walls and the Shaker blue milk-painted joinery provide a cool, understated backdrop that enhances the warm, natural wood finishes of the exquisitely made pieces of Shaker furniture. Notable Shaker colours include yellow ochre, olive green and earthy shades of terracotta and pink.

Paints: **Pre-18th century**

Before the 18th century, limewash was the favoured medium for decorating masonry and plaster surfaces (*see* opposite). Limewash was also sometimes applied to woodwork, although if it was mixed incorrectly it tended to rub off on to clothing if brushed against. Milk paint provided a more stable medium for woodwork and furniture (*see* page 290), and was in widespread use, particularly in rural areas. By the beginning of the 17th century, durable oil paints and egg tempera (powder pigments mixed with linseed oil, water and egg yolk) were also increasingly employed on internal woodwork and furniture. However, being more costly to mix and apply, they tended to be confined to wealthier urban houses. Polychromatic colour schemes were highly fashionable until the end of the 17th century. Primary colours – rich reds, yellows and blues – were much in evidence, as were various shades of green and brown. Pigments were mostly derived from earth, clays and vegetable matter, although diverse materials such as ox blood, cattle urine and beetle juice were also utilized by colourists who, since the Middle Ages, had belonged to specialist guilds that jealously guarded the secrets of pigment production.

1

2

3

4

DARKER HUES

Prior to the 18th century, most softwood wall-panelling and other joinery found in the reception rooms of residential houses was painted in dark colours. While milk paint was often employed in rural areas and less affluent households, the favoured medium in urban areas and grander homes was oil paint, mixed on site from boiled linseed oil, ground chalk (whiting), turpentine and ground pigment. Oil versions were invariably in earth colours (mostly browns, reds and greens) derived from clays, plants and metal oxides.

J.W. Bollom/Bromel Colour **earthenware 08C39 JWB421** Composition and finish *water-based:* **matt, silk** *oil-based:* **eggshell, gloss** Price ★★★ W C

The plasterwork and wooden panelling and mouldings in Dennis Severs's authentically restored 17th-century house in London, England, have been painted with a gloss-finish, dark green oil paint typical of the period.

1 **Cole & Son** Colour **Strawberry Hill** Composition and finish *water-based:* **matt, emulsion** Price ★ W C

2 **Auro Organic Paints** Colour **cranberry 15D** Composition and finish *water-based:* **matt** Price ★★ W F

3 **Auro Organic Paints** Colour **tobacco** Composition and finish *water-based:* **gloss, eggshell** Price ★★★

4 **Dulux/Heritage Colours** Colour **90RR22/227** Composition and finish *water-based:* **matt, silk, soft sheen** *oil-based:* **dead flat, eggshell, gloss** Price ★ W C

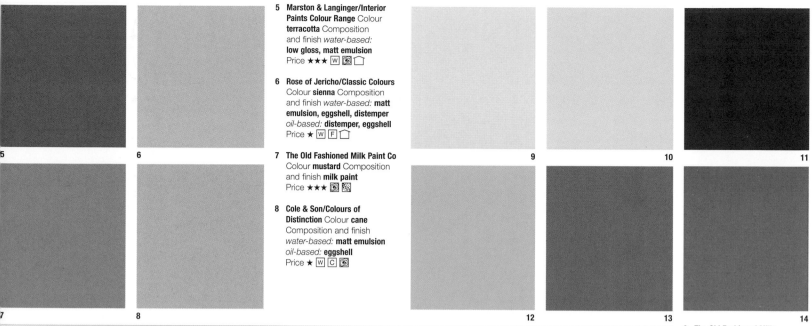

5 Marston & Langinger/Interior Paints Colour Range Colour **terracotta** Composition and finish *water-based:* **low gloss, matt emulsion** Price ★★★ Ⓦ ▣ ⌂

6 Rose of Jericho/Classic Colours Colour **sienna** Composition and finish *water-based:* **matt emulsion, eggshell, distemper** *oil-based:* **distemper, eggshell** Price ★ Ⓦ Ⓕ ⌂

7 The Old Fashioned Milk Paint Co Colour **mustard** Composition and finish **milk paint** Price ★★★ ▣ ▣

8 Cole & Son/Colours of Distinction Colour **cane** Composition and finish *water-based:* **matt emulsion** *oil-based:* **eggshell** Price ★ Ⓦ Ⓒ ▣

9 The Old Fashioned Milk Paint Co Colour **oyster white** Composition and finish **milk paint** Price ★★★ ▣ ▣

10 Sanderson/Spectrum Colour **pheasant's feather 2-23M** Composition and finish *water-based:* **matt, silk** *oil-based:* **eggshell, gloss** Price ★★ Ⓦ ⌂

11 Colourman Paints/Reproduction Colours Colour **100** Composition and finish *water-based:* **matt** Price ★★ Ⓦ ▣

12 Craig & Rose/Authentic Period Colours Colour **pale Medici blue** Composition and finish *water-based:* **eggshell, chalk emulsion** Price ★★ Ⓦ Ⓒ Ⓕ ⌂

13 Colourman Paints/Reproduction Colours Colour **115** Composition and finish *water-based:* **matt** Price ★★ Ⓦ ▣

14 Crown/RIBA Drawings Colour **Palladian 15** Composition and finish *water-based:* **matt emulsion, acrylic eggshell** Price ★★ Ⓣ Ⓦ Ⓕ ▣

LIMEWASH PAINTS

First used *c.* 8000 BC, white limewash is made by mixing lime putty with water and raw linseed oil. Coloured versions are created by adding earth or metallic pigments. Applied to masonry and to lime renders and plasters, limewash dries to an opaque "pure" white or colour that appears bright and luminous under strong light but darker and matt under poor light. It also has the advantage of allowing moisture in the underlying surface to evaporate, thereby preventing structural deterioration.

1 Liz Induni Colour **terracotta** Composition and finish **limewash, distemper** Price ★ Ⓦ ▣

2 Liz Induni Colour **pale pink** Composition and finish **limewash, distemper** Price ★ Ⓦ ▣

3 Rose of Jericho Colour **eau de Nil** Composition and finish **limewash, distemper, emulsion, flat oil, eggshell** Price ★★ Ⓦ Ⓕ ⌂

4 Cy-Près Colour **Alice Grace** Composition and finish **limewash, distemper** Price ★ Ⓦ Ⓕ ⌂ ▣

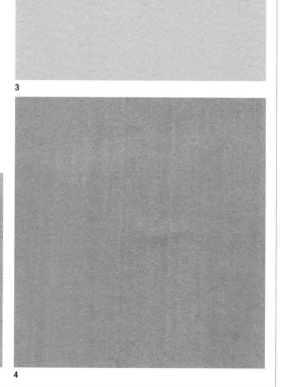

Paints: 18th century

In the 18th century, limewash (see page 289) and milk paint (see below) remained in widespread use on plasterwork and woodwork respectively. However, as the century progressed matt, mid-sheen and gloss oil paints became the most frequently used finishes for plaster and wooden surfaces in more affluent households. As far as choice of colours was concerned, from the 1750s there was a general move from darker to lighter hues (see opposite), with bright, vivid colours, such as citron, violet, turquoise, pea green and cerise, proving especially popular toward the end of the century.

Underpinning the new aesthetic was a growing understanding of colour theory. An influential publication on the subject was Moses Harris's *The Natural History of Colours* (1766), which explained how to mix more than 300 tints from 15 basic colours. The consequences of this were that a wider choice of colours opened up, and decorators were able to employ varying shades of the same basic colour on adjacent flat and moulded surfaces to emphasize subtly the architectural proportions and details of a room.

MILK PAINTS

Casein ("milk") paint was used on woodwork and furniture throughout Europe, Scandinavia and America from the 16th to the 19th centuries, especially in rural areas. Cheap and durable, it was made by tinting buttermilk or skimmed milk with earth or vegetable pigments, and a little lime was added to inhibit insect infestation and fungal growth. Milk paint dries to a subtle sheen (somewhere between matt and mid-sheen) and displays a clarity and opacity of colour that is rarely matched by modern paints. Today, milk paint is available from specialist manufacturers.

1 **Old Village Paints/ Williamsburg** Colour **Virginia clock blue** Composition and finish **milk paint** Price ★★★★

2 **The Old Fashioned Milk Paint Co** Colour **Lexington green** Composition and finish **milk paint** Price ★★★ W F

3 **Nutshell Natural Paints/ Casein Emulsion** Colour **turquoise** Composition and finish **milk paint** Price ★★ W

4 **The Old Fashioned Milk Paint Co** Colour **buttermilk** Composition and finish **milk paint** Price ★★★ W F

5 **Nutshell Natural Paints/ Casein Emulsion** Colour **iron oxide-red 110 "strong"** Composition and finish **milk paint** Price ★★

1 (caption)

3 (caption)

5 (caption)

1 **Cole & Son** Colour **Georgian grey** Composition and finish *water-based:* **matt, emulsion** *oil-based:* **eggshell** Price ★ W C

2 **Dulux/Heritage Colours** Colour **dark stone** Composition and finish *water-based:* **matt, silk, soft sheen** *oil-based:* **dead flat, eggshell, gloss** Price ★ W C

3 **Dulux/Heritage Colours** Colour **ash** Composition and finish *water-based:* **matt, silk, soft sheen** *oil-based:* **dead flat, eggshell, gloss** Price ★ W C

4 **Sanderson/Spectrum** Colour **almond cream/11-1P** Composition and finish *water-based:* **matt, silk** *oil-based:* **eggshell, gloss** Price ★★ W C

5 **Dulux/Heritage Colours** Colour **DH white 0105 Y10R** Composition and finish *water-based:* **matt, silk, soft sheen** *oil-based:* **dead flat, eggshell, gloss** Price ★ W C

6 **Sanderson/Spectrum** Colour **straw yellow 3-10M** Composition and finish *water-based:* **matt, silk** *oil-based:* **eggshell, gloss** Price ★★ W C

7 **Dulux/Heritage Colours** Colour **DH lemon 1643 YO5R** Composition and finish *water-based:* **matt, silk, soft sheen** *oil-based:* **dead flat, eggshell, gloss** Price ★ W C

8 **Paint Magic/Quality Emulsion** Colour **haystack** Composition and finish *water-based:* **matt** Price ★★ W

9 Dulux/Heritage Colours
Colour **DH pearl 1307G28Y**
Composition and finish *water-based:* **matt, silk, soft sheen** *oil-based:* **dead flat, eggshell, gloss** Price ★ W C 🖼 🏠

10 Farrow & Ball/National Trust
Colour **pea green** Composition and finish *water-based:* **distemper, matt** *oil-based:* **dead flat, eggshell** Price ★ W 🏠

11 Craig & Rose/Authentic Period Colours Colour **deep Adam green** Composition and finish *water-based:* **eggshell, chalk emulsion** Price ★★ W C F 🏠

12 Fired Earth/V&A Museum/ Historic Colours Colour **terre vert 16** Composition and finish *water-based:* **emulsion, eggshell, distemper,** *oil-based:* **gloss** Price ★★ W C 🖼 🏠

13 Colourman Paints/Reproduction Colours Colour **104** Composition and finish *water-based:* **matt** Price ★★ W 🖼

9

10

11

12

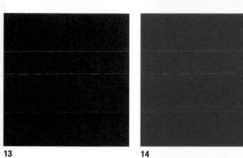

13

14

14 Crown/Non-drip and Liquid Gloss Colour **Scottish pine** Composition and finish *oil-based:* **gloss** Price ★★ 🖼 🏠

15 Craig & Rose/Authentic Period Colours Colour **pompadour** Composition and finish *water-based:* **eggshell, chalk emulsion** Price ★★ W C F 🏠

16 The Old Fashioned Milk Paint Co Colour **Federal blue** Composition and finish **milk paint** Price ★★★ F 🖼

17 Pratt & Lambert/Interior Wall & Trim Colour **princely blue 1148** Composition and finish *water-based:* **matt, satin, eggshell, semi-gloss, gloss** Price ★★ W F 🖼

18 Colourman Paints/ Reproduction Colours Colour **126** Composition and finish *water-based:* **matt** Price ★★ W 🖼

19 Paint and Paper Library/David Oliver Colour **Sophie Rose** Composition and finish *water-based:* **flat emulsion, acrylic eggshell, basecoat** *oil-based:* **dead flat, eggshell, basecoat** Price ★★★ W F 🏠

20 Paint and Paper Library/ David Oliver Colour **bruno** Composition and finish *water-based:* **flat emulsion, acrylic eggshell, basecoat** *oil-based:* **eggshell, dead flat, basecoat** Price ★★★ W F 🏠

15

16

17

18

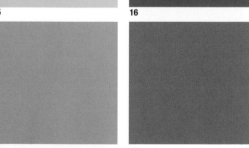

19

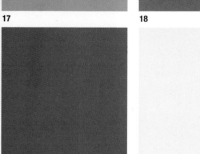

20

FROM DARK TO LIGHT

Lighter-coloured decorative schemes originated in the white-painted and gilded state rooms of French palaces during the late 17th century, but it took another 50 years for them to filter through to ordinary European, Scandinavian and American households. Consequently, for the first half of the 18th century, darker earth colours – muddy browns and greens ("drabs") – remained much in evidence on walls and joinery, but were gradually superseded by paler, brighter colours as the century progressed. Fashionable hues included pinks and light terracottas, pale greens and blues, and various yellows, such as "straw", "citron" and "Chinese".

1 Craig & Rose/Authentic Period Colours Colour **Swedish blue** Composition and finish *water-based:* **eggshell, chalk emulsion** Price ★★ W C 🏠 F

2 Berger Colour **pale lemon** Composition and finish *water-based:* **matt** Price ★★ W C

1

2

Subtly contrasting shades of pale lemon on the walls and ceiling complement the fine mahogany furniture, accentuate natural light and contribute to a general sense of spaciousness in this late 18th-century drawing room.

Paints: Early to mid-19th century

From the early 19th century until the 1830s, the late 18th-century drift toward the use of lighter hues (*see* page 290–291) continued in a number of fashionable colour schemes that combined cream, or sometimes white, with pale greys or blues. For the most part, however, Regency interiors were characterized by the use of stronger, more vivid hues. Notable examples, which were employed in fabrics and wallpapers as well as flat-painted finishes, included saffron and sulphur-yellows; emerald green; lilac and turquoise; deep pink; and cherry-, orange-, crimson- and Pompeiian reds. In the grandest Regency households, gilding was also much in evidence, primarily on decorative mouldings.

Such colours, many of which became fashionable in America, too (*see* opposite), were invariably applied flat and opaque. "Distressing" or "broken colour" techniques, such as sponging and ragging (*see* page 305), were not practised: their use in late 20th- and early 21st-century reproductions of Regency colour were an inauthentic, modern conceit.

1

2

3

4

1 Craig & Rose/Authentic Period Colours Colour **Regency white** Composition and finish *water-based:* **eggshell, chalk emulsion** Price ★★ W C F ⌂

2 Crown/RIBA Drawings Colour **Regency 14** Composition and finish *water-based:* **emulsion, acrylic eggshell** Price ★★ W C ▣ ▨ T

3 Pratt & Lambert/Interior Wall & Trim Colour **osprey 1292** Composition and finish *water-based:* **matt, satin, eggshell, semi-gloss, gloss** Price ★★ W F ▣

4 Grand Illusions/Traditional Paints Colour **duck-egg blue** Composition and finish *water-based:* **matt** Price ★★ W F ▣

5 The Stulb Company Colour **Windsor Chair pink 81.2000.2** Composition and finish **milk paint** Price ★★★ W F ▣

6 Farrow & Ball/National Trust Colour **Eating Room red** Composition and finish *water-based:* **distemper, matt** *oil-based:* **distemper, dead flat, eggshell, gloss** Price ★★★ W ⌂

7 Fired Earth/V&A Museum/ Historic Colours Colour **Pompeiian red** Composition and finish *water-based:* **distemper, matt, eggshell** *oil-based:* **gloss** Price ★★ W C ▣

8 Dulux/Trade Colour Palette Colour **09YR 11/476** Composition and finish *water-based:* **matt, silk, soft sheen** *oil-based:* **dead flat, eggshell, gloss** Price ★ W C

9 J.W. Bollom/Bromel Colour **RAL 4005** Composition and finish *water-based:* **matt, silk** *oil-based:* **eggshell, gloss** Price ★★ W C ▣

10 Sanderson/Spectrum Colour **imperial purple 54-18U** Composition and finish *water-based:* **matt, silk** *oil-based:* **gloss** Price ★★ W C ▣ ⌂

5

6

7

8

9

10

GOTHIC REVIVAL

Led by the architect Augustus Pugin and decorators such as John Gregory Crace, the Gothic Revival style became the height of fashion in Britain during the 1830s and 1840s. Based on studies of medieval design and decoration, it was characterized by deep, rich red, green, blue and yellow paint colours. These were echoed in tapestries and heavy, woven drapes, enlivened by brass candlesticks and wall sconces, and complemented by dark, heavy, ecclesiastical-style furniture mostly made of oak or mahogany.

1

2

3

4

1 Cole & Son Colour **Pugin blue** Composition and finish *water-based:* **emulsion** *oil-based:* **eggshell** Price ★★★ W C ▣ ⌂

2 Crown/RIBA Drawings Colour **Gothic Revival 12** Composition and finish *water-based:* **emulsion, acrylic eggshell** Price ★★ W C ▣ ▨ T

3 Crown/RIBA Drawings Colour **Gothic Revival 3** Composition and finish *water-based:* **emulsion, acrylic eggshell** Price ★★ W C ▣ ▨ T

4 Crown/RIBA Drawings Colour **Gothic Revival 8** Composition and finish *water-based:* **emulsion, acrylic eggshell** Price ★★ W C ▣ ▨ T

11   **12**   **13**   **14**   **15**   **16**

17   **18**   **19**   **20**   **21**

THE FEDERAL PALETTE

During the 18th and 19th centuries, the colours employed in American interiors were strongly influenced by those that were fashionable at the time in Britain and France. This was especially so in the southern states of America, where rich plantation owners vied with one another to decorate their mansions in the most up-to-date Continental styles. Consequently, during the first half of the 19th century the "Colonial-Federal palette", which had combined earth colours, such as almond, rust-red and red-brown, with bright blues, greens and yellows, was gradually superseded by a later "Federal palette" that favoured terracottas, deep pinks, milky yellows, lavender and various stone colours, including several shades of grey.

1 **Old Village Paints/Vintage Colours** Colour **1752 lamplighter yellow** Composition and finish **milk paint** Price ★★★★ 🖼🖼⌂

2 **Sawyer Finn Natural Milk Paint/River Valley** Colour **terracotta** Composition and finish **milk paint** Price ★★★ W C F 🖼

Milky-yellow painted walls provide the backdrop to a late 1830s, flame-cut mahogany settee in the Old Merchant's House, New York, USA. Yellow walls enlivened with gilt-framed paintings were particularly fashionable in the mid-19th century.

11 Finnaren & Haley/Shades of '76 Colour **Saybrook ivory 520800** Composition and finish *water-based:* **matt, satin, semi-gloss, gloss** *oil-based:* **semi-gloss** Price ★★★ W 🖼⌂

12 The Stulb Company Colour **Fancy Chair yellow 74.2000.1** Composition and finish **milk paint** Price ★★★ W F 🖼

13 Sherwin Williams/Preservation Palette Colour **rookwood clay SW2823** Composition and finish *water-based:* **matt, satin, semi-gloss** *oil-based:* **semi-gloss** Price ★★ W 🖼

14 Sherwin Williams/Preservation Palette Colour **Downing sand SW 2822** Composition and finish *water-based:* **matt, satin, semi-gloss** *oil-based:* **semi-gloss** Price ★★ W 🖼

15 Finnaren & Haley/Shades of '76 Colour **marblehead 520183** Composition and finish *water-based:* **matt, satin, semi-gloss, gloss** *oil-based:* **semi-gloss** Price ★ W 🖼⌂

16 Craig & Rose/Authentic Period Colours Colour **Sung yellow** Composition and finish *water-based:* **eggshell, chalk emulsion** Price ★★ W C F ⌂

17 Dulux/Heritage Colours Colour **French grey 16BB50066** Composition and finish *water-based:* **matt, silk, soft sheen** *oil-based:* **dead flat, eggshell, gloss** Price ★ W C 🖼⌂

18 Grand Illusions/Traditional Paints Colour **fresco pink** Composition and finish *water-based:* **matt** Price ★★ W F 🖼

19 Farrow & Ball/National Trust Colour **ointment pink** Composition and finish *water-based:* **distemper** *oil-based:* **distemper, dead flat, eggshell, gloss** Price ★★ W ⌂

20 The Old Fashioned Milk Paint Co Colour **slate** Composition and finish *water-based:* **milk paint** Price ★★★ W 🖼⌂

21 Sherwin Williams/Preservation Palette Colour **Queen Anne lilac SW 0021** Composition and finish *water-based:* **matt, satin, semi-gloss** *oil-based:* **semi-gloss** Price ★★ W 🖼

19th century

Paints: Mid- to Late 19th century

Most of the deeper, richer colours promoted by the Gothic Revival movement in the 1830s and 1840s (*see* page 292)) remained in vogue during the third quarter of the 19th century, and could still be found in many households 20 years later. In some respects this "High Victorian" palette was as much to do with technical innovation as fashionable aesthetics. The mid-century invention of aniline dyes derived from coal tar produced sharp yellows, deep blues, acid greens, lurid purples and mustards of an intensity not seen before – their sheer novelty an attractive quality in its own right. More traditional earthy reds and browns were still liked, but even these were usually brightened by eye-catching juxtapositions of gold or yellow. Not surprisingly, a reaction to this strong, eclectic and sometimes lurid palette soon set in – initially under the Aesthetic movement, and soon after among proponents and followers of the Arts and Crafts movement (*see*, respectively, below and opposite).

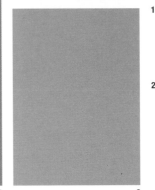

1 Craig & Rose/Authentic Period Colours Colour **Kashmir beige** Composition and finish *water-based:* **eggshell, chalk emulsion** Price ★★ W C F ⌂

2 Craig & Rose/Authentic Period Colours Colour **Winchester** Composition and finish *water-based:* **eggshell, chalk emulsion** Price ★★ W C F ⌂

AESTHETIC COLOURS

The richer and brighter hues favoured by the mid-to-late 19th-century Aesthetic movement (*see* above) included lustrous grape purples, plum-red, burgundy and lemon yellow. However, these were largely confined to soft furnishings. For painted woodwork and unpapered walls, paler or flatter colours were preferred. Flat olive green (known as "greenery-yallery") is probably the signature colour for Aesthetic woodwork, but white, ivory, stony greys and China blue were also popular, with shades of two or more often combined in the same room.

3 Craig & Rose/Authentic Period Colours Colour **tapestry green** Composition and finish *water-based:* **eggshell, chalk emulsion** Price ★★ W C F ⌂

4 Craig & Rose/Authentic Period Colours Colour **jasper cane** Composition and finish *water-based:* **eggshell, chalk emulsion** Price ★★ W C F ⌂

5 Dulux/Heritage Colours Colour **crimson** Composition and finish *water-based:* **matt, silk, soft sheen** *oil-based:* **dead flat, eggshell, gloss** Price ★ W C 🖼 ⌂

6 Crown/RIBA Drawings Colour **Victorian eclectic** Composition and finish *water-based:* **emulsion, acrylic eggshell** Price ★★ W C 🖼 ▦ T

7 Craig & Rose/Authentic Period Colours Colour **Osborne maroon** Composition and finish *water-based:* **eggshell, chalk emulsion** Price ★★ W C F ⌂

8 Dulux/Heritage Colours Colour **yellow ochre** Composition and finish *water-based:* **matt, silk, soft sheen** *oil-based:* **dead flat, eggshell, gloss** Price ★ W C 🖼 ⌂

9 Craig & Rose/Authentic Period Colours Colour **grate black** Composition and finish *water-based:* **eggshell, chalk emulsion** Price ★★ W C F ⌂

1 Craig & Rose/Authentic Period Colours Colour **moonstone grey** Composition and finish *water-based:* **eggshell, chalk emulsion** Price ★★ W C F ⌂

2 Morris & Co Colour **ivory** Composition and finish *water-based:* **matt emulsion** *oil-based:* **eggshell** Price ★ W C 🖼 🖼

3 Morris & Co Colour **olive** Composition and finish *water-based:* **matt emulsion** *oil-based:* **eggshell** Price ★★ W C 🖼 🖼

4 Fired Earth/V & A Museum/Historic Colours Colour **china blue** Composition and finish *water-based:* **emulsion and eggshell** Price ★★ W C 🖼

10

11

12

13

14

15

ARTS AND CRAFTS MOVEMENT

Also partly a reaction to the stylistic eclecticism and rich palette of many High Victorian interiors (*see* page 294), the late 19th-century Arts and Crafts movement promoted a more coherent, generally lighter approach to decoration. The palette drew for inspiration on a number of sources, including medieval ones, but was ultimately characterized by the colours of flowers and plants indigenous to the English countryside. Notable among these were "greenery-yallery" (*see* Aesthetic colours, opposite) on woodwork, and old rose, burgundy red and hyacinth blue on walls.

1

2

3

1 **Morris & Co** Colour **rose** Composition and finish *water-based:* **matt emulsion** *oil-based:* **eggshell** Price ★ w c

2 **Fired Earth/V&A Museum/ Historic Colours** Colour **Morris green** Composition and finish *water-based:* **emulsion, eggshell,** *oil-based:* **gloss** Price ★★ w c

3 **Morris & Co** Colour **mineral** Composition and finish *water-based:* **matt emulsion** *oil-based:* **eggshell** Price ★ w c

Designed in the 1890s by Philip Webb, Standen House in Sussex, England, is a showpiece of the Arts and Crafts movement preserved by the National Trust. Its dining-room chimneypiece is painted sea green – another classic Arts and Crafts colour.

10 **Fired Earth/V&A Museum/ Historic Colours** Colour **Indian red** Composition and finish *water-based:* **emulsion, eggshell,** *oil-based:* **gloss** Price ★★ w c

11 **Morris & Co** Colour **wine** Composition and finish *water-based:* **matt emulsion** *oil-based:* **eggshell** Price ★ w c

12 **Morris & Co** Colour **lichen** Composition and finish *water-based:* **matt emulsion** *oil-based:* **eggshell** Price ★ w c

13 **Holkham Linseed Paints** Colour **wild sage** Composition and finish **linseed paint** Price ★★★ w c f

14 **Morris & Co** Colour **woad** Composition and finish *water-based:* **matt emulsion** *oil-based:* **eggshell** Price ★ w c

15 **Crown/RIBA Drawings** Colour **Arts and Crafts 14** Composition and finish *water-based:* **emulsion, acrylic eggshell** Price ★★ w c t

Paints: Early 20th century

From the start of the 20th century to the outbreak of the First Word War, an element of continuity with late 19th-century Aesthetic colours was evident in Art Nouveau interiors (*see* below). However, the first four decades of the 20th century were largely dominated by three other, more innovative palettes. The first and most enduring of these centred on a fashion for "all-white" interiors, which emerged in the early 1900s and has coexisted alongside various other palettes to this day (*see* Quite White, page 300). The second palette, which largely consisted of pale, sophisticated hues, such as buff, beige, coffee, pastel blues and pinks and eau de Nil, became fashionable during the 1930s and in some respects was a forerunner of postwar–1950s' colour schemes (*see* page 298). In complete contrast, the third dominant palette – the height of fashion in Art Deco interiors of the late 1920s and 1930s – comprised striking combinations of hot, vivid colours (*see* opposite).

1

2

3

4

5

6

7

8

9

1 **Sherwin Williams/Preservation Palette** Colour **Burma jade SW 2862** Composition and finish *water-based:* **matt, satin, semi-gloss** *oil-based:* **semi-gloss** Price ★★ W C 🖾

2 **Dulux/Heritage Colours** Colour **eau de Nil 2127G36Y** Composition and finish *water-based:* **matt, silk, soft sheen** *oil-based:* **dead flat, eggshell, gloss** Price ★ W C 🖾 ⬜

3 **Dulux/Heritage Colours** Colour **turquoise blue** Composition and finish *water-based:* **matt, silk, soft sheen** *oil-based:* **dead flat, eggshell, gloss** Price ★ W C 🖾 ⬜

4 **Dulux/Heritage Colours** Colour **peacock blue** Composition and finish *water-based:* **matt, silk, soft sheen** *oil-based:* **dead flat, eggshell, gloss** Price ★ W C 🖾 ⬜

5 **Crown/Emulsion for Walls and Ceilings** Colour **misty rose** Composition and finish *water-based:* **matt, silk** Price ★★ W C

6 **Fired Earth/V&A Museum/Art Nouveau** Colour **Cranston pink** Composition and finish *water-based:* **emulsion, eggshell** Price ★★ W C 🖾

7 **Fired Earth/V&A Museum/Art Nouveau** Colour **Glasgow grey** Composition and finish *water-based:* **emulsion, eggshell** Price ★★ W C 🖾

8 **Jane Churchill** Colour **primrose 12 grey** Composition and finish *water-based:* **matt** Price ★ W F 🖾

9 **Fired Earth/V&A Museum/Art Nouveau** Colour **Brussels orange** Composition and finish *water-based:* **emulsion, eggshell** Price ★★ W C 🖾

ART NOUVEAU

In many respects the palette for painted surfaces in Art Nouveau interiors (*see* above) can be seen as an extension of that of the Aesthetic movement (*see* page 294). Core colours included olive and sage green, pale blueish hues such as lilac and violet, pale yellow, and white and cream – both of the latter being particularly prevalent on walls in Charles Rennie Mackintosh interiors. However, stronger yellow-mustard and quirkier brown-mustard colours, and even black, were also sometimes used on woodwork.

1 **Fired Earth/V&A Museum/Art Nouveau** Colour **tearoom pink** Composition and finish *water-based:* **emulsion, eggshell** Price ★★ W C 🖾

2 **Fired Earth/V&A Museum/Art Nouveau** Colour **thistle** Composition and finish *water-based:* **emulsion, eggshell** Price ★★ W C 🖾

3 **Fired Earth/V&A Museum/Art Nouveau** Colour **maison jaune** Composition and finish *water-based:* **emulsion, eggshell** Price ★★ W C 🖾

4 **Fired Earth/V&A Museum/Art Nouveau** Colour **tervuren green** Composition and finish *water-based:* **emulsion, eggshell** *oil-based:* **gloss** Price ★★ W C 🖾 ▨ ⬜

2

3

1

4

10 Dulux/Heritage Colours Colour **light buff** Composition and finish *water-based:* **matt, silk, soft sheen** *oil-based:* **dead flat, eggshell, gloss** Price ★ W C 🔲 🏠

11 Sanderson/Spectrum Colour **44-22M London grey** Composition and finish *water-based:* **matt, silk** *oil-based:* **eggshell, gloss** Price ★★ W C 🔲 🔳 🏠

12 Fired Earth/V&A Museum/Art Deco Colour **Silver screen** Composition and finish *water-based:* **metallic** Price ★★ W 🔲 S 🏠

13 Dulux/Heritage Colours Colour **battleship grey** Composition and finish *water-based:* **matt, silk, soft sheen** *oil-based:* **dead flat, eggshell, gloss** Price ★ W C 🔲 🏠

14 Dulux/Heritage Colours Colour **slate** Composition and finish *water-based:* **matt, silk, soft sheen** *oil-based:* **dead flat, eggshell, gloss** Price ★ W C 🔲 🏠

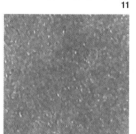

10
11
12

HOT COLOURS

While predominantly white colour schemes have proved popular throughout the 20th century, there has also been a significant and contrasting vogue for employing combinations of hot, vivid colours. This can be traced back to the *Exposition des Arts Décoratifs*, held in Paris, France, in 1925, which launched the Art Deco movement internationally. Colours on show at the exhibition included ultramarine, sea green, deep blue, turmeric yellow, black, crimson, burnt orange and hot pink – tints that have remained fashionable ever since.

J.W. Bollom Colour **mandarin 06E51 JWB74** Composition and finish *water-based:* **matt, silk** *oil-based:* **eggshell, gloss** Price ★ W C 🔲

John Oliver Colour **kinky pink** Composition and finish *water-based:* **matt** *oil-based:* **eggshell, gloss** Price ★★ W 🔲

This living room is painted and furnished in pink, beige, orange and black. The scheme is 1990s, but the colour combination originated in 1920s' Art Deco interiors.

15 Fired Earth/V&A Museum/Art Deco Colour **ocean liner** Composition and finish *water-based:* **emulsion, eggshell** Price ★★ W C 🔲

16 Sherwin Williams/Preservation Palette Colour **pink flamingo SW0080** Composition and finish *water-based:* **matt, satin, semi-gloss** *oil-based:* **semi-gloss** Price ★★ W C 🔲

17 Auro Organic Paints Colour **plum** Composition and finish *water-based:* **gloss, eggshell** Price ★★★ W C 🔲 🔳 🔲 🏠

18 Fired Earth/V&A Museum/Art Deco Colour **flapper pink** Composition and finish *water-based:* **emulsion, eggshell** Price ★★ W C 🔲

19 Fired Earth/V&A Museum/Art Deco Colour **cabaret red** Composition and finish *water-based:* **emulsion, eggshell** Price ★★ W C 🔲

20 Dulux/Heritage Colours Colour **brilliant green** Composition and finish *water-based:* **matt, silk, soft sheen** *oil-based:* **dead flat, eggshell, gloss** Price ★ W C 🔲 🏠

21 Crown/RIBA Drawings Colour **Art Deco 15** Composition and finish *water-based:* **emulsion, acrylic eggshell** Price ★★ W C 🔲 🔳 T

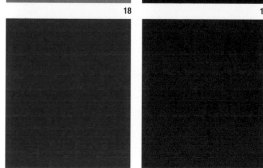

13
14
15
16
17
18
19
20
21
22
23
24
25

22 Fired Earth/V&A Museum/Art Deco Colour **jazz yellow** Composition and finish *water-based:* **emulsion, eggshell** Price ★★ W C 🔲

23 Fired Earth/V&A Museum/Art Deco Colour **glamour gold** Composition and finish *water-based:* **metallic** Price ★★ W 🔲 S 🏠

24 Crown/RIBA Drawings Colour **Art Deco 10** Composition and finish *water-based:* **emulsion, acrylic eggshell** Price ★★ W C 🔲 🔳 T

25 Crown/RIBA Drawings Colour **Art Deco 9** Composition and finish *water-based:* **emulsion, acrylic eggshell** Price ★★ W C 🔲 🔳 T

Paints: Mid-20th century

Underpinning the decorative styles that developed after 1945 was a universal need to leave behind the privations and gloom of the war years. This desire for a fresh start was strongly reflected in the colours favoured by decorators and homeowners. Initially, many looked back to the earlier years of the 20th century for inspiration – to bright, airy all-white or off-white schemes, and to the softer, paler colours of the 1930s (see pages 296 and 300).

By the 1960s and early 1970s, though, there was a widespread Art Nouveau revival, in which stronger Nouveau colours, such as peacock blues and greens, figured prominently (see page 296). Others took their inspiration from even earlier periods. For example, in some grander houses during the late 1950s and 1960s, late 18th- and early 19th-century schemes were recreated using opulent Neo-classical palettes (see pages 290–293). Far more innovative were the 'Op Art' interiors of the late 1950s and 1960s – notably those of influential designer David Hicks, who boldly combined an 18th-century sense of scale and form with saturated, contrasting colours, such as crimson, deep blue and violet.

THE 1950S PALETTE

For much of the 1950s, walls in many style-conscious homes were painted white. However, the chimneybreasts (or chimneybreast wall in its entirety) was invariably treated separately: either painted in a strongly contrasting primary colour, or lined with tongue-and-groove boards, usually of pine or stained in imitation of a darker wood. When white was not employed, fashionable alternatives included soft pinks, greens, blues and yellows, or pale, dusty reds, browns and greys.

1 **Crown/RIBA Drawings** Colour **50s sketchbook 1** Composition and finish *water-based:* **emulsion, acrylic eggshell** Price ★★ W C 🔲 🔲 T

2 **Crown/RIBA Drawings** Colour **50s sketchbook 4** Composition and finish *water-based:* **emulsion, acrylic eggshell** Price ★★ W C 🔲 🔲 T

3 **Crown/RIBA Drawings** Colour **50s sketchbook 9** Composition and finish *water-based:* **emulsion, acrylic eggshell** Price ★★ W C 🔲 🔲 T

4 **Crown/RIBA Drawings** Colour **50s sketchbook 11** Composition and finish *water-based:* **emulsion, acrylic eggshell** Price ★★ W C 🔲 🔲 T

5 **Crown/RIBA Drawings** Colour **50s sketchbook 15** Composition and finish *water-based:* **emulsion, acrylic eggshell** Price ★★ W C 🔲 🔲 T

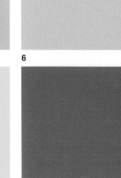

1 **Holkham Linseed Paints** Colour **custard** Composition and finish **linseed paint** Price ★★★ W C F 🔲 🔲 🔲 🔲 🔲

2 **Holkham Linseed Paints** Colour **antique gold** Composition and finish **linseed paint** Price ★★★ W C F 🔲 🔲 🔲 🔲 🔲

3 **Sawyer Finn** Colour **peach** Composition and finish **milk paint** Price ★★★ W C F 🔲

4 **Crown/RIBA Drawings** Colour **50s sketchbook 8** Composition and finish *water-based:* **emulsion, acrylic eggshell** Price ★★ W C 🔲 🔲 T

5 **Rose of Jericho/Classic Colours** Colour **Pozzuoli red** Composition and finish **limewash** *water-based:* **matt emulsion, distemper, eggshell** *oil-based:* **flat oil, distemper, eggshell** Price ★ W C 🔲 🔲 🔲

6 **Grand Illusions/Country Living** Colour **708 Chinese leaf** Composition and finish *water-based:* **matt, acrylic** Price ★★ W 🔲

7 **Grand Illusions/Country Living** Colour **706 tourmaline** Composition and finish *water-based:* **matt, acrylic** Price ★★ W 🔲

8 **Crown/RIBA Drawings** Colour **50s sketchbook 14** Composition and finish *water-based:* **emulsion, acrylic eggshell** Price ★★ W C 🔲 🔲

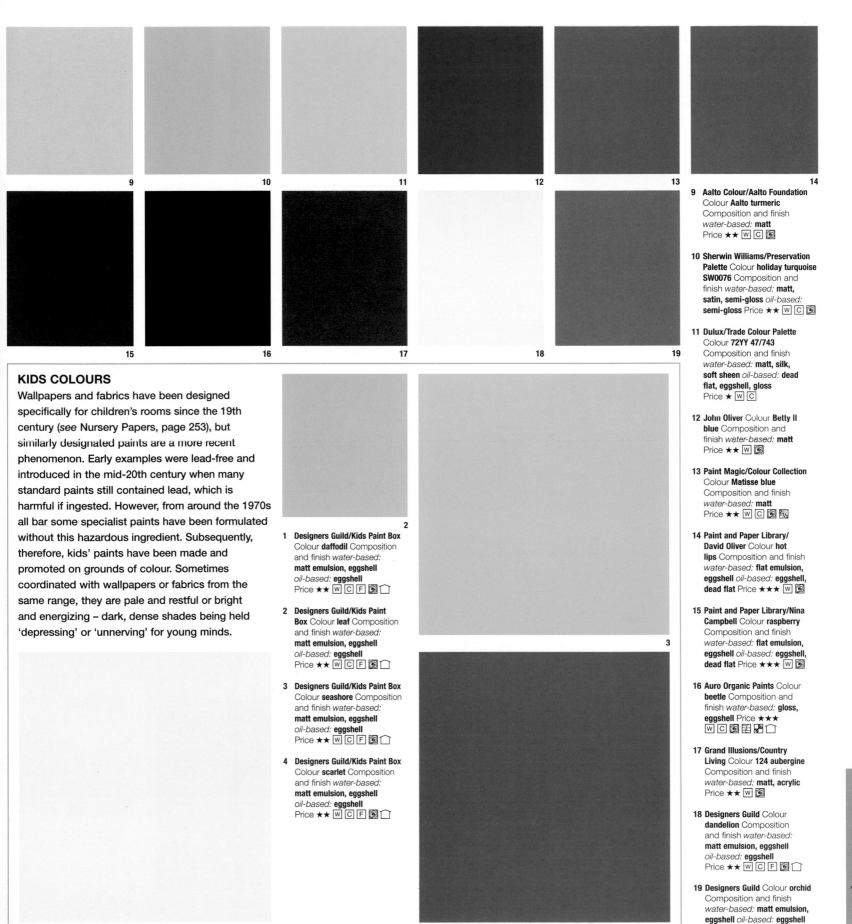

KIDS COLOURS

Wallpapers and fabrics have been designed specifically for children's rooms since the 19th century (*see* Nursery Papers, page 253), but similarly designated paints are a more recent phenomenon. Early examples were lead-free and introduced in the mid-20th century when many standard paints still contained lead, which is harmful if ingested. However, from around the 1970s all bar some specialist paints have been formulated without this hazardous ingredient. Subsequently, therefore, kids' paints have been made and promoted on grounds of colour. Sometimes coordinated with wallpapers or fabrics from the same range, they are pale and restful or bright and energizing – dark, dense shades being held 'depressing' or 'unnerving' for young minds.

1 Designers Guild/Kids Paint Box Colour **daffodil** Composition and finish *water-based:* **matt emulsion, eggshell** *oil-based:* **eggshell** Price ★★ W C F 📷 🏠

2 Designers Guild/Kids Paint Box Colour **leaf** Composition and finish *water-based:* **matt emulsion, eggshell** *oil-based:* **eggshell** Price ★★ W C F 📷 🏠

3 Designers Guild/Kids Paint Box Colour **seashore** Composition and finish *water-based:* **matt emulsion, eggshell** *oil-based:* **eggshell** Price ★★ W C F 📷 🏠

4 Designers Guild/Kids Paint Box Colour **scarlet** Composition and finish *water-based:* **matt emulsion, eggshell** *oil-based:* **eggshell** Price ★★ W C F 📷 🏠

9 Aalto Colour/Aalto Foundation Colour **Aalto turmeric** Composition and finish *water-based:* **matt** Price ★★ W C 📷

10 Sherwin Williams/Preservation Palette Colour **holiday turquoise SW0076** Composition and finish *water-based:* **matt, satin, semi-gloss** *oil-based:* **semi-gloss** Price ★★ W C 📷

11 Dulux/Trade Colour Palette Colour **72YY 47/743** Composition and finish *water-based:* **matt, silk, soft sheen** *oil-based:* **dead flat, eggshell, gloss** Price ★ W C

12 John Oliver Colour **Betty II blue** Composition and finish *water-based:* **matt** Price ★★ W 📷

13 Paint Magic/Colour Collection Colour **Matisse blue** Composition and finish *water-based:* **matt** Price ★★ W C 📷 🎨

14 Paint and Paper Library/ David Oliver Colour **hot lips** Composition and finish *water-based:* **flat emulsion, eggshell** *oil-based:* **eggshell, dead flat** Price ★★★ W 📷

15 Paint and Paper Library/Nina Campbell Colour **raspberry** Composition and finish *water-based:* **flat emulsion, eggshell** *oil-based:* **eggshell, dead flat** Price ★★★ W 📷

16 Auro Organic Paints Colour **beetle** Composition and finish *water-based:* **gloss, eggshell** Price ★★★ W C 📷 ▦ ✄ 🏠

17 Grand Illusions/Country Living Colour **124 aubergine** Composition and finish *water-based:* **matt, acrylic** Price ★★ W 📷

18 Designers Guild Colour **dandelion** Composition and finish *water-based:* **matt emulsion, eggshell** *oil-based:* **eggshell** Price ★★ W C F 📷 🏠

19 Designers Guild Colour **orchid** Composition and finish *water-based:* **matt emulsion, eggshell** *oil-based:* **eggshell** Price ★★ W C F 📷 🏠

Paints: Late 20th–early 21st century

The decorative styles fashionable during the late 20th and early 21st century have been highly eclectic. This has resulted in a diverse range of colours being employed. As in the early and mid-20th century, white and off-white schemes have been in vogue (*see* below and pages 296–299). The practice of importing decorative palettes traditionally associated with the vernacular architecture of other countries or regions has also been prevalent, especially during the 1990s. Notable sources of inspiration have included cooling North African palettes; the hot, candy hues of the Mexican countryside; and the pure, vital metallic- and earth-pigment colours of the Mediterranean. At the same time, recreating and reinterpretating colour schemes from previous centuries has continued unchecked. Almost all periods have been referenced, although the medieval and Neo-classical periods (*see*, respectively, pages 288–289, and 290–293) have proved particularly rich mines for inspiration. Ultimately, this has been possible because of increased research into authentic period colours, and a dramatic increase in the range of colours produced by manufacturers following the development of new synthetic pigments and ever more sophisticated methods of manufacture.

1   **2**   **3**

4   **5**   **6**

QUITE WHITE

All-white colour schemes, or predominantly white schemes offset with stone colours, have been consistently in vogue during the late 20th and early 21st century. However, the fashion for them actually began around the turn of the 20th century. In 1904 English decorators Cowtan & Sons noted: "We seem to have done everything flatted white or enamelled white paint", while in the late 1920s Syrie Maugham created the influential "All-White Room" at her London home and Elsie de Wolfe produced similar interiors in America. The enthusiasm for white increased under the Modern movement and, subsequently, as manufacturers have produced increasingly "pure" brilliant whites. This enduring fashion is also underpinned by the gradual reduction of fossil-fuel-generated air pollution, which means whites no longer dirty as quickly as in the past'

Paint and Paper Library/David Oliver Colour **York stone** Composition and finish *water-based:* **emulsion, eggshell,** *oil-based:* **eggshell, oil, dead flat acrylic** Price ★★★ Ⓦ Ⓒ

Crown/Emulsion Colour **pure brilliant white** Composition and finish *water-based:* **matt, silk** Price ★★ Ⓦ Ⓒ

White-painted walls and ceilings provide an unobtrusive, neutral background for the natural colours and textures of a collection of functional and decorative wooden artefacts in designer Ivy Rosequist's 20th-century, cliffside Californian home.

1 **Dulux/Heritage Colours** Colour **0710 Y10R** Composition and finish *water-based:* **matt, silk, soft sheen** *oil-based:* **dead flat, eggshell, gloss** Price ★ Ⓦ Ⓒ 🎨 🏠

2 **Farrow & Ball/Off-Whites** Colour **blackened** Composition and finish *water-based:* **emulsion, eggshell, distemper** *oil-based:* **gloss, flat** Price ★★ Ⓦ 🎨 🗂 🏠

3 **Farrow & Ball/Off-Whites** Colour **clunch** Composition and finish *water-based:* **emulsion, eggshell, distemper** *oil-based:* **gloss, flat** Price ★★ Ⓦ 🎨 🗂 🏠

4 **Jane Churchill** Colour **oatmeal** Composition and finish *water-based:* **emulsion, eggshell** Price ★★ Ⓦ 🎨

5 **Auro Organic Paints** Colour **ash** Composition and finish *water-based:* **gloss, eggshell** Price ★★★ Ⓦ Ⓒ 🎨 🗂 📑 🏠

6 **Auro Organic Paints** Colour **mid-grey** Composition and finish *water-based:* **gloss, eggshell** Price ★★★ Ⓦ Ⓒ 🎨 🗂 📑 🏠

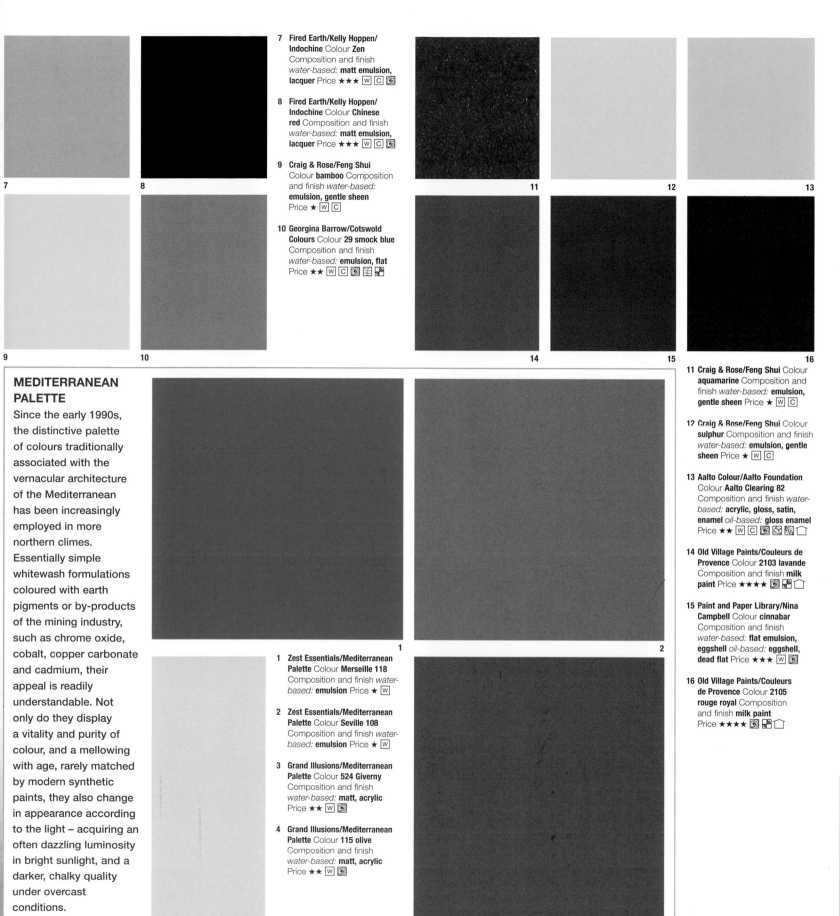

7 Fired Earth/Kelly Hoppen/Indochine Colour **Zen** Composition and finish *water-based:* **matt emulsion, lacquer** Price ★★★ W C ▣

8 Fired Earth/Kelly Hoppen/Indochine Colour **Chinese red** Composition and finish *water-based:* **matt emulsion, lacquer** Price ★★★ W C ▣

9 Craig & Rose/Feng Shui Colour **bamboo** Composition and finish *water-based:* **emulsion, gentle sheen** Price ★ W C

10 Georgina Barrow/Cotswold Colours Colour **29 smock blue** Composition and finish *water-based:* **emulsion, flat** Price ★★ W C ▣ ▣ ▦ ▨

11 Craig & Rose/Feng Shui Colour **aquamarine** Composition and finish *water-based:* **emulsion, gentle sheen** Price ★ W C

12 Craig & Rose/Feng Shui Colour **sulphur** Composition and finish *water-based:* **emulsion, gentle sheen** Price ★ W C

13 Aalto Colour/Aalto Foundation Colour **Aalto Clearing 82** Composition and finish *water-based:* **acrylic, gloss, satin, enamel** *oil-based:* **gloss enamel** Price ★★ W C ▣ ▨ ▨ ⌂

14 Old Village Paints/Couleurs de Provence Colour **2103 lavande** Composition and finish **milk paint** Price ★★★★ ▣ ▨ ⌂

15 Paint and Paper Library/Nina Campbell Colour **cinnabar** Composition and finish *water-based:* **flat emulsion, eggshell** *oil-based:* **eggshell, dead flat** Price ★★★ W ▣

16 Old Village Paints/Couleurs de Provence Colour **2105 rouge royal** Composition and finish **milk paint** Price ★★★★ ▣ ▨ ⌂

MEDITERRANEAN PALETTE

Since the early 1990s, the distinctive palette of colours traditionally associated with the vernacular architecture of the Mediterranean has been increasingly employed in more northern climes. Essentially simple whitewash formulations coloured with earth pigments or by-products of the mining industry, such as chrome oxide, cobalt, copper carbonate and cadmium, their appeal is readily understandable. Not only do they display a vitality and purity of colour, and a mellowing with age, rarely matched by modern synthetic paints, they also change in appearance according to the light – acquiring an often dazzling luminosity in bright sunlight, and a darker, chalky quality under overcast conditions.

1 Zest Essentials/Mediterranean Palette Colour **Merseille 118** Composition and finish *water-based:* **emulsion** Price ★ W

2 Zest Essentials/Mediterranean Palette Colour **Seville 108** Composition and finish *water-based:* **emulsion** Price ★ W

3 Grand Illusions/Mediterranean Palette Colour **524 Giverny** Composition and finish *water-based:* **matt, acrylic** Price ★★ W ▣

4 Grand Illusions/Mediterranean Palette Colour **115 olive** Composition and finish *water-based:* **matt, acrylic** Price ★★ W ▣

Specialist Paints & Waxes

Whether hand-mixed by 18th-century itinerant craftsmen or mass-produced in 21st-century factories, the majority of paints have been designed to cover plaster, masonry or wooden surfaces with a smooth, opaque film of colour. In other words, most paints are simply used to decorate and protect a surface, and even though they mask the underlying material they do not disguise what it is, nor are they meant to.

However, there are some specialist paints and waxes that are intended visually to transform masonry, plaster or wood into a different material, or replicate another decorative medium. These include metallic paints and gilt creams, which simulate base or precious metals; liming pastes, which reproduce the bleaching effects of quick-lime on wood; textured paints that mimic decorative plasterwork; multi-coloured paints that resemble stonework or ceramics; and "broken colour" applications that imitate the fugitive pigmentation of early paints or the effects of ageing, or simply confer an abstract pattern upon a surface.

LEFT The built-in storage cupboard in the bathroom of this 19th-century townhouse in London, England, would have been painted originally or grained to match the woodwork. It now boasts a silver metallic paint finish more in keeping with the 1990s. The silver also works harmoniously with the wall mirror, serving to brighten the room.

ABOVE Set against a dark, terracotta-coloured, limewashed wall, this fire surround has been given a painted *faux*-marble finish. During the last quarter of the 20th century, many paint manufacturers produced paint kits (supplied with specialist applicators) for producing *faux*-marble, *faux*-porphyry and woodgrained finishes on plaster and wood.

ABSTRACT FINISHES

During the late 20th century, "broken colour" techniques – such as spattering, ragging, sponging, stippling, dragging and combing – were all the rage. Derived from fine art, they involve distressing paints and glazes applied over a contrasting-coloured ground to produce subtle patterns and gradations of colour. Manufacturers often supply paints and application tools specifically designed for the purpose. This example is an abstract pattern; others may simulate stone.

KEY PAINT EFFECTS

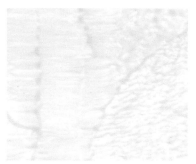

1 Many manufacturers supply paints designed to reproduce distressed finishes, such as ragging and rag-rolling, or to simulate materials such as porphyry.

2 Textured paints have been available since the early 20th century, and are mostly used to simulate the appearance of rustic plasterwork.

3 Gilt creams and waxes have been used since the Renaissance as an easy alternative to the traditional method of gilding wooden furniture and joinery with metal leaf or metallic powders.

4 Paints that produce a coating that imitates beaten and hammered metal became very popular during the late 20th century. They are available in a range of colours and finishes.

1 Dulux/Duette Colour **coral cascade** Composition and finish *water-based:* **matt** Price ★★ ⓦ ⓒ

2 Berger/Textures Colour **heavy texture with marble chips** Composition and finish *solvent-based:* **marble/stone** Price ★★★ ⓦ ⓒ

3 Liberon Waxes Colour **Fontainebleau** Composition and finish *spirit-based:* **satin sheen** Price ★★★★

4 Trimite/Hammer Finishes Colour **stoving red 811** Composition and finish *water-based:* **metallic** Price ★★

ABOVE The *chinoiserie* decoration on this four-poster bed has been executed in shades of gold metallic paint on a black oil-painted ground. The soft, flat finish was achieved by applying clear matt polyurethane varnish, lightly rubbed with fine-grade wire wool.

Specialist Paints & Waxes

Metallic paints can be used on metal, wood and plaster, and are available in a wide range of colours. They are also produced in a range of different textures, including "smooth", "hammered" and "metallic cloth". Gilt creams and waxes, on the other hand, are always burnished smooth; used on mouldings, they replicate leaf- or powder-gilding. Colours include copper and shades of gold and silver.

Liming kits are available as hard waxes and soft pastes: the former are used on open-grained hardwoods, such as oak and ash; the latter on close-grained softwoods, such as pine. Some contain lime, which bleaches the wood a grey-white hue; others mimic this by depositing flecks of whiting in the grain.

Textured paints are mainly used to disguise cracked plaster, and are patterned with a serrated tool in imitation of the random swirls of rustic plasterwork. Similarly, most paints that mimic the appearance of ceramics (notably earthenware) and decorative stones (such as porphyry), or simulate the breakdown of pigments seen in pre-20th-century paints, are distressed with a specialist tool, or a brush or rag (*see* opposite). However, a few are supplied with an applicator that spatters colours randomly on top of one another.

1

2

3

4

5

6

1 Aalto Colour/Aalto Precious Metals Colour **Aalto void 14** Composition and finish *water-based:* **enamel** Price ★★★★ Ⓦ Ⓒ ▨ ▤ ▨ ▨ ◻

2 Tor Coatings/Ardenbrite Colour **old penny bronze 35** Composition and finish *spirit-based:* **satin** Price ★★★★ ▨ Ⓢ ▨ ▨ ◻

3 Aalto Colour/Aalto Precious Metals Colour **Aalto void 4** Composition and finish *water-based:* **enamel** Price ★★★★ Ⓦ Ⓒ ▨ ▤ ▨ ▨ ◻

4 Aalto Foundation/Aalto Precious Metals Colour **Aalto starling 11** Composition and finish *water-based:* **enamel** Price ★★★★ Ⓦ Ⓒ ▨ ▤ ▨ ▨ ◻

5 Liberon Waxes Colour **gilt cream chantilly** Composition and finish *spirit-based:* **satin sheen** Price ★★★★ ▨ ▨

6 Aalto Foundation/Aalto Precious Metals Colour **Aalto zip 28** Composition and finish *water-based:* **enamel** Price ★★★★ Ⓦ Ⓒ ▨ ▤ ▨ ▨ ◻

7

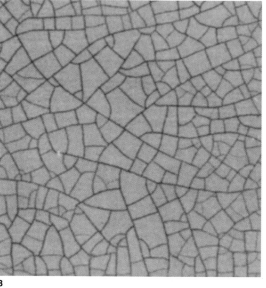

8

9

FAUX-STONE FINISHES

"Broken-colour" techniques such as ragging, sponging, stippling and spattering can be used to create abstract patterns in paint. However, since ancient Greek and Roman times these techniques have also been employed to simulate stones such as marble, limestone, granite and porphyry. *Faux*-stone finishes are used on architectural fixtures and fittings, and on furniture, when the natural material is unavailable, too expensive or structurally unsuitable. In the past, the authenticity of the finish was dependent on the skills of the decorator, but the specialist *faux*-stone paint kits now available have helped to guarantee effective results.

10

Paint Magic/Textures & Speciality Plasters/Marmorino Colour **white base (tint to colour)** Composition and finish *lime,* **marble** Price ★★★★ Ⓦ Ⓒ ▨

7 **Berger/Luxatile Epoxy Polyurethane System** Colour **white** Composition and finish *solvent-based:* **high sheen, gloss** Price ★★ Ⓦ Ⓒ ▦ ⌂

8 **Paint Magic/Textures & Speciality Plasters/Craquelure** Colour **clear** Composition and finish *water-based:* **antique cracked varnish** Price ★★★★ Ⓦ

9 **Berger/Textures** Colour **stoneshield** Composition and finish *solvent-based:* **marble/stone** Price ★★★ Ⓦ Ⓒ ▨ ⌂

10 **Trimite/Hammer Finishes** Colour **dark green 828** Composition and finish *water-based:* **metallic** Price ★★ ▨ ▨

11 **Artex/Decorative Textured Finishes** Colour **white** Composition and finish *water-based:* **textured** Price ★ Ⓦ Ⓒ ▨

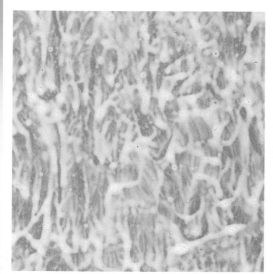

Dulux/Duette Classic Colour **springwater** Composition and finish *water-based:* **matt** Price ★★ Ⓦ Ⓒ

The Stencil Store/Paint Effects Colour **earthenware pink** Composition and finish *water-based:* **matt** Price ★★★ Ⓦ

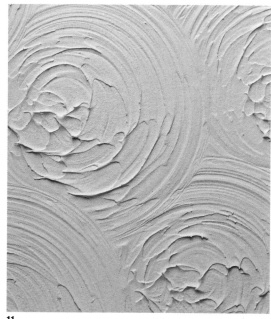

11

PAINTS & FINISHES: *SPECIALIST PAINTS & WAXES*   **305**

Pre-17th century

17th century

18th century

19th century

20th & 21st century

Wood Finishes

Unless they are heavily diluted, most paints dry to an opaque finish, and so obliterate the natural appearance of any wooden surface. For this reason, decorators have traditionally favoured translucent and semi-translucent stains and varnishes when highlighting the figuring and grain of a wood. This is particularly true in the case of hardwoods, such as walnut, oak and mahogany, which usually display more attractive markings than their softwood counterparts, which include pine and fir.

Wood stains are available in various formulations (*see pages 308–309*). Some are intended for use on external woodwork, others for internal wood and furniture. Some offer protection against moisture and general wear and tear in a single coat, while others require an additional application of varnish or shellac and wax. However, the real versatility of wood stains lies in the colours available, which range from "natural" hues, such as brown or red mahogany, ebony and pine, to "non-naturalistic" tones, such as several shades of blue, green and grey.

LEFT An 18th-century chest of drawers, made of mahogany, has been restored using a dark brown, water-based mahogany stain that has then been shellacked and polished – the traditional finish. The half-height wall-panelling – typical of both Georgian and later Arts and Crafts interiors – has been treated in the same manner.

KEY FINISHES

1 Oil-based stains produce pure, transparent colours on timber, and since the 1970s have often been formulated to allow moisture to evaporate rather than remain trapped in the wood.

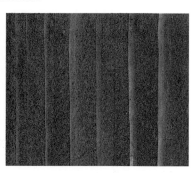

2 Many water-based stains require additional varnishing to make timber waterproof. However, those designed for exterior use are water-repellant and have anti-fungal properties.

3 Many chemical-based stains produce colour by reacting with the tannic acid that is present in wood. This light oak stain is designed for exterior use and formulated to resist cracking, peeling and flaking.

4 Nowadays, manufacturers often incorporate pigments in solvent- or spirit-based stains that help to filter out ultraviolet rays, thereby reducing the problem of fading in darker colours constantly exposed to sunlight.

---

1 Auro Organic Paints//Woodstains Colour **NR160-55 ultramarine blue** Composition and finish *oil-based:* **semi-translucent satin** Price ★★★ 🗐 ▢

2 Protim Solignum/Fencetone Colour **golden cedar** Composition and finish *water-based:* **matt** Price ★★★ 🗐 ▢

3 Dacrylate Paints/Nordac Wood Shades Colour **light oak** Composition and finish *chemical-based:* **natural** Price ★★ 🗐 ▢

4 Dulux/Weathershield Exterior Wood Stain Colour **ebony** Composition and finish *solvent-based:* **transparent satin** Price ★★★ 🗐 ▢

ABOVE The cupboard, mirror surround, tongue-and-groove dado cladding and butt-jointed floorboards in this bathroom are made of pine. They have been coated with clear varnish to protect them from the effects of moisture. The contrasting wooden rim of the bath has been mahogany-stained and clear-varnished.

RIGHT This late 20th-century dining table stands on lightly limed, butt-jointed pine floorboards in the principal living area of a converted malt house built in the early 19th century in Somerset, England. The table is made of elm and has a clear beeswax-polish finish that allows the natural colour and figuring of the wood to show through.

Wood Finishes

There are four basic types of wood stain: water-, oil-, spirit- and chemical-based. Water-based stains produce clear, vivid colours that are well suited to light, close-grained woods, such as beech and pine. They raise the grain of the wood, which then needs sanding before varnishing, or treating with shellac and waxing.

Oil-based stains do not raise the grain of the wood, nor do they have to be varnished or treated with shellack; they also produce more even and transparent coloration on both hardwoods and softwoods. If the stains are spirit-based, the colours are usually muted and the grain raised. Spirit-based stains are best suited to oily or hard, fine-grained woods (especially before French polishing).

Chemical stains are many and varied. Notable types include biochromate of potash, which turns beech a light tan and walnut a pale yellow; and blue copperas, which gives most woods a light grey hue. However, exact coloration is unpredictable since it is affected by the level of tannic acid in the wood.

1. **Ronseal/All-in-One Quick & Simple/Woodstain** Colour **walnut** Composition and finish *oil-based:* **satin, gloss** Price ★★★ 🖼☐

2. **Cabot Stains/O.V.T. Solid Color Stains** Colour **oracle sun** Composition and finish *oil-based:* **matt** Price ★★ 🖼☐

3. **Cabot Stains/O.V.T. Solid Color Stains** Colour **chesapeake** Composition and finish *oil-based:* **matt** Price ★★ 🖼☐

4. **Auro Organic Paints/Woodstain** Colour **NR160-74 grau** Composition and finish *oil-based:* **semi-translucent satin** Price ★★★ 🖼☐

5. **Protim Solignum/Timbertone** Colour **petrol blue** Composition and finish *oil-based:* **translucent matt, translucent sheen** Price ★★★ 🖼☐

6. **Liberon/Liming Wax** Colour **white** Composition and finish *water-based:* **matt** Price ★★★ 🖼

7. **Dulux/Protective Woodstain** Colour **elderberry** Composition and finish *solvent-based:* **transparent satin** Price ★★★ 🖼☐

1

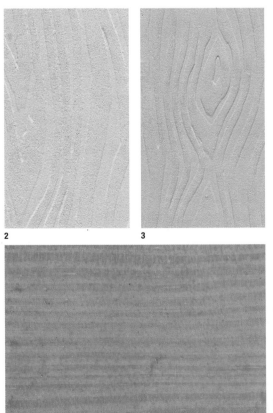

2

3

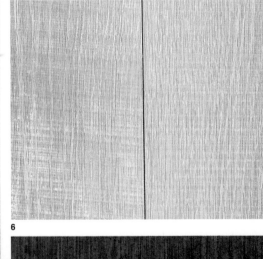

6

4

5

7

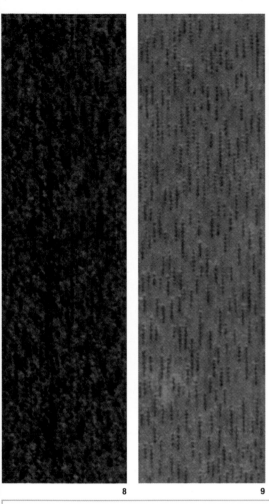

8 **Old Village Paints/Paste Woodstain** Colour **brown mahogany** Composition and finish **milk paint** Price ★★★★ 🖼️ 🖼️ 🏠

9 **Old Village Paints/Paste Woodstain** Colour **fruit wood** Composition and finish **milk paint** Price ★★★★ 🖼️ 🖼️ 🏠

10 **Auro Organic Paints/ Woodstains** Colour **orangerot 80% NR160-26, 20% 160-33** Composition and finish *oil-based:* **semi-translucent satin** Price ★★★ 🖼️ 🏠

12

13

14

11 **Dulux/Weathershield Exterior Woodstain** Colour **antique pine** Composition and finish *solvent-based:* **matt** Price ★★★ 🖼️ 🏠

12 **Dulux/Protective Woodstain** Colour **watermelon** Composition and finish *solvent-based:* **transparent satin** Price ★★ 🖼️ 🏠

13 **Rustins/Colorglaze Transparent Satin Colours** Colour **grey** Composition and finish *oil-based:* **satin** Price ★★ 🖼️ 🏠

14 **Rustins/Colorglaze** Colour **yellow** Composition and finish *oil-based:* **satin** Price ★★ 🖼️ 🏠

MICROPOROUS WOOD STAINS

Anyone wishing to produce a durable, decorative finish on wooden surfaces has to contend with the fact that timber readily absorbs moisture from the atmosphere and from any material with which it is in contact. When the weather is warm and humidity levels fall, the moisture evaporates, causing traditional stains and varnishes that seal the surface to "bubble" and eventually to lift off. Fortunately, manufacturers have recently found ways to formulate microporous stains and varnishes that let moisture evaporate through them without causing damage.

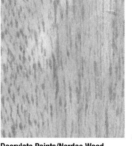

Dacrylate Paints/Nordac Wood Shades Colour **pine** Composition and finish *chemical-based:* **natural** Price ★★ 🖼️ 🏠

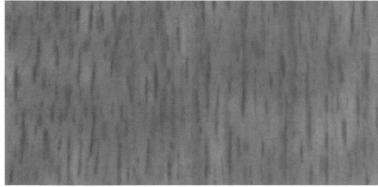

Dacrylate Paints/Nordac Wood Shades Colour **mahogany** Composition and finish *chemical-based:* **natural** Price ★★ 🖼️ 🏠

Tiles

Plain Tiles

ABOVE This bathroom in the Rockcliffe Mansion in Hannibal, Missouri, USA is typical of a luxury bathroom installation of the late 19th century. It features plain white tiles that have been laid in brick fashion with relief-moulded capping. Similar arrangements of tiles were popular until the mid-1930s.

LEIGHTON HOUSE
Early mosaics, made up of thousands of small plain tiles, often featured Islamic-inspired patterns. The mosaic panel shown here, with a geometric floral pattern, is in the entrance hall of Leighton House in London, England. The artist Lord Leighton displayed his large collection of Islamic tiles in the "Arab Hall". The walls and ceiling were clad with original 16th- and 17th-century Iznik tiles, with the reproductions made by his friend William de Morgan to complete damaged panels.

During the mid-12th century, plain tiles were laid in large numbers on the floors of churches, cathedrals and royal palaces throughout Europe. Most were made locally using red-firing clays, often with a honey-coloured lead glaze to minimize wear. This was sometimes applied over a layer of white slip to produce yellow tiles, while the addition of a little copper to the glaze gave a range of greens.

Unglazed plain quarry tiles were very popular during the 18th and 19th centuries, but these were superseded by the flatter, smoother tiles produced by Herbert Minton using the dust-pressing technique invented by the Englishman Richard Prosser in 1840. Initially conceived as a method of making ceramic buttons from dried clay, this technique, Minton realized, could also be used to form ceramic *tesserae* and larger tiles. Plain tiles have been popular ever since. Art Nouveau schemes favoured pastel-shaded tiles, while red and black were dominant in Art Deco interiors of the late 1920s and the 1930s. More recently, the plain "rustic" tile has once again become fashionable.

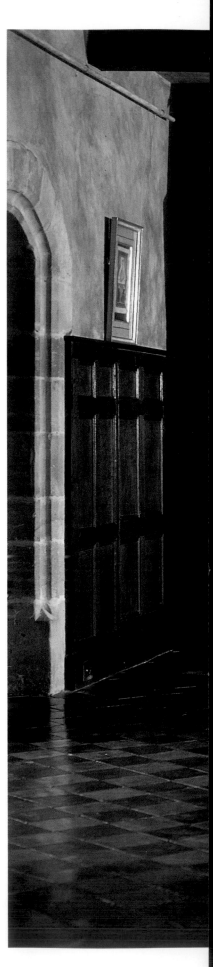

RIGHT A simple but effective floor pattern has been achieved here by using just two colours of plain tile, laid alternately. This style of floor has its origins in Medieval cathedrals across Europe and was often re-created during the Renaissance using black and white marble.

1 Natural stone has always been used as a flooring material. Reclaimed limestone tiles and ceramic tiles imitating natural materials have recently become popular.

2 Geometric pavements, often consisting of combinations of triangular, hexagonal or rectangular plain tiles, have limitless permutations of patterns.

3 The humble, unglazed quarry tile has been used for centuries as a hard and durable floor covering. Plain terracotta tiles have become highly desirable in homes over the past few years.

4 Glazed tiles, with an uneven, slightly translucent appearance, were much liked in the mid-19th century. The Victorians favoured this "hand-made" look on their mass-produced tiles.

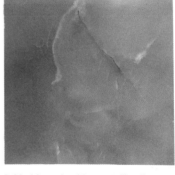

5 Light-reflective, easy-to-clean white tiles were widely seen during the mid-19th century, and have become almost universally popular in recent years.

6 Marble, a durable crystalline limestone, is available in an array of colours and patterns. Decorative and practical, it has remained a popular floorcovering.

---

1 Stonell/Bamboo Colour **grey with rust streak** Alt. colours **yes** Composition **slate** Size **40 x 40 x 1.2cm/15¾ x 15¾ x ½in** Price ★★★ F ⊞

2 Elon/Carrillo Plain Colours Colour **natural** Alt. colours **yes** Composition **ceramic** Size **30 x 30cm/11¾ x 11¾in** Price ★ F W

3 Elon/Saltillo Square Colour **terracotta** Alt. colours **no** Composition **terracotta** Size **30 x 30 x 2cm/11¾ x 11¾ x ¾in** Price ★ F ⊞

4 Winchester Tile Co/Colours Colour **lime green** Alt. colours **yes** Composition **ceramic** Size **10.5 x 10.5cm x 7mm/4 x 4 x ¼in** Price ★ W ⊞

5 H. & R. Johnson/Cotswold COTS 13 Colour **white gloss** Alt. colours **yes** Composition **ceramic** Size **15 x 15cm x 7mm/6 x 6 x ¼in** Price ★ W ⊞

6 Pisani/Onyx Green Colour **green** Alt. colours **yes** Composition **marble** Size **30.5 x 30.5 x 1cm/12 x 12 x ⅜in** Price ★★★★★ special order F ⊞

Plains: **Pre-20th century**

Most early plain tiles were single-coloured, hand-made products, formed from local clays. A glaze was often applied to make a more durable surface or to add to the limited range of colours. These tiles were used on the floors of abbeys, cathedrals and parish churches throughout Europe.

In 1840, in England, the dust-pressing technique was invented by Richard Prosser. The technique used dry clay, which was ground into a fine powder, moistened with water and pressed into shape in a tile press. International interest in this process stemmed from the fact that tiles could now be produced with smoother surfaces and more accurate dimensions. A greater range of colours was also made possible, as pigments could be added much more easily to dry clay. Huge quantities of dust-pressed tiles were produced for constructing geometric pavements, which relied on the many different and newly available colours for their decorative effect.

The mid-19th century saw a large increase in the production of plain-glazed wall tiles. This was triggered by the construction of railway stations and by new demands for hygiene in hospitals, which created a need for light-reflective, easy-to-clean, durable surfaces.

1

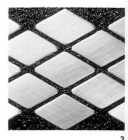

3

2

5

6

7

4

8

9

1 Fired Earth/Venetian Marble (2 tiles) Colour **Rosso** Alt. colours **yes** Composition **marble** Size **10 x 10cm/4 x 4in** Price ★ ☐F☐

2 Kievel Stone/Fossil Stone Colour **cream** Alt. colours **no** Composition **limestone** Size **40 x 20cm/15¾ x 8in** Price ★★★★★ ☐F☐ ☐⊞☐

3 Walker Zanger/Metallismo/ Rhomboid Finish 877 611 0199 Colour **smooth** Alt. colours **yes** Composition **metal** Size **2 x 4cm/¾ x 1½in** Price ★★★★★

4 Fired Earth/VM Travertino Colour **travertino** Alt. colours **yes** Composition **Venetian marble** Size **10 x 10cm/4 x 4in** Price ★ ☐F☐ ☐⊞☐

5 Fired Earth/Turin Stone/Aosta Green Colour **green** Alt. colours **yes** Composition **terracotta** Size **15 x 15cm/6 x 6in** Price ★ ☐F☐

6 Marble Flooring Specialists/ Labrador Blue Pearl Colour **blue pearl** Alt. colours **no** Composition **granite** Size **30 x 30cm/11¾ x 11¾in** Price ★★ ☐F☐ ☐⊞☐

7 Kirkstone/Pavia Toscana Colour **roman light** Alt. colours **yes** Composition **Itallian travertine** Size **40 x 40cm/15¾ x 15¾in** Price ★★★★★ ☐⊞☐

8 Original Style/Skirting Tile G9903 Colour **royal blue** Alt. colours **yes** Composition **ceramic** Size **15 x 15cm/6 x 6in** Price ★ ☐W☐

9 Stonell/Mountain Green Slate Colour **mountain green** Alt. colours **no** Composition **slate** Size **30 x 30cm/11¾ x 11¾in** Price ★ ☐F☐ ☐⊞☐

10

11

12

13

14

10 **Fired Earth/Valencia Dado** Colour **cream** Alt. colours **yes** Composition **ceramic** Size **12 x 5cm/4¾ x 2in** Price ★★ [W]

11 **Fired Earth/Antique Reclaimed Terracotta/Classic Melange Hexagonals** Colour **natural** Alt. colours **yes** Composition **terracotta** Size **various** Price ★★★★★ (£/m²) [F]

12 **Elon/Natural Marble** Colour **snow white** Alt. colours **yes** Composition **marble** Size **30 x 30cm/11¾ x 11¾in** Price ★ ⊞

13 **Paris Ceramics/Antique Parrefeuille Terracotta** Colour **terracotta** Alt. colours **no** Composition **terracotta** Size **35 x 21cm/ 13¾ x 8¼in** Price ★★★★★ (special order) [F]

14 **Fired Earth/Roman Mosaic Natural Floor** Colour **natural** Alt. colours **yes** Composition **stone** Size **20 x 20cm/8 x 8in** Price ★★ [F] ⊞

NATURAL STONE

The colours available to the tile-maker were once limited to those of the natural materials at hand. These materials had a wealth of subtle tones and natural patterning that are still appreciated today. Stone provides a rich variation of subtle hues according to locality, from dark slate or granite to pale, warm sandstones. Marble, with its distinctive, veined appearance, is a more costly alternative. In the case of stone and marble, most of the durable materials are of neutral, earthy tones, while naturally occurring clays generally fire to a red or a buff colour.

Villeroy & Boch/Villostone/Indian Stone Colour **2104 8335** Alt. colours **yes** Composition **porcelain stonework** Size **30 x 30cm/11¾ x 11¾in** Price ★★★★ [F]

15

16

17

18

19

20

21

15 **Fired Earth/Pre-sealed Encaustic** Colour **olive** Alt. colours **yes** Composition **encaustic** Size **20 x 20cm/8 x 8in** Price ★ [F]

16 **Elon/Carrillo Plain Colours** Colour **terracotta** Alt. colours **yes** Composition **ceramic** Size **20 x 20cm/8 x 8in** Price ★ [W] [F] ⊞

17 **Froyle Tiles/Vellum** Colour **vellum** Alt. colours **yes** Composition **stoneware** Size **10 x 10cm/4 x 4in** Price ★ [W] [F] ⬜ 🗖 ⊞

18 **Winchester Tile Co/Colours** Colour **yellow** Alt. colours **yes** Composition **ceramic** Size **12.5 x 12.5cm/5 x 5in** Price ★★ [W] ⊞

19 **Original Style/Victorian Floor Tiles/Conway Triangle** Colour **buff** Alt. colours **no** Composition **ceramic** Size **5 x 3.5cm/2 x 1⅜in** Price ★★ ⬜ [F] ⊞

20 **Original Style/KK5903** Colour **foxglove** Alt. colours **yes** Composition **ceramic** Size **14 x 10cm/5½ x 4in** Price ★ [W]

21 **H. & R. Johnson/Minton Hollins/Victoria Blue Border Tile MH1B** Colour **blue** Alt. colours **yes** Composition **ceramic** Size **15 x 7.5cm/ 6 x 2⅞in** Price ★ [W] [F] ⊞

Plains: 20th–early 21st century

At the beginning of the 20th century, the Art Nouveau influence began to manifest itself in tile design. Most Art Nouveau tiles were individual designs that were intended to be set among plain tiles within a scheme. However, by the 1920s the plain tiles had become dominant and entire rooms were decorated with these in pastel shades, sometimes with a narrow row of simple black and white geometric border tiles set at dado height. Highly glazed tiles gradually became less popular, and manufacturers responded by producing eggshell and matt-glazed plain tiles.

Stronger colours, including red and black, were used in the late 1920s and early 1930s as Art Deco schemes became increasingly favoured. The popularity of strong colours on plain tiles was further enhanced as tile-makers employed chemists to develop new glaze colours and effects. During the 1960s and 1970s, there was a move towards using not only strong colours but textures and mottling in the decoration of tiles.

During the late 20th and early 21st century, "rustic" plain tiles, made by hand or in imitation of hand-production, have become popular, the variations in shape and shade extending the range of plain tiles available.

4

5   6

7

4 **Kenneth Clark Ceramics/Plain Colours** Colour **honey** Alt. colours **yes** Composition **ceramic** Size **10 x 10cm/ 4 x 4in** Price ★ ⊞

5 **Domus Tiles/Interni Ghiaccio Satin Finish** Colour **white** Alt. colours **yes** Composition **ceramic** Size **10 x 10cm x 7mm/4 x 4 x ¼in** Price ★ F ⊞

6 **Winchester Tile Co/Colours** Colour **grey** Alt. colours **yes** Composition **ceramic** Size **10.5 x 10.5cm x 7mm/ 4 x 4 x ¼in** Price ★★ W

7 **Elon/Carrillo Plain Colours** Colour **red** Alt. colours **yes** Composition **ceramic** Size **10 x 10cm x 7mm/4 x 4 x ¼in** Price ★ W F

8 **H. & R. Johnson/Pennines/ Profile Strip** Colour **yellow** Alt. colours **yes** Composition **ceramic** Size **10 x 5cm/4 x 2in** Price ★ W

1

1 **Saloni/Eternity/Vidriado** Colour **miel** Alt. colours **yes** Composition **porcelain ceramic** Size **30 x 30cm/ 11¾ x 11¾in** Price ★★★★★ W F ⊞

2 **Elite Tiles/Porcelain Tile** Colour **polish** Alt. colours **yes** Composition **porcelain** Size **30 x 30cm x 9mm/ 11¾ x 11¾ x ⅓in** Price ★★★★ F

3 **Cinca/Arquitectos/Azulejo de Faianca/Vidruda de Parta/Branca Matt 0190** Colour **beige** Alt. colours **yes** Composition **white biscuit** Size **15 x 15cm/6 x 6in** Price ★★★ W ⊞

2

3

8

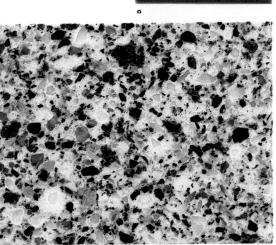

9 **Villeroy & Boch/Non-Vitreous Walls/Granicolour 0016 D341** Colour **green** Alt. colours **yes** Composition **non-vitreous ceramic** Size **15 x 15cm/6 x 6in** Price ★★★★ W

10 **Marble Flooring Specialists/Marghestone Grigio Plata M234** Colour **multi** Alt. colours **yes** Composition **marble** Size **60 x 40 x 2cm/23¾ x 15¾ x ¾in** Price ★ F ⊞

11 **Winchester Tile Co/Colours** Colour **turquoise** Alt. colours **yes** Composition **ceramic** Size **10.5 x 10.5cm x 7mm/ 4 x 4 x ¼in** Price ★ W ⊞

12 **Winchester Tile Co/Colours** Colour **amethyst** Alt. colours **yes** Composition **ceramic** Size **10.5 x 10.5cm x 7mm/ 4 x 4 x ¼in** Price ★★ W ⊞

13 **Carocim/Palette U15** Colour **violet** Alt. colours **yes** Composition **cement/ marble (encaustic)** Size **20 x 20 x 1cm/8 x 8 x ⅜in** Price ★ W F ⊞

14 **Simmy Ceramics/Crackle Glaze** Colour **ice** Alt. colours **yes** Composition **ceramic** Size **10 x 10cm/4 x 4in** Price ★★★★★ F

15 **Daltile/Semi-Gloss** Colour **vermilion** Alt. colours **yes** Composition **ceramic** Size **10.8 x 10.8cm x 7mm/ 4 x 4 x ¼in** Price ★ W ▣ ⊞

16 **Elon/Carrillo Plain Colours** Colour **lime green** Alt. colours **yes** Composition **ceramic** Size **10 x 10cm x 7mm/4 x 4 x ¼in** Price ★ W F

17 **Original Style/Ocean Deep/Midwater Tile 6773A** Colour **blue** Alt. colours **no** Composition **ceramic** Size **15 x 15cm/6 x 6in** Price ★★★ F

Motif Tiles

ABOVE This view of the hallway of Hall Place in London, England, indicates just how strong the Gothic Revival influence was on interior design in the mid-19th century. The inlaid tiles on the floor of the room enhance the Gothic look. They feature striking, Islamic-inspired medieval motifs.

TILED STOVES

In Eastern Europe and Scandinavia, tiled stoves were very common from the 15th century onward. The tiles were functional as well as decorative, helping to retain the heat and distributing it evenly to the room. Although such tiled stoves were not particularly common in England, A.W.N. Pugin designed one in 1850 for the Minton Company to display at the Great Exhibition of 1851. After the exhibition, the stove was destroyed, leaving behind only a few tiles and a contemporary engraving.

Symbolism was an essential component of medieval art, and many tiles of the period reflected this in the motifs chosen for inlaid patterns. Large numbers of motif tiles were used in churches, and featured the religious symbols that would be familiar to their congregations. Arabesques were common motifs on delftware tiles from the late 16th century to the mid-17th century, but gradually gave way to the more simply painted corner motifs that are a feature of later tiles.

In the 1770s, with the rise of interest in Neo-classicism, swags, drapes and urns all appeared on tiles. The Gothic Revival of the 1830s and 1840s brought about a return to the symbolism of medieval tiles but in an updated form, while the Aesthetic movement in the 1860s saw the use of prunus blossom and Chinese *mons* on tiles. Military or musical emblems became popular images on tiles during the 1880s.

By the 1920s motifs were seldom used in tile design owing to the influence of the Art Deco movement, which relied on strong geometric images. The late 20th and early 21st century has seen a return to motif-decorated tiles, with traditional designs being produced alongside "New Age" motifs, such as the sun, the moon and the stars.

ABOVE The use of natural materials pressed into an unfired clay tile has its origins in the animal footprints that are sometimes found on Roman roof tiles. The example shown here is modern, although the technique was first used by J. & J.G. Lowe in America in the 1880s.

LEFT The floor tiles in this bathroom in a house in Suffolk, England, feature strongly Islamic-inspired motifs. They form the perfect foil for the plainer, Victorian-style sanitary ware and wall tiles.

KEY DESIGNS

1 In the 1830s and 1840s, architects were inspired by motifs on medieval tiles, such as those on this Gothic Revival design panel.

2 Corner motifs are a particular feature of tin-glazed and delft tiles. When placed together, the corner patterns join to form another design.

3 Neo-classical imagery, such as this scrolling leaf pattern, has been popular on tiles since the 1770s. Swags, trophies and drapes have also been much used.

4 Tiles for cast-iron hearth surrounds proliferated in the late 19th century. This floral and foliate motif example is by Arts and Crafts designer William de Morgan.

5 Floral motifs on tiles have been popular since the Middle Ages. Monochromatic examples have been fashionable since the mid-19th century.

6 Of all the floral motifs, the fleur-de-lis, or Burgundian lily, is perhaps the most widely recognized. In the Middle Ages, it was a symbol of the Holy Trinity.

1 **Original Style/Gladstone 6260 (4-tile panel)** Colour **blue/brown** Alt. colours **yes** Composition **ceramic** Size **15 x 15cm/ 6 x 6 in** Price ★★★★ F

2 **Winchester Tile Co/English Delft/Ship and House W.DE1519HP** Colour **blue and white** Alt. colours **no** Composition **ceramic** Size **12.5 x 12.5cm/ 5 x 5in** Price ★★★★★ W F

3 **Candy/Vivaldi Florentine CAN32316** Colour **grey** Alt. colours **yes** Composition **ceramic** Size **20 x 10cm/8 x 4in** Price ★ W

4 **Kenneth Clark Ceramics/Hermitage/William de Morgan/Wightwick** Colour **green blue** Alt. colours **yes** Composition **ceramic** Size **15 x 15cm/6 x 6in** Price ★★★★ W

5 **Craven Dunnlll Jackfield/Leighton** Colour **cream** Alt. colours **yes** Composition **ceramic** Size **15 x 15cm/6 x 6in** Price ★ W

6 **Daltile/Metal Signatures/Fleur de Lis MS10** Colour **aged iron** Alt. colours **yes** Composition **Questech™** Size **5 x 5cm/2 x 2in** Price ★★ W

Motifs: **Pre-19th century**

The tradition of motifs on tiles began in the Middle Ages, when symbolism was used as a way of educating the people and focusing their thoughts on God. As a result, the motifs that adorned early tiles were strongly based on Christian beliefs and ideals. Typical examples from the period were the fish (a mystical symbol of the church), the fleur-de-lis (representing the Holy Trinity) and the circle (symbolizing eternity). Following on from this, certain symbols also became strongly associated with heraldry.

As Islamic influences spread across Europe via Spain, arabesques, which had originated as cloud scrolls on Chinese porcelain, became popular motifs. By the early 17th century, these had been reduced to a simple corner motif on the delftware tiles produced in the Netherlands, Germany, England and other European countries. There are a great many variations of these corner motifs, rejoicing in such names as spider's head, ox-head, fleur-de-lis and oak leaf. Delftware tiles, imported from the Netherlands, were equally successful in colonial America. The popularity of classical ornamentation in Europe during the late 18th century was reflected in tile design; many classical motifs, including urns and birds, were to be found as decorative designs on tiles.

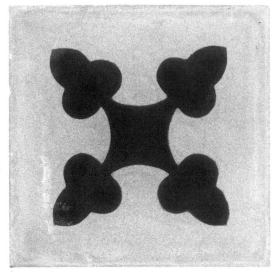

6

7

8

1

2

9

1 **Daltile/Metal Signature/ Floral Dot MS10** Colour **aged iron** Alt. colours **yes** Composition **Questech** Size **5 x 5cm/2 x 2in** Price **★★** W

2 **Fired Earth/Roman Mosaic/ Wave Scroll Border** Colour **black** Alt. colours **yes** Composition **stone/ceramic** Size **10 x 40cm/4 x 15¾in** Price **★★★★** F

3 **H. & R. Johnson/Cotswold Fairford (4-tile panel)** Colour **multi** Alt. colours **no** Composition **ceramic** Size **20 x 20cm/8 x 8in** Price **★★** W

4 **Daltile/Passagio/Universal Stone Corner PA40** Colour **natural** Alt. colours **yes** Composition **glazed porcelain** Size **15 x 15cm/ 6 x 6in** Price **★** W F

5 **Villeroy & Boch/Athos/Border Corner 2349-VA6100 1077** Colour **55C6** Alt. colours **yes** Composition **polished porcelain stone** Size **30 x 30cm/11¾ x 11¾in** Price **★★★★** W

6 **Carocim/Gothic** Colour **red and blue** Alt. colours **yes** Composition **cement/ marble (encaustic)** Size **20 x 20cm/8 x 8in** Price **★** W F ⊞

7 **Fired Earth/Antieke Delft/ Fish 4** Colour **blue and white** Alt. colours **no** Composition **ceramic** Size **13 x 13cm/5 x 5in** Price **★★★** W

8 **Ann Sacks/Batchelder Lion** Colour **stoneware** Alt. colours **yes** Composition **ceramic** Size **10 x 10cm x 9mm/4 x 4 x ⅛in** Price **★★★** W

9 **Elon/Carillo Wall Tiles/ Anita B** Colour **blue** Alt. colours **no** Composition **ceramic** Size **10 x 10cm/ 4 x 4in** Price **★** W ⊞

10 **H. & R. Johnson/Ravenna/ Mariona** Colour **natural** Alt. colours **yes** Composition **ceramic** Size **33 x 25cm/ 13 x 9¾in** Price **★★** W

11 **Walker Zanger/Avignon/ Décoratif/Fleur de Lis** Colour **chamois** Alt. colours **yes** Composition **ceramic** Size **13 x 13cm/5 x 5in** Price **★★** W F ⊞

3

10

4

5

11

12 Walker Zanger/Venezia Di Pinto/Duomo Liner Colour **natural** Alt. colours **no** Composition **stone** Size **31 x 9.5cm/12 x 3¾in** Price ★★★★ W

12

13 Carré/Sols/Terres Cuites/Antiquare/2733 Série C Colour **red and cream** Alt. colours **no** Composition **terracotta** Size **13 x 13 x 1.5cm/5 x 5 x ⅝in** Price ★ W

14 Winchester Tile Co/English Delft/Boats/Trinitie of London W.DE1527HP Colour **blue and white** Alt. colours **no** Composition **ceramic** Size **12.5 x 12.5cm/5 x 5in** Price ★★

15 Fired Earth/Puebla/Damask B Colour **blue and white** Alt. colours **no** Composition **terracotta** Size **10 x 10cm/4 x 4in** Price ★ W

13

14

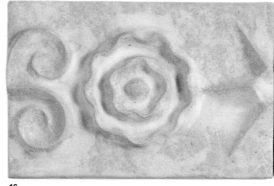

16

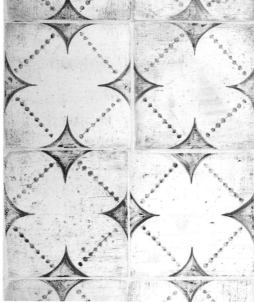

17

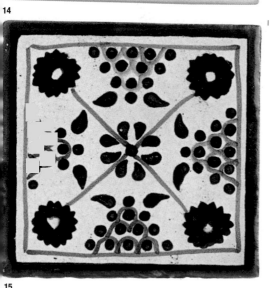

15

18

19

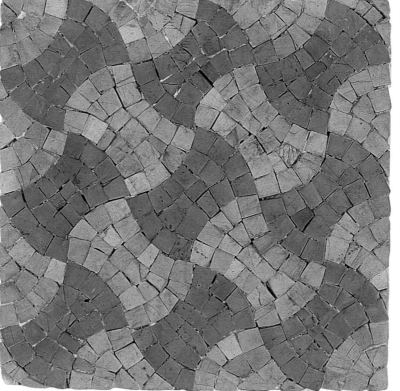

20

16 Lowitz & Co/Talisman Panel Beginnings Border (2 tiles) Colour **white** Alt. colours **yes** Composition **ceramic** Size **15 x 10cm x 7mm/6 x 4 x ¼in** Price ★★★ W ⌂

17 Paris Ceramics/Thera Star/Hand Decorated Colour **pale blue, russet and cream** Alt. colours **yes** Composition **ceramic** Size **15 x 15cm/6 x 6in** Price ★★★★ W

18 Walker Zanger/Venezia Di Pinto/Medici Border Colour **natural** Alt. colours **no** Composition **stone** Size **41 x 9.5cm/16 x 3¾in** Price ★★★★ W F

19 Walker Zanger/Intarsio Romano/Villa Nova Corner/Deco Colour **natural** Alt. colours **no** Composition **stone** Size **13.5 x 13.5cm/5¼ x 5¼in** Price ★★★★★ W F

20 Fired Earth/Roman Mosaic/Green Butterfly Colour **green** Alt. colours **yes** Composition **stone/ceramic** Size **20 x 20cm/8 x 8in** Price ★★★★ F

TILES: *MOTIFS*   **321**

Motifs: **19th century**

By the mid-19th century, A.W.N. Pugin and other Gothic Revival architects were finding inspiration in the Christian and heraldic symbols used on medieval tiles. Such motifs became icons for these architects, and they soon added new symbols of their own to the repertoire; these included the chalice and wafer, the Paschal Lamb and the Alpha and Omega.

The opening up of trade routes to the Orient led to an influx of porcelain and metal goods from the Far East that was to serve as a source of inspiration for the followers of the Aesthetic movement later in the century. Tiles featuring motifs such as the *prunus* blossom, often as a background to Japanese *mons* or armorial seals, proved particularly popular. Also widely used as a highly stylized motif in tile decoration was the sunflower, which was to become one of the Aesthetic movement's chief symbols (*see* page 332). The fan, too, was a favourite symbol on tiles, and inspired a variety of different designs. Toward the end of the century, the use of very stylized military or musical motifs became a trend throughout Europe and America. These were often combined with stylized swags or ribbons that served to unify the image and provide an extra, decorative element.

3

1

2

5

4

7

8

1 **Original Style/Victorian Border Tile 6034** Colour **colonial white** Alt. colours **no** Composition **ceramic** Size **15 x 15cm x 7mm/6 x 6 x ¼in** Price ★ W

2 **New Castle Delft/Gallery/ Coat-of-Arms** Colour **blue and white** Alt. colours **yes** Composition **ceramic** Size **13 x 13cm/5 x 5in** Price ★★ W

3 **Tiles of Stow/Gothic Reliefware/Fleur de Lys** Colour **cream** Alt. colours **yes** Composition **terracotta** Size **13 x 13cm x 11mm/ 5 x 5 x ¼in** Price ★★★

4 **H. & R. Johnson/Babylon/ Nineveh Inset** Colour **natural** Alt. colours **no** Composition **ceramic** Size **15 x 15cm/6 x 6in** Price ★ W

5 **Winchester Tile Co/Ironbridge Rope Moulding W.AN1217** Colour **anthracite** Alt. colours **yes** Composition **ceramic** Size **25 x 21.5cm/ 9¾ x 8½in** Price ★ W

6 **Walker Zanger/Venezia Di Pinto/Cascina Liner** Colour **natural** Alt. colours **no** Composition **stone** Size **31 x 4.5cm/12 x 1¾in** Price ★★★ W F

7 **Original Style/Victorian Floor Tiles/Liverpool 6283** Colour **white/buff** Alt. colours **yes** Composition **ceramic** Size **15 x 15cm/6 x 6in** Price ★ W ⬚

8 **Walker Zanger/Venezia de Pinto/Pompeii Medallion** Colour **natural** Alt. colours **no** Composition **stone** Size **93 x 93cm/36 x 36in** Price ★★★★★ W F

9

12

9 Original Style/Victorian Floor Tiles/Elgin Border 6582 Colour **blue on white** Alt. colours **yes** Composition **ceramic** Size **15 x 7.5cm/6 x 2¾in** Price ★★ W ⌂ F

10 The Arts & Crafts Home/ Pugin Floor Colour **multi** Alt. colours **yes** Composition **ceramic** Size **15 x 15cm x 7mm/6 x 6 x ¼in** Price ★★★ W F

11 Kenneth Clark Ceramics/ William de Morgan/Ruby Lustre/Winged Serpent Colour **ruby lustre** Alt. colours **no** Composition **ceramic** Size **15 x 15cm/ 6 x 6in** Price ★★★★★ W

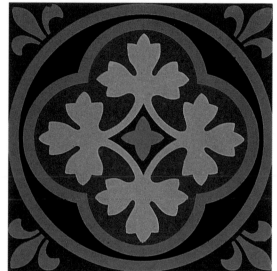

10

13

14

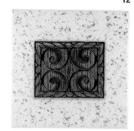

15

16

12 Kenneth Clark Ceramics/ William de Morgan/Ruby Lustre/Galleon West and Galleon East (2 tiles) Colour **ruby lustre** Alt. colours **no** Composition **ceramic** Size **15 x 15cm/ 6 x 6in** Price ★★★★★ W

13 H. & R. Johnson/Malverns Newland/Newland Inset Colour **marine, blue and platinum** Alt. colours **yes** Composition **ceramic** Size **15 x 15cm x 6.5mm/6 x 6 x ¼in** Price ★ W

14 Original Style/Victorian Floor Tiles/Wellesley 6568 Colour **green on buff** Alt. colours **yes** Composition **ceramic** Size **15 x 15cm/6 x 6in** Price ★★ F ⌂

15 H. & R. Johnson/Papyrus Idfu Colour **beige** Alt. colours **yes** Composition **ceramic** Size **15 x 15cm/6 x 6in** Price ★ W

16 Original Style/Evening Reverie 6046 Colour **multi** Alt. colours **no** Composition **ceramic** Size **15 x 4cm x 7mm/6 x 1½ x ¼in** Price ★ W

ARTS AND CRAFTS DESIGNS

In 1860, when William Morris was looking for tiles for his new home "Red House" in Kent, England, he lamented the fact that no company in England was manufacturing hand-made tiles. He decided to buy hand-made, white, glazed Dutch tiles and decorated them with the enamels he used for stained glass. The tile shown below is based upon one of Morris's own designs, known as "Swan". Not currently reproduced, it is often available from antique and reclaimed tile merchants.

11

Swan Repeat Colour **blue** Alt. colours **yes** Composition **ceramic** Size **15 x 15cm x 7mm/6 x 6 x ¼in** W

Motifs: **Early 20th century**

Perhaps as a reaction to the designs of the Art Nouveau movement, some tile manufacturers returned to Neo-classical imagery at the beginning of the 20th century. However, as labour costs rose, manufacturers sought methods of production that were cheaper and faster than the traditional printing and hand-colouring, and this led to the development of machine-moulded relief tiles. Tiles moulded with drapes, wreaths, bowls or baskets of fruit, shells and other still-life compositions were arranged as borders along the tops of walls, the remainder of the tiling being plain. Moulded tiles were used in commercial buildings, especially butcher's shops and dairies, as well as in domestic halls and porches.

In the 1920s and 1930s, many companies – such as Carter & Co in Dorset, England – produced tiles that featured small motifs, to be used in conjunction with their pictorial tiles; subjects might be a clump of grass or a bunch of flowers. During this period in America, companies such as Malibu Tiles and Gladding McBean were making tiles decorated with a range of boldly coloured, Catalan-inspired motifs, designs that were frequently in relief. In addition, the influence of Art Deco in Europe and America inspired graphic, linear motifs based on objects such as fans and stylized flowers.

5

1

3

4

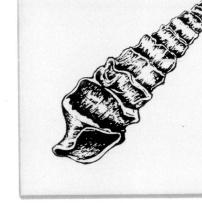

6

7

1 Ann Sacks/Topiary Tree
Colour **SW05** Alt. colours **yes** Composition **ceramic** Size **15 x 7.5cm/6 x 2¾in** Price ★★★ Ⓦ

2 Original Style/Shell Frieze 6991B (2 tiles) Colour **multi** Alt. colours **no** Composition **ceramic** Size **15 x 7.5cm/6 x 2¾in** Price ★★ Ⓦ

3 Fired Earth/Cherry Colour **red, cream and green** Alt. colours **no** Composition **ceramic** Size **11 x 11cm/4¼ x 4¼in** Price ★★★ Ⓦ 🗗

4 Walker Zanger/Ceramica Alhambra/Chaparral Border Colour **natural** Alt. colours **no** Composition **ceramic** Size **10 x 10cm/4 x 4in** Price ★★★ Ⓦ

5 Winchester Tile Co/Designer Flowers/Stem Vase W.HP1490 Colour **off-white** Alt. colours **no** Composition **ceramic** Size **21 x 10.5cm/8¼ x 4in** Price ★★★ Ⓦ

6 Kenneth Clark Ceramics/ Shells S3 Colour **black on white** Alt. colours **yes** Composition **ceramic** Size **10 x 10cm/4 x 4in** Price ★ Ⓦ 🗗 ⊞

7 Winchester Tile Co/ Cockerel WHP1052 Colour **white** Alt. colours **yes** Composition **ceramic** Size **10.5 x 10.5cm x 8mm/4 x 4 x ⅓in** Price ★★ Ⓦ

8

8 Walker Zanger/Ceramic Alhambra/Alamedilla Deco Border Colour **multi** Alt. colours **no** Composition **ceramic** Size **10 x 10cm/ 4 x 4in** Price ★★★ F

9 Winchester Tile Co/Cherry Border WHP1052 Colour **off-white** Alt. colours **yes** Composition **ceramic** Size **10.5 x 10.5cm/4 x 4in** Price ★★ W

10 Fired Earth/Anita B Colour **blue** Alt. colours **yes** Composition **ceramic** Size **10 x 10cm/4 x 4in** Price ★ W F +

11 Minton Hollins/Baroque ANFI Colour **blue** Alt. colours **yes** Composition **ceramic** Size **15 x 15cm/6 x 6in** Price ★ W

12

9

10

12 Fired Earth/Puebla Wall Tiles/Guadalajara Colour **multi** Alt. colours **no** Composition **terracotta** Size **10 x 10cm/4 x 4in** Price ★ W

13 Ann Sacks/Celtic Deer Colour **springwheat** Alt. colours **yes** Composition **ceramic** Size **10 x 10cm/4 x 4in** Price ★★★ W

14 Kenneth Clark Ceramics/ Doves Relief Colour **primrose yellow** Alt. colours **yes** Composition **ceramic** Size **15 x 7.5cm/6 x 2¾in** Price ★★ W

13

11

14

20th century

Floral Tiles

Floral designs have been a recurrent theme on tiles from earliest times. Styles have varied over the years, ranging from the simple lotus and daisy patterns of ancient Egypt to the elaborate flowers on Islamic tiles that were echoed in the 19th century by the Arts and Crafts designer William de Morgan. Flowers have featured as backgrounds in Islamic calligraphic tiles, as borders and corner ornaments and as individual specimen varieties on delftware tiles, and as vases or pots of flowers on large Dutch and Portuguese tile panels. They have also been seen as repeating designs on late 18th- and 19th-century tiles, in highly stylized form on Art Nouveau tiles and as posies and bunches on mid-20th century tiles.

Designs have been taken from a variety of sources including nature itself, herbals and florilegia in the late Middle Ages, and even bulb growers' catalogues, a source much used by the early 17th-century delftware painters. Flowers featured have ranged from the naturalistic to the highly stylized, where the original species is indeterminable.

LEFT The light, uncluttered style of this typically Swedish tiled stove was especially popular in Scandinavia. While the tiles on most Eastern European stoves were decorated with darker, lead-based glazes, the Scandinavian stoves invariably featured tiles based on white tin-glazes, similar to those used on delft tiles.

ABOVE A corner of a bathroom in La Heredia near Malaga, Spain, which, although decorated in the late 20th century, captures the spirit of a 16th-century Spanish tiled interior. There is an almost unbroken history of the manufacture of these richly glazed tiles, decorated with bold floral motifs, both in and around Seville.

BATHROOM TILING

In the late 19th century, bathrooms in wealthier homes often contained elaborate mahogany-panelled baths decorated with insets of tiles. These tiles were sometimes arranged in large panels of naturalistic or stylized floral patterns. Wash-basins were often housed in matching mahogany cabinets, with a marble surround and tiled splashbacks echoing those set behind the bath. The example shown here includes tiles set into the doors and a tip-up basin, which is inverted to dispose of the water.

KEY DESIGNS

1 The image of a flower as a botanical specimen was popular on early delftware tiles, the inspiration for which was often taken from bulb growers' catalogues.

2 Abstract designs – where the flower is depicted as a geometric pattern – have been frequently used on tiles since the Victorian era.

4 Flowers have frequently featured as ornament on border tiles. This is largely thanks to their form being suitable for both vertical and horizontal extension.

3 Floral designs in particular lend themselves to the imagination of the designer, and stylization reached its height during the Art Nouveau period in the late 19th century.

5 Floral tile designs have been taken from both nature and printed sources, with some naturalistic images rendered in the style of botanists' drawings.

6 Magnificent arrangements of flowers in vases or pots either on a single tile or a large panel of tiles were popular in 17th-century Portugal and the Netherlands, as well as on some English delft tiles.

1 **Fired Earth/Antieke Delft Tulips 3** Colour **blue, white, red, and green** Alt. colours **no** Composition **ceramic** Size **13 x 13cm/5 x 5in** Price ★★★★ Ⓦ

2 **Elon/Seville B** Colour **B** Alt. colours **yes** Composition **ceramic** Size **10 x 10cm/4 x 4in** Price ★ Ⓦ ⊞

3 **Craven Dunnill Jackfield/Art Nouveau/Iris (2 tiles)** Colour **violet on merganser** Alt. colours **yes** Composition **ceramic** Size **15 x 15cm/6 x 6in** Price ★★ Ⓦ

4 **Winchester Tile Co/Red Clover Border WKHP1356** Colour **multi** Alt. colours **yes** Composition **ceramic** Size **20 x 10cm/8 x 4in** Price ★ Ⓦ

5 **Welbeck Tiles/English/Flora 3** Colour **charcoal** Alt. colours **yes** Composition **ceramic** Size **13.5 x 13.5cm/5¼ x 5¼in** Price ★★ Ⓦ

6 **H. & R. Johnson/Minton Hollins/Lilies TRP1 (2 tile panel)** Colour **ivory** Alt. colours **yes** Composition **ceramic** Size **15 x 15cm/6 x 6in** Price ★★★ Ⓦ

Florals: **Pre-19th century**

The flower was an important element of early Egyptian culture, and fragments of tile dating from about 1370BC have been excavated from Tell-el-Amarna (north of Thebes) bearing lotus-blossom and daisy patterns. Floral themes recur on Islamic tiles from about AD1200, when they were used as a background for calligraphic inscriptions.

Tulips, carnations, daisies and leaf shapes were predominant themes on Iznik pottery (*see opposite*) of the 15th to 17th centuries. Tulips also appear on early polychrome delftware tiles, but, by 1625, the fashion for coloured ceramics declined as the trade in Chinese blue-and-white porcelain brought about a change in taste. A few large tile panels featuring vases of flowers were made toward the end of the 17th century; some fine examples can be seen in the kitchens at the Rambouillet Palace in France. Small quantities of polychrome, purple or blue-and-white flower-vase tiles were produced in Liverpool, Bristol and London in England, as well as in some areas of Germany, during the mid-18th century.

1

1 Fired Earth/Margarite B/Y Colour **yellow and green** Alt. colours **yes** Composition **ceramic** Size **10 x 10cm/ 4 x 4in** Price ★ Ⓦ

2 Fired Earth/Puebla/Bouquet Colour **multi** Alt. colours **no** Composition **terracotta** Size **10 x 10cm/4 x 4in** Price ★ Ⓦ

3 Fired Earth/Early English Delft/Daisy Colour **blue/ white** Alt. colours **no** Composition **ceramic** Size **13 x 13cm/5 x 5in** Price ★★★ Ⓦ

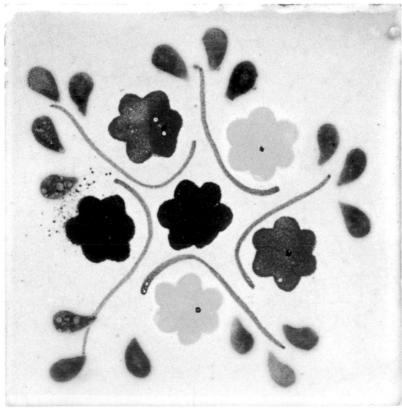

2

3

4

5

7

8

4 Fired Earth/Delft Archive Carnation Colour **blue and white** Alt. colours **yes** Composition **ceramic** Size **11 x 11cm/4¼ x 4¼in** Price ★★★ Ⓦ

5 Fired Earth/Iznik/Adana Silk Border A09L2 Colour **blue, green and red** Alt. colours **no** Composition **ceramic** Size **20 x 10cm/8 x 4in** Price ★★ Ⓦ

6 Winchester Tile Co/Swag Flower Border W.HP1234 Colour **rosa** Alt. colours **yes** Composition **ceramic** Size **21.5 x 7.5cm/8½ x 2¾in** Price ★★★ Ⓦ

7 Carré/Aquarelle/Les Majoliques Paniers cx 5254 Colour **blue** Alt. colours **yes** Composition **alabaster** Size **14 x 14cm/5½ x 5½in** Price ★★ Ⓦ Ⓕ

8 Marlborough Tiles/Georgian Flowers Colour **blue on ivory** Alt. colours **yes** Composition **ceramic** Size **11 x 11cm/4¼ x 4¼in** Price ★★ Ⓦ

9 Fired Earth/Foundry Art/Lotus Colour **white bronze** Alt. colours **no** Composition **bronze** Size **7.5 x 7.5cm/2⅞ x 2⅞in** Price ★★★★★ Ⓕ

SEALING-WAX RED

Probably some of the finest examples of the tile-maker's art were the beautiful floral tiles produced in Iznik, the modern-day Turkish town of Nicea, between about 1575 and 1600. One of the most striking features of these tiles is the rich sealing-wax red, so called because it stands proud of the surface of the glaze. The secret ingredients of this colour are still unknown and elude modern potters, although contemporary glazes have achieved a good approximation to the distinctive, rich red.

Fired Earth/Izmir Border Colour **multi** Alt. colours **no** Composition **ceramic** Size **20 x 5cm x 8mm/8 x 2 x ⅓in** Price ★★ Ⓦ

9

TILES: *FLORALS*   **331**

Florals: 19th century

Floral designs were seldom used on tiles in the late 18th and early 19th centuries, but they enjoyed a renaissance in the 1860s as designers were inspired by the new Aesthetic movement that drew heavily upon Japanese and other oriental designs and forms. William de Morgan, the English Arts and Crafts potter and friend of William Morris, revived interest in Islamic-influenced floral designs in the 1870s. It also became fashionable to make realistic drawings of flowers such as sunflowers from which to create more abstract decorative motifs; this can be seen in the work of tile designers such as C.F.A. Voysey in England, J. & J.G. Low in America and Rafael Bordallo Pinheiro in Portugal.

Floral tiles were used in cast-iron fireplaces. Traditionally, each side of the fireplace held five tiles, and many panels depicting a pot or vase of flowers were designed to suit this specification. These tiles were usually transfer-printed, but hand-painted versions were available for wealthier clients. Toward the end of the century, relief-moulded tiles gave a three-dimensional look to floral designs.

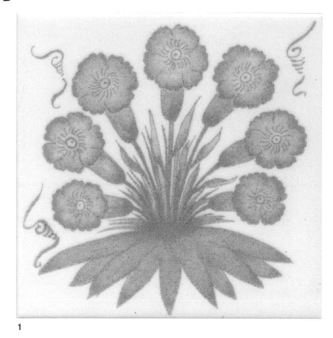

1

2

3

4

1 **Kenneth Clark Ceramics/ William Morris/Primrose**
Colour **green** Alt. colours **yes** Composition **ceramic** Size **15 x 15cm/6 x 6in** Price ★★ Ⓦ

2 **Kenneth Clark Ceramics/ William Morris/Columbine**
Colour **blue** Alt. colours **yes** Composition **ceramic** Size **15 x 15cm/6 x 6in** Price ★★ Ⓦ

3 **Original Style/Floral Garland/ Meadow Cranesbill 5962**
Colour **clematis** Alt. colours **no** Composition **ceramic** Size **10 x 10cm/4 x 4in** Price ★★★ Ⓦ

4 **Kenneth Clark Ceramics/ William Morris/Findon Daisy**
Colour **green** Alt. colours **yes** Composition **ceramic** Size **15 x 15cm/6 x 6in** Price ★★★★ Ⓦ

5

5 H. & R. Johnson/Minton Hollins/Persia/Persepolis Border Colour **multi** Alt. colours **no** Composition **ceramic** Size **15 x 2.5cm/ 6 x 1in** Price ★★ W

6 H. & R. Johnson/Minton Hollins/Kew/White Border Colour **white** Alt. colours **yes** Composition **ceramic** Size **15 x 7.5cm/6 x 2¾in** Price ★ W

7 H. & R. Johnson/Minton Hollins/Blenheim/Ivory Inset Colour **ivory** Alt. colours **yes** Composition **ceramic** Size **15 x 15cm/6 x 6in** Price ★ W

6

7

10

8

9

8 H. & R. Johnson/Minton Hollins/Transfers/Poppies Colour **multi** Alt. colours **yes** Composition **ceramic** Size **15 x 15cm/6 x 6in** Price ★★ W

9 Original Style/Blue Iris 6080A (5-tile panel) Colour **multi** Alt. colours **no** Composition **ceramic** Size **15 x 15cm x 7mm/6 x 6 x ¼in** Price ★★★★ W

10 Original Style/Rose and Trellis 6970A (2 tiles) Colour **multi** Alt. colours **no** Composition **ceramic** Size **15 x 15cm x 7mm/ 6 x 6 x ¼in** Price ★ W

TILES: *FLORALS* **333**

19th century

Florals: **Early 20th century**

With the advent of the Art Nouveau movement, the floral tile became increasingly abstract and stylized in its design. In Continental Europe, Art Nouveau-style tiled panels were used to create complete interiors, while in America and England such floral designs tended to be on individual tiles or arranged as small panels up to dado height. In the early 20th century, many tiles were produced by tube-lining. In this technique the linear elements of a design are applied to stand out from the surface of the tile, enabling designers to create fluid, sinuous shapes with positive outlines separating the coloured glazes.

In Portugal, Spain, Belgium and the Netherlands, highly elaborate Art Nouveau floral panels were often used to cover the façades of buildings, while in Britain tiles were largely confined to interiors. By the 1920s, floral tiles were becoming noticeably less stylized once again; naturalistic flowers were frequently shown in small posies or within larger arrangements. Many floral tiles in this style were made by Carter & Co in England, closely echoing the brightly coloured pots made at Poole Pottery in Dorset, England. Meanwhile, in America, the Rookwood Pottery (based in Cincinatti, Ohio), which was also well known for its pots, produced a wide range of spectacular floral tiles and tile panels.

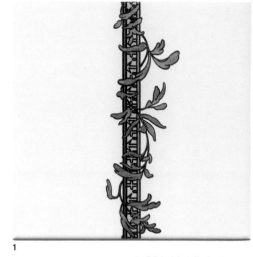

1

2

3

4

5

6

7

1 **Original Style/Spring Border 6062** Colour **lilac** Alt. colours **no** Composition **ceramic** Size **15 x 15cm x 7mm/ 6 x 6 x ¼in** Price ★ W

2 **Kenneth Clark Ceramics/ Tubeline Flowers GTF1** Colour **green** Alt. colours **yes** Composition **ceramic** Size **10 x 10cm x 6mm/4 x 4 x ¼in** Price ★★★ W ⊞

3 **Fired Earth/Bluebells** Colour **multi** Alt. colours **no** Composition **ceramic** Size **15 x 15cm x 8mm/6 x 6 x ⅜in** Price ★★★ W

4 **Minton Hollins/Kew/ Marguerite** Colour **multi** Alt. colours **no** Composition **ceramic** Size **15 x 15cm/ 6 x 6in** Price ★★ W

5 **Welbeck Tiles/Platinum/ Botanicals 4** Colour **black on cream** Alt. colours **yes** Composition **ceramic** Size **13.5 x 13.5cm/5¼ x 5¼in** Price ★★★ W

6 **Craven Dunnill Jackfield/ Victorian/Claverley** Colour **burgundy** Alt. colours **yes** Composition **ceramic** Size **30 x 10 x 1.5cm/11¾ x 4 x ⅝in** Price ★★ W

7 **Tiles of Newport & London/ Decorated Tozzetto TNL414A** Colour **multi** Alt. colours **no** Composition **ceramic** Size **4 x 4cm x 7mm/1½ x 1½ x ¼in** Price ★ W

8 Original Style/Rose and Bud (5-tile panel) Colour **colonial white** Alt. colours **no** Composition **ceramic** Size **15 x 15cm x 7mm/6 x 6 x ¼in** Price ★★★★ W

9 Craven Dunnill Jackfield/ Victorian/Hope Colour **cream** Alt. colours **yes** Composition **ceramic** Size **7.5 x 7.5cm/2¾ x 2¾in** Price ★ W

10 Original Style/Sunflower KHP5826B Colour **clematis** Alt. colours **yes** Composition **ceramic** Size **10 x 10cm x 7mm/4 x 4 x ¼in** Price ★★★ W

11 Original Style/Orchid (Orchidée) 1902 6054 Colour **multi** Alt. colours **no** Composition **ceramic** Size **15 x 15cm x 7mm/ 6 x 6 x ¼in** Price ★ W

8

9

10

11

ART NOUVEAU

The opening of the shop L'Art Nouveau in Paris, France in 1896 heralded the beginning of a new style movement that was to shape the decorative arts for the next 25 years. This was a period of highly stylized, curvilinear designs, which were often based on sinuous floral motifs and glamorous female figures. Such designs lent themselves particularly well to tube-lining, a technique similar to piping icing on to a cake. The raised lines give a three-dimensional appearance to the design as well as containing the coloured glazes used.

Kenneth Clark Ceramics/Tubeline Tulip Border Colour **green** Alt. colours **yes** Composition **ceramic** Size **10 x 10cm/ 4 x 4in** Price ★★★ W ⊞

20th century

Florals: Late 20th–early 21st century

Government restrictions in Britain, and to some extent in Continental Europe, inhibited the production of decorative tiles in the years following the Second World War. At this time, most building construction was government-commissioned and plain tiles, rather than decorated ones, were considered more appropriate, given limited resources. In Europe, this restriction affected some countries more than others but, overall, this period saw a temporary lull in the production of decorative tiles.

By the 1960s, tile production in Europe and America was increasing rapidly but was chiefly in the hands of a few large companies, such as Villeroy & Boch in Germany and H. & R. Johnson in England, which specialized in mass-production. Floral tiles tended to be simple, pastel-coloured designs that could be made quickly and easily by screen-printing or wax-resist techniques. Perhaps spotting a gap, many small companies emerged during the 1980s, 1990s and early 2000s in both Europe and America specializing in hand-made and decorated tiles. At the same time, the colourful tiles traditionally used in European countries, notably Spain and Italy, became more widely sought after, and were exported to other European countries and America.

4

1

2

1 **Tiles of Stow/Summer Flowers Border** Colour **multi** Alt. colours **yes** Composition **ceramic** Size **15 x 15cm/6 x 6in** Price ★★ [W]

2 **Tiles of Stow/Summer Flowers** Colour **multi** Alt. colours **yes** Composition **ceramic** Size **15 x 15cm/6 x 6in** Price ★★★ [W]

3 **Tiles of Stow/Fleur Antique Border** Colour **multi** Alt. colours **yes** Composition **ceramic** Size **10 x 10cm/4 x 4in** Price ★ [W]

4 **Carocim/Glamour Fleur M432 (4 tiles)** Colour **U4** Alt. colours **yes** Composition **cement/marble (encaustic)** Size **20 x 20cm/8 x 8in** Price ★ [W] [F]

5 **Elon/Carillo/Bouquet** Colour **multi** Alt. colours **no** Composition **ceramic** Size **10 x 10cm/4 x 4in** Price ★ [W]

3

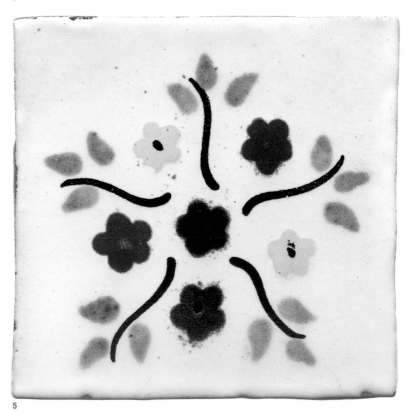

5

6

7

8

6 Winchester Tile Co/Clematis and Fuschia WHP1336 Colour **pure white** Alt. colours **yes** Composition **ceramic** Size 10.5 x 10.5cm/4 x 4in Price ★★ W

7 Original Style/Wild Rose 5964 Colour **clematis** Alt. colours **no** Composition **ceramic** Size 10 x 10cm/4 x 4in Price ★★★ W

8 Original Style/La Belle/Dried Bouquet Plaque KHP5698B Colour **clematis** Alt. colours **no** Composition **ceramic** Size 20 x 30cm/8 x 11¾in Price ★★★★★ W

9 Fired Earth/Impressions/ Flowers/Amaryllis Colour **cream** Alt. colours **yes** Composition **ceramic** Size 13 x 13cm/5 x 5in Price ★★★ W

10 Kenneth Clark Ceramics/ Hydrangea Border Colour **rosemary** Alt. colours **yes** Composition **ceramic** Size 15 x 15cm/6 x 6in Price ★★

9

10

Pictorial Tiles

Since the earliest times, pictorial tiles have been an important element of the tile-maker's repertoire. Displaying mythical creatures and warriors in tile work on the walls of the city of Babylon, built in about 580BC, was intended to frighten potential invaders. The medieval romance and hunting scenes on many 13th- and 14th-century tile installations reflect the lifestyle of the noblemen who were the tile-makers' patrons.

In the deeply religious countries of Spain and the Netherlands, tiles often depicted saints and biblical scenes. The tile-makers of the Netherlands, influenced by the nation's connections with the sea, also created maritime scenes on their tiles.

By the mid-19th century, there was a great interest in literary subjects, reflected in the numerous series of tiles presenting scenes from the works of writers and artists such as William Shakespeare and Albrecht Dürer. The advent of photography provoked a new enthusiasm for pictorial subjects, and many tile companies reproduced actual photographs on their tiles.

LEFT In Italy during the 15th and 16th centuries, tin-glazed tiles were commonly used on the floors as well as the walls of wealthy homes. On the floors, pictorial designs or motifs were often interspersed with areas of plain tiling. On the walls, pictorial panels, often featuring mythological subjects, were common.

ABOVE An original 18th-century tiled stove sits in Lars Sjoberg's home at Odenslunda in Stockholm, Sweden. The individual tiles are quite big, and combine to form an impressive pictorial design. Swags feature at the top and bottom of the stove, while the central image is that of a large urn.

POWDER-GROUND

The English delft tiles shown here were made in London between 1730 and 1750. They surround a niche decorated in plain tiles and marble. The border on the octagonal tiles is known as a powder- ground and was produced by spattering pigment through a metal stencil. Most of powder- ground tiles have a purple border produced from manganese ore, but occasionally English delft tiles are found with red, green or blue borders. These colours were never used on Dutch powder- ground tiles.

1 Ancient cultures have proved a rich source of imagery for tiles. Typical examples include scenes from ancient Greece, Rome and Egypt.

2 Marine-themed tiles were loved among the seafaring Dutch, and were a favourite subject for the Arts and Crafts potter William de Morgan.

3 Pictorial scenes of children's games and sporting activities have been popular since the 17th century, especially on delft tiles. Allegorical and symbolic designs were much used in the 19th century.

4 Landscape tiles and tile panels (often featuring people) have been widely seen since the 17th century. In the Victorian era, stylized imagery as well as naturalistic scenes were common.

5 Since the middle of the 19th century, tiles depicting scenes from literary works, such as this *Alice in Wonderland* design, have remained fashionable.

6 Animals have long been a favourite subject for tile designers. This late 20th-century kitchen tile is typical of a modern, cartoon-like scene.

1 **Original Style/Egyptian Wedding Banquet KHP5475** Colour **black on terracotta** Alt. colours **no** Composition **ceramic** Size **20 x 20cm/8 x 8in** Price ★★★ Ⓦ

2 **Original Style/Viking Longship 6966B** Colour **multi** Alt. colours **no** Composition **ceramic** Size **15 x 15cm/6 x 6in** Price ★★ Ⓦ

3 **Fired Earth/Delft Archive/Golfing/St. Andrews** Colour **sepia** Alt. colours **yes** Composition **ceramic** Size **11 x 11cm/4¼ x 4¼in** Price ★★★ Ⓦ

4 **Winchester Tile Co/English Delft/Lady and Mansion WDE1512** Colour **blue and white** Alt. colours **no** Composition **ceramic** Size **12.5 x 12.5cm/5 x 5in** Price ★★★★ Ⓦ

5 **The Arts and Crafts Home/Voysey "Alice"** Colour **multi** Alt. colours **no** Composition **ceramic** Size **15 x 15cm/6 x 6in** Price ★★★★ Ⓦ

6 **Tile Productions/Farmyard: Sheep** Colour **multi** Alt. colours **yes** Composition **ceramic** Size **11 x 11cm/4¼ x 4¼in** Price ★★ Ⓦ

Pictorials: **Pre-19th century**

In the 13th century, many inlaid floor tiles were produced with designs that depicted dogs, stags and huntsmen. Although made as individual tiles, they were often laid in groups to give the effect of a chase. In about 1500, the potter Francisco Niculoso moved from Pisa in Italy to Seville in Spain, where he introduced the art of painting ceramics in tin-glaze. From Spain the art spread to the Low Countries and, by the 17th century, many fine picture tiles and tile panels were being produced in Antwerp, Rotterdam and Delft. The tin-glaze technique gave the tile-maker a wider palette of colour, facilitating freer, more realistic designs.

Large-scale panels consisting of 400 to 500 tiles – such as those by the Dutch artist Cornelis Bouwmeester (1651–1733), best known for his shipping scenes – were expensive, but even the most humble of homes were decorated with single pictorial tiles. In 1756, in Liverpool, England, Sadler and Green perfected a method of transferring an image from a printing plate to a tile by means of a transfer tissue, to allow consistent reproduction of very fine detail. The majority of Sadler and Green's output was pictorial, with designs taken mainly from Rococo prints. In colonial America, delftware tiles imported from the Netherlands were favoured, particularly those showing figures or moral or religious themes.

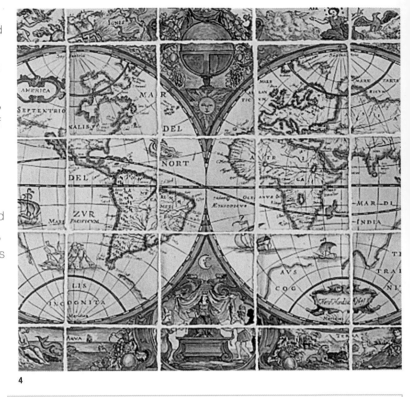

4

1

2

3

1 **Simmy Ceramics/Cherubs (6-tile panel)** Colour **blue on white** Alt. colours **yes** Composition **ceramic** Size **20 x 20cm/8 x 8in** Price ★★★★★ W ⊞

2 **Winchester Tile Co/Balloon 6 W.HP1418** Colour **off-white** Alt. colours **yes** Composition **ceramic** Size **12.5 x 12.5cm/5 x 5in** Price ★★★ W

3 **Fired Earth/Early English Delft/Fisherman** Colour **blue and white** Alt. colours **no** Composition **ceramic** Size **13 x 13cm/5 x 5in** Price ★★★ W

4 **Paris Ceramics/Hand-Painted Decorative/Mappa Mundi (35-tile panel)** Colour **multi** Alt. colours **no** Composition **ceramic** Size **12.5 x 12.5cm/5 x 5in** Price ★★★★★ F ♣

DELFTWARE

These tiles usually feature a central picture framed by a decorative border and a small ornamental motif at each corner. The delft tile-painter faces a task akin to painting a watercolour on blotting paper. After the tile has been biscuit-fired, it is dipped in a liquid tin-glaze; the tile absorbs the moisture, leaving a thin layer of powdered glaze. The outline is marked on this glaze by dabbing powdered charcoal through a pricked paper pattern, and the tile-painter then follows this outline, using a very fine brush to apply the colour.

1

2

1 **Fired Earth/Delft/Windmill 2** Colour **blue and white** Alt. colours **no** Composition **ceramic** Size **13 x 13cm/5 x 5in** Price ★★★ W

2 **Fired Earth/Early English Delft/Pottery** Colour **blue and white** Alt. colours **no** Composition **ceramic** Size **13 x 13cm/5 x 5in** Price ★★★ W

5 **Walker Zanger/Deruta/Pergola Border** Colour **multi** Alt. colours **no** Composition **ceramic** Size **15 x 15cm/6 x 6in** Price ★★★★★ W

6 **Original Style/Masterpiece/Botticelli, Birth of Venus 6364** Colour **multi** Alt. colours **yes** Composition **ceramic** Size **36 x 56cm/14 x 22in** Price ★★★★★ W

7 **Winchester Tile Co/King of Diamonds** Colour **multi** Alt. colours **no** Composition **ceramic** Size **15 x 10.5cm/6 x 4in** Price ★ W

8 **Welbeck Tiles/English/Figures 10** Colour **charcoal** Alt. colours **yes** Composition **ceramic** Size **13.5 x 13.5cm/5¼ x 5¼in** Price ★★★★ W

9 **Winchester Tile Co/English Delft/Exotic Birds/Bird in Tree W.DE1522** Colour **multi** Alt. colours **no** Composition **ceramic** Size **12.5 x 12.5cm/5 x 5in** Price ★★ F

10 **Fired Earth/Natural History/Crab Apple (12 tile panel)** Colour **multi** Alt. colours **no** Composition **ceramic** Size **40 x 30cm/15¾ x 11¾in** Price ★★★★★ W

11 **Fired Earth/Antieke Delft/Childrens Games 2** Colour **blue/white** Alt. colours **no** Composition **ceramic** Size **11 x 11cm/4¼ x 4¼in** Price ★★★ W

12 **Reptile/Birds and Bees** Colour **multi** Alt. colours **no** Composition **ceramic** Size **15 x 15cm/6 x 6in** Price ★★★ W ⊞

7

8

9

10

11

12

TILES: *PICTORIALS*   **341**

Pictorials: **19th century**

Comparatively few tiles were made in the first 40 years of the 19th century, but by 1845 the master British ceramicist Herbert Minton had introduced his first series of picture tiles, based on the romantic paintings of the French artist Jean-Antoine Watteau. These were so successful that they were still in production in the early 20th century. By the 1870s, his company, Minton China Works of Stoke-on-Trent, was one of the largest commercial potteries in the world.

Also produced in the 19th century were pictorial tiles in the style of the Aesthetic movement, echoing the renewed interest in the Orient. These tiles were all mass-produced, which was anathema to William Morris and the other leaders of the Arts and Crafts movement in Britain and America. Morris made tiles himself for a few years, before turning to his friend William de Morgan to make and paint decorative tiles for his company. Galleons, and real and mythical animals, such as sea monsters, all appear on the de Morgan tiles, which were painted in monochrome, full colour or his own wonderful lustres. Meanwhile, in America, tile-makers such as Henry Chapman Mercer and William H. Grueby, who formed part of the American Arts and Crafts movement, achieved an interesting range of pictorial relief tiles, including the distinctive floor tiles made by Mercer for Wellington House in New York.

1 H. & R. Johnson/Natural Selection/Cotswold Kelmscott Colour **mushroom** Alt. colours **yes** Composition **ceramic** Size **30 x 20cm/11¾ x 8in** Price ★★ Ⓦ

2 Winchester Tile Co/De Morgan/Fish Frieze W.HP1261/2 (2-tile panel) Colour **multi** Alt. colours **no** Composition **ceramic** Size **10.5 x 10.5cm/4 x 4in** Price ★★ Ⓦ

3 Fired Earth/Heritage/Hare and Hound (2 tiles) Colour **natural** Alt. colours **no** Composition **ceramic** Size **11 x 6cm/4¼ x 2½in** Price ★★ Ⓦ

4 New Castle Delft/Gallery/Stein-bass (18 tiles) Colour **blue and white** Alt. colours **yes** Composition **ceramic** Size **20 x 10cm/8 x 4in** Price ★★ Ⓦ

1

2

4

3

5

6

7

8

9

5 **Original Style/Masterpiece/ Alma-Tadema, Silver Favourites 6360** Colour **multi** Alt. colours **yes** Composition **ceramic** Size **56 x 38cm/22 x 15in** Price ★★★★★ W

6 **Fired Earth/Natural History/ Fish/Chetodon/Maille** Colour **natural** Alt. colours **no** Composition **ceramic** Size **10 x 10cm/4 x 4in** Price ★★★ W

7 **Original Style/Nocturnal Slumber 6042 (3-tile panel)** Colour **multi** Alt. colours **no** Composition **ceramic** Size **15 x 15cm/6 x 6in** Price ★★★ W

8 **Welbeck Tiles/Victorian Jelly** Colour **cream crackle** Alt. colours **no** Composition **ceramic** Size **13.5 x 13.5cm/5¼ x 5¼in** Price ★★★ W

9 **Winchester Tile Co/Animals and Bugs/Cow W.HP1293** Colour **brown on white** Alt. colours **no** Composition **ceramic** Size **10.5 x 10.5cm/4 x 4in** Price ★★ W

10 **Original Style/Cameo Carousel 6006 (5-tile panel)** Colour **imperial ivory** Alt. colours **no** Composition **ceramic** Size **15 x 15cm/6 x 6in** Price ★★★★ W

11 **Original Style/Exotic Birds (Left) 6968A (3-tile panel)** Colour **multi** Alt. colours **no** Composition **ceramic** Size **15 x 15cm/6 x 6in** Price ★★★ W

12 **Original Style/Peacock Border 6960A (2-tile panel)** Colour **multi** Alt. colours **no** Composition **ceramic** Size **15 x 7.5cm/6 x 2¾in** Price ★★ W

10

11

19th century

12

Pictorials: 20th–early 21st century

The Art Nouveau movement generated a wealth of wonderful tiled interiors, particularly in Belgium and France – many in the style of the graphic illustrations by Czech artist Alphonse Mucha. In Britain, few pictorial tiles were made until the 1920s and 1930s when Carter & Co produced several series of brightly coloured, hand-painted picture tiles in the Art Deco style, covering a number of subjects ranging from "Nursery Rhymes" to "Water Birds". Packard and Ord, established in London in 1935, specialized in hand-painted pictorial sets.

In America, the influence of the Arts and Crafts movement continued, and many small tile-makers offered striking relief landscapes and other pictorial tiles. In more recent years, tile murals, often in *trompe l'oeil* form, have regained their popularity. There is also a trend for manufacturers to commission fashion houses, such as Fendi and Kenzo, to provide ideas for tiles – hence Fendi's white-on-white relief-tile series, "Astrologia".

1

2

1 Winchester Tile Co/Copper Engravings/Sunbather W.1850HP Colour **off-white** Alt. colours **no** Composition **ceramic** Size **10.5 x 10.5cm/ 4 x 4in** Price ★★ W

2 Original Style/Laurel (Le Laurier) 6052 Colour **multi** Alt. colours **no** Composition **ceramic** Size **15 x 15cm/6 x 6in** Price ★★ W

3 Paris Ceramics/Four Seasons/ Summer Colour **multi** Alt. colours **no** Composition **ceramic** Size **25 x 25cm/9¾ x 9¾in** Price ★★★★★ W

4 Fired Earth/Natural History Crab Apple (2-tile panel) Colour **natural** Alt. colours **no** Composition **ceramic** Size **20 x 10cm/8 x 4in** Price ★★★★ W

5 Ann Sacks/Algonquin Tent Colour **earthenware** Alt. colours **yes** Composition **ceramic** Size **10 x 10cm/ 4 x 4in** Price ★★★ W

6 Reptile/4 Fishes No. 21 Colour **multi** Alt. colours **yes** Composition **ceramic** Size **15 x 15cm/6 x 6in** Price ★★★ W ⊞

7 Surving Studios/Vine Tree Frog Triptych (3-tile panel) Colour **green** Alt. colours **yes** Composition **ceramic** Size **10 x 10cm/4 x 4in** Price ★★★★★ W

8 Tiles of Stow/Sixpence Bird Colour **multi** Alt. colours **yes** Composition **ceramic** Size **15 x 15cm/6 x 6in** Price ★★★ W

3

4

5

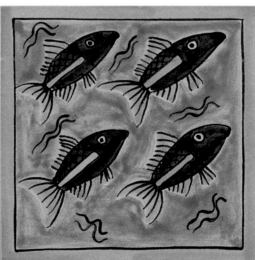

6

7

8

9 Reptile/Seal No. 17 Colour **multi** Alt. colours **yes** Composition **ceramic** Size **15 x 15cm/6 x 6in** Price ★★★ W ⊞

10 Candy/Reflection Marine Inset CAN32569 Colour **blue** Alt. colours **no** Composition **ceramic** Size **25 x 20cm/ 9¾ x 8in** Price ★★ W

11 Kenneth Clark Ceramics/ Magic Lantern/Animal Assembly Colour **multi** Alt. colours **yes** Composition **ceramic** Size **10 x 10cm/4 x 4in** Price ★★★ W ⊞

10

11

12

16

13

12 Kenneth Clark Ceramics/ Tubeline Tiles/Boats Colour **multi** Alt. colours **yes** Composition **ceramic** Size **10 x 10cm/4 x 4in** Price ★★★ W ⊞

13 Winchester Tile Co/Sweetcorn and Mushroom W.HP1085 Colour **multi** Alt. colours **no** omposition **ceramic** Size **10.5 x 10.5cm/4 x 4in** Price ★★ W

14

14 Simmy Ceramics/The International Restaurant Range Colour **white** Alt. colours **yes** Composition **ceramic** Size **20 x 20cm x 8mm/8 x 8 x ⅛in** Price ★★★★ W ⊞

15 Carocim/Dé Jeté H.M.C. 08 Colour **green** Alt. colours **yes** Composition **cement/ marble (encaustic)** Size **20 x 20cm/8 x 8in** Price ★ W F ⊞

15

16 Original Tiles/Fruits Exotiques/Star Fruit to Melon Border KHP5737B Colour **multi** Alt. colours **no** Composition **ceramic** Size **20 x 7.5cm/8 x 2⅞in** Price ★★ W ♣

17 Original Style/A La Ferme/ Geese Border KHP5797B Colour **clematis** Alt. colours **no** Composition **ceramic** Size **20 x 5cm/8 x 2in** Price ★★ W

18 Kenneth Clark Ceramics/ Magic Lantern/Elephant Colour **ML2** Alt. colours **no** Composition **ceramic** Size **10 x 10cm/4 x 4in** Price ★★ W ⊞

19 Tiles of Stow/Grasslands Tiger Colour **white** Alt. colours **yes** Composition **ceramic** Size **13 x 13cm/5 x 5in** Price ★★★ W

TILES & ADVERTISING

Because of their durability and ease of cleaning, tiles have frequently been used to advertise products and services. It was once common to see butcher's shops and dairies with tile panels depicting sheep, cattle and poultry, although many of these have now disappeared behind modern laminated surfaces. In the 1920s and 1930s, W.H. Smith, the English stationer and bookseller, used a number of Carter & Co's tiles to advertise their products, while the Santa Fe Railroad in America used tiled logos on its principal stations.

Rye Tiles/Rooster Panel (12-tile panel) Colour **multi** Alt. colours **yes** Composition **ceramic** Size **11 x 11cm/4¼ x 4¼in** Price ★★★★★

17

18   **19**

Overall Pattern Tiles

By their very nature, tiles make an overall pattern when laid. Even when the design extends across a large number of tiles, the basic grid pattern is visible in the joints. To try to hide this, delft tile-painters used various forms of corner ornament to carry the design to adjacent tiles; so that the corners themselves create an additional element in the overall pattern.

Individual tiles have also been designed with an overall pattern. By covering the tile with a repeated pattern of small motifs, often organic and vegetal in nature, an effect approaching that of wallpaper is achieved. The application of printing techniques to tile manufacture in the 1750s enabled such overall designs to be produced accurately and cheaply. Marble effects were also very popular on tiles, particularly in the Netherlands. These finishes subsequently reappeared in modified form during the 1920s and 1930s as the mottled tiles so beloved of fireplace manufacturers. The advent of Pop Art in the 1950s and 1960s brought a wave of tiles with simple designs that consisted of dots, squiggles, lines and other patterns; many of these are designed by computer today.

ABOVE This modern fireplace incorporates tiles that are essentially based on traditional designs and patterns. The inspiration is derived from the "Masters of Tabriz", from the dado of the Muradiye in Edirne, Turkey, which dates from the middle of the 15th century. The border tiles in the fireplace are based on later Iznik tiles of the 17th century.

RIGHT The strong geometric shapes in Charles Jencks's Post-Modernist home are characteristic of the Art Deco period. The patterns in which the simple, mottled tiles are laid in the bathroom reflect this style. Brightly coloured tiles of this kind were a particular feature of Art Deco schemes. The stepped window surround is also in keeping with the distinctive feel of the room.

KEY DESIGNS

1 Tile designs have often imitated architectural features. This is particularly true of border tiles where the overall pattern simulates plaster or stone mouldings.

2 The repeated use of a small floret or other motif can create an overall effect that almost produces the impression of "ceramic wallpaper".

3 Earthenware tiles with *faux* finishes were first seen in the Netherlands in the 17th century. This *faux* stone porcelain tile is a modern example.

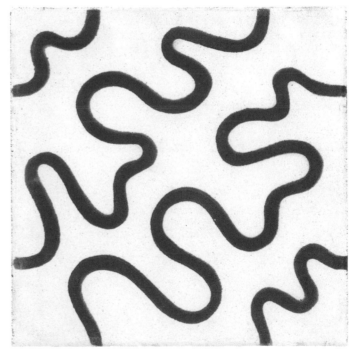

4 Dots, squiggles and a variety of other small-scale decorations have often been used since the mid-20th century as a background for a feature tile or tile panel, and also as patterns in their own right.

1 **Candy/Suzy Florentine 32583 (2 tiles)** Colour **dusk** Alt. colours **yes** Composition **ceramic** Size **20 x 10cm/8 x 4in** Price ★ W

2 **Elon/Terracotta Frieze** Colour **terracotta** Alt. colours **yes** Composition **ceramic** Size **10 x 10cm/4 x 4in** Price ★ W

3 **Daltile/La Costa/ColorBody Porcelain/Field** Colour **rust LC04** Alt. colours **yes** Composition **porcelain** Size **15 x 15cm/6 x 6in** Price ★ W F ⊞

4 **Carocim/Souleiado-Tortillon S510** Colour **blue** Alt. colours **yes** Composition **ceramic** Size **20 x 20cm/8 x 8in** Price ★ W F ⊞

OVERALL PATTERN TILES **347**

Overall Pattern: **Pre-20th century**

Early ceramic tiles rarely featured overall patterns, largely because of the difficulty of producing regular designs by hand-painting. Some medieval tiles did feature overall patterns, but the tiles were invariably divided up into panels of four, nine or 16 by additional lines of plain tiles.

In the Netherlands, a number of tiled rooms still exist that show how the corner ornaments on 17th- and 18th-century delft tiles created a cohesive pattern when used *en masse*. The marble patterns that appear on delft tiles from the end of the 17th century were produced before the tiles were fired, by splashing pigments on to the surface or by swirling colour into the glaze with a comb. The printing technique developed by Sadler and Green in England during the 1750s lent itself to the production of tiles with repeated small motifs and patterns, similar to those seen on wallpapers.

During the 19th century, more heavily patterned designs were used on tiles, many of them based on stylized, rhythmical, organic and vegetal forms. This was particularly true of the second half of the 19th century, and reflected the generally busy, cluttered feel of Victorian interiors. Classical patterns such as scrollwork also remained popular.

1

2

3

5

6

4

7

1 **Fired Earth/Ironbridge Spinney** Colour **Prussian blue** Alt. colours **yes** Composition **ceramic** Size **15 x 7.5cm/6 x 2¾in** Price ★★ Ⓦ

2 **Fired Earth/Roman Mosaic Rope Border** Colour **black** Alt. colours **yes** Composition **stone** Size **40 x 10cm/15¾ x 4in** Price ★★★★ Ⓕ

3 **Walker Zanger/Alhambra Algiers Border** Colour **multi** Alt. colours **yes** Composition **ceramic** Size **10 x 10cm/4 x 4in** Price ★★ Ⓦ

4 **Carocim/Victoria** Colour **black and white** Alt. colours **yes** Composition **cement/marble (encaustic)** Size **20 x 20cm/8 x 8in** Price ★ Ⓦ Ⓕ ⊞

5 **Tiles of Stow/Tozetto Inset** Colour **blue on white** Alt. colours **yes** Composition **ceramic** Size **4 x 4cm/1½ x 1½in** Price ★★ Ⓦ Ⓕ

6 **Candy/Cararra Troy CAN32767** Colour **white** Alt. colours **no** Composition **ceramic** Size **25 x 10cm/9¾ x 4in** Price ★★ Ⓦ

7 **Fired Earth/Iznik/Arabesque (4 tiles)** Colour **multi** Alt. colours **no** Composition **ceramic** Size **20 x 20cm/8 x 8in** Price ★★ Ⓦ

MEXICAN TILES

Although there had been an indigenous pottery industry in Mexico for many centuries, the Spanish Conquistadores introduced the technique of painting on tin-glaze. Colourful tiles were produced during the 17th and 18th centuries combining Spanish and native Mexican designs, and were used to decorate the façades of churches. The traditional centre for tile-making was Puebla, where there has been a recent revival of the craft. Most of the Spanish influence has now disappeared and modern production has a more traditional feel.

Elon/Carrillo Arbor G Colour **Mexican white and green** Alt. colours **no** Composition **ceramic** Size **10 x 10cm x 8mm/4 x 4 x ½in** Price ★ Ⓦ

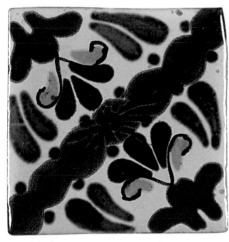

Elon/Carillo Wall/Martha Colour **multi** Alt. colours **yes** Composition **ceramic** Size **10 x 10cm/4 x 4in** Price ★ Ⓦ

12

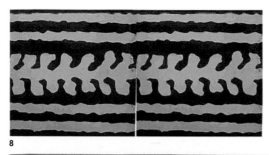

8

9

10

11

13

8 **Carocim/Souleiado/Ronce Frieze S507 (2 tiles)** Colour **U2/U8** Alt. colours **yes** Alt. colours **yes** Composition **cement/marble (encaustic)** Size **20 x 20cm/8 x 8in** Price ★ Ⓦ Ⓕ

9 **Daltile/Village Bend/Decorative Border** Colour **olive VB04** Alt. colours **yes** Composition **glazed ceramic** Size **31 x 15cm/12 x 6in** Price ★ Ⓦ Ⓕ

10 **Original Style/Cornice K9904** Colour **Baltic blue** Alt. colours **yes** Composition **ceramic** Size **15 x 7.5cm/6 x 2¾in** Price ★ Ⓦ

11 **Winchester Tile Co/Acanthus Leaf Moulding Trim W.SF1214** Colour **saffron** Alt. colours **yes** Composition **ceramic** Size **21.5 x 19cm/8½ x 7½in** Price ★★ Ⓦ

12 **Candy/Suzy Florentine CAN32286** Colour **dawn** Alt. colours **yes** Composition **ceramic** Size **20 x 10cm/8 x 4in** Price ★ Ⓦ

13 **Fired Earth/Anatolia 2** Colour **blue and white** Alt. colours **no** Composition **ceramic** Size **17.5 x 17.5cm/7 x 7in** Price ★★ Ⓦ

14 **Kenneth Clark Ceramics/William de Morgan/Ruby Lustre/Berries and Leaves** Colour **ruby lustre** Alt. colours **no** Composition **ceramic** Size **15 x 15cm/6 x 6in** Price ★★★★★ Ⓦ

14

TILES: *OVERALL PATTERN* **349**

Overall Pattern: **20th–early 21st century**

The use of overall tile patterns declined markedly at the beginning of the 20th century; this was largely as a result of the Art Nouveau movement sweeping across Europe, and to some extent, America. In keeping with this movement, plain tiles were preferred for room schemes, with patterned tiles being restricted to a mere dado-height row or a random insert.

By the 1920s, plain tiles had given way to mottles, often produced in the newly developed matt or eggshell glazes. Tile-makers began to investigate the chemistry of glazes, so that new and varied glazes were developed – many having small random crackle or star-burst effects. These and the mottled tiles were popular choices for decorating fireplaces, but they were also used to cover entire walls, especially in bathrooms and kitchens.

Increased mechanization in the 1950s and 1960s led to the simplification of tile design and the subsequent introduction of the many bland and repetitive patterns that swamped the market during the 1970s. Overall pattern designs featuring small floral motifs, in the style of Laura Ashley, were produced during the late 1970s and early 1980s, while in recent years computer-generated tile designs have become commonplace, although hand-made tiles have retained their appeal.

3

4

1

2

1 **Kenneth Clark Ceramics/ Border Tiles/Blue Waves**
Colour **blue** Alt. colours **yes** Composition **ceramic** Size **10 x 10cm/4 x 4in** Price ★ W

2 **Original Style/Laurel Quarter Tile** Colour **multi** Alt. colours **no** Composition **ceramic** Size **15 x 4cm/6 x 1½in** Price ★ W

3 **Tile Productions/Wave Border** Colour **multi** Alt. colours **yes** Composition **ceramic** Size **11 x 11cm/4¼ x 4¼in** Price ★★★ W

4 **Kirkstone/Minoan Liner** Colour **avalon** Alt. colours **no** Composition **glass** Size **19.5 x 6.5cm/7¾ x 2½in** Price ★★★★ W

5 **Carocim/Poétique Foncé M282** Colour **U9** Alt. colours **yes** Alt. colours **yes** Composition **cement/ marble (encaustic)** Size **20 x 20cm/8 x 8in** Price ★ W F

5

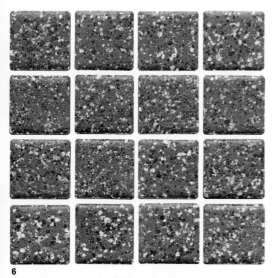

6

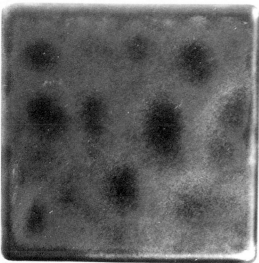

6 **Daltile/Keystones** Colour
corallin Alt. colours **yes**
Composition **ceramic**
Size **5 x 5cm/2 x 2in**
Price ★ W F C ⊞ ▣ ⬠

7 **Fired Earth/Planets/Jupiter**
Colour **browntone** Alt.
colours **yes** Composition
ceramic Size **10 x 10cm/4 x
4in** Price ★ W

8 **Winchester Tile Co/Leaf
Border WHP.1051** Colour
white Alt. colours **yes**
Composition **ceramic**
Size **10.5 x 10.5cm/4 x 4in**
Price ★★ W

9 **Candy/Silver Leaf CAN31364**
Colour **blue** Alt. colours
yes Composition **ceramic**
Size **20 x 7cm/8 x 2¾in**
Price ★★ W

10 **Carocim/Music** Colour **yellow
and black** Alt. colours
yes Composition **cement/
marble (encaustic)** Size
20 x 20cm/8 x 8in
Price ★ W F ⊞

11 **Fired
Earth/Heritage/Sunflower
Leaves** Colour **green** Alt.
colours **no** Composition
ceramic Size **11 x 11cm/4¼ x
4¼in** Price ★★★ W

12 **Carocim/Asie Mineure F551**
Colour **U8** Alt. colours **yes**
Alt. colours **yes** Composition
cement/marble (encaustic)
Size **20 x 20cm/8 x 8in**
Price ★ W F

10

8

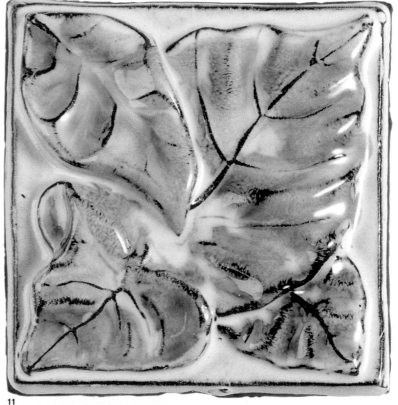

11

9

12

Geometric Tiles

Tiles are essentially geometric in form and, even when the design extends across a number of them, the geometric pattern of the tiling is still evident.

Since medieval times, geometry has also been a basis for tile decoration, often in the form of checks, trellises and overlapping circles. Designs of this nature are fundamental to Islamic culture and this is reflected in the tiles and mosaics of Spain, North Africa and the Middle East.

In 18th-century Portugal, so-called "pombaline" tiles, which have a diagonal pattern of foliage, were placed together to form a trellis pattern. Geometric patterns were also very popular on the tin-glazed tiles produced in France, and to a lesser extent in the Netherlands, toward the end of the 19th century. At the same time, pavements composed of geometrically shaped tiles in various colours were thought appropriate for hallways, porches and public buildings throughout Europe. In the 20th century movements such as Pop Art expanded the possibilities of geometrically patterned tiles.

RIGHT Designs composed of overlapping circles have been used on tiles since medieval times, and relieve the square effect of the tile itself. This 18th-century-style Spanish kitchen is an excellent example of this. Such geometric patterns have appeared in many eras, notably in Art Deco interiors of the early 20th century.

ABOVE The tiles positioned around the cooking range in the Scottish home of Annie and Lachlan Stewart have all been hand-made and hand-painted. The ever-popular tartan pattern, here in various shades of green, fits in perfectly with the style of this farmhouse kitchen, with its Aga and painted woodwork.

ZILLIJ DESIGNS

Zillij is the name given to traditional North African cut-mosaic tilework. Originally, large square tiles were cut after firing into the individually shaped pieces required to make up these elaborate patterns. However, nowadays the pieces are shaped before firing and glazing. The shapes of the pieces and the arrangements of the colours are traditional and have varied surprisingly little over the past 500 years.

KEY DESIGNS

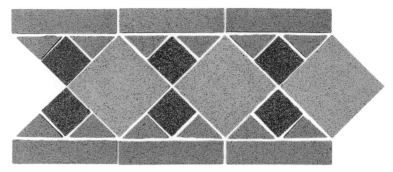

1 The use of interlocking shapes dates back to the medieval period, but it reached its height in Moorish Spain when extremely complex patterns were produced from very simple geometric shapes.

2 Some tiles give the illusion of having interlocking components, such as this geometric *trompe l'oeil* design. The visual effect is heightened when several tiles are placed together.

3 Perhaps the simplest and most popular of geometric designs is the square arranged in alternating colours, either straight or diagonally as a diamond pattern.

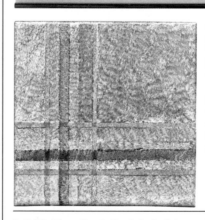

4 Some modern tiles are trimmed top and bottom with a contrasting material. The result, as on this chrome-trimmed 21st-century border tile, is a strongly defined linear pattern.

5 Tartan designs have been popular since the 19th century, and are still employed by tile designers in the 21st century – often updated with new colour combinations.

1 **H. & R. Johnson/Kerastar/Puzzle Border** Colour **grey and white** Alt. colours **no** Composition **porcelain** Size **30 x 15cm/11¾ x 6in** Price ★★★ F 🗑 ⬜

2 **Carocim/Cube Moyen M063** Colour **U1** Alt. colours **yes** Alt. colours **yes** Composition **cement/marble (encaustic)** Size **20 x 20cm/8 x 8in** Price ★ W F

3 **Carocim/Petit Carré M201** Colour **U2** Alt. colours **yes** Alt. colours **yes** Composition **cement/marble (encaustic)** Size **20 x 20cm/8 x 8in** Price ★ W F

4 **Saloni/Alesia/Stella Border/Celta** Colour **green** Alt. colours **yes** Composition **rectified porcelain** Size **30 x 5cm/11¾ x 2in** Price ★ ⊞ W F

5 **Tiles of Stow/Check** Colour **green and purple** Alt. colours **yes** Composition **ceramic** Size **10 x 10cm/4 x 4in** Price ★★★ W

Geometrics: **Pre-19th century**

During the period of the Roman Empire, geometric mosaic floors were laid in domestic buildings as well as in public ones, particularly in Britain and Italy. From the 10th century, the use of cut geometric mosaics was brought to Spain by the Moors from North Africa during their 500-year occupation. This style still survives in such buildings as the 14th-century Alhambra in Granada.

In the early 13th century, a number of abbeys in the north of England were tiled with elaborate pavements of geometrically shaped interlocking tiles. By the end of that century, however, these had been superseded by inlaid tiles, often with intricate geometric patterns, which were used in abbeys and churches across Europe. Owing to the difficulty of producing cut geometric mosaics, these designs were soon reproduced on tiles. Painted geometric tiles were used on walls in many Portuguese interiors during the 14th and 15th centuries, often creating a *trompe l'oeil* three-dimensional box effect. By the 17th century, the Portuguese were also applying tiles to the exteriors of buildings, often to resemble ornate trelliswork.

1

1 **H. & R. Johnson/Natural Selection/Chilterns Checkendon** Colour **sand** Alt. colours **yes** Composition **ceramic** Size **15 x 15cm/6 x 6in** Price ★ W

2 **Candy/Suzy Diamond Border/CAN33931** Colour **dawn** Alt. colours **yes** Composition **ceramic** Size **20 x 7cm/8 x 2¾in** Price ★ W

3 **Walker Zanger/Intarsio Romana/Tarquina Border** Colour **natural** Alt. colours **no** Composition **stone** Size **30 x 13.5cm/11¾ x 5¼in** Price ★★★★ W F

4 **Saloni Ceramics/Ocana Blanco** Colour **multi** Alt. colours **no** Composition **ceramic** Size **25 x 5cm/9¾ x 2in** Price ★ W

5 **Carré/Sols/Terres Cuites/ Antiquaire/Damiers 2736** Colour **red terracotta and cream** Alt. colours **no** Composition **terracotta** Size **13 x 13cm/5 x 5in** Price ★ W F

2

4

3

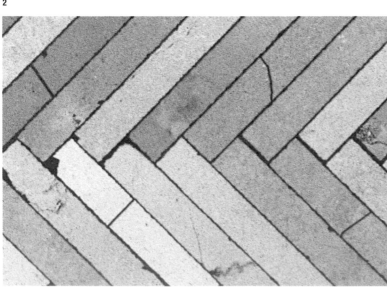

5

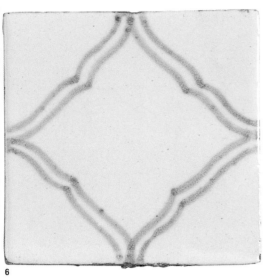

6

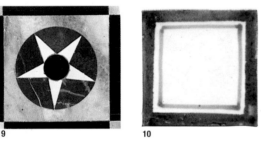

7

8

9

10

6 Elon/Trellis G Colour **green and cream** Alt. colours **yes** Composition **ceramic** Size **10 x 10cm/4 x 4in** Price ★ W

7 Candy/London Chelsea Cream Field CAN34297 Colour **cream** Alt. colours **yes** Composition **ceramic** Size **33 x 25cm/13 x 10in** Price ★★ W

8 Winchester Tile Co/Painted Edge Lines Colour **red** Alt. colours **yes** Composition **ceramic** Size **10.5 x 10.5cm/4 x 4in** Price ★ W ⊞

9 Walker Zanger/Intarsio Romano/Viejo Deco Colour **natural** Alt. colours **no** Composition **stone** Size **12 x 12cm/4¾ x 4¾in** Price ★★★★ W

10 Elon/Daisy May II G Colour **green** Alt. colours **yes** Composition **ceramic** Size **10 x 10cm/4 x 4in** Price ★ W

11 Carocim/Grec Colour **brown and white** Alt. colours **yes** Composition **cement/ marble (encaustic)** Size **20 x 20cm/8 x 8in** Price ★ W F ⊞

12

13

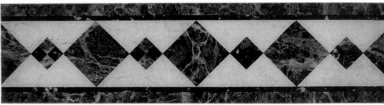

14

12 Carocim/Tanger Colour **multi** Alt. colours **yes** Composition **cement/ marble (encaustic)** Size **20 x 20 cm/8 x 8in** Price ★★ W F ⊞

13 Villeroy & Boch/Villostone/ Geometric Border Electra 2154 845G Colour **green and beige** Alt. colours **yes** Composition **porcelain stoneware** Size **30 x 7.5cm/11¾ x 2¾in** Price ★★★ W F

14 Candy/Tripoli Rombi CAN33382 Colour **cream** Alt. colours **yes** Composition **ceramic** Size **25 x 8cm/ 9¾ x 3in** Price ★ W

15 Carocim/Petit Latti M172 Colour **blue and black** Alt. colours **yes** Composition **cement/marble (encaustic)** Size **20 x 20 cm/8 x 8in** Price ★ W F ⊞

11

15

Geometrics: **19th century**

When the Gothic Revival took place in the early 19th century, architects in Britain and elsewhere in Europe rediscovered the geometric designs of the Middle Ages. Chief among these in England was A.W.N. Pugin, who collaborated with the potter Herbert Minton to create a range of encaustic tiles based on Gothic designs. Many of these were strongly geometric in form. In 1840 Herbert Minton purchased the rights to Richard Prosser's patent for dust-pressing clay products (*see* page 314) and realized that the process could be used to form ceramic *tesserae* and tiles. He was soon able to produce hundreds of geometric shapes based on fractions of a 15cm/6in square. The technique also made it easier to stain the clay different colours, and the tiles were used to create elaborate geometric pavements suitable for public as well as residential buildings. In France, intricate geometric patterns were stencilled on to tin-glazed tiles, particularly in the Pas de Calais region toward the end of the century.

1

1   **Carré/Les Classiques/Carré Bleu 3891** Colour **blue and white** Alt. colours **yes** Composition **glazed stoneware** Size **11 x 11cm/4¼ x 4¼in** Price ★★ W F

2   **Original Style/Royal Stewart Tartan Border 6795A** Colour **multi** Alt. colours **no** Composition **ceramic** Size **15 x 7.5cm/ 6 x 2¾in** Price ★ W

3   **Original Style/Culloden Stirling Tartan Border 6791A** Colour **multi** Alt. colours **no** Composition **ceramic** Size **15 x 7.5cm/ 6 x 2¾in** Price ★ W

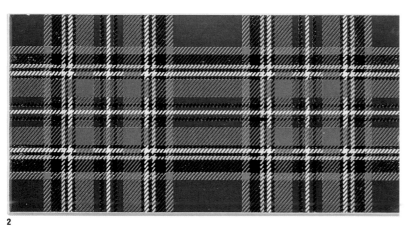
2

3

4

5

4   **Kenneth Clark Ceramics/ Gingham** Colour **black and white** Alt. colours **yes** Composition **ceramic** Size **15 x 7.5cm/6 x 2¾in** Price ★ W

5   **Daltile/Tajah/Natural Slate Borders/Autumn Mist** Colour **California gold TS91** Alt. colours **yes** Composition **slate** Size **23 x 13cm/9 x 5in** Price ★★ F W

6

7

8

9

6 Tiles of Stow/English Lattice
Colour **blue** Alt. colours
no Composition **ceramic**
Size **15 x 15cm/6 x 6in**
Price ★ W

7 Original Style/Melbourne Border 6680 Colour **black spot** Alt. colours **yes**
Composition **ceramic**
Size **15 x 2.5cm/
6 x 1in** Price ★ F

8 Carocim/Grand Carré M191
Colour **U4/U2** Alt. colours **yes**
Alt. colours **yes** Composition
cement/marble (encaustic)
Size **20 x 20cm/8 x 8in**
Price ★ W F

9 Carocim/Pliage Mariella Frieze F063 (3 tiles) Colour
U2/U4, U6/U9 Alt. colours
yes Composition **cement**
Size **20 x 20cm/8 x 8in**
Price ★ F

10 Carocim/Petit Carré M201
Colour **red and yellow** Alt.
colours **yes** Composition
cement/marble (encaustic)
Size **20 x 20cm/8 x 8in**
Price ★ W F ⊞

10

11

**11 Kenneth Clark Ceramics/
Fircone** Colour **various
(4 tiles)** Alt. colours **yes**
Composition **ceramic**
Size **10 x 10cm/4 x 4in**
Price ★ W

**12 Kenneth Clark Ceramics/
Stripes/Verdant Stripes
(4 tiles)** Colour **multi** Alt.
colours **yes** Composition
ceramic Size **15 x 15cm/
6 x 6in** Price ★★ W ⊞

**13 Carocim/Game/Corner
F202 (2 tiles)** Colour **U8** Alt.
colours **yes** Composition
cement/marble (encaustic)
Size **20 x 20cm/8 x 8in**
Price ★ W F

**14 Carocim/Game/Frieze
F202 (3 tiles)** Colour **U8**
Alt. colours **yes** Alt. colours
yes Composition **cement/
marble (encaustic)** Size **20 x
20cm/8 x 8in** Price ★ W F

12

13

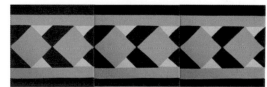

14

Geometrics: **20th–early 21st century**

Perhaps as a reaction to the excesses of Victorian design, early 20th-century tiles were often plain or simply moulded with a geometric effect that resembled bricks in a wall. During the 1920s and 1930s, bold geometric shapes in tilework were often applied to Art Deco buildings. This style was hugely popular in America, and was also used to decorate a number of buildings in England – for example, the Hoover Building in Perivale designed by the architects Wallis, Gilbert & Partners, which opened in 1933. Not only did tiles form dramatic designs on the exteriors of such buildings, they were used inside as well.

On a smaller scale, some geometric tube-lined tiles were produced for domestic use around fireplaces – by the English firm of Maw & Co, for example. Geometric designs became even more desirable during the 1950s and 1960s with the advent of Pop Art, with its designs of squares, circles and triangles that were often overlaid and printed in bright colours. The recently developed technique of screen-printing on tiles lent itself particularly well to this style of decoration. In the late 20th and early 21st century, geometric tiles have often featured a single design element, such as a diagonal line or a quadrant, which can be combined in different ways to create a wide range of patterns.

1

2

3

4

5

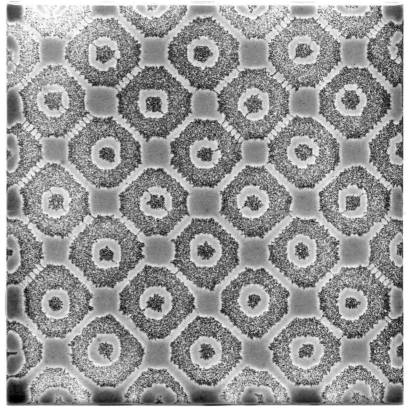

6

1 **Carocim/Horta** Colour **purple and white** Alt. colours **yes** Composition **cement/ marble (encaustic)** Size **20 x 20cm/8 x 8in** Price ★ Ⓦ Ⓕ ⊞

2 **Kenneth Clark Ceramics/ Squares/Mellow Squares** Colour **peach and white** Alt. colours **yes** Composition **ceramic** Size **10 x 10cm/ 4 x 4in** Price ★★ Ⓦ ⊞

3 **Carocim/Souleiado/Madras Frieze S514 (2 tiles)** Colour **U15/U3/U9** Alt. colours **yes** Composition **cement/marble (encaustic)** Size **20 x 20cm/ 8 x 8in** Price ★ Ⓦ Ⓕ

4 **Mosquito/Dichroic Sparkle Tile** Colour **turquoise** Alt. colours **yes** Composition **ceramic/glass** Size **20 x 20cm/8 x 8in** Price ★★★★★ Ⓦ ⊞

5 **Carocim/Casson M221** Colour **multi** Alt. colours **yes** Composition **cement/ marble (encaustic)** Size **20 x 20cm/8 x 8in** Price ★ Ⓦ Ⓕ ⊞

6 **Kenneth Clark Ceramics/ Peppercorn Sands** Colour **multi** Alt. colours **yes** Composition **ceramic** Size **15 x 15cm/6 x 6in** Price ★★ Ⓦ

7 **Winchester Tile Co/Little Snap Pattern** Colour **blue and white** Alt. colours **no** Composition **ceramic** Size **15 x 10.5cm/6 x 4in** Price ★ Ⓦ

8

**8 H. & R. Johnson/Alpine
White/Metallica Inset
MET 1D** Colour **platinum**
Alt. colours **no** Composition
ceramic body, chrome coating
Size **20 x 20cm/8 x 8in**
Price ★ W

9

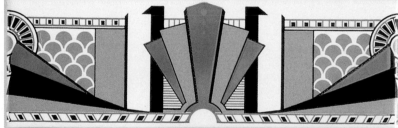

10

**9 Candy/Jazz Bebop/Satin
Gloss/CAN33177** Colour **blue**
Alt. colours **no** Composition
ceramic Size **20 x 7.5cm/
8 x 2¾ in** Price ★ W

**10 Original Style/Manhattan
Border 6490** Colour
multi Alt. colours **no**
Composition **ceramic**
Size **15 x 5cm/6 x 2in**
Price ★ W

**11 Fired Earth/Glass Art/Optics/
Decor 5** Colour **multi** Alt.
colours **no** Composition
glass Size **14.5 x 14.5cm/5¾
x 5¾in** Price ★★★★ W

11

12

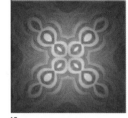

13   14

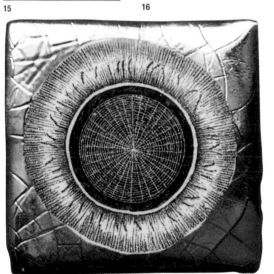

15   16

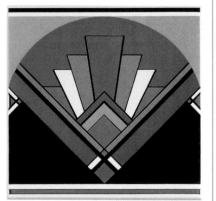

17

**12 Candy/Reflections Geo
CAN32552** Colour **black** Alt.
colours **no** Composition
ceramic Size **20 x 7.5cm/8 x
2¾in** Price ★ W

**13 The Digitile Showroom/
Dominic Crinson/Glitz/
Glaterre 5** Colour **blue** Alt.
colours **yes** Composition
ceramic Size **15 x 15cm/
6 x 6in** Price ★★ W ⊞

**14 Original Style/Satin Glazed
Decorative/Odeon Border/
Double Diamond** Colour
salmon Alt. colours **yes**
Composition **ceramic**
Size **15 x 8cm/6 x 3in**
Price ★ W

**15 Tiles of Stow/Kingham
Border** Colour **blue** Alt.
colours **yes** Composition
ceramic Size **15 x 15cm/6 x
6in** Price ★ W

**16 Tiles of Newport & London/
Check** Colour **yellow**
Alt. colours **yes**
Composition **ceramic**
Size **20 x 20cm/8 x 8in**
Price ★ W

**17 Fired Earth/Shadows/
Spirits 5** Colour **grey/silver**
Alt. colours **no** Composition
ceramic Size **6.5 x 6.5cm/2½
x 2½in** Price ★★★ W

ART DECO DESIGNS

The Art Deco movement was
particularly influential in Germany,
Austria and America, where it was
a major source of inspiration in the
architecture of the day. Tiles were
designed with bold geometric
patterns, often based on objects
including fans, bows and flowers.
The origin of the pattern is not
always apparent at first glance,
especially if the tiles are viewed
en masse. The tile shown here is
based on a fan but, when placed
with other tiles, a zig-zag effect is
the result.

Original Style/Salmon 6481 Colour **multi** Alt. colours
no Composition **ceramic** Size **15 x 15cm/6 x 6in**
Price ★★ W

Flooring

Wooden Flooring

The use of wood as a flooring material predates the classical civilizations of ancient Greece and Rome. However, before the late 17th century wooden boards were usually confined to upper storeys; thereafter they were increasingly employed at ground level as well. Until the 16th century, the types of wood used were generally restricted to locally available species, but subsequently the expansion of international trade enabled housebuilders to use imported timber as well.

Fashionable alternatives to plain, solid boards have included marquetry (*see* page 369), which originated in Persia and was brought to Europe in the 14th century, and parquetry (*see* opposite), a cheaper and more practical alternative. Favoured patterns include lozenges and diamonds. Stencilled patterns have also been much in evidence, especially during the 18th and 19th centuries. In the 20th century and early 21st, hardwood and softwood laminates have provided more affordable alternatives to solid wooden flooring, although reclaimed solid floors are now much sought after.

LEFT The hall of Richard Jenrette's house in New York State, USA, is dominated by a sweeping staircase and an inlaid wooden floor. Copied from a floor in the Tsar's Palace in St Petersburg, Russia, the design has big octagonal motifs and an Islamic-inspired geometric border. The furniture and colour scheme complete the early 19th-century look.

ABOVE The wide, uneven oak floorboards in this American kitchen typify the rustic simplicity of the Colonial look. Usually, boards of varying widths were laid, with the widest in the middle and the narrowest at the edges. Simple and practical, these boards were neatly tacked down with headless nails.

PARQUET FLOORS

Parquetry originated in France in the 17th century, and was first applied to small areas such as half-landings and stair treads. It involves the use of hardwood blocks arranged in geometric patterns, echoing the three-dimensional and *trompe l'oeil* effects of inlaid and paved stone. The parquet floor in this 18th-century French interior consists of a basic geometric pattern, although lozenge arrangements were very popular in France at this time. Other patterns include stars, diamonds and latticework.

KEY DESIGNS

1 These butt-jointed boards are made with reclaimed Bordeaux oak. Reclaimed wood has become increasingly popular as much for its period authenticity as for environmental reasons.

2 Basic geometric parquetry patterns have been popular since the early 17th century. This configuration, in walnut, has been one of the most popular parquet patterns since the early 20th century.

3 Marquetry patterns inlaid into wooden floors can consist of many different types of wood in addition to other materials, such as ivory and pewter, offering the decorator a choice of designs.

4 By the early 20th century, floorboards of the same width were usually laid in each room. A more recent alternative consists of a thin top layer of laminated hardwood glued to a plank of softwood.

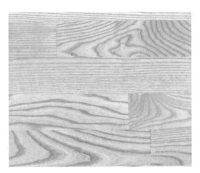

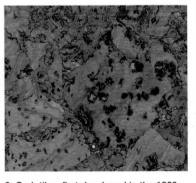

5 The chevron, or herringbone, pattern is a popular parquet design. In Europe Rhodesian teak was used extensively for this at the end of the 19th century and beginning of the 20th.

6 Cork tiles, first developed in the 1920s, are made from the bark of the cork oak. The bark is stripped every nine years, granulated, then made into blocks from which the tiles are cut.

1 LASSCO/Bordeaux Oak (Patinated) OB020 Colour **natural** Alt. colours **no** Composition **oak** Width **15cm/6in** Repeat – Price ★★★★ ⊞

2 Historic Floors of Oshkosh/Marie Antoinette 151 Colour **natural** Alt. colours **yes** Composition **walnut** Width **76cm/30in** Repeat – Price **on application** ⊞

3 Historic Floors of Oshkosh/Border 149 Colour **natural** Alt. colours **yes** Composition **red oak, maple, walnut and Brazilian cherry** Width **11.5cm/4½in** Repeat – Price **on application**

4 Boen Parkett/Ash Sheet Colour **natural** Alt. colours **yes** Composition **ash** Width **14cm/5½in** Repeat – Price ★★

5 LASSCO/Herringbone Colour **natural** Alt. colours **yes** Composition **antique Rhodesian teak** Width **to order** Repeat – Price ★★★ ⊞

6 Siesta Cork Tiles/Harlequin Colour **green** Alt. colours **yes** Composition **cork** Width **30 x 30cm/11¾ x 11¾in (tile)** Repeat – Price ★

Wooden Flooring: **Pre-19th century**

The choice of wood as a flooring material stemmed as much from its availability as its intrinsic beauty. Initially, wide boards were used, although they were often covered by matting or loose rushes. It was not until the 17th century that ornate designs in wood became common in Europe. Parquet flooring (*see* page 363) was popular in grander houses in the mid-17th century, particularly in France. This brought about the use of more unusual woods, and resulted in an increase in the importation of exotic woods – such as mahogany from the West Indies – into Europe. In the early 18th century, floorboards were sometimes decorated by painting or stencilling, a practice thought to have originated in Scandinavia. More elaborate designs often imitated the patterns and *trompe l'oeil* effects of marble, stone paving or garden parterres.

During the 17th and 18th centuries in America, floors were considered to be strictly functional, and floorboards were invariably left bare. Pine was laid in broad planks, and was scrubbed, not waxed or polished. Occasionally, the boards were painted or stencilled with floral patterns, animals or folk-art motifs. At this time in both Europe and America, fine parquet floors were still considered to be the preserve of the wealthy.

4

4 **Sinclair Till/Greek Key Border** Colour **natural** Alt. colours **yes** Composition **walnut and maple** Width **28.5cm/11in** Repeat – Price ★★

5 **Historic Floors of Oshkosh/ Medallion 306** Colour **natural** Alt. colours **yes** Composition **American cherry, walnut, red oak and mahogany** Width **to order** Repeat – Price **on application**

6 **Berti Pavimenti Legno/Bonfadini Border** Colour **natural** Alt. colours **yes** Composition **jatoba and maple** Width **to order** Repeat – Price ★★★★★

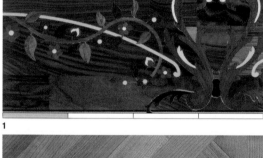
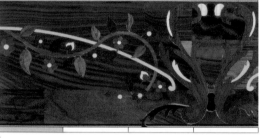
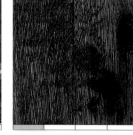

1

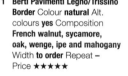

2

1 **Berti Pavimenti Legno/Trissino Border** Colour **natural** Alt. colours **yes** Composition **French walnut, sycamore, oak, wenge, ipe and mahogany** Width **to order** Repeat – Price ★★★★★

2 **Fired Earth/Planche Antique de Quercy** Colour **natural** Alt. colours **no** Composition **oak** Width **14cm/5½in** Repeat – Price ★★★ ⊞

3 **Historic Floors of Oshkosh/ Marseille 145** Colour **natural** Alt. colours **yes** Composition **American cherry** Width **to order** Repeat – Price **on application**

5

3

6

7

9

8

7 **Historic Floors of Oshkosh/Rose Border 130** Colour **natural** Alt. colours **yes** Composition **bubinga, mahogany, walnut, green poplar and maple** Width **to order** Repeat **10.5cm/4in** Price **on application**

8 **Historic Floors of Oshkosh/ Château 152** Colour **natural** Alt. colours **yes** Composition **ipe** Width **to order** Repeat – Price **on application**

9 **Berti Pavimenti Legno/ Giustinian Border** Colour **natural** Alt. colours **yes** Composition **walnut, ipe, maple and oak** Width **to order** Repeat – Price ★★★★★

10 **Berti Pavimenti Legno/ Todeschini Border** Colour **natural** Alt. colours **yes** Composition **doussie, walnut, gatambu and wenge** Width **to order** Repeat – Price ★★★★★

11 **Historic Floors of Oshkosh/ Louve 154** Colour **natural** Alt. colours **yes** Composition **white oak** Width **to order** Repeat – Price **on application**

12 **LASSCO/Baltic Pine PN101** Colour **natural** Alt. colours **no** Composition **pine** Width **20cm/8in** Repeat – Price ★★ ⊞

13 **Historic Floors of Oshkosh/ Fontainebleau** Colour **natural** Alt. colours **yes** Composition **red oak and white oak** Width **to order** Repeat – Price **on application**

10

11

12

MAHOGANY

Since the 16th century, mahogany has been recognized as one of the world's finest timbers for flooring and cabinet-making. Less subject to shrinking, swelling or warping than many other hardwoods, it ranges in colour from a light tan to a dark reddish-brown and displays aesthetically pleasing grain and figuring. The latter varies – curly, wavy, speckled or "ostrich-plume", depending on how it is cut. In the 17th and 18th centuries it was mostly imported from the West Indies and Cuba.

Pergo/PO 26001 Colour **Mahogany Blocked** Alt. colours **no** Composition **mahogany** Width **19.5cm/7¾in** Repeat – Price ★★

13

17th century

18th century

Wooden Flooring: **19th century**

During the 19th century in Europe and America, narrower floorboards came into use, especially in wealthier homes. Such floorboards were often only 10cm (4in) in width – in contrast to the 23cm- (9in-) wide floorboards used in poorer homes. In the 1820s, tongued-and-grooved wooden boards were introduced. As the century progressed, these were increasingly prepared by machine and, as a result, became more even in width.

In America, the practice of painting wooden floors developed into a popular craft, although plain-coloured versions were as liked as stencilled ones. In Europe, the tradition of floor painting continued, as did the trend for staining wood with different oils. However, now that carpets had become more common, floors were generally painted or glazed in a single colour, and the designs for parquet floors became simpler. At the same time, it was discovered that thin boards could be glued, nailed or screwed down on to a solid backing to produce a good imitation of a floor composed of solid wood blocks. This was the forerunner of the modern parquet floor. By the end of the 19th century, American manufacturers were offering intricate, ready-made examples consisting of oak blocks glued to cloth or softwood in a closely woven pattern.

Historic Floors of Oshkosh/110 and 106 Colour **natural** Alt. colours **yes** Composition **plainsawn white oak and walnut** Width **30.5 x 30.5cm/12 x 12in (panel)** Repeat – Price **on application**

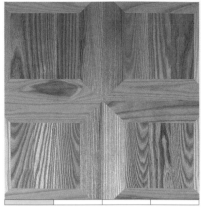

Historic Floors of Oshkosh/Monticello 155 Colour **natural** Alt. colours **yes** Composition **ash** Size **25.5 x 25.5cm/10 x 10in (panel)** Repeat – Price **on application**

Boen Parkett/Ship's Deck Colour **natural** Alt. colours **yes** Composition **merbau** Width **14cm/5½in** Repeat – Price ★★★

LASSCO/Norse Oak NS009 Colour **dark oil stain** Alt. colours **yes** Composition **oak** Width **2m/2¼yd** Repeat – Price ★★

Kentucky Wood Floors/Trinity Colour **natural** Alt. colours **yes** Composition **oak** Width **to order** Repeat – Price ★★★★★ (special order)

Historic Floors of Oshkosh/Border 137 Colour **natural** Alt. colours **yes** Composition **Santos mahogany, maple and red oak** Width **to order** Repeat – Price **on application**

Historic Floors of Oshkosh/Border 135 Colour **natural** Alt. colours **yes** Composition **ash, mahogany, bubinga and walnut** Width **to order** Repeat – Price **on application**

Historic Floors of Oshkosh/Wave Border 168 Colour **natural** Alt. colours **yes** Composition **red oak, maple and American cherry** Width **11.5cm/4½in** Repeat – Price **on application**

LASSCO/Re-Milled Bordeaux Oak Colour **natural** Alt. colours **no** Composition **oak** Width **to order** Repeat – Price ★★★★ ⊞

The Hardwood & Natural Stone Flooring Company/Antiqued English Oak Colour **antiqued** Alt. colours **yes** Composition **oak** Width **17cm/6¾in** Repeat – Price ★★★

LASSCO/Burmese Teak Parquet Colour **natural** Alt. colours **yes** Composition **teak** Width **23cm/9in** Repeat – Price ★★★ ⊞

Kentucky Wood Floors/Florentine Colour **natural** Alt. colours **yes** Composition **Brazilian cherry, walnut, bird's-eye maple and brass** Width **to order** Repeat – Price ★★★★★

FLOORING: *WOODEN FLOORING*   **367**

Wooden Flooring: 20th–early 21st century

Although parquet borders were popular in the early 20th century as an accompaniment to loose-laid carpet, it was not until the 1930s that complete parquet floors enjoyed a resurgence in Europe; this was to last until the 1950s. The designs were extremely basic, with the polished hardwood blocks or strips being laid in clear, simple patterns.

By the 1970s, a revival of appreciation for the qualities of wood sparked a fashion for revealing and restoring old wooden floorboards, as well as laying new ones. This led to the development of new types of wooden flooring systems that catered to a growing international market. By the 1990s, the different options included prefinished floors of oiled wood planks and floors with a wooden laminate surface laid over a high-density fibreboard or chipboard base. Wood-laminate flooring is easy to lay, as it is glued at the tongue-and-groove and does not need to be secured to the sub-floor. In addition, tongued-and-grooved parquets are available in many different woods of various colours, grades and thicknesses. Marquetry designs have remained popular, and replicas of old parquet floors – made by gluing thin panels of oak, beech or birch to a solid backing – have also become widely available.

7

1

2

3

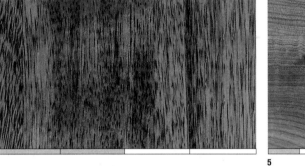

4

5

6

8

9

10

1 **Boen Parkett/Natural Dark Beech** Colour **dark** Alt. colours **yes** Composition **beech** Width **14cm/5½in** Repeat – Price ★★

2 **Westco/C480012** Colour **natural** Alt. colours **no** Composition **Rhodesian teak** Size **47.5 x 47.5cm/18¾ x 18¾in (panel)** Repeat – Price ★

3 **Natural Wood Floor Co/African Walnut Planks** Colour **natural** Alt. colours **yes** Composition **African walnut** Width **9cm/3½in** Repeat – Price ★ ⊞

4 **Junckers/Merbau Plank 065300-189** Colour **natural** Alt. colours **yes** Composition **merbau** Width **13cm/5in** Repeat – Price ★★★

5 **LBC/Solid Elm Planks** Colour **natural** Alt. colours **yes** Composition **elm** Width **to order** Repeat – Price ★★

6 **Historic Floors of Oshkosh/ Oxford 150** Colour **natural** Alt. colours **yes** Composition **Santos mahogany, ipe, maple and American cherry,** Width **to order** Repeat – Price **on application**

7 **Historic Floors of Oshkosh/ Nautical Compass 319** Colour **natural** Alt. colours **yes** Composition **wenge, jatoba, purple heart, maple and brass** Width **to order** Repeat – Price **on application**

8 **LBC/Pitch Pine Planks** Colour **natural** Alt. colours **no** Composition **pine** Width **10cm/4in** Repeat – Price ★★ ⊞

9 **Kahrs/Alder Monte Carlo** Colour **natural** Alt. colours **no** Composition **alder** Width **20cm/8in** Repeat – Price ★★

10 **Kahrs/Rotterdam Diagonal Pattern 3215 OB 50** Colour **natural** Alt. colours **yes** Composition **birch and oak** Width **15cm/6in** Repeat – Price ★

11 Bruce Hardwood/Dakota Plank E-153 Colour **harvest** Alt. colours **yes** Composition **oak** Width **7.5cm/2¾in** Repeat – Price ★★

12 Bruce Hardwood/Dakota Plank E150 Colour **toast** Alt. colours **yes** Composition **oak** Width **7.5cm/2¾in** Repeat – Price ★★

13 Wicanders/LS06 & LS13 Colour **ruby and coal** Alt. colours **yes** Composition **cork** Width **30.5 x 30.5cm/12 x 12in (tile)** Repeat – Price ★

14 Pergo/PC 14592 Colour **green maple** Alt. colours **no** Composition **maple** Width **20cm/8in** Repeat – Price ★

11

12

MARQUETRY

The skilled art of inlaying wood with pieces of wood or other materials, such as ivory and metal, to form mosaics, arabesques or pictures is the basis of marquetry. First seen in Italy in the 14th century, marquetry was mainly used to decorate furniture. By the early 17th century, it was widespread in France and the fashion rapidly spread to the rest of Europe. Today, many marquetry firms use a laser beam to cut the veneer, thus ensuring a precision previously attained only through the very time-consuming hand-cutting of wooden shapes.

Historic Floors of Oshkosh/Medallion 340 Colour **natural** Alt. colours **yes** Composition **maple and ipe** Width **to order** Repeat – Price **on application**

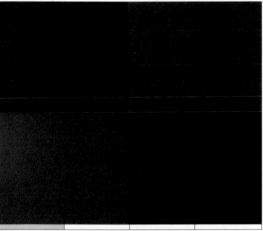

13

14

15

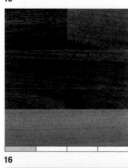

16

17

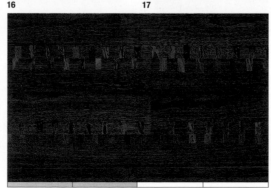

18

19

15 Junckers/Sylvaket Plank Colour **natural** Alt. colours **yes** Composition **sylvaket** Width **13cm/5in** Repeat – Price ★★

16 Wicanders/Walnut 3 Strip PT57 Colour **natural** Alt. colours **yes** Composition **walnut** Width **13cm/5in** Repeat – Price ★★

17 Boen Parkett/Oak Dutch Pattern Colour **natural** Alt. colours **yes** Composition **oak** Width **14cm/5½in** Repeat – Price ★★

18 Pergo/PO 25401 Colour **Bali walnut** Alt. colours **no** Composition **walnut** Width **19.5cm/7¾in** Repeat – Price ★★

19 Seri Parquet/Bamboo Light Colour **natural** Alt. colours **yes** Composition **bamboo** Width **17.5cm/7in** Repeat **2.2m/2⅜yd** Price ★★

Matting

ABOVE This medieval-style room features an elegant coir-matting floor covering. Coir is harvested in two main seasons: the freshwater season, when the fibre lying in the lagoons is washed daily, and the saltwater season. The fibre is then beaten from the coconut husks before being spun and woven into patterns such as this herringbone design.

GRASSES

The different grasses used in matting depend on where it is produced. Sisal is the fibre produced from the leaf of the Mexican agave plant, coir is harvested from the husks of coconuts, while jute is derived from the stalk of a herb of an Indian *Tiliaceae* family. With the expansion of maritime trade, these fibres gradually replaced the rush (shown here) as the traditional component of matting in Europe. All can be woven into a variety of patterns and are particularly suitable for early period homes.

Matting evolved from the spreading of rushes, straw and herbs over floors for both insulation and comfort. By the 17th century in Europe, braided rush strips sewn together to cover the whole floor were common in wealthier houses, although the matting was often covered by oriental carpets. As trade with North Africa opened up in the 17th century, more lightweight mattings – made from narrow strips of braided bullrushes – became popular. These finely woven and delicately patterned floor coverings were known as Africa, Barbary or Portugal mats and largely superseded the traditional European rush matting, which was heavy and needed replacing every few years. The introduction of mass-produced carpets led to a decline in the use of matting, although it was still laid in informal areas of houses. In America, matting was popular in the early 19th century, as importers brought in mats from India and Africa.

Contemporary production techniques mean matting can be machine-woven and given a latex backing. This has increased its durability and made it reasonably stain-proof.

RIGHT Forms of rush matting have been woven for centuries. The ancient Egyptians used bullrushes from the Nile to weave floor-coverings. Today, methods have changed little and rush matting is equally suited to contemporary interiors.

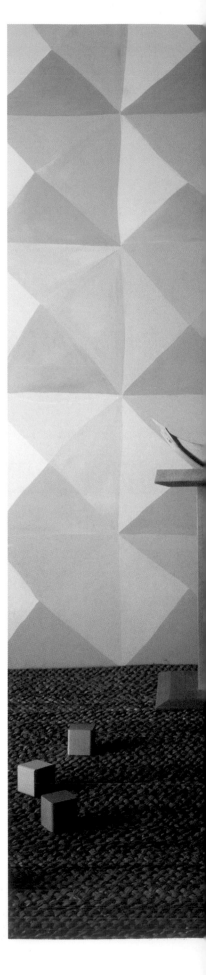

KEY DESIGNS

1 Jute has been used as a floor covering since the 18th century. Once harvested, it is tied together, soaked in water and then pounded with wooden mallets. This provides a very soft matting.

2 Wool is often mixed in varying proportions with durable but coarser sisal to give the matting a softer texture underfoot. The 80/20 per cent ratio of wool to sisal in this example is typical.

3 As well as having a wide variety of weaves, sisal is available in numerous colourways. Blues, reds and greens have proved very fashionable in the late 20th and early 21st century.

4 Throughout the years, matting has been decorated with different patterns – such as this medieval design – using either paints or dyes, and it can be printed, stencilled or hand-painted.

5 Modern weaving techniques make it easier for different materials and colours to be combined. The mixture of coir and sisal shown here displays an appealing abstract-motif repeat.

6 Coir matting, produced from coconut fibre that is spun and then woven, varies in colour depending on the time at which it is harvested. It became very popular in the late 20th century.

---

1 Carpet Innovations/Panama Jute Colour **natural** Alt. colours **yes** Composition **100% jute** Width **3.9m/4½yd** Repeat **–** Price ★

2 Fired Earth/Hungerford/Ribbed Colour **natural** Alt. colours **yes** Composition **80% wool, 20% sisal** Width **4m/4½yd** Repeat **–** Price ★★

3 Crucial Trading/Accents/Fine Bouclé C712 Colour **blue** Alt. colours **yes** Composition **100% sisal** Width **4m/4½yd** Repeat **–** Price ★★

4 Sinclair Till/Wrought Iron Colour **black** Alt. colours **yes** Composition **100% sisal** Width **to order** Repeat **–** Price ★★★

5 Ruckstuhl/Pur/Dots Colour **727** Alt. colours **yes** Composition **48% coir, 52% sisal** Width **2m/2⅛yd** Repeat **–** Price ★★

6 Reeve Flooring/Herringbone Colour **natural** Alt. colours **yes** Composition **100% coir** Width **4m/4½yd** Repeat **–** Price ★

Matting

Thick rush matting (*see* opposite), which was common in Europe in the 16th century, was largely replaced during the 17th century by imported North African matting. During the 1970s and 1980s plant-fibre matting, especially varieties made from sisal and coir, and mostly in natural colours (*see* pages 370–371), became hugely fashionable. Indian matting was tremendously popular in the late 18th and early 19th centuries. Made of reeds or grass, it was often woven into yard-wide strips and then bound with linen twill. In the latter part of the 19th century, mats from China and Japan were widespread. They were made from grass but had a jute warp, and they invariably featured tight chevron patterns in bright colours with the ends bound with oil cloth.

In the early part of the 20th century, popular colours for matting included natural, white, olive, and red-and-white checks. More recently, there has been a renewed interest in plant-fibre matting, including varieties made from sisal and coir.

1 **Crucial Trading/Coir/Herringbone Contrast HBC** Colour **natural** Alt. colours **yes** Composition **100% coir** Width **4m/4½yd** Repeat – Price ★

2 **Crucial Trading/Accents/Big Bouclé E680** Colour **black** Alt. colours **yes** Composition **100% sisal** Width **4m/4½yd** Repeat – Price ★★

3 **Ruckstuhl/Pur/Step** Colour **726** Alt. colours **yes** Composition **100% sisal** Width **2m/2⅛yd** Repeat – Price ★★★

4 **Crucial Trading/Papa/Papaflat PFN** Colour **natural** Alt. colours **yes** Composition **100% paper** Width **3.6m/4yd** Repeat – Price ★★

5 **Ruckstuhl/Fondato/Jaipur** Colour **50038** Alt. colours **yes** Composition **100% sisal** Width **2m/2⅛yd** Repeat – Price ★★★

6 **Ruckstuhl/Webside/Upside** Colour **20303** Alt. colours **no** Composition **100% sisal** Width **4m/4½yd** Repeat – Price ★★

1

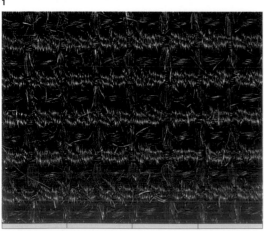

2

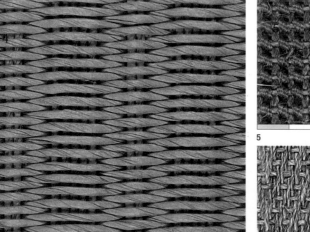

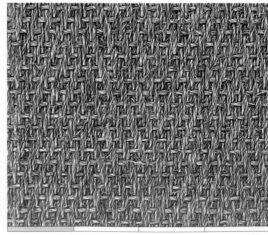

4

5

6

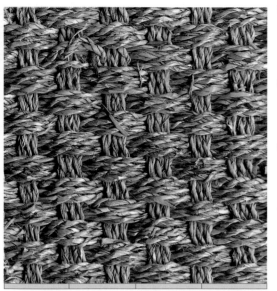

7 **The Alternative Flooring Co/Buckingham Basketweave AFC 102** Colour **natural** Alt. colours **no** Composition **100% seagrass** Width **4m/4½yd** Repeat – Price ★★

8 **Carpet Innovations/Tecwoven** Colour **603** Alt. colours **yes** Composition **90% polyester, 10% wool** Width **4m/4½yd** Repeat – Price ★

9 **Sinclair Till/Giraffe** Colour **giraffe** Alt. colours **yes** Composition **100% sisal** Width **to order** Repeat – Price ★★★

10 **Carpet Innovations/Recife** Colour **chestnut** Alt. colours **yes** Composition **100% sisal** Width **4m/4½yd** Repeat – Price ★★

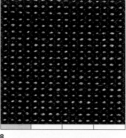

8

9

10

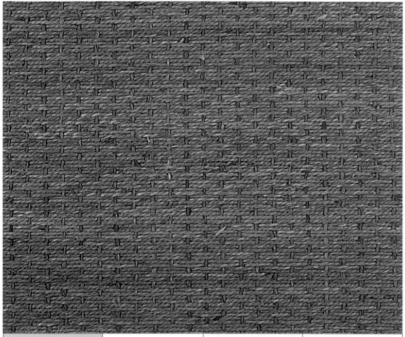

11

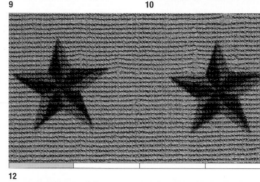

12

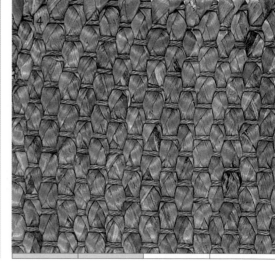

13

11 **Fired Earth/Rousham Seagrass** Colour **natural** Alt. colours **no** Composition **100% seagrass** Width **4m/4½yd** Repeat – Price ★

12 **Sinclair Till/Stars** Colour **black and blue** Alt. colours **yes** Composition **100% sisal** Width **to order** Repeat – Price ★★★

13 **The Alternative Flooring Co/Sisal Panama AFC 503** Colour **Donegal** Alt. colours **yes** Composition **100% sisal** Width **4m/4½yd** Repeat – Price ★★

14 **Stark/Water Hyacinth/Andiamo** Colour **natural** Alt. colours **yes** Composition **100% water hyacinth** Width **to order** Repeat – Price ★★★★★

TRADITIONAL RUSH MATTING

Used since Medieval times, rush matting is still manufactured in the traditional way. The rushes are soaked in cold water to make them pliable, squeezed dry, then plaited into strips, each consisting of 9 strands. (This is known as a 9-ply weave.) These strips are then sewn together with string using a sailmaker's curved needle. The use of string is the only deviation from traditional methods. Edged with a finer, 11-ply strip, the matting must be sprinkled with water every 6–8 weeks in order to keep it supple.

Waveney Rush Industry/Rush Medieval Matting Colour **natural** Alt. colours **no** Composition **100% rush** Width **to order** Repeat – Price ★★★★

14

Matting

Since the 1990s, matting has become an increasingly fashionable alternative to fitted carpets, although it is often augmented with loose-lay kilims and rugs. Pure sisal and coir weaves have remained popular choices, but other materials have also figured prominently. Notable examples include seagrass, and hard, durable bamboo-strip matting – the latter, reasonably resilient to water and moisture, has been much employed in shower rooms and bathrooms. Compositional matting, in which different fibres and materials are combined, has also become more prevalent. These include paper and viscose; paper, wool and goathair; and wool and sisal – the two latter combinations providing a softer texture underfoot particularly suited to bedrooms.

Plain, solid colours, most notably natural hues and shades of red, blue and green, have remained in vogue, although there has been a discernible increase in patterned examples. Invariably geometric designs, they are mostly two-tone, but occasionally polychromatic.

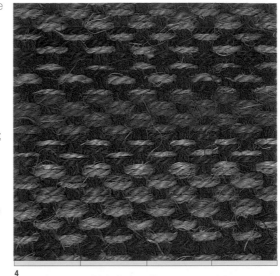

4

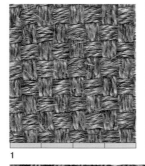
1

2

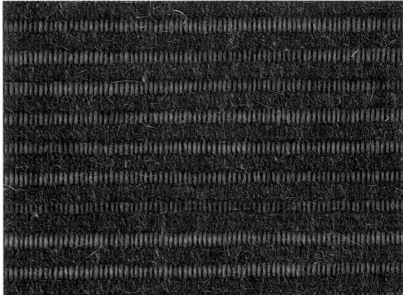
5

3

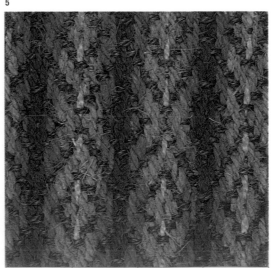
6

1 **Crucial Trading/Basket/ Basket T300** Colour **gold** Alt. colours **yes** Composition **100% sisal** Width **4m/4½yd** Repeat – Price ★★

2 **Crucial Trading/Bamboo/ Bamboo for Rugs BBN** Colour **natural** Alt. colours **yes** Composition **100% bamboo** Width **2m/2½yd** Repeat – Price ★★

3 **Ruckstuhl/Webside/Check** Colour **395** Alt. colours **yes** Composition **66% sisal, 34% linen** Width **4m/4½yd** Repeat – Price ★★

4 **Carpet Innovations/Multicolor Coir** Colour **M7 candy stripe** Alt. colours **no** Composition **100% coir** Width **2m/2½yd** Repeat – Price ★★

5 **Ruckstuhl/Spirit/Capra** Colour **283** Alt. colours **yes** Composition **30% wool, 30% goathair, 40% paper** Width **2m/2½yd** Repeat – Price ★★★★

6 **Carpet Innovations/Diamond Coco** Colour **712** Alt. colours **no** Composition **100% coir** Width **2m/2½yd** Repeat – Price ★★

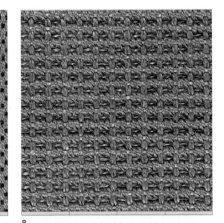

7

8

Pre-17th century

17th century

18th century

19th century

20th & 21st century

7 Ruckstuhl/Webside/Fresco
Colour **361** Alt. colours **yes**
Composition **100% sisal**
Width **4m/4½yd** Repeat –
Price ★★

8 Carpet Innovations/Santorini
Colour **3045** Alt. colours **yes**
Composition **100% sisal**
Width **4m/4½yd** Repeat –
Price ★

9 Ruckstuhl/Webside/One One
Colour **251** Alt. colours **yes**
Composition **100% sisal**
Width **4m/4½yd** Repeat –
Price ★★

10 Ruckstuhl/Fondato/Jaipur
Colour **10098** Alt. colours
yes Composition **100% sisal**
Width **2m/2½yd** Repeat –
Price ★★★

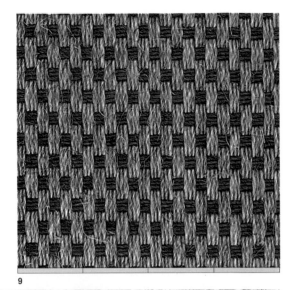

9

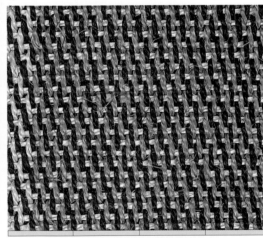

10

11

12

11 Ruckstuhl/Fondato/Manila
Colour **20155** Alt. colours
yes Composition **100% sisal**
Width **2m/2½yd** Repeat –
Price ★★★

12 Carpet Innovations/Tree Bark
Colour **maize** Alt. colours
no Composition **100%
seagrass** Width **4m/4½yd**
Repeat – Price ★

13 Ruckstuhl/Pur/Scotch
Colour **234** Alt. colours
yes Composition **100%
sisal** Width **1.68m/1¾yd**
Repeat – Price ★★★

14 Ruckstuhl/Spirit/Shine
Colour **271** Alt. colours **no**
Composition **70% paper,
30% viscose** Width **2m/2½yd**
Repeat – Price ★★★

15 Fired Earth/Woodstock Colour
Blenheim Alt. colours **no**
Composition **100% sisal**
Width **4m/4½yd** Repeat –
Price ★★

13

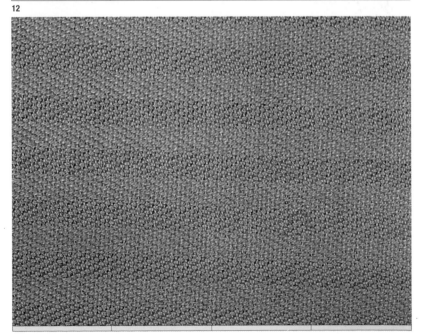

14

15

Carpets

ABOVE This carpet in Richard Jenrette's house in New York State, USA, combines strong, symmetrical lines with simple motifs, a combination that epitomizes the American Empire style in carpets. This mirrors the French Empire and English Regency styles, but lacks the opulence and elaboration that characterizes European carpets of the period.

Carpets are highly decorative textiles manufactured on a horizontal or vertical loom. A knotting technique is used to create an artificial pile that hides the supporting grid of horizontal and vertical strands. The yarns and fibres used range from wool, silk and cotton to modern synthetics, such as nylon and viscose.

The earliest known knotted carpet, the Altai carpet, was found preserved in the ice of Siberia and dates from approximately 500BC. From the 11th century, carpets were used in Europe to cover walls, chairs and tables, but it was only in the late 17th century that they began to be used regularly as a floor covering. During the 16th century, European imitations of oriental carpets, such as "turkeywork" (*see* page 378), emerged, but it was the development of European and American looms in the 19th century that made carpets widely available. By the mid-20th century, fitted wall-to-wall carpets were widespread.

Designs and decorative motifs have varied throughout the centuries, although abstract or stylized geometric designs have remained consistently popular.

WILTON CARPET

Developed from Brussels carpet, Wilton has a velvety surface formed by the cutting of the looped pile. It was first produced in the mid-18th century in Wilton, England, but the method soon spread to Europe and America. Wilton carpets were woven in 69cm/27in strips with repeating patterns so the pieces could be laid wall-to-wall. The introduction of the Jacquard loom in 1805 meant that Wilton soon became cheaper than hand-knotted carpets and as a result much more widespread.

RIGHT The principal staircase in Sir John Soane's London, UK, house is covered by a sumptuous, deep red-and-gold stair runner. The scrolling leaf border in gold and the red moiré-effect pile reflect the influence of the French Neo-classical movement.

1 Small, symmetrical motif patterns are typical of North African carpets and have often been adopted in European carpets. Many of the motifs were originally ancient tribal and religious emblems.

2 Stylized and naturalistic floral designs originated in Persia and India in the 16th century and have always been popular. Here, small floral vignettes are interspersed among strips of geometric motifs.

3 Geometric diaper patterns are a recurring design on carpets. The patterns include trelliswork, latticework and strapwork, and often enclose floral motifs or plant-form imagery.

4 When introduced in the 1860s, chemical dyes produced only strong, often virulent solid colours, but nowadays they can create softer tones previously given only by traditional vegetable dyes.

5 The pile in this monochromatic tufted carpet consists of long strands of wool stitched into a prewoven backing. Deep-pile carpets have proved particularly popular in the 20th century.

6 The mottled colouring of this carpet is typical of the late 20th and early 21st century. In this example synthetic (nylon) fibres have been woven to create a texture similar to that of woollen fibres.

---

1 Stoddard/Cathiness/Traditional Axminster 4/4556 Colour **zanzibar** Alt. colours **no** Composition **80% wool, 20% nylon** Width **91cm/35¾in** Repeat **81cm/32in** Price ★★ ⊞

2 Ulster Carpets/Glenmoy/Persian Garden Colour **10-2160** Alt. colours **no** Composition **80% wool, 20% nylon** Width **3.66m/4yd** Repeat **91.5cm/36in** Price ★★ ⊞

3 Stoddard Templeton/Midnight Embroidery Colour **4** Alt. colours **no** Composition **80% wool, 20% nylon** Width **3.66m/4yd** Repeat **76cm/30in** Price ★★

4 Ollerton Hall/Solid Extra Colour **7510** Alt. colours **yes** Composition **100% danaklon** Width **4m/4½yd** Repeat – Price ★

5 Ollerton Hall/Shag Pile Colour **pink** Alt. colours **yes** Composition **100% wool** Width **3.66m/4yd** Repeat – Price ★

6 Mannington/Aspects II Modular Colour **bellflower** Alt. colours **yes** Composition **100% DuPont nylon** Width **3.66m/4yd** Repeat – Price ★★ ◻ ⊞ Ⓣ

Carpets: **Pre-19th century**

In Europe during the Middle Ages, oriental carpets were the preserve of the wealthy. However, during the 15th and 16th centuries English workshops were producing "turkeywork", a cheap hand-knotted pile cloth used for chair upholstery and tablecloths. Some of these were later introduced into America by British settlers. Embroidered carpets were commissioned in America, featuring heraldic motifs and floral patterns.

By the middle of the 18th century, the carpet industry was thriving in Europe, the two main centres for carpet production being Britain and France. In Britain, the Earl of Pembroke gave his patronage to the Wilton factory in 1740; the carpet weavers Thomas Whitty and Thomas Moore were working in Axminster and London respectively; and there was great activity in Scotland, the north of England and Kidderminster. In France at this time, Henry IV supported Pierre Dupont in establishing a workshop in the Louvre to produce carpets in "the manner of the Orient". This later moved to the Savonnerie site. At Aubusson, the long-established tapestry weavers turned their skills to producing tapestry carpets, which were less costly than Savonneries. With their delicate floral patterning, these carpets became extremely popular during the reigns of Louis XV and Louis XVI.

5

1

2

3

6

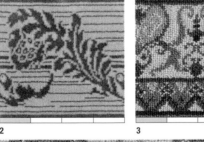

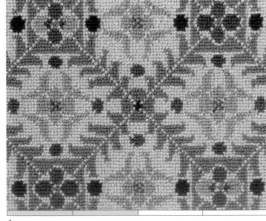

4

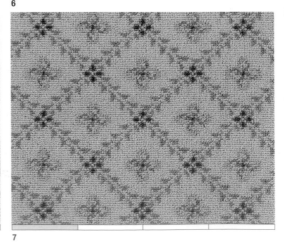

7

1 **Stark/Dartmouth** Colour **multi** Alt. colours **no** Composition **100% wool** Width **68.5cm/ 27in** Repeat **35cm/13¾in** Price ★★★★

2 **Stark/Brissac Border** Colour **white and gold** Alt. colours **yes** Composition **80% wool, 20% viscose** Width **23cm/ 9in** Repeat **22cm/8½in** Price ★★★

3 **Stark/Czardis Border** Colour **spice** Alt. colours **no** Composition **100% wool** Width **17cm/6¾in** Repeat **16cm/6¼in** Price ★★

4 **Stark/Czardis** Colour **spice** Alt. colours **no** Composition **100% wool** Width **372cm/12ft 2in** Repeat **30.5cm/12in** Price ★★★★

5 **Axminster Carpets/Turkish Splendour 380/01803** Colour **oriental gold** Alt. colours **yes** Composition **100% wool** Width **3.66m/4yd** Repeat **91cm/35¾in** Price ★★ ⊞

6 **Stark/Dover** Colour **stock** Alt. colours **yes** Composition **100% wool** Width **3.66m/ 4yd** Repeat **30.5cm/12in** Price ★★★★

7 **Hugh Mackay/Ribbon 100089- 910953** Colour **multi** Alt. colours **yes** Composition **100% wool** Width **69cm/ 27in** Repeat **11cm/4¼in** Price ★★

8 Stoddard Templeton/Cathiness
1/4558 Colour **turkey red**
Alt. colours **no** Composition
80% wool, 20% nylon Width
91cm/35¾in Repeat 41cm/16in
Price ★★ ⊞

9 Brintons/Flake 1/2455 Colour **1**
Alt. colours **yes** Composition
80% wool, 20% nylon Width
4m/4½yd Repeat 50cm/19½in
Price ★★★ ⊞

10 Hugh Mackay/Fleur de Lys
126893-910063 Colour **multi**
Alt. colours **yes** Composition
80% wool, 20% nylon Width
69cm/27in Repeat 9cm/3½in
Price ★★★ ⊞

11 Brintons/Regina International
16/19714 Colour **coronet
apricot** Alt. colours **yes**
Composition 80% wool,
20% nylon Width 3.6m/
4yd Repeat 23cm/9in
Price ★★ ⊞

12 Hugh Mackay/Balmoral 99956-
910984 Colour **multi** Alt.
colours **yes** Composition
100% wool Width 69cm/
27in Repeat 43cm/16¾in
Price ★★

13 Stark/Brissac Colour **white/
gold** Alt. colours **yes**
Composition 80% wool,
20% viscose Width 68.5cm/
27in Repeat 53cm/21in
Price ★★★★

8

CLASSICAL WREATHS

Used in ancient Rome and Greece to laud the
achievements of emperors, heroes, poets and
athletes, the wreath symbolizes eternity,
sovereignty, honour and glory. It usually consists
of a garland of leaves (usually laurel, but oak
or olive are also seen), often bound with ribbon.
Wreaths became popular in carpet designs in
the mid-18th century as the Neo-classical style
spread throughout Europe.

Brintons/Wreath 9/13710 Colour **9** Alt. colours **yes** Composition
80% wool, 20% nylon Width **4m/4½yd** Repeat **50cm/19½in**
Price ★★★ ⊞

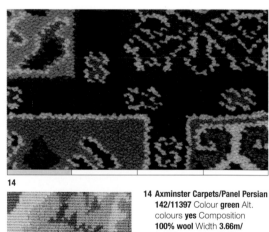

9

10

11

14

14 Axminster Carpets/Panel Persian
142/11397 Colour **green** Alt.
colours **yes** Composition
100% wool Width **3.66m/
4yd** Repeat **91cm/35¼in**
Price ★★ ⊞

15 Stark/Filigrane et Fleurs
Colour **pastel** Alt. colours
yes Composition **100%
wool** Width **101cm/39¾in**
Repeat **131cm/51¼in**
Price ★★★★★

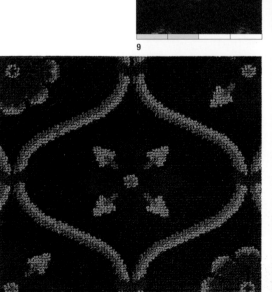

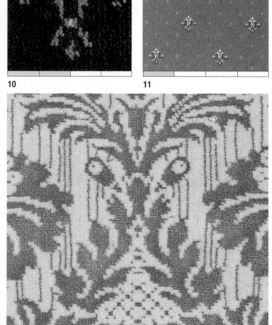

12

13

15

Carpets: **Early 19th century**

The early 19th century saw Jacquard machines largely supplanting the old hand looms, and greatly expanding carpet production. In Britain, Kidderminster remained the major manufacturing centre, with at least 1,000 carpet looms in operation. Brussels carpet, where a worsted warp is brought to the surface to form a pile, and Wilton, where the looped pile is cut to create a more velvet-like surface, were especially popular at this time, being both versatile and cheap. In America, non-pile, reversible carpets, such as "ingrain" and "Scotch", were being produced in large numbers. These were made in strips and laid to cover the whole room.

Desirable designs sought after in America and Europe at this time included those based on architectural panels, as well as paisley and Indian motifs, naturalistic floral designs and *verdure* patterns of ferns, foliage and palms. Heraldic motifs were also popular. In France, delicate floral carpets in soft colours became fashionable.

5 Chatsworth/Buckingham Colour **constitution gold** Alt. colours **yes** Composition **100% wool** Width **4m/4½yd** Repeat **90cm/35½in** Price ★★★

6 Stark/Houles Colour **floral black** Alt. colours **yes** Composition **100% wool** Width **3.66m/4yd** Repeat **99cm/39in** Price ★★★★

7 Stark/Fontainebleau Ribbon Border Colour **creme** Alt. colours **yes** Composition **100% wool** Width **35cm/13¾in** Repeat **44cm/17in** Price ★★★

8 Stark/Clichy Colour **yellow** Alt. colours **yes** Composition **100% wool** Width **101cm/39¾in** Repeat **25cm/9¾in** Price ★★★★

9 Hugh Mackay/142974–7282 Colour **multi** Alt. colours **yes** Composition **100% wool** Width **91cm/35¾in** Repeat **86cm/33¼in** Price ★★ ⊞

5

1

2

1 Stark/Summer Flowers Border Colour **yellow** Alt. colours **no** Composition **100% wool** Width **23cm/9in** Repeat **6cm/2⅜in** Price ★★★★★

2 Stark/Kingston Border Colour **blue** Alt. colours **yes** Composition **100% wool** Width **17cm/6¾in** Repeat **18cm/7in** Price ★★

3 Brintons/Annabelle Classique 136/16668 Colour **summer spray harvest** Alt. colours **yes** Composition **80% wool, 20% nylon** Width **3.6m/4yd** Repeat **91cm/35¾in** Price ★★ ⊞

4 Woodward Grosvenor/Emblem 36/5681 Colour **36** Alt. colours **yes** Composition **100% wool** Width **4m/4½yd** Repeat **13cm/5in** Price ★★★

6

7

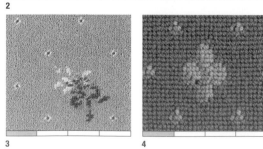

3

4

8

9

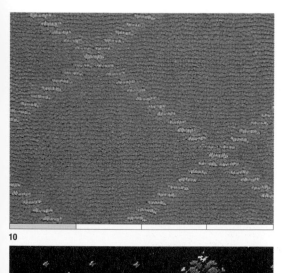

10

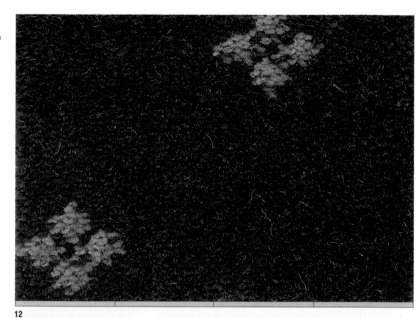

12

10 **Hugh Mackay/Brampton 7426**
Colour **62273** Alt. colours **yes**
Composition **100% wool** Width
91cm/35⅜in Repeat **12cm/4¾in**
Price ★★★ ⊞

11 **Brintons/Regina International
44/19784** Colour **rosette
green** Alt. colours **yes**
Composition **80% wool,
20% nylon** Width **3.66m/
4yd** Repeat **45cm/17½in**
Price ★★ ⊞

12 **Zoffany/Richmond RIC21004**
Colour **speedwell** Alt. colours
yes Composition **80% wool,
20% nylon** Width **4m/4½yd**
Repeat **–** Price ★★★ ⊞

13 **Stark/Navarre Border**
Colour **olive** Alt. colours
no Composition **100% wool**
Width **17cm/6¾in** Repeat
17cm/6¾in Price ★★

11

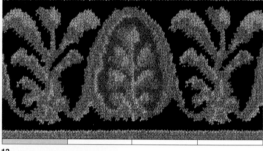

13

15

14

14 **Stoddard Templeton/Cathiness
4/4540** Colour **midnight
embriodery** Alt. colours **no**
Composition **80% wool,
20% nylon** Width **91cm/
35⅜in** Repeat **78cm/30¾in**
Price ★★ ⊞

15 **Stark/Small Star** Colour
cobalt blue Alt. colours
yes Composition **100%
wool** Width **3.66m/4yd**
Repeat **15cm/6in**
Price ★★★

16 **Stark/Small Star Border**
Colour **cobalt blue** Alt.
colours **yes** Composition
100% wool Width **17cm/
6¾in** Repeat **29.5cm/
11½in** Price ★★

17 **Bosanquet Ives/Icicles**
Colour **01** Alt. colours
yes Composition **100%
wool** Width **69cm/27in**
Repeat **–** Price ★★

18 **Stark/Kingston** Colour **blue**
Alt. colours **yes** Composition
100% wool Width **372cm/
12ft 2in** Repeat **8cm/3in**
Price ★★★★

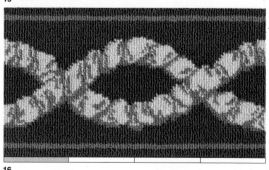

16

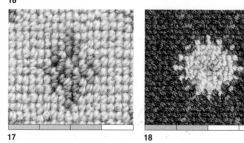

17   **18**

FLOORING: *CARPETS*   **381**

Carpets: Late 19th century

Factors such as the development of synthetic dyes and the power loom, along with the increased wealth of the middle class, gave great impetus to the British and American carpet industries. Engineers in America developed the Axminster loom, and Brintons of Kidderminster, England, introduced the Gripper version in 1890. The Kleitos Axminster Broadloom, brought from America and patented by Tomkinson Ltd in Kidderminster in 1896, enabled the production of large carpets with no colour limitation, giving full rein to the floral chintz that became a hallmark of the British industry. A mid-19th-century exhibition of oriental carpets in Berlin triggered a revival in Persian and Indian designs. Many carpets were based on Baroque themes using crimsons and blues. Other influences at this time were Owen Jones's *Dictionary of Ornament* (1856) and Christopher Dresser's *Principles of Design* (1879). The Great Exhibition of 1851 in Britain inspired carpet designs by Morris and Company, C.F.A. Voysey, and other members of the Arts and Crafts movement. William Morris's floral designs, such as the acanthus and poppy Axminsters of the 1870s, were reinterpretations of Persian designs. In America, the Arts and Crafts designs of Frank Lloyd Wright and Greene & Greene were more restrained.

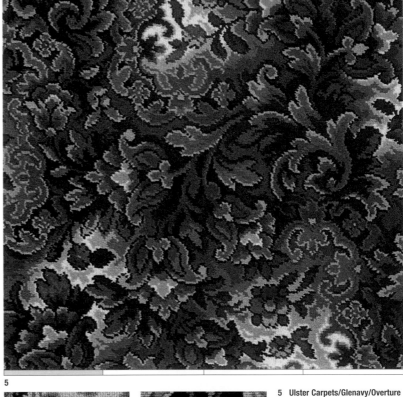

5

1

1 Stark/Winford Rose Border
Colour **yellow** Alt. colours **no** Composition **100% wool** Width **23cm/9in** Repeat **61cm/24in** Price ★★★★★

2 Woodward Grosvenor/Pearl Damask 26/5687 Colour **26** Alt. colours **yes** Composition **100% wool** Width **4m/4⅓yd** Repeat **74.5cm/29¼in** Price ★★★

3 Stark/Chambone Border
Colour **stock** Alt. colours **no** Composition **100% wool** Width **23cm/9in** Repeat **47cm/18½in** Price ★★★

4 Stark/Flanders Border
Colour **stock** Alt. colours **no** Composition **100% wool** Width **23cm/9in** Repeat – Price ★★★

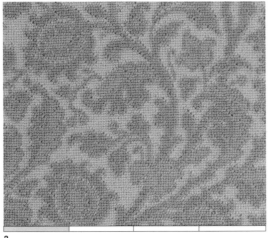

2

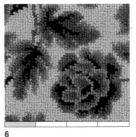

6

7

5 Ulster Carpets/Glenavy/Overture Colour **2-2162** Alt. colours **no** Composition **80% wool, 20% nylon** Width **3.66m/4yd** Repeat **94cm/36½in** Price ★★

6 Stark/Buisson des Roses Colour **stock** Alt. colours **no** Composition **100% wool** Width **101cm/39¾in** Repeat **11.5cm/4½in** Price ★★★★

7 Stark/Fontaine de Bleu Colour **black and white** Alt. colours **no** Composition **100% wool** Width **69cm/27in** Repeat **85cm/33½in** Price ★★★★

8 Axminster Carpets/Torbay 100/Silk Chintz 152/11008 Colour **shadow green** Alt. colours **yes** Composition **100% wool** Width **3.66m/4yd** Repeat **91cm/35¾in** Price ★★ ⊞

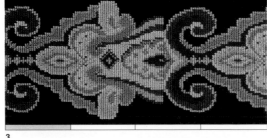

3

4

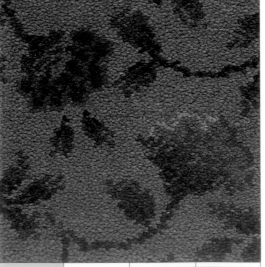

8

9 **Bosanquet Ives/Wool Linen** Colour **multi** Alt. colours **yes** Composition **80% wool, 20% linen** Width **4m/4½yd** Repeat – Price ★

10 **Stark/Villandry** Colour **green and peach** Alt. colours **yes** Composition **100% wool** Width **69cm/27in** Repeat **76cm/30in** Price ★★★★★

11 **Stark/Kenshire** Colour **gold/green** Alt. colours **yes** Composition **100% wool** Width **68.5cm/27in** Repeat **18cm/7in** Price ★★★★

12 **Stark/Petite Diagonal Border** Colour **navy blue** Alt. colours **yes** Composition **100% wool** Width **23cm/9in** Repeat **55cm/21½in** Price ★★★★

13 **Stark/Polo** Colour **stock** Alt. colours **no** Composition **100% wool** Width **68.5cm/27in** Repeat **18cm/7in** Price ★★★★

14 **Stark/Chambone** Colour **stock** Alt. colours **no** Composition **100% wool** Width **101cm/39¾in** Repeat **105cm/41¼in** Price ★★★★★

15 **Woodward Grosvenor/21/7051** Colour **red** Alt. colours **yes** Composition **100% wool** Width **69cm/27in** Repeat – Price ★★

16 **Woodward Grosvenor/19–7050** Colour **green** Alt. colours **yes** Composition **100% wool** Width **69cm/27in** Repeat **29.5cm/11½in** Price ★★★

9

10

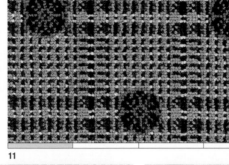

11

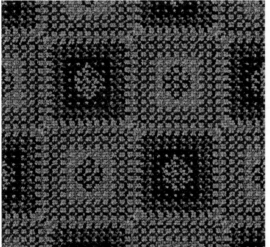

13

14

15

16

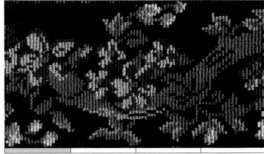

12

DESIGN PAPERS

Carpets have traditionally been designed using "point-paper". Point-paper is divided into inch squares, each redivided into tiny blocks representing one tuft. The transferring of the design to the paper has to be precise, and applied in a semi-transparent form so that each square can be counted (so as to calculate the exact amount of yarn for each colour). In spite of computerization, which is now universal, many companies retain the services of a designer who understands these techniques.

The design paper shown above was used to produce the carpet shown below, which is an interpretation of an historic Persian design.

Stoddard Templeton/Antiquarian 1/8312 Colour **multi** Alt. colours **no** Composition **80% wool, 20% nylon** Width **137cm/54in** Repeat **93cm/36in** Price ★★ ⊞

Carpets: **Early 20th century**

In Britain the transition from Art Nouveau to Art Deco can be seen most clearly in the work of Charles Rennie Mackintosh, who stripped away gratuitous ornament and pointed the way to cleaner, simpler lines. This simplicity was reflected in carpet designs of the early 20th century. Geometric patterns, reflecting the Modernist preoccupation with the machine, were particularly favoured, as were plain, wall-to-wall carpets. In Britain, Scotland and America, brilliantly coloured abstracts were woven for the new cinemas and department stores. Large hotels and ocean liners were treated to soft, muted designs with large repeats, intended to create a mood of calm. In France, highly formal, stylized floral carpets were in demand.

More inspiration for designs on both sides of the Atlantic came from the Ballet Russe, the discovery of the tomb of Tutankhamun and the popularity of African art. However, at the same time, the tradition of Persian, Turkish and chintz designs also remained an important part of carpet ranges (*see* opposite).

1 **Stark/Navarre** Colour **olive** Alt. colours **yes** Composition **100% wool** Width **372cm/ 3ft 2in** Repeat **10cm/4in** Price ★★★★

2 **Bosanquet Ives/Trellis** Colour **olive and khaki** Alt. colours **yes** Composition **100% wool** Width **69cm/27in** Repeat – Price ★★★

3 **Stark/La Seine** Colour **cocoa** Alt. colours **no** Composition **100% wool** Width **372cm/ 3ft 2in** Repeat **93cm/36in** Price ★★★★

4 **Axminster Carpets/Honeycomb 40/2505** Colour **champagne** Alt. colours **yes** Composition **100% wool** Width **3.66m/ 4yd** Repeat **23cm/9in** Price ★★ ⊞

1

2

3

4

5 **Ulster Carpets/Glenmoy/Royal Stewart** Colour **10-2754** Alt. colours **no** Composition **80% wool, 20% nylon** Width **3.66m/4yd** Repeat **45.5cm/ 17¾in** Price ★★ ⊞

6 **Stark/Floral Vine** Colour **azure yellow** Alt. colours **yes** Composition **100% wool** Width **4m/4½yd** Repeat – Price ★★★★★

7 **Stoddard Templeton/Cathiness 2/4541** Colour **lorenzo green** Alt. colours **no** Composition **80% wool, 20% nylon** Width **91cm/35¾in** Repeat **88cm/34½in** Price ★★ ⊞

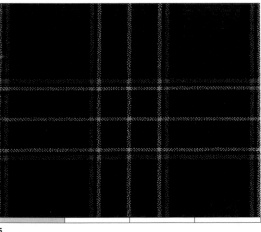

5

6

7

8

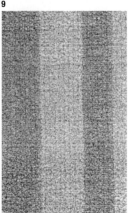

9

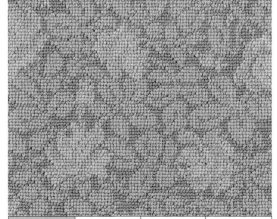

10   11

8 Bosanquet Ives/Woodlands Colour **multi** Alt. colours **yes** Composition **100% wool** Width **69cm/27in** Repeat **–** Price ★★★

9 Woodward Grosvenor/Strata 26/5677 Colour **26** Alt. colours **yes** Composition **100% wool** Width **4m/4½yd** Repeat **10cm/4in** Price ★★★

10 Stark/Bristol Border Colour **sienna gold** Alt. colours **yes** Composition **100% wool** Width **17cm/6¾in** Repeat **–** Price ★★

11 Woodward Grosvenor/Rambling Rose 16/5684 Colour **16** Alt. colours **yes** Composition **100% wool** Width **4m/4½yd** Repeat **43cm/16¾in** Price ★★★

12 Ulster Carpets/Glenavy/White Shirzar Colour **1-2467** Alt. colours **no** Composition **80% wool, 20% nylon** Width **3.66m/4yd** Repeat **94cm/36½in** Price ★★ ⊞

13 Stark/Havorford Colour **black and white** Alt. colours **no** Composition **100% wool** Width **3.66m/4yd** Repeat **30cm/11¾in** Price ★★★★★ ⊞

14 Stark/Nouvelle Colour **stock** Alt. colours **no** Composition **100% wool** Width **68.5cm/27in** Repeat **11.5cm/4½in** Price ★★★★

15 Stark/Calla Lilies Colour **red** Alt. colours **no** Composition **100% wool** Width **3.66m/4yd** Repeat **15cm/6in** Price ★★★★★

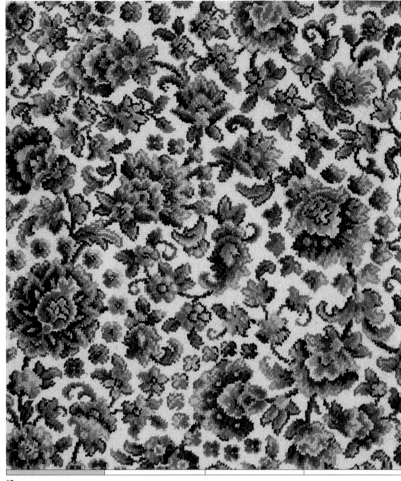

12

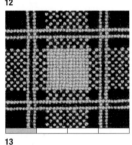

13   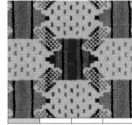 14    15

PERSIAN INFLUENCE

The influence of richly coloured Persian carpets on contemporary European and American designs has been profound. Although Art Deco and Modernist schemes largely eschewed the complex Persian-style designs, such carpets were arguably more popular in the early 20th century than ever before. Carpets from Sarouk in Persia – which were salmon pink in colour and featuring geometric or floral decoration – were particularly loved in America at this time.

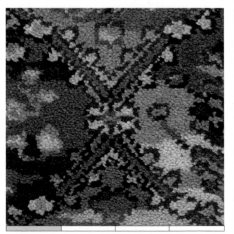

Stoddard Templeton/Cathiness 20/4520 Colour **Persian lattice** Alt. colours **no** Composition **80% wool, 20% nylon** Width **91cm/35¾in** Repeat **57cm/22½in** Price ★★ Ⓣ ⊞

Carpets: **Mid-20th century**

From the mid-20th century onward, there has been a great increase in the use of man-made fibres. Although wool has always been the traditional fibre for carpet (owing to its natural resilience and ability to absorb dye), it is comparatively more expensive than man-made fibres. Wool is frequently blended with nylon in a ratio of 4:1 to improve durability, and synthetic fibres are also blended in various combinations.

In terms of patterning, there was a new range of influences on carpet design in the mid-20th century. In 1951 the Festival of Britain had a profound impact on the industry, which produced for the first time delicate, linear "spot" designs. In the late 1950s and 1960s there was a noticeable response to the leading painters and designers, with, for example, the painter Jackson Pollock greatly influencing domestic Axminster and Gripper ranges. At this time, Middle Eastern and African ornament – including animal-print patterns – was fashionable in Europe and America, but plain carpets were also popular.

Ollerton Hall/Berber Colour **sea green** Alt. colours **yes** Composition **100% wool** Width **4m/4½yd** Repeat **–** Price ★ ⊞

Ollerton Hall/Sovereign Colour **106250** Alt. colours **yes** Composition **100% polypropylene** Width **4m/4½yd** Repeat **–** Price ★ ⊘⊞

Brintons/Bell Twist 9582 Colour **dianthus** Alt. colours **yes** Composition **80% wool, 20% nylon** Width **3.66m/4yd** Repeat **–** Price ★★ ⊞

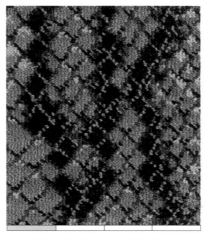

Hugh Mackay/Indian River Snake 1377/7152 Colour **multi** Alt. colours **yes** Composition **80% wool, 20% nylon** Width **69cm/27in** Repeat **30cm/11¾in** Price ★★★

Zoffany/Paintbox Border Colour **sable with porridge** Alt. colours **yes** Composition **80% wool, 20% Woolbond** Width **12cm/4¾in** Repeat **–** Price ★

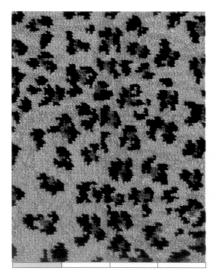

Stark/Somali Panther Colour **stock** Alt. colours **no** Composition **100% wool** Width **3.66m/4yd** Repeat **1.87m/2yd** Price ★★★★★

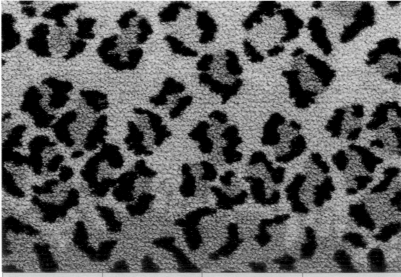

Chatsworth/Leopard Skin Colour **multi** Alt. colours **no** Composition **100% nylon** Width **3.66m/4yd** Repeat **90cm/35½in** Price ★★

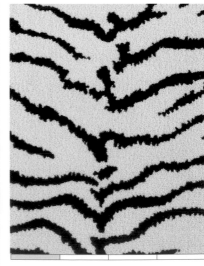

Chatsworth/White Tiger Colour **black and white** Alt. colours **no** Composition **100% nylon** Width **3.66m/4yd** Repeat **90cm/35½in** Price ★★

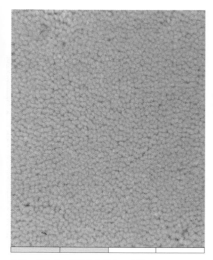

Zoffany/Windsor WIN0000 Colour **4** Alt. colours **yes** Composition **100% wool** Width **4m/4½yd** Repeat **–** Price ★★★

Ulster Carpets/York Wilton/Paprika Colour **Y1025** Alt. colours **yes** Composition **80% wool, 20% nylon** Width **3.66m/4yd** Repeat **–** Price ★★

Ollerton Hall/Graphics Colour **dark blue** Alt. colours **yes** Composition **100% polypropylene** Width **4m/4½yd** Repeat **–** Price ★ ⊙

Mannington Carpets/Sorata RERI Colour **red river** Alt. colours **yes** Composition **100% nylon** Width **3.66m/4yd** Repeat **5.5cm/2¼in** Price ★ ⊞

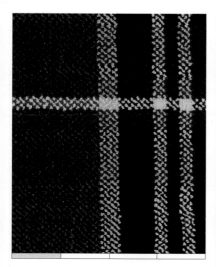

Hugh Mackay/MacBeth Tartan 1389-7104 Colour **multi** Alt. colours **yes** Composition **80% wool, 20% nylon** Width **69cm/27in** Repeat **69cm/27in** Price ★★★

Brintons/Zenith Club Class Calypso 23/12740 Colour **multi** Alt. colours **no** Composition **80% wool, 20% nylon** Width **69cm/27in** Repeat **85cm/33½in** Price ★★ Ⓣ

Stoddard/New England 3/8334 Colour **multi** Alt. colours **no** Composition **80% wool, 20% nylon** Width **3.66m/4yd** Repeat **65cm/25¼in** Price ★★ ⊞

Ollerton Hall/Princess 6TCP Colour **burgundy** Alt. colours **yes** Composition **80% wool, 20% nylon** Width **4m/4½yd** Repeat **–** Price ★★ ⊞

Hugh Mackay/Wilton 210455 Colour **308891** Alt. colours **yes** Composition **100% wool** Width **91m/35¾in** Repeat **–** Price ★★★ ⊞

Axminster Carpets/French Impressions 232/15020 Colour **Erica pink** Alt. colours **yes** Composition **100% wool** Width **3.66m/4yd** Repeat **91cm/35¾in** Price ★★ ⊞

Hugh Mackay/127864-942416 Colour **multi** Alt. colours **yes** Composition **80% wool, 20% nylon** Width **69cm/27in** Repeat **–** Price ★★ ⊞

Carpets: Late 20th–early 21st century

The majority of carpets are now mass-produced using a tufting process; the machines that create them resemble gigantic sewing machines with hundreds of needles. Unlike woven carpet, where the backing is an integral part of the cloth, tufted yarn is machine-sewn to a ready-woven backing that is then covered with latex. The continuing development of synthetic fibres, an expanding range of textures and industry computerization have all contributed to the success of such carpets. They are often produced in soft, modulated colours, achieved by using space-dyed yarns or screen-printing. There has been experimentation recently with injection dyeing, which involves each tuft receiving its own jet of dye; this provides complete freedom for designers and can produce highly colourful ranges.

Lately, too, the popularity of the loose carpet square – available in sizes as large as a square metre or yard – has provided designers with many opportunities. Contemporary designers in Europe and America have continued to draw inspiration for the patterning of carpets from the bold influences of Africa, India and South America and from a wide range of styles from the past, as well as creating exciting new designs and experimenting with colours and patterns.

1

2

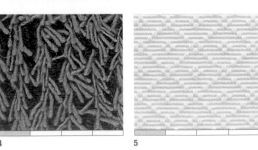

3

4

5

6

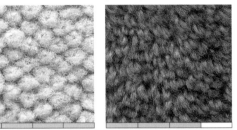

7

8

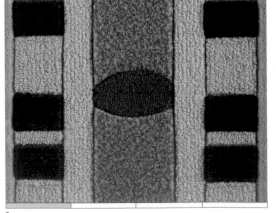

9

1 Chatsworth/Pebbles Colour **silver grey** Alt. colours **yes** Composition **100% wool** Width **4m/4½yd** Repeat – Price ★★★★★ ⊞

2 Stark/Broadway Colour **ocean** Alt. colours **yes** Composition **80% wool, 20% nylon** Width **4m/4½yd** Repeat – Price ★★★

3 Chatsworth/Keyboard Colour **multi** Alt. colours **yes** Composition **100% wool** Width **to order** Repeat – Price ★★★★★

4 Ruckstuhl/Jack Lenor Larsen/ Get Up Colour **486** Alt. colour **yes** Composition **100% wool** Width **4m/4½yd** Repeat – Price ★★★

5 Zoffany/Pastiche Colour **spin drift** Alt. colours **yes** Composition **100% wool** Width **4m/ 4½yd** Repeat **5cm/2in** Price ★★

6 Bosanquet Ives/Sinfonie Colour **54** Alt. colours **yes** Composition **100% wool** Width **4m/4½yd** Repeat – Price ★★★★

7 Ollerton Hall/Ultimate Shag Pile Colour **pink** Alt. colours **yes** Composition **100% wool** Width **to order** Repeat – Price ★★

8 Atlas Carpet Mills/Tintoretto TT01 Colour **Danube** Alt. colours **yes** Composition **100% nylon** Width **3.66m/ 4yd** Repeat **4cm/1½in** Price ★★

9 Chatsworth/Dakee SP121 Colour **multi** Alt. colours **yes** Composition **100% wool** Width **to order** Repeat – Price ★★★★★

10 **Chatsworth/Link Border
(carved)** Colour **blue and green**
Alt. colours **yes** Composition
100% wool Width **to order**
Repeat **–** Price ★★★★

11 **Bosanquet Ives/Woollen Chord**
Colour **multi** Alt. colours **yes**
Composition **100% wool**
Width **to order** Repeat **–**
Price ★★

12 **Ulster Carpet/Metro/Hemp**
Colour **11-2987** Alt. colours
yes Composition **80% wool,
20% nylon** Width **3.66m/4yd**
Repeat **91.5cm/36in**
Price ★★ ⊞

13 **Chatsworth/Foresta 8520**
Colour **white** Alt. colours **yes**
Composition **100% wool**
Width **to order** Repeat **–**
Price ★★★★

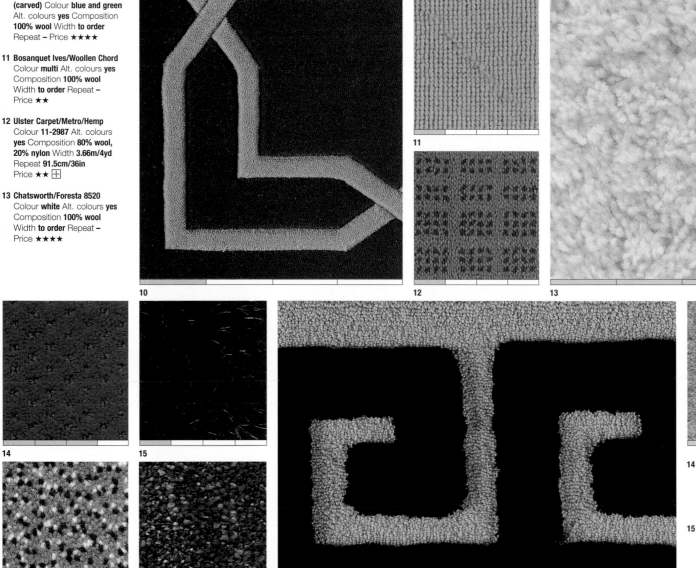

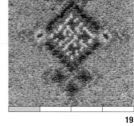

14 **Atlas Carpet Mills/Cipriani 35**
Colour **R947 Lapis** Alt. colours
yes Composition **100% nylon**
Width **3.66m/4yd** Repeat
2cm/¾in Price ★★

15 **Ruckstuhl/Jack Lenor Larsen/
Diva** Colour **179** Alt. colours
yes Composition **97% wool, 3%
lurex** Width **2m/2⅕yd** Repeat **–**
Price ★★★★★

16 **Westbond/8L** Colour **curry,
Bastille grey, white Russia**
Alt. colours **yes** Composition
100% nylon Width **50 x 50cm/
19½ x 19½in (tile)** Repeat **–**
Price ★★ ⊞

17 **Mannington Carpets/Strategies
ZENI** Colour **zenith** Alt. colours
yes Composition **100% nylon**
Width **3.8m/4⅛yd** Repeat
47cm/18½in Price ★★

18 **Chatsworth/Greek Key Border**
Colour **black and beige** Alt.
colours **yes** Composition
100% wool Width **to order**
Repeat **–** Price ★★★★★

19 **Brintons/Marrakesh 22/11894**
Colour **22** Alt. colours **yes**
Composition **80% wool,
20% nylon** Width **3.66m/
4yd** Repeat **18cm/7in**
Price ★★ ⊞

COMBINATION WEAVES

Owing to the increased
sophistication of looms and
tufting machines, a very wide
range of textures is now available
in carpets. For example, high
and low piles, cut and uncut
loops, and "carved" effects
can all be employed within a
single carpet, giving it a mixture
of several different textures.
New yarns can also provide
"pebble" surfaces, while space-
dyed yarns provide a speckled
effect. Modern tufted carpets
are extremely hardwearing,
and any number of colours
can be used.

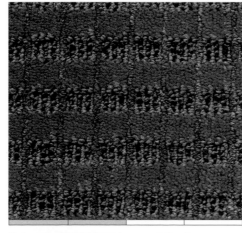

Monterey/Presidio 6021-384 Colour **general** Alt. colours **yes**
Composition **100% nylon** Width **3.66m/4yd**
Repeat **–** Price ★★

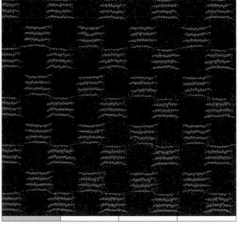

Hugh Mackay/Brampton 210482 Colour **308904** Alt. colours **yes**
Composition **100% wool** Width **91cm/36in**
Repeat **4cm/1½in** Price ★★★ ⊞

20th & 21st century

Sheet Flooring

Sheet flooring refers to a wide range of highly practical floor coverings. These include floorcloths, linoleum, vinyl and rubber.

Floorcloths first appeared in the late 17th century as groundsheets for marquees, but they were soon integrated in interiors as an economical and decorative means of covering floors. Often made from oil cloth, they came into use as a result of the availability of large expanses of sailcloth from the shipbuilding industry. Stemming from the older practice of painting floorboards, the patterns often simulated stone and marble pavings.

The rapid growth of industrial mass-production in Britain during the 19th century brought with it the invention of linoleum (*see page 393*). Made from relatively cheap materials, it remained the most popular form of domestic sheet flooring until the mid-20th century. The social changes since have brought an increased demand for easy-to-clean, mass-produced flooring. Major developments in the plastics industry led, in the 1950s, to the introduction of vinyl and resin floorings that imitated wood, stone and terracotta. The late 20th and early 21st century has seen a move into the domestic market of contract flooring materials such as rubber and metal.

1 Popular since the middle of the 19th century, linoleum is now available in a wide range of colours. However, the traditional colours – browns, reds and yellows – are still very fashionable.

2 Rubber is a highly durable 20th-century floor covering. Particularly suitable for public areas and airports, it can now be produced in a variety of colours and textures thanks to new technology.

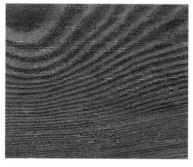

3 Traditional stone or terracotta slabs are just one of the styles imitated by vinyl flooring. Available as rolls or tiles, this can simulate most natural materials; modern abstract designs are also used.

4 Composite laminates that imitate wood are a durable, easy-care and cheaper alternative to natural boards. A wide range of different grains, colours and board sizes is available.

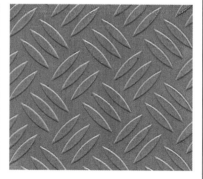

5 Modern techniques can reproduce the look of natural stone to a highly accurate degree, as seen on this *faux*-stone vinyl. The benefits of this include ease of installation and lower cost.

6 Metal sheet flooring became increasingly popular in the late 20th century. Being both durable and stylish, it is now found in domestic as well as commercial settings.

ABOVE Modern vinyl flooring can replicate the most intricate of designs found on traditional floor coverings, and can be coloured to complement any interior. This bold geometric design is based on a classical pattern.

LEFT The white vinyl floor tiles in this modern interpretation of a 17th-century interior give the appearance of a polished marble floor, yet provide a surface that is easy to clean and warm to the touch.

FAR LEFT Cushion vinyl, invented in America in 1963, cleverly simulates a wood finish in this modern interior. Today, cushion vinyl is produced in many different designs and textures. It also has the advantage of being much quieter underfoot than its wooden equivalent.

1 **Armstrong DLW/Linoleum/Marmorette 121** Colour **48** Alt. colours **yes** Composition **linoleum** Width **2m/2⅕yd** Repeat – Price ★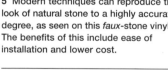

2 **Dalsouple/Uni** Colour **pêche** Alt. colours **yes** Composition **rubber** Width **34 x 34cm/ 13⅓ x 13⅓in (tile)** Repeat – Price ★★

3 **Westco/Cobble Gold Embossed** Colour **cobble gold** Alt. colours **yes** Composition **PVC** Width **30.5 x 30.5cm/12 x 12in (tile)** Repeat – Price ★

4 **Armstrong DLW/Scala/Scala Wood 20040** Colour **52** Alt. colours **yes** Composition **synthetic** Width **91.5 x 7.5cm/36 x 2¾in (tile)** Repeat – Price ★★

5 **Armstrong DLW/Scala/Scala Stone 20258** Colour **85** Alt. colours **yes** Composition **synthetic** Width **30.5 x 30.5cm/12 x 12in (tile)** Repeat – Price ★★

6 **Deralam/Footplate AD866** Colour **pewter tone** Alt. colours **no** Composition **aluminium laminate** Width **122cm/48in** Repeat – Price ★

Sheet Flooring: **Pre-20th century**

In the 18th century, floors were often covered by painted, stencilled or printed floorcloths. Canvas was stretched and nailed down so that it would hold its shape; it was then soaked with water, primed and painted several times on each side with finely ground ochres or leads and linseed oil to give it a base coat before being decorated. Much employed in imposing Neo-classical entrance halls, floorcloths were either painted one colour or decorated – much as were painted floorboards – to look like stone or marble paving or mosaic. Other patterns popular in the 18th century included the simulation of elaborate Roman floors. The patterns of Eastern carpets were also copied, while in America geometric chequer patterns were common.

In Britain, painted floorcloths were being mass-produced in factories by the late 18th century. The introduction of a printing process in about 1770, as well as improvements in colouring pigments, made more elaborate designs possible. Although waterproof, painted floorcloths were quite fragile and could not withstand a great deal of wear and tear. However, in spite of the advent of harder-wearing linoleum in 1860 (*see* opposite), production of floorcloths continued until after the First World War.

1

2

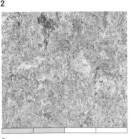

3

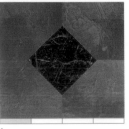

4

5

6

7

1 **Sinclair Till/Tartan** Colour **multi** Alt. colours **yes** Composition **linoleum** Width **to order** Repeat – Price ★★

2 **Sinclair Till/Chequerboard with Inlaid Stars** Colour **multi** Alt. colours **yes** Composition **linoleum** Width **to order** Repeat – Price ★★★

3 **Armstrong DLW/Linoleum/ Marmorette 121** Colour **70** Alt. colours **yes** Composition **linoleum** Width **2m/2⅕yd** Repeat – Price ★ ▧ ⊞

4 **Karndean/Desert Clay Terracotta and Midnight Black Marble T74** Colour **red and black** Alt. colours **yes** Composition **vinyl** Width **30.5 x 30.5cm/ 12 x 12in (tile)** Repeat – Price ★

5 **Karndean/Carrara Marble and Diamond T90 & B300 Border** Colour **white and black** Alt. colours **yes** Composition **vinyl** Width **30.5 x 30.5cm/ 12 x 12in (tile)** Repeat – Price ★

6 **Armstrong DLW/Linoleum/ Granette 111** Colour **59** Alt. colours **yes** Composition **linoleum** Width **2m/2⅕yd** Repeat – Price ★ ⊞ ▧

7 **Sinclair Till/Inlaid Curlicue and Star Border** Colour **multi** Alt. colours **yes** Composition **linoleum** Width **to order** Repeat – Price ★★

8

9

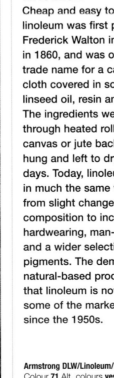

12

8 Jane Knapp/Fossil Stone Marble Floorcloth Colour **multi** Alt. colours **yes** Composition **paint on canvas** Width **to order** Repeat – Price ★★★★★

9 Amtico/Norwegian Slate SN36 Colour **silver** Alt. colours **no** Composition **vinyl** Width **30.5 x 30.5cm/12 x 12in (tile)** Repeat – Price ★★★ ⊞

10 Armstrong DLW/Linoleum/ Linodur 151 Colour **42** Alt. colours **yes** Composition **linoleum** Width **2m/2⅙yd** Repeat – Price ★ ⊞ ▧

11 Karndean/Granite Dove and Raven D202/D203 Colour **grey** Alt. colours **yes** Composition **vinyl** Width **30.5 x 30.5cm/ 12 x 12in (tile)** Repeat – Price ★

12 Marley/Leaf Border Colour **MBF4MPC** Alt. colours **yes** Composition **vinyl** Width **15cm/6in** Repeat **90cm/35½in** Price ★

10   11

LINOLEUM

Cheap and easy to produce, linoleum was first patented by Frederick Walton in Scotland in 1860, and was originally the trade name for a canvas floor cloth covered in solidified linseed oil, resin and kauri gum. The ingredients were pressed through heated rollers on to the canvas or jute backing, then hung and left to dry for several days. Today, linoleum is made in much the same way, apart from slight changes in the composition to incorporate hardwearing, man-made fibres and a wider selection of pigments. The demand for natural-based products means that linoleum is now reclaiming some of the market lost to vinyl since the 1950s.

Armstrong DLW/Linoleum/Marmorette 121 Colour **71** Alt. colours **yes** Composition **linoleum** Width **2m/2⅙yd** Repeat – Price ★ ⊞ ▧

Sheet Flooring: **20th–early 21st century**

The first half of the 20th century saw little change in the sheet-flooring market. Floorcloths were factory-produced until after the First World War, while linoleum continued to dominate the market until the introduction of vinyl-based products in the 1950s. The Art Deco and Modernist movements influenced linoleum design in the 1940s and early 1950s, and soon inspired designs on vinyl. Imitation brick, tile, wood and even carpet designs were all possible on vinyl, and this resulted in a reduction in sales of linoleum. The new vinyl sheet flooring was sound- and shock-absorbent, slip-resistant, gave good heat insulation and was easy to clean. In the late 20th century, a small, specialist market for floorcloths appeared, with designs based on traditional as well as modern patterns. There has also been a renewed interest in linoleum – its use of natural ingredients making it desirable again in the environmentally aware 21st century. Other types of sheet flooring have emerged, including traditional contract floorings (such as rubber) which have been adapted slightly to offer designs suited to domestic use. Such flooring became the keynote of the late 1970s' and early 1980s' high-tech style (*see page 397*). Metal sheet flooring in a variety of finishes has also become fashionable in recent years, as have resin laminates.

1

2   3   5

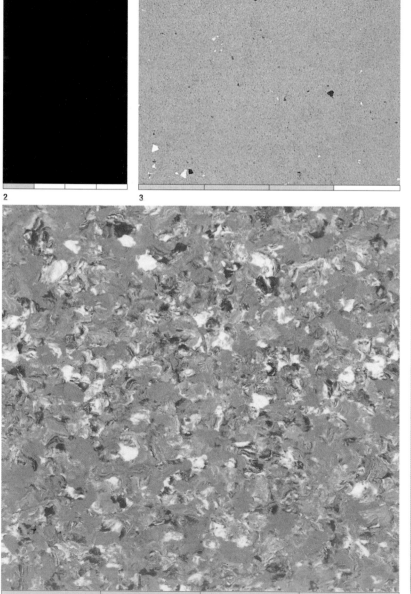

4   6

1 **Armstrong DLW/Linoleum/ Linorette 124** Colour **18** Alt. colours **yes** Composition **linoleum** Width **2m/2⅕yd** Repeat – Price ★ ⊞ ▧

2 **Westco/Aristocrat** Colour **London brick** Alt. colours **yes** Composition **PVC** Width **30.5 x 30.5cm/12 x 12in (tile)** Repeat – Price ★

3 **Armstrong DLW/Linoleum/ LinoArt Star 144** Colour **72** Alt. colours **yes** Composition **linoleum** Width **2m/2⅕yd** Repeat – Price ★ ⊞ ▧

4 **Marley/Eclipse BEF528** Colour **sunflower** Alt. colours **yes** Composition **vinyl** Width **2m/2⅕yd** Repeat – Price ★★★★ ⊞

5 **Armstrong DLW/Scala/Scala Wood 20015** Colour **65** Alt. colours **yes** Composition **synthetic** Width **91.5 x7.5cm/ 36 x 2¾in (tile)** Repeat – Price ★ ⊞

6 **Karndean/Knight Plank D504** Colour **beech** Alt. colours **yes** Composition **vinyl** Width **91.5 x 10.5cm/36 x 4in (tile)** Repeat – Price ★

20th & 21st century

7

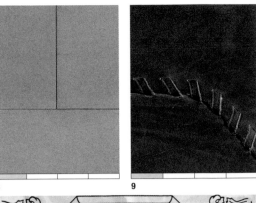

8

9

7 Bonar Floors/Newlyn 146010 Colour **ocean spray** Alt. colours **yes** Composition **flotex flooring** Width **2m/2⅙yd** Repeat – Price ★★ 🔲 T

8 Bill Amberg/Leather Floor (Tile) Colour **light tan** Alt. colours **yes** Composition **leather** Width **to order** Repeat – Price ★★★★★

9 Bill Amberg/Leather Floor (Stitch) Colour **tan** Alt. colours **yes** Composition **leather** Width **to order** Repeat – Price ★★★★★

10 Westco/Floral Colour **multi** Alt. colours **no** Composition **PVC** Width **30.5 x 30.5cm/12 x 12in (tile)** Repeat – Price ★

10

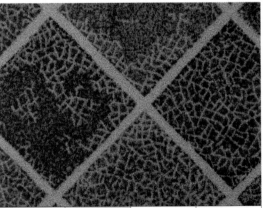

11

12

11 Bonar Floors/Orkney 120020 Colour **summer sand** Alt. colours **yes** Composition **flotex flooring** Width **2m/2⅙yd** Repeat – Price ★★ 🔲

12 Armstrong DLW/Scala/Scala Stone 20045 Colour **43** Alt. colours **yes** Composition **synthetic** Width **30.5 x 30.5cm/ 12 x 12in (tile)** Repeat – Price ★★ ⊞

13 Armstrong DLW/Scala/Scala Metal 20063 Colour **06** Alt. colours **yes** Composition **synthetic** Width **30.5 x 30.5cm/ 12 x 12in (tile)** Repeat – Price ★★ ⊞

14 Amtico/Tilewood TW 714 Colour **warm maple** Alt. colours **yes** Composition **vinyl** Width **30.5 x 30.5cm/ 12 x 12in (tile)** Repeat – Price ★★★ ⊞

15 Armstrong DLW/Heterogeneous/ Protech 518 Colour **223** Alt. colours **yes** Composition **heterogeneous vinyl** Width **2m/2⅙yd** Repeat – Price ★ 🔲 ⊞ 🔲

16 Westco/Diamond Black Embossed Colour **diamond black** Alt. colours **yes** Composition **PVC** Width **30.5 x 30.5cm/12 x 12in (tile)** Repeat – Price ★

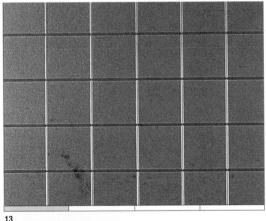

13

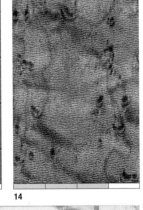

14

15

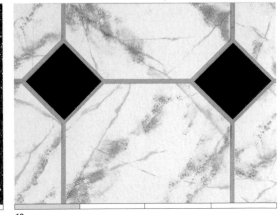

16

FLOORING: *SHEET FLOORING*

Sheet Flooring: 20th–early 21st century

During the late 20th and early 21st century, patterns on sheet flooring have often been derived from classical designs, such as the ancient Greek key pattern. Some manufacturers provide ready components, including borders and key squares, for constructing formal classical patterns. Recent designs have also included 1950s' café-revivalist flooring; semi-flexible PVC tiles with sparkling silica quartz; and sheet flooring consisting of coloured vinyl chips suspended in clear vinyl to produce a three-dimensional effect.

The art of mimicking other, more costly materials in synthetic flooring has become increasingly sophisticated in the early 21st century. Imitation wood is produced using a material with a fibreboard core, laminated with a wood-textured photoprint overlay and bonded with melamine resin. Marble, granite and terracotta are still extremely popular effects, as they were on floorcloths, and offer the look of the original material but with the added advantages of being hardwearing and washable.

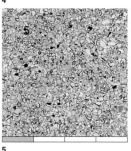

1

2

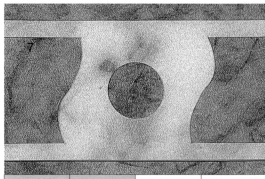

3

4

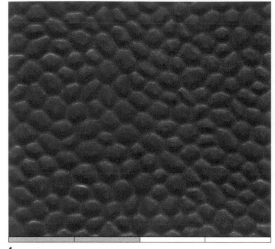

5

6

1 Dalsouple/Martelé Colour **rose indien** Alt. colours **yes** Composition **rubber** Width **68cm/26¾in** Repeat – Price ★★

2 Deralam/Antique Copper CD490 Colour **copper** Alt. colours **no** Composition **copper laminate** Width **122cm/48in** Repeat – Price ★★★★

3 Deralam/Copper Relief CD710 Colour **green/black** Alt. colours **no** Composition **copper laminate** Width **122cm/48in** Repeat – Price ★★★★

4 Deralam/Stainless Steel Wheels SS600 Colour **stainless steel** Alt. colours **no** Composition **stainless steel laminate** Width **102cm/40in** Repeat – Price ★★★★

5 Armstrong DLW/Homogeneous/ Conductive/Pastell LG2 2815 Colour **40** Alt. colours **yes** Composition **synthetic** Width **1.8m/2yd** Repeat – Price ★

6 Armstrong DLW/Homogeneous/ Conductive/Royal LG1/LG2 1422/2422 Colour **41** Alt. colours **yes** Composition **synthetic** Width **1.8m/2yd** Repeat – Price ★★

7 Armstrong DLW/Scala/Scala Borders/Stream 2 23206/23106 Colour **60** Alt. colours **yes** Composition **synthetic** Width **91.5 x 7.5cm/36 x 2¾in** Repeat – Price ★

8 Jaymart/Fishface Colour **black** Alt. colours **no** Composition **rubber** Width **100cm/39¼in** Repeat – Price ★★★ 🔲 ⊠

9 Armstrong DLW/Scala Borders/Cube 1 23204/12104 Colour **40** Alt. colours **yes** Composition **synthetic** Width **91.5 x 7.5cm/36 x 2¾in** Repeat – Price ★

10 Amtico/Treadplate Colour **silver** Alt. colours **yes** Composition **vinyl** Width **30.5 x 30.5cm/12 x 12in (tile)** Repeat – Price ★★★ ⊞

11 Armstrong DLW/Scala/Scala Uni 20023 Colour **30** Alt. colours **yes** Composition **synthetic** Width **30.5 x 30.5cm/12 x 12in (tile)** Repeat – Price ★

12 Jaymart/Astroturf Colour **classic green** Alt. colours **yes** Composition **vinyl** Width **91cm/35¾in** Repeat – Price ★★ 🔲

8

9

10   11   12

13

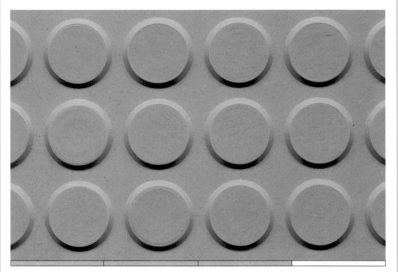

RUBBER FLOORING

First produced in the 1930s, sheet rubber flooring has been used regularly in the contract market. It is tough, hardwearing and easy to clean, and, thanks to developments in the 1990s, available in virtually any colour. Popular designs include terrazzo effects as well as a variety of studded surfaces. The high-tech style of the late 1970s and early 1980s introduced rubber into a domestic setting. "Ecologically friendly" rubber flooring has also been produced recently using recycled car tyres.

Dalsouple/Metro Colour **vert pomme** Alt. colours **yes** Composition **rubber** Width **68 x 68cm/26¾ x 26¾in (tile)** Repeat – Price ★★ 🔲 ⊠

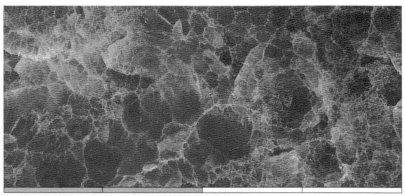

14

13 Armstrong DLW/Scala/Scala Metal 20052 Colour **20** Alt. colours **yes** Composition **synthetic** Width **30.5 x 30.5cm/12 x 12in (tile)** Repeat – Price ★

14 Amtico/Florentine NM-97 Colour **blue** Alt. colours **yes** Composition **vinyl** Width **30.5 x 30.5cm/12 x 12in (tile)** Repeat – Price ★★★ ⊞

15 Armstrong DLW/Heterogeneous/Contract Interior Acoustic/Strata 333 Colour **61** Alt. colours **yes** Composition **heterogeneous vinyl** Width **2m/2¼yd** Repeat – Price ★

15

Glossary

★ Asterisked terms have a separate entry

A

acanthus Foliage ornament based on the serrated leaves of the *Acanthus spinosus* plant. Similar to thistle, parsley or poppy leaves and sometimes used for *scrolling foliage. Originally used in *Classical Greek and Roman architecture and ornament.

Adam style A *Neo-classical style pioneered by the English Adam brothers during the late 18th century, inspired by *Classical Roman and Greek and *Renaissance ornament. Characterized by motifs such as *swags, *guilloche*, *friezes, *anthemia and *palmettes.

Aesthetic movement *See* p.43.

aniline dyes Synthetic dyes made from coal tar. Formulated in the late 1820s, but not developed for general use until the 1850s.

anthemion A floral motif similar to the *palmette and primarily associated with the Classical vocabulary of ornament. Based on either the flower of the *acanthus, the flower and leaf of the honeysuckle or the Egyptian lotus.

appliqué Technique of applying cut-out patterns of fabric on to a ground cloth using either plain or embroidery stitches.

arabesque A stylized, interlaced foliage pattern of Near-Eastern origin, probably based on laurel leaves. In Western ornament often combined with *bandwork or *strapwork. In the 18th century, French designers used the term to describe panels of *grotesque designs incorporating figures, bandwork and *scrolling foliage.

Art Deco *See* pp.49–51.

Art Nouveau *See* p.46.

Arts and Crafts movement *See* pp.42–48.

Aubusson French town where, in the "Royal Manufactury", flat-weave tapestries were made from *c.*1665, and thick- and short-pile carpets were made from c.1742.

Axminster English town where Thomas Whitty established a carpet factory in 1755 (the factory moved to Wilton in 1835). Before 1860 it made hand-woven, woollen pile carpets ("Axminsters"); later, machine-woven equivalents were also produced.

B

bandwork An 18th-century term for *strapwork.

Baronial style Mock-*Gothic style of architecture and decoration inspired by the castles and manor houses of medieval feudal overlords, the barons. Popular during the late 19th and early 20th centuries.

Baroque Style of architecture and ornament prevalent during the 17th century. A *Classical style characterized by elaborate sculptural forms, painted decoration, marble inlays, carved gilding, and architectural elements applied purely ornamentally. Typical motifs included human figures, angels, *putti, scrolls, *swags, urns and flaming torches.

batik *See* Indonesian style p.126.

Bauhaus School of arts and crafts founded at Weimar in Germany in 1906, and moved to Berlin in 1932. Closed by the German Nazi party in 1933. Initially inspired by the *Arts and Crafts movement, but from the 1920s focused on industrial designs characterized by a stark, cubic simplicity.

bed-hangings Collective term for fabrics draped above or around beds. Includes canopies, valances, drapes and coronas.

Biedermeier *See* p.29.

"black stitch" *Embroidery worked in black thread on a white or ivory-coloured ground fabric. Also known as "blackwork".

block-printing *See* *hand-blocking.

braid Decorative woven ribbon made of almost any fibre. Used for trimming and edging seams, especially on upholstered furniture.

brocade Heavyweight fabric with elaborately figured patterns raised against a ground cloth by the addition of supplementary *wefts.

brocatelle A variant of *damask, with raised areas of pattern.

Brussels carpet A flat-weave carpet woven from *linen and *worsted with a looped, uncut pile. Typically decorated with bold patterns in two or three colours (but sometimes more).

bullion fringe *See* p.197.

buttonhole stitch A looped outline stitch used to finish the raw edges of fabric, and to create straight or curved lines in embroidery patterns.

C

calico A *plain-weave cotton fabric, originally from India but also produced in the West from the 17th century. Naturally cream-coloured, but can also be bleached white, dyed and printed with motifs and patterns.

cambric A fine, slightly stiff, plain-weave cotton fabric.

campaign fringe *See* p.191.

canvas A coarse, hardwearing fabric woven from fibres of hemp or flax. It can be unbleached, bleached white or dyed.

cartouche A decorative panel consisting of a scroll-shaped frame with a plain, decorated or inscribed centre. Much used in *Renaissance, *Baroque and *Rococo decoration.

casein paint *See* *milk paint.

chenille "Caterpillar" in French. A velvet-like fabric woven from a soft, fuzzy-textured woven yarn of natural or synthetic fibre.

chequer A geometric pattern consisting of regularly spaced squares of alternating colour.

chevrons V-shaped motifs, traditionally symbolizing water and lightning. Usually stacked singly in a vertical series or strung together horizontally to form a zig-zag.

chiaroscuro Originally a fine-art technique employing shades of black, grey and white to introduce areas of light and shade (and therefore a sense of depth and perspective) into a painting. Since the 17th century also used on fabrics and wallpapers.

chiffonier A wooden cupboard with twin doors, surmounted by drawers and a flat top sometimes supporting one or two shelves.

chimera A fire-breathing creature from classical mythology with the head, mane and legs of a lion, the body of a goat, the tail of a dragon and the wings of an eagle.

chinoiserie Western adaptations of traditional Chinese artefacts and styles of ornament.

Classical style Revivals of the principles and forms of ancient Greek and Roman architecture and ornament. There have been numerous reinterpretations and revivals, beginning with the late 14th- to late 16th-century *Renaissance, when illustrated treatises, engravings and pattern books of the monuments and ruins of the Roman Empire first became widely available. Notable and influential 17th-century examples include the architecture of Perrault and Mansart in France, and Inigo Jones in England – the latter inspired by the work of Palladio (*see* *Palladianism). During the 18th century, the classical vocabulary was expanded (and better understood) following excavations at Pompeii and Herculaneum. This resulted in the *Neo-classicism of *Adam style, *Empire style, *Federal style and the *Greek Revival. Late 19th- and early 20th-century Classicism took the form of various *Renaissance, *Baroque and *Empire revivals, while 20th-century *Modernism was also partly inspired by classical forms.

coir Fibre made from coconut husks and woven into matting.

Colonial style The styles of architecture and decoration prevalent in the North American colonies during the 17th and 18th centuries. The primary sources of inspiration were contemporary or recent English and, to a lesser extent, European designs (*see* pp.14–21).

combing A *distressed paint finish that involves dragging a comb through a wet *glaze to produce vertical, horizontal or wavy stripes that allow a contrasting-coloured ground coat to ghost through. Sometimes employed in woodgraining.

Constructivism An early 20th-century Russian style of architecture and design, based on the principles of utilitarian simplicity and logical use of materials, notably glass and metal, in construction and decoration.

cord A form of rope, of various thicknesses, made from twisted threads (of any fibre). Primarily used for *tie-backs and as a trim on upholstered seating.

corduroy A pile fabric (*see* pp.70–75) with regularly spaced, parallel ridges (or ribs).

cornice A decorative moulding used to cover the join between the walls and the ceiling.

cotton Lightweight fabric woven from spun fibres from the boll (the fruit) of the cotton plant.

cotton duck *See* p.59.

crewelwork *See* p.113.

Cubism Abstract art movement of the early 20th century that analysed the interrelation of forms. In practice, several views of the subject were combined and superimposed on one another to provide an account of the entire structure of the subject, rather than simply one view of it.

cypher *See* p.93.

D

dado Lower section of a wall, running from floor to waist height, the latter often defined by a wooden or plaster dado rail. Also *see* *tripartite division.

damask *See* pp.76–85.

damascening A decorative technique, originally applied to metalwork, in which gold, silver and copper are inlaid in *arabesque patterns into base metal. Developed in the Near East, it was brought in the 15th century to Europe where the patterns were also applied to other decorative media.

deal Collective term for softwoods (pine and fir) used in the construction of furniture and architectural fixtures and fittings.

delftware Pottery made in England from the late 17th century, in imitation of the Dutch *tin-glazed earthenwares named after the town of Delft, the principal centre of production. Typical decoration included *chinoiserie* and European (mostly Dutch) landscapes.

dentils *Classical ornament consisting of a row of small, regularly spaced blocks. Originally applied along a *cornice, but from the early 17th century also applied to furniture.

Deutscher Werkbund An association of manufacturers, architects, artists and designers founded in Munich, Germany, in 1907. Its purpose was to create a national style of art, architecture and design without any stylistic imitation and based on sound principles of construction. Their ideas were taken over by the *Bauhaus during the 1920s.

diaper patterns Collective term for patterns incorporating a geometric framework, such as *latticework or *trelliswork.

distemper Alternative English term for whitewash: a water-based paint made from whiting (ground chalk) and animal glue. Forerunner of modern latex emulsion paints.

distressed finishes Collective term for paint finishes, mostly derived from fine art, in which semi-translucent paints or *glazes are applied over a contrasting-coloured, opaque ground coat, and then distressed while wet to produce patterns and subtle gradations of colour over a surface. *See*: *combing, *dragging, *ragging, *spattering, *sponging and *stippling.

dobby A mechanical attachment for a loom that facilitated the production of patterns made up of regularly repeated small motifs, particularly geometric shapes. Invented in the early 19th century.

documentary fabrics *See* p.117.

dogtooth A star-shaped motif, developed from the *nailhead, applied in regular repeats and popular in *Gothic and *Renaissance decoration.

dragging A *distressed paint finish that involves dragging a brush through a wet glaze in parallel sweeps to produce a striped finish in simulation of the figuring and grain of wood.

drawboy Type of loom, named after the weaver's assistant (a young boy) who operated the harness that raised the *warp threads when weaving patterns. Introduced into Europe from the Near East during the *Middle Ages, and a forerunner of the *Jacquard loom.

E

earthenware Porous (unless glazed) pottery produced by firing earth or clays at low temperatures.

egg-and-dart A decorative moulding consisting of alternating egg and V shapes. Originated in *classical Greek architecture.

egg tempera A paint made by mixing powder pigments with linseed oil, water and egg yolk. Primarily used on furniture.

embroidery Decorative stitching applied to the surface of a fabric.

Empire style *See* pp.29–33.

encaustic tiles *Earthenware tiles patterned with inlays of coloured clay *slips.

enfield An *heraldic beast, with the body of a dog, the head, hindquarters and tail of a fox and the claws of an eagle.

F

Federal style The predominant style of architecture and decoration in America between 1776, following the Declaration of Independence, and *c.*1830. Initially based on *Adam style, but superseded by the adoption of *Empire style – in turn, gradually supplanted by the *Greek Revival.

felt A dense cloth made from compressed wool or animal fur.

fêtes galantes Pictorial decoration showing fashionably dressed men and women in romantic landscapes. Originated in mid-18th-century France, and widely used in *Rococo style.

field The section of a wall that extends down from the *cornice or *frieze to the top of the *dado. Also *see* *tripartite division.

flame stitch *See* p.155.

fleur-de-lis A stylized three- or five-petal lily. Originally a symbol of purity, the motif has been used since the early *Middle Ages, notably in *heraldic ornament.

flock Wallpaper with a raised, textured pattern formed by sprinkling fine particles of *wool (or other fibres) over the paper. These stick to an adhesive applied to the paper in the shape of the pattern.

floorcloth A floorcovering made from *canvas stiffened with linseed oil, and then either painted or *stencilled (often to resemble more expensive floorcoverings such as carpet, *parquet or tiles).

formalized *See* *stylized.

French knots Decorative embroidery knots worked on the show side of a fabric to create textured dots of colour.

frieze Section of wall extending from the ceiling or *cornice down to the top of the *field. Also *see* *tripartite division.

fringe A trimming for upholstery and curtains. Consists of threads or decorative shapes made from materials such as fabric, wood, glass or metal, hung from a heading (such as *braid).

fustian Collective term for a group of coarse, usually patterned fabrics woven from *wool, *worsted, or *cotton and wool.

G

gaufrage French for stamping, and a method of embossing patterns on to the surface of fabrics with heated metal rollers. Often applied to velvets.

galloon A decorative tape or ribbon primarily used to disguise the stitched or glued seams between joined sections of fabric.

gimp A type of *braid traditionally made from strands of *silk, *worsted or *cotton, plaited or twisted around a cord or wire.

gingham A light *cotton fabric with a geometric check pattern of two alternating colours on a white or off-white ground.

glaze In ceramics, a clear or coloured vitreous coating fired over the body of the object. In painting, a semi-translucent paint applied over an opaque ground. (Also *see* *distressed finishes.)

Gothic The predominant style of architecture and ornament during the *Middle Ages. Also *see* p.13.

Gothic Revival A late 18th- and 19th-century revival of *Gothic architectural forms and ornament.

Gothick *See* p.19.

grass cloth *See* p.207.

Greek key pattern A regular repeat of interlocking right-angled and vertical lines. Used as a border ornament in *Classical architecture and decoration.

Greek Revival *See* p.61.

grisaille A *trompe l'oeil* technique in which figures and patterns are rendered in shades of black, grey and white to produce a three-dimensional effect.

grotesques Decorations based on ancient Roman wall paintings (*grottesche*) discovered in buried ruins in Rome in the late 15th century. Subsequently also applied to ceramics, fabrics and wallpapers. Typical motifs included animals, birds and fishes. Grotesques provided the inspiration for 18th-century, Neo-classical *arabesques.

grotto ornament Decorative elements, including stalactite- and shell-encrusted ceilings and walls, water cascades and pools of ornamental fishes, frogs, lizards and snakes. Originally used in ancient Roman grottoes. Revived in the 17th and 18th centuries.

guilloche A decorative repeat of interlacing curved bands, sometimes forming circles embellished with floral motifs. Used in *Classical ornament.

H

hand-blocking *See* p.235.

half-tester A bed with an overhead canopy extending from the headboard to partway along the bed.

hemp Coarse fabric woven from fibres of plants such as *Cannabis sativa*. The fibres can also be twisted and plaited into rope.

heraldic motifs *See* p.95.

herbals Illustrated accounts of plants. Circulated in Europe during the late *Middle Ages and the *Renaissance.

herringbone Geometric pattern consisting of alternating diagonal lines similar in appearance to the spine and ribs of a herring fish.

hieroglyphics Picture characters developed by the ancient Egyptians and accommodated within Classical Roman ornament.

holland Generic term for fine-woven linen cloth, available unbleached, bleached white, dyed or patterned (usually with stripes), and glazed or unglazed. Produced since the 16th century, notably for upholstery and window blinds.

I, J

ikat Indonesian fine cotton or silk fabric decorated with blocks, circles or stripes softened by a vegetable-dyeing process that blends the edges of the colours into one another.

indiennes *See* p.132.

Iznik pottery *Earthenware of Turkish origin. Either *tin-glazed or coated with white *slip. Decorated with brightly coloured designs.

Jacquard loom A mechanical loom, invented in the early 19th century. Did away with the need for a *drawboy by employing a system of punch-cards (similar to a piano roll) to control the harness mechanism that raised the *warp threads during weaving. Now often computer-controlled.

japonaiserie English, European and American furniture, ceramics, metalwares, wallpapers and fabrics decorated in the style of imported Japanese equivalents. Typical motifs include blossoms, chrysanthemums, bamboo, exotic birds and animals, and *diaper patterns. Especially fashionable during the last quarter of the 19th century.

jewelled strapwork *See* *strapwork.

jute Fibre derived from Asian plants. Woven into a floor matting.

L

lacquerware *Oriental furniture and wooden artefacts coated with numerous polished layers of sap of the lacquer tree. Untreated, the lacquer dries to a lustrous black colour. However, it can also be dyed various colours, notably red, and inlaid with shells or decorative powders. European and American pieces have also been produced, in imitation of the oriental originals.

lambrequin A stiff, shaped *pelmet similar in shape to a horse's harness. First used in the 17th century; in the 18th and 19th, it was often extended over halfway down the sides of the window.

latticework A grid-like design made up of open diamond shapes. The pattern for leading in late 16th-century glazed windows. Also worked in stone or wood as an architectural and furniture embellishment, and used as a pattern on ceramics, fabrics, wallpapers and metalwares.

limewash *See* p.289.

linen Strong fabric woven from fibres of flax plant stalks. Mostly used for bedsheets, pillowcases, tablecloths and upholstery.

linenfold panelling Wooden panelling in which the individual panels are carved to resemble the vertical folds of draped linen.

lit-en-bateau French term meaning "boat bed". A bed with outwardly curving wooden head- and foot-boards (of equal height), their shape approximating to the bow and stern of a boat.

lustreware Ceramics or glass wares with a metallic sheen, produced by firing them with a thin coating of metallic *glaze.

M

madras Brightly coloured checked and *plaid *cotton or *silk cloth from Madras in India.

Manchester velvet A *cotton velvet with a pile that simulated the sheen of expensive silk velvets. Made in a wide range of colours and patterns (woven or *gaufrage*). Manufactured in Manchester, England, during the late 18th century and for most of the 19th. Popular in Britain, Europe and America.

marquetry *See* p.369.

matelassé *See* p.85.

medieval style *See* pp.12–13.

Middle Ages Historical period extending from the fall of the Western Roman Empire in the 5th century AD to the beginning of the Renaissance in the 15th century.

milk paint *See* p.290.

mille fleurs French for a thousand flowers. A flower-studded pattern originally used on medieval pictorial tapestries. Favoured flowers, naturalistically depicted, include roses, anemones, pinks and violas.

Modernism *See* pp.49–52.

moiré *See* p.65.

monochrome One-colour (or shades of one colour).

moquette A woollen velvet, either plain or patterned, the patterns either woven or *gaufrage*. Used for upholstery and carpeting.

moresques Alternative name for *arabesque patterns from the late 16th to the early 17th centuries.

mosaic A pattern constructed from small pieces of coloured stone, ceramic or glass. Originally used in Roman architecture.

mottle tiles Tiles decorated with spots of varying shades of colour. Introduced in the 1920s.

mullions Vertical bars used to divide windows into sections.

muslin A lightweight, *plain-weave cotton gauze. Either left plain or patterned with motifs.

N, O

nailheads Small pyramid-shaped motifs, often regularly repeated to create an overall pattern.

naturalistic Realistic depictions of organic or inorganic forms.

Neo-classical style *See* p.22.

noil *Silk fabric with a shimmery surface created by the presence of tiny balls made from the waste products of spun silk mixed with *cotton or wool.

ogival Pointed arch formed by pairs of serpentine-shaped curves.

oil cloth *See* *floorcloth.

Op Art A 20th-century style of art and decoration in which geometric forms are precisely arranged so that the movement of the observer's eye, or loss of focus, creates an illusion of movement in the painting or pattern.

organza A fine, *plain-weave, sheer *cotton fabric. Produced either plain or printed with motifs.

oriental Collective term used in the West for Eastern artefacts and styles of decoration and ornament. Includes Arabian, Chinese, Indian, Japanese, Persian and Turkish styles.

P, Q

paisley *See* p.154

Palladianism *See* pp.18–23.

palmette Foliate motif loosely based on a formalized palm leaf. Often indistinguishable from the *anthemion and much used in *Classical decoration.

parquetry *See* p.363.

passementerie Collective term for decorative trimmings applied to soft furnishings. Includes, ribbons, bows, braids, tassels and fringes.

pastoral Romanticized imagery of life in the countryside. Also *see* *Picturesque.

paterae Oval- or circular-shaped form or motif based on dishes or wine holders used in religious ceremonies. Usually decorated with a stylized flower and/or fluting. In Neo-classical ornament often designed as *rosettes.

pelmet Fabric-covered wooden fitting, or a stiffened section of fabric, fixed above a window and designed to conceal the curtain pole and the tops of the curtains.

petit point Form of *embroidery using very fine, small stitches.

photogravure A method of machine-printing wallpaper using metal rollers photochemically engraved with tiny cells or dots that together make up the design. Coloured inks are scraped into the cells and the paper is then forced between the rollers and a rubber cylinder, which forces the surface of the paper into the cells to take up the inks.

picot A decorative furnishing trim that is made up of small loops of thread.

Picturesque A late 18th- and early 19th-century taste for *pastoral imagery combined with theatrical architectural forms (especially *Gothick).

plaid A *plain- or *twill-weave cloth, such as Scottish tartan, with a pattern of intersecting stripes in both the *warp and the *weft.

plain weave A simple weave in which the *warp and the *weft yarns cross at right angles to each other, are spaced at roughly equal intervals and the wefts are passed alternately over and under the warps in one direction and vice versa in the other direction. Also known as "tabby" weave.

plush A velvet-like fabric, but with a longer, less dense pile. Mostly used for upholstery.

point-paper Paper used for designing carpets. Divided into small squares, these being further divided into tiny blocks – each block representing one tuft in the pile of the carpet.

Pointillism Style of painting, developed in France during the late 19th century, in which images are gradually built up through the application of small dots of colour. In the 20th century, also applied to fabrics and wallpapers.

polychromatic Multi-coloured.

polyester Durable, crease-resistant, synthetic fibre.

pombaline A form of tile decoration prevalent in Portugal during the 18th century, in which individual tiles are decorated with a diagonal band of foliage so that a *trellis pattern is formed when the tiles are placed together.

Pop Art An art movement of the 1960s, producing graphic images of everyday figures and objects using techniques employed in film, television and advertising.

poplin Lightweight fabric traditionally woven with fine *silk *warps covering coarser *worsted *wefts to produce a ribbed effect.

portière A curtain designed to be hung over an archway or door.

Post-Modernism An architectural and design movement that began in the mid-1960s as a reaction to the plain, unadorned forms of Modernism, and revived traditional *Classical forms of ornament.

powder ground Tile decoration created by *spattering fine sprays of pigment through a stencil.

powdered ornament Patterns consisting of evenly spaced scatterings of small motifs such as flower sprigs and stars. Originated in *heraldic ornament.

print room *See* p.245.

putti Images of children based on cherubs and the infant attendants of Cupid or Eros (gods of classical mythology).

quarries Small panes of glass, usually diamond-shaped, supported by *latticework leading in 16th-century glazed windows.

quarry tile An unglazed floor tile made from fired clay.

R

ragging or **rag-rolling** A *distressed paint finish that involves brushing a semi-translucent glaze over an opaque, contrasting-coloured ground coat and dabbing it with a rag to remove random patches of glaze.

Regency *See* pp.29–35.

relief tiles Tiles decorated with a moulded pattern that stands proud of the surface.

Renaissance Historical period and a term used to describe the movement in art, architecture, design and ornament that originated in Italy in the late 14th century and spread across Europe during the course of the next 200 years. At its heart lay a revival of the architecture and ornament of ancient Rome and Greece (*see* *Classical style).

rep *Plain-weave, ribbed fabric mainly used for upholstery. Made from *silk, *wool, or silk and wool, and sometimes *cotton.

rocaille A form of ornament prevalent in *Rococo style. Based on asymmetrical rock and shell forms found in *grotto decoration.

Rococo *See* p.19.

rosette A circular, formalized floral ornament of Mesopotamian and ancient Greek origin, widely employed in *Classical decoration since the Renaissance. Also used to describe any circular ornament with decorative elements, such as fluting, radiating from its centre.

rush Grass-like, marshland plant, the dried stalks of which are plaited into strips and sewn together to form floor matting.

S

sanitary papers *See* p.263.

sash window A window made of glazed wooden frames (sashes) that slide up and down in vertical grooves by means of counterbalanced weights.

saturated colour Dense, opaque colour, as opposed to thin, semi-transparent colour.

screen printing A method of transferring a design on to fabric or paper by squeezing dyes or inks through a mesh screen placed on the surface. The screen is masked in those areas where a colour is not required for the design.

scrolling foliage Naturalistic plant forms presented in abstract, curving lines (*see* p.147).

seersucker Originally an Indian striped fabric of mixed *silk and *cotton, but from the 17th century also manufactured in the West. Characterized by a rippled or puckered texture formed by weaving the cotton *warps at a looser tension than the silk *wefts.

shellac A transparent varnish with a red-brown tint, made from a resin secreted on the twigs of trees by Asian lac insects.

silk Luxury cloth woven from the shiny, smooth filaments spun from the cocoons of the silkworm.

singerie From the French for monkey, and a style of pictorial decoration showing monkey figures engaged in human activities (often set within *scrolling foliage or *bandwork). Popular in *Rococo interiors.

sisal A fibre produced from the leaf of the Mexican agave plant. Woven into rope or floor matting.

slip A creamy mixture of clay and water used to decorate pottery. Also a fascia, usually of marble or glazed tiles, set into a fireplace.

slub silk Raw silk fabric with a textured surface produced by incorporating small flecks of the silkworm cocoon in the weave.

Spanish stitch Embroidery characterized by naturalistic floral, fruit and insect patterns.

spattering A *distressed paint finish that involves flicking flecks of wet *glaze from the bristles of a brush over an opaque, contrasting-coloured ground coat to create a pattern of random specks of colour. Used to simulate stones such as porphyry and granite.

sponging *Distressed paint finish that involves dabbing a sponge over a *wet glaze applied to a contrasting coloured ground coat. The resulting pattern of random specks and gradations of colour is often incorporated in *faux* marble and stone finishes.

stem stitch An overlapping embroidery stitch particularly suited to producing curving lines, and so often employed for plant-form patterns (especially florals).

stencilling A technique for applying motifs and patterns to a surface by dabbing paints, glazes or dyes through cut-outs made in a stencil (a thin card usually made of oiled paper, but sometimes wood, metal or plastic).

stippling *Distressed paint finish that involves tapping the bristle tips of a brush over wet glazes applied to an opaque, contrasting-coloured ground coat. Used to blend different coloured glazes and to create subtle shading and gradations of colour.

strapwork Form of ornament consisting of twisted and intertwined bands (similar in appearance to strips of leather or ribbons). Sometimes combined with *arabesques or serving as the framework for *grotesques. Also often studded with *rosettes, *nailheads or faceted jewel-like forms – the latter known as jewelled strapwork.

strié A mottled effect produced on the surface of a fabric by dyeing the yarns with two different colours before weaving.

stucco A fine cement or plaster made from sand, slaked lime and gypsum. Applied to the surface of walls, mouldings and other architectural ornaments. By the 19th century, generally used as a term for exterior rendering.

stylized Non-*naturalistic depictions of organic or inorganic forms, the original subject matter merely providing inspiration for the final design.

swag Both a loop of drapery and a pendant garland made up of, or depicting, flowers, vegetables, fruit, leaves or shells.

swag-and-tail A style of hanging curtains in which the main body of the fabric is looped horizontally along the top of a window or door, and the ends, or tails, are allowed to hang down at the sides.

Swedish style In the 20th-century, a simple style of interior decoration characterized by the use of muted colours such as cobalt blue, grey and white, restrained ornamentation and the extensive use of natural materials, notably wood and glass. However, in the 18th century, Swedish "Gustavian" style based on *Rococo was far more elaborate.

T

taffeta A firm, closely woven *silk or *linen fabric with an identical glossy surface on both sides.

tassel *See* p.192-195.

terracotta A red-coloured *earthenware, usually unglazed.

terrazzo A decorative finish for walls and floors, made of chips of marble or other stones set into mortar and then polished smooth.

tesserae The small cubes of coloured stone, ceramic or glass used to make *mosaic patterns.

ticking *See* p.161.

tie-back A length of rope, *cord or fabric used to secure a curtain to one side of a window.

tin-glaze A glassy white *glaze made by adding tin oxide to lead glaze. Used to decorate pottery such as *delftware.

toile de Jouy *See* p.135.

tongue-and-groove A method of jointing boards, in which the edge of one board has a tongue, or lip, that fits into a groove cut into the edge of the next board.

tours de cheminées Plain or decorative lengths of fabric hung from the leading edge of the mantelshelf of a fireplace.

transfer printing A method of printing designs on ceramics by first printing an engraved design on paper, using an oil-based ink. The paper is then laid over the body of the ceramic and burnt off during firing, to leave an outline design (which can be coloured in by hand).

Tree of Life An English pattern developed during the late 16th century, possibly from ancient Persian or Indian ornament, and symbolizing the life force. Much used on fabrics, it usually consisted of a central trunk, branches, sinuous stems and tendrils, fantastical flowers and exotic fruits, all woven around exotic birds and insects.

trelliswork A crisscross wooden support for plants, and a decorative pattern devised in imitation of it. Notably popular in *medieval, *Regency and *Arts and Crafts decoration.

tripartite division The horizontal division of a wall into three sections – *frieze, *field and *dado – for the purposes of decoration.

triquetra A three-lobed, triangular motif made up of interlaced crescent shapes. Of Celtic origin.

triskele A Y-shaped sun motif, originally used in ancient Greek and Celtic ornament.

trompe l'oeil French for "trick the eye". A decorative technique in which paints or dyes are applied to stone, plaster, wood, fabric or paper to create the appearance, form (and often texture) of three-dimensional scenes or objects. Typical examples included marbling, woodgraining, **grisaille* and architectural components or vistas rendered in perspective.

tube-lining A method of decorating tiles in which raised lines of *slip are piped on to the surface through a thin tube. The lines define the pattern by separating subsequently applied coloured glazes.

tufting A technique used in the mass-production of carpets, in which a pile is created by sewing tufted yarn on to a ready-woven backing fabric (the backing is then coated in latex to secure the yarn).

tulle Fine, *muslin-like material made of silk. First produced in France during the 18th century.

turkeywork An inexpensive woollen pile fabric produced in imitation of expensive Turkish and Persian carpets. Used for upholstery and table and floor coverings during the 17th century.

tweed A coarse-textured, *twill-weave cloth made from different coloured woollen yarns.

twill-weave A variation of a *plain-weave. Has a diagonal grain produced by floating the *weft threads diagonally over and under groups of, rather than alternating, *warps.

V, W, Y, Z

valance A short, soft curtain, either used at the top of a window to hide the curtain pole and the tops of the main curtains, or hung from the canopy or base of a bed.

velour Heavyweight, velvet-like fabric with a thick pile that lies in one direction. Woven from wool, cotton or synthetic fibres.

verdure French for "greenness", and for tapestry with a green colour cast and displaying predominantly plant-form imagery.

vinyl A man-made polymer used in resin form to produce sheet flooring. Also used for vinyl wallpapers (*see* p.243).

voile A fine, crisp, sheer fabric woven from *cotton, *silk, *wool or synthetic fibres.

warp The threads that run lengthways in a piece of cloth. They are set and spaced on a loom and the *wefts are woven through them from side to side.

water leaf A motif consisting of a broad, blade-shaped leaf with crimped edges and curling tip. Probably based on the waterlily leaf and widely used in *Gothic and *Neo-classical ornament.

weft The threads in a piece of cloth that are woven from side to side through the *warps.

Wiener Werkstätte A studio founded in Vienna, Austria, in 1907. Specialized in hand made fabrics, furniture and metalwork in the *Art Nouveau style.

Wilton Generic name for a type of carpet first produced in Wilton, England, in the mid-18th century. Similar to *Brussels carpet, but with a cut pile.

wool A yarn spun from the fibrous coat of an animal, most often a sheep or a goat.

worsted Smooth, strong woollen cloth made from carded and combed wool yarn.

ypotryll An *heraldic beast with the head of a boar, the body of an antelope and the tail of a lion.

zillij Traditional North African *mosaic tile work.

Directory

All items featured in the book are available from a store, a distributor or by mail order. Some manufacturers will ship overseas. If a supplier in your area is not listed, please contact the company for details of local availability. Company websites offer a wealth of information and some provide online ordering. Before visiting suppliers, it is recommended that you telephone or check the website, as not all outlets are open to the public, and some may have limited hours or require an appointment.

For assistance in locating an interior designer, contact:

American Society of Interior Designers
608 Massachusetts Avenue NE
Washington DC 20002-6006
Tel: (202) 546 3480
Fax: (202) 546 3240
www.asid.org

Canadian Decorators' Association (CDECA)
565 Bryne Drive
Barrie ON L4N 9Y3
Toll-free: 1 866 878 2155
Fax: (705) 722 8355
www.cdeca.com

The Interior Design Society
3910 Tinsley Drive, Suite 101
High Point NC 27265
Toll-free: 1 800 888 9590
Fax: (336) 801 6110
www.interiordesignsociety.org

Interior Designers of Canada
220-6 Adelaide Street East
Toronto ON M5C 1H6
Tel: (416) 594 9310
Fax: (416) 921 3660
www.interiordesigncanada.org

International Interior Design Association (IIDA)
222 Merchandise Mart, Suite 1540
Chicago IL 60654
Tel: (312) 467 1950
www.iida.org

Design Centers

Design centers host a number of manufacturer and designer showrooms in one place. They are generally for trade only, though some allow the public to visit if accompanied by a member of the design trade or by special permission and with an appointment. Prior to visiting a designer showroom, check the website or contact directly for more information.

Canada

AnneStarr Agencies
3–611 Alexander Street
Vancouver BC V6A 1E1
Tel: (604) 254 3376
Fax: (604) 254 3336
annestarr@telus.net
and
160 Pears Avenue, Suite 110
Toronto ON M5R 3P8
Tel: (416) 921 3334

Bilbrough & Co. Ltd.
Designers Walk, Building 2
326 Davenport Road
Toronto ON MR5 1K6
Toll free Tel: 1 800 563 5716
Tel: (416) 960 1611
Fax: (416) 960 5742
www.bilbroughs.com

Designers Gallery
354 Davenport Road
Toronto ON M5R 1K6
Tel: (416) 964 3714
Fax: (416) 964 2015

Designers Walk
168 Bedford Road
Toronto ON M5R 2K9
Toll-free: 1 888 707 9255
Tel: (416) 961 1211
Fax: (416) 928 9683
www.designerswalk.com

Gala/Crescendo
Les Papiers Peints et Tissus Crescendo Inc.
4271 Rue Ste-Catherine West
Montreal QC H3Z 1P7
Tel: (514) 933 0067
Fax: (514) 989 2944
www.crescendogala.com

Primavera
160 Pears Avenue, Suite 210
Toronto ON M5R 1T2
Tel: (416) 921 3334
Fax: (416) 921 3227
www.primavera.ca

Télio & Cie
219 Dufferin Street
Toronto ON M6K 1Y9
Tel: (4160) 532 9444
Fax: (416) 532 0683
www.telio.com
and
1407 rue de la Montagne
Montreal QC HG3 1Z3
Toll-free: 1 800 361 0375
Tel: (514) 842 9116
Fax: (514) 842 3728
and
160 Pears Avenue, Suite 400
Toronto ON M5R 3P8

Tessuti Uno
Designer's Walk, Building 2
320 Davenport Road
Toronto ON M5R 1K6
Tel: (416) 922 0126
Fax: (416) 922 0441

United States

California

Design Pavilion
At 200 Kansas:
200 Kansas Street
San Francisco CA 94103
Tel: (415) 552 2290
Fax: (415) 864 5561
and
At 251 Rhode Island:
251 Rhode Island Street
San Francisco CA 94103
Tel: (415) 558 9925

L.A. Mart
1933 South Broadway
Los Angeles CA 90007
Toll-free: 1 800 526 2784
Tel: (213) 763 5800
Fax: (213) 763 5881
www.lamart.com

Laguna Design Center
23811 Aliso Creek Road
Laguna Niguel CA 92677
Tel: (949) 643 2929
Fax: (949) 643 8316
www.lagunadesigncenter.com

Pacific Design Center
8687 Melrose Avenue, M60
West Hollywood CA 90069
Tel: (310) 657 0800
Fax: (310) 652 8576
www.pacificdesigncenter.com

San Francisco Design Center
Two Henry Adams Street
San Francisco CA 94103
Tel: (415) 490 5800
Fax: (415) 490 5885
www.sfdesigncenter.com

San Francisco Mart
1355 Market Street
San Francisco CA 94103
Tel: (415) 241 7958
Fax: (415) 658 0580
www.sfmart.com

Showplace Square West
550 15th Street
San Francisco CA 94103
Tel: (415) 626 8257
Fax: (415) 626 8265
www.showplacesquarewest.com

Colorado

Denver Design Center
595 S. Broadway
Denver CO 80209
Tel: (303) 733 2455
Fax: (303) 777 6104
www.denverdesign.com

Denver Merchandise Mart
The Interior Resource Center
451 East 58th Avenue
Denver CO 80216
Tel: (303) 292 6278
Fax: (303) 297 8473
www.denvermart.com

Florida

Design Center of the Americas (DCOTA)
1855 Griffin Road
Dania Beach FL 33004
Tel: (954) 920 7997
Fax: (954) 920 8066
www.dcota.com

Miami Inter Design Centre I
4100 NE 2nd Avenue
Miami FL 33137
Tel: (305) 576 7571
info@miamiDesignCentre.com

Miami Inter Design Centre II
4141 NE 2nd Avenue
Miami FL 33137
Tel: (305) 576 5515
Fax: (305) 573 9931
info@miamiDesignCentre.com

Trade Only Design Library, Inc.
1150 Kapp Drive
Clearwater FL 33765
Toll Free: 1 800 631 3111
Tel: (727) 441 2060
Fax: (727) 4412065
www.todl.com
(Trade-only online product research and specification database.)

Georgia

Americas Mart Atlanta
240 Peachtree Street NW
Atlanta GA 30303
Tel: (404) 220 3000
Fax: (404) 220 3030
www.americasmart.com

Atlanta Decorative Arts Center
349-351 Peachtree Hills Avenue NE
Atlanta GA 30305
Tel: (404) 231 1720
Fax: (404) 239 9109
www.adacdesigncenter.com

Illinois

The Merchandise Mart, Chicago
Chicago IL 60054
Toll-free: 1 800 677 6278
www.merchandisemart.com

Massachusetts

Boston Design Center and Outlet
One Design Center Place
Boston MA 02210
Tel: (617) 338 5062
Fax: (617) 482 8449
www.bostondesign.com

Michigan

Michigan Design Center
1700 Stutz Drive
Troy MI 48084
Tel: (248) 649 4772
Fax: (248) 649 1224
www.michigandesign.com

Minnesota

Minneapolis Design and Home Furnishings Mart
International Market Square
275 Market Street
Minneapolis MN 55405
Tel: (612) 338 6250
Fax: (612) 338 1813

Nevada

Las Vegas Design Center
World Market Center
495 S. Grand Central Parkway
Las Vegas NV 89106
Toll-free: 1 888 416 8600
Fax: (702) 380 0917
www.lasvegasmarket.com

New York

The A&D Building
150 East 58th Street
New York NY 10155
Tel: (212) 644 6555
Fax: (212) 750 1934
www.merchandisemart.com/kbnewyork
(Open to the public.)

The D&D Building
979 Third Avenue
New York NY 10022
Tel: (212) 759 5408
Fax: (212) 751 8130
www.thedanddbuilding.com

Forty-One Madison
The New York Merchandise Mart
41 Madison Avenue
New York NY 10010
Tel: (212) 686 1203
Fax: (212) 779 7105
www.41madison.com

New York Design Center
200 Lexington Avenue
New York NY 10016
Tel: (212) 679 9500
Fax: (212) 447 1669
www.nydc.com

North Carolina

High Point Market Square
305 W. High Street
High Point NC 27260
Tel: (336) 821 1500
Fax: (336) 821 1581
www.mmart.com/highpoint

Ohio

Longworth Hall Design Center
700 West Pete Rose Way
Cincinnati OH 45203
Tel: (513) 721 6000
Fax: (513) 345 8794

Ohio Design Centre
23533 Mercantile Road
Beachwood OH 44122
Tel: (216) 831 1245
Fax: (216) 831 3770
www.ohiodesigncentre.com

Pennsylvania

Marketplace Design Center
2400 Market Street
Philadelphia PA 19103
Tel: (215) 561 5000

Fax: (215) 561 0225
www.marketplacedc.com

Metro Design Center
1206 N. Sherman Street
Allentown PA 18103
Tel: (610) 434 0161
Fax: (610) 437 9111
www.metrodesigncenter.com

Texas

Dallas Design Center
1025 North Stemmons Fwy.
Dallas TX 75207
Tel: (214) 747 2411
Fax: (214) 741 1550

Decorative Center Dallas
1400 Turtle Creek Boulevard
Dallas TX 75207
Tel: (214) 698 1300
Fax: (214) 698 1301
www.decorativecenterdallas.com

Decorative Center of Houston
(Design Center Houston/DCH)
5120 Woodway Drive
Houston TX 77056
Tel: (713) 961 9292
Fax: (713) 963 8603
www.decorativecenter.com

The Resource Center
7026 Old Katy Road
Houston TX 77024
Tel: (713) 864 4735
Fax: (713) 864 2760
www.resourcecenterhouston.com

Washington

Seattle Design Center
5701 Sixth Avenue South
Seattle WA 98108
Toll-free: 1 800 497 7997
Tel: (206) 762 1200
Fax: (206) 767 9162
www.seattledesigncenter.com

Washington D.C.

The Washington Design Center
300 D Street, SW
Washington DC 20024
Tel: (202) 646 6100
Fax: (202) 488 3711
www.merchandisemart.com/dcdesigncenter

United Kingdom

Chelsea Harbour Design Centre
Chelsea Harbour
London SW10 0XE
United Kingdom
Tel: +011 (44) 20 7225 9100
Fax: +011 (44) 20 7352 7868
www.designcentrechelseaharbour.co.uk

A

Aalto Country Colours
8 Railway Street
Newmarket Auckland
New Zealand
Tel: +011 (64) 9 522 2019
Fax: +011 (64) 9 522 2149
www.aaltocolour.com
(Ships worldwide.)

Abbott & Boyd
1/22 Chelsea Harbour
  Design Centre
Chelsea Harbour
London SW10 0XE
United Kingdom
Tel: +011 (44) 20
  7351 9985
Fax: +011 (44) 20
  7823 3127
www.abbottandboyd.co.uk
*(Distributed in USA by
Brunschwig & Fils. Contact
for more details.)*

Ace Hardware Corporation
Paint Division
2200 Kensington Court
Oak Brook IL 60523-2100
Tel: (630) 990 6600
www.acehardware.com
(See website for retailers.)

**Acme Slate & Tile
  Company**
21 Golden Gate Court
Scarborough ON M1P 3A4
Tel: (416) 293 3664
Fax: (416) 293 3232
(Distributor of Kirkstone.)

**Akzo Nobel Decorative
  Coatings Ltd.)**
(see Crown)

Alexander Beauchamp
The Printworks, Hall Lane
Rhos
Wrexham LL14 1TG
United Kingdom
Tel: +011 (44) 19
  7884 4442
Fax: +011 (44) 19
  7884 4448
www.alexanderbeauchamp.com
  and
Alexander Beauchamp
  Wallpapers
Watkins & Fonthill
The D&D Building
Suite 1732
979 Third Avenue
New York NY 10022
Tel: (336) 299 7377
info@fonthill-ltd.com
*(Distributed in USA by
Fonthill. Contact for
Canadian availability.)*

**Allback Organic Linseed
  Paints from Sweden**
(Viking Sales, Inc.)
7710 Victor-Mendon Road
Victor NY 14564
Tel: (585) 924 8070
www.solventfreepaint.com

*(Online shopping only.
Product similar to Holkham
Linseed Paints.)*

The Alternative Flooring Co.
Unit 3b, Stephenson Close
East Portway Industrial Estate
Andover
Hampshire SP10 3RU
United Kingdom
Tel: +011 (44) 12 6433 5111
Fax: +011 (44) 12 6433 6445
www.alternative-flooring.co.uk

Altfield Limited
2/22 Chelsea Harbour
  Design Centre
Chelsea Harbour
London SW10 0XE
United Kingdom
Tel: +011 (44) 20 7351 5893
Fax: +011 (44) 20 7376 5667
www.altfield.com
*(Distributor of van Schelle &
Gurland, Maya Romanoff,
Blumenthal. Exports
worldwide.)*

Amtico International Inc.
The Amtico Studio
6480 Roswell Road
Atlanta GA 30328
Toll-free: 1 800 268 4260
Tel: (404) 267 1900
Fax: (404) 267 1901
www.amtico.com
(See website for distributors.)

**Andrew Martin
  International Ltd.**
D&D Annex, Suite 111
222 East 59th Street
New York NY 10022
Tel: (212) 688 4498
www.andrewmartin.co.uk
(Also distributed by Lee Jofa.)

AnneStarr Agencies
3–611 Alexander Street
Vancouver BC V6A 1E1
Tel: (604) 254 3376
Fax: (604) 254 3336
annestarr@telus.net
  and
160 Pears Avenue, Suite 110
Toronto ON M5R 3P8
Tel: (416) 921 3334
*(Distributor of David Oliver,
Colefax & Fowler, Cowtan &
Tout, Jane Churchill, Larsen,
Manuel Canovas, Osborne &
Little, Designers Guild,
Liberty, Lorca, Nina
Campbell, Chelsea, Malabar,
Pierre Frey, Nancy Corzine,
Hollly Hunt, Scalamandre.)*

Anna French
343 Kings Road
London SW3 5ES
United Kingdom
Tel: +011 (44) 20 7351 1126
Fax: +011 (44) 20 7351 0421
www.annafrench.co.uk
*(Distributed in USA by
Sanderson, in Canada by
AnneStarr Agencies.)*

Ann Sacks Tile and Stone
5 East 16th Street
New York NY 10003
Toll-free: 1 800 278 8453
Fax: (212) 463 0067
www.annsacks.com
*(See website for products
and showrooms. Distributed
in Canada by Yaletown
Tileworks.)*

Anne and Robert Swaffer
Bakewell Road
Orton Southgate
Peterborough PE2 6WQ
United Kingdom
Tel: +011 (44) 17 33 37127
Fax: +011 (44) 17 33 371247
www.swaffer.co.uk
*(Distributed in Canada by
Bilbrough & Co. Contact for
other suppliers.)*

Annie Sloan Practical Style
117 London Road
Headington
Oxford OX3 9HZ
United Kingdom
Tel: +011 (44) 18
  6576 8666
www.anniesloan.com
*(Online shopping. Ships
overseas.)*

Anta Interiors (Scotland)
Fearn, Tain
Ross-shire IV20 1XW
United Kingdom
Tel: +011 (44) 18
  6283 2477
Fax: +011 (44) 18
  6283 2616
Trade Tel/Fax:
  +011 (44) 131 220 1693
www.anta.co.uk
(Online shopping.)

Antico Setificio Fiorentino
50124 Firenze
Via L. Bartolini 4
Italy
Tel: +011 (39) 55 21 38 61
Fax: +011 (39) 55 21 81 74
www.anticosetificio
  fiorentino.it

Anya Larkin
39 West 28th Street
8th Floor
New York NY 10001
Tel: (212) 532 3263
Fax: (212) 532 2854
www.anyalarkin.com

Appel Ltd.
321 Davenport Road
Toronto ON M5R 1K5
Tel: (416) 922 3935
Fax: (416) 921 7029
*(Distributor of Sandberg
Tapeter AB and Ian
Sanderson.)*

Apenn Fabrics
33 Kensington
Park Road
London W11 2EU

United Kingdom
Tel: +011 (44) 20 7792 2457
Fax: +011 (44) 20 7727 4719
(Contact for supplier details.)

Armstrong World Industries
2500 Columbia Ave.
P.O. Box 3001
Lancaster PA 17604
Toll-free: 1 800 233 3823
www.armstrong.com
(See also Bruce Hardwood.)
  and
Armstrong World Industries
  (Canada)
6911 Decarie Blvd.
Montreal PQ H3W 3E5
Toll-free: 1 800 233 3823

Artex
(aka CertainTeed
  Corporation)
P.O. Box 860
750 East Swedesford Road
Valley Forge PA 19482
Tel: (610) 341 7000
Fax: (610) 341 7777
www.bpb-na.com
www.bpbartex.co.uk

Artistic Tile
520 Secaucus Road
Secaucus NJ 07094
Fax: (201) 605 0850
www.artistictile.com
(Online store locator.)
  and
Artistic Tile
New York Showroom:
79 Fifth Avenue
New York NY 10003
Tel: (212) 727 9331
Fax: (212) 727 9883

The Arts & Crafts Home
25a Clifton Terrace
Brighton BN1 3HA
United Kingdom
Tel: +011 (44) 12 7332 7774
Tel: +011 (44) 77 755 3 3453
www.achome.co.uk
(Web-based company.)

Atlas Carpet Mills
2200 Saybrook Avenue
Los Angeles CA 90040
Toll-free Tel: 1 800 367 8188
Toll-free Fax: 1 800 272 8527
Tel: (323) 724 9000
Fax: (323) 724 4526
www.atlascarpetmills.com

Auro Organic Paints
1340-G Industrial Avenue
Petaluma CA 94952
Toll-free: 1 888 302 9352
Tel: (707) 763 0662
Fax: (707) 769 7342
www.auroorganic.co.uk
www.aurousa.com
*(Product similar to Holkham
Linseed Paints.)*

Axminster Carpets Ltd.
6th Floor, 150 East 55th Street
New York NY 10022
Toll-free: 1 800 356 5013

Tel: (212) 421 1050
Fax: (212) 935 6690
www.axminster-carpets.com

B

Baer & Ingram
*(Ceased business in July
2007. Contact by post or
e-mail only.)*
Dragon Works
Leigh on Mendip
Radstock BA3 5QZ
United Kingdom
sales@baer-ingram.co.uk
*(Distributed in USA by Davan
Port Ltd.)*

(H.T.) Barnes Co., Inc.
P.O. Box 1327
Foley AL 36536
Toll-free: 1 800 211 5018
Fax: (251) 943 8310
www.htbarnes.com
*(Supplier of Conso trim,
including Imperial Collection,
Wendy Cushing trims, and
British Trimmings.)*

Beaumont & Fletcher
Unit C21, The Old Imperial
  Laundry
71 Warriner Gardens
London SW11 4XW
United Kingdom
Tel: +011 (44) 207 352 5594
Fax: +011 (44) 207 352 3546
www.beaumontandfletcher.com
*(Distributed in USA by
F. Schumacher & Co.)*

Beauport Wallcoverings
(Blue Mountain
  Wallcoverings Inc.)
1400 Graham Bell
Boucherville QC J4B 6E5
Tel: (450) 641 4477
Fax: (450) 641 4585
  and
Blue Mountain
  Wallcoverings Inc.
15 Akron Rd
Toronto ON M8W 1T3
Toll-free Tel (Canada):
  1 800 219 2424
Toll-free Fax (Canada):
  1 800 741 2083
Toll-free Tel (USA):
  1 866 563 9872
Toll-free Fax (USA):
  1 800 741 2083
Tel: (416) 251 1678
Fax: (416) 251 8968
www.blmtn.com

Belinda Coote Tapestries
(see Watts of Westminster)

Bellbridge Carpets
5401 Industrial Way
Benicia CA 94510
Toll-free Tel: 1 800 227 3408
Tel: (707) 747 7208
www.bellbridge.com
*(See website to locate
dealers in Canada and USA.)*
  and

Maeve Fegan
767 Lexington Avenue
Suite 402
New York NY 10021
Tel: (212) 355 7053
Fax: (212) 355 6722
  and
Wes Friesen & Associates
31265 Wheel Avenue
Suite 206
Abbotsford BC V2T2X1
Tel: (604) 855 5186
Fax: (604) 855 6071

Bennett Silks
Crown Royal Park
Higher Hillgate
Stockport SK1 3HB
United Kingdom
Tel: +011 (44) 16
  1476 8600
Fax: +011 (44) 16
  1480 5385
www.bennett-silks.co.uk
*(Distributed in USA by Elijah
Slocum, in Canada by
Bilbrough & Co.)*

Bennison Fabrics
The Fine Arts Building
232 East 59th Street
New York NY 10022
Tel: (212) 223 0373
Fax: (212) 223 0655
www.bennisonfabrics.com
  and
Bennison Fabrics
8264 Melrose Avenue
Los Angeles CA 90046
Tel: (323) 653 7277
Fax: (323) 653 723
*(Also distributed by Ainsworth
Noah, De Sousa Hughes,
George Cameron Nash,
Monica James, and John
Brooks. Contact for
Canadian suppliers.)*

Bentley & Spens
1–2 Mornington Street
London NW1 7QD
United Kingdom
Tel/Fax: +011 (44) 20
  7387 7374
www.fabenglish.com
*(Online catalog. Distributed in
USA by Christopher Hyland
and Bergamo. Will ship
overseas.)*

Bergamo Fabrics Inc.
256 Washington St.
3rd Floor
Mount Vernon NY 10553
Tel: (914) 665 0800
Fax: (914) 665 7900
www.bergamofabrics.com
*(Distributed in USA by Holly
Hunt, Donghia, I.D.
Collection, John Brooks and
others. See website.
Distributor of Bentley &
Spens, Maya Romanoff,
Sahco Hesslein. See website
for all showroom locations.)*
  and
New York Showroom:

The D&D Building
Suite 1705
979 Third Avenue
New York NY 10022
Tel: (212) 888 3333
Fax: (212) 888 3837

Berger Paints
Berger House
129 Park Street
Kolkata 700017
India
Tel: +011 (91) 33
  2229 9724
Fax: +011 (91) 33
  2249 9009
www.bergerpaints.com
  and
Lewis Berger Overseas
  Holdings
77 Marlowes
Hemel Hempstead
Hertfordshire HP1 1LF
United Kingdom
Tel: +011 (44) 1442 260075
Fax: +011 (44) 1442 254600
www.apaints.com/
  BergerInternational.jsp
*(Limited distribution. Contact
for details.)*

Bernard Thorp & Co.
53 Chelsea Manor Street
London SW3 5RZ
United Kingdom
Tel: +011 (44) 20
  7352 5745
Tel: +011 (44) 20
  7352 5457
Fax: +011 (44) 20
  7376 3640
www.bernardthorp.co.uk
*(Distributed in USA by Stark
Carpet Corporation.)*

Berti Pavimenti Legno
Via Rettilineo 81
35010 Villa del Conte
Padova
Italy
Tel: +011 (39) 49 93 25011
Fax: +011 (39) 49 93 23639
www.berti.net
*(Contact for details. See
website for USA distributors.)*

Bilbrough & Co.
Designers Walk, Building 2
326 Davenport Road
Toronto ON M5R 1K6
Tel: (416) 960 1611
Fax: (416) 960 5742
www.bilbroughs.com
*(Distributor of Wm. Bennett
Silks, Borderline, Busby &
Busby, Gainsborough Silk
Weaving, Henry Newbery
Trimmings, Imperial, Jason
D'Souza, Malabar Cotton
Company, Marvic Textiles,
Textra, Timney Fowler.)*

Bill Amberg
The Shop
10 Chepstow Road
London W2 5BD
United Kingdom

Tel: +011 (44) 20
7727 3560
Fax: +011 (44) 20
7727 3541
www.billamberg.com

BioShield Paint Co.
3215 Rufina Street
Santa Fe NM 87507
Toll-free: 1 800 621 2591
Fax: (505) 438 0199
www.bioshieldpaint.com
*(Product similar to Holkham
Linseed Paints. Catalogue;
ships in USA and to
Canada.)*

Blackstone Carpets & Rugs
1401 Oak Lawn Avenue
Dallas TX 75207
Tel: (214) 748 1570
Fax: (214) 761 1418
www.blackstonecarpets.com
*(Distributor of Stoddard
carpets, European Wiltons
and others.)*

Blumenthal Printworks
905 S. Broad Street
New Orleans LA 70125-1493
Toll-free USA:
1 800 535 8590
Toll-free Canada:
1 800 654 4832
Fax: (504) 822 2147
www.blumenthalprintworks.com

Boen Hardwood Flooring
Boen Bruk AS
4658 Tveit
Norway
Tel: +011 (47) 3806 6600
Fax: +011 (47) 5806 6601
*(Distributed in USA by
Centaur, in Canada by
Floorworks International,
Nova Hardwood and Coast
Hardwood Floors. Contact
for other suppliers.)*
and
BOEN National Sales (USA)
Toll-free: 1 888 897 0800
and
BOEN Hardwood Flooring
(Canada)
Tel: (276) 638 3723

Bonar Floors Inc.
London Business Centre
Suite 105, The Tea Building
56 Shoreditch High Street
London E1 6JJ
United Kingdom
Tel: +011 (44) 207 033 0335
www.bonarfloors.com
and
365 Walt Sander
Memorial Drive
Newnan GA 30265
Tel: (770) 252 4890
Fax: (770) 252 4894
www.bonarfloors.com

Borderline
Unit 12, 3rd Floor
Chelsea Harbour

Design Centre
London SW10 OXE
United Kingdom
Tel: +011 (44) 20 7823 3567
Fax: +011 (44) 20 7351 7644
www.borderlinefabrics.com
*(Distributed in USA by
Classic Revivals, in Canada
by Bilbrough & Co. See
website for retailers.
Distributor of Lewis & Wood.)*

Bosanquet Ives
Bank Chambers
29 High Street
Ewell
Surrey KT17 1SB
United Kingdom
Tel: +011 (44) 7768
815 745
www.bosanquetives.co.uk
enquiries@bosanquetives.co.uk

Bradbury & Bradbury
940 Tyler St., Studio 12
P.O. Box 155
Benicia CA 94510
Tel: (707) 746 1900
Fax: (707) 745 9417
www.bradbury.com

Brian Yates (Interiors) Ltd.
Lansil Way
Caton Road
Lancaster LA1 3QY
United Kingdom
Sales Tel: +011 (44)
1524 35035
Sales Fax: +011 (44)
1524 32232
Export Tel: +011 (44)
1524 381161
Export Fax: +011 (44)
1524 842233
www.brian-yates.co.uk
*(Distributes Sheila Coombes
collection internationally. Also
distributed in USA by
Sanderson, in Canada by
Télio & Cie.)*

Brintons US Axminster
1856 Artistry Lane
Greenville MS 38702-0827
Tel: (662) 332 1581
Fax: (662) 332 1594
and
Brintons US Axminster
150 East 58th Street
New York NY 10155
Toll-free: 1 800 941 9884
Tel: (212) 832 0121
Fax: (212) 980 1505
www.brintonsusax.com

British Ceramic Tiles
Heathfield
Newton Abbot
Devon TQ12 6RF
United Kingdom
Tel: +011 (44) 1626
834774
Fax: +011 (44) 1626
834775
www.bctltd.co.uk
*(Distributor of Laura Ashley,
Hemingway "Wet", Candy*

*Dartmoor Naturals. Contact
for suppliers.)*

Briwax
Toll-free: 1 800 274 9299
Tel: (212) 504 9299
www.briwax.com
*(Product similar to Rustins.
Online shopping. See
website for retailers selling
product.)*

**Bruce Hardwood and
Laminates**
Armstrong World
Industries, Inc.
P.O. Box 3001
Lancaster PA 17604
Toll-free: 1 800 233 3823
www.bruce.com
*(See website for store
locations.)*

Brunschwig & Fils Inc.
75 Virginia Road
North White Plains
NY 10603
Tel: (914) 684 5800
Fax: (914) 684 5842
www.brunschwig.com
*(See website for
showrooms.)*

Burnside Flooring
31 Sterns Court
Dartmouth NS B3B 1W7
Tel: (902) 468 5576
www.burnsideflooring.com
*(Distributor of Kentucky
Wood Floors.)*

Busby & Busby
The Old Stables
Winterbome Whitchurch
Blandford Forum
Dorset DT11 9AW
United Kingdom
Tel: +011 (44) 1258 881211
Fax: +011 (44) 1258 881351
www.busbyfabric.com
(Contact for distributors.)

Cabot Stains
33360 Central Avenue
Union City CA 94587
Toll-free: 1 800 877 8246
Fax: (978) 462 2720
www.cabotstain.com
(Online dealer locator.)

Candy Tiles
(see British Ceramic Tiles)

Carocim
BP 10
1515, route du Puy Sainte
Réparade — CS 70040
13089 Aix-en-Provence
Cedex 2
France
Tel: +011 (33) 4 4292 2039
Fax: +011 (33) 4 4292 2096
www.carocim.com
(Contact for distributors.)

Carpet Design Solutions
42 Heath Street East
Toronto ON M4T 1S3
Tel/Fax: (416) 966 3332
*(Distributor of Ulster Carpet
Mills.)*

Carpet Innovations
(Clodan Carpets Inc.)
588 Broadway, Space 803
New York NY 10012
Tel: (212) 966 9440
Fax: (212) 941 8467
www.carpetinnovations.com

Carré Tiles
91 quai de Valmy
75010 Paris
France
Tel: +011 (33) 146 07 03 26
Fax: +011 (33) 146 07 37 61
www.ceramiques-carre.com
and
Briare Tile, Inc.
50-I Corbin Avenue
Bayshore NY 11706
Tel: (631) 492 2195
Fax: (631) 492 2196
www.emauxdebriare.com

Cath Kidston
9a Penzance Place
London W11 4PE
United Kingdom
Tel: +011 (44) 20
7221 4248
Fax: +011 (44) 20
7221 4388
www.cathkidston.com
www.cathkidston.co.uk
*(Ships worldwide. Distributed
outside the UK by Designers
Guild.)*

Celia Birtwell
71 Westbourne Park Road
London W2 5QH
United Kingdom
Tel: +011 (44) 20
7221 0877
Fax: +011 (44) 20
7229 7673
www.celiabirtwell.com
(Ships worldwide.)

Centaur Floor Systems
135 Chapala Street
Santa Barbara CA 93101
Tel: (805) 957 0182
Fax: (805) 957 0125
www.centaurfloors.com
*(Supplier of Boen Hardwood
Flooring.)*

**Ceramic Tile Distributors
Association**
800 Roosevelt Road
Building C, Suite 312
Glen Ellyn IL 60137
Toll-free Tel: 1 800 938 283)
Fax: (630) 790 3095
www.ctdahome.org

Cercan Tile Inc.
Designers Walk Building 2
320 Davenport Road
Suite 105

Toronto ON M5R 1K6
Tel: (416) 413 9008
Fax: (416) 413 9652
and
Michigan Design Centre
1700 Stutz Drive
Suite 92-94
Troy MI 48084
Tel: (248) 643 6520
Fax: (248) 643 6523
www.cercantile.com
*(Distributor of Winchester
Tiles. See website for other
locations.)*

Charles Rupert Designs
107-401 Garbally Road
Selkirk Waterfront
Victoria BC V8T 5M3
Tel: (250) 592 4916
Fax: (250) 592 4999
www.charles-rupert.com
Trade only:
www.charlesrupert.biz
*(Distributor of Craven Dunnill
Jackfield, Charles Rupert,
Voysey, William Morris,
Mackintosh and other
Victorian, Arts & Crafts, Art
Nouveau and similar designs.
Distributed in Canada by
Charles Rupert, AnneStarr
Agencies, and Suzanne
Brown and Assoc. Online
catalog. Ships worldwide.)*

Chase Erwin
River House
53 Lydden Grove
London SW18 4LW
United Kingdom
Tel: +011 (44) 20
8875 1222
Fax: +011 (44) 20
8875 1444
www.chase-erwin.com
*(Distributed in USA by
Zoffany.)*

Chatsworth Carpets
(with Club Rugs)
Unit 3
The Trident Centre
Imperial Way
Watford WD24 4YX
United Kingdom
Tel: +011 (44) 2075
841 386
Fax: +011 (44) 1923
222 210
www.club-rugs.com

Chatsworth Carpets
Showroom:
532a Hornsey Road
London N19 3QN
United Kingdom
Tel: +011 (44) 20
7263 8846
Fax: +011 (44) 20
7263 8985
www.chatsworthcarpets.co.uk
jim@chatsworthcarpets.co.uk

Chelsea Textiles
13 Walton Street
London SW3 2HX

United Kingdom
Tel: +011 (44) 20
7584 5544
Fax: +011 (44) 20
7584 4844
www.chelseatextiles.com
and
Chelsea Textiles
The D&D Building
Suite 914
979 Third Avenue
New York NY 10022
Tel: (212) 319 5804
Fax: (212) 319 1492

Christopher Hyland, Inc.
The D&D Building
Suite 1710
979 Third Avenue
New York NY 10022
Tel: (212) 688 6121
Fax: (212) 688 6176
www.christopherhyland.com
*(See website for showrooms.
Distributed in Canada by
AnneStarr Agencies.
Distributor of Bentley &
Spens.)*

Christopher Norman Inc.
41 West 25th Street
10th Floor
New York NY 10010
Tel: (212) 647 0303
Fax: (212) 647 0369
www.christophernorman.com
*(Distributor of De Gournay,
Hodsoll McKenzie, Watts of
Westminster.)*

Christy Trading
4 Danbury Court
Winford Wood
Milton Keynes MK14 6PL
United Kingdom
Tel: +011 (44) 1908
308 777
Fax: +011 (44) 265
224
www.christy-carpets.co.uk
*(Distributor of Atlas and
Monterey Carpet Mills.)*

Cinca
Rua Principal 39
Apartado 12
P-4509-908 Fiães VFR
Portugal
Tel: +011 (351) 22
747 6400
Fax: +011 (351) 22
747 6490
Export Tel: +011 (351) 22
747 6462
Export Fax: +011 (351) 22
747 6494
www.cinca.pt
and
Cinca USA
P.O. Box 411085
Melbourne FL 32941
info@cincausa.com

**Claremont Furnishing
Fabrics Company**
1059 3rd Avenue, 2nd Floor
New York NY 10021

Tel: (212) 486 1252
Fax: (212) 486 1253
www.claremont
furnishing.com
*(Distributor of George
Spencer and Nicholas
Herbert 'Corinthia 109'.)*
and
636 North Almont Drive
West Hollywood CA 90069
Tel: (310) 248 3841
Fax: (310) 248 3842

Clarence House
The D&D Building
Suite 205
979 Third Avenue
New York NY 10022
Toll-free: 1 800 221 4704
Toll-free: 1 800 632 0076
Tel: (212) 752 2890
Fax: (212) 755 3314211
www.clarencehouse.com
*(See website for all
showroom locations.
Distributed in Canada by
Télio & Cie.)*

Classic Revivals
1 Design Centre Place
Suite 534
Boston MA 02210
Tel: (617) 574 9030
Fax: (617) 574 9027
www.classicrevivals.com
*(Distributor of Borderline, Guy
Evans, John Boyd, Mauny,
Stark Wallcovering. Agent for
Lennox Money Antiques.)*

Clodan Carpets
(see Carpet Innovations)

Coast Hardwood Floors
Unit 2, 6531 148th Street
Surrey BC V3S 3C5
Tel: (604) 592 5551
Fax: (604) 590 7002
www.coasthardwood
floors.com
*(Supplier of Boen Hardwood
Flooring.)*

Cole & Son
Lifford House
199 Eade Road
London N4 1DN
United Kingdom
Tel: +011 (44) 20
8442 8844
Fax: +011 (44) 20
8802 0033
www.cole-and-son.com
*(Distributed by Lee Jofa and
Kravet.)*

Colefax and Fowler
19–23 Grosvenor Hill
London W1K 3QD
United Kingdom
Tel: +011 (44) 20
7493 2231
Fax: +011 (44) 20
7499 9910
www.colefax.com
*(Distributor of Colefax &
Fowler, Cowtan & Tout, Jane*

Churchill, [Jack Lenor] Larsen, Manuel Canovas. Distributed in USA by Cowtan & Tout, Jane Churchill, [Jack Lenor] Larsen, Manuel Canovas, in Canada by AnneStarr Agencies, Primavera. See also website.)

Coloroll
(CWV Group Ltd.)
P.O. Box 15
Talbot Road, Hyde
Cheshire SK14 4EJ
United Kingdom
Tel: +011 (44) 161
    368 4000
Fax: +011 (44) 161
    368 3430
and
CW Textiles Ltd.
The Courtyard
Royd Ings Avenue
Keighley
West Yorkshire
BD21 4BZ
United Kingdom
Tel: +011 (44) 1535
    617300
Fax: +011 (44) 1535
    616900
(Contact for distributors.)

Colourman Paints
The Bowjy
Trevowhan, Morvah
Penzance
Cornwall TR20 8YT
United Kingdom
Tel: +011 (44) 1736 787420
Fax: +011 (44) 1736 788518
(For similar products, see also Old Fashioned Milk Paint Co., Nitty Gritty Reproductions, Old Village Paints, Homestead House Paint Company.)

(G.) Comoglio
22 rue Jacob
Paris 75006
France
Tel: +011 (33) 143 54 65 86
Fax: +011 (33) 140 51 70 56
contact@comoglio.fr
www.comoglio.fr

Compass Flooring Ltd.
The Flooring Technology
    Centre
6580 Kestrel Road
Mississauga ON L52 123
Tel: (905) 564 1330
Fax: (905) 564 0750
www.compassfloor.com
(Distributor of Marley Floors.)

Concepts International
83 Harbour Road
Port Washington NY 11050
Tel: (516) 767 1110
Fax: (516) 767 3019
(Distributor of Crucial Trading.)

Country Swedish
22 Elizabeth Street
S. Norwalk CT 06854
Toll-free: 1 888 807 9333
Tel: (203) 855 1106
Fax: (203) 855 0181
www.countryswedish.com
(Distributor in USA of Sandberg Tapeter AB.)
and
The D&D Building
Suite 1409
979 Third Avenue
New York NY 10022
Tel: (212) 838 1976
and
Country Swedish
    Showroom:
The Chicago
    Merchandise Mart
1621 Merchandise Mart
Chicago IL 60654
Tel: (312) 644 4540

Cowtan & Tout
111 Eighth Avenue
Suite 930
New York NY 10011
Tel: (212) 647 6900
Fax: (212) 647 6906
www.cowtan.com
(Distributor of Colefax and Fowler, Cowtan & Tout, Jane Churchill, Larsen, Manuel Canovas. Distributed in Canada by AnneStarr Agencies, Colefax & Fowler, Primavera. See website for showrooms.)
and
Cowtan & Tout Larsen
20 Vandam Street
New York NY 10013
Tel: (646) 638 4201
(Distributor of [Jack Lenor] Larsen.)

Craig & Rose
Unit 16/17 Stewartfield
Newhaven Road
Edinburgh EH6 5RQ
United Kingdom
Tel: +011 (44) 131
    555 3773
Fax: +011 (44) 131
    555 5777
www.craigandrose.com
(Distributor of Cath Kidston, Opulence, Holly Hopper, 1829, Craig & Rose paints. Contact for locations.)

**Craven Dunnill
    Jackfield Ltd.**
The Encaustic and
Decorative Tile Works
Ironbridge Gorge
Shropshire TF8 7LJ
United Kingdom
Tel: +011 (44) 1952
    884 124
Fax: +011 (44) 1952
    884 487
www.cravendunnill
    -jackfield.co.uk
(Distributed by Charles Rupert Designs.)

Création Baumann Fabrics
Création Baumann USA Inc.
114 North Centre Avenue
Rockville Centre
New York NY 11570
Trade Tel: (516) 678 6770
Trade Fax: (516) 678 6848
Retail toll-free:
    1 800 727 6770
Retail Fax: (516) 678 6848
www.creationbaumann.com
(See website for USA showrooms. Distributed in Canada by Tessuti Uno.)

Creekside Tile Co.
161 West 2nd Avenue
Vancouver BC V5Y 1B8
Tel: (604) 876 4900
Fax: (604) 876 4902
www.creeksidetile.com
(Distributor of Surving Studios.)

Crescendo
(See AnneStarr Agencies.)

Crown
(Akzo Nobel Decorative
    Coatings Ltd.)
Crown House
P.O. Box 37
Hollins Road, Darwen
Lancashire BB3 0BG
United Kingdom
Tel: +011 (44) 1254 704951
Fax: +011 (44) 1254 774414
www.crownpaint.co.uk
and
Akzo Nobel Decorative
    Coatings Inc.
117 Brush Street
Pontiac MI 48341
Tel: (248) 253 2495
Fax: (248) 333 8775
www.akzonobel.com

Crown Wallpaper & Fabrics
88 Ronson Drive
Etobicoke ON M9W 1B9
Tel: (416) 245 2900
Fax: (416) 245 0760
and
Crown Wallpaper & Fabrics
303-611 Alexander St
Vancouver BC V6A 1E1
Tel: (604) 736 4541
Fax: (604) 736 4955
and
Crown Wallpaper & Fabrics
4269 Ste-Catherine West
Suite 701
Westmount QC H3Z 1P7
Tel: (514) 935 3591
Fax: (514) 935 6524
www.crownwallpaper.com
(Distributor of Old World Weavers.)

Crowson
Crowson House
Bellbrock Park
Uckfield
East Sussex TN22 1QZ
United Kingdom
Tel: +011 (44) 1825 761044
Fax: +011 (44) 1825 764283

www.crowsonfabrics.com
(Distributor of Crowson, Monkwell, The Design Archives, Hill & Knowles, Monkwell and Dovetail Fabrics. Distributed in USA by Lee Jofa, in Canada by Télio & Cie. See also Monkwell, The Design Archives.)

Crucial Trading
P.O. Box 10469
Birmingham B46 1WB
United Kingdom
Tel: +011 (44) 1675 743747
Fax: +011 (44) 1675 433521
www.crucial-trading.com
(Distributed by Concepts International and Stark Carpet.)

Cuprinol
Wexham Road
Slough
Berkshire SL2 5DS
United Kingdom
Tel: +011 (44) 1753 550555
www.cuprinol.co.uk

Cy-Près
14 Bells Close
Brigstock
Kettering
Northamptonshire NN14 3JG
United Kingdom
Tel: +011 (44) 1536 373158
Tel: +011 (44) 1536 373431
Fax: +011 (44) 1536 373223

D

Dacrylate Paints
Lime Street
Kirkby in Ashfield
Nottingham NG17 8AL
United Kingdom
Tel: +011 (44) 1623 753845
Fax: +011 (44) 1623 757151
www.dacrylate.co.uk
(Contact for distributors.)

Dalsouple Direct Ltd.
P.O. Box 140
Bridgewater
Somerset TA5 1HT
United Kingdom
Tel: +011 (44) 1984 667233
Fax: +011 (44) 1984 667366
www.dalsouple.com
(Mail order available from some suppliers. Contact for details.)

Daltile
7834 CF Hawn Freeway
Dallas TX 75217
Tel: (214) 398 1411
Fax: (214) 309 4480
www.daltile.com
and
Daltile (Canada)
470 Rowntree Dairy Road
Woodbridge ON L4L 8H2
Tel: (905) 850 4390
Fax: (905) 850 4398

Davan Port Ltd.
(Dorian Bahr)
Decorative Center Houston
Suite 130
Houston TX 77056
Tel: (713) 599 0900
Fax: (713) 599 0905

David Oliver Ltd.
(Paint & Paper Library)
5 Elystan Street
London SW3 3NT
United Kingdom
Tel: +011 (44) 20
    7823 7755
Fax: +011 (44) 20
    7823 7766
www.paintlibrary.co.uk
(Online shopping. Distributed in USA by Fonthill and Hinson & Company.)

De Gournay
143 West 29th Street
7th Floor
Chelsea, New York
NY 10001
Tel: (212) 564 9750
Fax: (212) 564 9067
www.degournay.com
(Also distributed in USA by Christopher Norman.)

De Le Cuona Designs
Mistress Page's House
13a High Street, Windsor
Berkshire SL4 1LD
United Kingdom
Tel: +011 (44) 1753
    830 301
Fax: +011 (44) 1753
    620 455
www.delecuona.co.uk
(Contact for suppliers.)

Dedar
Via della Resistenza
3-22070 Appiano Gentile (Co)
Milano, Italy
Tel: +011 (39) 31 2287511
Fax: +011 (39) 31 2287533
www.dedar.com
www.dedar-usa.com
info@dedar.com
Toll-free (USA):
    1 800 493 2209
(Distributed in Canada by Tessuti Uno. See website for USA showrooms.)

Deralam Laminates
[manufactured by]
Kronospan Ltd.
Chirk, Wrexham LL14 5NT
United Kingdom
Tel: +011 (44) 1691 773361
Fax: +011 (44) 1691 773292
sales@kronospan.co.uk
www.kronospan.co.uk

Derr Flooring Co.
525 Davisville Road
P.O. Box 912
Willow Grove PA 19090
Toll-free: 1 800 523 3457
Tel: (215) 657 6300
Fax: (215) 657 9830

www.derrflooring.com
(Distributor of Oshkosh Flooring. See website for locations.)

The Design Archives
Crowson House
Bellbrock Park, Uckfield
East Sussex TN22 1QZ
United Kingdom
Tel: +011 (44) 1825 761044
Fax: +011 (44) 1825 764283
www.monkwell.com
(See also Monkwell. Distributor of Design Archives, Monkwell, and Crowson. Distributed in USA by Lee Jofa, in Canada by Télio & Cie.)

Designers Guild
3 Olaf Street
London W11 4BE
United Kingdom
Tel: +011 (44) 20
    7243 7300
Fax: +011 (44) 20
    7243 7320
www.designersguild.com
(Distributed in USA by Osborne & Little. Distributor of Cath Kidston outside the UK)

Designer Stencils
c/o The Stencil Shoppe Inc.
3364 Silverside Road
Wilmington DE 19810
Toll-free: 1 800 822 7836
Fax: (302) 477 0170
www.designerstencils.com
(Online shopping, custom stencils.)

De Sousa Hughes
2 Henry Adams Street, #220
San Francisco CA 94103
Tel: (415) 626 6883
Fax: (415) 626 2489
www.desousahughes.com
(Distributor of Bennison, George Spencer, Galbraith & Paul, Création Baumann.)

**Domestic Marble and
Stone Corporation**
145 Hudson Street
New York NY 10013
Tel: (212) 343 3300
Fax: (212) 343 3301
(Distributor of Kirkstone.)

Domus Tiles
3 Molesey Business Centre
Central Avenue
West Molesey
Surrey KT8 2QZ
United Kingdom
Tel: +011 (44) 20
    8481 9500
Fax: +011 (44) 20
    8481 9501
www.domustiles.co.uk
www.domustiles.com
(Contact for distributors.)

Donghia
256 Washington Street
Mount Vernon NY 10553
Tel: (914) 662 2377
Fax: (914) 662 2307
mail@donghia.com
www.donghia.com
(Distributor of Anya Larkin, Création Baumann, Donghia, Maya Romanoff. Distributed in Canada by Télio & Cie and William Switzer. See website for showrooms.)

Dulux Paints
925 Euclid Avenue
Cleveland OH 44115
Tel: (216) 344 8000
www.dulux.com
www.iciduluxpaints.com

E

Elijah Slocum
5924 Blackwelder Street
Culver City CA 90232
Toll-free: 1 800 310 8011
Tel: (310) 280 9098
Fax: (310) 280 9077
www.elijahslocum.com
(Distributor of Bennett Silks. See website for showrooms.)

Elite Tiles
Elite House
The Broadway
London NW9 7BP
United Kingdom
Tel: +011 (44) 20
    8202 1806
Fax: +011 (44) 20
    8202 8608
www.elite-tiles.co.uk
enquiries@elite-tiles.co.uk
(Contact for distributors.)

Elizabeth Eaton
85 Bourne Street
Chelsea
London SW1W 8HF
United Kingdom
Tel: +011 (44) 20
    7730 2262
Fax: +011 (44) 20
    7730 7294

Elon
12 Silver Road
White City
London W12 7SG
United Kingdom
Tel: +011 (44) 20
    8932 3000
Fax: +011 (44) 20
    8932 3001
www.elon.co.uk
(Contact regarding delivery outside the U.K.)

F

F. Schumacher & Co.
79 Madison Avenue
New York NY 10016
Tel: (212) 213 7900
and
Customer Service Center

1325 Old Cooches Bridge Road
P.O. Box 6002
Newark DE 19714
Tel: (302) 454 3200
and
The D&D Building
Suite 832
New York NY 10022
Tel: (212) 415 3900
Fax: (212) 415 3907
www.fschumacher.com
(Supplier of Schumacher and Patterson, Flynn & Martin, Waverly, Beaumont & Fletcher and John Boyd. Distributed in Canada by AnneStarr Agencies and Bilbrough & Co. See website for showrooms)

Fabric Unlimited
158 North Third St.
Danville KY 40422
Tel: (859) 238 2289
www.fabric-unlimited.com
(Online mail order. See also Primavera and Golia Color Centre.)

Fardis
Omnova Solutions France SA
Touranjou/Fardis
1, avenue Molière
92600 Ansières
France
Tel: +011 (33) 49 07 86 20
Fax: ı011 (33) 49 06 02 77
www.fardis.fr
info@omnova.fr

Farrow & Ball
249 Fulham Road
London SW3 6HY
United Kingdom
Tel: +011 (44) 20
　7351 0273
USA Toll free:
　1 888 511 1121
www.farrow-ball.com
nasales@farrow-ball.com.
(See website for showrooms and approved retailers.)
and
The D&D Building
Suite 1519
979 Third Avenue
New York NY 10022
Tel: (212) 752 5544
and
1054 Yonge Street
Toronto ON M4W 2L1
Toll-free: 1 877 363 1040
Tel: (416) 920 0200
Fax: (416) 920 1223

Finnaren & Haley
901 Washington Street
Conshohocken PA 19428
Tel: (610) 825 1900
Fax: (610) 825 1184
www.fhpaint.com

Fired Earth Company
Twyford Mill
Oxford Road

Adderbury
Oxon OX17 3HP
United Kingdom
Tel: +011 (44) 1295 812088
Fax: +011 (44) 1295 812189
www.firedearth.com
(Online shopping. Distributor of [and see also] Froyle Tiles and Lowitz & Company.)

Floor Supply Distributing
N1802 Langley
Spokane WA 99212
Tel: (509) 535 9707
Fax: (509) 535 0558
www.floor-supply.net
(Distributor of Marley Floors.)

Floorworks International Ltd.
365 Dupont Street
Toronto ON M5R 1W2
Tel: (416) 961 6891
Fax: (416) 961 3881
www.floorworks.ca
(Supplier of Boen Flooring. Distributed by Nova Hardwood and Coast Hardwood.)

Fonthill Ltd. (Stark Fabric)
The D&D Building
10th Floor
979 Third Avenue
New York NY 10022
Tel: (212) 752 9000
Fax: (212) 758 4342
www.fonthill-ltd.com
www.starkfabric.com
(Distributor of Old World Weavers, Fonthill, Lelièvre, Etro, Ottilie Stevenson, Thomas Dare, Alexander Beauchamp, Neisha Crosland, Paint and Paper Library, Wendy Cushing, David Oliver, Stark Fabric. See website for showrooms and distributors.)

Froyle Tiles
Froyle Pottery
Lower Froyle
Alton
Hampshire GU34 4LL
United Kingdom
Tel: +011 (44) 1420 23693
Fax: +011 (44) 1420 22797
www.froyletiles.co.uk
(Distributed in USA by Paris Ceramics. Contact for others. See also Fired Earth.)

G

G.P. & J. Baker
2 Stinsford Road
Poole
Dorset BH17 0SW
United Kingdom
Tel: +011 (44) 1202
　266 700
Fax: +011 (44) 1202
　266 701
www.gpjbaker.co.uk
(Distributor of Parkertex. Distributed by Lee Jofa.)

Gaetano, Ltd.
186 Sherman Avenue
Berkeley Heights NJ 07922
Tel: (908) 508 9006
Fax: (908) 508 9797
www.gaetano-usa.com
(Distributor of Today Interiors, including Pippa & Hale.)

Gainsborough Silk Weaving
Alexandra Road
Sudbury
Suffolk CO10 2XH
United Kingdom
Tel: +011 (44) 1787 372081
Fax: +011 (44) 1787 881785
(Distributed in USA by Travers & Company and Lee Jofa, in Canada by Bilbrough.)

Galbraith & Paul
116 Shurs Lane
Philadelphia PA 19127
Tel: (215) 508 0800
Fax: (215) 508 0866
www.galbraithandpaul.com
(See website for retailers.)

Garin 1820
C/Quart 45–49 Moncada
CP 46113 Valencia
Spain
Tel: +011 (34) 96 130 90 23
Fax: +011 (34) 96 139 58 64
www.garin1820.com
(Contact for distributors in USA and Canada.)

Gaskell Mackay Carpets
(Formerly Hugh Mackay Carpets)
Whitestone House
Whitestone Business Park
Saltwells Road
Middlesbrough TS4 2ED
United Kingdom
Tel: +011 (44) 1642
　242 423
Tel: +011 (44) 1642
　757 600
Fax: +011 (44) 1642
　757 620
www.gaskell.co.uk
(Part of the Whitestone Weavers Group. Distributor of Axminster, Wilton and tufted carpets. Relocating to Hartlepool in 2008.)
and
Whitestone Weavers
Tel: +011 (44) 1642 242423
Fax: +011 (44) 1642 757628
info@whitestone.co.uk
(See Bellbridge Carpets for Maeve Fegan, Wes Friesen & Associates and Bellbridge Carpets.)

George Cameron Nash
150 Dallas Design Center
1025 North Stemmons Freeway
Dallas TX 75207
Tel: (214) 744 1544
Fax: (214) 748 3255
and

5120 Woodway, Suite 140
Houston TX 77056
Tel: (713) 892 5710
Fax: (713) 892 5721
www.georgecameronnash.com
(Distributor of Today Interiors, including Pippa & Hale.)

George Spencer Designs
29 Chapel Street
London SW1X 7DD
United Kingdom
Tel: +011 (44) 20
　7235 1501
Fax: +011 (44) 20
　7235 1502
www.georgespencer.com
(Distributed in USA by Claremont. Distributor of Ornamenta.)

Glant Textiles
P.O. Box 84228
Seattle WA 98124
Toll-free: 1 800 88 5268
Tel: (206) 725 4444
Fax: (206) 725 5544
www.glant.com
(See website for distributors.)
and
Hines & Company
The D&D Building
Suite 1010
979 Third Avenue
New York NY 10022
Tel: (212) 754 5880
Fax: (212) 758 4881

The Gold Leaf Company
27 Fort Place, 2nd floor
Staten Island NY 10301
Tel: (718) 815 8802
Orders Fax: (718) 720 7027
www.goldleafcompany.com
(Distributor of Liberon products.)

Graham & Brown
Harwood Street
Blackburn
Lancashire BB1 3BR
United Kingdom
Tel: +011 (44) 1254 661122
Fax: +011 (44) 1254 680849
www.grahambrown.com
(Online shopping. Will ship overseas.)

Grand Illusions
41 Crown Road
St Margaret's
Twickenham TW1 3EJ
United Kingdom
Tel: +011 (44) 20 8607 9446
Fax: +011 (44) 20 8744 2017
www.grandillusions.co.uk
(See website for distributors.)

Guy Evans, Inc.
82585 Showcase Parkway
Indio CA 92203
Toll-free: 1 888 434 3667
Tel: (760) 262 6300
(Facilities in California and Nevada. Contact for availability and distributors.)

H

H. & R. Johnson
Harewood Street
Tunstall
Stoke-on-Trent ST6 5JZ
United Kingdom
Tel: +011 (44) 1782 575575
Fax: +011 (44) 1782 577379
www.johnson-tiles.com
(Distributor of Minton Hollins. Online shopping. Distributed in USA by W. May & Co.)

Hamilton Weston Wallpapers
18 St Mary's Grove
Richmond
Surrey TW9 1UY
United Kingdom
Tel: +011 (44) 20 8940 4850
Fax: +011 (44) 20 8332 0296
www.hamiltonweston.com
(Distributed by Classic Revivals.)

The Hardwood & Natural Stone Flooring Company
Fisherton Mill
59–61 Fisherton Street
Salisbury
Wiltshire SP2 7SU
United Kingdom
Tel: +011 (44) 1722 415000
Fax: +011 (44) 1722 414816
www.woodstonefloors.co.uk
(Online shopping; overseas delivery.)

Hardwood Flooring Supplies
Unit 1, Goldsworth Park Trading Estate
Kestrel Way
Woking GU21 3AZ
United Kingdom
Tel: +011 (44) 870
　770 4322
Fax: +011 (44) 870
　770 4340

Harlequin USA
5100 Highlands Parkway
Smyrna GA 30082
Tel: (678) 303 9999
Fax: (678) 303 8250
www.harlequin.uk.com
(Distributed in Canada by Beauport.)

Henry Newbery & Co.
18 Newman Street
London W1T 1AB
United Kingdom
Tel: +011 (44) 20 7636 5970
Fax: +011 (44) 20 7436 6406
www.henrynewbery.com
(Distributed in USA by Christopher Hyland and Lee Jofa, in Canada by Bilbrough & Co.)

Hill & Knowles
(see Crowson Fabrics)

Hinson & Company
Space B-690

8687 Melrose Avenue
Los Angeles CA 90069
Tel: (310) 659 1400
Fax: (310) 659 0104
(Distributor of David Oliver.)

Historic Floors of Oshkosh
911 East Main Street
Winneconne WI 45986
Tel: (920) 582 9977
Fax: (920) 582 9971
www.oshkoshfloors.com
(Also distributed by Derr Flooring. See website for dealers.)

Hoboken Floors
70 Demarest Drive
Wayne NJ 07470
Toll Free: (800) 222 1068
Tel: (973) 694 2888
Fax: (973) 694 6885
www.hobokenfloors.com
and
The D&D Building, Suite 820
979 Third Avenue
New York NY 10022
Tel: (212) 759 5917
Fax: (212) 593 0268
(See website for regional showrooms and distributors.)

Hodsoll McKenzie
52 Pimlico Road
London SW1W 8LP
United Kingdom
Tel: +011 (44) 20
　7254 9940
Fax: +011 (44) 20
　7254 2033
www.hodsollmckenzie.com
(Distributed in USA by Christopher Norman.)

Holkham Linseed Paints
The Clock Tower
Longlands
Holkham Park
Wells-Next-The-Sea
Norfolk NR23 1RU
United Kingdom
Tel: +011 (44) 1328
　711 348
Fax: +011 (44) 1328
　710 368
www.holkhamlinseedpaints.co.uk
(Online shopping, but no overseas delivery. For similar products, see Allback Organic Linseed Paints, Auro Organic Paints and BioShield Paints.)

Holly Hunt Collection
801 West Adams
Chicago IL 60607
Tel: (312) 329 5999
www.hollyhunt.com
and
The D&D Building
Suite 605
979 Third Avenue
New York NY 10022
Tel: (212) 755 6555
Fax: (212) 755 6578
(Distributor of Bennison

Fabrics and Bergamo. See website for showrooms.)

Homestead House Paint Company
95 Niagara Street
Toronto ON M5V 1C3
Tel: (416) 504 9984
Fax: (416) 504 9984
www.homesteadhouse.ca
(Product similar to Colourman Paints.)

Howe
93 Pimlico Road
London SW1W 8PH
United Kingdom
Tel: +011 (44) 20
　7730 7987
Fax: +011 (44) 20
　7730 0157
www.howelondon.com
(Will ship overseas.)

Hugh Mackay Carpets
(see Gaskell Mackay Carpets)

I

Ian Mankin
109 Regents Park Road
London NW1 8UR
United Kingdom
Tel: +011 (44) 20
　7722 0997
Fax: +011 (44) 20
　7722 2159
www.ianmankin.com
(Catalogue mail order.)

Ian Sanderson
P.O. Box 148
Newbury
Berkshire RG15 9DW
United Kingdom
Tel: +011 (44) 1635 33188
Fax: +011 (44) 1635 45070
www.iansanderson.co.uk
(Distributed in USA and Canada by Appel Ltd.)

The Imperial Home Décor Group (IHDG)
(Now trading as Blue Mountain Wallcoverings Inc.)
15 Akron Road
Toronto ON M8W 1T3
Toll-free Tel (Canada):
　1 800 219 2424
Toll-free Tel (USA):
　1 800 866 563 9872
Toll-free Fax (Canada and USA): 1 800 741 2083
www.ihdg.com
(Distributed in Canada by Bilbrough & Co.)

Interdesign UK Ltd.
G30 Chelsea Harbour Design Centre
Chelsea Harbour
London SW10 0XE
United Kingdom
Tel: +011 (44) 20
　7376 5256
Fax: +011 (44) 20
　7376 3020
www.interdesignuk.com

I.D. Collection
1025 North Stemmons
Freeway
Suite 745
Dallas TX 75207
Tel: (214) 698 0226
Fax: (214) 698 8650
and
I.D. Collection
5120 Woodway, Suite 4001
Houston TX 77056
Tel: (713) 623 2344
Fax: (713) 623 2105
www.interiordesign
collection.com
(Online showroom.
Distributor of Bergamo,
Création Baumann,
Designers Guild, Malabar,
Majilite, Old World Weavers,
Osborne & Little,
Renaissance, Rubelli, Sacho
Hesslein, Stark.)

The Isle Mill Ltd.
(a division of Macnaughtons)
Tower House
Ruthvenfield Road
Inveralmond
Perth PH1 3UN
United Kingdom
Tel: +011 (44) 1738 609000
Fax: +011 (44) 1738 604010
www.islemill.com
(Sales by mail order through
Macnaughtons.)
and
Macnaughtons of Pitlochry
Mail Order Department
Station Road
Pitlochry
Perthshire
Scotland PH16 5AF
United Kingdom
Tel: +011 (44) 1796 472722
Fax: +011 (44) 1796 474266
www.macnaughton
-group.com
(Mail order for The Isle Mill
Ltd. by mail order. Distributor
of Thomas Dare.)

Ivo Prints
Unit 3 Trident Way
International Trading Estate
Southall
Middlesex UB2 5LF
United Kingdom
Tel: +011 (44) 20
8574 7943
Fax: +011 (44) 20
8571 7664
sales@ivo.co.uk
www.ivo.co.uk

J

J. Robert Scott
500 North Oak Street
Inglewood CA 90302
Tel: (310) 680 4300
Toll-free: 1 800 322 4910
Fax: (310) 680 4424
www.jrobertscott.com
and
The D&D Building
Suite 220
979 Third Avenue

New York NY 10022
Tel: (212) 755 4910
Fax: (212) 755 4957
(Distributed in Canada by
Télio et Cie.)

J.R. Burrows & Company
P.O. Box 522
Rockland MA 02370
Toll-free: 1 800 347 1795
Tel: (781) 982 1812
Fax: (781) 982 1636
www.burrows.com
(Distributor of Woodward
Grosvenor. See website for
stores in MA, NY, KS, VA.)

J.W. Bollom
Bollom House
P.O. Box 78
Croydon Road
Beckenham
Kent BR3 4BL
United Kingdom
Tel: +011 (44) 20
8658 2299
Fax: +011 (44) 20
8658 8672
www.bollom.com

JAB International
Furnishings Ltd.
1/15–16 Chelsea Harbour
Design Centre
Chelsea Harbour
London SW10 0XE
United Kingdom
Tel: +011 (44) 20
7349 9323
Fax: +011 (44) 20
7349 9282
and
JAB Anstoetz Inc.
326 Davenport Road
Toronto ON M5R 1K6
Tel: (416) 927 9192
Showroom: (416) 920 3020
Fax: (416) 927 7510
www.jab.de
jab-canada@jab.de
(Distributed in USA by
Stroheim & Romann, in
Canada by JAB Anstoetz.
See wesbsite for more
distributors.)

Jack Lenor Larsen
(see Larsen)

Jane Churchill
(Part of the Colefax Group.)
19-23 Grosvenor Hill
London W1K 3QD
United Kingdom
Tel: +011 (44) 20
7318 6000
Fax: +011 (44) 20
7499 9910
www.janechurchill.co.uk
(Distributed in USA by
Colefax and Fowler, in
Canada by Primavera. See
website for showroom
locations.)

Jane Knapp Ltd.
6 Chatham Row

Bath BA1 5BS
United Kingdom
Tel/Fax: +011 (44) 1225
463 468
www.janeknapp.com
(Online ordering. See also
www.walcot.com)

Jason D'Souza
1/6 Chelsea Harbour
Design Centre
Chelsea Harbour
London SW10 0XE
United Kingdom
Tel: +011 (44) 20
7351 4440
Fax: +011 (44) 20
7351 4396
www.jasondsouza.co.uk
(Distributed in USA by Nancy
Corzine, in Canada by
Bilbrough & Co.)

Jaymart Rubber &
Plastics Ltd.
Woodlands Trading Estate
Eden Vale Road
Westbury
Wiltshire BA13 3QS
United Kingdom
Tel: +011 (44) 1373 864926
Fax: +011 (44) 1373 858454
Jaymart@compuserve.com
(Contact for suppliers.)

Jim Thompson
(The Thai Silk Company
Limited)
96 Soi Pungmee 29
Sukhumvit 93 Road
P.O. Box Onnuch 88
Bangchak, Prakanong
Bangkok 10260
Thailand
Tel: +011 (662) 762 2600
Fax: +011 (662) 762 2609
office@jimthompson.com
www.jimthompson.com
(Distributed in Canada by
Telio & Cie. See website for
USA distributors.)

Joanna Wood
(see Lewis & Wood)

John Boyd Textiles
Higher Flax Mills
Castle Cary
Somerset BA7 7DY
United Kingdom
Tel: +011 (44) 1963 350451
Fax: +011 (44) 1963 351078
www.johnboydtextiles.co.uk
(Distributed in USA by
Classic Revivals,
Schumacher & Co.,
Scalamandré, Stark Carpet,
Lee Jofa and Brunschwig &
Fils, in Canada by William
Switzer and Télio & Cie.)

John Brooks, Inc.
601 South Broadway
Suite L
Denver CO 80209
Tel: (303) 698 9977
Fax: (303) 698 9797

www.johnbrooksinc.com
and
2732 North 98th Street
Suite 1
Scottsdale AZ 85257
Tel: (480) 675 8828
Fax: (480) 675 7722
(Distributor of Bennison,
Bergamo, Maya Romanoff,
William Morris & Co. See
website for locations.)

John Oliver Ltd.
33 Pembridge Road
Notting Hill
London W11 3HG
United Kingdom
Tel: +011 (44) 20
7221 6466
Fax: +011 (44) 20
7727 5555
www.johnoliver.co.uk

John Wilmans
(see Wilman Interiors)

Junckers Hardwood, Inc.
95 Grand Street, Unit 3
New York NY 10013
Toll-free: 1 800 878 963
Tel: (212) 334 8060
Fax: (212) 334 8062
information@junckers
hardwood.com
www.junckershardwood.com
and
Junckers Hardwood, Inc.
4920 E. Landon Drive
Anaheim CA 92807
Tel: (714) 777 6430
Fax: (714) 777 6436

K

Kährs Wood Flooring
940 Centre Circle
Suite 1000
Altamonte Springs FL 32714
Toll-free: 1 800 800 5247
Tel: (407) 260 9910
Fax: (407) 260 9933
www.kahrs.com
(See website for showrooms
in USA and Canada.)

Karndean International
LLC
Bushy Run Corporate Park
1100 Pontiac Court
Export PA 15632
Toll-free Tel: 1 888 266 4343
Toll-free Fax: 1 800 887 7043
Tel: (724) 387 2056
Fax: (724) 387 2057

Keimfarben
Export Department
Keimstraße 16
86420 Diedorf
Germany
Tel: +011 (49) 82
148 02 109
Fax: +011 (49) 82
148 02 173
www.keimfarben.de
(Limewash, mineral-based
and non-allergenic paints.
Distributed in USA and

Canada; contact for details.
See also Portola Paints and
U.S. Heritage Paints.)

Kenneth Clark Ceramics
The North Wing
Southover Grange
Southover Road, Lewes
East Sussex BN7 1TP
United Kingdom
Tel: +011 (44) 1273 476761
Fax: +011 (44) 1273 479565
www.kennethclark
ceramics.co.uk
(Mail order available.)

Kentucky Wood Floors
15412 Highway 62
Charlestown IN 47111
Tel: (502) 451 6024
Fax: (502) 451 6027
www.kentuckywood.com
(Distributed in Canada by
Burnside Flooring.)

Kievel Stone
Lower Farm, Lower Farm Lane
Ampfield
Hants SO51 9BP
United Kingdom
Tel: +011 (44) 1794 368 865
Fax: +011 (44) 1794 368 914

Kirkstone Quarries Ltd.
Skelwith Bridge
Ambleside
Cumbria LA22 9NN
United Kingdom
Tel: +011 (44) 1539 433296
Fax: +011 (44) 1539 434006
www.kirkstone.com
(Distributed in USA by Walker
Zanger and Domestic Marble
and Stone, in Canada by
Acme Slate & Tile.)

Knowles & Christou
116 Lots Road
London SW10 0RJ
United Kingdom
Tel: +011 (44) 20
7352 7000
Fax: +011 (44) 20
7352 8877
www.knowles-christou.com
(Distributed in USA by Stark
Wallcovering.)

Kravet Inc.
225 Central Avenue South
Bethpage NY 11714
Toll-free: 1 888 266 4343
Toll-free Fax: 1 800 887 7043
Tel: (516) 293 2000
Fax: (516) 293 2737
Trade Toll-free Tel:
1 800 535 3434
Trade Toll-free Fax:
1 800 221 6981
www.e-designtrade.com
www.kravet.com
and
Kravet Canada
3600-B Laird Road, Suite 6
Mississauga ON L5L 6A7
Toll-free Tel: 1 800 535 3258
Toll-free Fax: 1 800 355 3434
www.kravetcanada.com

(Distributor of Andrew Martin
International, Kravet, Laura
Ashley, Lee Jofa, Cole &
Son. See websites for
showrooms, retailers and
contact details.)

L

Langevin & Forest
Les Connaisseurs de Bois
9995, boul Pie IX
Montreal QC H1Z 3X1
www.langevinforest.com
Tel: (514) 322 9330
Fax: (514) 322 0943
(Distributor of Libéron.)

Larsen
(previously known as Jack
Lenor Larsen)
Supplier information:
+011 (44) 20 8877 6400
(Distributed by Cowtan &
Tout, Colefax and Fowler.)

LASSCO
30 Wandsworth Road
Vauxhall
London SW8 2LG
United Kingdom
Tel: +011 (44) 20
7394 2100
Fax: +011 (44) 20
7501 7797
www.lassco.co.uk
(Online catalog. Contact for
shipping details.)

Laura Ashley Ltd.
Freepost SY1225
P.O. Box 19
Newtown
Powys SY16 1DZ
United Kingdom
Customer Service: +011
(44) 871 9835 999
Tel: +011 (44) 870
562 2116
Fax: +011 (44) 1686
622 183
www.lauraashley-usa.com
(Fabrics and trimmings
distributed by Kravet. See
website for distributors and
retailers of other Laura Ashley
products.)

LBC Hardwood Flooring
Unit 9, Knutsford Way
Sealand Road
Chester CH1 4NS
United Kingdom
Tel: +011 (44) 1244 377811
Fax: +011 (44) 1244 373678

Lee Jofa
201 Central Avenue South
Bethpage
Long Island NY 11714
Tel: (516) 752 7600
Fax: (516) 752 7623
www.leejofa.com
(Distributor of Andrew Martin,
Cole & Son, Crowson,
Design Archives, G. P. & J.
Baker, Gainsborough Silk
Weaving, Henry Newbery &

Co., Hill & Knowles, John
Boyd, Monkwell, Mulberry
Home, in Canada by Kravet.
See website for showrooms.)
and
The D&D Building
Suite 234
979 Third Avenue
New York NY 10022
Tel: (212) 688 0444
Fax: (212) 759 3658
and
Lee Jofa Canada
Donovan & Associates Inc.
Designers Walk, Suite 200
320 Davenport Road
Toronto ON M5R 2K9
Tel: (416) 921 1262
Fax: (416) 921 7875

Lelièvre
13, rue du Mail
Paris 75002
France
Tel: +011 (33) 1 43 16 88 00
Fax: +011 (33) 1 40 20 08 08
www.lelievre.eu
(Online catalog. Distributed in
USA by Stark Carpet/Old
World Weavers and in
Canada by Télio & Cie.)

Lennox Money
Antiques Ltd.
93 Pimlico Road
London SW1W 8PH
United Kingdom
Tel: +011 (44) 20
7730 3070
Fax: +011 (44) 20
7259 9563
(USA agent is Classic
Revivals.)

Lewis & Wood
(also known as Joanna
Wood)
5 The Green
Uley
Gloucestershire GL11 5SN
United Kingdom
Tel: +011 (44) 1453
860 080
Fax: +011 (44) 1453
860 054
www.lewisandwood.co.uk
(Distributed by Borderline.)

Liberon
(Distributed in USA by Sepp
Leaf US, in Canada by
Langevin & Forest. For similar
products, see Briwax and
The Gold Leaf Company. For
orders by mail, see Star
Wood Finish Supply.)

Liberty Furnishings
(see Osborne & Little)

Liz Induni Traditional Paints
11 Park Road
Swanage
Dorset BH19 2AA
United Kingdom
Tel: +011 (44) 1929 423776
induni@tesco.net

(For similar products, see Allback Paints, Auro Organic Paints, Portola Paints, Keimfarben, and U.S. Heritage Paints.)

Louis de Poortere
World Headquarters
Louis De Poortere SA
Rue de la Royenne, 45
7700 Mouscron
Belgium
Tel: +011 (32) 56 393 393
Fax: +011 (32) 56 393 317
www.louisdepoortere.com
(Distributed in USA and Canada by Prestige Mills.)

Lowitz & Company
4401 N. Ravenswood Avenue
Chicago IL 60640
Tel: (773) 784 2628
Fax: (773) 784 2656
www.lowitzandcompany.com
(Talisman, Foundry Art and Bronzework Studio designs. Distributed in USA by Ann Sacks. Contact for Canadian suppliers.)

M

Macnaughtons of Pitlochry
(see The Isle Mill)

The Malabar Cotton Co. Ltd.
31–33 The South Bank
Business Centre
Ponton Road
London SW8 5BL
United Kingdom
Tel: +011 (44) 20
7501 4200
Fax: +011 (44) 20
7501 4210
For USA suppliers, call
toll-free: 1 877 625 2227
www.malabar.co.uk
(Distributed in Canada by Bilbrough & Co.)

Manningtons International
1844 US Highway 41 S.E.
Calhoun GA 30701
Toll-free: 1 800 482 0466
Tel: (706) 629 7301
Fax: (706) 629 0705
www.mannington.com

Manuel Canovas
19-23 Grosvenor Hill
London
W1K 3QD
United Kingdom
Tel: +011 (44) 20
8874 6484
Fax: +011 (44) 20
8877 6420
www.manuelcanovas.com
(Distributed in USA by Colefax and Fowler, in Canada by Primavera. See website for showroom locations.)

Marble Flooring Specialists
Verona House
Filwood Road
Fishponds
Bristol BS16 3RY
United Kingdom
Tel: +011 (44) 117
965 6565
Fax: +011 (44) 117
965 6573
www.marbleflooring.co.uk

Marlborough Tiles
Elcot Lane
Marlborough
Wiltshire SN8 2AY
United Kingdom
Tel: +011 (44) 1672 512422
Fax: +011 (44) 1672 515791
www.marlboroughtiles.co.uk

Marley Floors
(see Tarkett SA)

Marston & Langinger
117 Mercer Street
New York NY 10012
Tel: (212) 575 0554
Tel: (212) 965 0434
Fax: (212) 840 0236
www.marston-and
-langinger.com

Marthe Armitage
(Hamilton Weston Wallpapers)
18 St. Mary's Grove
Richmond
Surrey TW9 1UY
United Kingdom
Tel: +011 (44) 20
8940 4850
Fax: +011 (44) 20
8332 0296
www.hamiltonweston.com
(Contact for distributors in USA and Canada.)

Marvic Textiles
Unit 11 Westpoint Trading
Estates
Alliance Road
London W3 0RA
United Kingdom
Tel: +011 (44) 20
8993 0191
Fax: +011 (44) 20
8993 1484
(Distributed in USA by Roger Arlington Inc., in Canada by Bilbrough & Co.)

Mauny
(Distributed by Classic Revivals.)

The Maya Romanoff Corporation
1730 West Greenleaf
Chicago IL 60626
Tel: (312) 465 6909
Fax: (312) 465 7089
www.mayaromanoff.com
(Distributed in USA by Donghia, Bergamo, John Brooks, in Canada by Télio & Cie. See website for showrooms.)

Minton Hollins
(Distributed in UK by H. & R. Johnson, with international export. See also www.tessellations.org.uk, a national database of historic tile designs for antique Minton Hollins tiles.)

Monica James & Co.
Miami Design District
140 N.E. 40th Street
Miami FL 33137
Tel: (305) 576 6222
Fax: (305) 576 0975
www.monicajames.com
(Distributor of Bennison Fabrics.)

Monkwell
Crowson House
Bellbrook Park
Uckfield
East Sussex TN22 1QZ
United Kingdom
Tel: +011 (44) 1825 747901
Fax: +011 (44) 1825 764517
xenquiries@monkwell.com
Monkwell (USA)
Tel: (516) 752 7600
(Distributor of Design Archives, Crowson, Monkwell, Hill & Knowles. Distributed in USA by Lee Jofa, in Canada by Télio & Cie.)

Monterey Carpet Mills
(Tandus US Inc.)
3030 South Susan Street
Santa Ana CA 92704
Toll-free: 1 800 678 4640
Fax: (714) 557 0292
Trade samples, toll-free:
1 800 248 2878
www.montereycarpets.com
www.tandus.com
(Monterey, C & A and Crossley carpets. See website for USA showrooms.)
and
Tandus Canada
2820 Argentia Rd., Unit 5
Mississauga ON L5N 8G4
Tel: (905) 542 0229
Fax: (905) 542 1206

Montgomery Tomlinson Ltd.
Broughton Mill Road
Bretton
Cheshire CH4 0BY
United Kingdom
Tel: +011 (44) 1244 661363
Fax: +011 (44) 1244 661167
www.montgomery.co.uk
(Contact for distributors.)

Mosquito Design by Amy Cushing
62 Lower Ham Road
Kingston-upon-Thames
Surrey KT2 5AW
United Kingdom
Tel: +011 (44) 20
8715 5611

Tel: +011 (44) 7957
258 620
Fax: +011 (44) 20
8949 4490
www.mosquito-design.com
amy.cushing@mosquito
design.com
(Contact for distributors.)

Mulberry Home
322 Kings Road
London SW3 5UH
United Kingdom
Tel: +011 (44) 20
7823 3455
Fax: +011 (44) 20
7823 3329
www.mulberry.com
(Distributed in Canada and USA by Lee Jofa.)

N

Nancy Corzine
256 West Ivory Avenue
Inglewood
Los Angeles CA 90302
Tel: (310) 672 6775
Fax: (310) 672 7160
www.nancycorzine.com
(Distributor of Jason D'Souza. See website for locations.)

National Wood Flooring Association
111 Chesterfield Industrial
Boulevard
Chesterfield MO 63005
Toll-free (USA):
1 800 422 4556
Toll-free (Canada):
1 800 848 8824
Tel: (636) 519 9663
Fax: (636) 519 9664
www.woodfloors.org
(Sources to find products and professionals.)

Natural Wood Floor Co.
20 Smugglers Way
Wandsworth
London SW18 1EQ
United Kingdom
Tel: +011 (44) 20
8871 9771
Fax: +011 (44) 20
8877 0273
www.naturalwoodfloor.co.uk

New Castle Delft
Charles S. Allen
25b Hoult's Estate
Walker Road
Newcastle upon Tyne
NE6 1AB
United Kingdom
Tel: +011 (44) 1388
517 727
Tel: +011 (44) 7946
423 296
www.newcastledelft.com

Nice Irma's
Unit 2
Finchley Industrial Centre
879 High Road
London N12 8QA

United Kingdom
Tel: +011 (44) 20
8343 9766
Fax: +011 (44) 20
8343 9590
www.niceirmas.co.uk
(Online shopping.)

Nicholas Herbert
118 Lots Road
London SW10 0RJ
United Kingdom
Tel: +011 (44) 20
7376 5596
Fax: +011 (44) 20
7376 5572
www.nicholasherbert.com
(Distributed in USA by Travers & Co.)

Nina Campbell
318–26 Wandsworth Bridge
Road
London SW6 2TZ
United Kingdom
Tel: +011 (44) 20
7471 4270
Fax: +011 (44) 20
7471 4274
www.ninacampbell.com
(Online shopping. Distributed by Osborne & Little; distributor of Galbraith & Paul.)

Nitty Gritty Reproductions
170 King Street East
Toronto ON M5A 1J4
Tel: (416) 364 1393
Fax: (416) 364 1170
www.nittygritty.ca
(For milk paints and related products similar to Colourman Paints.)

Nobilis
29 rue Bonaparte
75006 Paris
France
Tel +011 (33) 143 29 21 50
Fax +011 (33) 143 29 77 57
www.nobilis.fr
and
Nobilis Inc.
3006 Emrick Blvd
Bethlehem PA 18020
Tel: (610) 866 8320
Fax: (610) 866 8322
nobnj@aol.com
and
Nobilis Inc.
The D&D Building
Suite 508
979 Third Avenue
New York NY 10022
Tel: (212) 980 1177
Fax: (212) 980 7988
(Distributed in Canada by Télio & Cie. See website for other USA distributors.)

Northwood Design & Interiors Ltd.
(previously known as Northwood Designs)
(Fiona S. Finlay)
Grantully Castle

by Aberfeldy
Perthshire
Scotland PH15 2EG
United Kingdom
Tel: +011 (44) 1887 840 488
Fax: +011 (44) 1887 840 477
www.northwooddesign.co.uk
info@northwooddesign.co.uk

Nova Hardwood Flooring
170 Akerley Blvd.
Burnside Industrial Park
Suites 4 & 5
Dartmouth NS B3B 1Z5
Tel: (902) 468 5154
Fax: (902) 468 1917
www.atyp.com
novahardwood
(Supplier of Boen Hardwood Flooring.)

Nutshell Natural Paints
P.O. Box 72
South Brent
Torquay TQ10 9YR
United Kingdom
Tel: +011 (44) 1364 73801
Fax: +011 (44) 1364 73068
www.nutshellpaints.com
(Online ordering. Contact for overseas delivery.)

Nya Nordiska Textiles
An den Ratswiesen
D 20451 Dannenberg
Germany
Tel: +011 (49) 5861 809 0
Fax: +011 (49) 5861 809 10
nya@nya.com
www.nya-nordiska.de
(Distributed in USA by Randolph & Hein, in Canada by Tessuti Uno.)

O

The Old Fashioned Milk Paint Co.
436 Main Street
P.O. Box 222
Groton MA 01450
Tel: (978) 448 6336
Fax: (978) 448 2754
www.milkpaint.com
(For milk paints and related products similar to Colourman Paints.)

Old Village Paints
P.O. Box 1030
Fort Washington PA 19034
Toll-free: 1 800 498 7687
Tel: (215) 234 2400
www.old-village.com
(Distributor of Stulb's Paints.)

Old World Weavers
(Stark Fabrics)
(See Stark Fabrics for USA distributors. Distributed in Canada by Crown Wallpaper and Fabric.)

Olicana
Brook Mills
Crimble, Slaithwaite
Huddersfield
West Yorkshire HD7 5BQ
United Kingdom

Tel: +011 (44) 1484 847666
Fax: +011 (44) 1484 847735
www.olicana.co.uk
sales@olicana.co.uk
(Distributed in USA by ZG Design. Contact for other suppliers.)

Les Olivades
Chemin des Indienneurs
13103 Saint Etienne-
du-Grès
France
Tel: +011 (33) 490 491919
Fax: +011 (33) 490 491920
www.les-olivades.com
(Distributed in USA by Pierre Deux.)

Ollerton Hall Decor
Ollerton
Knutsford
Cheshire WA16 8SF
United Kingdom
Tel: +011 (44) 1565 650222
Fax: +011 (44) 1565 754411
www.ollertonhalldiscount
carpets.co.uk

Original Style
Falcon Road
Sowton Industrial Estate
Exeter
Devon EX2 7LF
United Kingdom
Tel: +011 (44) 1392 474011
Fax: +011 (44) 1392 473003
www.originalstyle.com
(The parent company of Winchester Tiles. Distributed in USA by Roma Tile Company, in Canada by Cercan Tile.)

Ornamenta (by Jane Gordon Clark)
The Ornamenta Studio
South Kensington
London
United Kingdom
enquiries@ornamenta.co.uk
Tel: +011 (44) 20
7591 0077
Fax: +011 (44) 20
7584 3002
www.ornamenta.co.uk
(Distributed in USA by Stark Wallcovering. Contact for others.)

Osborne & Little
Riverside House
26 Osiers road
London SW18 1NH
United Kingdom
Tel: +011 (44) 20
8812 3000
Tel (Sales): +011 (44) 20
8812 3030
Fax: +011 (44) 20
8877 7500
and
The D&D Building
Suite 520
979 Third Avenue
New York NY 10022
Tel: (212) 751 3333

Fax: (212) 752 6027
www.osborneandlittle.com
(Distributor of Osborne &
Little, Liberty Furnishings,
Nina Campbell and
Designers Guild. Distributed
in Canada by Primavera. See
website for distributors.)

Osmose, Inc.
1016 Everee Inn Road
Griffin GA 30224
Toll-free Tel: 1 800 585 5161
Fax: (770) 229 5225
Tel: (716) 882 5905
Fax: (716) 882 5134
www.osmose.com
info@osmose.com
In Canada:
Tel: (905) 854 2244
Fax: (905) 854 0834
info@timberspecialties.com
(Wood preservation
products. North American
subsidiary of Protim
Solignum.)

Ottilie Stevenson
18 St. Paul's Place
London N1 2QF
United Kingdom
Tel: +011 (44) 20
    7288 2727
www.ottiliestevenson.co.uk
(Distributed by Fonthill.)

P

Paint and Paper Library
5 Elystan Street
London SW3 3NT
United Kingdom
Tel: +011 (44) 20
    7823 7755
Fax: +011 (44) 20
    7823 7766
www.paintlibrary.co.uk
(Distributed by Fonthill and
Hinson & Company. Online
shopping.)

Paint Magic
(Desmond International)
412 Pebble Creek Court
Pennington NJ 08534
Tel: (609) 730 0445

Paper Moon
The Paddocks
29 Bragbury Lane
Bragbury End
Hertfordshire SG2 8TJ
United Kingdom
Tel: +011 (44) 1438
    211770/1
Fax: +011 (44) 1438
    211772
www.papermoon.co.uk
(Online ordering available.)

Paris Ceramics
150 East 58th Street
7th Floor
New York NY 10155
Tel: (212) 644 2782
Fax: (212) 644 2785
www.parisceramics.com
(Distributor of Froyle Tiles.)

Pergo Inc.
P.O. Box 1775
Horsham PA 19044
Toll-free: 1 800 337 3746
www.pergo.com
(Online showroom. See
website to find showrooms in
USA and Canada.)

Pierre Deux
40 Enterprise Avenue
Secausus NJ 07094
Tel: (201) 809 2500
Fax: (201) 319 0719
www.pierredeux.com
(Online and catalogue
shopping. See website for
locations. Distributor of Les
Olivades. Distributed by
Kravet.)

Pierre Frey France
47 rue des Petits-Champs
75001 Paris
Tel: +011 (33) 1 44 77 36 00
Fax: +011 (33) 1 42 96 85 38
contact@pierrefrey.com
www.pierrefrey.com
(Distributed in Canada by
Primavera. See website for
USA showrooms and
distributors.)
    and
The D&D Building
Suite 1611
979 Third Avenue
New York NY 10022
Tel: (212) 421 0534
Fax: (212) 826 9236
    and
Pierre Frey Customer Service
1692 Chantilly Drive NE
Suite C
Atlanta GA 30324
Toll-free: 1 866 707 1524
Tel: (678) 904 2009
Fax: (404) 835 1102
contact.usa@pierrefrey.com

Pippa & Hale
(Distributed by Today Interiors
Ltd.)

Pisani Ltd.
Unit 12, Transport Avenue
Great Western Road
Brentford
Middlesex TW8 9HF
United Kingdom
Tel: +011 (44) 20
    8568 5001
Fax: +011 (44) 20
    8847 3406
www.pisani.co.uk

Portola Paints & Glazes
12442 Moorpark Street
Studio City CA 91604
Tel: (818) 623 9053
Fax: (818) 623 9210
www.portolapaints.com
(For limewash paints and
related products similar to Liz
Induni and Rose of Jericho.
See also Keimfarben and
U.S. Heritage Paints.)

Pratt & Lambert Paints
101 W. Prospect Avenue
Cleveland OH 44115
Toll-free: 1 800 289 7728
Fax: (216) 566 1655
www.prattandlambert.com

Prestige Mills
Prestige Mills, Inc.
34-01 38th Avenue
Long Island City NY 11101
Toll-free Tel: 1 866 537 7847
Toll-free Fax: 1 866 537 2329
ehollier@prestigemills.com
(Distributor of Louis de
Poortere in USA and
Canada.)

Primavera
160 Pears Avenue
Suite 210
Toronto ON M5R 1T2
Tel: (416) 921 3334
Fax: (416) 921 3227
www.primavera.ca
(Distributor of David Oliver,
Colefax & Fowler, Cowtan &
Tout, Jane Churchill, Larsen,
Manuel Canovas, Osborne &
Little, Designers Guild,
Liberty, Lorca, Nina
Campbell, Chelsea, Malabar,
Pierre Frey, Nancy Corzine,
Hollly Hunt, Scalamandré.
See also AnneStarr Agencies
for regional showrooms.)

Protim Solignum
(Osmose UK)
Fieldhouse Lane
Marlow
Buckinghamshire SL7 1LS
United Kingdom
Tel: +011 (44) 1628 486644
Fax: +011 (44) 1628 476757
www.protimsolignum.com
(For similar products see
Osmose, Inc.)

R

Ramm, Son & Crocker
Chiltern House
The Valley Centre
Gordon Road
High Wycombe
Buckinghamshire HP13 6EQ
United Kingdom
Tel: +011 (44) 1494 446555
Tel: +011 (44) 1494 603555
Fax: +011 (44) 1494 464664
www.ramm.co.uk
www.robertallendesign.com
(Owned and distributed by
Robert Allen. See website for
showrooms and distributors.)
    and
Robert Allen/Beacon Hill
The D&D Building
Suite 301
979 Third Avenue
New York NY 10022
Tel: (212) 759 5408

Randolph & Hein
2222 Palou Centre
San Francisco CA 94124
Toll-free Tel: 1 800 844 9922

Tel: (415) 864 3371
Fax: (415) 864 2185
Sales Tel: (310) 967 6165
Sales Fax: (310) 360 1406
www.randolphhein.com
(Distributor of Nya Nordiska.
See website for showrooms.)

Reed Harris
Riverside House
27 Carnwath Road
London SW6 3HR
United Kingdom
Tel: +011 (44) 207
    736 7511
Fax: +011 (44) 207
    751 2988
www.reedharris.co.uk
(Online tile design feature.)

Reeve Flooring
Valley Farm
Brancaster Staithe
Norfolk PE31 8DB
United Kingdom
Tel: +011 (44) 1485 210754
Fax: +011 (44) 1485 210910
www.reeveflooring.com

Reptile Tile & Ceramics
(Carlo Briscoe & Edward
Dunn)
Gwaith Meyn
Llanglydwen
Whitland
Carmarthenshire SA34 0XP
United Kingdom
Tel/Fax: +011 (44)
    1994 419402
Tel: +011 (44)
    7796 793362
www.reptiletiles.co.uk
(Available worldwide by mail
order. Commissions
worldwide.)

Robert Allen
225 Foxboro Boulevard
Foxboro MA 02035
Toll-free Tel: 1 800 333 3777
Toll-free Fax: 1 800 332 8256
(Parent company and
distributor of Ramm, Son &
Crocker. See website for
showrooms.)
    and
Robert Allen (Canada)
2880 Argentia Road, Unit 11
Mississauga ON L5N 7X8
Toll-free Tel: 1 800 363 3020
Toll-free Fax: 1 800 463 0339

Roger Arlington, Inc.
30-10 41st Avenue, 2 R
New York NY 11101
Tel: (718) 729 5554
Fax: (718) 729 5556
    and
The D&D Building
Suite 1411
979 Third Avenue
New York NY 10022
Tel: (212) 752 5288
Fax: (212) 935 5195
(Distributor of Marvic
Textiles.)

Roma Tile Company Inc.
400 Arsenal Street
Watertown MA 02472
Tel: (617) 926 5800
www.romatile.com
(Distributor of Winchester
Tiles.)

Ronseal Ltd.
Thorncliffe Park
Chapeltown
Sheffield S35 2YP
United Kingdom
Tel: +011 (44) 114
    246 7171
Fax: +011 (44) 114
    245 5629
www.ronseal.co.uk
(Online ordering available.)

Rose of Jericho
Horchester Farm
Holywell
Dorchester
Dorset DT2 0LL
United Kingdom
Tel: +011 (44) 1935 83676
Fax: +011 (44) 1935 83903
www.rose-of-jericho
    .demon.co.uk
(Limewash and distemper
paints. For similar products
see also Keimfarben, Portola
Paints and U.S. Heritage
Paints.)

Roses Mill
14 Stoneygate Road
Newmilns
Ayrshire KA16 9AL
United Kingdom
Tel/Fax: +011 (44)
    1560 322285
www.rosesmill.co.uk
(Online shopping available.)

Rubelli
H.A. Percheron Ltd.
202 The Chambers
Chelsea Harbour
London SW10 0XF
United Kingdom
Tel: +011 (44) 20
    7349 1590
Fax: +011 (44) 20
    7349 1595
info@rubelli.com
www.rubelli.com
(Distributed in USA by
Bergamo, in Canada by Télio
& Cie. See website for
showrooms.)
    and
Bergamo Fabrics, Inc.
The D&D Building
Suite 1705
979 Third Avenue
New York NY 10022
Tel: (212) 888 3333
Fax: (212) 888 3837
    and
Rubelli (USA)
Tel: (914) 665 0800
Fax: (914) 665 7900
www.bergamofabrics.com

Rucksthul
St. Urbanstrasse 21

4901 Langenthal
Switzerland
Tel: +011 (41) 62 919 86 00
Fax: +011 (41) 62 922 48 70
www.ruckstuhl.net
    and
Ruckstuhl USA Ltd.
P.O. Box 50
Allendale NJ 07401
Tel: (239) 573 3400
Fax: (239) 573 3415

Rustins
Waterloo Road
London NW2 7TX
United Kingdom
Tel: +011 (44) 20
    8450 4666
Fax: +011 (44) 20
    8452 2008
www.rustins.co.uk
(See Briwax for similar
product.)

Ryalux Carpets Ltd.
Ensor Mill
Queensway
Castleton
Rochdale
Lancashire OL11 2NU
United Kingdom
Tel: +011 (44) 1706 716000
Fax: +011 (44) 1706 860618
www.ryalux.com

Rye Tiles
(Rye Pottery Ltd.)
The Old Brewery
Wishward
Rye
East Sussex TN31 7DH
United Kingdom
Tel: +011 (44) 1797 223038
Fax: +011 (44) 1797 224834
www.ryetiles.co.uk

S

Sahco Hesslein
Sahco Hesslein
    GmbH & Co. KG
Kreuzburger Str. 17–19
D-90471 Nürenberg
Germany
Tel: +011 (49) 911 99 87 0
Fax: +011 (49) 911 99 87 480
info@sahco.de
www.sahco-hesslein.com
(Distributed in USA by
Bergamo, in Canada by Télio
& Cie. See website for all
showrooms.)

Saloni Ceramica
Carretera Alcora 12130
San Juan de Moro
12080 Castellon
Spain
Tel: +011 (34) 96 434 3434
Fax: +011 (34) 96 434 3473
www.saloni.com
(See website for all
showrooms in USA and
Canada.)

Sandberg Tyg & Tapet AB
Box 69
Hesters Industriomrâde

52322 Ulricehamn
Tel: +011 (46) 321 531 660
Fax: +011 (46) 321 531 661
www.sandbergtapeter.com
(Distributed in USA by
Country Swedish Showroom,
in Canada by Appel.)

Sanderson
(Arthur Sanderson & Sons)
Chalfont House
Oxford Road
Denham
Middlesex UB9 4DX
Tel: +011 (44) 1895
    830 044
Fax: +011 (44) 1895
    830 055
www.sanderson-uk.com
www.william-morris.co.uk
    and
Arthur Sanderson & Sons Ltd.
100 Acres
Sandersons Road
Uxbridge UB8 1DH
Middlesex
Tel: +011 (44) 1895
    238 244
Fax: +011 (44) 1895
    231 450
    and
Sanderson (USA)
Zoffany Showroom
The D&D Building
Suite 409
979 Third Avenue
New York NY 10022
Tel: (212) 319 7220
Fax: (212) 593 6184
    and
Corporate Office:
285 Grand Avenue
3 Patriot Centre
Englewood NJ 07631
Toll-free Tel: 1 800 894 6185
Toll-free Fax: 1 800 894 6098
(Major distributor for William
Morris & Co. archive.)

Sawyer Finn Company
1600 Genessee
Kansas City MO 64102
Tel: (816) 421 3321
richo@primenet.com
(For similar products, see
also Old Fashioned Milk
Paint Co., Nitty Gritty
Reproductions, Old Village
Paints, Homestead House
Paint Company.)

Scalamandré
Head office:
300 Trade Zone Drive
Ronkonkoma NY 11779
Toll-free: 1 800 932 4361
Tel: (631) 467 8800
Fax: (631) 467 9448
Fax: (631) 467 8909
www.scalamandre.com
    and
The D&D Building
Suites 110/210/310
979 Third Avenue
New York NY 10022
Tel: (212) 980 3888
Fax: (212) 688 7531

(Distributed in Canada by AnneStarr Agencies and Primavera. See website for all showrooms.)

Sepp Leaf US
381 Park Avenue South
Suite 1301
New York NY 10016
Toll-free: 1 800 971 7377
Tel: (212) 683 2840
Fax: (212) 725 0308
sales@seppleaf.com
www.seppleaf.com
(Distributor of Libéron.)

Seri Parquet
BP60ZI du Centre 12300
Decazeville
France
Tel: +011 (33) 565 430574
Fax: +011 (33) 565 433980
www.parquets-du
-rouergue.eu
adv.export@seriparquet.fr
(Contact for distributors.)

Sheila Coombes
(see Brian Yates Interiors)

Sherwin Williams
101 Prospect Street
Cleveland OH 44115
Tel: (216) 566 2000
Fax: (216) 566 2318
www.sherwin-williams.com
and
Sherwin Williams (Canada)
170 Brunel Road, Unit A
Mississauga ON L4Z 1T5
Tel: (905) 507 0166
Fax: (905) 507 4198

Siesta Cork Tile Co
Unit 21 Tate Road
Gloucester Road
Croydon Surrey CR0 2DP
United Kingdom
Tel: +011 (44) 20
8683 4055
Fax: +011 (44) 20
8683 4480
www.siestacorktiles.co.uk

Sigma Coatings USA
1401 Destrehan Avenue
Harvey LA 70058
Tel: (504) 347 4321
Fax: (504) 341 9120
www.sigmacoatings.com

The Silk Gallery
G25 Chelsea Harbour
Design Centre
Chelsea Harbour
London SW10 0XE
United Kingdom
Tel: +011 (44) 20
7351 1700
Fax: +011 (44) 20
7376 4693
www.thesilkgallery.co.uk
(Mail order available.)

Simmy Ceramics
Sayer House
Oxgate Lane

London NW2 7JN
United Kingdom
Tel: +011 (44) 20
8208 0416
Fax: +011 (44) 20
8450 1140
www.simmyceramics.com
(Online shopping.)

Sinclair Till Flooring Company
793 Wandsworth Road
London SW8 3JQ
United Kingdom
Tel: +011 (44) 20
7720 0031
Fax: +011 (44) 20
7498 3814
www.sinclairtill.co.uk
(Contact for more information.)

Stark Carpet Corporation
(Fonthill Ltd.)
The D&D Building
11th Floor
979 Third Avenue
New York NY 10022
Tel: (212) 752 9000
Fax: (212) 752 9013
www.starkcarpet.com
(See website for showroom locations. Also distributes Bernard Thorp & Co., Crucial Trading and John Boyd.)

Stark Fabrics
The D&D Building
10th Floor
979 Third Avenue
New York NY 10022
Tel: (212) 752 9000
Fax: (212) 758 4342
www.stark.com
www.old-world-weavers.com
(Distributor of Lelièvre.)

Stark Wallcovering
The D&D Building
10th Floor
979 Third Avenue
New York NY 10022
Tel: (212) 355 7186
Fax: (212) 753 3761
www.starkwallcovering.com
(Distributor of Ornamenta, Knowles & Christou, Alexander Beauchamp.)

Star Wood Finish Supply
P.O. Box 86
Mendocino CA 95460
Tel: (707) 962 9480
Fax: (707) 962 9484
www.woodfinishsupply.com
(Sells Liberon by mail.)

The Stencil Store
4a Horsegate Road
Chorleywood
Hertfordshire WD3 5BL
United Kingdom
Tel: +011 (44) 1923 285577
Tel: +011 (44) 1923 285588
Fax: +011 (44) 1923 285136
www.stencilstore.com

(Online shopping. See also Designer Stencils.)

Stoddard Carpets Ltd
P.O. Box 11080
Boulder CO 80301
Toll-free: 1 800 742 1244
Tel: (303) 516 9620
Fax: (303) 527 1662
www.stoddardcarpet.com

Stonell
Forstal House
Beltring, Paddock Wood
Kent TN12 6PY
United Kingdom
Tel: +011 (44) 189
283 3500
Fax: +011 (44) 189
283 3600
www.stonell.com

Stroheim & Romann, Inc.
30–30 47th Avenue
New York NY 11101
Tel: (718) 7067000
Fax: (718) 361 0159
www.stroheim.com
(Distributor of JAB International. See website for showroom locations.)

Stuart Interiors
Barrington Court
Barrington
Ilminster
Somerset TA19 0NQ
United Kingdom
Tel: +011 (44) 146
024 0349
Fax: +011 (44) 146
024 2069
www.stuart-interiors.com
(On-site work. Contact for details.)

Stulb's
(Distributed by Old Village Paints.)

Surving Studios
17 Millsburg Road
Middletown NY 10940
Toll-free: 1 800 768 4954
Tel: (845) 355 1430
Fax: (845) 355 1517
www.surving.com
(Distributed in Canada by Creekside Tile Co. and World Mosaic Inc. See website for showroom locations in USA.)

Suzanne Brown and Associates
354 Davenport Road
Toronto ON M5R 1K6
Tel: (416) 944 8311
Fax: (416) 944 8312
suzanne.brown@
sympatico.ca
(Distributor of Zuber & Cie.)

T

Tarkett SA
2, rue de l'Egalité
F-92748 Nanterre Cedex
France

Tel: +011 (33) 1 41 20 43 86
Fax: +011 (33) 1 41 20 47 05
and
Tarkett-Marley Floors Ltd.
Lenham, Maidstone
Kent ME17 2QX
United Kingdom
Tel: +011 (44) 1 622
854040
Fax: +011 (44) 1 622
854520
www.marleyfloors.com
and
Tarkett, Inc.
(Tarkett-Marley Floors Ltd.)
2728 Summer Street
Houston TX 77007
Toll-free: 1 800 877 8453
www.tarkett-floors.com
(Distributed in USA by Floor Supply Distributing, in Canada by Compass Flooring. See website for dealer locations in USA and Canada.)

Télio & Cie
Montreal Office:
625 Deslauriers
Montréal QC H4N 1W8
Toll-free: 1 800 361 0375
Tel: (514) 271 4607
Fax: (514) 807 8808
www.telio.com
(Distributor of Brian Yates, Clarence House, Crowson, Design Archives, J. Robert Scott, John Boyd, Lelièvre, Maya Romanoff, Nobilis, Sahco Hesslein, Sanderson.)
and
Montreal Showroom:
1407 rue de la Montagne
Montreal QC I IG3 1Z3
Tel: (514) 842 9116
Fax: (514) 842 3728
deco@telio.com
and
Toronto Showroom:
160 Pears Avenue
Suite 400
Toronto ON M5R 3P8
Tel: (416) 968 2020
Fax: (416) 968 7298
orders@telio.com

Terrazzo, Tile and Marble Association of Canada
Eastern Branch:
163 Buttermill Avenue, Unit 8
Concord ON L4K 3X8
Toll-free: 1 800 201 8599
Tel: (905) 660 9640
Fax: (905) 660 0513
www.ttmac.com
and
Western Branch:
108-3650 Bonneville Place
Burnaby BC V3N 4T7

Tel: (604) 294 6885
Fax: (604) 294 2406

Tessuti Uno
Designer's Walk Bldg 2
320 Davenport Road
Toronto ON M5R 1K6

Tel: (416) 922 0126
Fax: (416) 922 0441
(Distributor of Création Baumann, Dedar, Nya Nordiska, Zimmer + Rohde, Zoffany.)

Textra Limited
8 Station Yard
Steventon
Oxfordshire OX13 6RX
United Kingdom
Tel: +011 (44) 1235 823100
Fax: +011 (44) 1235 823101
www.textra.co.uk
(Contact for ordering information. See also Pierre Frey for flame-retardant fabrics.)

Thomas Dare
Tower House
Ruthvenfield Road
Perth PH1 3UN
Scotland
Tel: +011 (44) 1738 609000
www.thomasdare.com
(A division of the Macnaughton Group. Distributed in USA by Fonthill.)

Tile Productions
Technique House
New Garden Street
Blackburn
Lancashire BB2 3RE
United Kingdom
Tel/Fax: +011 (44)
1254 673003
www.tileproductions.co.uk

Tiles of Newport & London
320 Chepstow Road
Newport
South Wales NP19 8NP
United Kingdom
Tel: +011 (44) 1633 273399
Fax: +011 (44) 1633 270404
www.tilesofnewport.co.uk

Tiles of Stow
Langston Priory Workshops
Station Road
Kingham OX7 6UP
United Kingdom
Tel: +011 (44) 1608 658993
Fax: +011 (44) 1608 658951
www.tilesofstow.co.uk
(Catalogue available.)

Timney Fowler
355 King Street
London W6 9NH
United Kingdom
Tel: +011 (44) 20 8748
3010 for US suppliers.
Fax: +011 (44) 20 8748
3007
(Distributed in Canada by Bilbrough & Co.)

Today Interiors Ltd.
Hollis Road
Grantham
Lincolnshire NG31 7QH
United Kingdom

Tel: +011 (44) 1476 574401
Fax: +011 (44) 1476 590208
www.todayinteriors.com
(Distributor of Pippa & Hale. Distributed by Gaetano Ltd.)

Tor Coatings Ltd.
Portobello Industrial Estate
Birtley
Chesterle Street
Co. Durham DH3 2RE
United Kingdom
Tel: +011 (44) 191
410 6611
Fax: +011 (44) 191
492 0125
www.tor-coatings.com

Travers & Company
504 East 74th Street
New York NY 10021
Tel: (212) 772 2778
Fax: (212) 888 7800
(Distributor of Gainsborough Silk Weaving.)

Trimite Powders Inc.
5680 North Blackstock Road
Spartanburg SC 29303
Toll-free: 1 800 866 8666
Fax: (864) 587 6152

Tritex Fabrics Ltd.
106–611 Alexander Street
Vancouver BC V6A 1E1
Tel: (604) 255 4242
Fax: (604) 255 9255
www.tritexfabrics.com
(Exclusive distributor of Kravet in British Columbia.)

Turnell & Gigon
Chelsea Harbour
Design Centre
Lots Road
London SW10 0XE
Tel: +011 (44) 20 7259 7280
Fax: +011 (44) 20 7259 7283
www.tandggroup.com

U

Ulster Carpet Mills (N.A.) Inc.
81 Whitlock Avenue
Marietta GA 30064
Tel: (770) 514 0707
Fax: (770) 514 1006
(Distributed in Canada by Carpet Design Solutions.)

U.S. Heritage Paints
3516 N. Kostner
Chicago IL 60641
Tel: (773) 286 2100
Fax: (773) 286 1852
(Premixed Old-World European limewash by mail-order. Online catalogue.)

V

V. V. Rouleaux
54 Sloane Square
Cliveden Place
London SW1W 8AW
United Kingdom

Tel: +011 (44) 20
7730 3125
Fax: +011 (44) 20
7730 9985
www.vvrouleaux.com
(Online ordering available.)

van Schelle & Gurland
50 Cambridge Mansions
Cambridge Rd, Battersea
London SW11 4RX
United Kingdom
Tel: +011 (44) 020
7223 6485
(Distributed by Altfield Limited.)

Villeroy & Boch
The House of Villeroy & Boch
901 Broadway
New York NY 10003
Tel: (212) 505 1090
Fax: (212) 505 3739
www.villeroy-boch.com

Vymura (now CWV Ltd)
No 1, The Beehive
Shadsworth Business Park
Lions Drive
Blackburn
Lancashire BB1 2QS
United Kingdom
Tel: +011 (44) 1254
222 800
Fax: +011 (44) 1254
222 972
www.wallpapers-uk.com
enquiries@cwvgroup.com
(Shop online or contact for distributor locations.)

W

Walcot Inc.
(see Jane Knapp.)

Walker Zanger
8901 Bradley Avenue
Sun Valley CA 91352
Tel: (818) 504 0235
Fax: (818) 504 2057
www.walkerzanger.com
(Distributed in Canada by World Mosaic. Distributor of Kirkstone.)

Warner Fabrics
(Distributed by Zimmer + Rohde Ltd.)

Warwick
Hackling House
Bourton Industrial Park
Bourton-on-the-Water
Gloucestershire GL54 2EN
United Kingdom
Tel: +011 (44) 1451 833383
Fax: +011 (44) 1451 822369
www.warwick.co.uk
(Contact for distributors.)

Watts of Westminster (Belinda Coote)
The Granary
Wernddu, Pontrilas
Herefordshire HR2 0ED
United Kingdom

Tel: +011 (44) 1873 860314
Fax: +011 (44) 1873 860342
www.wattsofwestminster.com
*(Distributed in USA by
Christopher Norman.
Contact for other suppliers.)*

**Waveney Rush
  Industry Ltd.**
The Old Maltings
Caldecott Road
Oulton Broad
Lowestoft
Suffolk NR32 3AH
United Kingdom
Tel: +011 (44) 1502 538777
Fax: +011 (44) 1502 538477
www.waveneyrush.co.uk
*(Online ordering; overseas
delivery.)*

Welbeck Tiles
Treriefe Park, Units 2 & 3
Treriefe
Penzance
Cornwall TR20 8TB
United Kingdom
Tel/Fax: +011 (44) 1736
  762000
www.welbeck-tiles.co.uk
*(Mail order catalogue
available. Ships overseas.)*

Wemyss (Houlès)
Houlès USA
8687 Melrose Avenue
Suite B256
Los Angeles CA 90069
Tel: (310) 652 6171
Fax: (310) 652 8370
  and
Houlès Canada
P.O. Box 11281
Station Centreville
Montreal QC H3C 5G9
Toll-free Tel: 1 800 654 9116
Toll-free Fax: 1 800 654 9143
www.houles.com
*(See website for USA
showrooms. Distributed in
Canada by Télio & Cie,
Annestarr Agencies, and see
website for others.)*

Wendy Cushing Trimmings
P.O. Box 51435
74 Millmead Business Centre
London N17 9YS
United Kingdom
Tel: +011 (44) 208
  885 0300
Fax: +011 (44) 208
  885 0304
www.wendycushing.com
*(Distributed in USA by
Fonthill Ltd. Contact for
others.)*

Westbond
Cortonwood Drive
Cortonwood Business Park
Brampton
Barnsley S73 0UF
United Kingdom
Tel: +011 (44) 1226
  757 757

Fax: +011 (44) 1226
  757 759
www.westbond-carpets.com

Westco
Penarth Road
Cardiff
Wales CF1 8YN
United Kingdom
Tel: +011 (44) 29
  203 76700
Fax: +011 (44) 29
  203 83573
www.westcofloors.co.uk

Wicanders Cork Flooring
Amorim Flooring
  North America
7513 Connelley Drive
Suite M
Hanover MD 21076
Tel: (410) 553 6062
Fax: (410) 553 6123
info@amorimus.com
For USA trade and retail,
see: www.wicanders.com
For Canada trade, see:
www.shnier.ca
For Canada retail, see:
www.floorsfirst.com
*(See websites for distributors
and retail showrooms.)*

William May & Co.
P.O. Box 234
Brielle NJ 08730
Tel: (732) 528 2248
Fax: (732) 528 2249
toffeemad1@aol.com
*(Distributor of H. & R.
Johnson tiles.)*

William Morris & Co.
*(See Sanderson, which
distributes the majority of the
William Morris & Co. archive.
See also www.william-
morris.co.uk for USA
distributors. Distributed in
Canada by Télio & Cie.)*

**William Switzer &
  Associates**
6–611 Alexander Street
Vancouver BC V6A 1E1
Tel: (604) 255 5911
Fax: (604) 255 5931
www.williamswitzer
  collection.com
*(Distributor of William Switzer,
Christopher Norman, John
Boyd Textiles, Donghia, Maya
Romanoff, Bergamo, John
Brooks. See website for
showrooms in Canada and
USA.)*

Wilman Interiors
(John Wilmans)
Wilman Interiors Customer
  Services
Unit 1, Farrington Place
Farrington Road
  Industrial Estate
Burnley
Lancashire BB11 5TY
United Kingdom

Tel: +011 (44) 845
  271 7333
Fax: +011 (44) 845
  271 7334
www.wilmaninteriors.com
*(Contact for distribution
details.)*

Winchester Tile Co.
Falcon Road
Exeter
Devon EX2 7LF
United Kingdom
Tel: +011 (44) 1392
  474011
Fax: +011 (44) 1392
  219932
www.winchestertiles.com
*(See Original Style for
distributors. See also Cercan
Tile Inc. and Roma Tile.)*

Woodward Grosvenor
Stourvale Mill
Green Street
Kidderminster
Worcestershire DY10 1AT
United Kingdom
Tel: +011 (44) 800 526696
Tel: +011 (44) 1562 820020
Fax: +011 (44) 1562 820042
www.woodward
  grosvenor.co.uk
*(Distributed in USA by J.R.
Burrows & Company.)*

World Mosaic (B.C.) Ltd.
1665 West 7th Avenue
Vancouver BC V6J 1S4
Tel: (604) 736 8158
Fax: (604) 736 9908
  and
World Mosaic Stone & Tile
Designer's Walk
354 Davenport Road
Suite 101
Toronto ON M5R 1K6
Toll Free: 1 877 768 1555
Tel: (416) 929 1555
www.worldmosaic.ca
(Distributor of Walker Zanger.)

Y

Yaletown Tileworks
1009 Cambie Street
Vancouver BC V6B 5L7
Tel: (604) 682 3060
Fax: (604) 681 5997
*(Distributor of Ann Sacks
Tiles.)*

Z

Zest Essentials
(formerly Brats Paints)
38 Upper Street
Islington
London N1 OPN
United Kingdom
Tel: +011 (44) 20
  7226 6138
Fax: +011 (44) 20
  7226 7001
www.zestessentials.com
*(Online ordering; overseas
shipping.)*

ZG Design
(Zina Glazebrook)
East Hampton New York
Tel: (631) 749 5058
www.zgdesign.com
Zina@ZGdesign.com
*(Online catalog. Distributor of
Olicana. See website for
locations.)*

Zimmer + Rohde Ltd.
15 Commerce Road
Stamford CT 06902
Tel: (203) 3271400
Fax: (203) 327 7722
www.zimmer-rohde.com
*(Online shopping. See
website for USA distributors.
Distributed in Canada by
Tessuti Uno.)*
  and
The D&D Building
Suite 1616
979 Third Avenue
New York NY 10022
Tel: (212) 593 9787
Fax: (212) 753 4372

Zoë Barlow Passementerie
17 Oak Road
Hale
Altrincham
Cheshire WA15 9JA
United Kingdom
Tel: +011 (44) 161
  929 1255

Zoffany
Chalfont House
Oxford Road
Denham UB9 4DX
United Kingdom
www.zoffany.com
  and
The D&D Building
Suite 1403
979 Third Avenue
New York NY 10022
Tel: (212) 593 9787
Fax: (212) 593 9771
*(Distributed in Canada by
Tessuti Uno. Distributor of
Chase Erwin in the USA.)*

Zuber
21 rue Zuber
BP 1
68171 Rixheim Cedex
France
Tel: +011 (33) 3 89 44 13 88
Fax: +011 (33) 3 89 65 52 22
www.zuber.fr
  and
Zuber Inc.
200 East 59th Street
New York NY 10022
Tel: (212) 486 9226
Fax: (212) 754 6166
  and
(Stark Carpet)
Pacific Design Center
8687 Melrose Avenue
Suite B-629
Los Angeles CA 90069
Tel: (310) 657 8275
Fax: (310) 657 2191

Index

H

H. & R. Johnson 313, 315, 316, 320, 322, 323, 329, 333, 336, 342, 353, 354, 359

Hamilton Weston 119, 214, 215, 216, 217, 219, 220, 231, 232, 234, 235, 237, 245, 247, 258, 260, 261, 264, 272, 273, 274, 275, 276, 277, 279

hand–blocking 206, 234, 235

Hardwood & Natural Stone Flooring Company, The 367

hardwoods 14, 23, 40, 306, 362

Harlequin 63, 64, 65, 67, 83, 93, 95, 107, 108, 205, 207, 209, 225, 226, 227, 229, 266, 268, 282, 283

Harris, Moses *The Natural History of Colours* 290

Hay, D. R. *Original Geometric Diaper Designs* 278

Henry Newbery & Co. 191, 192, 193, 194, 195, 196, 198, 199, 200, 201

Hepplewhite, George 26, 64

heraldic style 13, 14, 94, 95, 138

Herculaneum 23, 136, 214

herringbones 62, 63

Heywood, Higginbottom & Smith 263

Hicks, David 298

Hill & Knowles 104, 105, 170, 182, 186, 187

Historic Floors of Oshkosh 363, 364, 365, 366, 367, 368, 369

Hodsoll McKenzie 65, 71, 72, 73, 81, 96, 103, 112, 114, 115, 116, 119, 121, 152, 169, 170, 218, 236, 237, 263, 274

Holkham Linseed Paints 295, 298

Honiton, England 180

Hoover Building, Perivale, England 358

horsehair fabric 64

Howe 153

Huguenots 78, 190

Huquier, J. G. *Nouveau Livre de Trophées de Fleurs Etrangers* 150

I

Ian Mankin 63, 65, 161, 168, 172, 173

Ian Sanderson 64, 67, 72, 75, 78, 97, 166, 176, 183, 197, 201

IHDG 222, 265, 269

ikat 174

Inca influence 176

India 14, 37, 94, 112, 114, 128, 132, 136, 138, 140, 144, 150, 154, 166, 170, 180

indiennes 17, 110, 112, 114, 128, 132

Indonesia 128, 130, 170, 174

industrial espionage 129

Interdesign 180, 182, 187, 188

Ipswich, Massachusetts 180

Ireland 76, 78

Iribe, Paul 104

iron 40

Islam 94, 149, 320, 328, 330, 332

Isle Mill, The 97, 161, 165, 171, 173, 175

Italy 14, 76, 78, 82, 180

Ivo Prints 144

Iznik, Turkey 331

J

J. & J. G. Lowe 319, 332

J. Robert Scott 105, 126

J. W. Bollom 211, 292, 297

Jab 63, 66, 67, 75, 79, 82, 85, 100, 114, 165, 173

Jack Lenor Larsen (see *Larsen* in directory) 186, 187

Jackson, John Baptist 232, 244

Jacobean Revival 87, 90, 104, 111, 142, 156, 172, 252

Jacquard loom 82, 86, 380

Jane Churchill 112, 117, 121, 125, 145, 173, 183, 210, 217, 227, 231, 232, 236, 240, 241, 242, 261, 268, 279, 280, 281, 296, 301

Jane Knapp 393

Japan 43, 57, 122, 170, 186

japonaiserie 140

Jason D'Souza 94, 111, 113, 115, 148, 162

Jaymart 397

Jencks, Charles 53, 346

Jenrette, Richard 362, 376

Jim Thompson 121, 123, 140, 159, 169, 176

Joanna Wood (see *Lewis & Wood* in directory) 262, 277

John Boyd Textiles 64, 162, 170, 171, 172, 175, 177

John Lewis 89

John Oliver 299

John Wilman (see *Wilman Interiors* in directory) 77, 81, 164, 165, 264

Jones, Owen 152, 218, 220, 236, 262

Jones, Owen *Grammar of Ornament* 37, 170, 276, 278, 382

Jones, Robert 274

Jouy-en-Josas, France 129, 134

Junckers 368, 369

K

Kahrs 368

Karndean 392, 393, 394

Kashmir 100, 154

Kenneth Clark Ceramics 316, 319, 323, 324, 325, 326, 327, 332, 334, 335, 337, 344, 345, 349, 350, 356, 357, 358

Kentucky Wood Floors 366, 367

Kenzo 344

Kievel Stone 314

Kirkstone 314, 350

Knowles & Christou 106, 150, 158, 159, 177, 180

Kravet 102

L

lace 17, 32, 40, 178–89

antiquing 179

lacquer 49

Lafon, Françoise 47

Larsen 65, 177, 180, 187, 188, 189

LASSCO 363, 365, 366, 367

Laura Ashley 98, 126, 127, 180, 186, 213, 215, 216, 219, 221, 225, 227, 237, 239, 241, 242, 255, 271, 350

LBC 368

Le Corbusier, C. E. 49

Le Moyne De Morgues, *Jacques La Clef des Champs* 110

leather 17

Lee Jofa 93, 104, 115, 119, 120, 122, 123, 125, 131, 135, 142, 143, 157, 176

Leeds Castle, Kent, England 13

Leighton House, London 312

Lelièvre 71, 72, 77, 98, 99, 111, 123, 126, 159

Lennox Money 116, 117, 152, 154

leno 178, 180

Leonardo da Vinci 167

Les Olivades 94

Lewis & Wood 245, 246

Liberon Waxes 303, 304, 308

Liberty Furnishings 55, 68, 69, 103, 109, 113, 123, 142, 147, 155, 179, 185, 189

limewash 13, 14, 286, 288, 289, 290

waxes 304

linen 63, 76, 78, 80, 84, 86, 114

brown Holland 64

linoleum 37, 239, 390, 393, 394

looms 82, 86, 380, 382, 386, 389

loose covers 63

Louis XI of France 93, 244

Louis XIV of France 102, 120

Lowitz & Co. 321

Lurçat, Jean 90

Lyons, France 78, 82

M

Mackintosh, Charles Rennie 384

madras 168, 174

mahogany 26, 32, 40, 306, 364, 365

Malabar 64, 69, 106, 109, 157, 181, 186, 189

Malibu Tiles 324

Manchester velvet 70, 72

Mannington Carpets 377, 387, 389

mantels 40

Manuel Canovas 109, 125, 126, 127, 129, 157, 161, 167, 172

maple 32

marble 14, 37, 40, 315

Marble Flooring Specialists 314, 317

marbling 32, 40

Marie Antoinette 116

Marlborough Tiles 331

Marley 393, 394

marquetry 14, 362, 368, 369

Marston & Langinger 289

Marthe Armitage 253, 254, 265, 266

Marvic Textiles 65, 68, 81, 90, 91, 97, 114, 123, 129, 135, 136, 138, 140, 151, 153, 155, 159, 168, 169, 172, 175, 184, 187

Mary Fox Linton 101, 170

Mary, Queen of Scots 14

matelassé 85

Matisse, Henri 242, 252

matting 13, 17, 19, 47, 370–5

types 371

Maugham, Syrie 300

Mauny 211, 240, 241, 252, 253, 280, 281

Maw & Co. 358

Maya Romanoff 205, 206, 266, 269

Mechlin 180

medieval 12–13, 14, 37, 43, 54, 170, 300, 318

Mediterranean 57, 300, 301

Mercer, Henry Chapman 342

Mesopotamia 149

metallic finishes 268, 302, 303, 304

metalware 46

Mexico 57, 300, 349

Middle East 128

Milan, Italy 180

milk paints 286, 288, 290

Miller, Philip *Figures of the Most Beautiful and Uncommon Plants* 150

Milner, Janet 129

Minimalism 57, 74

Minton Company 318

Minton Hollins 325, 334

Minton, Herbert 312, 342, 356

Miró, Jean 252

Modernism 49, 53–4, 74, 124, 142, 174, 194, 198, 204, 206, 208, 222, 228, 280, 394

carpets 384, 385

mohair 70, 74

moirés 62, 69

Monet, Claude 242

Monkwell 66, 71, 106, 130, 131, 156, 158, 174

Monmouth House, Natchez, Mississippo, USA 39, 244

monograms 13

Montagu, Lady Mary Wortley 132

Monterey 389

Montgomery (Tomlinson) 107, 109, 149, 153, 163

Moore, Thomas 378

Moorish (moresque) 43, 100, 132, 220

moquette 70, 72

Morris & Co. 111, 122, 155, 250, 257, 294, 295, 382

Morris Jumel Mansion, New York 28, 29, 229

Morris, William 43, 68, 108,122, 123, 124, 126, 220, 238, 262, 266, 323, 332, 342, 382

Acknowledgments

I would very much like to thank the editorial, design and production team for all the long hours, dedication and skill they have committed to the new *Style Sourcebook*: Emma Clegg for calmly and efficiently overseeing this complex project from start to finish; Catherine Emslie for her editorial skills, co-ordinating with suppliers and design and, especially, for her unflagging good humour and encouragement in her constant dealings with this author; Caroline Dyas for researching a wealth of detailed information on the samples shown; Libby Willis for her eagle-eyed proof-reading; Helen Snaith for her essential index; and Juanne Branquinho for contacting suppliers. Also many thanks to Auberon Hedgecoe for overseeing the design; Peter Gerrish and John Round for transforming an enormous volume of fresh material into an informative visual treat; Roger Dixon for excellent new photography; Emma O'Neil for researching new interiors pictures; and Gary Hayes and Julie Young for marshalling the complex process of production.

I would also like to acknowledge again the team who created the first *Style Sourcebook* over five years ago. Their pioneering work still resonates in our new title: Emma Boys, Kenny Grant, Estelle Bayliss, Penelope Cream, Julia North, Claire Musters, Anna Nicholas, Patrick Evans, Steve Tanner, Judith More, Janice Utton, Samantha Gray, Jane Royston, Hilary Bird, Jo Wood, Glen Watkins, and the late and much-missed Arlene Sobel.

Heartfelt thanks to the following for kindly allowing location photography: Lee Anderson; Andrew Lowe House; Sue Andrews; Roger Banks-Pye; Cornelia Bayley; Alison & Kip Bertram; Calhoun Mansion; Cedar Grove; Château de Compiègne; Comoglio Showroom; Colline Covington; Clifford Ellison; John Evert; Ruth Fane; Garth Woodside Mansion; Geffrye Museum; Christophe Gollut; Jacques Granges; Richard Gray; Paul & Lisa Grist; Richard Hampton Jenrette; Amelia Handegan; Michael Harris; Thierry & Agnès Hart; La Heredia; Jonathon Hudson; Charles Jencks; Mr & Mrs Michael Keehan; Wendy Kidd; Lyn von Kirsting; Leeds Castle; Ian Lieber; Linley Sambourne House; Lord & Lady McAlpine; The Malt House; Marshall Schule Associates; Justin Meath Baker; Jim & Debbie Millis; Janet Milner; Issey Miyake; Morris Jumel Mansion; Monmouth Mansion; Françoise Lafon; Nathaniel Russell House; The Old Merchant's House; Eileen O'Neill; Jaime & Janetta Parlade; Parham House; Tom Parr; Jack & Tasha Polizzi; Rockliffe Mansion; Rosalie Mansion; Ivy Rosequist; Jackl Sadoun; Dennis Severs; Shaker Museum; Lars Sjöberg; Keith Skeel; Sir John Soane Museum; Annie & Lachlan Stewart; Eric & Gloria Stewart; St Mary's, Bramber; Temple Newsam House; Maryse and Michel Trama; David Warbeck; West Green House; Louis de Wet; Lillian Williams.

Picture Credits

Andrew Martin International (74 bc, p95 br); Attica (37, 338); Baumann (146–7); Bradbury & Bradbury (44–5 [Jeremy Samuelson], 212 [Ron Mitchell], 251 box br [Douglas Keister]); Tommy Candler (6); De Gournay (249 box); Designers Guild (70); Dulux (286–7, 297, 303 bl, 370–1); Fired Earth (318–9 t, 346); James Merrell (328, 339 tl); Osborne & Little (54, 178, 256 tl, 339 b); Naim (390, 391 t); The National Trust Photographic Library/Mike Caldwell (295); (Octopus Publishing Group Limited/Bill Batten (125)/Paul Bricknell (222)/Tim Clinch (57 b, 58–59)/Geoff Dann (256 bl)/Peter Marshall (1204, 205 b)/James Merrell (12, 13 t/b, 14 t/b, 15, 16, 17, 18, 19, 20, 21, 22, 23 t/b, 24, 26 l, 28, 29 t/b, 30–1, 32 l, 33, 34–5, 36, 37 t, 38, 39, 40, 41 t/b, 42, 43 t/b, 46 l/r, 47, 48, 49, 50, 51, 52, 53 t/b, 56, 57 t, 62, 63 t/b, 71 t/b, 76 t/b, 77 l, 86, 87 bl/br/tl, 92 t/b, 93, 110 t/b, 111 t/b, 128, 129, 146 t/b, 159, 160, 161 t/b, 179 bl/tl, 190, 191 t/b, 205 t, 213 t/b, 228, 229, 244, 245 b/t, 256 tr/bl, 271 t/b, 286 t/b, 288, 291, 293, 300, 303 t, 306, 307 br, 312 t/b, 313, 318 bl/tl/b, 329 t/b, 346, 352, 353 t/b, 362, 363 t/b, 370 t/b, 376 b, 377, 390–1 b)/Kim Sayer (376 t)/Steve Tanner (10–11, 60–1, 202–3, 284–5, 310–1, 360–1)/Andrew Twort (303 r)/Simon Upton (55, 270, 302, 307); Red Cover/Michael Reeves (1)/Emy Herbosch (2–3)/Alex Ramsay (4–5); Sanderson (27, 54).